Oracle Press™

Oracle Developer Starter Kit

Robert Muller

Osborne/**McGraw-Hill**

Berkeley New York St. Louis San Francisco
Auckland Bogotá Hamburg London Madrid
Mexico City Milan Montreal New Delhi Panama City
Paris São Paulo Singapore Sydney Tokyo Toronto

Osborne/**McGraw-Hill**
2600 Tenth Street
Berkeley, California 94710
U.S.A.

For information on translations or book distributors outside the U.S.A., or to arrange bulk purchase discounts for sales promotions, premiums, or fund-raisers, please contact Osborne/**McGraw-Hill** at the above address.

Oracle Developer Starter Kit

1234567890 AGM AGM 90198765432109

ISBN 0-07-212047-9

Publisher
   Brandon A. Nordin

**Associate Publisher and
Editor-in-Chief**
   Scott Rogers

Acquisitions Editor
   Jeremy Judson

Project Editor
   Madhu Prasher

Editorial Assistant
   Monika Faltiss

Technical Editor
   Claire Dessaux

Copy Editor
   Judith Brown

Proofreader
   Carol Burbo

Indexer
   Valerie Robbins

Computer Designer
   Ann Sellers
   Roberta Steele
   Gary Corrigan

Illustrator
   Beth Young
   Robert Hansen
   Brian Wells

Series Design
   Jani Beckwith

This book was composed with Corel VENTURA.

About the Author

Robert J. Muller, Ph.D., is Chief Information Officer at ValueStar, Inc. (www.valuestar.com), the consumer service rating company. He has worked with the ORACLE database management system since version 3 in 1983, and with Oracle Forms since 1984. He has a Ph.D. from the Massachusetts Institute of Technology and has published several papers on relational database and CASE applications as well as books on database design, managing object-oriented software projects, and testing object-oriented software.

*To M'Linn and Theo,
my own starter kits for life*

Contents

PART I
Building Applications

PART II
A Tutorial for Oracle Developer

PART III
Programming with Developer

PART IV

Advanced Tools

PART V

Reference

Acknowledgments

I want to thank several people from Oracle Corporation, where I first learned how to use the Interactive Application Facility. Larry Ellison, of course, was always inspirational; my real thanks to him are for guiding Oracle and its products to become the terrific success that it has become. Jenny Overstreet always helped to get things done. Kathryn Daugherty and Mary Winslow taught me most of what I learned at Oracle. Bill Friend, the inventor of Forms, was always helpful, as were Sohaib Abbassi and Peter Clare. Gary Berlind let me go beyond Forms to understanding the bigger picture. For this book, I would like to specifically thank Paul Zola, my technical editor for the first edition; Steve Illingworth, my Oracle guide for the second edition; Carl Zetie, my technical editor for the second edition; and Claire Dessaux, my technical editor for the new Starter Kit version of the book. Their hard work complements my own and makes the book work.

I want to thank George Koch for giving me the opportunity to become a writer. Revising his first edition of *ORACLE: The Complete Reference* was a key experience in discovering this new horizon. I also want to thank George and the crew at KOCH Systems Corporation (especially Ann Steele, Baxter Madden, and Lynn Healy) for showing me what ORACLE could do in the real world. I'd like to thank Jim Stein of ValueStar for letting me show him what Oracle can do in the real world of consumer services and for being patient while I finished the book.

At Osborne/McGraw-Hill, I'd like to thank my editor, Jeremy Judson, who had faith in the book's ideas and market; Madhu Prasher, project editor; Judith Brown, copy editor, who sharpened the prose wonderfully; and last but not least Monika Faltiss, Editorial Assistant, who made sure everything got to the right people at the right time. I'd also like to thank Jani Beckwith, Gary Corrigan, Micky Galicia, Ann Sellers, and Roberta Steele, all of whom had the Herculean task of integrating and arranging the massive bitmap illustration load that this book required. The Augean stables have nothing on this book.

It is customary to apologize to one's family for taking time on weekends and vacations to do the book. This edition was a challenge due to balancing executive responsibilities at ValueStar with early morning and weekend writing and editing, and we all breathed a sigh of relief when the last diagram was drawn and proof proofed. The support of my wife, M'Linn Swanson, and our son Theo's ability to create random joy in my life enabled me to finish the book.

Introduction

t is not really very hard to write a book like this, but as with writing software, the writing of the book is a pebble on the tip of the iceberg. I would like to draw a small, metaphorical picture in the hopes of conveying a deeper understanding of the architectural underpinnings of this book.

Everyone should read the article in a recent issue of *IEEE Software* magazine, "Architectural Mismatch: Why Reuse Is So Hard," by David Garlan, Robert Allen, and John Ockerbloom (*IEEE Software,* Volume 12 Number 6, November 1995, pages 17-26). This article makes explicit some of the things that have formed my way of thinking about using tools such as Developer to develop applications. Reuse, of course, is the Holy Grail of software architecture, and as yet there are no Galahads capable of finding that grail. The article details some of the reasons why this is so, the main one being that so-called reusable systems simply do not match the situations in which designers try to use them.

While it may seem logical to many to pursue the grail, I am convinced that most of us in the software industry are not Galahads, pure of heart and soul and ready to leave this vale of tears once we find perfection. Most of us simply need to get our jobs done and to contribute as much value to our customers as possible in the process. As a purely practical matter, it makes perfect sense to construct software that is as reusable as possible—but *not more so.*

We design tools for specific purposes. If you go to any large hardware store, you will find a plethora of saws designed for every possible situation. You have different saws for different kinds of wood. You have different saws for cutting wood in different directions. You have different saws for different locations of wood (cutting wood that is attached to something, as in being part of a wall, requires a special saw: you cannot move the wall to the table saw). You have different saws for different power sources. You even have different saws that vary purely in an economic sense (competing brands, international trade, local preferences). And the world is not static; new situations (new building materials, new locations, new vendors) arise every day, adding to the need for new tools. To choose the right saw for the right job is a skill requiring years of direct experience with tools, building materials, and situations, not to mention a largish cash flow.

The practical builder does not choose the tool solely by its intended use. By experience, he or she has learned how to apply tools to situations beyond those envisioned by their designers. The art of *using* tools (as opposed to *designing* them) requires just as much knowledge and creativity. But there are limits, and you cannot press a design into use beyond its intended limits.

Developer is also a tool, like a saw. Over the twelve or so years of its existence, it has grown to be an extraordinarily capable, broad-ranging tool for developing applications. As with any tool, Developer has its limits and shortcomings, and it makes specific assumptions that are basic to its design intentions—go beyond these assumptions at your peril.

NOTE
This book covers Developer version 2.1. The bulk of the examples use the product versions in the following table. I used the Windows 98 operating system with a Workgroup Oracle version 7.3 database. If you are working with Forms 4.5 or Reports 2, please consult the second edition of this book, which covers both release 1 of Developer and release 2.

Product	Version
Form Builder	6.0.5.0.2
Report Builder	6.0.5.28.0
Graphics Builder	6.0.5.8.0
Procedure Builder	6.0.5.0.0
Project Builder	6.0.5.7.0
Query Builder	6.0.5.6.0
Schema Builder	6.0.5.6.0
Translation Builder	6.0.3.0.3

My contention has always been that software tools need to be extensible and easy to use to allow them to fit the very different situations they must confront. Oracle Developer is such a system. When you find yourself, however, spending hours trying to get that very capable tool to do something that it was not intended to do, you are wasting your time. In writing this book, I have tried repeatedly to clarify the whys of Developer, so that you understand what it does. The reverse of this is to understand, clearly, what it does not do. The best way to use this tool is to build applications in a straightforward, competent manner that accomplishes your requirements and adds value to your customer's lives.

—Bob Muller
  San Francisco, California, July 1999

PART I

Building Applications

CHAPTER

1

Introducing Developer

racle Developer is a highly productive integrated development environment that lets you build scalable database applications for the Internet or for client/server systems. Oracle Developer Server is an application server specialized and optimized for deploying your Oracle Developer applications to the Internet. This book teaches you everything you need to know to develop powerful, reusable, and useful applications that give you access to the data in your database.

Overview of Building Applications

An *application* is a computer program that does some task. A *database application* is a program that manages data in a database management system such as Oracle8i. Database applications move data in and out of the database, either by displaying the data or by letting the user add to or modify the data in the database.

There are many ways to build application systems. You can use a full-scale programming language such as COBOL, C, C++, or Java. There are many such languages, each with its advantages and disadvantages. Programming with these languages gives you a great deal of flexibility and control and performance, but you must work hard to take advantage of that flexibility. You must work even harder to ensure that the application performs and scales in the face of ever-expanding use. It is quite easy to make errors or to inadvertently program in such a way that you crash or slow the program down rather than speed it up.

Oracle Developer is a *declarative* tool that lets you build applications mainly through telling the database what you want instead of telling it how to give it to you. With just a few statements or filled-in properties, you can easily generate scalable database applications for running your business on the Web. With some additional coding in PL/SQL, you can do pretty much anything you want.

Today, applications deployed to the Internet consist of a rich graphical user interface with menus, toolbars, dialog boxes, and windows that display the application objects, whatever they might be. The three kinds of objects of interest are forms, reports, and graphics. Oracle Developer provides modules for each of these three kinds of objects: Oracle Forms, Oracle Reports, and Oracle Graphics.

But developing an application doesn't mean much unless you can deploy it effectively. In the old days, deploying an application meant figuring out a way to use SneakerNet to get the application installed on all the client machines in your shop. Today, with intranets and extranets and the Internet, deployment is much easier, but scaling up is harder. Anyone with a Web browser can run today's applications, as long as there is a server somewhere that runs them. That's the job of application servers, such as the Developer Server, which executes the business logic of your applications on the server while connecting to a browser to display forms, reports, and graphics.

Form Applications

To understand Oracle Developer, you need to understand a few of the terms it uses to refer to the objects in an application.

A *form* application is an application that presents data in an online format consisting of a series of items laid out in one or more windows. Items can be enterable fields, graphics, buttons, check boxes, or any number of other kinds of objects. Here is a sample form application:

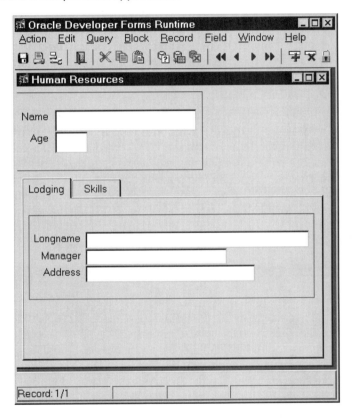

As you can see, the form provides a good way to view the information from the database. Forms also provide a way of entering and changing that information. You can type data into the form fields or change the data that is in them, depending on what the application lets you do.

An application can have just one form, or it can have many forms, depending on the tasks it has to accomplish and the architecture required to run it. Form design, as with paper forms, is an art: you have to display information in just the right format or the form becomes difficult to use and error prone. Breaking it into sections is a common way to reduce the complexity of a very large and complicated form. The same approach works with an online application. Simple forms correspond to a *record type*, which is a series of data fields—a single row of data. The form can display a single record at a time, or it can display several at once. The tools in a form let you manage the records and interact with the displayed information (query, insert, update, delete, scroll, and so on).

There is a particular kind of form called a *master-detail* form that automatically manages the relationship between a parent record and several child records. This situation is so common that Oracle Developer handles it as a specific option for building the form, along with the more common single-record option. The Departments section of the form is the master record. When you select a department, the form automatically displays the employee records that correspond to that department.

Report Applications

A *report* is a page-oriented display of data. Whereas a form provides an interactive tool for managing data, the purpose of a report is to format a large amount of data in a readable fashion, not to let you manage data. You still have data laid out in records and fields, but you do not have interactive tools such as scroll bars to deal with the records. The records are all laid out on pages, and the tools you have let you deal with the pages—print them, scroll through them, or whatever the format permits—rather than deal with the data blocks. Oracle Developer Reports Builder gives you very powerful report generation capabilities.

This is a report that represents ledger entries grouped by person:

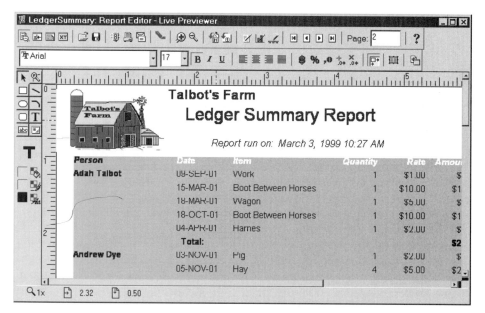

This report closely resembles what you would see in a paper ledger. The report has multiple pages with footers, headers, and all the other accoutrements of a page-oriented report.

Oracle Developer provides you with many different kinds of reports, and a single report can combine different types.

- *Tabular:* A simple table of data

- *Mailing label:* A series of regularly repeating records formatted on each page in a certain area (mailing labels, get it?)

- *Form letter:* Boilerplate text surrounding data from a record that fills in blanks in the text, such as recipient's name and address

- *Master-master:* Two groups of unrelated records displayed together

- *Master-detail:* A master record with two or more related detail records displayed together

- *Matrix or crosstab:* A cross-tabulation of two columns showing some aggregate or other value for the combination of each value from each column

- *Data file:* A comma-separated or other variety of delimited data file; you use this to transfer data into other tools (there are easier ways, usually)

- *Graph:* A report that includes a chart or graph of the data in addition to or in place of displaying the data itself

NOTE
Oracle Reports is quite capable of standing on its own. In fact, Oracle sells Oracle Reports as a standalone product along with the Oracle Report Server.

Graphics Applications

Graphics are pictorial representations of data. The term *chart* also refers to this kind of data representation. Line charts, pie charts, and bar charts in all their variations let you visualize data rather than just displaying it. Oracle Developer gives you a sophisticated set of tools for both creating standalone graphics applications and for including graphics in your forms and reports. This is a graphics application depicting a pie chart:

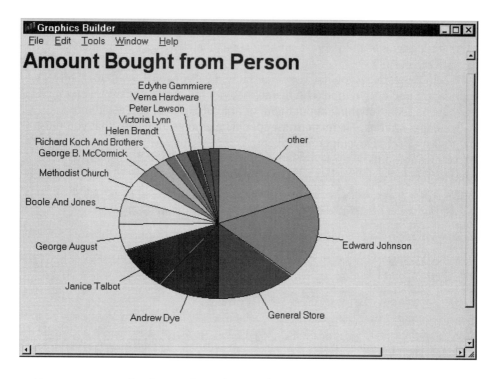

You can even make the graphs active, so the user can manipulate them. For example, take a graph that represents some kind of aggregation such as revenue by salesperson. You can create the ability for the user to drill down to see a graph with the detail for a single salesperson, breaking it down by city. This capability is particularly powerful when you embed the graphic in a form application. See Chapter 8 for details on drill-down graphics.

What Is Different About Database Applications?

What makes a database application so special? How does it differ from the ordinary, everyday application?

Database management engines provide data protection against the vicissitudes of life (*recovery*); support multiple users (*concurrency*), multiple applications, and *referential integrity*; protect you from unauthorized use of your data (*security*); and isolate you from the details of managing data on a particular platform (*portability*). SQL and relational or object-relational data modeling give you a strong, reliable paradigm for data access. Finally, database management engines are tightly interfaced and integrated with tools that let you use all these database features and efficiently maintain your data.

Oracle Developer automatically handles the details of database management for you. In fact, Oracle Developer handles so many of the gory details that you might never have to learn anything about them, or at least not until you get to more advanced applications. There are some specific elements, however, that you must know to use Oracle Developer effectively.

If you want to follow up on how the Oracle Internet Database Server works behind the scenes, look in the Oracle documentation or a book on Oracle database administration and programming, such as *Oracle8: The Complete Reference*, by George Koch and Kevin Loney (Osborne/McGraw-Hill, 1997), or *Oracle8 DBA Handbook*, by Kevin Loney (Osborne/McGraw-Hill, 1998).

A *transaction* is a logical unit of work. The transaction begins with a data-related action and ends with a successful-termination command (*commit*) or an unsuccessful-termination command *(rollback)*. These limits essentially set up a sequence of data operations that you can undo if needed by rolling back the changes in the database.

The one thing your Oracle Developer application does need to worry about is signaling to the database engine when your transaction ends, usually with the SQL COMMIT WORK statement or the ROLLBACK WORK statement. This has some implications for application design.

The first choice you must make is whether to make the decision to commit or rollback accessible to your end user. You do this with a menu choice, keypress, or tool button. This gives the end user total control over the progress of the work in the database. He or she can perform one small change or many large changes— whatever is appropriate.

The next choice is to decide what constitutes a logical unit of work. Even if you give end users control over commit and rollback, your application will still need to offer those choices at appropriate points. For example, you might allow commits or rollbacks after both the deletion of a row and of the rows that depend on the row. If you allowed end users to commit after the deletion but before the dependent deletion, you would violate referential integrity (discussed shortly). Ask yourself what the database engine should restore in the event of a disk crash. If the material to be restored includes more than one operation, package all the operations involved into one transaction.

Now, the good thing about Oracle Developer is that it fully understands all of these issues and automatically takes care of them for you. It automatically handles commit and rollback requests from end users at appropriate points in the application logic. It automatically generates the commit and rollback commands in your interface. It gives you ways to include supporting operations in each transaction as part of its basic application structure.

Referential integrity is the ability of the database to make sure that when a row refers to another row, that second row exists. Oracle and other database management systems let you manage most referential integrity in the database through integrity constraints on the tables or through triggers that fire on common events such as insert, update, and delete. Where possible, you should move this kind of validation to the database server so that all applications share it. What's left becomes your application validation code.

Every table has or should have a primary key. The *primary key* is one or more columns with values that uniquely identify each row of the table. The nature of relational databases represents logical relationships between tables through data references to the primary key of another table. The referring column is a *foreign key*, and it refers to the primary key of the foreign table. Most table joins involve matching the foreign key to the primary key.

Given that, you can see how important it is to maintain the integrity of these data pointers. In a relational database, the pointers are data, not physical pointers that can get fouled up. But you still have the problem of making sure that when there is a data reference, it does map to a primary key value somewhere. You also have the reverse problem for some relationships of making sure that for every primary key value, there is a foreign key referring to it. Finally, you need to make sure that the primary key does uniquely identify the rows of the table.

Portability is the capability of running on different systems. It applies to operating systems; it also applies to windowing systems, application frameworks, and any other platform of services. This includes the database management platform. Most applications have to deal with portability in several different ways. Your requirements for an Oracle Developer application may include running the same application on different database management systems or on different operating systems.

Database portability is how independent the application is of its underlying database engine. The *interface* or set of interfaces—the specific method(s) by which you access the database manager—can be an issue. The decision you must make here is the extent to which your application must run against more than one database platform. Does your client require the application to run on both Oracle8i and Informix? Sybase? If so, you immediately drastically limit yourself to the standard SQL, which is a *minimal* standard to say the least.

ODBC helps somewhat with this, but its main contribution is to standardize the interface to different databases available in the marketplace. ODBC (the *Open Data Base Connectivity standard*) provides a uniform SQL language and programming interface for any database that cares to write a driver for it. There are vendor or third-party ODBC drivers for every database of any interest (see Chapter 15 for details on using the ODBC interface with Oracle Developer). By using ODBC, you can switch databases at runtime without recompiling your code.

Operating system (OS) portability is the portability of the tools and database manager itself. If you want to run your application on different platforms (Internet,

Windows, Macintosh, and UNIX, for example—a common combination these days), either you must port the application to different database managers, or your database manager and tools must be able to run on different operating systems using the same interfaces. Increasingly, ODBC plays this role as ODBC drivers become available on different operating systems, as well as for different database managers.

While it isn't absolutely necessary to know SQL to use Oracle Developer, you will find such knowledge useful as you get into more advanced uses of the product. If you do not already know SQL, you should get training or read one of the many good books on the language, such as *Oracle8: The Complete Reference*, by Koch and Loney (Osborne/McGraw-Hill, 1997); or the *SQL: The Complete Reference* by Groff and Weinberg (Osborne/McGraw-Hill, 1999).

Finally, Oracle Developer delivers on its promise of enabling high-quality, scalable applications working in a three-tier environment. A *two-tier* application is one that runs on a workstation and accesses a database server. A *three-tier* application is one that runs mainly on an application server, which in turn accesses a database server, and which manages only user-interface functions through the client workstation. With Developer Server, you can now build robust, high-performing applications for large numbers of clients and very large databases.

What Is Different About Internet Database Applications?

The progress of the Internet in application development is nothing short of amazing. In just a few years, the Internet has completely changed the way we think about applications. This is just as true for database applications as for any other kind. Internet computing requires that application development environments do more than was required before, however.

Internet database applications must be

- Reliable

- Secure

- Highly available

- Scalable

Reliability is important because companies now rely on Internet applications to run their business. A company that makes products or services available on the Web must be assured that the applications for delivering those products and services work reliably. Mistakes in such a competitive environment can cost the company both in lost revenue and lost good will.

Many Internet applications deal with money or with private information or trade secrets. Such applications require full security to protect the valuable data and privacy of the system's users.

The new area of e-commerce puts extreme demands on database applications deployed over the Internet. Such applications must be available around the clock. You may be asleep, but your customers, wherever in the world they might be, are not. Your database application can't be, either!

Finally, if the last few years have shown us little else, it is the requirement for scalability. No one could have imagined the dramatic growth in the Internet. When companies put their products and services on the Internet, they usually find they have underestimated demand for access. If your Internet database application can't handle rapid increases in the number of users, you'll be in trouble very quickly.

These requirements are just as important for enterprise-wide applications deployed within a company as for worldwide applications deployed outside the company. Oracle Developer provides a strong solution for all these applications. The challenge of such applications to the development tools is high: networks can bottleneck data flow, servers can provide poor performance, and many layers of software and scalability requirements can exceed the skills of your developers.

Oracle Developer Server is an application server specialized and optimized for Oracle Developer applications. It lets you deploy new and existing Oracle Developer applications to the Internet without changing the application code.

The good news is that Oracle Developer Server automatically scales and performs over any network and automatically delivers native services and built-in functionality to ensure reliable, secure, available, and scalable performance.

Oracle Developer gives you the integrated development environment you need to create scalable, mission-critical database applications. Oracle Developer Server delivers a specialized and optimized application server for deploying your Oracle Developer applications to the Internet. This book guides you on how to use Oracle Developer and Oracle Developer Server, with several tutorials that focus on the essential characteristics of the products. It also provides a complete reference to the details of the products. Combining the tutorials with the reference gives you a complete guide to using Oracle Developer to build high-performance database applications.

With the overview of the development process complete, the next chapter gives you some details about the objects you'll be creating in Oracle Developer applications.

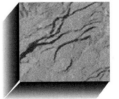

CHAPTER
2

Overview of Oracle Developer Objects

hat are the specific tools you get with Oracle Developer? This chapter gives you an overview of the tools and the objects with which you can create your applications. With this summary, you will have a basis for the tutorials in the following chapters. Figure 2-1 shows the overall structure of the Oracle Developer system.

The Project Builder is the primary interface for working with Oracle Developer modules. You do not need to use it, but if you are working with more than a couple of forms, it can make your life significantly easier by organizing your modules into projects. You can set up a default login to the Oracle Database Server for each project so that you don't make mistakes or waste time accessing the wrong development database. You can generate and regenerate your modules with a single

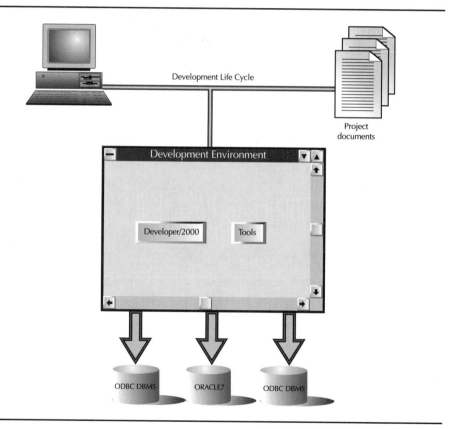

FIGURE 2-1. *Structure of Oracle Developer*

button click rather than by tediously going through each module. You can set up your Project Builder toolbar to give you access to all your tools, and you can write macros that let you automate various building procedures.

The Project Builder lets you organize and automate your building process. The real work of creating an Oracle Developer application, however, is in the individual builders—Form, Report, and Graphics Builders. These tools let you create the building blocks for your applications: forms, reports, and graphics. Each of these three tools has a corresponding Compiler, which lets you recompile the modules without the overhead of the full builder environment. You also have helper tools: Procedure Builder, Query Builder, Schema Builder, and Translation Builder. The Procedure Builder helps with creating stored procedures on your Oracle Database Server or with building client PL/SQL code. Query Builder helps you to create SQL SELECT statements using a graphical interface. Schema Builder helps you to create relational database schemas. Translation Builder lets you localize your forms, reports, and graphics by adding translations for the various strings you use.

These components make up the Oracle Developer environment that you use to build applications. When you are ready to deploy your applications, you install the Oracle Developer Server, which comprises the Forms, Reports, and Graphics Servers. These three servers work with the Oracle Application Server to let you deploy your applications to the Internet (or your local intranet).

NOTE
The Oracle Developer Server comes on its own CD-ROM to facilitate server installation and deployment. You should also be aware that Oracle sells the Oracle Reports product separately, comprising the Report Builder and the Reports Server.

The rest of this chapter introduces you to the scope and structure of the individual modules you create with these tools.

Forms

The Forms component of Oracle Developer is the part of the development environment in which you develop, not surprisingly, form modules. It also provides the software framework for developing menu and PL/SQL client library modules. A *framework* is a reusable system of objects that work together to define the basic abstractions required by a particular application domain—in this case menus and forms. You build forms and menus with the Form Builder.

The Form Module

The form module is the main component of your database application. It is also the richest module in terms of internal structure, containing many different types of objects. Figure 2-2 shows the hierarchy of objects that make up a form module. The box labeled "Programming Objects" summarizes a group of objects; you'll see what these are in the "Reusable Objects" section later in this chapter.

Triggers

A *trigger* is a block of PL/SQL code you attach to another object: a form, a data block, or an item. This code represents the business logic you want to attach to the

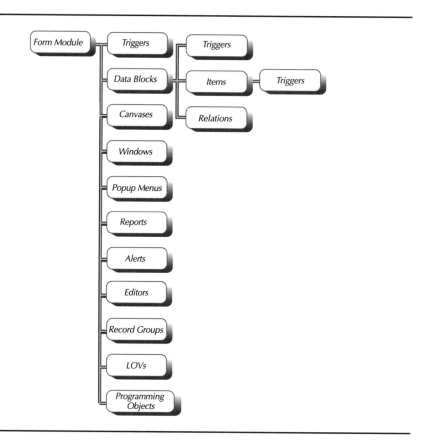

FIGURE 2-2. *Object hierarchy for a form module*

object. You can also have triggers attached to property classes (you'll learn more about this in the "Reusable Objects" section, later in the chapter). The trigger "fires," or executes, when certain events occur: the event triggers the code.

Triggers in a form application contain the working code that you add to the application, apart from the code you put into separate program units or libraries. Creating triggers and their business logic takes up most of the effort of form design and coding. Chapter 6 contains detailed activity diagrams showing the structure of the different forms scenarios and how triggers fire in those scenarios. Examples of triggers and their associated PL/SQL code appear in most of the following chapters.

Most triggers you use are built-in triggers that the Oracle Developer framework provides. These triggers come in several categories, as Chapter 5 details. Each trigger has a specific name—When-Button-Pressed, Post-Query, On-Delete, Key-Help, Pre-Update, for example—that you choose from a list of predefined names. If you define the same name at different levels—data block and item, for example—Oracle Developer executes the one at the lowest level by default. For example, you can define a trigger for 2 of the 20 items in a data block and the same trigger at the data block level. For events on the 2 triggered items, the item trigger executes; otherwise, the data block trigger executes. You can change this behavior with the Execution Style property of the trigger. The default behavior is Override; you can change this to Before or After in a higher-level trigger to have the trigger fire before or after the lower-level one. You can thus combine behavior in several triggers, as well as replace behavior.

You can also add your own user-defined triggers and fire them explicitly. This feature was more useful in previous versions of forms; now, with the flexibility of PL/SQL, it is not as important, and Oracle plans to eliminate it in the near future.

A running form has two main modes: Normal mode and Enter Query mode. Normal mode lets you insert, update, and delete information in the database. Enter Query mode lets you create an example record to use to specify a query of data from the database by example. The query-by-example approach of Oracle Developer gives you many features for data retrieval with little or no coding on your part.

NOTE
Some triggers are not available in Enter Query mode (see the following section, "Data Blocks"), because the actions they take relate to data manipulation and therefore make no sense in that mode.

A certain class of triggers, *key triggers*, fire when you press a key combination in the user interface. Adding key triggers lets you reprogram your keyboard to take actions different from the standard keypress definitions. Because these are nonstandard, the trigger definition lets you display a description of the key in the list of keys available through the Help menu in the standard menu bar.

Data Blocks

The *data block* is the intermediate building unit for forms. You can think of a data block in two ways: as a collection of items or as a collection of records, each of which has the same structure. You specify the number of records to display at once, and you specify whether to display the records horizontally or vertically.

There are two kinds of data blocks. A *base-table data block* corresponds to a relational table, an object table, or a view in the database and manages some number of records corresponding to rows in the table or view. A base-table data block can also represent a stored procedure. A *control block* does not correspond to a table, view, or stored procedure, and its records do not correspond to database rows. Usually, control blocks represent a collection of single-valued items, effectively having only a single record. For example, if you need to keep track of an aggregate value for a set of records, such as a total or an average, you create an item in a control block to represent that value. There is only one value for that item and control block, compared to a set of records in a base-table data block.

The data block display has two special characteristics relating to being a container of records. The data block can have a scroll bar that lets the user manage a set of records larger than what the canvas can display. It can also have a special set of visual attributes, which the "Reusable Objects" section later in this chapter will cover. These attributes define a different display for the *current record*—the record on which the cursor currently rests.

Navigation within the data block normally proceeds in the order in which you define the items in a record. The runtime system has functions to move from record to record, from item to item, and from data block to data block. When you navigate out of the last item in a record, you normally return to the first item in the same record. The Form Builder lets you redefine this default behavior so that you go to the next record (or previous record if you back up from the first item). It also lets you navigate to the next or previous data block when you move from the last or first item, respectively. You can set specific data blocks to be the next block or previous block, creating a linked list of blocks. You can also tell Forms to enter the data block name in the block menu, which lets you navigate to a data block by choosing its name from a list.

The primary function of the base-table data block is to provide an interface to a relational or object table or a stored procedure in the database. Oracle Developer provides a Data Block Wizard that helps you build these blocks from the database schema. That wizard also helps you to create master-detail data blocks. These are data blocks that relate to one another in a parent-child relationship, such as an invoice and its items.

Oracle Developer manages data in the database automatically by constructing SQL statements based on data blocks and their structure. The data block thus has several properties that manage the construction of these SQL statements:

■ *Enforce Primary Key and Key Mode:* By default, Forms uses the *rowid*—a unique Oracle internal identifier—to identify the row in SQL statements that it generates. The Enforce Primary Key property tells Forms to use instead items and their values to identify the row, corresponding to the columns that make up the primary key in the database table. The Key Mode property tells Forms whether to include primary key values in the UPDATE statement; some database managers do not permit you to update primary key values.

■ *<Operation> Allowed:* You can disable specific SQL statements—SELECT, INSERT, UPDATE, or DELETE—for the data block. For example, to prevent users from deleting rows, set Delete Allowed to No.

■ *WHERE Clause:* This is a SQL fragment that Forms adds to the SELECT statement it generates for a query. See the section "Entering a Query" in Chapter 5 for details.

■ *ORDER BY Clause:* This is a SQL fragment that Forms uses as the ORDER BY clause in the SELECT statement it generates for a query. See Chapter 5.

■ *Optimizer Hint:* Forms appends this Oracle SQL fragment to the SELECT statement to use the special optimization features of Oracle to speed up a query.

■ *Update Changed Columns Only:* Forms includes only changed columns in the UPDATE statement it generates if this property is Yes; otherwise, it updates all columns in the row whether the values have changed or not. You should generally leave this set to No.

■ *Locking Mode:* This property determines whether to lock a row immediately when you change a value in the row, or to lock it only when you commit the changes you make to the database.

■ *Data Source and DML Target:* This property determines what kind of data source to use to supply data for the data block or to which to write data: a FROM clause, a table name, a stored procedure, or transactional triggers.

■ *DML Array Size:* This property determines the number of records to insert, update, or delete at once.

Data blocks also provide the interface for the query-by-example features of the form. As a user, you can place the data block in Enter Query mode, then enter query criteria into the fields of the special example record. When you execute the query, Forms then automatically builds a SQL SELECT statement from these values. In combination with the WHERE Clause and ORDER BY Clause properties, this gives you a comprehensive query facility. You can also enter your own additional SQL for the WHERE clause while in Enter Query mode. You can specify the number of records to buffer in memory as well as the maximum query time and the maximum number of records to fetch at a time into the form.

Items

An *item* is the primary building unit of the form. An item has many properties—so many that it is really difficult to summarize here. This section provides a summary of the functions of an item without going into gory detail on its specific properties. You refer to item values using a special dot-separated syntax: *<data block>.<name>*, where *<data block>* is the name of the data block that owns the item, and *<name>* is the name of the item. The item's name is unique within the data block.

Table 2-1 describes the different types of items. The description mentions any special properties relevant only to the particular type of item.

Item Type	Description
ActiveX Control	Displays an ActiveX control; see Chapter 15
Bean Area	Displays the output of a Java Bean you have integrated with your form; See Chapter 15
Chart Item	Displays a chart from a graphics display module
Check Box	Lets the user turn a Boolean value on or off
Display Item	"Read-only" text items that display data without allowing changes by the user
Hierarchical Tree	Displays a tree structure similar to the Windows Explorer or the Object Navigator tree and lets you manipulate data through the tree
Image	Displays a bitmap or vector image
List Item	A list of text lines you can display as a pop-up list, a fixed-size list, or a combo box
OLE Container	Displays an OLE object; see Chapter 15
Push Button	Lets the user execute a trigger you associate with the button (When-Button-Pressed)

TABLE 2-1. *Item Types and Their Purpose in Forms*

Item Type	Description
Radio Group	Lets the user turn on one of a series of buttons while turning all other buttons off; this object owns a set of radio button items that all work together, each representing a particular value for the radio group item, which in turn represents a column in the database
Sound	Displays an icon representing a sound, which plays when you click on the icon
Text Item	Displays text in a single- or multiple-line display field
User Area	Displays anything under the sun that you can fit into the space with a program
VBX Control	Displays a VBX (16-bit) control

TABLE 2-1. *Item Types and Their Purpose in Forms* (continued)

Each specific type has a set of properties. For example, text items may have scroll bars. Radio groups may have an Other Values property, which lets you define what happens on querying the database when the value is not one of the radio button values.

Because items are data values, several properties relate to the properties of the data the item holds. Table 2-2 lists the different data types that Developer Forms supports. Some types exist only for backward compatibility with previous versions of Forms (such as EDATE, JDATE, RMONEY, and so on) and do not appear in Table 2-2. You should avoid using these types whenever possible to ensure that your items map directly to the correct Oracle native data types. You should only use the data types specified in Table 2-2.

Data Type	Description	Avoid or Use
Alpha	Any alphabetic character—uppercase, lowercase, or mixed case	Avoid
Char	Any alphabetic or numeric character (corresponds to VARCHAR2 type in Oracle)	Use
Date	A valid date and time (corresponds to an Oracle DATE type)	Use

TABLE 2-2. *Item Data Types in Forms*

Data Type	Description	Avoid or Use
DateTime	A valid date and time (corresponds to an Oracle DATE type)	Use
Int	Any integer value, signed or unsigned	Avoid
Long	An extended-length character string	Use
Number	Fixed or floating-point numbers, signed or unsigned, with or without exponential/scientific notation (corresponds to an Oracle NUMBER column)	Use

TABLE 2-2. *Item Data Types in Forms* (continued)

Several properties let you control the format and validation of item values:

- *Format mask:* One of a wide variety of value specifications that let you format the output to display or to validate input

- *Default value:* A value to assign to the item when you create it

- *Copy value:* Another item from which to copy an initial value when you create an item

- *Length and Range:* The maximum length or range of the data

- *Must Enter:* A setting to determine whether the user must enter a value

- *LOV:* A list of values associated with the item that constrains the data entered to be one of a specific set of values (see the section "Record Groups and LOVs," later in this chapter)

- *Editor:* A text editor object to use to enter the item value

Items have all kinds of visual attributes: fonts, colors, fills, bevels, and so on. A key attribute is whether to display the item at all: you can have an item that doesn't appear anywhere but holds a value. You can use these items as variables in your PL/SQL code. A specific use lets you retrieve values into these items from the database, then compute other displayed items from those values. You can also write tool tips that the system will display when you move the mouse over the item.

Another key display property for the item is the name of the canvas on which to display it (see the "Canvases and Windows" section below). By changing the canvas name, you have complete control over where and how the item appears on your display. There is also a tab property that lets you position the item on a particular tab in a tab canvas view. You'll see more about this shortly.

Every item has a *prompt*—a string that displays next to the item on a canvas. The prompt properties include the location of the prompt (left of the item, right, top, or bottom), distance from the item, and display attributes of the prompt (font, color, and so on). The prompt follows the item around on the canvas when you move it, so you don't have to worry about creating boilerplate text on the canvas and managing that separately when you rearrange the items on the canvas.

You can disallow navigation into an item, either disabling it completely or just allowing navigation by mouse click instead of allowing a user to move from item to item. You can also link the item to other items and force navigation to occur in an order different from the order of definition of the items.

A series of properties affect the way Oracle Developer Forms uses the item in building SQL statements. The most important one is whether the item corresponds to a column in the data block's base table. Other properties let you control query behavior, data manipulation behavior, and locking behavior.

The Implementation Class property lets you override the behavior of the control with a Java Bean. You can specify Implementation Class (the name of the Java Bean class) for item types ranging from Bean Area to Check Box, List Item, Push Button, Radio Group, or Text Item types. See Chapter 15 for a detailed example of a Java Bean control.

Finally, there is a group called Calculation. This group contains properties that let you transform an item into a calculated field, either through a formula or by summarizing the value from another item. You can thus create totals, summary fields, or all kinds of interesting calculated fields that are automatically maintained without your having to write any triggers. See Chapter 6 for an example of a calculated item.

Relations

A *relation* is a special object that Oracle Developer Forms uses to structure master-detail forms. The relation object, which belongs to the master data block, expresses the relationship of the master record to its detail records. The main properties of the relation are the name of the detail data block and the join condition that Forms uses to manage the relationship.

You can also specify some special behavior regarding deletion of master records (whether to delete detail records) or the insertion or update of detail records when there is no master record. Chapter 6 discusses these properties and settings related to the automatic display of detail records.

Canvases and Windows

A *canvas* is the background on which you place boilerplate text and items. Each item refers to exactly one canvas in its property sheet. You can divide a data block's items between different canvases. That is, a data block can display its items on different canvases, not just on a single canvas.

A canvas does not stand alone as an interface object. To see it and its items, you must display the canvas in a *window*—a rectangular area of the application display surrounded by a frame and maintained by the GUI platform. Oracle Developer makes these separate objects and lets you build windows that provide a *view* of the canvas: a rectangle within the window that covers part or all of the canvas. The part of the canvas that you can see through the window is the view. The window may have horizontal and vertical scroll bars that let you scroll around the canvas to see different views.

There are five types of canvases:

- *Content:* Displays the basic content of a window

- *Tabbed:* Displays the basic content of a window in a series of overlapping canvases with labeled tabs

- *Stacked:* Displays over other canvases to show conditional or separable contents; you can specify whether to display the stacked canvas immediately on displaying its window or to leave it invisible until you need it

- *Vertical toolbar:* Holds tool icons for display in a vertical toolbar along the left side of a window; the window specifies the canvas to use in its toolbar by name

- *Horizontal toolbar:* Holds tool icons for display in a horizontal toolbar along the top of a window; the window specifies the canvas to use in its toolbar by name

Not only can you scroll windows around canvases, but you can also display multiple canvases in the same window through the stacked canvases. Each stacked canvas can have its own scroll bars, letting you move them around while leaving the other canvases where they are. See the discussion of stacked canvases in Chapter 6 for more details on how to use this feature.

You can define a canvas to have a series of tab pages. This gives you the ability to create a tab dialog box—a box with multiple views that you access by clicking on a tab—as shown here:

The tab canvas view lets you organize a large number of items into a single window in a clear and usable way. All of this is very easy to create through the Layout Wizard, which guides you through the process of creating or modifying the canvas layout of the data blocks you create.

Windows can be modal or modeless. A *modal window* requires the user to respond and dismiss the window before doing anything in any other window in the application. A *modeless window* lets you move to another window without dismissing the first one. Often, modal windows have distinguishing characteristics such as lack of scroll bars, fixed size, and an inability to be minimized to an icon.

You can also tell Developer to hide a modeless window when you navigate to an item in another window. Developer, however, defines its two window types not in terms of modality but by what they do:

- *Document:* A generally modeless window that displays an application "document" object, usually a content canvas related to a major part of the application

- *Dialog box:* A generally modal window that displays options or other ways to control application operation

Usually dialog boxes are modal by their nature, although you can have modeless dialog boxes that continue to exist while you are doing other things in the application.

The canvas object specifies the name of the window that displays it, establishing the relationship between canvas and window. The window object specifies by name its primary content canvas, which it tries to display when you first open the window. You can set the height and width of the canvas rectangle. If you want to display different items and stacked canvases, you can modify the height and width of window and canvas, and you can use scroll bars to allow the user to move the canvas and window around.

You have all the standard visual attributes available for the canvas and the window. You can iconify or *minimize* a window, which results in displaying the window as an icon, and you can specify the icon to display. You can also specify whether to display horizontal and/or vertical scroll bars for windows (although usually only for modeless windows).

Chapter 6 has a complete discussion of windows and canvases.

Pop-up Menus, Alerts, and Editors

Oracle Developer gives you several minor objects to address specific needs. First, a *pop-up menu* is a floating menu that pops up when you click the right mouse button on a canvas or item. Pop-up menus are a relatively recent innovation in Windows but have a longer history in other windowing systems. These menus let you put behavior onto the objects in your application in a natural, accessible way. They let the user quickly fire off some action relevant to the location of the mouse in the application.

An *alert* is a special dialog box that displays a message with an icon and up to three buttons, such as OK and Cancel, Yes and No, or whatever. You can also specify one of these three buttons as the default button. You could build this as a window with a canvas, but the alert object lets you quickly put the dialog box together without going through all the fuss. There are three types of alert: Stop, Caution, and Note. These are the usual categories of simple messages that applications display.

An *editor* is a simple text-editor dialog box that lets you enter lines of text into a text item. The editor object lets you specify the window size, visual attributes, editor title, and other properties of the window. This lets you create editors with different appearances for different text fields.

Record Groups and LOVs

A *record group* is a special data structure that resembles a table, with rows and columns. A record group can be a query record group or a static record group. You define a query record group with a SQL SELECT statement. The SELECT list of the query gives the record group its column structure. You define a static record group with a column specification you enter through a special dialog box. There are several built-in subprograms that let you manipulate record groups at runtime. You can use record groups for LOVs (see the following paragraph and Chapters 4 and 6), for data parameters to pass records to reports or graphics displays (see Chapter 15), or as PL/SQL data structures.

TIP
A record group lets you retrieve data from the Database Server into client memory. You can then use the data just as though you were referring to a database table, but the table is in client memory. This makes access very fast and reduces network traffic. You can use record groups in this way to optimize applications.

An *LOV* (list of values) is a special dialog box that displays a record group and lets you choose a row of the group, returning a single value. You use an LOV as a way to choose from a specific set of values. You can, for example, associate an LOV with a text item both to provide an easier way to input values and to provide a list of values against which to validate the user's data entry. The autoselection feature lets the end user enter a string pattern to search automatically for an item in the list. Again, you could build this dialog box using standard windows and canvases, but the LOV object gives you a shortcut and a way to get LOV behavior in fields automatically without any programming. The LOV Wizard simplifies this and lets you use the Query Builder to create the SQL query for the LOV values. Chapter 4 shows you how to use LOVs in forms.

Reusable Objects

Under the rubric of "reusable objects," this section summarizes several objects that you use to structure your application components. These objects apply equally to form and menu modules, and some of them (attached libraries and program units) apply to library modules as well.

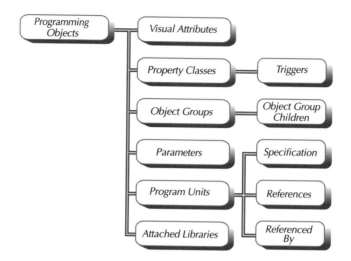

A *named visual attribute* is a collection of display properties such as font or background and foreground colors attached to an object (item, canvas, data block). You can refer to these visual attribute objects from other objects. If you do so, the properties of the visual attribute override the properties of the object. If you change a property in the visual attribute, the property changes in all the objects that inherit the property from the visual attribute.

The *property class* is a set of object properties—any object properties—aimed at being attached to an object. Just as with a visual attribute, when you attach a property class to an object, you get all the properties of that class that make sense for the kind of object you are defining. Again, when you change the property class, the objects to which the property class is attached may or may not inherit these new values depending on whether the property value has been overridden at the object level.

You can create subclasses from property classes, or you can subclass any other object. This feature lets you add new attributes or methods to the object or change the ones it already has.

The *object group* lets you package your reusable objects for later copying or subclassing. An object group collects a set of objects in the module under a single heading. By copying or subclassing the object group, you get all the objects it contains. You can group any objects down to the block level, but you cannot group items within a block; you have to include the entire data block in the object group.

The *object library* is a module that lets you collect reusable sets of objects by dragging them to the library module and dropping them. To reuse an object in an object library, you open the library and drag the object into your application and drop it. The library lets you organize the objects in one or more tab folders. An object library can include individual objects, such as blocks, windows, alerts, property classes, and so on, but also object groups.

Chapter 10 explains the details of named visual attributes, property classes, object groups, and object libraries. It also shows you how to use them effectively to build reusable components and to impose standard sets of properties on your applications.

A *parameter* is a form, menu, report, or display data object that you define at the level of the module. You can use the parameter as a variable in any PL/SQL program unit in the scope of the module. A parameter has a data type, a default initial value, and a maximum length. You can set a parameter by passing in a value when you start up the form, either by putting the parameter on the command line (PARAM="value") or by passing the parameter in a parameter list (see Chapter 15).

The *program units* of a module are the PL/SQL packages, procedures, and functions you define in the scope of that module. All the Developer modules permit you to define program units as part of the module. The library module is somewhat special: it packages the program units as a module and makes them available to other modules through the *attached-library* object. This is a reference to a library you have defined as a module. You can call any program unit the module defines from PL/SQL in that module; you can also call any program unit in a library you have attached to the module. You cannot call any program unit defined in other modules or libraries that you have not attached.

Each subprogram program unit shows its *specification* (the procedure or function parameters, or function return type). Each package program unit shows its *subprograms* (the package subprograms). Each program unit also shows what program units the unit refers to (References objects), and which program units refer to the current one (Referenced By objects). Chapter 12 explains the details of program units (packages, procedures, and functions).

The Menu Module

The menu module is much simpler than the form module, as you can see:

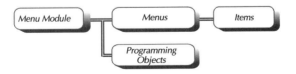

It consists of a set of programming objects (the same ones the preceding section describes) and a set of menus. Each menu in turn consists of a set of items. Chapter 6 shows you how to customize menus in detail.

Menu items can be plain items, or they can be one of several special menu item formats:

- *Check:* A menu item with a check mark beside it; these items let you enable and disable options through menus instead of through dialog boxes

- *Radio:* A menu item that is one of a group of mutually exclusive options; if you select one, you deselect the others

- *Separator:* A do-nothing menu item that separates other items, usually a space or a line on the menu

- *Magic:* A special menu item for a platform, such as Cut, Copy, Paste, Undo, or Help

Each menu item has a command that Developer executes when you choose the item. This can be one of several things:

- *Null:* Does nothing; a separator must have a null command.

- *Menu:* The menu displays a submenu.

- *PL/SQL:* The menu executes a PL/SQL block, including Run_Product and Host, to execute other Developer programs or operating system commands.

You can also associate a menu item with one or more security roles. Chapter 10 gives details on security and menus.

The Library Module, Built-in Packages, and Database Objects

Several of the objects you see in Developer appear in all the components: library modules, built-in packages, and database objects.

The library module is quite simple compared to other modules. It consists only of a set of program units and a set of attached libraries. See Chapter 12 for details on libraries and on the program units they contain. You can store libraries in the file system or in the database, as with any module. This is the structure for library modules:

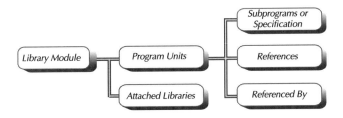

All the Developer builders have access to a series of built-in PL/SQL packages, though the packages differ with each product. These packages give you a broad array of tools for manipulating the modules and other objects in that component (Forms, Reports, or Graphics). Each package has a specification that lists the subprograms in the package along with their specifications (parameters and function returns). Each package has extensive documentation in the product reference manual, and you should consult that documentation to see package types and exceptions, as well as the details of using the different subprograms.

Also, all the builders let you access the objects in the database to which you connect. The following diagram shows the object hierarchy for the database objects. The builders list all the users in the database. For each user, you can see the accessible stored program units, libraries, tables, and views. You only see the ones that you can access through the user name with which you logged on. For example, if you log on as a user who does not have privileges to use a particular table, you will not see that table listed among the database objects. Libraries are library modules you store in the database as opposed to the file system.

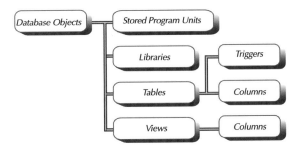

Tables also show the *database triggers* for the table. These triggers are PL/SQL blocks that execute when a particular event occurs in the database, such as an

INSERT or DELETE. Although similar to the triggers in Developer code, database triggers respond to database events rather than to application events. Tables and views also show their columns, with data types.

You can create stored program units by dragging program units from other modules into the database objects section for stored program units. This lets you move the processing for that subprogram or package into the database, permitting you to develop multiple-tier architectures. You can often improve performance or reliability by moving code in this way.

Reports

The Reports component of Developer is the part of the development environment in which you develop reports modules. You can refer to external query objects, and you can set and store debugging objects in this environment. The Report Builder also includes libraries and database objects.

A report module has a complex structure, as shown in Figure 2-3. The basic components of a report are its data model, parameter form, report triggers, and layout. Chapter 7 describes the different features of the report module. It can also have program units and attached libraries, as discussed in the section "Reusable Objects," earlier in this chapter.

The report *data model* is the structure of data and its different representations in the report. You create the data model in a special graphical editor.

Parameter objects are module variables that you can refer to in PL/SQL code and anywhere else that accepts data values as input. *System parameters* are the parameters that Reports defines automatically; user-defined parameters are those you define. You have a default form for setting parameters at runtime, or you can create a completely different one as a *parameter form* object in the report. The Reports runtime program runs this form when you run the report to prompt the user to set the parameters you specify. Chapter 10 goes into detail on report parameters, default parameter forms, user-defined parameter forms, and all the ways you can use parameters to make your report reusable.

A *query* is a SQL statement that returns the data values that are the basis for the report. You can embed the query in the report, or you can use an *external query* object: this is simply SQL text in a separate file that you can share between applications. The *group* identifies the records the queries return as a repeating group of records in the report, and there is a hierarchy of groups that represents the nesting of records within each other. The *database columns* are the columns from the query SELECT list. The *formula columns* are special columns you compute using PL/SQL blocks. The *summary columns* are special columns that accumulate summary information for multiple records in the report, such as subtotals or grand totals. These columns go in a group at a higher level than the records they summarize. The *placeholder columns* are columns you define to fill in from a trigger, formula, or

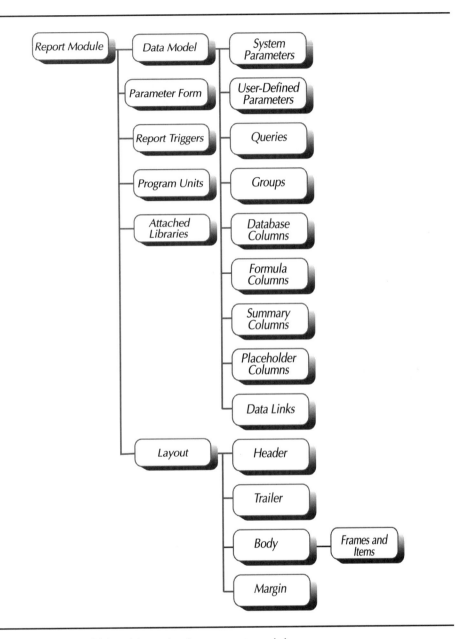

FIGURE 2-3.   *Object hierarchy for a report module*

user exit instead of from data or standard summarization. For example, you can derive special report fields that report the region with the highest sales among a set of regional rows. The *data links* are links you use in master-detail reports (see Table 2-3) to link one group of rows to another group of rows.

The *layout* of the report is its graphical structure. The *header* pages come first, followed by the *body* pages, followed by the *trailer* pages. The report margin is the area on the page outside the text boundaries of the header, trailer, and body. The body contains all the repeating frames and report items that graphically structure the data model into a formatted report. The header and trailer contain whatever data elements or boilerplate make sense preceding and following the body, respectively. You can manipulate most of these objects through the Live Previewer, which hides the messy details of the object structure in a user-friendly interface for report formatting.

There are several varieties of report layout, as Table 2-3 summarizes. Each layout may have specific requirements for the accompanying data model.

Chapter 4 gives an introduction to creating data models and layouts for reports, which Chapter 7 continues in more detail. Each layout has options that let you do an amazing number of things with the relatively few basic report layouts. The Report Wizard helps you to build these reports through a series of interactive dialogs.

The *report triggers* are blocks of PL/SQL code that execute at well-defined points: before the report, after the report, between the pages, before the parameter

Report Layout Type	Description
Tabular	The default, this structures a series of rows of data with a repeating column heading on each page
Master-Detail	Structures two or more groups into related, nested sets of rows; the purpose is to display a set of rows for each row of the outer group
Form	Structures data like a form, with one row of data formatted onto several lines, with labels to the left of the individual fields
Form Letter	Intermixes boilerplate text with fields of data, with each row from the data model repeating the boilerplate; the purpose is to generate multiple copies of the form, one for each row
Mailing Label	Prints repeating groups of fields in fixed-size boxes on each page
Matrix	Better known as a crosstab report, this displays a grid of data with row and column headings

TABLE 2-3. *Report Layouts in Developer*

form, and after the parameter form. There are other triggers in reports, but these are not separate, named objects the way they are in forms. You access these triggers through the items that own them. Chapter 5 details the way report triggers fire and the specifics of how to write them.

The Report Builder also integrates debugging information into the objects available. It lets you create debug actions (breakpoints that you can set in your PL/SQL code) that persist between debugging sessions. It also contains a representation of the calling stack you see at runtime. See Chapter 13 for details on debugging reports and using these objects in the PL/SQL debugger.

Graphics

The Graphics component of Developer is the part of the environment in which you develop display modules. A display module may be one or more charts you derive from database data, or it may contain any combination of graphic elements with or without reference to the database. You can use display modules strictly for business graphics display of data, or you can use them as a graphics drawing tool, or both.

As you can see in Figure 2-4, the structure of a graphics display is simple in object terms. A display module contains a layout, sets of templates, queries,

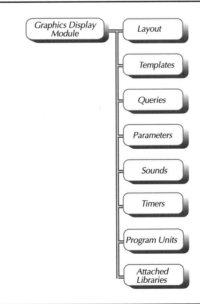

FIGURE 2-4. *Object hierarchy for a graphics display module*

parameters, sounds, and timers, and the same program units and attached library objects that the other modules contain.

The layout contains the graphic elements of the display in a hierarchy that represents their relationships. It also relates those elements to the columns of a query. Several specific types of chart are available as part of the Graphics product, as Table 2-4 shows.

A *chart template* is a customized set of options that lets you build several charts with identical formatting, possibly in the same display. For example, you could build a series of pie charts that all use one template to make them consistent. Chapter 10 has details on how to build templates that let you reuse chart definitions.

A query, as in a report module, is a SQL SELECT statement that defines a set of data to display as a chart. You construct the query to return the data in exactly the format you want to chart. For example, the pie chart does not summarize the data for the slices; you must use a GROUP BY and a SUM function to do this. Chapter 4 shows you how to build a query of this kind.

Chart Type	Description
Column	Shows data groups as vertical bars
Pie	Shows data groups as slices of a circular pie
Bar	Shows data groups as horizontal bars
Table	Shows data values in a tabular format
Line	Shows data values as a line relating x and y values
Scatter	Shows data values as points relating x and y values
Mixed	Shows data values as both points and a line relating x and y values
High-Low	Shows each data element as a combination of three values: high, low, and close; you can use this to display stock market prices, for example
Double-Y	Shows two y-axis data values for each x-axis value, with both the scales showing; you can use this to display two variables that differ over time, for example
Gantt	Shows horizontal bars that represent start and end values; usually represents a schedule, with the x-axis representing time and the y-axis representing the set of tasks in the schedule

TABLE 2-4. *Chart Types for a Graphics Display*

The parameters, as for reports, are module variables that you define and use throughout the module in PL/SQL code. You can set the parameters on the command line or through passing a parameter list from another program such as Forms or Reports. Chapter 10 has the details.

Besides visual elements, your displays can also integrate sound objects to create full multimedia displays.

A special timer object in graphics displays acts as a kind of alarm clock for the display. You specify an interval of time at the end of which the timer executes some PL/SQL code. You can achieve all kinds of special effects with timers.

The Graphics Builder also integrates the same kind of debugging information that the Report Builder does. It lets you create debug actions—breakpoints that you can set in your PL/SQL code that persist between debugging sessions. It also contains a representation of the calling stack you see at runtime. Chapter 14 gives details on debugging graphics displays and using these objects in the PL/SQL debugger.

The Nuts and Bolts

Each object, taken by itself, is a powerful contribution to building your applications. Developer is more than just the objects it comprises, however. It is a system that glues together all of these objects into a working whole. Not only do all these objects work together, but you can also work with objects from other applications and with data from database managers other than Oracle.

The primary glue for Developer is PL/SQL, the programming language you use in triggers, program units, and other program objects in Developer. By accessing items and parameters (or even global data), PL/SQL is what makes things happen, binding together all the objects. Using the built-in subprograms for each component of Developer, you can manipulate the objects in the other components:

- Embedding graphics displays in reports and forms

- Passing form or report data to graphics

- Producing reports from graphics displays or forms

- Reading parameter values from graphics displays into a form

Specific subprograms in each component let you interact with things outside the standard Oracle and Developer environment. You can use the Host procedure to call other programs through the operating system command interface. On the Windows platform, you can use OLE2, ActiveX controls, and DDE to manipulate objects from other applications. You can also use the Open Client Adapter to access database managers other than Oracle, using ODBC drivers for those database managers. You may use these to replace Oracle entirely, both in the design environment and in the runtime environment. Or you can develop under Oracle but use another database manager in your runtime environment, letting users keep their data in a SQL Server, Sybase, or Informix database, for example.

All of these options make Developer a strong environment for developing well-structured, robust, and open Internet applications. Parts II and III of this book go into detail on how to prototype, design, code, test, debug, and deploy applications to end users. Part IV gives you a complete reference to all the different objects you can use in your Developer applications.

PART
II

A Tutorial for Oracle
Developer

CHAPTER

3

Databases, Forms, and Reports Working Together

his first chapter in Part II prepares the way for the tutorials in the next few chapters. It sets up the database the tutorials use and then gives you an introduction to some of the rules for setting up forms, reports, and graphics in Oracle Developer.

Setting Up Talbot's Database and Applications

Before we create the database, let's look at some history. Talbot's farm, a historic and not necessarily apocryphal venture in New Hampshire, was a working farm at the turn of the century. The farm was in a rural area of southwestern New Hampshire near the towns of Keene and Edmeston. A previous book (*ORACLE: The Complete Reference*, by George Koch and Kevin Loney, Osborne/McGraw-Hill, 1996) used Talbot's farm as part of its set of examples. The example suits the needs of a Developer tutorial very well.

The example came from an old ledger book found by George Koch, with entries dating from 1896 through 1905 (Figure 3-1). This book was the general ledger for Dora Talbot's farm, kept by (possibly) her son, George B. Talbot.

This ledger contained sales and purchases, laborers paid, and materials bought: all the transactions of a working business in serial form. It also contained other useful information, such as a list of the addresses of the casual laborers who worked on the farm.

This ledger struck George Koch as a fine example of how people kept books before there were relational databases—and as an illustration of the similarities between old-fashioned ledger entries and those in current relational databases. He used the ledger as an example of a small but essential relational database that would support a small business. The ledger could easily be a relational table, as could the table of addresses. The original database provided a coherent example for how to write SQL; this book takes this idea a step further and uses Talbot's ledger to develop applications with Oracle Developer.

ORACLE: The Complete Reference was not really concerned with the tasks of developing applications, just with teaching SQL and Oracle. The examples in that book, although perfectly useful, did not adhere to the process and design suggestions this book advocates. So, here you'll see a more complete version of the Talbot database, with full integrity constraints, that will serve as a comprehensive example for the suggestions in this book.

This book also takes the liberty of extending the anachronism to make something out of Talbot's farm that it was not: an expanding, modern business with expanding, modern data processing needs. The Talbot operation may deal in cows and hire people to dig graves or shoe horses, but this book sees it as an example of

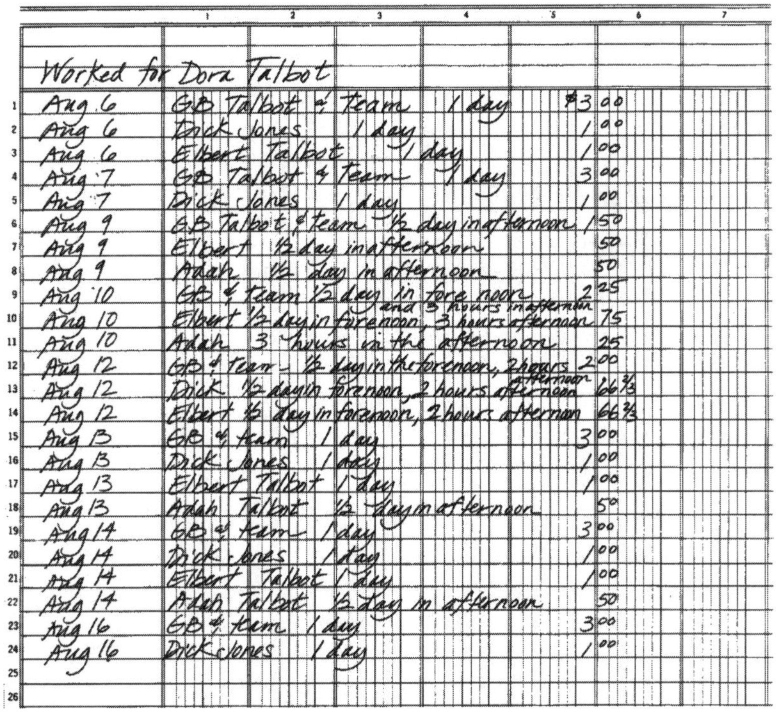

Worked for Dora Talbot

1	Aug 6	GB Talbot & Team 1 day	$3	00
2	Aug 6	Dick Jones 1 day	1	00
3	Aug 6	Elbert Talbot 1 day	1	00
4	Aug 7	GB Talbot & Team 1 day	3	00
5	Aug 7	Dick Jones 1 day	1	00
6	Aug 9	GB Talbot & team ½ day in afternoon	1	50
7	Aug 9	Elbert ½ day in afternoon		50
8	Aug 9	Adah ½ day in afternoon		50
9	Aug 10	GB & team ½ day in fore noon and 3 hours in afternoon	2	25
10	Aug 10	Elbert ½ day in forenoon, 3 hours afternoon		75
11	Aug 10	Adah 3 hours in the afternoon		25
12	Aug 12	GB & Team – ½ day in the forenoon, 2 hours afternoon	2	00
13	Aug 12	Dick ½ day in forenoon, 2 hours afternoon		66 ⅔
14	Aug 12	Elbert ½ day in forenoon, 2 hours afternoon		66 ⅔
15	Aug 13	GB & team 1 day	3	00
16	Aug 13	Dick Jones 1 day	1	00
17	Aug 13	Elbert Talbot 1 day	1	00
18	Aug 13	Adah Talbot ½ day in afternoon		50
19	Aug 14	GB & team 1 day	3	00
20	Aug 14	Dick Jones 1 day	1	00
21	Aug 14	Elbert Talbot 1 day	1	00
22	Aug 14	Adah Talbot ½ Day in afternoon		50
23	Aug 16	GB & team 1 day	3	00
24	Aug 16	Dick Jones 1 day	1	00
25				
26				

FIGURE 3-1. *Sample page from Talbot's ledger*

a modern corporate farm looking toward the next century—whatever century that might be. Talbot's is growing, and its customers and suppliers are all over the world now, requiring global approaches to global problems. Talbot's is expanding into Internet access. So, suspend historical disbelief and let Talbot's illustrate how to use Oracle Developer effectively in your own business; with any luck, it will survive. (Just make sure to hide away at least one of your Oracle Developer applications for discovery in 2095 for use as an example of organic or quantum databases, or whatever technology they'll have then.)

Talbot's Requirements

Any database application project starts with requirements from the users of the application system. Talbot's requirements center on two clusters of query and maintenance functions: the ledger and the list of people who work at Talbot's along with their addresses and skills.

NOTE
In the real world, the requirements process would uncover many, many possible requirements beyond these. The ins and outs of requirement definition are beyond the scope of the tutorials and reference material in this book. The material in this chapter provides a sample of the kind of requirements and data you would see in a real system, but only enough to present the various tutorials in the next few chapters. Also, an enterprise-wide development process would use more complex requirements definition technology such as FHD diagrams in Oracle Designer. See Chapter 15 for a basic description of Oracle Designer and its use with Oracle Developer.

The first step is to assess the feasibility of the project. With the limited set of requirements and the focus of the requirements on a central database, there is every reason to believe that a straightforward Developer database application system will fully satisfy Talbot's requirements. There do not appear to be any unusual technological requirements, so Oracle Developer (an enterprise tool capable of building very large systems) can easily handle the requirements.

The next step is to get a problem statement. The short answer to this need is the ledger book illustrated in Figure 3-1, which contains the data and business logic developed during several years of keeping Talbot's books. Though the technology is different, this book represents what Talbot's sees as its current requirements for information processing. Why change something that works? Talbot's Farm is not standing still; they are in the midst of a rapid expansion into the agricultural industry, acquiring farms and agricultural processing businesses to expand their global reach. A manual ledger system works for a single farm, but not for a global farming enterprise. The problem, therefore, is to automate the manual ledger system to support an enterprise resource planning approach with much greater capacity than the current system. What are some of the specific pieces of this new system?

Talbot's needs to maintain and use a database that contains cash transactions: amounts of goods bought and sold, hours of labor paid for, and amounts received. Talbot's needs to maintain and use a database that lists the people who work at Talbot's and their addresses and skills. How does this translate into functions? This section gives you some idea of the kind of requirements that a company such as Talbot's would have and what kind of information you need to get. The process followed here is not as exhaustive as a real requirements analysis.

An initial guess might be that ledger transactions are central to the database. In a way, that's true; Talbot's cares very much about keeping track of amounts spent and received. However, if you probe more deeply, you begin to realize the importance of the people involved in both the transactions and the personnel applications. People tie together the financial and human resource sides of the system. An early decision was to represent people in a central way, putting laborers together in a single table with people who have entered into transactions with Talbot's.

First let's list the functions our software application will need to address.

- *Function:* To represent all the people and organizations with which Talbot's interacts in a central list available to accounting and personnel for query and maintenance.

  For this function, it is essential for this list to be available to both accounting and personnel. It also is essential that anyone with whom Talbot's does monetary business be on the list. It is desirable that the application make it easy to correct mistakes in the list.

- *Function:* To track all monetary transactions that involve Talbot's, including the kind of transaction (bought, sold, paid, received), description of the item, the number of units, the rate for each unit, and the amount of the transaction. This information must be available for query and must be available for auditing.

  To enable auditing, it is essential that all transactions exist in the database and that corrections are separate transactions. It is essential that no transaction change or disappear at any time for any reason. It is desirable for the application to calculate the amount of the transaction automatically from the quantity and rate. It is desirable for the user to be able to sort queried transactions by any data element.

- *Function:* To maintain a list of the addresses of the laborers for contact and payment purposes.

  It is essential that addresses be current and correct. It is desirable to be able to produce mailing labels for all laborers.

- *Function:* To maintain a list of the skills and competencies of the laborers for work assignment purposes.

  It is desirable that all laborers have skill entries and that each entry evaluates their competence at that skill.

There is also a deployment requirement: the applications must be available to a global network of farms and subsidiaries of Talbot's Farm. The IT department at Talbot's believes that deploying the applications through the company's intranets and through the global Internet would satisfy the need for a wide area network. Therefore, all the applications developed must be suitable for deployment on the Internet.

Now, given these requirements, you can proceed to designing your database.

A Sample Database

Without a database design, you will find it difficult to visualize the forms, reports, and graphics, because they all reflect the basic purpose of Oracle Developer: allowing the end users to manipulate database information. A database design states the problem in a clear, formal statement that you will find essential in defining your forms, reports, and graphics. Having a sample database also makes developing a working prototype much easier.

Appendix A has the complete database with data definition statements and all the data. This section explains the database design and gives you what you need to interpret the SQL and data in the following chapters.

Figure 3-2 shows the Unified Modeling Language (UML) diagram that defines the Talbot database. If you have never seen a UML class diagram before, here are the graphical conventions:

- *Classes* (the boxes) represent the tables in the database, with the rows in the table representing the object of the class. The class name appears in the top section; the class properties appear in the bottom section.

- *Associations* (the lines) represent the relationships between classes; some associations also represent database tables (many-to-many associations and associations with their own properties, for example). The little black diamond on the association from Address to Lodging represents ownership (*composite aggregation* is the formal UML term): a Lodging row owns an Address row, so if you delete a Lodging row, you must also delete the Address row.

- *Properties* (the text in the boxes) represent the data properties of the objects.

- *Roles* (the names on each side of an association line) represent the role the class plays in the association.

- *Role multiplicity* (the 1 and * labels) represents the number of objects, one or many, that relate to the other entity in the relationship.

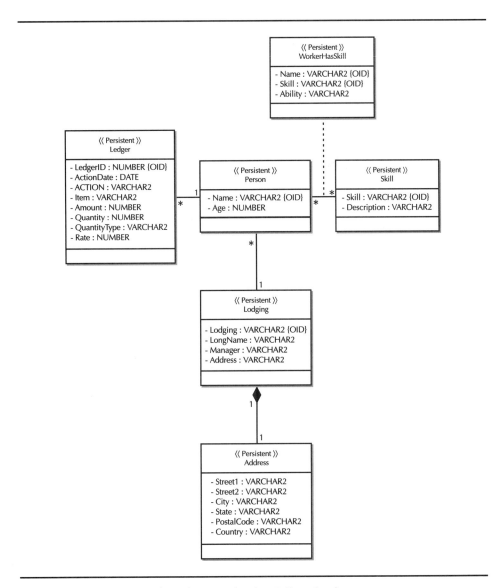

FIGURE 3-2.   *UML class diagram for the Talbot database*

There are five classes of object:

- *Ledger:* The entries in the ledger, each object referring to a single transaction of some kind, identified by a unique number (the Ledger ID)

- *Person:* The people that Talbot deals with, identified by name

- *Lodging:* The place where certain people live, identified by lodging name

- *Address:* The postal mail information for the lodging

- *Skill:* A person's skill, identified by skill name

There are four associations in the model:

- *refers to:* Relates a ledger entry to a person; the ledger entry refers to the person as the seller or buyer or payee or payor

- *lives at:* Relates a person to a lodging; the person lives at the lodging

- *has address:* Relates a lodging to a postal mail address

- *worker has skill:* Relates a person to one or more skills and a skill to one or more people; has a single attribute, Ability, that represents the ability of the worker with respect to the skill, a *relationship attribute*

The first two associations are optional one-to-many relationships. A ledger entry refers to exactly one person, and you can refer to a person by more than one ledger entry. A person lives at a single lodging, and a lodging may have more than one person living at it. In a relational database, the person row contains a foreign key column relating it to the lodging, and the ledger row contains a foreign key column relating it to the person. In an object-relational database, you can either have foreign keys or references (REF columns) linking the rows. See Appendix A for complete schema information for both approaches.

The third relationship is a required one-to-one relationship. A lodging has exactly one address, and each address applies to exactly one lodging. In a relational database, you would most likely move the columns from Address into the Lodging table. In an object-relational database, you would create an Address type and a column of that type in the Lodging type. See Appendix A for complete schema information for both approaches.

The fourth relationship is an optional many-to-many relationship. A person may have several skills, and a skill may apply to more than one person. The skills apply only to people who are workers—a fact that this particular database does not represent because it detracts from the clarity of the example.

Transforming this to a relational or object-relational database requires the following steps:

1. Create one table or object type for each entity (Ledger, Person, Lodging, Address, and Skill tables), creating the columns from the attributes and giving them the primary key columns (Ledger ID, Name, Lodging, Lodging, and Skill, respectively).

2. Create one table or object type for each many-to-many relationship (Worker Has Skill), creating any columns (Ability) and giving the table the primary key of the two primary keys of the entities that participate in the relationship (Name and Skill from Person and Skill, respectively).

3. Add a column for each one-to-many relationship to the table on the many side of the relationship that refers to the primary key on the one side (Person in the Ledger table referring to the Person table, Lodging in the Person table referring to the Lodging table), either with a standard foreign key for a relational database or with a reference (REF) column for an object-relational database.

4. For one-to-one relationships between tables, the transformation is a little involved. First, decide which of the two tables is the owner of the relationship. For example, in the sample Talbot database, the lodging owns the address (that's what the little black diamond in Figure 3-2 means). To create the relational Lodging table, you move the columns from Address into the Lodging table, and you have no separate Address table. To create an object-relational version of this structure, you create Lodging and Address object types, then create a LodgingAddress column in the Lodging table of type Address.

In this sample database, these rules are sufficient to create the relational or object-relational database. In a more complex database, there are some additional things to worry about, such as relationships with more than two entities, and one-to-many relationships with attributes. There are also more constraints to worry about, and the data types to consider, as well. See my book *Database Design for Smarties* (Morgan Kaufmann, 1999) for a full discussion of these issues.

If you look at the SQL in Appendix A, you will see that it creates an additional object: a sequence. Oracle provides the ability to declare a *sequence,* which is a tool that generates a unique integer in series. Talbot's database uses this sequence to generate the Ledger IDs in the INSERT statements for the Ledger table. If it were a requirement for Talbot's to be portable to other database managers, the database would not contain this sequence, as it is nonstandard. You could not depend on having the CREATE SEQUENCE statement or the NEXTVAL pseudo-column to return the next sequence number. Talbot's has made a major commitment to use only Oracle, so it can take full advantage of the many nonstandard features of the Oracle database manager.

NOTE
If you're interested in using UML to design databases, please consult my book Designing Databases for Smarties: Using UML to Design Databases *(Morgan Kaufmann, 1999) or Paul Dorsey's book,* Oracle8 Design Using UML Object Modeling *(Oracle Press, 1999). The Oracle Designer tool now supports UML for schema definition, so you should also consult* The Designer/2000 Handbook *by Dorsey and Koletzke (Oracle Press, 1998).*

Oracle Developer Project Management

Before doing anything else, you should set up a project using the Project Builder component of Oracle Developer.

Creating a Project with Project Builder

The Project Builder is a component of the Oracle Developer tool set. It lets you organize your files into projects and gives you the tools you need to manage them.

For Talbot's system, we will set up two projects, one for the Ledger system and one for the Worker Skills system. Deciding your project boundaries depends on many factors, including the timing of the applications, how your organization allocates people to the tasks, how much new software development gets shared between projects, and so on. We'll assume that these two applications are separate, one being developed by the Information Services (IS) group for Financial Services, and the other being developed within Human Resources at Talbot Farms.

1. To create a project, your best bet is the Project Wizard. Double-click on the Project Builder icon to see the following dialog box:

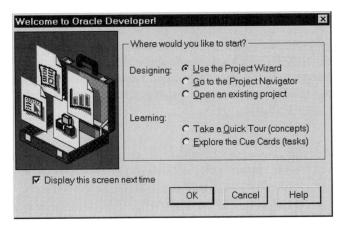

2. Click on OK to start the Project Wizard. After the welcome screen, you see a Wizard dialog box that prompts you to enter the name of the project registry file. This file contains all the information about your project files and dependencies between them. Enter a filename.

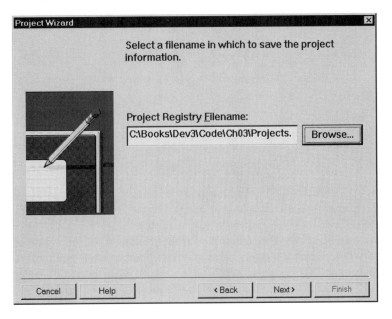

NOTE
When you have some projects defined, the Project Wizard will insert a screen that asks you whether you want to create a standalone project or a subproject. Using subprojects, you can build a hierarchy of projects that can increase your ability to manage changes across a whole range of related projects. You should experiment with this feature to see how it benefits your particular situation.

3. Click on Next. The next screen lets you enter a project title and the folder in which to save the project information. This is the folder that contains the Oracle Developer project registry, which in turn contains the information for all your projects. Enter the name of the folder.

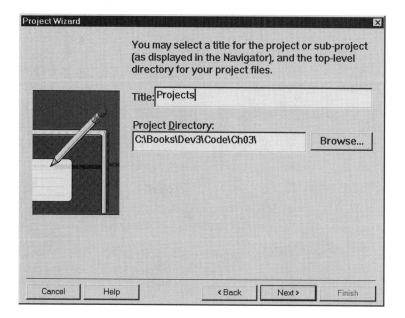

4. Click on Next. The Project Wizard now displays the Connection screen, which prompts for a connection to add to the project repository. A connection is an Oracle username, password, and service name that you will be using to connect through all the tools. A good choice is your

development database; in the case of the Talbot example, this is talbot, as this illustration shows:

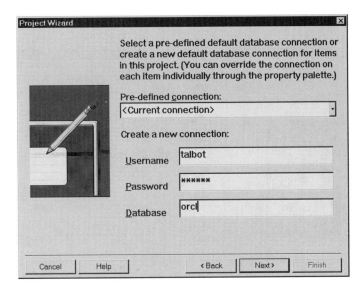

5. Click on Next. This action takes you to the next screen, which lets you put in the author's name (yours, the project manager's, or whomever) and the default connection for the project if any. You can also enter a comment describing the project here.

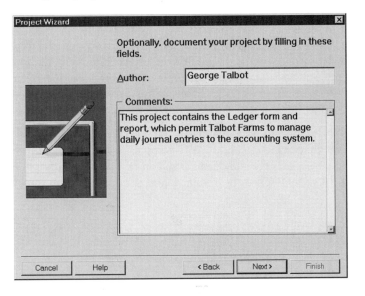

6. Click on Next to see the final Wizard screen. This one gives you three choices about what to put into the project: nothing, a set of files that you select from an Open dialog box, or all the files in the project folder you previously selected.

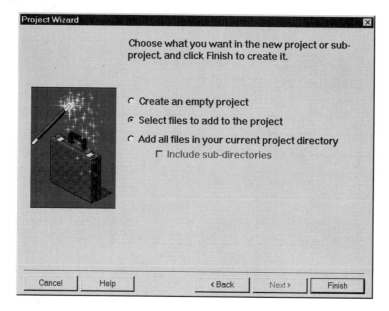

7. Click on Finish to create the project.

You can share files between projects by just adding the file to as many projects as you want. The project registry contains a link to the file; it doesn't copy or move the file under your project directory. All the files in your project can be anywhere you like—on the network, distributed around many different directories, or whatever. The project gives you a way to manage the files in one place even though they aren't in one place.

The Project Wizard now displays a standard file-opening dialog box that lets you choose files to add. We're going to find and select the standard object library and the standard PL/SQL library, which Talbot IS has created to hold standard application objects and code.

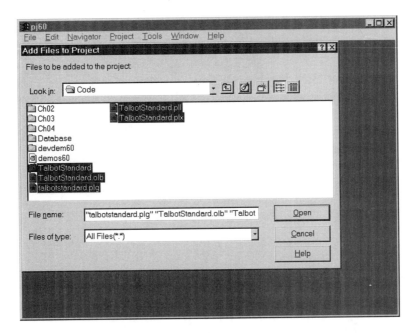

8. Click Open. The Project Builder now adds the files to the project. At this
point, you have a project ready and waiting for your new applications.

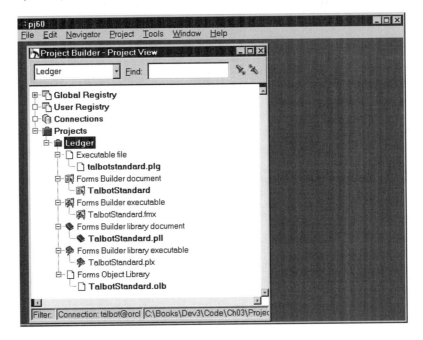

To add a second project, you just double-click the Projects node to start another session with the Project Wizard.

How the Project Builder Helps You

The Project Builder helps you manage your project in several ways:

- It lets you launch the various Builders, either by clicking on the Builder tool in the toolbar on the side of the Project Builder window or by double-clicking on a file you have previously created and added to the project.

- It lets you organize your files without constraining you by the directory structure of the underlying operating system. Files can be anywhere—on the network, on your hard disk, or anywhere else to which you have access.

- It provides an interface to your configuration management tools, such as PVCS, ClearCase, or Starteam.

- It lets you automate the creation of multiple files by giving you a way to specify which files depend on what other files. You can change a PL/SQL library, for example, and with one command, you can rebuild all the forms, reports, and displays that depend on code in that library.

- It automates the deployment process through the Deliver action, which you can program to do the appropriate things, such as zipping up the executables into a deliverable file.

- Because it is fully programmable, it lets you add file types and any kind of action for new and existing types, which means you can completely customize the environment to automate whatever you want. This book does not cover customization; see the Project Builder documentation for details.

Developing Forms

This section shows you how to approach the initial design for the various forms and reports based on the requirements.

The first form is the Ledger form, which addresses the ledger-related functionality. This form will serve the accounting department as the main interface to the ledger table. This form must accomplish the following tasks:

- The form must permit a bookkeeper to enter accounting transactions. Each transaction must have a date, an item description, an action, a quantity and its unit type, a rate, and an amount.

- The form must generate Ledger IDs to identify each transaction.

- The transaction must link to a person already present in the database through the name of the person.

- The form must calculate the value of the amount as the quantity multiplied by the rate.

- The form must prevent anyone from updating or deleting transactions in the database.

- The form must allow an accountant to retrieve the transactions using a query-by-example functionality.

- The form should allow ad hoc sorting of the transactions by the different data elements.

- The form must follow guidelines that make it suitable for Internet deployment.

The fields in the form represent the structure of the Ledger table in an accessible format. The first choice to make is whether to lay out the form to handle one transaction at a time or several. The maintenance requirements would indicate one transaction, whereas the query requirements would indicate multiple transactions. The single-transaction screen would have the fields distributed around the form window; the multiple-transaction screen would have a spreadsheet-style grid of fields and rows. In this case, the choice is to go with the multiple-transaction screen. This accommodates both query and maintenance in one form, because the size and shape of the spreadsheet can fit into the required window size. If there were more fields, or if the fields needed to be bigger, it might make sense to build two forms, one for query and one for maintenance.

You can satisfy the requirement for linking to people by creating a List of Values (LOV) dialog box or drop-down list on the Person field in the entry table.

The second form is the Enter Worker Skills form. This form shows the second major kind of form, the master-detail form. The function of this form is to maintain the database of laborer skills and to give managers a way to query those skills for individual workers. A reference report could also perform the latter part of the task; the following section gives an example in the Ledger Summary report.

Because of the diversity of requirements and the many-to-many association, the best solution is to maintain each table (Person, WorkerHasSkill, and Skill) in a separate form. The Person form will have the Person columns, the Skill form will have the Skill columns, and the WorkerSkill form will have the relationship columns (the keys from Person and Skill and the Ability column). In the WorkerSkill form, there is no need to include the person's age. Looking at the Skill and Description column values, the primary key is descriptive enough to serve as a short description for the WorkerSkill form. You probably do not need to display the Skill Description either. That leaves the Person Name, the Ability, and the Skill as the three fields to display on the form.

Because the form represents a relationship, you use the master-detail relationship to create a natural hierarchy for entry. The master record is read-only; you query it to find the person to whom you want to assign a skill. The detail records then link multiple skills to the person. You could also do this by having two List of Values dialog boxes or drop-down lists on the fields. That would mean displaying the same person multiple times, as well as allowing multiple people to get skills assigned at the same time, which seems confusing. The hierarchical arrangement is more natural, less confusing, and less complex to implement. It also looks simpler to the user, because the Person field by itself and the associated two-column table of skill information looks less complicated than a spreadsheet-style table of people and skill information would.

Other forms might include the Person form with a master-detail relationship to the Lodging table and the Skill form with a simple table for entering skills. It may be possible during the form design to combine these into a more general purpose human resources form that lets Talbot managers manipulate all the person-related information with multiple master-detail relationships to Person. This form could simplify its interface by using *tab canvases,* a user interface technique that lets you put several elements into a single view and move between them by clicking on folder tabs.

In the process of creating these forms, you begin to realize that you require standards to ensure that all the forms present a consistent interface to the users. Here are some examples:

- Each form represents a basic function. Use the form title to summarize this function, and put the title in the window title.

- Place scroll bars for data blocks on the right side of the block to conform to the usual format for scrolling windows.

- Use LOVs rather than drop-down lists to represent choice selection in multiple-row tables.

- Adhere to the user interface standards for font, prompt placement, and other visual features to produce the best result for Internet deployment of the form.

Developing Reports

Although the Ledger form is adequate for ad hoc querying of transaction data, the different users of the ledger information need a more accessible accounting that summarizes the information in the ledger. This calls for a report rather than a form, although the distinction is a fine one. Generally, you use reports when you want to query information from the database in a standard format, but there is no need to allow manipulation of the data (changing it or adding new data, for example). Using Oracle Developer Server, you can deploy reports across the Internet as easily as you can deploy forms, so when users need up-to-date information through queries, think about reports, and when they need to add or change information, think about forms.

Looking at the current accounting reports done by Talbot's outside accountants, the Talbot designers can easily produce similar reports automatically without spending any more money on the yearly accounting audit than is necessary for verification of the numbers. Their accountants will no longer need to produce the reports (and to charge for producing the reports) that they need to do their work.

These reports summarize the ledger by the person affected by the transaction. The auditing accountants need to see the individual transactions by person, listed in chronological order, and a total for each person.

The accounts payable department pays workers at their home addresses. This indicates the need for a report because Personnel also wants the ability to mail company newsletters and other information to workers' home addresses. To do this, Talbot's needs to generate mailing labels from the Person and Lodging tables.

The only major decision you need to make for a mailing label report is the label size. Mailing labels now come in laser-printer sheets that contain a uniform layout of labels, usually in two or three columns per page. The Talbot Lodging Mailing Label report thus needs a layout showing how Personnel wants the names and lodging addresses to appear on the label pages. You might want to be able to specify the size of labels as a parameter to the report so that you can use the report with labels of different sizes.

Some Rules for Setting Up Forms and Reports

Forms and reports seem as natural to anyone in business as a book is to a reader. Anyone who has tried to write a book will tell you it is not quite so simple to write one as to read one. Form and report design is an art that requires much experience and thought about how people use these things. This section outlines some of the major principles and issues in designing Oracle Developer forms and reports, particularly if you are deploying them on the Internet or on your internal intranet.

There are five essential principles of design relevant to forms and reports:

- A form or report must convey information or *communicate* to the user in as efficient a manner as possible.

- A form or report must be *flexible* enough to adapt to the different needs, levels of experience, and levels of knowledge of its intended users.

■ A form or report must be as *simple* as possible, but no simpler (attributed to Albert Einstein in a slightly different context).

■ A form or report must *perform* to match the flow and speed of human response.

■ A form or report must provide *assistance* to its users through feedback at the appropriate level, help as necessary, and the ability to undo errors.

Most of these principles apply as much to paper forms and reports as they do to online forms and reports. Reference to a tax form (*any* tax form except perhaps for the ones with which you enclose a check) will demonstrate that the state of the art is nowhere near its acme. The following suggestions for design may help you see how to make your forms better. The best way to learn this sort of design is by studying some good design books, then doing it and observing how easy it is for your clients to use the results.

These three elements sum up form and report design: *understanding, learning,* and *cohesion.* The ability to understand the form or report promotes the passing of information and derives from the innate simplicity of the form or report. The ability to learn how to use a form or report stems from its flexibility, its simplicity, and the way the form or report renders assistance. How the report or form hangs together promotes information flow and performance, particularly by letting the user enter information quickly and reliably. These elements are all aspects of the interlocking design principles, each of which contributes its part in a broad system of user interaction.

Forms and reports are of course different in many ways, but the logic of their layout and design is quite similar. They differ in that forms are by nature interactive, whereas reports have a repetitive page structure, but otherwise, they are the same. The design elements here that pertain to data entry apply only to forms; the other elements apply both to reports and forms.

Communication

To communicate effectively, a form or report needs to present only the information required—no more and no less. To do this, you must first decide what exactly that information is and how the user will use it. You will sometimes find that by breaking up a requirement into two parts, you lose nothing in communication and gain in simplicity. This in turn improves communication by making it easier for the user to understand the information you are conveying.

There are several techniques for effective communication: minimize the use of jargon, use graphics when possible, use captions or labels, avoid redundancy, and be consistent.

Minimize Jargon

Avoid code words, acronyms, and malapropisms. Use plain English (or whatever your native language is) in both your form or report and in the data in your database. If you allow anyone to input data to the database, you will probably have to provide some kind of editing to render the input data into something that communicates well.

Use Graphics

Use pictures and graphics instead of text and tables if they communicate the right amount of information at the right level of presentation. The "Effectively Using Graphics" section in Chapter 8 provides a more detailed discussion.

Use Labels

Use captions or labels to give meaning to the data in your form or report. Some data or graphics may stand alone and communicate well, but this is rare. More often, you will find a few words in a caption will immediately communicate the purpose and nature of the picture or data to the user.

Minimize Redundancy

Check your form for any redundant information and minimize the number of paths that a user must follow to get data into or out of a form or report. Redundancy improves communication when it ensures the receipt of the whole picture; it obscures communication when it makes it difficult to absorb the information in a message. The length and complexity of the paths you must take to move data into a database or to understand the content of your report will often determine the level of communication. If you have to leave a trail of bread crumbs behind you, go back to the drawing board.

Add Variety Sparingly

Use difference sparingly to emphasize important data or instructions. Using a different font (boldface, for example, or a different point size or typeface) can distinguish a caption or label from the associated data, as can the graphical layout (beveled three-dimensional fields, for example). However, too much difference leads to increased complexity and a diminished ability to absorb information or learn relationships. Having many different typefaces, colors all over the place, or funny symbols and icons bouncing around the screen may entertain the user (briefly) but does not communicate effectively. Also, each platform has style requirements that limit the extent to which things can appear different, and being too different usually makes your application look out of place on platforms with conflicting styles.

Flexibility

Flexibility is the degree to which users with different needs can adapt your application to their intended use. Requirements do not constrain a *truly* flexible system. That is, it really does not matter what you intended users to be able to do; they can do whatever they want.

In the real world of the database application, things are too complex to permit true flexibility. You only get true flexibility with programming languages or other similar levels of complexity that are not options for most users. If you are willing to use C or COBOL, you can do anything you want, within certain limits. But an end user cannot do this because the skills are beyond his or her knowledge and capabilities.

The form or report provides a carefully structured, much less flexible interface for the end user. Within the limits of this careful structuring, however, you should try to give the user the ability to use the application flexibly.

The primary flexibility issue to consider is *experience*. What level of knowledge does your target user have, and does the application scale in usability as the user learns more about using it? Often, the levels of simplicity and helpfulness appropriate to less experienced or less knowledgeable users just get in the way of the experienced user. You should offer methods of helping the experienced user, such as the ability to turn off features, use direct entry as opposed to entry through accessing lists of possibilities, special keypresses, and so on. If you cannot do this through a single application, build more than one for the different levels of knowledge. Make them consistent so that when a new user becomes more experienced, he or she can quickly adapt to the experienced-user application.

The other major flexibility issue to consider is the potential for *different* paths through the network of possibilities. People view things differently, and you should try not to constrain people where it is not necessary to do so. If the order of entering information is unimportant, you should make it possible to enter data in any order. If there are several ways to enter a value (for example, a date in any of its multifarious formats), do not constrain the user to a single format just because you can easily check it for accuracy. Provide options so that different users can do things the way they want instead of the way you want.

Simplicity

By reducing complexity, you increase simplicity, and vice versa. There are many different principles that you can apply to reduce complexity:

- You can *hide* levels of complexity from the user in hierarchies of windows and dialog boxes.

- You can make the *common things* that the user needs to do simple and easy, even at the expense of making less common things hard.

- You can *limit* the number of elements in your interface using the limits on human cognitive ability as a guide (seven elements plus-or-minus two).

- You can make interface elements as *consistent* as possible to improve the ability of the user to perceive those elements.

- You can make the interface elements *cohesive*, grouping elements by consistent principles and keeping all data the user needs in one place.

- You can minimize *redundancy* and the *complexity* of paths, which also improves communication.

- You can use *standards* for layout and formatting to guide users to the right place, making it seem a natural process.

- You can automate data entry to improve reliability through validation and structured entry techniques (list of values, defaults, and intelligent triggers, for example).

Layout Standards

Your forms and reports should follow the natural layout conventions of the language and culture of the user. For English-speaking cultures, this means positioning the fields beginning at the upper left of the page or screen and continuing from left to right, top to bottom.

Forms should follow the layout standards that apply to the platform. For example, most graphical user interfaces place the form title in the top center of the window. Most platforms have a standard location for a scroll bar and a status bar, as well.

You should settle on a few major conventions for emphasis and use them sparingly in your layout. Remember that the more you emphasize, the less important your emphasized text will seem. Also, use different layout options to distinguish different elements of the form or report. Make captions and labels differ from data, and distinguish summaries and totals from the data they summarize.

Use mixed case (normal capitalization, just as you see in this sentence) in text; it is easier to read. You can use uppercase text in captions or labels, but this book advises against it. Keep text on one line in captions and titles. Avoid abbreviations and contractions.

Cohesion and Consistency

Keep your form and report layout cohesive by grouping elements and by balancing them on the screen or page.

Grouping elements lets you bind the elements together according to some principle. Choose your principle carefully, and then adhere to it consistently throughout your groupings to make your layout easily understandable:

- *Frequency*: Group your items by the frequency with which the user refers to them or enters them. Put the most frequently used items in the "first" location, such as the upper left for layouts in English.

- *Sequence*: If the items form a natural sequence of some kind, lay them out in the natural order according to the cultural sequence layout (left-to-right in English, for example).

- *Importance*: Place the more important items together.

- *Function*: Place the items that relate to a specific function together.

Balancing elements is a graphical device for making the user feel comfortable with the layout. Align fields and other items with one another for a regular, even appearance. Make fields of similar sizes despite varying requirements for actual text length. Having many fields of different sizes tends to distract the user by drawing the eye to different locations, diminishing the value of your grouping strategy. The exception to this is to use ragged text justification in multiple-line text fields if you have them. Having a ragged right margin is more readable with most computer text layouts. Imperfections in the use of proportional fonts can make justified text look silly, and the ragged-right appearance leaves more white space for the user's eye. Finally, make the center of your form or page the center of gravity of your fields and boilerplate text. This makes the layout more comfortable for the eye.

Automated Data Entry in Forms

You can automate form data entry almost endlessly with Oracle Developer, but there are some specific techniques that you should consider.

First, try to arrange your data entry fields in forms to promote reliability. You can use grouping strategies (see the previous section, "Cohesion and Consistency") to make entry a more natural process. You can also use validation (see Chapter 5) to provide immediate feedback on entered data.

Second, where possible, provide default values. Having the user press the ENTER key to accept a value is a lot more reliable and faster than any other kind of data entry. If you choose the defaults wisely, the user might need to enter just a few items, then save the entry.

Third, use lists of values to provide acceptable entries for inexperienced users. Oracle Developer makes it easy to associate a list dialog box with a field or to provide a drop-down list or combo box for entering values.

Fourth, use item triggers to make your fields more intelligent. One technique is to fill out different fields based on an entry in one field that precedes them. This works well with field-grouping strategies, for example. Another technique is to provide experienced users with shortcuts to entering values through intelligently interpreting the entry. For example, you can write reasonably generic code in PL/SQL that will take a few characters and look up a value in a table or record group. This kind of "quick-pick" approach appears increasingly in user interfaces and is not hard to do with elementary SQL WHERE clauses. You can extend this kind of thinking in many inventive ways to improve the speed and reliability of your data entry capabilities.

Performance

The basic standard for performance in a form or report is to match the speed and flow of the form or report with the human response.

Data entry in forms is a critical performance component. If you add much PL/SQL code in triggers that fire during navigation or validation events, make sure your performance matches human response. If users navigate out of a field, they should see results of validation in reasonably quick order. If you have performance issues with such triggers, try to move the offending code to commit processing or to a trigger that fires on explicit demand rather than automatically. Most users have lower performance expectations for the commit stage, and you can set expectations appropriately for on-demand actions through feedback messages. Considering the application as a whole, you should generally make delays predictable to the user. Making slight delays consistent is better than having many variable delays that the user cannot predict.

Query in forms is not really an issue because you can set the user's expectations. You should avoid certain situations if possible, however:

- When the user executes the Execute_Query function to query all the data instead of entering a query by example, the application should not go away for a long time. Construct your default query for a form so that it will retrieve a small set of data if possible. You can also use a pre-query trigger to add a query term to the query if it has none.

NOTE
Many platforms offer the capability of interrupting a query, such as by using CTRL-C in Windows or Windows 95. You may have to set an environment variable to do this; see your installation documentation for details.

■ Try to prevent the system from giving users an unreasonable or unclear response. Make sure your ad hoc query capabilities provide reasonable responses under most circumstances. Think about what will happen if the user adds a specific field to a query. Use a pre-query trigger to warn the user if there might be a slow response to the query.

Reports come in three varieties: interactive, ad hoc, and batch. *Interactive reports* use buttons to provide drill-down behavior that lets you make an interactive application out of a report. The performance of the navigation and display of the drill-down reports should match response expectations. *Ad hoc reports* are reports that you generate when you need them; again, performance on these reports should match expectations, generally requiring reasonably quick responses. *Batch reports* are things you fire off before you go home for the evening or through timer mechanisms available in your operating system. The only performance requirement for batch reports is that they not take longer than the period over which you repeat the reports. In other words, if you have a daily batch report, the report had better format and print in less than a day. Make sure you understand your requirements.

Assistance

The user almost always welcomes a helping hand in an application. You have several ways to do this. Most of the layout techniques in previous sections help by making it easier or more natural for the user to work with the form or report. But there are more specific things you can do to help out.

One of the most important things you can do in interactive forms is to give the user immediate *feedback* on the results of his or her actions. This means that there should be as little time as possible between the user's action and a message or response. Oracle Developer usually provides basic feedback, telling you when it is working or doing something with the database. You can go far beyond this default behavior. Two specific areas that you should consider are validation and performance feedback.

If the user takes some action that results in an error condition, you should inform the user of the error immediately. Sometimes this is harder than it might appear. For example, if the user violates security by changing data without privileges to do so, Oracle Developer will not automatically catch the error until you commit and send the data to the server. You can use various options and techniques to move the feedback closer to the action; Chapter 9 describes this in more detail. Make sure your application always confirms or invalidates the result of a user's action to the user. You can rely on Oracle Developer to do this for the most part, but you may need to go further in certain cases.

You should always provide enough information to the user online to enable him or her to understand what is happening. Oracle Developer gives you extensive *help* capabilities on almost every object you can think of, such as tool tips on items.

Make use of them. If you can, interpret common errors for users rather than just giving them the raw error messages. Provide online documentation for your application using any of the commonly available help or interactive document tools.

Finally, *you* need to understand clearly how the user can undo mistakes. The best techniques for dealing with mistakes prevent them in the first place—that is the purpose of validation and reliability techniques. However, few applications achieve the peak of never permitting the user to make a mistake. If they did, they would probably be unusable. Make sure you understand how the user can correct an error; then make it clear to the user.

Oracle Developer applications use transaction management to finalize changes in the database. Up to the point of committing data, you can correct any problems; after committing, you need to change the data in the database. Provide the user with tools for identifying and correcting problems in the database if there are any necessary holes in your consistency and integrity strategy.

This chapter has taken you through the initial steps of building an application and has given you some basic guidelines about what works and what does not. It also introduced you to the Talbot Farms example and used it to illustrate the first steps in building your application. The next chapter moves you into the first tutorial.

CHAPTER

4

Forms, Reports, and Graphs Basics

ou have now laid the basis for developing your first application. Using the Oracle Developer Builders and Layout Editors with the database that Chapter 3 created (see Appendix A), this chapter tutors you in generating the forms, reports, and graphics that satisfy the Talbot requirements. After creating the forms, you then create reports with the report Layout Editor and link them into the form through report objects. Then you can add graphs to illustrate the forms and reports.

It is simple to create forms and reports with a sophisticated appearance and even more sophisticated behavior. You can easily create form applications that let you display and manipulate data from the database with full data integrity. You can very easily create standard reports. You can create menus and connect them to forms, dialog boxes, and reports, and easily add basic graphs and charts to your application.

Getting even the simplest C or C++ program to do anything that you can do in Oracle Developer takes much more work. To bring in a cooking metaphor, this is the difference between cooking your basic meal (easy) versus cooking a gourmet meal (harder) versus raising the animals and growing the vegetables yourself, transforming them into food products (including documenting all the ways you did that), and then supervising the 16 line chefs needed to produce the meal in a restaurant (C++ programming—and that's *with* CASE tools!). If you have programmed with a programming language, you probably understand the point; if you have not, try it.

The difference is in the style of development. Oracle Developer emphasizes declarative application building over procedural coding. Many first-time users of Oracle Developer (and previous editions of this book) start out wondering when they're going to learn about all the coding techniques they need to know to make things work. There is a reason this book does not teach PL/SQL programming until Chapter 11: you don't need it to do 99 percent of the work you will do in building Oracle Developer applications. This chapter shows you how to build basic forms and reports, with graphics, without having to write any code at all (or at least not much). This, again, is the primary reason why Oracle Developer is a win-win tool: you win on productivity because you're not writing code, and you win on quality because you get tons of sophisticated tools to help you develop your applications.

NOTE
The Forms tool in particular makes many assumptions about what a database application looks like and how it behaves. If you want to lower your productivity and create work for your development and quality assurance teams, use different assumptions, whether from an aesthetic judgment or from a desire for increased performance. For example, trying to build forms that violate the way Forms handles transactions in its blocks; or building reports that look like spreadsheets, grid and all; or trying to develop a complicated, graphical application using Forms and Graphs: all of these are just likely to get you into trouble. Use Oracle Developer the way Oracle intended it, and you can reap large rewards in value and productivity. Most developers will find that Oracle Developer gives them the tools they need to do the job, and to do it quite satisfactorily.

The Chapter 3 section "Creating a Project with Project Builder" set up two projects, one for the WorkerSkill application and one for the Ledger application. This chapter works with both of those projects. The following tutorial assumes you are using the Project Builder as your main entry point into the development process. If you are not, you must start the Builders using the standard group of icons where the following sections tell you to click on the tool button for one of the tools.

A Forms Tutorial

This tutorial develops the WorkerSkill application from Chapter 3 that lets you associate skills with workers. There are many illustrations in this section that introduce the various tools; you can familiarize yourself with those tools by experimenting with them as you go.

After completing this tutorial, you will have learned these skills:

- How to launch the Form Builder
- How to set up your development environment with a standard object library
- How to connect to the database from the Form Builder
- How to build a form with the Data Block Wizard and the Layout Wizard
- How to use database tables and columns in your form
- How to build using a form layout
- How to build using a multirecord block layout with scroll bars
- How to build a master-detail form
- How to create a drop-down list for data entry in a form
- How to use the tools of the Layout Editor to adjust the form layout
- How to use SmartClasses from a standard object library to format form objects
- How to save a form to a module file or to the database
- How to add your form to the Project Builder Projects tree
- How to compile your form into a runtime module
- How to run your form

Launching

The first thing you must do is to start up the development environment in which you will build the form.

1. Launch the Form Builder by clicking on the icon in the Project Builder launcher.

   The Builder displays a Welcome dialog box. Choose the "Build a new form manually" radio button to open the Navigator, as you need to do some things to initialize your development environment before building your first form. Ordinarily, you would use a wizard to start building your form.

NOTE
I uncheck the Display at startup check box so that I don't see this Welcome screen again. For me, it just slows down the development process. This is purely a matter of personal preference.

When the Form Builder window displays the Object Navigator window, you will see a default form, MODULE1, as the only form in the window.

Now, open the standard Talbot object library module. As Chapter 10 discusses in detail, a Forms object library module provides you with a set of Forms objects. You can use these objects through subclassing or copying to set the properties and behavior of the new objects you create. Most development projects will set up at least one standard object library to standardize the appearance of items, windows, canvases, alerts, and so on. This chapter assumes that Talbot Farms has done just that with an object library called TalbotStandard. This object library contains SmartClasses for the main types of data block items, document windows, content and toolbar canvases, property classes, and named visual attributes. During the prototyping process, you will use these standard objects to subclass the objects you create for your prototype.

2. Use the Open File button to find the library in your code directory, and open it.

In the future, whenever you start up the Form Builder, it will open this library or whatever object library you opened last. You only have to do this once to access all the library SmartClasses for the rest of your project.

Creating a Master-Detail Form

The first form the tutorial creates is a master-detail form. This form illustrates the two basic types of form layout—form and tabular. The form layout style lays out the screen as a single record. The tabular layout style lays out the screen as a grid or spreadsheet with multiple records. The master-detail form usually displays a single record as the master and a set of records in a tabular layout as the detail. In this tutorial, the form displays a single person, the Worker, and then lists all the skills the worker possesses as the details for the Worker master.

1. Select the form object in the Object Navigator.

2. Click on the object name, Module1.

3. Type in the new name: WorkerSkill.

Notice that the Form Builder translates everything you type to uppercase. You now have a WorkerSkill form module! However, it doesn't do anything yet, so let your breath out.

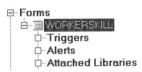

You are creating the form manually rather than going right into the Data Block Wizard, because you need to set up the form's Coordinate System property, as Chapter 5 recommends, using inches instead of points. This enables you to use the TalbotStandard object library, which uses a similar coordinate system. This gives the tutorial the opportunity to show you some things that you wouldn't see if you just used the wizards.

4. Select the form object and display the Property Palette, either by double-clicking the form icon or by right-clicking and choosing Property Palette from the pop-up menu.

5. Scroll down to the Physical property group, and then double-click on the Coordinate System property or on its More button to see the Coordinate Info dialog box, which Chapter 5 will describe in more detail.

6. Set the Coordinate System to Real and the Real Unit to Inches.

TIP

The TalbotStandard object library has a coordinate system based on Inch. You must change the Coordinate System property in each application that uses objects from the library to Inch. The Width and Height numbers, for example, in objects you subclass from the object library, are in inches; but if the Forms coordinate system is Points, it interprets the numbers as points, not inches, yielding results unlikely to be useful. You should also note that the standard object libraries that Oracle ships with Oracle Developer assume a point-based coordinate system, which may or may not be appropriate to your specific situation. If you have no concerns about operating system or user interface portability, you may find it easier to accept the default coordinate system. You won't have to go through creating the form manually each time if you do, but you sacrifice some portability.

You now have set up your standard environment and the basic elements of your first form. The next phase of the tutorial creates the details of the form. To create the form, you will go through these steps:

■ Create the Worker data block that displays a single-person record from the Person table.

■ Create the WorkerHasSkill data block that displays several skill records from the WorkerHasSkill table, and make it a detail block linked to the master Worker block.

■ Add a drop-down list to provide the possible skills from the Skill table so you do not have to type in the skill but instead just choose it from the list.

■ Clean up the appearance of the form.

■ Save and run the application to verify that it will serve as a prototype.

Before starting work, connect to the database. Choose File|Connect and enter the user name, password, and server alias for your database (talbot, george, and orcl for the examples here).

NOTE
There are several points at which you access the database during your development process using Oracle Developer. Until reaching one of these points, you need not connect. At any point that requires connection to the database, Oracle Developer automatically prompts you with the Connect dialog box if you haven't connected.

Creating the Worker Data Block

The Worker data block corresponds to the Person table in the database. By querying the records in this block, you can scroll through all the Person records in the database. The WorkerSkill application lets you assign a particular skill to a person. The first thing you have to do is find the person in the database to whom you want to assign a skill. In this case, all you need is a single field for the Worker name.

First, start up the Data Block Wizard. If you had chosen the Wizard option when you first entered the Form Builder, this would have happened automatically. Since you are building the form manually, you must start the Wizard yourself.

I. Pull down the Tools menu and select the Data Block Wizard item. The Builder displays the Data Block Wizard welcome screen.

You also get to this screen directly from the Form Builder Welcome screen if you choose the option in that screen to build a form using the wizards.

2. Click on Next; you see the screen that lets you choose between basing the data block on a table or on a stored procedure. Choose the Table or View option, as Figure 4-1 illustrates.

TIP

See the Chapter 6 section "Procedural Encapsulation" for details on building data blocks using stored procedures. Using stored procedures lets you have more control over access to the data and improves performance by minimizing network traffic. You can only use this approach when you use Oracle as your database server, however. You can also start the Data Block Wizard by creating a new data block. Select the Data Block label in the Object Navigator and click on the Create tool. Oracle Developer will prompt you whether to use the Wizard or to build the data block manually.

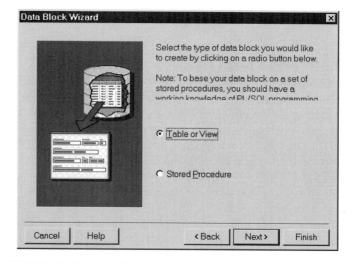

FIGURE 4-1. *The Data Block Wizard type screen*

The Data Block Wizard now displays the table screen. It asks you to enter the table or view name and to select which columns from the table or view you wish to add to the block.

3. The Browse button lets you browse the data dictionary for tables. Click on it. The Builder displays the Tables dialog box, which asks what you want to see (Tables, Views, or Synonyms) and from what schema (Current user, Other users). It then displays a list of objects from which you can choose. Choose tables for the current user:

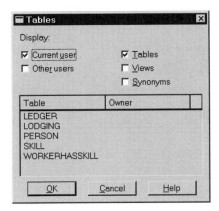

4. Select the table name you want to enter into the Base Table field, "Person." Just click on that row and click OK.

You are now in the data block screen of the Wizard, as Figure 4-2 illustrates. The Data Block Wizard assumes you want the same name for the data block as the table you chose, so you can't change it here. Keeping the name the same makes it easier to understand what's going on later and is highly recommended. The data block screen lists the columns for the table. In this case, the columns include the Name and Age columns plus two separate Lodging columns. The Lodging column in the Person table is actually an Oracle8 REF column that points to a row in the Lodging table. Oracle Developer understands this kind of relationship. The first Lodging column in the list is a lookup of the columns in the Lodging table. You can click on the + to expand this list, and you can include any of these columns as an item in your data block. If you do this, you'll notice that there is in turn another REF, this time to the Address table, and you can incorporate any of the Address columns in your data block as well. Oracle Developer thus gives you access to the full power of the object features of Oracle8 through the Data Block Wizard.

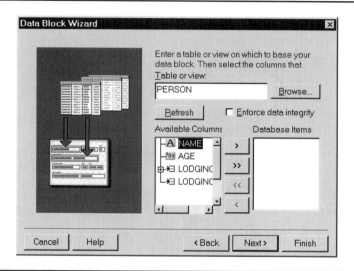

FIGURE 4-2. *The Data Block Wizard data block screen*

TIP
Databases can change without your knowing it. You can use the Refresh button to ensure that you see all the available columns if you are returning to this screen after doing work in the Form Builder rather than just entering it for the first time.

   5. Using the > and >> buttons, you can move the columns into the Database Items list, which is the list of items you want to create in the data block. You want only the Name column, so click on that column to select it, and then click on the > button to move it into the list of Database Items, or double-click on the Name column. Click Finish.

   6. Oracle Developer now starts the Layout Wizard, displaying the welcome screen. Click on Next to see the canvas screen, shown in Figure 4-3. By default, this screen creates a new content canvas for the block, which is what you want.

   7. Click on Next to move to the data block screen. You see the NAME item in the list of Available Items. Double-click it to tell the Wizard you want to display this column. This activates the Item Type field, which is Text Item by default, as shown in Figure 4-4. Click on Finish.

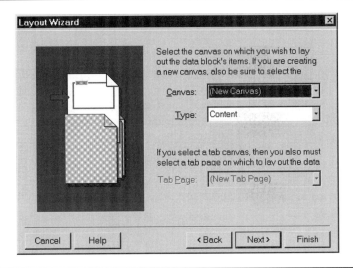

FIGURE 4-3. *The Layout Wizard canvas screen*

The Worker block now appears in the Object Navigator under the WorkerSkill form. The Layout Editor displays the new layout. Congratulations: you have your first block!

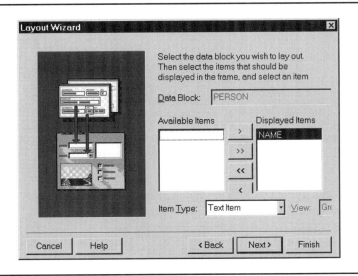

FIGURE 4-4. *The Layout Wizard data block screen*

Creating the WorkerHasSkill Data Block

Now, create the WorkerHasSkill data block that lets the user query and enter worker skills for a particular worker. This is a detail block to the Worker master block.

1. Find the Person data block in the Object Navigator and select it; then click the Create button in the toolbar. This tells the Form Builder that you want to create an object of the same type as the Person object, a data block, so the Form Builder displays a small dialog box that asks whether to create the block manually or to use the Data Block Wizard. Choose the latter radio button.

2. Choose the WorkerHasSkill table as the base for the data block and use the >> button to move all the columns into the Database Items list in the table dialog box.

3. Click on Next to display the master-detail screen. This box appears only if there are other data blocks that could serve as a master for the one you're creating. You didn't see it when you created the first block in your form.

4. Click on the Create Relationship button to display a list of the available master data blocks—in this case, Person.

5. Click on OK in the list. The Builder fills in the rest of the fields with the default join condition, linking the person with the worker's skill by the person's name, as shown in Figure 4-5. Click Finish to complete the data block and to start the Layout Wizard.

6. The Layout Wizard's canvas screen displays the canvas you created for the Person data block, CANVAS2. This tells Oracle Developer to create the WorkerHasSkill items on the same canvas, which is what you want to do.

7. Click on Next to proceed to the displayed items screen.

8. Use the > button or double-click on the SKILL and ABILITY items from the Available Items list to transfer them to the Displayed Items list, as shown in Figure 4-6. Leaving the NAME item out of the Displayed Items list means that you won't see it on the canvas. You already see the name in the Person data block; you don't need to see it again in the detail data block.

9. Click on Next to proceed to the item screen. This screen lets you modify the prompts, width, and height of the items you chose to display. In this case, you can leave everything alone. When the database table column names are not natural-language words that produce easy-to-understand prompts, you change them into such prompts here.

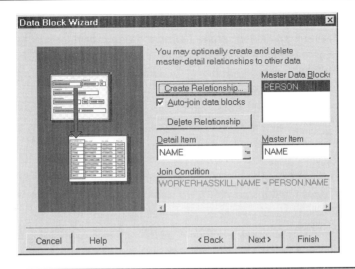

FIGURE 4-5. *The Data Block Wizard master-detail screen*

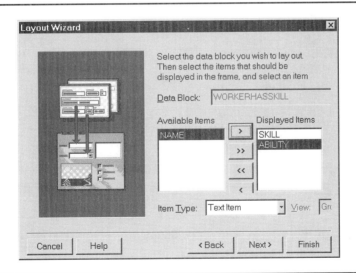

FIGURE 4-6. *The Layout Wizard items screen for the WorkerHasSkill data block*

TIP
I've found it better to wait until later to modify the width and height. You often set the height through subclassing or a property class (discussed in Chapter 10) with a standard height. The width depends on your ultimate arrangement of fields, which you can better see in the Layout Editor. There you can just drag the item's edges to a better width in a graphical drawing environment.

10. Click on Next; this brings you to the choice between a Form and a Tabular layout (radio buttons). In this case, choose Tabular, which results in a grid of records.

11. Click on Next; you now see the frame dialog box shown in Figure 4-7. The *frame* groups the set of items you are displaying on the canvas. Later, you will be able to modify the items with the Layout Wizard by selecting the frame.

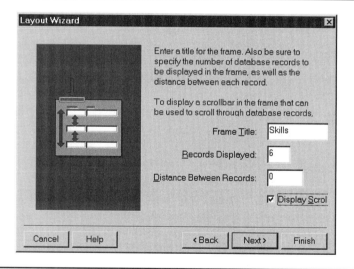

FIGURE 4-7. *The Layout Wizard frame dialog box for the WorkerHasSkill data block*

12. Enter a frame title, "Skills," and set Records Displayed to 6. Also, check the Display Scrollbar check box to display a scroll bar next to the six records on the tab page, which will let the user scroll if there are more than six skills. Click on Finish, and you have a master-detail form in the Layout Editor without having coded a single program statement!

NOTE
The Distance Between Records setting lets you spread the records apart on the canvas by a standard amount between each two records. The main use for this feature is to allow wrapped records—records that wrap around to display several items on several lines instead of on just one line. By leaving space between the lines, you can move the groups of items so they overlap. Place the items on the second line of the record right below the items on the first line of the record. This lets you display long records in a relatively small horizontal canvas. Experiment with these settings here and in the Property Palette to see the effect of this relatively specialized feature. Take a look at the prompt properties in each item to reposition the item labels to your satisfaction; labels are properties of the item, not freestanding boilerplate text on the canvas.

The Skills List
To finish off the first form, you will now put a list into the WorkerHasSkill block to help users to enter skills. There are several different ways to do this, but the most effective is to make the Skill item in the WorkerHasSkill block a list item.

The list item presents the user with a list of values from which to choose. With the list available, the user doesn't need to remember the exact value to type in. This improves productivity because it prevents typing errors and the consequent corrections. You can build such a list in two ways: either by entering the values directly into the form or by arranging for the form to query the values from the database. The latter approach is much more flexible, since you can add new values, change existing ones, or delete values from the database without recompiling the forms that use them. You can build this kind of dynamic list either as a GUI-standard drop-down list of items or as an Oracle Developer list of values (LOV) object. Here, because the list is relatively short, I have chosen the drop-down list format.

TIP

See the section "Using the LOV Wizard" later in this chapter for an example that uses the LOV Wizard to build an LOV for a more extensive list. LOVs have a very nice pattern-matching search capability, which makes them ideal for lengthy lists of choices. The user just enters one or two characters of the choice, and the LOV finds it. LOVs are thus the tool of choice for lengthy lists, even though they are not standard GUI controls.

This approach requires using a bit of standard code from the standard PL/SQL library for Talbot Farms, so you must first attach that library to the form.

1. Find the Attached Libraries node in the Object Navigator and double-click on it to attach a library to the form.

2. Enter the library name, "TalbotStandard," into the Library field.

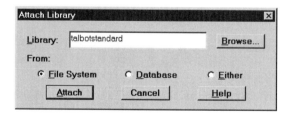

3. Click the Attach button. Oracle Developer searches the standard search path FORMS60_PATH in the System Registry (see the Note that follows this paragraph). You then will find the TALBOTSTANDARD library and its subprograms under the Attached Libraries node. Talbot Farms has a simple procedure called Set_Up_List that handles setting up a database-driven list.

NOTE
*You will need to add the path to the library
to the registry before attaching the library.
Find the TALBOTSTANDARD.PLL file and
note the folder path to it. Edit the registry key
FORMS60_PATH under the HKEY_LOCAL_
MACHINE\SOFTWARE\ORACLE registry folder to
include that path. If you are unfamiliar with editing
the registry, consult a book on Windows or a
knowledgeable Windows expert. On operating
systems other than Microsoft Windows, please
check your operating-system-specific documents for
information about setting these environment
variables. You can also put the full path into the
Library field, but this is bad practice. If you later
move the file to another directory, you will have to
change the path and recompile the form. If you
don't specify the path, this extra work disappears.*

You now need to subclass the item.

4. Find the Skill item under the WorkerHasSkill data block set of items.

5. Open the Property Palette by double-clicking on the item's icon.

6. Click on the Subclass Information property twice to make Skill a subclass.

7. In the Subclass Information dialog box, set the Module name to
   TALBOTSTANDARD from the drop-down list. Then set the Object Name to
   LIST and click OK to make the list a subclass of the standard list object from
   the TalbotStandard library:

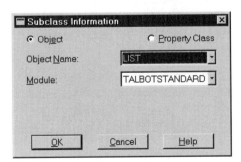

The next step in setting up the Skills list is to create the record group. A record group is a tablelike object that contains multiple records of items. In this case, you use the record group as an in-memory storage area for the items to display in the list. You want Oracle Developer to build this record group by querying the skills from the Skill table in the database when the form starts up. When the user pulls down the Skills list, the list item must access these records in the record group to generate the list of items to display in the drop-down list.

8. Find the Record Groups heading in the Object Navigator and double-click it to create a new record group. When you do this, Oracle Developer prompts you for a query.

9. Enter this SQL SELECT statement to query all the skills from the Skill table:

```
SELECT Skill, Skill
  FROM Skill
 ORDER BY 1
```

The SQL statement must be in a specific format because you are going to use it for filling in a list. The list has two values for each list element: a value and a label. The list element *label* is what you see in the drop-down list; the list element *value* is what Oracle Developer puts into the database. This lets you display a readable text string but put a number code or some other value into the database instead of the full text string. See the section "Lists" in Chapter 6 for full details.

The SQL statement thus cannot just retrieve a single set of values. It must retrieve both a set of labels and the corresponding values as the two columns of the SELECT list, in that order. Because the Skill table represents the skills with text strings, you can use the same column for both the label and the value. The SELECT list thus retrieves the Skill column twice—the first time for the label and the second time for the value. The SELECT also orders the results by the first column, the label, so the list of labels will display in alphabetical order. When you click OK, Oracle Developer parses the SQL statement to ensure that you have it right, then creates the record group. You should also rename the record group for readability by clicking on the name and entering "SKILL."

The last step in this process is to connect the record group with the list item and to enter data into the group. That's the job of the Set_Up_List procedure, which takes two arguments: the name of the list and the name of the record group. But where do you call it?

You will usually set up your list items when you start the form. The place to put calls to PL/SQL procedures to run at startup is thus in a form trigger.

10. Select the Triggers heading right under the form.

11. Right-click the heading icon to pop up its menu, and choose SmartTriggers. You see several possibilities.

12. Choose the When-New-Form-Instance trigger item. Oracle Developer opens the PL/SQL editor and awaits your programming skills.

13. To enter a call to Set_Up_List, find the Attached Libraries node in the Object Navigator. Expand the TALBOTSTANDARD library.

14. Expand all the nodes for Set_Up_List with the Expand All tool in the toolbar.

15. Select the full specification under the Specification Heading.

16. Choose the Navigator|Paste Arguments menu item from the main menu.

17. Go back to the PL/SQL editor, and you see the procedure call you need.

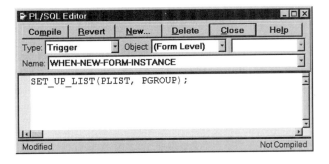

18. Replace the string PLIST with the name of the list item, 'WorkerHasSkill.Skill,' and the string PGROUP with the name of the record group, 'Skill'. Don't forget the single quotes around the string values. The single quotes indicate these are strings, not variables, and the case (upper, lower, or mixed) is irrelevant.

19. Click on Compile to verify that you've done everything correctly and to compile the code.

    Now when you run this form, the trigger will fire and automatically populate your drop-down list of skills.

NOTE

It is always a good idea to qualify an item name with its block name. In this case it is not strictly necessary because there is only one Skill item in the form at this time. If you later add another block with a Skill item, your code may not work as it did before.

Finally, you need to set up the various list item properties so the record group can populate the list.

20. First, click on the Elements in List property of the Skill item in the WorkerHasSkill data block. You see the single list element inherited from the object library, "Default value."

21. Change the List Item Value field to a valid value from the database table; in this case, enter "Work" and click OK.

22. Now enter the same value, "Work," in the Mapping of Other Values property.

A Form Is Born

You now have a form, but it still does not look much like your original concept. Oracle Developer makes some assumptions about appearance that do not necessarily match your requirements.

To see what the form looks like, open the canvas by double-clicking on the canvas icon under Canvases (Forms|WORKERSKILL|Canvases). The Builder displays the Layout Editor, showing you what the canvas looks like, as you can see in Figure 4-8.

To complete your form, you need to accomplish the following formatting changes in the canvas:

- Remove the frame lines and labels.

- Subclass the items from the standard object library.

- Change the name of the Name column label to "Worker."

1. To remove the line boxes and titles, select the frame in the Layout Editor by clicking on it.

2. First, make the frame tightly enclose the objects. Display the Property Palette for the frame object. To do this, you can double-click on the selected frame, or you can right-click on the selected frame to see the

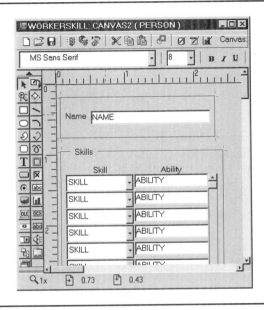

FIGURE 4-8.   *The default Layout Editor for the WorkerSkill canvas*

pop-up menu and click on Property Palette, or you choose Tools|Property
Palette from the main menu.

3. Find the Layout Frame Group. Set the following properties, as shown here:

▫ Horizontal Object Offset	0
◦ Vertical Object Offset	0
◦ Allow Expansion	Yes
▫ Shrinkwrap	Yes

- ■ Horizontal Margin: 0

- ■ Vertical Margin: 0

- ■ Horizontal Object Offset: 0

- ■ Vertical Object Offset: 0

- ■ Shrinkwrap: Yes

4. Reposition the frame so its corner is in the upper-right corner of the
canvas. This positions the Name field to occupy as little space as possible
on the canvas.

5. Now, find the Line Color tool at the bottom of the tool palette and click on it.

6. Find the No Line button at the bottom of the color palette that pops up, and click on it. This removes the line while leaving the frame in place.

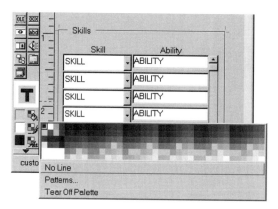

You see the frame as a blue, dashed line that will not appear when you run the application, as this illustration shows:

CAUTION

Under no circumstances should you delete the frame, although you can do so by pressing the DELETE key. You need to leave the frame in place to use the Layout Wizard on the frame's elements later. If you delete it, you can no longer change the data block or its layout using the wizard system, and you've disposed of one of the best features of Oracle Developer.

Repeat this for the Skills frame, positioning the frame directly under the Person frame. You also need to remove the frame title for the Skills frame.

7. Display the Property Palette for the frame.

8. Find the Frame Title heading and remove the "Skills" string in the Frame Title property. Looking back at the Layout Editor, you'll find the frame is now invisible and without a title.

NOTE
Removing the frame lines and titles is a matter of preference. In this case, the basic layout is so simple that the lines just take up space without adding any visual value. It's easy to distinguish the single name item from the grid of skills. For more complex pages and canvases, it makes sense to surround the data block's items with a visible frame to distinguish them from other data blocks on the same canvas. In design terms, you are visually distinguishing related clusters of information on the screen, giving the user a visual clue about data organization. In any case, become familiar with these properties, as you will need to understand how they affect your canvas under different circumstances.

To format items properly using Talbot-standard formatting, you will now subclass all the items you've created using SmartClasses. A SmartClass is an object in an open object library that the creator of the library has marked as a standard object (see Chapter 10 for details). When you select an object in the Object Navigator, Oracle Developer creates a list of the objects marked as SmartClasses in the open object libraries that are of the same type as the object you've selected. All you need to do to subclass the object is to pop up the menu with a right mouse click and choose from the set of SmartClasses.

9. For example, select the Name item in the Person Block.

10. Now right-click on the item and click on the SmartClasses menu item. You see several class names.

11. In this case, choose Text to make the object a character text item.

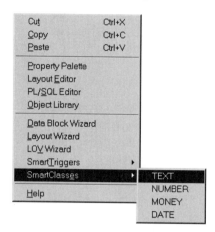

12. Repeat this for the Name and Ability items in the WorkerHasSkill data block. There is no real need to subclass the Name item in the WorkerHasSkill data block, but it's a good idea to subclass it anyway, in case there are specific properties that it inherits or will inherit in the future.

NOTE

What you see in the SmartClass menu depends entirely on the object libraries you have built and opened. In this example, the picture is showing three objects marked as SmartClasses in the Talbot Standard object library. You may see something different if you are using a different object library.

When you subclass the item, the various property values in the library object replace the corresponding values in the subclassed object. For example, if there is a standard width and height for text items, Oracle Developer resizes the item on the canvas to that width and height, regardless of the settings from the Layout Wizard. You can then override the subclass settings through the Property Palette or through the Layout Wizard. You may need to drag the frame vertically or horizontally to accommodate the newly resized object.

When you change a property you inherit from another object, the Property Palette shows a small icon telling you that the value overrides a property value you inherited from the parent object. You can always restore the inherited value with the Inherit tool at the top of the Property Palette. Select the property you want to inherit and click on the tool, and the value changes back to the value from the parent object.

13. To change the Name prompt, find the Name item again and display the Property Palette.

14. Find the Prompt heading and change the string in the Prompt attribute to "Worker." This changes the prompt in the Layout Editor.

NOTE
You may need to resize the frame slightly to accommodate the new prompt. Turn off the Shrinkwrap property of the frame; then select the frame in the Layout Editor and drag the frame out to the right beyond the text box. Before moving the components around, turn on the snap-to-grid feature of the Layout Editor with the View|Snap to Grid menu item. The Layout Editor assumes that a grid underlies the canvas, and it displays rulers at the top and left sides of the canvas. You can display the grid with the View|Grid menu item, although the background fill obscures it. With snapping on, when you move the various components, you can easily line them up to the pixel by looking at the rulers. Change the units of the grid with the Ruler Settings dialog box (View|Settings|Ruler menu item) to inches to conform to your coordinate system. I find a grid spacing of 0.25 and 4 snap points per grid spacing suits my applications style best. After you've finished pushing things around, restore the frame's Shrinkwrap property to Yes.

At the end of the process, the canvas should look like the one in Figure 4-9, depending on exactly how you went about changing things.

Saving Your Form

You now have a complete, working form that does the job laid out in Chapter 3. You can use the form to query, including queries of subsets of the data through query by example. You can use it to manipulate the data by adding new records,

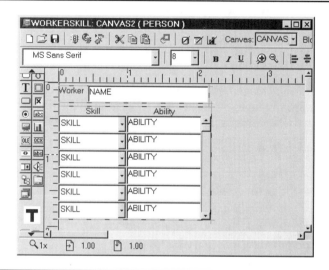

FIGURE 4-9. *The modified WorkerSkill canvas in the Layout Editor*

querying records, deleting records, or typing over values to change the data already in the database. And you did all this in just a few minutes of work!

It is time to save your work and run the application to see what it looks like in practice and to verify that it works as you think it should.

You can save a form module either in a module file or in the central application's database on your database server. I recommend that you take the former course. Here is an outline of some of the main issues to consider when making this decision:

- *Module accessibility*: If you have a relatively complex and large application environment, and you want to share your modules with other developers, saving the modules in a database accessible to all Oracle Developers scales up better than saving them in files. Shared files on a network are a possibility but can involve more complexity, especially in a wide area network.

- *Project management*: You can use Project Builder only to manage files, not modules in the database. That means you lose all the project management and deployment features of Project Builder if you store modules in the database.

- *Integrity*: As with any data, you have the basic issue of data integrity—that is, if there is a media failure or some other kind of data-corrupting event, you can lose your application module. Because a database provides strong integrity mechanisms, there is less risk if you store the modules in a database. Either way, back up your files or database regularly so you can restore lost data.

■ *Performance*: Saving to the database is slower than saving to files, and retrieving is also slower.

■ *Configuration management*: If you want to use a commercial configuration management system to manage your applications, you have to use files, because those systems do not yet work with a database.

■ *Convenience*: You can use standard file system utilities to manipulate your files, whereas the database tables and tools are much less flexible. You can use names of up to 30 characters for modules in the database.

■ *Portability*: You can store modules only in an Oracle database server. If you are developing on another database, you must use files to store the modules.

Because this book strongly recommends using Project Builder and a configuration management system as part of your risk management process, and because of various convenience and performance issues, it recommends using the file approach rather than saving in the database. Again, *you should always back up your files regularly*.

For now, if you want to save to the database, you need to enable saving to the database, because the Builders do not do that automatically.

1. Display the Preferences dialog box by choosing the Tools|Preferences menu item.

2. In the Access tab, find the Access section in the upper-left corner. Change the radio button from File to Database, or set it to Ask to have Form Builder prompt you every time you save.

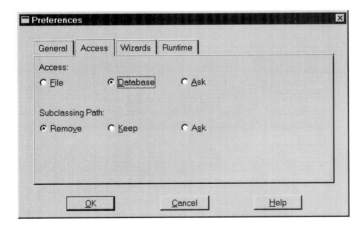

3. Now choose the File|Save menu item to save your work.

4. If you chose File/Database, Form Builder pops up a small dialog box called Filter that gives you the choice of Database or File System. Choose the File System radio button and click OK.

Form Builder will work for a few moments, saving the form module to your database or file. Run your form with the Program|Run Form|Client Server menu item or the Run tool on the vertical toolbar of the Builder or on the horizontal toolbar of the Layout Editor. Builder compiles the form, runs the Form Runtime program, and tells it to run the form. Figure 4-10 shows the resulting application.

NOTE
You can also use the Program|Run Form|Web menu item or the equivalent tool to run the form in a browser if you're developing the application for the Internet.

To verify the application, try some operations.

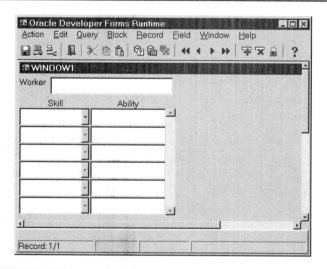

FIGURE 4-10. *The WorkerSkill application running*

5. Query all the workers with the Query Execute tool in the menu toolbar.

6. Use Record|Next to move down the list of people. Notice how, when you get to a person with skills, the form automatically fills out the Skill and Ability fields.

7. Now click on a Skill field and drop down the list.

8. Select a skill, click OK, and fill in the Skill field. Try typing in a skill that is not in the list; you cannot, as Oracle Developer just ignores what you type.

   When you complete your prototype test, close the application. Make any corrections to the form in the Form Builder. There's one more step: adding the file to the Project Builder project hierarchy.

9. Open Project Builder and select the project you created by clicking on its name.

10. Click the Add Files tool in the toolbar and find the WorkerSkill.FMB file in the resulting Add Files to Project dialog box.

11. When you click on Open to add the file, Project Builder adds a node under the Forms document node of the project for the WorkerSkill.FMB file:

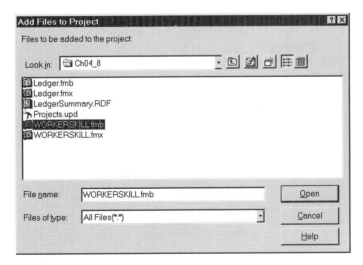

Project Builder is smart enough to also add the WorkerSkill.FMX file under the Forms executable node. The FMX file is an *implied item*—an item that is usually the result of a compilation or generation step. Project Builder automatically adds an implied item to the project when you add the *input item* from which you generate the implied item (an FMB file, in this case). When you use Project Builder to build one or more files incrementally with the Build Incremental tool, Project Builder understands the implied dependencies and recompiles any dependent files that are out-of-date.

Although Project Builder can infer many implied dependencies between objects, it cannot see dependencies in PL/SQL code or to object libraries. That means that when you change a PL/SQL or object library, Project Builder will not automatically rebuild all the applications that depend on them when you recompile all the files. Therefore, you must enter those dependencies explicitly when you create them.

12. First, to see the dependency relationships more clearly, change from the Navigator's project view to its dependency view by choosing the Navigator|Dependency View menu item. This displays all the files in dependency order.

13. Now select the FMX file and click on the Add Files tool again.

14. Find the TalbotStandard.OLB and TalbotStandard.PLX files in the Add Files to Project dialog box.

15. This time when you click on Open you will see the OLB and PLX files appear under the FMX file, indicating that the FMX file depends on those files.

Updating Project Builder with the form module and its dependencies lets you manage the files using the automated tools of the Project Builder in the future. If you are using configuration management tools, for example, you can check the files into the version control system now to create a prototype baseline (again, see Chapter 15 for details). Before modifying the form prototype, however, let's explore the world of reports.

Creating a Grid Form

The tutorial in the section "Creating a Master-Detail Form" created a form that used both the single-record form style and the multiple-record tabular style. This tutorial shows you some techniques specific to multiple-record grid forms and creates a basis for the next section, "Using the LOV Wizard."

The Ledger form presents the Ledger table (see Appendix A) in a grid layout. You would use this form for basic data entry and for querying ledger entries.

1. Select the Forms node in the Object Navigator and click on the Add tool to create a new form. Change the form's name to LEDGER, and then display the Property Palette and modify the Coordinate System to Real Inches as you did for the WorkerSkill form in the section "Creating a Master-Detail Form."

2. Select the Data Blocks node in the Object Navigator and click the Add tool. Choose to use the Data Block Wizard to create the new data block.

3. Click next in the welcome screen. Base the data block on a table in the data block type screen. Click the Browse button in the table screen and choose the LEDGER table. Use the > button to move all the basic columns (LEDGERID, ACTIONDATE, ACTION, ITEM, QUANTITY, QUANTITYTYPE, RATE, and AMOUNT) into the data block. Also move the Person.Name field into the data block, but leave the Person REF field. The Name stands in for the Person reference, and the form doesn't require any of the other Person columns. Click Next.

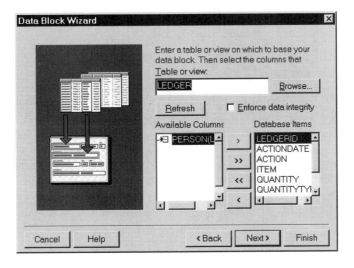

NOTE
*Using the lookup columns is a powerful feature you
have only when you're working with Oracle8. In
this case, the form doesn't need any of the
information. If it did, all you would need to do is to
include the referenced columns in the data block,
and the Form Builder would take care of all the
code needed to navigate the reference link to the
other object tables.*

The Data Block Wizard now displays a screen that asks you whether to
create a list of values (LOV) for the Person.Name item. It knows to do this
because the item is a lookup. Creating the LOV will enable you to update
the REF column in the database by selecting a name from the LOV.

4. Check the Person check box, then click on the ... button to browse the
   database for the lookup object table, PERSON. You see only the single table
   unless you have multiple object tables for the Person type. Click Finish.

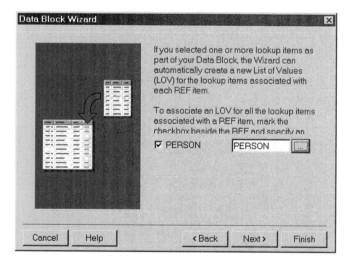

5. In the Layout Wizard, choose a new canvas and click Next.

6. Click on the >> button to display all the items and click Next.

7. Change a couple of the labels: make Ledgerid "ID," Actiondate "Date," and
   Quantitytype "Type." Click Next.

8. Choose the Tabular layout style and click Next.

9. Set the number of records to 10, leave the Frame name blank, and check the check box to display a scroll bar. Click Finish.

The Form Builder now displays your new canvas—a large grid displaying all the columns of the Ledger table.

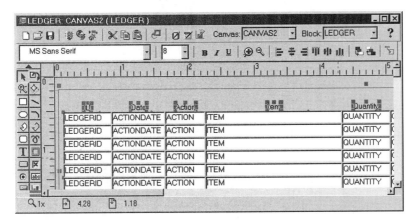

Next, we need to apply the standard SmartClasses to the items.

10. Go to the Object Navigator. For each item under the new Ledger data block, select the item and right-click to display the pop-up menu. Choose SmartClass and the appropriate class, such as Text.

NOTE
When you look at the items in the data block, you will see Person at the top of the list. The Data Block Wizard created both the Person REF item and the Person_Name item. If you look at the Person item properties, you will see that it has a Canvas property value of <null>, meaning no canvas displays the item. Users will update the item through the Person_Name item and its LOV. More on that in a few paragraphs.

11. As in the previous tutorial, remove the frame line, set the Frame size properties to 0, and set the Shrinkwrap property to Yes.

12. Run the form. Click the Execute Query tool to see what the data looks like. Figure 4-11 shows the result.

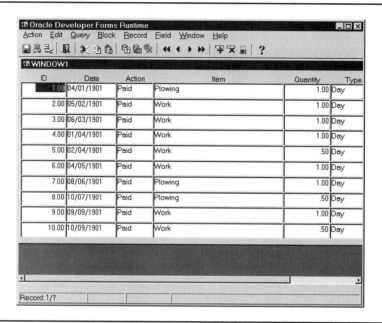

FIGURE 4-11. *The Ledger form*

13. Use the TAB key to move over to the last item, Person. It displays the Name for the person. If you look at the status bar, you see the list of values lamp lit. If you choose Edit|Display List, the Forms Runtime displays the LOV, listing all the people in the Person table:

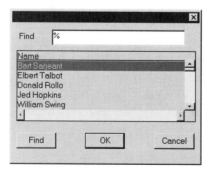

Using the LOV Wizard

The Data Block Wizard can easily create an LOV for you when you use a lookup value derived from a REF column. You will often want to create an LOV, however, in situations without REF columns. In the earlier section "The Skills List," you worked through the steps for creating a drop-down list. These lists are good for displaying a limited number of items, say, fewer than 10 or 15. With more items than that, you benefit from the features of the LOV: scroll bars and pattern matching. The Person LOV is the perfect example of this benefit.

With the drop-down list, you can type in the first letter of the choice, and the list positions the selection on the first item that begins with that letter. Type the letter again, and it goes to the next item beginning with that letter. In the LOV, you can type several letters, and the LOV positions the selection on the correct item the first time. Try it using the Ledger Person LOV to see how it works.

This section presents a tutorial on the LOV Wizard—a tool that makes it easy to create a LOV for an item. This tutorial teaches you the following skills:

- How to use the LOV Wizard to create a LOV

- How to specify the list items in the LOV

- How to associate the result of a LOV pick with a data block item

- How to create a title for the LOV

- How to use the LOV to validate a data block item

The tutorial adds a LOV that will present the values for the QuantityType item. Quantity types are ever expanding in the database, so Talbot's does not want to provide only a drop-down list here.

1. Choose the Tools|LOV Wizard menu item. The LOV Wizard starts up and asks you whether to base the LOV record group on a query or on an existing record group. Choose the former and click Next.

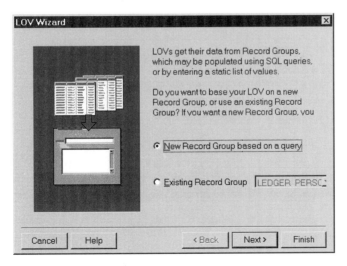

2. Enter this SQL statement into the query screen and click Next :

```
SELECT DISTINCT QuantityType
  FROM Ledger
ORDER BY 1
```

The DISTINCT qualifier tells Oracle to return only the set of distinct values from the Ledger table. The LOV will thus display all the values currently in the table. The ORDER BY displays the values in alphabetical order, which is the usual way to display values in a LOV.

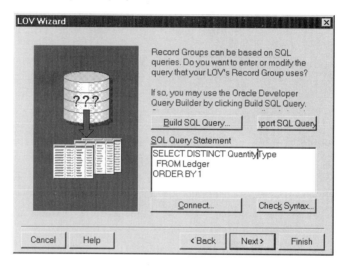

TIP

You will usually want a bit more control over the set of values. You can create a separate table to hold the set of values in Oracle, then base the LOV on a query from that lookup table. To add a new value to the LOV list, you enter it into the table. Just getting it from the actual data means you don't really control the set of values, which can cause problems under some circumstances.

3. The LOV columns screen lets you display one or more of the columns you've defined in the record group with your query. In this case, there is only one column, QuantityType, so double-click it to display it. Click Next.

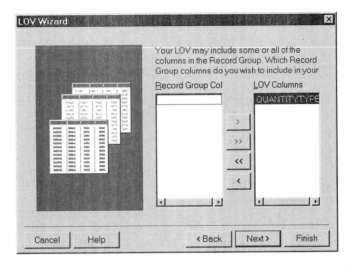

4. In the properties screen, specify a column title for the item, "Type." Click on the button toward the bottom of the screen (the label is not really readable, but it is "Look up return items"). Choose the item Ledger.QuantityType from the pick list and click OK. Click Next.

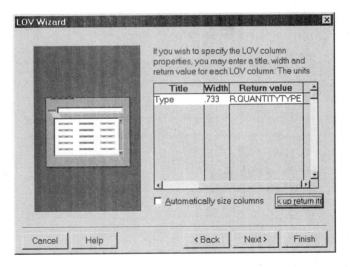

Setting the return type associates the value in the list with a specific data block and item. A later screen will use this value, so it is important to set it here.

5. In the LOV window screen, specify a title, "Quantity Type"; leave the width and height alone for now. Click Next.

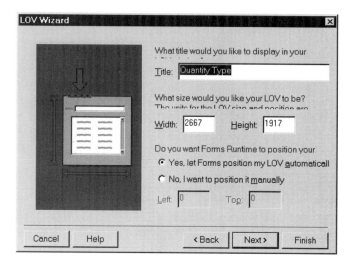

6. Click Next to accept all the advanced properties; then in the assigned item screen choose the QuantityType item as the assigned item. This assigns the return value to the QuantityType item. Click Finish.

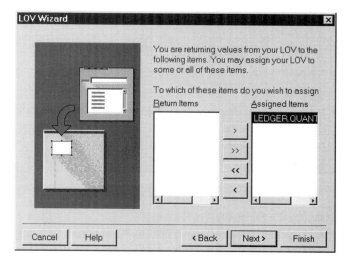

7. Find the new LOV in the Object Navigator and rename it to "QuantityType," and rename the corresponding Record Group to "QuantityType" as well.

8. Navigate to the Ledger.QuantityType item and display its Property Palette. Find the list of values (LOV) section. Set the Validate from List property to Yes.

▪ List of Values (LOV)	
▫ List of Values	QUANTITYTYPE
◦ List X Position	0
◦ List Y Position	0
▫ Validate from List	Yes

This last step tells the Forms Runtime to use the LOV values as a set of values against which to validate data entered into the field. Users are thus constrained to enter only values from the list. In this case, that means that the current values in the database constrain what users can enter.

9. Run the form, click on the Execute Query button, and tab over to the Type item. Use Edit|Display List to display the LOV.

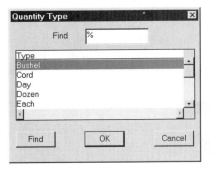

Developing a Simple Summary Report

Reports are as easy to set up as forms, but the follow-through tasks are different. Many of the tasks in building a report relate to formatting the report layout, as opposed to constructing objects to get things done.

A *tabular* report prints out a table of data from a single SQL SELECT statement. A *summary tabular* report adds subtotals and performs other aggregations. In building the Talbot Ledger Summary report, this section shows you how to quickly generate a summary report, the most common kind of report.

When you start Report Builder by clicking on the tool in the Project Builder launchpad, the Welcome dialog box asks whether to run the Report Wizard. Defining the summary report using the Wizard is a very simple process. Click on the Use the Report Wizard radio button to start the Wizard.

In this first report tutorial, you will learn these skills:

■ How to build a simple summary report with the Report Wizard

■ How to map database columns to report fields

■ How to generate simple groups and summary columns

■ How to use a standard report template to format the basic report

■ How to use the Live Previewer to rearrange the default report layout

■ How to add a title to the report in the Live Previewer

The Ledger Summary report shows the data from the Ledger table, sorted by person, with the action date, item description, and total amount spent or received. In the ledger, each person also has a subtotal showing the total amount bought or sold to that person.

Running the Report Wizard

After the Wizard welcome screen, you see the Report Wizard style screen, as in Figure 4-12. You choose which style of report you want here (see Chapter 7 for details on the different types of report). The Ledger Summary report is a Group Left report, with a grouping of records on the left side of the report.

1. Enter the report title, "Ledger Summary Report."

2. Click on the radio button Group Left, as you want a grouped summary report. Figure 4-12 shows the filled-in screen.

3. Click on Next.

   The next screen prompts for whether to use an SQL statement or an Express query. If you have an Oracle Express installation, this data mining tool can be very effective in developing queries. The tutorial uses a basic SQL statement.

4. Choose the SQL Statement radio button and click on Next.

   The next screen lets you enter the query on which to base the SQL statement, as shown in Figure 4-13. You will enter this query:

```
SELECT p.Name, l.ActionDate, l.Item,
       l.Quantity, l.Rate, l.Amount
  FROM Ledger l, Person p
 WHERE l.Person = REF(p)
```

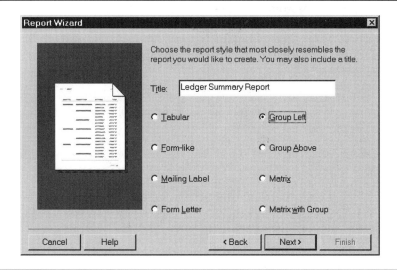

FIGURE 4-12.   *The Report Wizard report style screen set to a Group Left report*

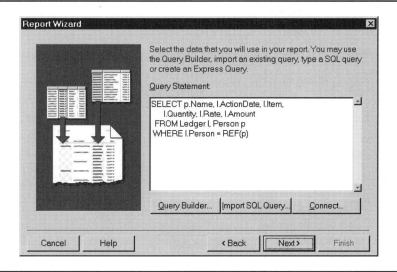

FIGURE 4-13.   *The Report Wizard SQL query screen with Ledger Summary query*

This query joins the Ledger and Person tables using the Person REF column. It returns the person's name from the Person table and the other five data elements for the report from the Ledger table. You can also use the graphical Query Builder to construct the query by clicking on the Query Builder button.

5. Click on the Connect button to connect to the database. You see the same connect dialog box that you saw in the Form Builder. Enter the user name, password, and host name.

6. Click on Next. The Wizard checks the query, then proceeds to the next screen.

   The next screen, shown in Figure 4-14, displays the available fields and asks you to specify which fields you want to use for grouping the report display. This particular report groups on the person's name.

7. Select the Name field and use the > button to move it across to the Group Fields list. Click on Next.

   The next screen, shown in Figure 4-15, displays your available report fields and lets you designate which ones to display in what order. You need not display all of the items, just ones with values that you want to see. The others might be in the report for use as the basis of calculated fields or for some other purpose.

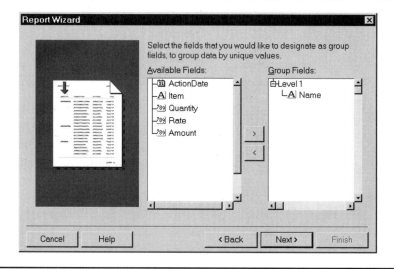

FIGURE 4-14.   *The Report Wizard group fields screen with Person group*

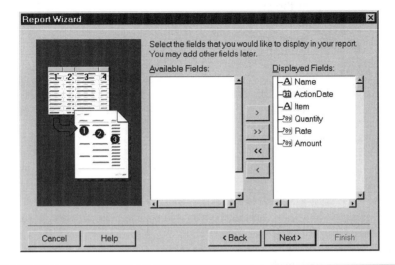

FIGURE 4-15.   *The Report Wizard fields screen with the Ledger Summary fields*

8. Click on the >> button to move all the items under the Available Fields list into the Displayed Fields list. Click on Next.

Now you see the totals screen, which lets you choose fields to aggregate using one of the aggregation functions (Sum, Average, Count, Minimum, Maximum, or %Total). The Ledger Summary report subtotals the amounts for each person.

9. Select the Amount field and click on the Sum > button. The Wizard creates a sum total for the Amount field, as shown in Figure 4-16. Click on Next.

The next screen lists the fields along with their labels and widths.

10. Change Actiondate to "Date." Change the second Total to "Grand Total." Figure 4-17 shows the changed field names. Click on Next.

This brings you to the template screen, which lets you associate a template with the report. You will use the standard Talbot template, as Figure 4-18 shows.

NOTE
You need to locate the standard Talbot template file, Talbot.tdf, from among the various files in your tutorial directory. Use the Browse button next to the Template file field to find it.

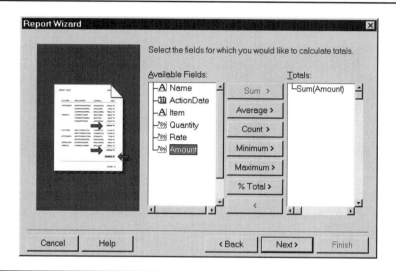

FIGURE 4-16. *The Report Wizard totals screen with sum field*

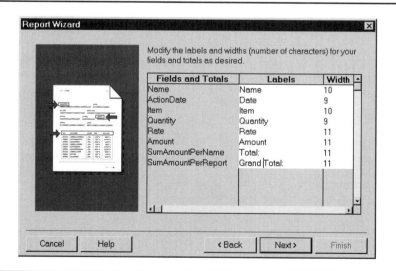

FIGURE 4-17. *The Report Wizard field names screen*

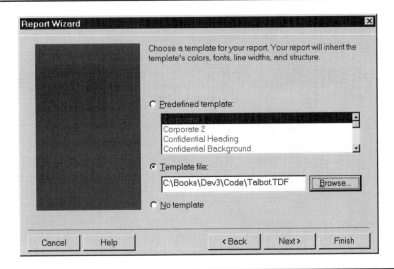

FIGURE 4-18.   *The Report Builder template screen with the Talbot template selected*

11. Choose the Template file radio button, and then fill in the Template file field by using the Browse button and selecting the Talbot.tdf file. Click Finish to create the report.

The Report Wizard now generates the report and displays the Live Previewer with the report, as shown in Figure 4-19. Although the basics are there, you may want to refine the look and feel of the report to present the data more effectively. You can accomplish much of this either with the Report Wizard or the Live Previewer.

Straightening Up After the Wizard

To refine the report into a well-structured report, you can use the Live Previewer to improve the formatting:

- Size the fields and rearrange them to take up less space; when they spread out too much on the page or when the fields are too short, it causes unnecessary wrapping within the field.

- Format the money fields.

- Add a title to the report.

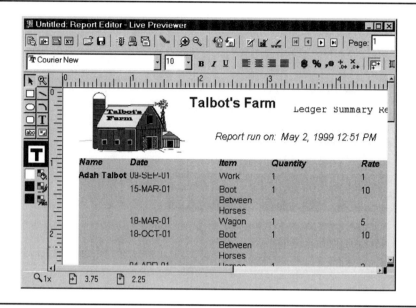

FIGURE 4-19. *The Live Previewer with the initial Ledger Summary report*

To size the fields, move them around in the Live Previewer. The Live Previewer is by default in Flex mode. This mode constrains fields to fit within the page and margins, so you can move the fields up to the point where something goes off the page. You can turn this off with the Flex Mode tool on the Previewer toolbar. If there is room on the page on the right, for example, when you drag a field to the right, the fields between that field and the right margin move over to accommodate the widening field. If there is no space, you can't widen the field. The arrangement is like one of those games where you have to rearrange the pieces, shifting them back and forth, to get them into the pattern you want.

For example, to widen the Person field, you have to reduce the sizes of the number fields to open up some space on the right.

1. Select the Quantity field by clicking on a value in that column.

2. Click on a drag handle on the right side of the column and drag it back toward the number value to reduce the size of the field.

   You see handles all over the place. You can drag the field wider by clicking on any of the side handles. If you get to somewhere the field can't go, such as making it too wide for the page, the mouse cursor turns to a "not" symbol. This is another of those things you need to experience to understand fully, so try it. Generally, you resize the field to fit either the data or the header. In the case of the Quantity field, the numbers are single or double digits, and the header "Quantity" is much longer.

3. Select the "Quantity" header by clicking on it. Double-click on the header to activate text editing, then change the header to "Qty."

The new header is much smaller but is still longer than the numbers underneath it.

4. Resize the Quantity field again to make it smaller.

5. Repeat the resizing process for Rate and Amount; there is no need to change these headers.

6. Drag the fields as far to the right as you can, and then drag Date and Item to the right as well.

7. Select the Person field; then click on a drag handle and drag the border to the right until it is about 1-3/4 inches long and none of the names in the column wrap.

8. To format the money fields, select the field, and then click on the formatting tools on the Live Previewer toolbar.

The $ tool adds a currency symbol, the comma tool adds a digit separator, and the plus tool adds a decimal place. Don't forget to format the totals fields as well as the Amount and Rate fields, including the grand total at the end of the report.

9. Make each of the three numeric fields right-justified by clicking on the Justify Right tool after selecting the field.

The report title appears in Courier type in the center of the upper margin. You need to modify both its location and font to make it appear consistent with the rest of the report.

1. Click on the title to select it.

2. Set the font to Arial 18 bold or some similar attractive font, using the font and size drop-down lists on the toolbar.

3. Resize the field using the sizing handles until the entire text displays nicely.

4. Rearrange the various elements in the report header to display the title in an attractive way.

TIP
By default, the Live Previewer displays the report with Destination Type Previewer. For whatever reason, this style displays the text in the Previewer in slightly incorrect typeface sizes, cutting off some of the text. You can fix this cosmetic issue by setting the Destination Type to Screen. Go to the Object Navigator and find the Reports|UNTITLED|System Parameters|DESTYPE object. Double-click the object to display its Property Palette. Find the Initial Value property and set it through the drop-down list to Screen. Now run the report with the Run tool to redisplay the report in the Previewer.

Saving and Running the Report

This is a good time to save your report. Use the Tools|Preferences menu item to access the Preferences dialog box and its Access tab to choose where to save the report (File, Database, or File/Database). The Builder uses the filename you supply as the report name. When you click on the Save tool in the Data Editor toolbar, the Builder saves the various parts of the report, prompts you for a filename, and updates the Object Navigator with the name you give to the report (in this case, LedgerSummary.RDF).

You can run the report to see what it looks like. Click on the Run button to display the Live Previewer.

Creating Reports for Web Display

At this point, you can generate a Web report in HTML and Adobe Acrobat formats to see what the report will look like online.

Creating an HTML Report
The Hypertext Markup Language (HTML) is an extension of the SGML standard markup language that lets you format documents in a Web browser. HTML provides many features for organizing active Web documents, including hypertext linking and active links that run various kinds of applications. Because HTML is a standard language that runs in any Web browser, you can run an HTML page on any platform that runs a Web browser. HTML is thus an ideal tool for presenting the report in a platform-independent and easy-to-use format.

The following tutorial teaches you these skills:

- How to use the Web Wizard to produce HTML reports
- How to add HTML bookmarks to a report
- How to add standard HTML headers and footers to a report

1. Click on the Web Wizard tool. You see the welcome screen, then the bookmark screen.

The bookmark screen lets you produce a bookmark outline in the report output. A bookmark is a string displayed to the side of the report. When you click on the bookmark, the browser positions you at the corresponding location in the report. The Web Wizard lets you use any group field as a bookmark generator.

2. Use the > button to use the Name group field as a bookmark generator, as Figure 4-20 shows.

The next screen lets you include HTML tags from a file at the beginning and end of your report. You can use this feature to display headers and footers or any other HTML formatting before and after your report displays in the Web page.

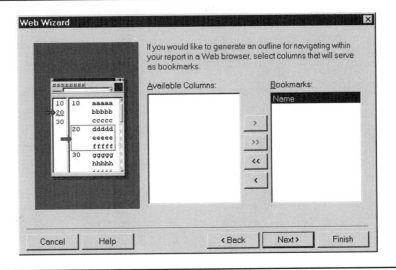

FIGURE 4-20. *The Web Wizard bookmark screen*

3. This report does not use any additional HTML, so click Next.

   This brings you to the final screen, shown in Figure 4-21, which lets you generate an HTML page, an HTML style sheet, an Acrobat PDF, or nothing. By checking the check box "Generate output to a Web browser," you can display the HTML page or PDF document in your default Web browser.

4. Check the "Generate output to a Web browser" check box. Click on the "Generate HTML output now" radio button to generate an HTML file.

5. Click on Finish to generate the report. First, you save the HTML file on disk. Figure 4-22 shows the report in a Netscape Web browser.

Creating an Adobe Acrobat Report

Adobe Acrobat is an extension of the Adobe PostScript language that lets you represent documents in online form exactly as they would appear in hard copy. Acrobat adds hypertext and table-of-contents (bookmark) capabilities to the document to make it an effective tool for online documents. You can also display an Acrobat document on any operating system or user interface that has an Acrobat Reader (most do). Because Oracle Developer reports are static documents, Acrobat is an ideal tool for presenting the report in a platform-independent and easy-to-use format.

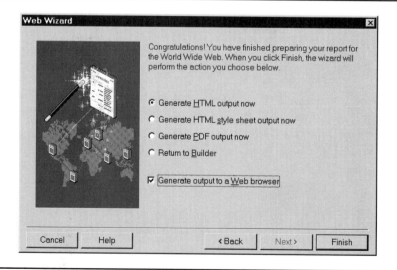

FIGURE 4-21. *The Web Wizard generation screen*

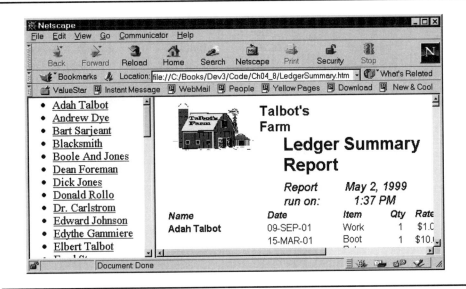

FIGURE 4-22.   *Ledger Summary report prototype in HTML*

The following tutorial teaches you these skills:

■ How to use the Web Wizard to produce Adobe Acrobat reports

■ How to define automatic bookmark production

1. Click on the Web Wizard tool. You see the welcome screen, then the bookmark screen.

   The bookmark screen lets you produce a bookmark outline in the report output. An Acrobat *bookmark* is a tag that shows up in a special bookmark pane in Acrobat. This pane, which Acrobat displays to the left of the document pane in the Acrobat window, gives you an interactive table of contents. When you click on the bookmark, Acrobat positions you to the corresponding location in the report. The Web Wizard lets you use any group field as a bookmark generator.

2. Use the > button to use the Name group field as a bookmark generator, as Figure 4-23 shows.

   The next screen lets you include HTML tags from a file at the beginning and end of your report. You can use this feature to display headers and footers

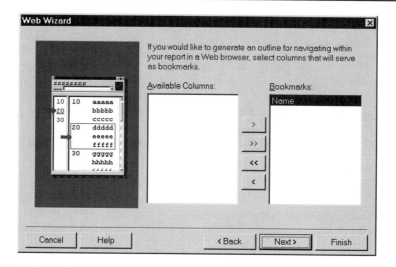

FIGURE 4-23. *The Web Wizard bookmark screen*

or any other HTML formatting before and after your report displays in the Web page.

3. Since this part of the tutorial produces a PDF file, not an HTML file, click Next.

   This brings you to the final screen, shown in Figure 4-24, which lets you generate an HTML page, an HTML style sheet, an Acrobat PDF, or nothing. By checking the check box "Generate output to a Web browser," you can display the HTML page or PDF document in your default Web browser.

4. Check the "Generate output to a Web browser" check box. Click on the "Generate PDF output now" radio button to generate an Acrobat file.

5. Click on Finish to generate the report. First, you save the PDF file on disk. Figure 4-25 shows the report in a Netscape Web browser running the Acrobat Exchange plug-in.

NOTE
You should have your Web browser running before attempting to generate and display the Acrobat file. If you don't, you get an error message saying that the program can't find the browser.

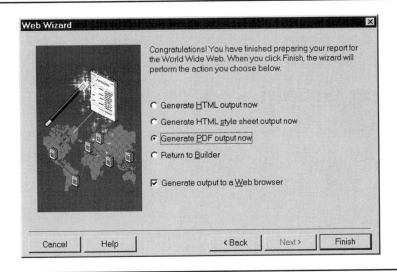

FIGURE 4-24.   *The Web Wizard generation screen for Acrobat*

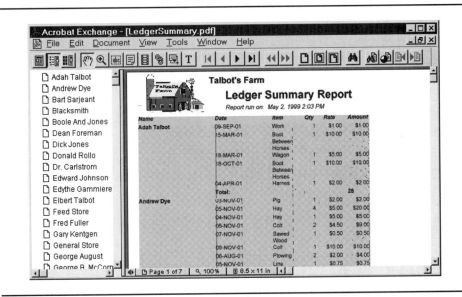

FIGURE 4-25.   *Ledger Summary report prototype in Acrobat*

You've stepped through several tutorials that have demonstrated the basic features of forms and reports. Now it's time to look at how to add some color to your applications with the third component of Oracle Developer, Oracle Developer Graphics.

Adding Graphics to Your Forms and Reports

The Ledger Summary report gives you summary information about each person with whom Talbot Farms does business. To make that report more useful to the customers of the report (probably Talbot executives), you can add simple graphics at the beginning of the report. Such graphics could display the distribution of the "Bought" or "Sold" ledger entries by person. You can also display this chart in your Ledger Entry form as a pop-up display.

Graphics are a full component of Oracle Developer, and you can run them separately if you want to do so. You can provide graphics as standalone applications running through the Oracle Developer Graphics Runtime module. You can make them available through a Web browser, which automatically lets users select from the available graphics. For most applications, however, you will want to embed the graphics and charts into forms and reports, and that is the route this section takes.

You do not have to run the Graphics Designer separately unless you want to build an independent graphics display module for later reuse in several places. Instead, you can use the Chart Wizard within the Form Builder or Report Builder.

NOTE

A graphic display may get data from either the embedding report or form or from the database directly through a separate query. The Chart Wizard assumes you wish to use data already in your form or report to generate the chart. If you want to use a SELECT statement to get data directly from the database, build the chart from scratch rather than use the Wizard, or build a separate data block or data model from which your graphic display can get its data.

Creating a Graphics Display in a Form

When you embed a chart in a form, you usually want that chart to complement and use the data in the form. For example, in the Ledger form, you might add a line chart to show the amounts over time or a pie chart to show the distribution of the totals. If you use the query-by-example features of the form, you want the chart to reflect the subset of data you select. This gives you a powerful tool for illustrating only the information you want to see.

The following tutorial teaches you these skills:

- How to create a graphics display in a form

- How to use the Form Builder Chart Wizard

- How to use data from a data block as graphics display data

- How to get aggregate data from the database to use as graphics display data

- How to position the graphics display in a canvas together with the data

- How to position the graphics display in a separate window available on demand through a button

- How to use navigation to activate and hide windows

- How to save the graphics displays as separate, reusable modules

The tutorial builds two charts in the Ledger application you developed in the section "Creating a Grid Form." The first chart is a line chart that graphs the amounts of transactions over time. This chart will show any trends toward larger transactions or temporary blips due to unusual transactions, for example. This chart will appear underneath the scrolling table of ledger entries and will take its data from that table. The second chart is a pie chart that graphs the distribution of amounts by type, showing how much of the transaction total is due to sales versus purchases. This chart appears in a separate window that you access on demand by clicking on a button above the ledger table.

NOTE
This tutorial assumes you are already familiar with the basic processes of building a data block, so it abbreviates the process a bit. Please go through the Form Builder tutorials if you are not totally familiar with the data-block-building process.

1. Open the Ledger form. Add a new data block named CHART by selecting the Data Blocks node in the Object Navigator, then clicking on the Add tool. Choose to build the data block manually, and then click on the default name and change it to CHART.

2. Make the CHART block a control block. Open the Property Palette for the data block, find the Database Data Block property, and set it to No.

3. Find the canvas in the Object Navigator and double-click on it to display the canvas in the Layout Editor. Drag out the canvas to leave some space under the Ledger grid in which to position the graphic item.

4. Click on the Chart Item tool in the Layout Editor. Draw a rectangle under the existing frame that contains the ledger table grid.

5. Oracle Developer asks whether to use the Chart Wizard; click on OK.

The next screen lets you enter a title for the chart and choose what kind of display you want. The first list contains the different kinds of charts. The second list changes based on your choice in the first one. Each element of the second list represents a subtype of the chart you chose in the first list.

6. Enter the title "Amount Trend." Choose the Line diagram and its Plain subtype in the chart type screen; then click Next.

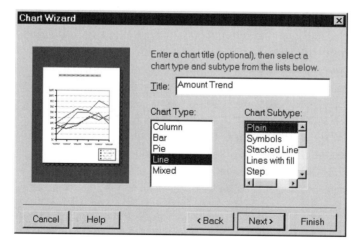

To identify the data for the graph, you first choose a data block as the data source through the data block screen of the Chart Wizard, as Figure 4-26 shows.

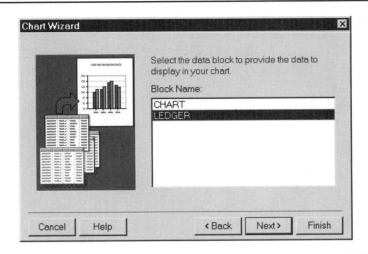

FIGURE 4-26.   *The Forms Chart Wizard data block screen*

7. Choose the Ledger block and click on Next. The Wizard displays the category, or *x*-axis, screen, as Figure 4-27 shows.

8. Choose the ActionDate field to use as the *x-axis—the time axis. Click on Next. The Wizard displays the value, or y-axis, screen, as Figure 4-28 shows.*

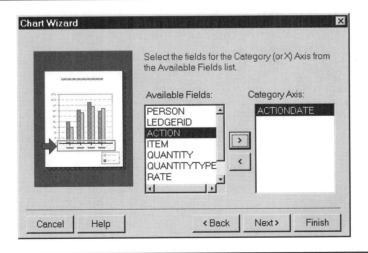

FIGURE 4-27.   *The Chart Wizard category screen*

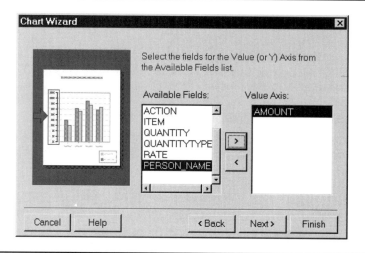

FIGURE 4-28. *The Chart Wizard value screen*

9. Choose Amount as the *y*-axis value—the quantity that the chart displays for each date. Click on Next. Figure 4-29 shows the final screen.

10. Save the chart as AmountTrend.OGD by clicking on Finish.

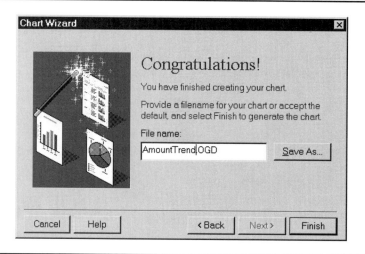

FIGURE 4-29. *The Chart Wizard save screen*

You now have an embedded line chart in your Ledger form. Unfortunately, it is an item in the Ledger data block. If you scroll down in the canvas, you see the graphic repeating. That's because there is one for each record in the Ledger grid. You need to move the graphic to the CHART data block to have it display only once.

11. Rename the chart item to "AMOUNTTREND." Drag it into the CHART data block.

If you run the form with the Run tool and execute a query in the ledger block with the Execute Query tool, you will see the chart populated with the data values, as in Figure 4-30.

Now create a pie chart that breaks down the amount by action and displays in a separate window. This part of the tutorial requires data from the database rather than data from the Ledger data block, as the chart aggregates information about the ledger transactions. That is, instead of using the raw data from the Ledger data block, you want to group the values by action and display the sums for each group. Since the Ledger data block has no calculated fields corresponding to this data, and since the records in that block do not correspond one-to-one with the items to

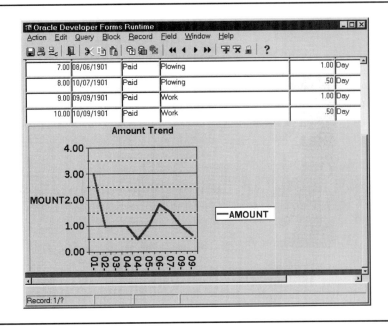

FIGURE 4-30. *The Ledger form with a graphics display*

display in the graphic, you must query the data separately. This requires a separate data block to hold the aggregate data plus some code to get the data on demand and display the chart.

The easiest way to get this kind of data is to create a view in the database with the appropriate aggregation, although there are ways to create a block based on an embedded query. Using a view lets you use the Data Block Wizard to create the block; it also moves the aggregation processing to the database server, which can improve performance and reduce network traffic.

NOTE

The creation of this data block and its corresponding canvas and window require using some advanced techniques that you will learn about in more detail in Chapter 6. For now, just follow the tutorial instructions exactly.

12. Create a view in the database with the following SQL run in SQLPLUS or another SQL execution tool as the Talbot user:

```
CREATE OR REPLACE VIEW ActionAmount (Action, Amount) AS
SELECT Action, SUM(Amount)
  FROM Ledger
 GROUP BY Action;
```

13. Add a new data block to the form by clicking on Ledger and clicking on the Add tool. Use the Data Block Wizard to find the ActionAmount view (don't forget to click the Views radio button to see the views in the browser) and the two columns. Select both columns to include in the block. This creates the ActionAmount data block.

14. Display the Property Palette for the ActionAmount data block. Find the Query All Records property and set it to Yes.

15. Double-click on the Triggers node under the new block. Add a When-New-Block-Instance trigger and type the following code into the PL/SQL Editor:

```
Execute_Query;
```

The When-New-Block-Trigger executes whenever you navigate into the data block. Putting the Execute_Query built-in subprogram call into this trigger forces the form to query the aggregate data every time you enter the block. The idea is to click on a button in the Ledger canvas that navigates to the graphic display item in the ActionAmount data block. This navigation fires the trigger, which queries all the aggregate data because the data block Query All Records property is set to Yes. The records then populate the graphic display.

16. Create a new canvas by selecting the Canvases node in the Object Navigator and clicking on the Add tool. Name the canvas PIECHARTCANVAS.

17. Display the empty PIECHARTCANVAS by double-clicking on the canvas object in the Object Navigator.

18. Click on the Chart Item tool in the Layout Editor for the PIECHARTCANVAS, and drag out a chart rectangle on the canvas. The Form Builder again displays the Chart Wizard.

19. Enter a display title of "Amount by Action." Choose the Pie chart with the Plain subtype and click Next.

20. Choose the ActionAmount data block as the data source and click Next.

21. Choose the Action item as the x-axis, or category data source, and click Next.

22. Choose the Amount item as the y-axis, or value data source, and click Next.

23. Save the graphics display as ActionSummary.OGD and click Finish.

24. Rename the chart item in the Object Navigator to "AMOUNTBYACTION" and move it to the CHART data block.

The final step in creating the ActionAmount data block is to add an OK button to that block that will serve two purposes. First, this button displays in the graphic window and lets you dismiss the window. If you didn't have the button, you wouldn't be able to dismiss the window. Second, the button serves as the single navigable item in the canvas that will hold the display. Without a navigable item to which to transfer the focus (see Chapter 5 for details on the concept of focus), you won't be able to display the window with its chart.

25. Click on the Button tool in the Layout Editor displaying the PIECHARTCANVAS canvas and draw a small button under the chart item you just added.

26. Double-click the button to display the Property Palette. Find the Label property and set it to "OK."

27. Find the button in the Object Navigator. Rename the button to "OKBUTTON." Move the button to be the first item in the ActionAmount data block. Double-click the Triggers node to add a trigger to the item and add a When-Button-Pressed trigger. Enter the following code into the PL/SQL Editor:

```
Go_Block('LEDGER');
Hide_Window ('CHARTWINDOW');
```

When the user presses the OK button, the Forms Runtime fires the When-Button-Pressed trigger. The Go_Block built-in subprogram navigates out of the current block (ActionAmount) to the Ledger block. This removes the focus from the chart window. The Hide_Window built-in subprogram then removes the window from the form so you can no longer see it. The effect is to close the window.

NOTE
While this approach may seem rather ornate, say, compared to calling the Close_Window built-in (which doesn't exist in Oracle Developer), all of the steps have a purpose. Chapter 6 goes into detail on the navigation processes and how they support moving the focus from data block to data block and window to window. This way of doing things synchronizes the window and canvas displays with the underlying data blocks in a rigorous way so that the Forms Runtime always has a single point of focus. It may seem confusing at first, but once you get the hang of it, it becomes second nature in Form Builder programming.

Next, you have to create a new window for the canvas.

28. Find the Windows node in the Object Navigator and click on the Add tool to add a new window. Name the window CHARTWINDOW by clicking on the default name.

29. Display the window's Property Palette by double-clicking on the window object. Find the Title property and set it to "Summary of Amount by Action."

30. Find the Primary Canvas property and select the PIECHARTCANVAS from the drop-down list.

This associates the canvas with the window. You also need to make sure the Window property of the canvas is set to the CHARTWINDOW.

31. Display the Property Palette for the canvas by right-clicking on the object and choosing Property Palette from the pop-up menu. Find the Window property and set it to CHARTWINDOW.

Now you must create the button to display the chart.

32. Display the Ledger canvas. Click on the Button tool and draw out a button rectangle on the canvas (here, it's just above the grid, which I've moved down to accommodate the button). Double-click on the button to display its Property Palette. Set the Label property to "Summarize." Go to the Object Navigator and move the button to the CHART data block.

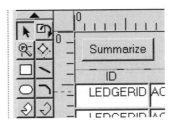

33. Find the button item in the Object Navigator. Find the Triggers node under the item and double-click it to create a new trigger. Add a When-Button-Pressed trigger. Enter the following code into the PL/SQL Editor:

```
Go_Item('ACTIONAMOUNT.OKBUTTON');
```

The Go_Item built-in subprogram navigates to a particular item, in this case the OK button you just created. This shifts the focus to the OK button, and in turn to its canvas, which also displays the pie chart. Be careful to use the single quotes, and don't misspell the name. You should always specify the item name prefixed with the data block name so that there is no possibility of ambiguity if you have the same item name in more than one data block.

When the user running the form clicks on the Summarize button, the Forms Runtime fires the When-Button-Pressed trigger, which then navigates the cursor to the OK button. This in turn causes the display of the pie-chart canvas in its default window, popping up the window over the Ledger window and displaying the pie chart.

When you compile and run the application, click on the button. You will now see the pie chart appear in a separate window, as in Figure 4-31.

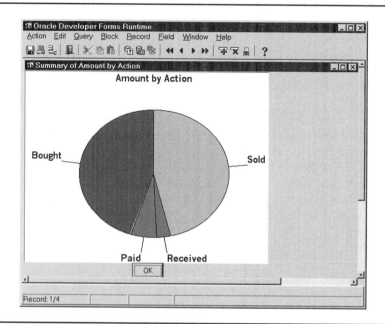

FIGURE 4-31. *Ledger form pie chart*

TIP
You can close the window by choosing the File|Exit menu item; you may want to make the window a dialog box and add an OK button (see Chapter 6) to close it, as well as implementing the standard window close button on the window's title bar.

Creating a Graphics Display in a Report

This tutorial teaches you the following skills:

- How to create a graphics display in a report

- How to use the Report Builder Chart Wizard

- How to use the summary information from the report to generate a graphic summary display

- How to position the graphics display in a report header

- How to save the graphics display as a separate, reusable module

The tutorial creates a pie chart that shows the distribution of ledger transactions among people. This chart lets you rank people by their impact on transactions in the ledger. The pie chart will appear in the *report header*—the page that comes before the repeating record pages of the report.

1. Open the Ledger Summary report, go to the Layout Editor by double-clicking the Layout Model node in the Object Navigator, and click on the Header Section tool.

2. Click on the Chart Wizard tool. The first screen after the welcome screen lets you both give your chart a title and choose what kind of chart to create (line, pie, bar, and so on), as Figure 4-32 shows.

3. Enter the title in the title field ("Amount Sold by Person") here. To create a pie chart for the Ledger form showing the distribution of amounts by person, click on Pie in the first column and Plain in the second. Click on Next.

   The next screen you see shows you the report fields. When creating a chart in report, the Chart Wizard assumes you want to display data from a data model in the report. The category fields screen in Figure 4-33 shows you a list of report fields that you can use in your graphics display.

4. Choose the Name field to identify the pie slices (the Category Axis). Click on Next to go to the next screen, the value field screen, shown in Figure 4-34.

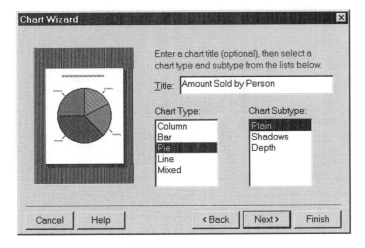

FIGURE 4-32. *The Chart Wizard chart type screen for the Ledger Summary report*

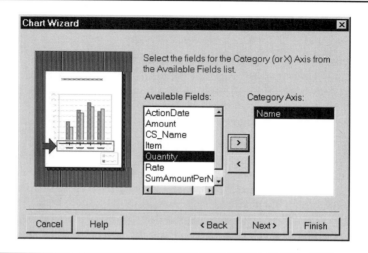

FIGURE 4-33. *The Chart Wizard category fields screen*

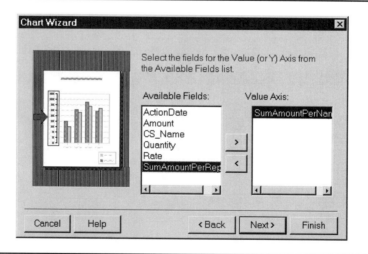

FIGURE 4-34. *The Chart Wizard value screen*

5. Choose SumAmountPerName as the *y*-axis value—the quantity the chart uses to calculate the size of the pie slices. You want the sum of the ledger entries for each person. Click on Next.

The next screen is the print frequency screen, shown in Figure 4-35. This screen lets you choose among several options for the placement of the chart on the report. In this case, you only want the chart to display once for the report.

6. Choose "at the beginning of the report" to place the graphic in the report header. Click on Next.

7. Save the display module as AmountByPerson.OGD in your project directory. Click on Finish to complete the chart.

8. Run the report; you see the graphic appear on the first page of the report, as Figure 4-36 illustrates.

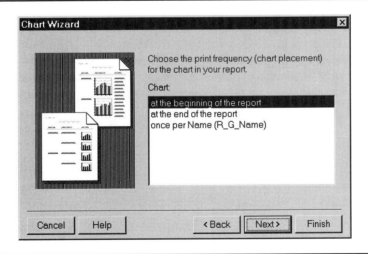

FIGURE 4-35.   *The Chart Wizard print frequency screen*

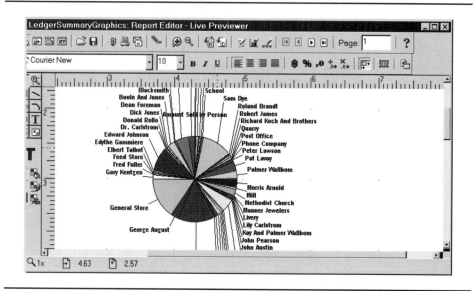

FIGURE 4-36.   *The Amount Sold by Person chart in the Ledger Summary report*

This particular pie chart is far from optimal in structure. To clean it up, you can open the chart in the Graphics Builder and use the tools there (see Chapter 8 for details on the Graphics Builder) to arrange the slices more neatly, to suppress many of the very small slices, and to rearrange the title.

You now have a complete, working prototype with forms, reports, and graphics! Now, it's time to get into some detail about how Oracle Developer accomplishes all this magic.

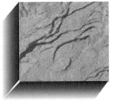

CHAPTER
5

Advanced Processes, Triggers, and Cross-Platform Design

he previous chapter exposed you to the broad strokes you make with Oracle Developer. This chapter examines the internal workings of the product. It shows you the specific processes and how they work to produce the effects you want. With knowledge of these processes, you will understand how to use the event-handling features of Oracle Developer in some detail, preparing you for the advanced tutorials in the next few chapters.

NOTE
The tutorials and examples in this chapter show you how and where to use PL/SQL programming in triggers to add your own logic to the Oracle Developer standard processes. Often, the standard processing is enough: Chapter 4 showed you how to build a working application with no coding at all. Chapters 11 and 12 go into PL/SQL programming in detail, so this chapter simply presents the example code without further discussion of programming details. These examples show you how to accomplish basic tasks in triggers; you can build on what you learn here and in Chapters 11 and 12 to build very sophisticated applications.

In the Unified Modeling Language (UML), activity diagrams represent processes. *Activity diagrams* show the flow of work through a process much as did the older flowchart diagram, but activity charts refer directly to the state of objects and the flow of control between them. They are very well suited to illustrating the process work flow of Oracle Developer forms, reports, and graphics at runtime. At the first drawing in the chapter, the text will explain activity diagramming in enough detail for you to understand it, giving examples from the drawing.

You also need to consider platform portability—how to get your application to run on more than one target computer platform. This chapter describes the issues associated with cross-platform application development in Oracle Developer. It shows you how to design your forms, reports, and graphics for maximum portability.

Oracle Developer Processes and Triggers: How It All Works

This section gives you an overview of how Oracle Developer performs its magic. Prior chapters have introduced some of the basic concepts of database applications and the objects in Oracle Developer. This chapter shows how these objects interact to behave as a system.

The most practical of all your low-level design decisions in an Oracle Developer application is *where* to put your code. Because you are not developing the application logic from scratch, you must fit your additions into the Oracle Developer logic. To do that, you need to understand where Developer runs your code, and what happens before and after your code executes. This section gives you a clear picture of where you can intervene in the Oracle Developer processes by showing what the processes are and where the triggers fire within those processes.

Oracle Developer applications are *event driven.* When you run an application, you interact with the runtime system to cause events, which in turn start various *form* processes. The form processes contain the preprogrammed *default behavior* for forms, reports, and graphs. As various internal events occur during this processing, the runtime system handles them by running the code you write in PL/SQL: it *fires triggers.*

You inherit at a high level the set of assumptions and behaviors the designers built into the product. Instead of having to analyze and design from the ground up, you start with a set of preprogrammed behaviors, giving you a dramatic head start on development. The processes in this chapter describe the default runtime behavior of an Oracle Developer application. Understanding these processes helps you to think like Oracle Developer rather than developing the whole system of behavior from scratch. You are much more likely to succeed with Oracle Developer if you work with it rather than against it.

Forms Processes and Triggers

Of the three parts of Oracle Developer, Forms has the most sophisticated process logic by far. This section gives you an overview of the different processes and triggers in Forms.

First, you must understand some basic concepts: navigation and scope.

Navigation

The user interface permits the user of the system to do work. Although this seems obvious, the consequences are fundamental for understanding the development structure of a form. Oracle Developer Forms is event driven, which implies that the user controls the processing through the user interface, rather than the application controlling it.

At any given time, the Oracle Developer Forms user interface permits the user to interact with a single object, such as a push button, a drop-down list, or a text field. This single object, a part of the user interface, is the user's *focus*. Another way of referring to the focus is to refer to the position of the *cursor*—a kind of virtual pointer that points to the object that has the focus. Like a unicorn, the cursor is a mythical beast that sometimes allows you to see it. For example, when the cursor appears in a text field, it usually appears as the text entry marker for the platform, such as the straight bar for Windows or the I-beam for the Macintosh. Other items, such as pictures or radio buttons, do not explicitly show a cursor. Using the term "focus" can avoid confusion, especially as the term "cursor" refers to at least three other things. It can refer to the mouse cursor, an SQL cursor, or the keyboard cursor itself that exists independently of your form.

NOTE

By "single object," I mean single application object. From the form process perspective, user interface objects such as windows and menus are irrelevant; only items on canvases count as things on which you can focus. From the user interface perspective, however, "focus" applies just as much to the window containing the application focus as it does to that object itself. So, for example, if the focus is on a text field, it is also on the window that contains the canvas on which the text field appears, and on the application's MDI window as well. The term "focus" in this book refers to application object focus, not window focus. You can also download a complete reference to the processes from the McGraw-Hill Web site, www.osborne.com, along with the code examples for this book.

The user interacts with the application by moving the focus from object to object. This movement is *navigation*. By navigating from item to item, record to record, block to block, or form to form, the user controls the tasks that make up the application. Navigation events (going to a different item, going to a different record, going to a different block, going to a different form) constitute the basic events of your form application. Many of the processes in subsequent sections either contain or are a result of such events.

In Oracle Developer Forms, the navigational objects are arranged in a hierarchy of *navigational units*. The form contains a series of blocks, each of which contains a set of records and a sequence of items. Part of the navigational behavior of Oracle Developer Forms is the automatic navigation that occurs because of user actions. If the focus is on an item in one block and you click on another item in the block, this action navigates from item to item. If the items are in different blocks, however, you also must navigate from data block to data block. If each data block has different records, you also navigate from record to record. Each of these navigational events has a different consequence, such as certain triggers firing (When-Validate-Item, When-Validate-Block, and When-Validate-Record, respectively, in this case).

This hierarchy of objects—item, record, block, form—results in a set of processes that refer to navigating to a level, such as Navigate to Form Level. The "Level" in the names of these form processes refers to the navigational unit in the object hierarchy:

- Navigate to the Form Level

- Navigate to the Block Level

- Navigate to the Record Level

- Navigate to the Item Level

Each of these form processes moves the focus from the current unit to the indicated object. The process identifies the next smaller subunit of the navigation unit that contains a target and "enters," or sets the focus to, that object.

The navigation process automatically *validates* the current navigation unit. For example, if you navigate to the form level from an item, you validate the item depending on which particular event is the cause of the navigation. Some events navigate without validation; most navigate with validation. Most of the time this depends on the validation unit—the level at which you set the form to validate through the form's Validation Unit property. The "Validation" section, later in this chapter, tells you the basics of validation processes.

Although most forms navigation is a result of user actions, a process can also cause navigation to occur. You can call built-in subprograms such as Go_Item, Go_Block, or Go_Record, for example, in many of the Oracle Developer Forms triggers. Later in the chapter, "Navigational Processing" gives more details on explicit navigation.

NOTE

Navigation is a key concept in Oracle Developer. Virtually everything you do relates to navigation. Although the concept and processes themselves are quite simple, their ubiquity combines in many interesting and sometimes unpredictable ways. More than anything else, navigation in Developer is where you must "go with the flow," both literally and figuratively. Trying to fool Developer's navigational structure will almost always result in problems.

Trigger Scope

You can define triggers in Oracle Developer Forms at the item, block, or form levels in the Object Navigator hierarchy. The *trigger scope* is the set of objects that fire the trigger; it consists of the object that owns that trigger and any objects belonging to that object. For example, if you attach a trigger to a block, events in all the items in that block fire that trigger.

NOTE
Those paying sharp attention may realize that the last paragraph does not mention record-level scope. Though there are record navigation triggers, you don't define those triggers on records. A record exists only at runtime; it is not available as an object in Form Builder, and you therefore cannot attach a trigger to a "record." Since the data block, seen one way, is a collection of records, it is most often the place where you'll attach the record-oriented triggers. These block triggers fire on the current record—the record that has the focus. Thus, there is no actual record trigger scope.

If there is more than one trigger with the same name in a particular scope, by default Oracle Developer fires the one attached to the object lowest in the hierarchy. For example, if you put a When-New-Item trigger on both an item and that item's block, Oracle Developer fires the trigger on the item and ignores the one on the block. You can change this behavior for a particular trigger by changing the Execution Style property of the trigger in the trigger's property sheet. The default is Override, but you can also choose Before or After. Before specifies that the trigger fire before any higher-level trigger, and After, that it fire after a higher-level trigger. The next-higher-level trigger fires with either choice along with the current trigger. You can set the properties in higher scoping levels to cause all the different triggers at those levels to fire before or after the item trigger.

TIP
Using Execution Style set to Before or After and having multiple triggers firing increases the complexity of your module dramatically. Unless you have a really strong reason to do it, you should avoid it to make your modules easier to understand, debug, and test.

Some triggers only make sense when you define them at a specific level. When-Validate-Record, for example, does not apply to individual items. You can define it only at the block and form levels. The SmartTriggers feature identifies the most likely triggers to define for a particular object. Right-click the object for which you want to define a trigger in the Object Navigator or the Layout Editor. The resulting pop-up menu contains a SmartTriggers item. Clicking on that item displays a submenu that lists the triggers that make the most sense for the object. Choose the appropriate item to display the PL/SQL editor for the trigger. The submenu also contains an Other item that displays the standard trigger choice dialog box listing all Oracle Developer triggers.

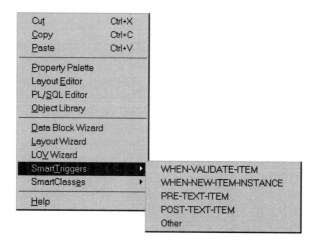

You can also inherit triggers through property classes, and you can include triggers by referring to an object group that has the trigger defined. The same rules apply to these triggers: only one trigger executes. If you override the Property-Class trigger with a trigger on the item, the item trigger executes. Object groups can only define form-level triggers; block and item triggers come along with their blocks and items.

NOTE

For simplicity's sake, the activity charts in this chapter do not show triggers with their decisions, but every trigger results in either a success or failure. If the trigger succeeds, the process continues as the diagram shows; if the trigger fails, the process stops with a failure return.

Now you've had an overview of navigation and have gained a basic understanding of how triggers work, how to use SmartTriggers, and how you can modify the default properties of a trigger. It's time to see what processes and triggers really do in practical terms.

Transaction Processing

A form *transaction* is a sequence of events, processes, and triggers that ultimately results in either committing data to the database or rolling back changes. This section describes the processing that underlies your actual work in transactions. The following sections cover the actual processes.

POSTING TO THE DATABASE   *Posting* to the database means writing any pending changes in a form to the database through a series of INSERT, UPDATE, and DELETE statements. Oracle Developer generates these statements as part of its default processing. Posting *does not commit the changes,* but it usually accompanies a commit or rollback as part of the default behavior. Part of the posting process is the firing of all the validation triggers, so every post to the database validates the stored data, whether committed or not.

By default, there is one post to the database followed by a commit or rollback to end the transaction; however, you can use the POST built-in procedure to post the changes without committing. The primary use for posting without committing is when you open a form from another form. In this situation, you may have uncommitted data in the first form, and the second form may exist for the purpose of adding more data to an ongoing transaction.

For example, you might be entering an item in an accounting transaction that requires adding some detailed information in a subsidiary table through a separate form. When you open a second form, Oracle Developer requires that all outstanding data be posted to the database to ensure data integrity. Thus, you call Post in the When-Validate-Item trigger code on the item.

NOTE
Chapter 10 gives a more complete discussion of multiple-form processing and the different techniques you can use to manage it.

Before going into detail on the posting process, here's a capsule lesson in interpreting activity diagrams. The rounded rectangles are *action states*—a state with an internal action and at least one outgoing transition. The activity diagrams in this chapter refer entirely to internal Oracle Developer Forms processes as action states, such as Savepoint or Clean up cursors. The arrows between action states represent *transitions*—movement from an action state to another state or decision. There are two special transitions. The transition originating in a black circle is an *entry transition* representing the beginning of the activities in the diagram. The transition ending in a black circle with an outer circle is an *exit transition* representing the end of the activities. Exit transitions are either "success" or "failure" depending on the result of the activities. The diamond shapes represent *decisions,* which split transitions based on guard conditions (if this condition is true, flow this way, and if this condition is true, flow that way). The text near each transition out of the decision is a *guard condition.*

Figure 5-1 is the simplified activity chart for the posting process.

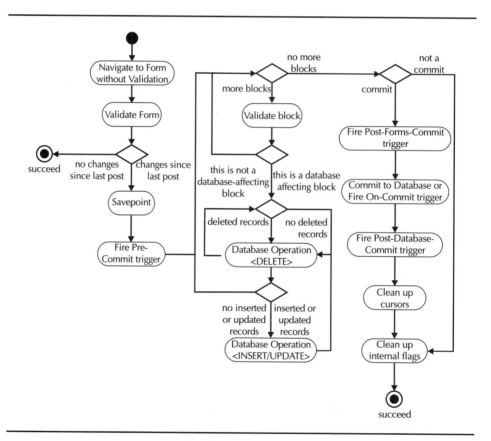

FIGURE 5-1. *A simplified UML activity diagram for the posting process*

Now, let's get into the details of the posting process. First, Oracle Developer navigates to the form level, then validates the form. If there are no changes that require posting, the process stops right there.

Oracle Developer then issues a savepoint before posting. The *savepoint* is a feature of Oracle that marks a point in a transaction to which you can roll back if necessary without rolling back the entire transaction. This permits Oracle Developer to post multiple times without rolling back all the posts—just the one that failed.

NOTE
The SAVEPOINT statement may not be available with database managers other than Oracle, so if you have a database portability requirement, you should not use the POST procedure. Also, Oracle Developer uses the SAVEPOINT when you call another form using the Open_Form or Call_Form built-in functions, so that if a commit fails in the called form, it rolls back only to the savepoint.

After issuing the savepoint, Oracle Developer fires the Pre-Commit trigger, then loops through the blocks. For each block, it validates the block, then determines whether the block has any changes that affect the database. If the block is a control block, it has no such changes. If the block's base table is a *nonupdateable view* (one with a join or other disqualifying condition), Oracle Developer only processes the block if there are transaction triggers defined in it. Finally, if the block has no changed records, Oracle Developer skips the block.

Block processing then proceeds in two parts: dealing with deleted rows and dealing with inserts and updates by looping through the records in the block. Figure 5-2 shows the details of database operation processing. Database operations consist of DELETE, INSERT, or UPDATE statements and include the Pre- and Post-operation triggers. You can replace the default operation with an On-<Operation> trigger if you need to control database operations (for example, in using database managers other than Oracle with differing syntaxes).

After processing all the blocks, if the process is a commit, not just a post, Oracle Developer fires the Post-Forms-Commit trigger, commits the changes (or fires the On-Commit trigger if there is one), and fires the Post-Database-Commit trigger. It then cleans up SQL cursors as required. Oracle Developer then cleans up the internal flags, including marking all the inserted records as database records and marking any changed items as Valid.

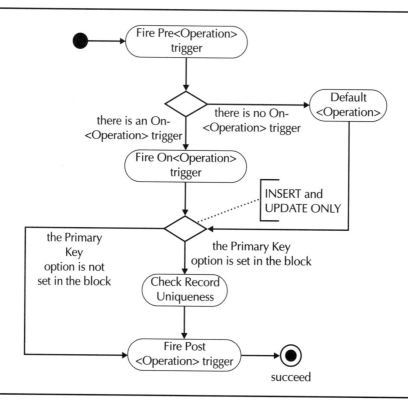

FIGURE 5-2. *A UML activity diagram for database operations*

NOTE

If you use any of the Pre- or Post-operation triggers to change database-related data in the form, it is possible for Oracle Developer to commit these changes to the database without validating them because it immediately marks everything as Valid. Revalidating might cause an infinite validation loop as triggers fire, changes get made, and more validation is required.

The most common triggers you will use in posting are the Pre-Insert, Pre-Update, Pre-Delete, Post-Insert, Post-Update, and Post-Delete triggers. These triggers contain the code you write to check multiple-table conditions or to manipulate data in other tables that depends on the changes you're posting to the database. They can also contain the auditing updates you add to your application to trace activity against specific tables.

NOTE
Many of the actions you might take in Pre- and Post-triggers may be more appropriately coded in server triggers. That is, you may want to add triggers to your database for pre- and post-operation actions. You would move these into application triggers when the triggers must refer to data that does not exist in the database, such as the value of an item in a control block or values in other data blocks that have not yet moved into the server database. Briefly, if you need to refer to a block and item in your PL/SQL code, you probably need to be coding a trigger in the application. Another reason to use these triggers is to move the message handling from the database server to the application to enable better and more informative messages.

For example, the Ledger form lets a Talbot Farms employee enter transactions in the daily journal. Before deleting a row, the Pre-Delete trigger contains code that looks up the security access level of the user with respect to deleting transactions. If the user doesn't have the appropriate security level, then the trigger fails and the system displays an error message telling the user that he or she does not have security privileges to delete transactions.

```
DECLARE
   v_Level NUMBER = 0; -- lowest security level as default
BEGIN
   SELECT SecurityLevel
     INTO v_Level
     FROM User_Security_Level
    WHERE User = :Control.Username AND Object = 'Transaction';
   IF v_Privilege < 5 THEN -- delete only for security level 5 and over
     Message('You must have level 5 security to delete transactions.');
     Form_Trigger_Failure;
   END IF;
END;
```

LOCKING   The Oracle database manager ensures integrity while permitting concurrent access to data through locking resources such as tables and rows. Locking is how Oracle implements transactions, or logical units of work. Some database applications lock entire tables; others lock physical pages of data. Oracle Developer, working with Oracle, uses the exclusive row lock, which is a lock on a specific row that prevents other transactions from updating or deleting the row by preventing them from acquiring locks on the row. Adding the FOR UPDATE OF clause to an Oracle SQL SELECT statement signals the need to acquire row locks.

By default, Oracle Developer acquires row locks under any of the following conditions:

- When the operator changes the value of a base table item in a database row, including a change from a NULL value to a non-NULL value.

- When the operator requests an explicit row lock for the current record through the Record|Lock menu item.

- When a trigger makes a change to the database through an UPDATE or DELETE statement.

- When a trigger calls the DELETE_RECORD, ENTER_QUERY(FOR_UPDATE), EXECUTE_QUERY(FOR_UPDATE), or LOCK_RECORD built-in functions.

- When a trigger contains an explicit SQL LOCK TABLE statement. Because this will usually seriously impact transaction performance in your application, you should not do it without an overwhelmingly good reason and several design reviews with people who understand the transaction behavior of the application.

If Oracle Developer cannot obtain a lock immediately, it tries to obtain the lock repeatedly for a fixed number of times, then asks you whether to proceed. If this happens a lot, have your database administrator monitor the database to figure out why the resources are unavailable. Often, this is a result of using explicit, exclusive table locks, which you should avoid when possible.

As with any transaction, when the transaction commits or rolls back, the database manager releases all the locks. Because Oracle Developer uses savepoints, it is possible to retain some locks after a rollback, permitting you to redo just the rolled back part after making necessary changes.

NOTE
If you explicitly lock queried rows in a trigger, you will need to query those rows again to reestablish the locks on the rows after a commit or rollback. Clearing a block or record does not release any row locks on rows that correspond to the record(s).

If you define an On-Lock trigger at any level, Oracle Developer fires that trigger whenever it tries to obtain a lock at that level. You can use this trigger to replace the default locking mechanism (if you have sufficient justification to do so).

CAUTION
Avoid using the On-Lock trigger when you are running the application against an Oracle database, as you are likely to degrade transaction throughput by replacing Oracle's locking strategies.

You control locking through the Locking Mode property on the block. The default setting of this property when you create the block is Immediate, meaning that Oracle Developer will automatically lock the current record if you change a base-table item in that record. You can change this to Delayed, meaning that Oracle Developer waits until just before committing to acquire the locks. Under some circumstances, this can improve transaction performance in high-volume applications by allowing other users to change the value while you're still looking at it. The risk is that such actions will invalidate any work the user does before he or she commits it, causing an error that requires additional work unexpectedly. This can be confusing and irritating if it happens often. When you are deploying your applications over the Internet, your best bet is to make use of the Oracle Developer Server's locking and transaction management capabilities. Application developers using these features don't need to worry about the difficult-to-manage locking and transaction management issues in their applications.

There is another property, Lock Record, on text items. You use this for text items that are not base-table items (that is, that do not correspond to columns in the underlying database table). Ordinarily, changing such an item does not invoke immediate locking, since you haven't really changed any item in the database row. Setting Lock Record to Yes for such a text item instructs Oracle Developer to attempt to lock the current record if you change the text for the item.

Validation

Validation is the process of making sure that an object satisfies all the constraints you put on it in defining the form. Oracle Developer automatically validates items, records, blocks, and forms when necessary. You can add additional constraints in triggers, either as part of the validation process (validation triggers) or as part of the transaction process (see the previous section). Validation happens when you navigate out of the object or when you press the ENTER key or call the Enter built-in procedure. Also, the posting process automatically validates the form when the user commits or when your code posts changes.

VALIDATION UNITS AND STATES   You can validate item, record, data block, or form objects. The automatic validation by default validates items, meaning that automatic validation fires off every time you navigate out of an item. You can set the validation unit to record, data block, or form to suppress automatic validation to a certain level. If you do this, Oracle Developer does not do any validation until you take an action that validates at the level you've specified. If you choose Form, for example, you validate only when you post changes, which in turn validates the form. Generally, you should leave the validation unit at item level for best results. You can change the validation unit through the Validation Unit property of the form object.

TIP

Oracle Corporation recommends that you change the Validation Unit property only when running the application against database managers other than Oracle.

Before getting into detail about dynamics, you need to understand the different trigger-related states of items and records in an Oracle Developer form application. An *object state* is the configuration of properties of the object at some point in the object's life cycle. Most Oracle Developer objects have many different properties, such as screen location, width, height, and so on. *Trigger-related* object state does not refer explicitly to these properties, only to the properties relevant to trigger behavior. This simplifies the object state considerably.

The following subsections build from the individual item all the way up to form. Each object refers to the state of other objects, usually down the hierarchy.

ITEM STATE AND VALIDATION   The state of an item has to do with the value of the item and what you have done to that value. An item can be New, Changed, or Valid. Figure 5-3 shows the activity diagram for the item validation

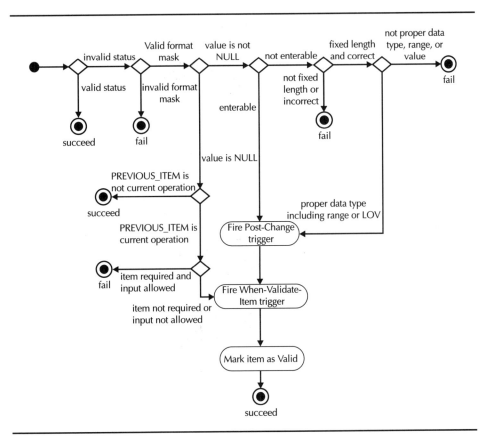

FIGURE 5-3.   *The activity diagram for the item validation process*

process. As you can see from this diagram, validation is mostly a series of decisions about validity of various kinds.

You can create an item in any of three ways:

- *Creating* a record creates the items in the record as New. Oracle Developer can fill in the value with a default value or copy it from another item in the process, but the item is still New.

- *Duplicating* a record—copying the values from the previous record into a New record—puts the items in the New record into any of the three substates New, Changed, or Valid. The exact state duplicates the state of the item in the previous record, from which Oracle Developer copies the item.

- *Fetching* the record immediately makes the items in the record Valid and executes the On-Fetch and Post-Change triggers for each item (the latter exists for compatibility; you should not use it). The "Fetching Records" section later in this chapter gives more details.

When you modify an item in any way, Oracle Developer marks the item Changed. Item validation happens only for New and Changed items. When you have a New or Changed item and the Validate Item process results in True, Oracle Developer fires the Post-Change and When-Validate-Item triggers, then marks the item Valid. When the Validate Item process results in False, the item remains as it was, and the cursor remains on the item.

TIP
You should not use the Post-Change trigger, as Oracle is phasing it out. Use the When-Validate-Item trigger instead.

Records own items, so the only way to get rid of a particular item is to clear the record; this can happen in any item state. You can always set the item to its default value through Clear_Item, but this does not remove the item from memory; only removing the record can do that.

When you validate an item, the process checks the following properties, as you saw in Figure 5-3:

- *Format mask:* The format of the item value for a text item (status can be Valid or Invalid).

- *Required and input allowed:* Whether the item value must exist.

- *Fixed length:* Whether the item value must be a certain length and is that length.

- *Data type:* The basic type of value, such as number or date.

- *Range:* The minimum and maximum values possible.

- *List of values:* The list of possible values in a list-of-values (LOV) object.

- *Formula:* If there is a formula on that field, the formula is calculated.

If everything validates, the process fires the Post-Change and When-Validate-Item triggers for the item to do any additional validation. The process marks the item as Valid if these triggers succeed.

If you consider the above list of validation properties for the item, you can see that there are really very few things you will need to code in a When-Validate-Item trigger. Consider, also, that your database will probably have CHECK constraints that validate individual items on insert and update with simple SQL expressions. Given all this built-in checking, what's left for the When-Validate-Item trigger?

Generally, you use a When-Validate-Item trigger for complex, multiple-item validation, usually some kind of business rule that involves more than one item or even a database lookup of some kind. For example, say the purchasing manager at Talbot Farms was entering the price for a Buy transaction. The accounting department could have a limit for each user on the price in a read-only database table, AuthorizedPurchaseLimit. You might then code a When-Validate-Item trigger on the price item that looks like this:

```
DECLARE
   vPriceLimit NUMBER = 0;
BEGIN
   SELECT PriceLimit
     INTO :vPriceLimit
     FROM AuthorizedPurchaseLimit
    WHERE USER = AuthorizedUser;
   IF :Purchase.Price > vPriceLimit THEN
     Form_Trigger_Failure;
END;
```

Another more sophisticated use for the When-Validate-Item trigger is in list programming for combo boxes. A combo box is an item that presents the user with a list of values but also lets the user enter a value not in the list. You can use the When-Validate-Item trigger to add the new value to the list using PL/SQL (the techniques are beyond the scope of this book).

RECORD STATE   A record has three validation states:

- *New:* When you Create Record, the record object is New.

- *Changed:* When you change any item (see the previous section for how this happens) in the record, the record becomes Changed.

- *Valid:* A record becomes Valid after Oracle Developer validates all the Changed or New items in a record and validates the record, or after it fetches the record from the database or commits the record to the database.

Duplicating a record copies the state of the source record.

Record validation and posting proceed only for Changed records. Figure 5-4 shows the activity diagram for the record validation process; see the earlier section "Posting to the Database" for the posting process.

The record validation process iterates through all the items in the record, validating them. If any item fails validation, the process stops with an error message. After validating all the items, the process marks any items changed through triggers to be valid without revalidating them. Then, if you have updated the record, the process locks the row (see the earlier section, "Locking," for details). The process then fires the When-Validate-Record trigger and marks the record as Valid.

The When-Validate-Record trigger is the logical place to put any business-rule checking that involves checking several different items that must have consistent values once the record becomes a database row. You can also use it to check the values of several items against tables in the database or against other records in the data block. As with the When-Validate-Item trigger, many such constraints are better expressed as CHECK or FOREIGN key constraints on the underlying tables rather than as code in the When-Validate-Record trigger. On the other hand, you do get the benefit of immediate feedback to users when they complete a record that is wrong in some way. The trigger fails, and you display a message that directly tells the user what is wrong instead of relying on cryptic DBMS errors about constraints failing.

FORM AND BLOCK VALIDATION   Validating a form means validating all the blocks in the form. After Oracle Developer completes validating the blocks, it checks whether there are any items or records with Changed status in the form due to triggers. If so, it marks those items and records as Valid without validating them further. This feature lets you do what you need to in the validation triggers without looping indefinitely. It does have the consequence of possible validation problems, so you should take care to get everything right in such triggers.

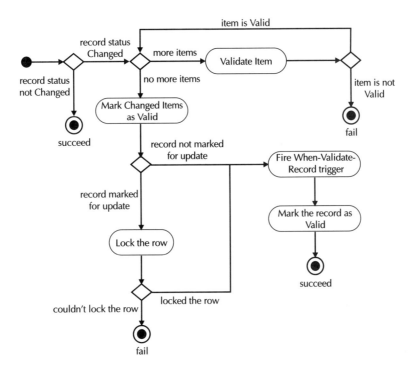

FIGURE 5-4.   *The activity diagram for the record validation process*

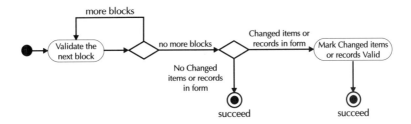

Validating a block differs slightly depending on the validation unit, which can be form, data block, record, or item. See the previous section "Validation Units and States." If the validation unit is data block or form, Oracle Developer validates all the records in the block. If the validation unit is item or record, it validates the current record only, as shown here:

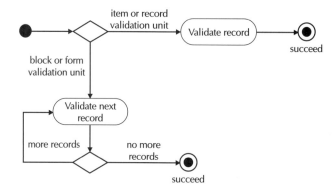

Query Processing

A *query* is a request for data from the database. An Oracle Developer form application has a built-in query process that gives you tremendous power and flexibility without making you write a line of code. This section helps you understand the logic of the different parts of the query process. This chart summarizes query processing in a form:

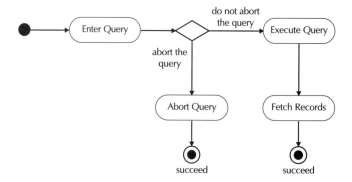

Creating a query means specifying the logical conditions you want to apply to the database. In Oracle Developer, to do this you create an example record in a block (that is, *enter a query*) that lets you enter conditions to attach to the default query. This way of specifying a query is called *query by example*, because it specifies the query by your supplying an example of the data you want to see. This query in turn contains a set of conditions and a default ordering specification. You can, if you wish, enter more complex SQL conditions through a special dialog box. You then *execute the query* and *fetch the records*, displaying them in the block.

These are the three main processes this section discusses; each has some subprocesses that it shares with other processes.

Also, you have these two processes:

■ *Count the query:* This process prepares the query and requests the server to tell you how many records the query will return in an informational message; the process fires the On-Count trigger, if there is one, replacing the counting process.

■ *Abort and close the query:* While entering the query, you may want to end it without executing it; the process fires the On-Close trigger, if there is one, which replaces the close process.

ENTERING A QUERY The SQL SELECT statement for a single-table query has four major clauses:

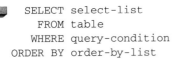

```
SELECT select-list
   FROM table
  WHERE query-condition
ORDER BY order-by-list
```

When you enter a query in an Oracle Developer form application, you are building a SELECT statement of this type by example. The *select-list* is the set of column names that correspond to your record items. The *table* is the base table that corresponds to the block. The *order-by-list* is a list of the columns in the select-list that specifies the order for the queried records. You specify the order-by-list through the ORDER BY clause block property or interactively through the Where dialog box.

The *query-condition* is the set of SQL expressions that specifies which records to return. This set of expressions has three parts:

■ *Default conditions:* The set of conditions you specify as the default WHERE clause as a block property, which you can also change at runtime through a trigger

■ *Column conditions:* Conditions you enter by filling out columns in the example record

■ *Special conditions:* Conditions you enter through the Where dialog box

You can base the query on a procedure, a transactional trigger, or an explicit FROM clause through the Query Data Source Type property of the data block. In the first two instances, Oracle Developer does not use the various conditions; instead, you supply arguments to the procedure or refer to items in the trigger. In the last instance, you still have all the conditions, but you can refer to any columns in the join. For more details about using procedures as your data source type, see "Procedural Encapsulation" in Chapter 6.

When the user enters a query, he or she can use relational operators (>, <, =, !=, and so on) and other SQL features as part of the column conditions. This allows some fairly complex queries without departing from the "by-example" approach. If necessary, though, the user can escape to a separate dialog and enter the WHERE clause SQL code directly.

When you are entering a query, Oracle Developer does not validate items or records, uses standard key definitions rather than executing key triggers, and disables various function keys (mainly record navigation and commit processing functions).

NOTE
You can set the "Fire in Enter-Query Mode" property of a key trigger to True if you want to be able to override a particular key. This can cause quite a lot of confusion, so when you do it, carefully test your form both in regular and Enter Query modes.

This is the flowchart for the process of entering a query:

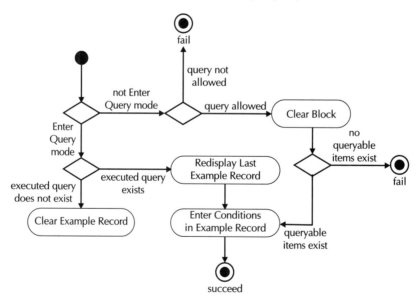

The Query Allowed property in the Block property sheet lets you disable a query for a block. You can specify a block to be a *control block*—a block without an underlying base table—by setting Database Data Block to No. Also, you must have at least one item in the block that comes from the base table in the database.

EXECUTING A QUERY   Once you have entered your query conditions, you then execute the query with the menu, toolbar, or whatever other interface you have created for executing a query. It is not quite that simple, of course. You can execute a query without having entered a query first; this means you want to retrieve all the rows using only the default WHERE clause or the query procedure. You can execute a query while there are changed records in the block; Oracle Developer asks you whether to commit the changes. There are also some complexities relating to the number of rows fetched that the following section discusses.

Figure 5-5 shows the execution of a query. For the sake of simplicity, the activity diagram does not illustrate the process of putting the cursor on the first records (or the error return if the fetch returns no records).

When you execute the query, Oracle Developer first checks whether the block allows queries (as discussed in the previous section). If so, it navigates to the block, validating any records not already validated. If there are Changed records in the block, it prompts whether to commit and commits or clears the changes as appropriate.

Oracle Developer then fires the Pre-Query trigger for the block. This trigger provides another place to specify WHERE column conditions. Oracle Developer now checks whether there is a base table for this block. Although this duplicates the first check of the block, you can get to this point in the process from other places, such as counting query rows, without having done that previous check. If the check succeeds, Oracle Developer builds the SELECT statement and fires the Pre-Select trigger. If there is an On-Select trigger, it executes it; otherwise, it executes the SELECT statement. It fires the Post-Select and When-Clear-Block triggers and flushes the example record from the block, then fetches the records.

NOTE

If for some reason the query you specify results in a mistaken and very long processing time, you can stop the query with the CTRL-C keys if you have set CNTL_BREAK=ON in the Windows Registry.

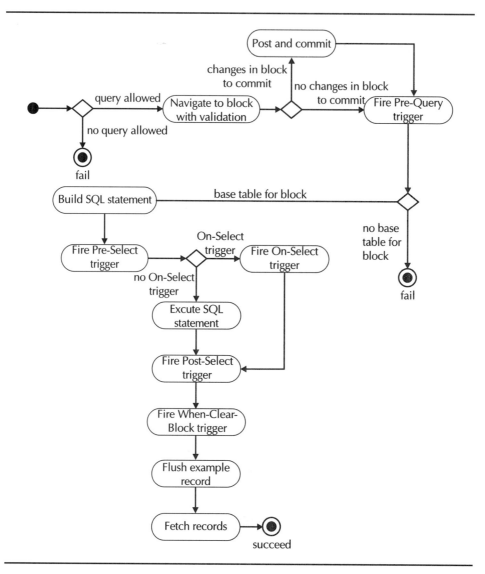

FIGURE 5-5. *An activity diagram showing the process of executing a query*

FETCHING RECORDS   After completing the process of executing the SQL query, Oracle Developer organizes the fetching of records. This is a complex process that retrieves rows from the database based on several variables:

- Whether you have turned on array processing

- The number of rows the query selects from the database

- The number of rows that are visible at once in the block

- The number of rows that the block stores in memory

- The operation causing the fetch (deleting records, scrolling, or any number of other candidates are possible)

If there is an On-Fetch trigger, Oracle Developer fires that trigger rather than fetching a row from the database into the record buffer.

Figure 5-6 shows the fetching process. First, the process checks the list of waiting rows in the buffer that you have already fetched. If there are such rows, the process creates a record and reads the current row in the list into that record. If there are no rows waiting, the process is just starting or needs to fetch more records from the server. If the current action is Clear Record, it means you need to fetch one additional row to fill in the space. Otherwise, you need to fetch the number of rows you've specified in the Query Array Size property of the block. The process sets the Records to Fetch property of the block with the appropriate value. If there is an On-Fetch trigger, the process executes it, and you can access the number of records to fetch in the block property Records to Fetch with Get_Block_Property. Otherwise, the process fetches the required number of records and creates a record, reading the first row in the new waiting list into that record.

After completing record creation, Oracle Developer loops through the non-null items in the new record, executing any Post-Change triggers. Because of restrictions on the processing in these triggers, and because they exist only for backward compatibility, you should avoid using them. Rely instead on the Post-Query trigger to accomplish any tasks for the fetched record such as validation or propagation of data to other items in the record. After all this item processing, the process marks all the items and the record as valid.

After marking the items valid, the process then executes the Post-Query trigger for the record. You use this trigger to set values in items that don't correspond to columns in the base table, for example, or to validate item and record conditions. If the Post-Query trigger fails, the process flushes the record, meaning that it will not show up in the displayed records. When this happens, the process restarts itself at the beginning for the next row to fetch.

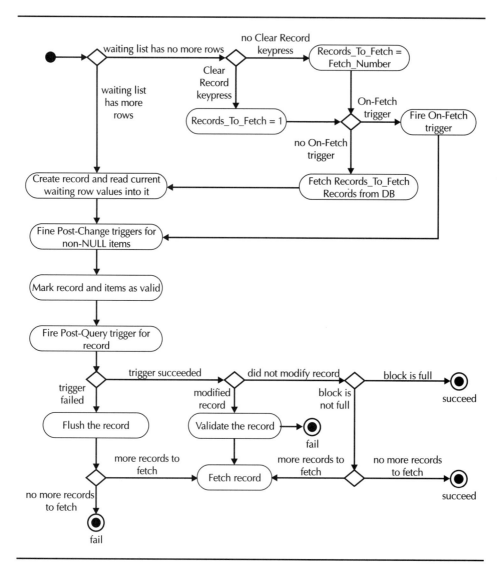

FIGURE 5-6. *An activity diagram showing the fetching of records*

NOTE
*Developer does not inform the user that it flushed
records without displaying them; it just does it
silently. This can be confusing. For example, if you
put validation code in your Post-Query trigger, and
validation fails for 10 records out of 50 in the
database, the user sees only the 40 records for which
the trigger succeeded. That means the user cannot
access these records for update. If that's what you
want, fine; otherwise, do something other than the
default of calling Form_Trigger_Failure on a
validation failure in this trigger. You can, for example,
display an error alert or log the error in a table.*

A major use for the Post-Query trigger is to fill in nondatabase items with values
you look up from tables in the database. For example, the address information for a
person consists of several columns in a nested object type within the Person table.
Instead of displaying all these columns separately, you may want to display the
information in a single field, concatenated and formatted according to envelope
address conventions. You also may want to suppress Street2 if there is only one line of
street address. You retrieve the individual values into items, but you don't display
them individually. Instead, you use the following code in a Post-Query trigger on the
Lodging block to fill in a nondatabase text item in the data block, DisplayAddress:

```
:Lodging.DisplayAddress := :Lodging.Street1 || CHR(10);
IF (:Person.Street2 IS NOT NULL) THEN – only show Street2 if it isn't null
   :Lodging.DisplayAddress := :Lodging.DisplayAddress || :Lodging.Street2 || CHR(10);
END IF;
:Lodging.DisplayAddress := :Lodging.DisplayAddress || :Lodging.City || ", " ||
   :Lodging.State || "  " || :Lodging.PostalCode;
```

TIP
*The ASCII code 10, a carriage return, breaks the line
between address components. The CHR function is
an Oracle function that returns the ASCII character
given its integer value.*

If the Post-Query trigger succeeds, then the process decides what to do based on whether the trigger modified the record. If it did, the process validates the record. A validation failure at this point stops the fetching process with an error message. Otherwise, the process continues to fetch more records.

If the block is full, meaning that it cannot hold any more records in memory due to the Number of Records Buffered property setting, the current fetching stops. If not, and there are more records to fetch, the process loops from the beginning to fetch the next record.

NOTE
It's really rare to exceed memory limitations unless you set Number of Records Buffered to something other than the default. You should leave this property alone unless you're willing to undertake the consequent intensive testing required to validate your approach.

Navigational Processing

There are several triggers that you can use for special effects when the user moves around the application. The trigger-firing processes contain various ways of creating defaults, such as creating a default New record when you enter a block for the first time.

Entering an object fires the Pre-navigational trigger for that object (Pre-Form, Pre-Block, Pre-Record, Pre-Text-Item). Leaving an object fires the Post-navigational trigger (Post-Form, Post-Block, Post-Record, Post-Text-Item).

Moving to a different object fires the When-New-<Object>-Instance trigger (When-New-Form-Instance, When-New-Block-Instance, When-New-Record-Instance, and When-New-Item-Instance). You will find these triggers very useful in situations that require initialization of some kind. They are really helpful to implement conditional navigation in a mouse environment, for instance. They are particularly useful for navigating somewhere when Forms instantiates the object, such as to an item on a stacked canvas or in a dialog box. This is because these triggers permit the use of restricted built-in subprograms such as Go_Item and Go_Block, whereas the navigational triggers do not. You'll hear more about this in the "Restricted Built-ins" section later in this chapter.

Oracle Developer fires the When-New-Form-Instance trigger when you start a new form. Specifically, it fires that trigger after completing navigation to the first navigable item in the first navigable block in the form. That means that all the navigation triggers (Post-Form, Post-Block, Pre-Form, Pre-Block, Pre-Text-Item, and so on) fire before When-New-Form-Instance, which fires before returning control to the user. The When-New-Form-Instance trigger fires just before letting the user enter data into the form.

A common task for the When-New-Form-Instance trigger in a top-level form is to control the size of the MDI window. For example, the following When-New-Form-Instance trigger code sets the window to 600x300 pixels if your coordinate system is pixels:

```
Set_Window_Property(Forms_MDI_Window, WINDOW_SIZE, 600, 300);
```

Oracle Developer fires the When-New-Block-Instance trigger when you navigate to an item in a different block. It fires the trigger after the navigational triggers but before returning control to the user for input. You use the When-New-Block-Instance trigger to initialize internal block elements such as lists or record groups not populated automatically from the database. You can also use it to control navigation after block validation, since leaving one block usually implies entering another one.

Oracle Developer fires the When-New-Record-Instance trigger when you move to a different record. You use this trigger on a block when you want something to happen whenever you move focus to a record in the block. The "New" in the trigger name really means "different" here. Oracle Developer fires the trigger whenever you move into the record, no matter how many times you move into it. The trigger fires after any navigational triggers but before returning control to the user for input. You can use When-New-Record-Instance to initialize internal elements of a record in a data block, or you can use it to navigate after validation of the previous record. A major use for When-New-Record-Instance is to navigate to a new form or another block or item after record validation. Since When-Validate-Record does not allow the use of restricted built-in procedures such as Go-Record, you must rely on the When-New-Record-Instance to control navigation. You can set a control item or global item, for example, in the When-Validate-Record trigger, then check it in the When-New-Record-Instance trigger, navigate, and reset the item.

Finally, Oracle Developer fires the When-New-Item-Instance trigger when you move to a different item as a final destination before getting input from the user. You use this trigger on an item when you want to fire the trigger whenever the input focus moves to this item. The trigger doesn't fire when you navigate *through* the item, just before you stop on the item to get input from the user. It also doesn't fire when you move to alert fields or menu items. You will find this trigger particularly useful for calling restricted built-ins after navigation completes. It gives you a very fine level of control over the behavior of the form.

Logon Processing

Logging in and out of an Oracle Developer form application fires triggers at several points. Logging into a form application sets various options, connects you to the database, and sets column security for all blocks in the current form. Figure 5-7 is the activity diagram for the logon process. The process checks whether you have already logged on and only proceeds if you have not. After firing the Pre-Logon

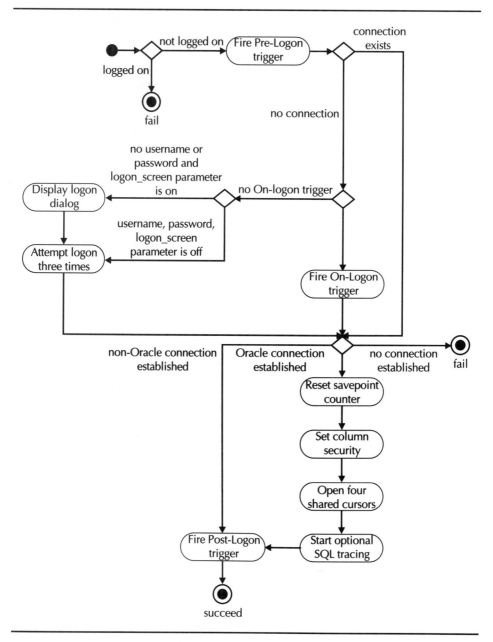

FIGURE 5-7. *An activity diagram for logging on*

trigger, the process checks for a valid connection. If there is no connection, it fires an On-Logon trigger if one exists. If no such trigger exists, it attempts to connect to the server, failing after three attempts.

If you are connecting to the Oracle database server, as opposed to some other database manager, Oracle Developer sets up the Oracle-specific client-side objects (savepoints, column security, shared cursors, and SQL tracing). The Oracle Client Adapter makes some of these features available for third-party database managers as well. See "Using Other Database Managers with ODBC" in Chapter 14 for more information.

After resetting the savepoint counter, the logon process goes through all the blocks in the form, checking columns for security restrictions. You enable this by setting the Column Security property to True for the blocks you want to restrict. In any such block, the operator must have column-level update privileges in the data dictionary on the server, or the logon process dynamically sets the Update Allowed property for the item off. You can define your own security process by defining an On-Column-Security trigger.

TIP

Oracle Corporation recommends against using these properties, as the consequence is to make your module much more complex.

After enforcing security, the process opens four shared cursors, starts tracing if you requested it, and fires the Post-Logon trigger.

Logging out of a form application is much simpler than logging in. Logging out cleans up the database-related memory and logs out of the database. First, the process fires the Pre-Logout trigger. It then closes the Oracle shared cursors. If there is an On-Logout trigger, the process executes that instead of logging off the server and firing the Post-Logout trigger.

A common task for client/server applications is to connect the application to a different user name. When you start an Oracle Developer application without a user name, password, or connect string, Oracle Developer displays an initial form prompting you for this information. After successfully connecting, you may want to permit the user to log off and connect to a different user name. This is not part of the default menu or set of actions available in Forms. You can code a trigger such as When-Button-Pressed on a toolbar button item with code similar to this:

```
DECLARE
    vUser     varchar2(80);
    vPassword varchar2(80);
    vConnect  varchar2(80);
```

```
BEGIN
   Logout;
   Logon_Screen;
   vUser := Get_Application_Property(USERNAME);
   vPassword := Get_Application_Property(PASSWORD);
   vConnect := Get_Application_Property(CONNECT_STRING);
   IF vConnect IS NOT NULL THEN
      Logon(vUser, vPassword||'@'||vConnect);
   ELSE
      Logon(vUser, vPassword);
   END IF;
END;
```

When the user clicks on the button, this trigger displays the standard Oracle Developer logon screen, gets a new user name, password, and connect string, and logs the user on as that user name. You can always substitute your own dialog box for the standard logon screen, especially if you want to do some error checking on the entered information.

NOTE
You must log out before attempting to log on to another user name because logon will fail if you are already logged on. Unfortunately, this means that if the user supplies a bad user name, password, or connect string, the application is no longer connected to the database. Ensure that the user understands this through some kind of alert or message, as in an On-Error trigger (see the upcoming section "Message Handling" for details).

Data Block and Record Processing

The data block is at the center of much of what happens in a form. A *data block* is an object that is the parent of a set of items. Most data blocks map to a single base table on the server, but you can also have control blocks (blocks that do not map to a database table). You use control blocks to add items to your form that do not come from the database and do not fit into database-linked blocks. In any case, the data block is the basic structure that contains items, and it provides a level of aggregation for the group of items it contains. You use this level for many different actions and effects.

Besides the extensive query facilities that the previous section discussed, there are some basic data-block processes that drive major parts of your application.

Creating a record is a fundamental process, though a simple one. This illustration shows the activity diagram for the process:

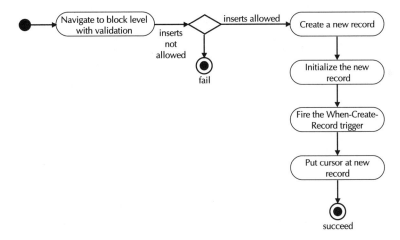

After navigating to the data-block level with validation, the process creates and initializes a new record (if the data block allows creation of new records). The process then fires the When-Create-Record trigger and positions the cursor at the new record. The process of *marking items and records changed* can happen in various ways. See the earlier section "Validation" for some of them. This process is central to transaction processing in Oracle Developer applications. This activity diagram follows the process:

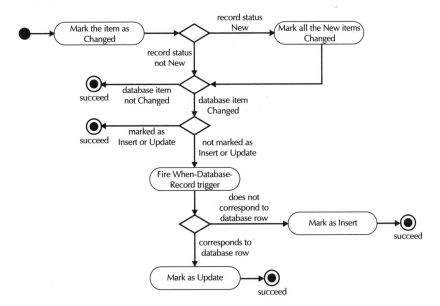

The process first marks the item as Changed. If the record is New, the process marks all the items in that record as Changed. It then checks for any database item marked as Changed. If such an item exists, and Oracle Developer has not yet marked the record as Insert or Update, the process fires the When-Database-Record trigger, then marks database rows (rows that came from the database through a query) as Update and other rows as Insert.

Clearing a data block validates the block and prompts you if there are changes to commit. If you wish, it posts and commits, and then it fires the When-Clear-Block trigger, flushes the current block, and puts the cursor at the current block.

Clearing a record has a relatively complex logic relating to rearranging the remaining records in the block and on the display. The firing of the When-Remove-Record trigger is the most important event in the process.

Interface and Key Event Processing

There are dozens of interface events in an Oracle Developer form application. Fortunately, there is little complex logic surrounding these events and their processes in the application. Usually, all that happens is that you raise the event (click the mouse, press the button, check the check box, close the window, and so on), and the trigger you associate with the event fires.

Using these triggers, you can define what happens for most interface events in a form application:

- *User interface controls:* You can define what happens for the different items in your block, such as images, buttons, check boxes, radio buttons, and lists.

- *Mouse events:* You can define the logic behind clicks, double-clicks, mouse-down, mouse-up, and so on.

- *Key events:* You can define what happens for the various function keys (Clear Block, Insert Record, Previous Block, Enter Query, and so on), and keyboard function keys (F0-F9).

NOTE

Use the Key-Others trigger to override any function keys that can have triggers but for which there are no such triggers defined at any level in the form. You can use this trigger to turn off all the key functions, for example, when the user is in a dialog box.

Master-Detail Coordination

A *coordination-causing event* is any event in a master block (of a master-detail pair) that makes a different record the current record in the master block. Oracle Developer handles all actual processing of the event through triggers that it generates by default: On-Clear-Details, On-Populate-Details, and On-Check-Delete-Master. Oracle Developer stacks the triggers and processes them as part of the stacked sequence of processes before the next event. This behavior is somewhat unusual compared to the rest of the logic in the form application. If you intend to modify the triggers to handle the coordination yourself, be prepared to experiment with the logic until you fully understand it.

Forms creates the On-Clear-Details trigger when you define the master-detail relationship. It automatically clears the detail block when a coordination-causing event occurs if the Auto-Query property of the relation is False.

Forms creates the On-Populate-Details trigger when you define the master-detail relationship. It automatically populates the detail block when a coordination-causing event occurs.

Forms creates the On-Check-Delete-Master trigger when you set the property Master Deletes to Non-Isolated in the relationship property sheet. This means you want to prevent deletion of the master record if there are details associated with it.

There is also some logic having to do with the Auto-Query setting, which permits you to defer populating the details until you navigate into the detail block.

TIP

As you rearrange your Forms data blocks, you may encounter problems with inconsistencies in these triggers. You can regenerate them at any point by deleting and recreating the relation using the Data Block Wizard. You can also create the relation object and enter the join condition directly through its property sheet rather than using the Wizard. You will of course have to do this manually if you are working outside a data block frame, since blocks without frames no longer can use the Data Block Wizard.

Message Handling

Two triggers affect message handling in an Oracle Developer form application: On-Error and On-Message. The former fires when Oracle Developer tries to display an error message; the latter fires when it tries to display an informational message.

You can use these triggers to handle errors and messages. In the trigger code, you can access built-in functions that return various parts of the message:

- *Error_Code or Message_Code:* Returns the error number

- *Error_Text or Message_Text:* Returns the text message

- *Error_Type or Message_Type:* Returns the kind of message

- *DBMS_Error_Code:* Returns the server error number, which may differ from the forms error number

- *DBMS_Error_Text:* Returns the server message, which may differ from the forms error message

If you must, you can extract any element of a message and use it in further processing, or provide your own error handling. The usual way to do this is to code On-Error and On-Message triggers at the form level. These triggers call a library procedure in your standard library to format and display the message. For example, here is an On-Message trigger that replaces standard Forms message handling:

```
IF Message_Type = 'FRM' THEN
   Handle_Forms_Message(Message_Code, Message_Text);
ELSE
   Handle_Database_Message(DBMS_Error_Code, DBMS_Error_Text);
END IF;
```

This trigger distinguishes the Forms messages from the database messages and calls the appropriate subprogram in the standard library with the appropriate message code and text. These subprograms can not only impose a standard format for your applications but also handle specific messages in special ways. For example, if you don't want to display the message "Database apply complete: <n> records applied OK" that comes from posting changes before you open another form, you might have a Handle_Forms_Message procedure like this:

```
PROCEDURE Handle_Forms_Message(pCode IN NUMBER, pText IN VARCHAR2) IS
BEGIN
   IF pCode = 40404 OR pCode = 40405 THEN
      null; -- do nothing for this message
   ELSE
      Message('Forms '||To_Char(pCode)||':  '||pText);  -- format message
      Message('');  -- stack message to display alert, clear status bar
      Synchronize;  -- display message
   END IF;
END Handle_Forms_Message;
```

This procedure ignores the 40404 and 40405 messages but displays any other message using a programming trick that displays an alert instead of a message on the message bar. If there is more than one message to display on the message stack, Forms pops up an alert with the first message, then displays the last message on the status bar. This lets the user see all the messages. This procedure takes advantage of this feature to force Forms to display all messages in alerts—something you may or may not want to do depending on your application programming style. The Synchronize built-in tells Forms to synchronize the display with the message stack; that is, to display the messages *now*.

There are three kinds of Forms messages: working messages, informative messages, and error messages. Consult the Forms online help for information about specific messages. You can suppress working messages with this line of PL/SQL code:

```
:SYSTEM.Suppress_Working := 'TRUE';
```

You handle informative messages with the On-Message trigger, and you have the message information in Message_Code, Message_Text, and Message_Type. You handle error messages with the On-Error trigger, and you have the error information in Error_Code, Error_Text, and Error_Type.

A slightly less fine-grained level of control over messages comes from using the System.Message_Level variable. The string values of this variable represent the different severity levels of Forms messages, as shown in Table 5-1.

Severity	Description	Example Message
0	Any message	
5	Obvious conditions	At first record.
10	Procedural mistakes (something done out of order)	Field is full. Can't insert character.
15	Design mistakes (something done that can't be done in the form by design)	You tried to update a field that does not allow updates.
20	Trigger failures or conditions that stop the user from proceeding	Cannot insert into or update data in a view.
25	Conditions that prevent the form from performing correctly	Update cannot be made due to prior rollback. Clear the record.
>25	Errors that Forms always displays	Out of memory.

TABLE 5-1. *Forms Message Severity Levels*

The value of this variable determines what messages Forms displays. It will display only messages above the message level you set here. If you set it to '5', for example, Forms suppresses messages with a severity of 0 or 5. Using this variable, you can turn off warning messages that you think will just confuse the user.

```
:System.Message_Level := '5';
```

You can turn messages on and off whenever you like using the appropriate triggers. Again, consult the online help to find the severity levels for different messages.

CAUTION
Don't set Message_Level greater than 0 for an extended sequence of operations. Try to limit the scope of this change only to eliminate confusing messages for a short period of time in which they are likely to occur. If you turn off messages for an extended period, you will find it very difficult to debug and fix problems that come up, as you may not be aware of the real cause due to lack of information.

Restricted Built-ins

The automatic navigating capabilities of Oracle Developer make your programming job much easier. The downside of Developer's sophisticated navigation and event-driven processing, however, is the potential for infinite loops. If you were able to navigate while Oracle Developer Forms was navigating for you, you could easily get stuck in a loop—you navigate, which causes Forms to navigate, which causes you to navigate, and on, and on. Fortunately, Oracle Developer recognizes this possibility and uses restricted built-ins to make it difficult for you to put yourself in this situation. At first glance, this feature may seem to make programming more difficult, but the reverse is really true.

A *restricted built-in* is a built-in subprogram that initiates navigation. Oracle Developer makes the use of restricted built-ins illegal in triggers that fire in response to navigation. In practice, this restriction usually results in runtime errors in your triggers and furious attempts to figure out what is going on and how to work around this "limitation" of Oracle Developer. A bit of reflection and familiarizing yourself with the restrictions can thus pay off in avoiding these problems.

Instead of trying to call restricted built-ins in navigating triggers, put the calls in triggers that fire separately from the ones that navigate. For example, you cannot call Go_Item to move the cursor to a different item in a Post-Query trigger. Instead, put the Go_Item call in a Key-EntQry trigger on the block, as shown here:

```
Enter_Query;
Go_Item ('Ledger.ActionDate');
```

When the user enters a query, this trigger fires instead of the default query-entering action. After the user executes the query and Forms fetches all the rows, control returns to this trigger, which forwards it to the Ledger.ActionDate item. Because you can take a similar action using just a keypress, you also need to define the Key-ExeQry trigger on the block.

```
Execute_Query;
IF :SYSTEM.MODE = 'NORMAL' THEN
Go_Item ('Ledger.ActionDate');
END IF;
```

If you'd like to do this, the best place to start is with the set of New-Instance triggers (When-New-Form-Instance, When-New-Block-Instance, When-New-Record-Instance, and When-New-Item-Instance). Acquiring a thorough understanding of the use of these triggers can save you quite a bit of time.

For example, say you have a validation issue that requires navigating to one or another item, depending on the current state of the record. The obvious place to do such validation processing is the When-Validate-Item trigger on the item (say, Ledger.Action). When validation occurs, you must move the focus to another item. But the When-Validate-Item trigger doesn't let you call Go_Item!

To handle this situation, you need to use a "global variable" style of programming. Set up a control block (a data block with its Database Data Block property set to No) and a text item you can use as a variable called vDestination. Size it to hold the name of any item. In the When-Validate-Item trigger on Ledger.Action, where you would ordinarily put the call to Go_Item, use this statement:

```
:Control.vDestination := 'ActionType.Action';
```

This variable will contain the name of the item on the dialog box's canvas (ActionType.Action in this case). In the When-New-Item-Instance trigger for the block or perhaps for the next item in sequence, you would have this code:

```
IF :Control.vDestination IS NOT NULL THEN
   Go_Item(:Control.vDestination);
   :Control.vDestination := '';
END IF;
```

When the user moves out of the Ledger.Action item, the When-Validate-Item trigger fires, setting the vDestination variable. Then the trigger successfully handles the situation, completing navigation and moving the focus to the next item. At that point, the When-New-Item-Instance trigger fires. This trigger goes to the named item (ActionType.Action), then resets the variable. This latter step ensures that you continue processing correctly for further navigation; otherwise, you would just pop back to the dialog box when you moved to the next item in the Ledger block.

This kind of logic allows some relatively fancy maneuvering. The example given here represents a simple case study of the Oracle Developer "way of thinking," if there is such a thing. Instead of trying to force the system to bend to your will, understand how its processes work and go with the flow—literally.

TIP

Another way to navigate without actually navigating: create an item to serve as an indicator flag, create a When-New-Item-Instance trigger at block or form level, then check the flag in the trigger and navigate to the indicated item. When you execute the validation trigger, you set the flag; navigation proceeds, and when the focus shifts to a new item, the When-New-Item-Instance trigger fires, you check the flag, and navigate to the indicated item.

CAUTION

One "solution" that does not work is the use of the When-Timer-Expired trigger. You can set this trigger to go off in a very short period so that it fires right after navigation stops. This trigger keeps coming back to haunt the Oracle Developer community because the trigger does not fire when navigation is under way. The timer trigger fires almost immediately after navigation stops. Almost, however, is not good enough. Anyone familiar with multithreading systems will tell you this is a terrible idea. If the system gets busy, other triggers can fire first, no matter how short your time interval. This is particularly a problem if you deploy on the Web, since each timer event requires a round-trip to the application server across the network. Use process logic, not tricks, to solve this particular programming problem.

Tables 5-2, 5-3, and 5-4 list the triggers that cannot use restricted built-in subprograms, those that can, and the set of restricted built-in programs, respectively.

On-Check-Delete-Master	Post-Block	Pre-Insert
On-Check-Unique-Trigger	Post-Change	Pre-Logon
On-Close	Post-Database-Commit	Pre-Logout
On-Column-Security	Post-Delete	Pre-Query
On-Commit	Post-Form	Pre-Record
On-Count	Post-Forms-Commit	Pre-Select
On-Delete	Post-Insert	Pre-Text-Item
On-Error	Post-Logon	Pre-Update
On-Fetch	Post-Logout	When-Clear-Block
On-Insert	Post-Query	When-Create-Record
On-Lock	Post-Record	When-Custom-Item-Event
On-Logon	Post-Select	When-Database-Record
On-Logout	Post-Text-Item	When-Image-Activated
On-Message	Post-Update	When-Remove-Record
On-Savepoint	Pre-Block	When-Validate-Item
On-Select	Pre-Commit	When-Validate-Record
On-Sequence-Number	Pre-Delete	
On-Update	Pre-Form	

TABLE 5-2.   *Triggers That Cannot Use Restricted Built-in Subprograms*

Key-<Whatever>	When-List-Changed	When-New-Item-Instance
Key-Fn	When-Mouse-Click	When-New-Record-Instance
Key-Others	When-Mouse-DoubleClick	When-Radio-Changed
On-Clear-Details	When-Mouse-Down	When-Timer-Expired
On-Populate-Details	When-Mouse-Enter	When-Window-Activated

TABLE 5-3.   *Triggers That Can Use Restricted Built-in Subprograms*

When-Button-Pressed	When-Mouse-Leave	When-Window-Closed
When-Checkbox-Changed	When-Mouse-Move	When-Window-Deactivated
When-Form-Navigate	When-Mouse-Up	When-Window-Resized
When-Image-Pressed	When-New-Block-Instance	
When-List-Activated	When-New-Form-Instance	

TABLE 5-3. *Triggers That Can Use Restricted Built-in Subprograms*

Block_Menu	Delete_Region	Help	Post
Call-Input	Down	Insert_Record	Previous_Block
Clear-Block	Do_Key	Last_Record	Previous_Form
Clear-EOL	Duplicate_Item	List_Values	Previous_Item
Clear_Form	Duplicate_Record	Main_Menu	Previous_Menu
Clear_Item	Edit_Text_Item	Menu_Next_Field	Previous_Menu_Item
Clear_Message	Enter	New_Form	Previous_Record
Clear_Record	Enter_Query	Next_Block	Scroll_Down
Close_Form	Execute_Query	Next_Form	Scroll_Up
Commit_Form	Execute_Trigger	Next_Item	Select_All
Convert_Other_Value	Exit_Form	Next_Key	Select_Records
Copy_Region	First_Record	Next_Menu_Item	Show-LOV
Count_Query	Go_Block	Next_Record	Terminate
Create_Queried_Record	Go_Form	Next_Set	Up
Create_Record	Go_Item	Open_Form	Update_Record
Cut_Region	Go_Record	Paste_Region	

TABLE 5-4. *Restricted Built-in Subprograms*

The Report Process and Triggers

The Oracle Developer report process is much simpler than the form processes the first part of the chapter discusses. Most of what you do with reports, and in particular the repetitive looping, you specify with a combination of data model group, repeating frame, and report type. See Chapter 7 for details on creating and programming reports. There are some special effects, particularly those involving conditional decisions, that you must do in custom programming in report triggers. Figure 5-8 shows the report process, which contains several trigger points. A major use for the Before and After triggers is to create processing tables the report uses. For example, you can create a temporary table, populate it with an SQL statement or PL/SQL code, then report on the values in the table. An example of this is a balance sheet report that builds a balance table and aggregates the account information from the initial balance table and the transaction tables.

The report process starts with the command line arguments you give the report runtime system. If you supply any arguments, Oracle Developer fires the Validation trigger you have entered through the Parameter property sheet to check and/or change the parameters for the report instance. The Runtime Parameter Form lets the user enter runtime options for the report. Oracle Developer fires a Before Form and After Form trigger, as well as potentially firing the Validation trigger again.

After setting up the parameters, Oracle Developer compiles the report and fires the Before Report trigger. The logic of executing the report is more complex than Figure 5-8 shows. The places you can intervene are in Format triggers you associate with any object in the report and in Between Page triggers that fire after printing each page except the last one.

After printing the last page, the report commits to end the transaction, then fires the After Report trigger.

You can run a report in the Previewer or just send the results to a destination. If you choose to preview the report, you have interactive access to the report. You can use certain triggers to do interactive things, particularly the Action trigger (more about this in the upcoming "Action Trigger" section). You can treat a report as an interactive application through this mechanism. You should realize that things such as forward references can cause triggers to fire in unexpected ways in the Previewer.

Report Triggers

The Report triggers (Before and After Report, Between Pages, and Before and After Form) give you procedural access to report processing at the report and page levels.

The Before Report trigger fires before any formatting of the report objects but after querying the data for the report. You can initialize things with this trigger. If the trigger fails, Oracle Developer displays an error message and returns.

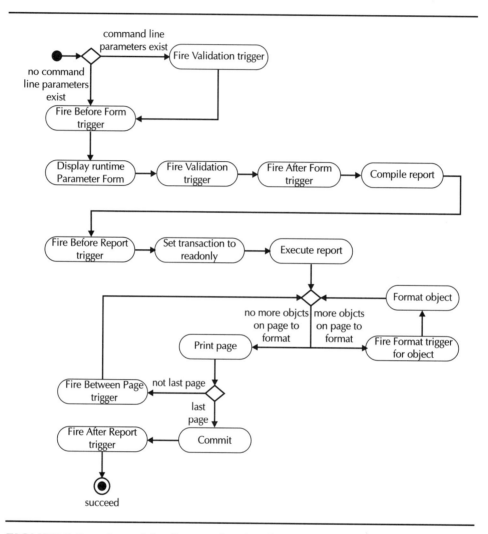

FIGURE 5-8. *An activity diagram showing the report process*

The After Report trigger fires after printing the report or exiting the Previewer. You can use this trigger to clean up anything you do not want left around after running the report. Even if triggers fail during the report, this trigger always fires. You have to explicitly display any error messages; the trigger does nothing if it fails.

You can use the Between Pages trigger for custom page formatting. In the Live Previewer, Oracle Developer fires this trigger only the first time you display the report page. If the trigger fails, Oracle Developer stops formatting pages and displays an error message.

Before Form and After Form triggers let you manipulate the parameters of the report. You cannot manipulate data model objects such as columns from these triggers. After Form always fires, whether or not you suppress the Runtime Parameter Form. If these triggers fail, Oracle Developer stops executing the report.

NOTE
Avoid DDL and DML statements in Before Report and After Report triggers and in Between Page triggers. Oracle Developer takes a snapshot of tables as it builds the report at runtime. If you execute DDL and DML statements, this snapshot will no longer reflect the correct data dictionary, and this can cause really mysterious runtime errors.

Format Trigger
When it formats an instance of the object, Oracle Developer calls a Format trigger you have associated with any object in a report. You can change borders, format masks, or format any other aspect of the object you can access through the SRW PL/SQL library package. You can skip processing within an object based on variable values.

As noted earlier, you should avoid DML and DDL statements in these triggers, as the firing of these triggers can be unpredictable. The triggers can fire many times during the formatting of a single object.

You can format cells in a matrix by putting a frame object around the field and associating a Format trigger with the frame.

Action Trigger
You can put buttons on reports in order to be able to do something interactive when you run the report in the Previewer. An Action trigger runs when you push the button. You can use this trigger to run another report in a separate Previewer, letting you drill down based on the current report values. See Chapter 7 for more details on these and other special-purpose reports.

The Graphics Process and Triggers
The Oracle Developer graphics process is also much simpler than the form processes. Most of what you do with graphics, and in particular the basic display object formatting and association with database data, you specify with a combination of Layout Editor, query, and chart type. See Chapter 8 for details on creating graphics. There are some special effects, particularly those involving drill-down graphics or conditional decisions, that you must do in custom programming in graphics triggers. Figure 5-9 shows the graphics process, which contains several trigger points.

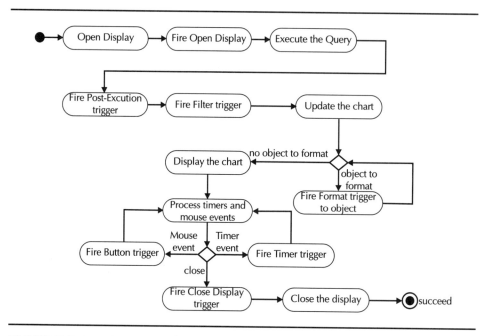

FIGURE 5-9. *An activity diagram showing the graphics process*

When you open a graphics display using the runtime graphics system, it fires the Open Display trigger for the display. The process then executes the query and fires the Post-Execution trigger, then fires the Filter trigger. The process then updates the chart, firing any Format triggers associated with the objects in the chart. If there is a timer, the timer fires the Timer trigger after a set time period passes. If there is a mouse event on an object that acts as a button (for a drill-down relationship, for example), the process fires the Button trigger.

You can build your own chart templates as a way to program a specific format and use it in multiple charts. You can use the various triggers to add special effects to a particular graphics display.

Graphics Triggers

Graphics triggers are all PL/SQL procedures (not anonymous blocks as for forms). You can link any procedure to a trigger in the Object Navigator through the property sheet for the object that owns the trigger. You have a special library package, OG, that contains functions for obtaining internal elements (the display, the query, the timer, and so on), for formatting objects, and for executing the different graphics processes.

If you need to initialize anything in the chart, such as setting up display layers, starting timers, or executing special queries, you can do that in the Open Display trigger. Both the Open Display and Close Display triggers are entries in the Display Object property sheet.

If you want to process query data in some way or set up something that depends on having done the query, you can use the Post-Execution trigger. You can create this in the Query property sheet.

If you want to format individual chart elements based on other elements or queried data relationships, you can do that with the Format trigger you associate with the chart element. Oracle Developer executes the Format trigger just before updating the display for the element. You can create the Format trigger from the object's property sheet.

Timers handle situations in which you want to update a display after some time interval. A common example is querying real-time transaction data to get a completely up-to-date graphic that shows the changes that occurred during the period. Timers are a bit complex, and you should experiment with them to become familiar with their behavior. You can automatically execute a query and/or execute the Timer trigger, for example, by associating a Timer trigger with a query or a timer object.

Button procedures are yet more complex. Oracle Developer automatically sets up the appropriate events and processing for drill-down for you; but if you want more complex events and graphics changes, you will need to associate Button triggers with chart objects. Oracle Developer Graphics handles the mouse events down, up, move down, and move up; you can set the object to receive these events. You can then test for the events in the trigger procedure. For example, you could set up a button procedure on a button graphic that turns off the timer that automatically updates the display. You can set up event reception and create the button procedure through the object's property sheet.

Finally, you can use the Close Display trigger to clean anything that needs to be cleaned up. You can commit changes to the database here if you have programmed other parts of the graphic to make such changes.

Now that you're acquainted with the basic processes of Forms, Reports, and Graphics, the rest of this chapter takes you through some of the basic design issues you'll face when using them. While the processes are the same on all platforms, other aspects of Oracle Developer are not. The next section introduces you to the issues of cross-platform design.

Designing for the Internet and Other Platforms

Having done your basic work, what do you need to do to make your application run anywhere? You may want to deploy your application in different Internet browsers, on Windows, X-Windows, and the Macintosh. How can you insure the application presents itself well in all the different browsers and user interfaces on which you want to run it? There are several issues with cross-platform development:

- *Control and menu standards:* What are the standards for controls such as buttons and menus on the target platform? Do you want to conform absolutely to all such standards? Is operational consistency across platforms more important than conforming to platform standards?

- *Colors and patterns:* How do colors and patterns translate between different platforms?

- *Fonts:* How do fonts translate to different platforms? What are the standard fonts on each platform? How do fonts display on different monitors and printers that the applications might use?

- *Platform-specific functionality:* Do you use any icons, user exits, or specific features of a platform, such as OLE or AppleEvents? Do you use external DLLs through ORA_FFI? Do you use any file path names specific to an operating system? Do you need to execute external programs to implement some features of an application? Do you use native platform context-sensitive help?

NOTE

If you need to run with character-mode applications, you are in a different world from these considerations. According to Oracle Corporation, Oracle Developer will discontinue support for character mode after this release. If you haven't already made arrangements to move your legacy applications into a graphical user interface, now is the time to start doing it.

You will find it easier to deal with these issues through planning and standardization than by dealing with the issues as they arise.

Control and Menu Standards

Each platform has specific graphical user interface guidelines that all applications should follow. Oracle Developer automatically translates the standard control objects (buttons, check boxes, radio buttons, and the like) to the appropriate format for the platform on which you design the application.

Please see the following references for the specific guidelines for each platform:

- *Windows 95/98 and NT 4:* Microsoft Corporation, *The Windows Interface Guidelines for Software Design*, Microsoft Press, 1995.

- *Macintosh*: Apple Computer, *Macintosh Human Interface Guidelines*, Addison-Wesley, 1992.

- *Motif*: Open Software Foundation, *The Motif Style Guide Release 1.2*, Prentice-Hall, 1992.

As far as I am aware, there is no accepted standard design guide for Internet applications—rather the reverse, if anything, as the Internet is full of just about any kind of design you can imagine! Other platforms may have their own style guides, which you should obtain and use as references.

Now, given these standards, you face your first big decision. Do you want to conform to these standards? Usually, the answer will be yes, but not always. If your users are themselves working across platforms, you may want to emphasize operational over platform consistency. That is, if your application users move from platform to platform, they will usually want the application to behave much the same on each platform. On the other hand, if users always use the same platform, but there are different users on different platforms, you probably want to conform to platform standards and let the application behave differently on the different platforms.

Consider menus, buttons, and icons, for example.

On Windows, MDI applications provide a single menu in the MDI window. On Motif, each window has its own menu. On the Macintosh, there is only one menu for all applications at the top of the screen. If you choose to adhere to platform standards, you've got your work cut out for you. You will need a separate Windows application to support the MDI approach, and your Motif and Macintosh versions will need some extra coding to work properly in each window. If, on the other hand, you want all the systems to work identically, you can make modifications to Motif and Macintosh versions to emulate the MDI application menu behavior.

Buttons are very different on different platforms. There are two basic differences: moats and navigability. Before you break out your drawbridge designs, a *moat* is the emphasis given to a button to indicate that it is the default choice that executes when you press ENTER, and *navigability* is the ability to move from control to control using the keyboard. The Windows moat is very small compared to the Motif and Macintosh moats, and buttons can look really odd when you move from one platform to another. If your goal is to adhere to platform standards, you must have a different set of buttons for each platform. Usually, you do this with a different stacked canvas that you show or hide depending on the platform. See the upcoming section "Platform-Specific Functionality" for details on accessing information about the operating system and graphical user interface.

Finally, icons illustrate a fundamental truth: a picture may be worth a thousand words, but not a thousand hours of effort. There is no standard icon format. Windows has its ICO files, Motif uses its own format, Web pages use GIF files, and the Macintosh compiles the icons into the application. If you use icons, you'll need to have separate libraries of icons for each platform. If you go with a standard platform interface, this helps you keep the implementations separate. If you decide to make the toolbars and iconic buttons the same on all platforms, you will have to work hard to get everything consistent.

Colors and Patterns

Color, even a splash, can make your applications come alive. Use too much or the wrong combination, and it will kill it. Application developers regularly get bug reports these days about the color combinations of the applications they develop. This is especially true when the applications run on monochrome monitors or when documentation people try to print pictures of the screens and key parts come out black, instead of that nice dark blue they saw on the screen. If a platform uses different standard colors, you can see controls such as progress bars disappear because they accidentally use the same color as the background controlled by the operating system. It's also important to realize that many Motif and Macintosh users have grayscale monitors and cannot readily distinguish colors at all. Colors should not carry information.

Unless you are a color expert with lots of experience on all your target platforms, restrain your use of color to three or four basic colors that work well together and that work in their monochrome, grayscale equivalents. Put these in your named visual attributes and templates to make sure all your applications start with the right effects. Test the color combinations on all the target systems to make sure they work.

The same rules apply to patterns. Use them sparingly, as they can differ dramatically on different displays.

Finally, although Oracle Developer gives you a 256-color palette, the actual colors that you see on a particular display may differ, sometimes greatly. Especially on Windows, this can be a real problem. Monitor resolutions and drivers affect the color palette. For controls and windows, Windows controls the color palette through the Control Panel desktop color settings. Again, limit your range of colors, and test them on your target displays to identify any problems.

Fonts

It is still quite difficult to translate fonts between platforms. Oracle Developer does all it can, but in the end it relies upon your specifying translations explicitly for portability.

The first thing you should do is to set up your coordinate system and grid. Ideally, you should put these settings in your template or set them up when you create a new form. Changing this setting later can cause problems in your established layout as Oracle Developer recalculates all the coordinates in new units. Use Real coordinates in centimeters or inches for maximum portability between platforms. You can also use points, which gives you the ability to compare control sizes to your text size, as Oracle Developer always expresses text size in points. I find it easier to use inches because I'm used to the measure. However, on Windows, which allows different screen resolutions, an inch doesn't mean much when you look at the application on monitors with wildly different resolutions. To set this option, select the form object and display its property sheet. Find the Coordinate System property, and click on the More button to display the Coordinate Info dialog box.

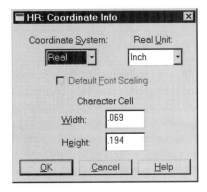

Set the Coordinate System to Real and the Real Unit to inches or centimeters. Using pixels makes it much harder to move your application between systems. Now, in each canvas, you need to set up your grid. For a relatively fine-grained grid, set it to a quarter-inch grid with four snap points in each cell. That means you can align background text to within a sixteenth of an inch, which is a reasonable margin of error for portability. To set up the grid ruler, display the canvas in the Layout Editor and select the Format|Layout Options|Ruler menu item. Choosing this item displays the Ruler Settings dialog box.

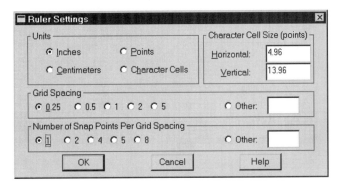

Set the Units for the ruler to the same units you picked for the coordinate system (inches or centimeters). Set Grid Spacing to 0.25 (a quarter inch) and Number of Snap Points Per Grid Spacing to 4 (4 snap points per quarter inch).

TIP

You can also use a Character coordinate system, but this can lead to difficulty in aligning the items and background text in your canvases because of the large-grained nature of characters. Where possible, use the system of prompt specification through the Prompt properties of the item, where you specify alignment as property values.

Now, choose a font palette: what typefaces do you want to use, in what type sizes and weights? A typeface is a particular style of type, such as Times Roman or Helvetica. Because of intellectual property issues, different systems and vendors provide essentially the same font with different names. For example, Apple Computer and Adobe Systems Adobe Type Manager provide the Helvetica font, whereas Windows 3.1 provides the system font Helv and the TrueType font Arial. There are minor differences in the typefaces, but generally this issue is not important in developing database applications. Typefaces become more important for applications such as World Wide Web pages that need to express individuality and creativity—unlike database applications, right? Well, if you want to develop some creative applications, try a book such as *Stop Stealing Sheep* by Erik Spiekermann and E. M. Ginger (Mountain View, CA: Adobe Press, 1993). But be aware that "creative" and "portable" may be mutually exclusive terms, at least with respect to font technology.

NOTE

Aside from applications such as word processors or other systems that are oriented toward displaying large amounts of text, most GUI applications use a simple typeface that is relatively standard for the platform. On the Macintosh, for example, you use Geneva; on Windows, MS San Serif. Usually, you want to use a type size that is standard as well, such as 10-point MS San Serif for Windows, 12-point Geneva for the Macintosh, and 10-point Helvetica on Motif.

You should also decide where and how to use font characteristics such as boldface, italics, and underlining. Most of the time, you should minimize the use of these font features. You should standardize the type size of different display text objects, making all labels 10 points, for example. This will help if you need to translate a font on a different platform. The best way to do this is to use Named Visual Attributes and subclassed object library objects. See Chapter 10 for details on using these reuse features of Oracle Developer.

You may find that a given font differs across platforms due to differences in the font technology. As with color, you should test your standard fonts on all your target platforms.

You can set your default font for boilerplate text in form applications with the variable FORM60_DEFAULT_FONT in the System Registry. Implement your standards decisions in named visual attributes and property classes to ensure that your applications conform to the standards.

If you need to translate fonts between platforms, you can use the Oracle Developer font alias files (UIFONT.ALI on Windows; the "Oracle Font Aliases" file in the System:Preferences folder on the Macintosh). These files simply map one font by name into another font. See the *Installation Guide* for the target platform for details on font mapping for the platform. Experiment with different font mappings until you are happy with the effects on your applications. Different styles of canvas item arrangement require different font mappings.

You may find it easier in the long run to use object libraries to manage platform differences, especially if you are using several different standard fonts for different objects. See Chapter 10 for details on using object libraries.

Platform-Specific Functionality

There are several things you can do in Oracle Developer that limit you to a single platform:

- Menus and status bars/console

- Icons

- User exits

- Platform-specific features

Each platform has its own quirky approach to menus. On Windows platforms, the MDI requires a single menu belonging to the MDI window that contains all the other windows. The MDI window also displays the *console,* or status bar. Motif windows (and Web windows) are independent, not contained within a larger window. Each window has its own menu, which may derive from a linked parent window. Macintosh windows have no menus; instead, they use a single menu at the top of the screen. When you switch the focus to a window, it replaces the top menu with a window-specific menu. See the Chapter 6 section "Menus" for more details.

Icons come from icon files in a platform-dependent format, so you need to have a complete set of icon files for each platform in the format appropriate to that platform. Windows has its ICO files, Motif uses its own format, Web pages use GIF files, and the Macintosh compiles the icons into the application.

User exits are compiled separately on each platform into the executable library format of the platform. If your application depends on user exits, you will need to port your code from platform to platform.

Finally, there are specific things you can use on each platform that are not available on other platforms:

- *Windows:* DDE, OLE, VBX, and ActiveX.

- *Macintosh:* AppleEvents.

- *All:* Anything you call through the HOST built-in procedure; user exits that manipulate the graphical user interface objects.

- *Internet:* All of the above, because standard Java doesn't permit use of these features, though this may change in the future for ActiveX. Other Web restrictions: no combo boxes (there is no Java equivalent for them), icons in GIF format, and no When-Mouse-Enter, When-Mouse-Leave, or When-Mouse-Move triggers (too much network traffic required). You should also avoid timer triggers and extensive use of images, both of which can cause network performance problems for Internet applications.

TIP

The online documentation that comes with Oracle Developer has an extensive discussion of Internet application development. You should definitely consult that documentation before designing your applications for the Internet.

One trick you can use in your trigger code is to refer to the application properties that determine portability issues. This lets you choose which property values to use at runtime by checking the values of these properties using the Get_Application_Property built-in function:

- *DISPLAY_HEIGHT and DISPLAY_WIDTH:* These variables tell you how big the current display is. The unit depends on how you have set up the form coordinate system, a property of the form module.

- *OPERATING_SYSTEM:* This variable tells you the name of the platform on which the application currently is running (MSWINDOWS, WIN32COMMON, MACINTOSH, SunOS, VMS, UNIX, or HP-UX).

- *USER_INTERFACE:* This variable tells you the name of the user interface technology on which the application currently is running (WEB, MOTIF, MACINTOSH, MSWINDOWS, MSWINDOWS32, PM, X, VARCHAR2MODE, BLOCKMODE, or UNKNOWN).

Standards and Planning

The one thing you must do to be portable is to specify which platforms you intend to support. If you can avoid certain very different platforms, such as character-mode terminals, you will find it much easier to achieve portability. If you can limit certain issues to certain applications, this can help too. For example, if your mobile sales force uses laptops for lead tracking and sales management applications, but everyone else uses 17-inch SVGA terminals, you can save yourself much pain by restricting the window size of only the two critical laptop applications. In any case, knowing the window size variations is essential in designing the layout of fixed forms and graphics. You can also use scrolling judiciously to accommodate smaller screens in some cases. Look at the capabilities of scrolling and stacked canvases as well in the next chapter.

Once you are clear on your platforms, put together a set of standards for user interface objects and properties that takes portability into account. If you make full use of named visual attributes, property classes, and graphics templates to make your standards easy to implement in working applications, you will find it much easier to move those applications to the different platforms. See Chapter 10 for details on increasing reusability of your code through object libraries, subclasses, named visual attributes, and property classes (and other methods).

To summarize the portability issues, it is relatively easy to build portable applications using Oracle Developer, but it takes some planning and standardization to do it effectively and efficiently.

Now you are ready to take your prototype to the next stage by using the advanced programming and development features of Oracle Developer. The next five chapters delve into even more advanced issues that will add dramatically to your productivity in generating safe and solid applications.

CHAPTER
6

Advanced Windows
and Menus

nce you understand the processes of the Form Builder component of Oracle Developer, you'll have a structure in which to expand the horizons of your form application. Two additional topics will round out your ability to design full-scale, complete applications with Oracle Developer: windows and menus. You can design with these Form Builder features using little or no programming.

In Chapter 4, the prototype form presented a single canvas in a single window. This chapter shows you how to expand your application into multiple windows using multiple canvases. These features give you the ability to build dialog boxes, toolbars, and alerts.

The default menu of the application in Chapter 4 is not the extent of what you can do with menus, either. You can build your own custom menu to integrate forms with reports and graphics or whatever else you want to call from a form.

Windows

Doing windows in Form Builder means one of two things: creating the contents of the window or creating and managing the window itself. The following discussion expands on the Chapter 4 tutorial to show you how to make full use of Oracle Developer canvases and windows as design features of your application.

Painting Canvases

Recall from Chapters 2 and 4 that you use a canvas to display your blocks and items. You edit the canvas in the Layout Editor, and it becomes the basis for much of the work you do in building your forms. What exactly, then, is a canvas?

A *canvas* is the background on which you place boilerplate text and items. Each item refers to exactly one canvas in its Property Palette. You can divide a block's items between different canvases.

A canvas does not stand alone as an interface object. To see it and its items, you must display the canvas in a window. Oracle Developer makes these separate objects to let you build windows that provide a *view* of the canvas: a rectangle that covers part or all of the canvas. For example, the Ledger application below shows a window that reveals a little more than half of the underlying canvas. The part of the canvas that you can see through the window is the view. The window has horizontal and vertical scroll bars that let you scroll through the canvas to see different views.

This separate-but-equal division of labor between display and content lets you build your forms independently of the size of the window that displays them. This widens your horizons but narrows your interface, literally. You may find that users who constantly need to scroll through their canvases express a dissatisfaction with the interface. Your best interface will show all the fields and other items on a canvas all the time. But, as with most aspects of life, sometimes you need to have more than you can show at once. Windows and canvases give you that flexibility.

Choosing the Right Background

To build on this flexibility, consider first the type of canvas to use. Certain canvases can do more for you than just letting you scroll around within a window. There are four types of canvases:

- ■ *Content:* A canvas that contains the "contents" of a window; every window has at least one content canvas, and usually only one.

- ■ *Stacked:* A canvas you display on top of another canvas, usually containing some items in a group separate from the items in the underlying content canvas.

- *Tabbed:* A content canvas that divides the contents of the window into tabbed pages; the user clicks on a tab on the canvas to see the items on that tab page.

- *Toolbar:* A canvas containing tool icon buttons that the window displays in horizontal and vertical bars at the top of or to the left side of a window, respectively.

Filling Up the Canvas

To set up a canvas, you first create a block, as demonstrated in Chapter 4. Oracle Developer automatically creates a content canvas with the name you specify in the New Block window or Layout Wizard. You can also start the Layout Editor in a new form to get a default content canvas. Otherwise, you must create a canvas in the usual way in the Object Navigator, by selecting the Canvases node and clicking on the Create tool. You can set the Canvas Type (default Content) and the Window that displays the canvas in the Property Palette for the canvas, as this illustration shows.

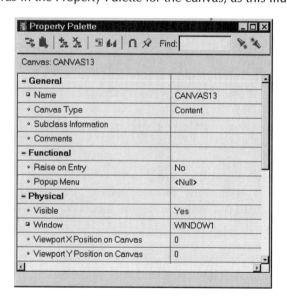

To see the canvas in the Layout Editor, double-click on the Object Navigator icon for the object. You saw in Chapter 4 how to use the Layout Editor to put items and boilerplate text on the canvas. The only difference here is that you are building the canvas from scratch rather than working with a canvas with a set of items that Oracle Developer generates when you create a block. You can create an item in the Object Navigator, then set the item's Canvas property to be the new canvas. You can also create the item in the Layout Editor and change the properties of the item through its Property Palette. You can create a second canvas and move items to it from the base canvas by changing the Canvas property in the items that already exist. If you set this property to NULL, the item appears in no canvas. This lets you define items that do not display their values.

You can control the display of the canvas background through the View|Show Canvas menu item, available when the Layout Editor is active. If you set this item off, you will see the background grid directly under the items. If you turn it back on, you will see the canvas with no grid. This menu item serves two purposes. First, a grid may help you in placing the items. Second, if you want to resize the canvas itself, you can do so by dragging the selection handle in the lower-right corner of the canvas. To see this, turn on the View|Show Canvas menu item, then click on the right or bottom edge of the canvas. You can also change the Width and Height attributes in the canvas Property Palette.

The View|Show View menu item lets you see the view. If you display the canvas in its window, the view is the area of the canvas you would see. The Layout Editor displays the view as a 1-point black rectangle with handles that you can use to resize the default window. You can also change the size by changing the window's Width and Height in its Property Palette. One common reason to do this is to set the window Width and Height to the same values as the Width and Height for the content canvas. This sizes the window so it just encloses the canvas. You can also move the view by dragging the rectangle or by changing the X/Y Position properties of the canvas. This lets you position the canvas within the window at a point other than the upper-left corner.

NOTE

For a stacked canvas, you have an additional view through the boundaries of the canvas. You can, for example, place a scroll bar on the stacked canvas and scroll it within the window. The next section, "Stacking Canvases," gives more details.

You use all these features to position the internal items and their canvases to greatest effect in the window that displays them. For example, you usually want the window to tightly enclose the canvas, and you want the canvas to be as small as possible given the item layout. Whenever feasible you want the user to be able to see all the items in a window without scrolling, which makes the form easier to use. To do this, you resize the canvas so it just encloses the item layout, then copy the canvas Width and Height properties to the corresponding window Width and Height properties. This sizes the window precisely to the canvas.

Users can resize the canvas by selecting an edge and dragging it, which means they can adjust both the window and the canvas to their screen display. You can thus size the initial window to scroll across a larger canvas to accommodate smaller video displays, and users with high-resolution displays can resize the canvas to see everything at once.

You delete the canvas in the Object Navigator by selecting it and clicking on the Delete tool. Oracle Developer cleans up any item references to the deleted canvas by setting their Canvas property to NULL.

The window, when you display it, automatically displays the base canvas for a window. You can control display of other canvases through the Show_View and Hide_View built-in subprograms in triggers.

Stacking Canvases

Stacked canvases allow you to create several special effects:

- You can create a group of buttons or other items in a separate cluster with a background that graphically distinguishes the cluster from the underlying content canvas.

- You can create a separable and reusable group of items, such as a button array, that you can reuse in different canvases by copying. (Chapter 10 gives the details on how to do this.)

- You can hide or display a stacked canvas programmatically to create a view that changes automatically when the user takes some action.

- You can display unchanging text and fields on top of multiple content canvases that change in and out dynamically, giving you a way to have recurring elements without producing multiple items.

- You can have a set of items in a multiple-record display remain on the screen while you scroll the underlying content canvas to see other items. For example, you can display the primary key in an unchanging column while you view the rest of the columns by scrolling. You always see the primary key no matter where you are in the canvas. This special effect behaves like a multiple-display view in a spreadsheet.

This last trick can help quite a bit with master-detail forms that have too many items to view at once in a reasonably sized window. For example, if your target display platform is a 640x480 VGA Windows display and your form is similar to the Ledger form, there will be no way to display several records with that many fields so the user can see them all. Window scrolling can handle this problem. Change applications to a person-oriented ledger display that shows all the ledger entries for a given person. The person information is at the top of the application, while the ledger information displays multiple records with multiple items below it. If you scroll the window, you lose the person information as it scrolls off the screen. The scrolling stacked canvas can help you deal with this situation.

1. Create the Person data block by clicking on the Create tool; use the Data Block Wizard and display only the Name column. In the Layout Wizard, create a new Content canvas and make the data block type a Form.

2. Create the Ledger data block by clicking on the Create tool after selecting the Person data block in the Object Navigator. Using the Data Block Wizard, add all the Ledger columns and the Person.Name lookup column.

3. In the Layout Wizard for the Ledger data block, create the canvas as a New Canvas and set the Type to Stacked. Set the data block type to Tabular and make it contain 5 rows of data with a scroll bar.

4. Save the new form as Person_Ledger.

5. Navigate to the Person block Relation node (Person_Ledger|Data Blocks|Person|Relations) in the Object Navigator and click the Create tool to create a master-detail relation. As in Chapter 4, create the relation based on the object reference between Ledger and Person.

6. Open the Person canvas view in the Layout Editor by double-clicking on its node in the Object Navigator.

7. To help see the relationship between the canvases, choose the View|Stacked Views menu item. This displays the Stacked/Tab Canvases dialog box, which lets you select the stacked canvas to display. This dialog box lists all the stacked canvases and lets you toggle them on and off, but in a relatively unusual way. Instead of clicking the canvases on and off with sequential clicks or double clicks, you click to select and CTRL-click to deselect a canvas. That is, click on the stacked canvas name to display it, and CTRL-click on it to remove it from the display.

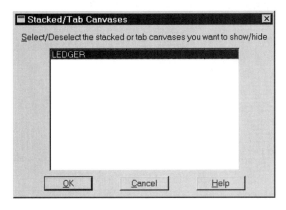

8. Clicking on OK displays or removes the stacked canvases from the Layout Editor. The resulting Layout Editor for the example Person-Ledger form shows the Ledger block completely obscuring the Person block.

The view of a stacked canvas is the portion of the canvas that is visible. Although the view of a content canvas relates to the window boundaries, the view of a stacked canvas has nothing to do with the window. You can see the boundaries of the stacked canvas by selecting the canvas in the Object Navigator, then displaying the Layout Editor. You see sizing handles at the boundaries of the stacked canvas, and the ruler for the canvas is the active ruler while the content canvas ruler is grayed out. Drag the handles to change the size of the view to show more or less of the stacked canvas.

The easiest way to position the stacked canvas is to set the viewport coordinates in the Property Palette for the canvas.

9. Select the Ledger canvas in the Object Navigator.

10. Display the Property Palette by choosing the Tools|Property Palette menu item or Property Palette on the pop-up menu you get by right-clicking the canvas object.

11. Find the Viewport header and the two properties for Viewport Position. Set the Y position to .8 inch, which puts the stacked view just below the Name item. Figure 6-1 shows the results in the Layout Editor. You see the stacked canvas ruler distinguished by shading.

NOTE
Do not confuse Viewport Y Position with the Viewport Y Position on Canvas property, which appears in the Physical property group. The latter positions the stacked canvas in the viewport, not the viewport itself. This lets you position the scrolling canvas somewhere other than at the leftmost side or top when you first display the stacked canvas. Also, you can try dragging the stacked canvas view directly in the Layout Editor instead of setting it through its properties. Sometimes the boundary of the stacked canvas cannot be seen, and it can be a bit of a challenge to find it to drag; look for the resize handles after clicking on the canvas background, then drag by clicking and holding somewhere close to a resize handle. I usually prefer to drag the canvas around until it is approximately where I want it, then position it exactly by setting the properties.

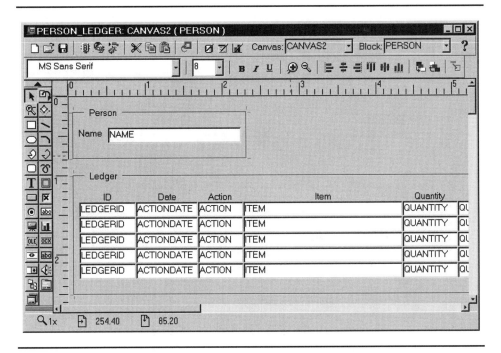

FIGURE 6-1. *The Layout Editor with a stacked canvas displayed within a content canvas*

12. Turn on the horizontal scroll bar by setting the Show Horizontal Scroll Bar property to Yes.

    This scroll bar appears under the bottom edge of the view, so you must size the view properly to get the scroll bar where you want it. For our example, the view will extend just past the bottom of the last row of the fifth ledger record. Then the scroll bar appears right under the block of records. You see the scroll bar in the Layout Editor for the content canvas, not in the one for the stacked canvas.

13. Finally, you must size the content canvas to contain its own items and the stacked canvas, and then you must size the window to contain the content canvas, either through the Layout Editor boundaries or through the canvas and window Property Palettes.

    Running the example now results in the display shown in Figure 6-2.

    Notice the two horizontal scroll bars in Figure 6-2. The lower one is the scroll bar associated with the window. This scroll bar only appears if the canvas extends beyond the window, which in this case it does by just a bit. The upper scroll bar is associated with the stacked Ledger canvas, and you can use it to scroll over to the Amount field and the record scroll bar.

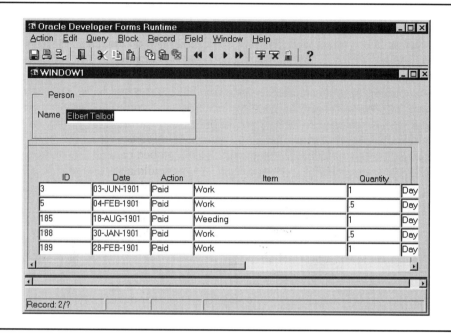

FIGURE 6-2. *The PersonLedger form with its scrolling view*

NOTE
If you don't see the stacked Ledger canvas, check a couple of things. First, make sure the Person canvas is first in order in the Navigator Canvases group. The first canvas displays first, the second canvas displays on top of it. If Person is second, it obscures the stacked canvas Ledger. Second, make sure the stacked canvas viewport positions the stacked canvas frame below the Person block frame (look at the dashed blue lines and the frame handles). Try moving the viewport down a bit and see what happens. If the stacked canvas items obscure the content items, even a tiny bit, the content canvas raises itself to show the entire obscured item when you navigate to it. This is the first thing your form does after displaying the canvases. You see the stacked canvas appear; then it disappears as if by magic!

Tabbed Canvases

A *tabbed* canvas displays its items on one or more tab pages. A *tab page* is a kind of minicanvas that resembles a tabbed file folder. You click on the labeled tab, and Oracle Developer displays that page. You use tabbed canvases to arrange items in groups. This permits you to show one group but to hide the others, simplifying the display for the user. You can use this feature to build forms that have many items but that offer them to the user in a highly structured and controlled way, making the form much easier to use. Not only that, but the tabbed canvas is fully portable to all the graphical user interfaces that Oracle Developer supports.

Chapter 4 showed the basic process of creating tabbed canvases. This section shows you how to treat a tabbed canvas just as you would a stacked canvas. This lets you combine a master content canvas with a series of detail tabbed canvases. For example, the WorkerSkill form in Chapter 4 linked a master person with a set of skills, with the person on one tab page and the skills on another. This has the disadvantage of removing the person from the display when you are looking at skills, and vice versa. Ideally, users could see the person information and skill information at the same time.

A more general version of the WorkerSkill form might be a HumanResources form that links lodgings and skills with people in a master-detail relationship. This form has three data blocks corresponding to the Person, Lodging, and WorkerHasSkills tables. The Person canvas has the person's name in a content canvas. When you lay out the other two data blocks, instead of choosing a content or stacked canvas, choose a single tabbed canvas with Lodging on one page and WorkerHasSkills on another. The first time through the Data Block Wizard, choose a new tabbed canvas; the second time through, select the one you created the first time through, then select a (New Tab Page). The Lodging canvas has a form layout, whereas the Skills page has a tabular layout listing several skills.

Once you've finished arranging and sizing the canvases and their item layouts, you can combine the two canvases in the same way you combined the Person canvas with the Ledger canvas using a stacked canvas.

1. Display the Layout Editor for the Person canvas and choose the View|Stacked Views menu item.

2. Select the tabbed canvas from the list of canvases in the Stacked/Tab Canvases dialog box. As before, selecting the canvas sets it down on top of the items in the content canvas.

3. Select the tabbed canvas and drag it down or change its Viewport Y Position to a value of around .25 inch or a little more.

This yields the layout shown in Figure 6-3 and the runtime form shown in Figure 6-4.

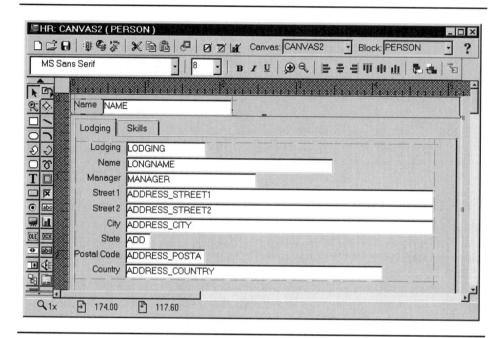

FIGURE 6-3. *The Layout Editor with a stacked tabbed canvas*

Once you've laid out the canvas, the next step is to display it through a window. The following section takes you through the different kinds of views you can create of your canvases through creative uses of the window.

Viewing Through Windows

The canvas structures the contents of your form; the window lets you see it. By adding windows and their canvases to your forms, you can create forms that are easy to understand and to use. Each window has at least one content canvas that defines the contents of the window.

Using Multiple Documents

The Microsoft Windows platform introduced the Multiple Document Interface (MDI), which structures the use of multiple windows in an application. Oracle Developer adopts the MDI architecture and extends it to other platforms by making specific assumptions and facilities available.

An MDI application has an *application window* that owns all the other windows in the application. The application window has no canvas but rather displays the other windows. The main menu belongs to the application window, and that

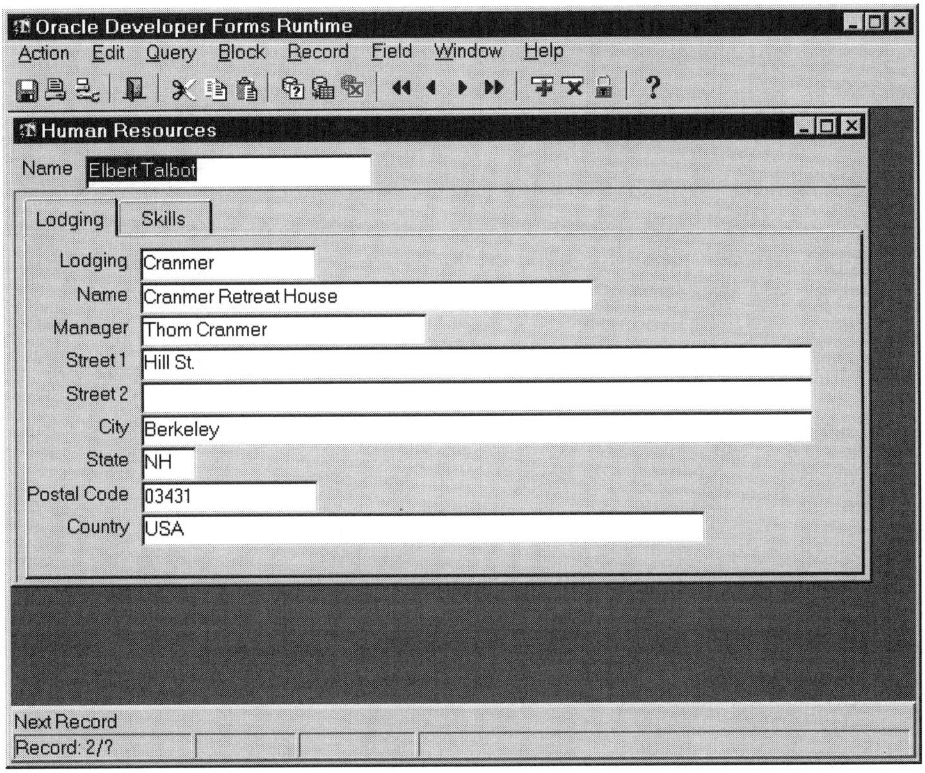

FIGURE 6-4. *The tabbed canvas at runtime*

window is always open. The form windows are children of this window and can be either document or dialog windows.

NOTE
Platforms other than Windows and NT do not use the MDI architecture; Motif and the Macintosh do not use it either.

A *document window* is a window contained entirely within the application window. If you move the document window beyond the application window, the portion of the document that you move beyond that window disappears. Usually, you display the document windows in an overlapping or tiled group in the application-window display area. You can also *maximize* a document window to take up the entire display area of the application window, or *minimize* the document window into an icon. The document window usually displays the central content of the application, such as the database table data and graphics.

NOTE

Some designers prefer to start their application without displaying a content window. Instead, they want the user to choose a window through the menus or through some other interface. You can achieve this effect by creating a small "parent" form as the form you run. This form can have a splash screen graphic or a set of buttons that open other forms. See the "Using Multiple Forms" section in Chapter 10 for hints on how to build effective multiple-form applications.

A *dialog box* is a window that is independent of the application window. You can move the dialog window outside the application window (if its properties allow this) without having the application window clip the dialog window. The dialog window typically contains fields that let the application interact with the user, such as collections of options or parameters for the application.

Another way to categorize windows is as modal or modeless. A *modal window* requires the user to respond and dismiss the window before doing anything in any other window in the application. Since the main function of a dialog box is to get information necessary to proceed, dialog boxes are usually modal. You can have modeless dialog boxes that continue to exist while you are doing other things in the application, if the dialog box information isn't part of subsequent processing. For example, a Find dialog that lets you search for a string can be modeless. A *modeless window* lets you move to another window without dismissing the first one. Often, modal windows have distinguishing characteristics such as lack of scroll bars, fixed size, and an inability to be minimized to an icon. On some platforms, the modality extends to other applications. That is, you must respond to the window and dismiss it before doing anything else in the system, not just the application (*system modal* as opposed to *application modal*).

In Oracle Developer applications, the application window corresponds to the currently executing form. The main menu for the application is the menu for the form. You can also have horizontal and vertical toolbars by specifying their canvases as the Horizontal MDI Toolbar or Vertical MDI Toolbar properties of the form.

You can set the application window's properties programmatically in trigger code by using the name FORMS_MDI_WINDOW in the Set_Window_Property built-in procedure.

Creating Windows

When you create a new form, you get a new window. Your first canvas uses this window automatically. When you want to create more windows, use the Object Navigator in the usual way: select the Windows heading and click on the Create tool.

   You determine almost everything to do with a window through the properties in the Window Property Palette. The "Functional" section lets you set up the basic interface capabilities of the window. These properties, shown in Table 6-1, are called hints because not all of them apply to all platforms.

   To set up the basic structure of the window, use the properties in Table 6-2.

NOTE
Oracle Developer scrolls a canvas in a window automatically when you navigate to an item in the canvas that is outside the current window. You can also control scrolling through triggers with the Set_Canvas_Property built-in procedure or by setting the X or Y Position on Canvas property of the canvas with Set_View_Property. You should use Set_Canvas_Property; Scroll_View is provided only for backward compatibility with previous releases of Oracle Developer.

   Oracle Developer makes it easy for you to display and close windows. It controls this automatically for you through navigation. When you navigate to an

Property	Description
Close Allowed	Whether you can close the window with the platform-specific Close command.
Resize Allowed	Whether the height and width of the window is fixed or the user can resize the window; Resize Allowed set to No is only valid with Maximize Allowed set to False.
Minimize Allowed	Whether the user can minimize the window to an icon.
Inherit Menu	Whether the window displays the form menu; not valid on Microsoft Windows.
Move Allowed	Whether the user can move the window.
Maximize Allowed	Whether the user can maximize or zoom the window with platform-specific operations; valid only if Resize Allowed is False.

TABLE 6-1. *Functional Forms Window Properties*

Property	Description
Primary Canvas	The name of the canvas to display in this window as the *primary context view*—the base view that the window always displays when you open it. This is optional but can be necessary if you use Show_Window to display the window or if you use stacked canvases and navigate directly to them.
Vertical Toolbar Canvas, Horizontal Toolbar Canvas	The canvas to display in the vertical or horizontal toolbar. See the upcoming section "Creating Toolbars."
Window Style	The kind of window, Document or Dialog.
Modal	Whether the window is modal.
Hide on Exit	Whether to close and deactivate a modeless window when you navigate out of it to another window; valid only if Modal is False.
Direction	The direction of flow of text. The Default setting is usually what you want, as it inherits the proper direction from the NLS setup in Oracle.
Icon Filename, Minimized Title	The name of the icon file and the title to display when the user minimizes the window; valid only if Iconifiable is True. The path and other characteristics of this icon file depend on the platform, and using icon files requires extra work to port the application to other platforms.
Show Horizontal Scroll Bar, Show Vertical Scroll Bar	Whether to display a horizontal and/or a vertical scroll bar, which lets you scroll the view over the canvas if the canvas is larger than the window; valid only for modeless windows.

TABLE 6-2.   *Structural Forms Window Properties*

item on a canvas that is not active, Oracle Developer displays the canvas in its associated window. When you navigate out of the canvas to another canvas in a different window, Oracle Developer automatically closes the first one only if you have the Remove on Exit property set to True. Otherwise, the window goes to the back but still displays.

NOTE

See the following section for modal window behavior; the Remove on Exit property does not apply to modal dialogs.

You can also open and close windows in triggers by navigating with built-in navigation subprograms or with the Show_Window and Hide_Window built-in procedures. If you do this for an inactive, displayed window behind the currently active window, Oracle Developer raises the inactive window to the top of the window stack and activates it. You can show and hide particular canvases in the same way, with navigation or with Show_View and Hide_View.

Creating and Closing Modal Dialog Boxes

To create a modal dialog box:

1. Set the Window Style to Dialog and set Modal to True.

2. Create the content canvas and the items that constitute the dialog box, along with their block, if necessary, and associate the canvas with the dialog box.

3. Most dialog boxes benefit from being a fixed size, so set the Fixed Size or Resize Allowed property to True and the window Width and Height properties to the size of the canvas. This ensures that the window displays the entire canvas.

4. It is also a good idea to make the dialog box smaller than the window or windows it will appear over; this keeps the user aware of the application's modal status.

You need to set up the displaying of the modal dialog box on the appropriate events. There are two simple ways to do this. First, you can arrange the item navigation order in such a way that the user navigates to an item on the dialog's canvas. You can do the navigation explicitly, without regard to navigation order, in a button trigger or menu command. In either case, Oracle Developer automatically displays the dialog box when the user navigates to the dialog item.

Second, you can call the Show_Window built-in subprogram from a button trigger or menu command. This procedure displays the window and navigates to the first item on the dialog box canvas.

The Modal property in Oracle Developer prevents the user from navigating out of the dialog box with the mouse. It does not, however, suspend keypresses; so the user can navigate out using the navigation keys. When the user does this, Oracle Developer closes the dialog box automatically. However, this behavior is not what users expect from dialog boxes. Modal dialog boxes should remain on the screen as the active window until a positive user action dismisses them, usually by clicking on an OK or Cancel button.

There are several ways to turn off the keypress navigation keys:

■ Set the Previous Navigation Block and Next Navigation Block properties for the blocks with items in the dialog box to the block itself, making navigation circular. If you do this, you should have separate blocks with all items appearing in the dialog box canvas.

■ Create a Key-Others trigger on the block that owns the items you are displaying that contain a single null statement:

```
NULL;
```

This turns off all keys except those keys for which you define a key trigger. You need to minimally define Key-Next-Item and Key-Previous-Item to allow tabbing between the dialog items.

You then need to set up the triggers on the OK and Cancel buttons, or whatever alternative ways you have of instructing Oracle Developer to close the dialog box. Oracle Developer closes the dialog box automatically when you navigate out of the window with, for example, the When-Button-Pressed trigger. You must navigate to an item in a modeless window with its block outside the dialog canvas.

You can open another modal dialog box from a modal dialog box. For example, you can have an Options button that displays a second dialog box of extended options. You can also achieve some fancy effects such as having an Extended button that replaces the current dialog box with a second, larger dialog box. Experiment.

Creating Toolbars

A *toolbar* is a strip of icons along the top or left side of a window. To create one, you must first create a toolbar canvas (the canvas types Horizontal Toolbar or Vertical Toolbar) that contains the button items and boilerplate graphics. See the preceding sections on creating canvases.

1. Specify the window that will display the toolbar as the Window property for the canvas.

2. Set the width and height to values that give you a toolbar optimally sized for the application you're designing. For example, you want the width of the toolbar canvas for the horizontal toolbar to be the same as the window's width, and the height to just encompass the icons.

3. The next step is to set the Horizontal Toolbar or Vertical Toolbar properties for the window object to the name of the appropriate canvas. This tells the window to display the toolbars in the appropriate locations.

NOTE
In Microsoft Windows, you can also display MDI application window toolbars through the Horizontal or Vertical MDI Toolbar properties of the form object. Oracle Developer ignores the Window property of the toolbar canvas for these toolbars.

You can have multiple toolbar canvases for a single window. Oracle Developer uses the standard rules for displaying these. You just navigate to the first item on the toolbar to display it instead of the original toolbar. Usually, toolbars that change dynamically are *not* a good idea, as this kind of change tends to confuse the user. You could use this feature to disable and enable tools on the toolbar by substituting a different icon for the disabled tool (dimmed, grayed, or crossed out, for example).

Because the items in the toolbar are just that—items in a block—you must take some special measures to ensure that these items don't behave just as any other item on the form, especially with regard to navigation. Generally, it's a good idea to put the button items for the toolbar into a separate block. Take this block out of block navigation by setting the Next Navigation Data Block property of the previous block to point at a block other than the toolbar block; do this with the Property Palette. Turning off block navigation to the block prevents the user from accidentally navigating to a tool.

4. For each item, set the Keyboard Navigable and Mouse Navigate properties to No in the Property Palette. Turning these properties off prevents the clicking of a tool on the toolbar from causing the cursor to navigate into the toolbar block. Users stay firmly in the block they're in when they click on a tool.

NOTE
If you run an MDI application without substituting your own menu for the standard Oracle Developer menu, you will see a toolbar appear under the main menu at the top of the MDI window. This is the special menu toolbar. The default menu toolbar contains icons that correspond to the common menu items such as Enter Query, Next Record, and so on. You cannot change this toolbar, nor can you remove it, without supplying your own entire main menu module. See the "Menus" section later in the chapter for details on adding custom menus.

Creating Alerts

An *alert* is a modal window that displays a message or asks a simple question that elicits a yes/no type of response from the user. Oracle Developer has a special object for alerts to simplify programming for these very common windows.

NOTE
Oracle Developer automatically displays an alert when you use the Message function in PL/SQL code, or when a built-in message occurs and there are multiple messages. Ordinarily, the messages appear on the status bar. If there are multiple messages, the user would see only the last one and would miss interim messages. Instead, Oracle Developer displays the interim messages as special alerts. You can sometimes avoid these by using the Synchronize built-in subprogram to display the message immediately in your PL/SQL code right after the call to the Message built-in. A better way is to replace the messaging system entirely by using explicit alert objects for errors. You can build a set of reusable alert objects for standard errors and package them in your standard object library, for example.

To create an alert, select the Alerts heading in the Object Navigator and click on the Create tool in the usual way.

There are three kinds of alert. You specify which type to use through the Alert Style property in the alert's Property Palette:

- *Stop:* Displays a stop sign icon with the message.

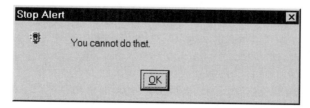

- *Caution:* Displays an exclamation point icon with the message.

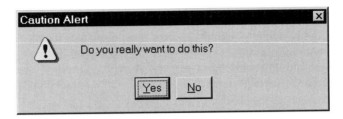

■ *Note:* Displays an information icon with the message.

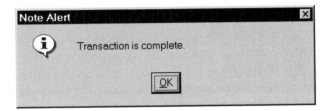

The Message property lets you enter a message to display in the alert. You can enter up to 200 characters (although not all platforms can display the full number of characters).

The Button 1, Button 2, and Button 3 fields in the Property Palette let you label the buttons the alert displays. If you do not enter a label, the alert does not display the button. For example, if you use the default OK and Cancel settings, you get an alert with two buttons labeled "OK" and "Cancel." If you delete the Cancel setting for Button 2, you get a single button with "OK." You must label at least one button. You also should designate one button as the default button; when the user presses ENTER, Oracle Developer selects the default button.

You display an alert from trigger code using the Show_Alert built-in subprogram. This subprogram returns the number ALERT_BUTTON1, ALERT_BUTTON2, or ALERT_BUTTON3 depending on which button the user selects. You can then test the returned number and take the appropriate action in your trigger code. For example, the following code prompts the user with the Caution alert to decide whether to continue with the trigger or not. Button 1 is Yes and button 2 is No.

```
DECLARE
  vAlertButton NUMBER;
BEGIN  -- Initial processing
  vAlertButton := Show_Alert('Caution');
  IF vAlertButton = ALERT_BUTTON1 THEN
    NULL; -- Continue processing
  END IF;  -- do nothing for button 2
END;
```

With a bit of coding, you can also create reusable alert objects and alerts that display dynamic messages that refer to specific values or objects. For example, you can create a single informational alert with just an OK button. By setting the message text at runtime, you can reuse this single object instead of creating a separate alert for each message. You could build a simple procedure in a library with this code:

```
PROCEDURE Show_Info_Alert(pText IN VARCHAR2) IS
  vAlertID ALERT := Find_Alert('GenericInfoAlert');
  vDummy NUMBER;
BEGIN  Set_Alert_Property(vAlertID, ALERT_MESSAGE_TEXT, pText);
  vDummy := Show_Alert(vAlertID);
END;
```

You then just pass in a message string as the text parameter to the procedure call to display the GenericInfoAlert alert with that message. The procedure deliberately ignores the return code from Show_Alert.

You could also build more complex, reusable functions that accept arguments for the message, build the message text by concatenating the arguments, display the dynamic message, and return the appropriate button number. Again, you should put the function in a library for reuse in other modules.

```
FUNCTION Show_Info_Alert(pText1 IN VARCHAR2, pText2 IN VARCHAR2)
        RETURN NUMBER IS
  vAlertID ALERT := Find_Alert('GenericInfoAlert');
  vMessage VARCHAR2(200);
BEGIN
  vMessage := 'The '||pText1||' is '||pText2||'.';
  Set_Alert_Property(vAlertID, ALERT_MESSAGE_TEXT, vMessage);
  RETURN Show_Alert(vAlertID);
END;
```

Data Blocks

Oracle Developer provides several special features relating to blocks and their items. You can dramatically improve the usability of your forms with these features. If you use lists, you can construct them in several different formats for different purposes. Using radio buttons lets you create mutually exclusive choices easily. Using a calculated field makes the job of automatically showing totals and other calculations on your form much easier. Using the right format masks for dates can drastically reduce the errors relating to dates and times in your database. Finally, you can use procedural encapsulation in combination with the Data Block Wizard to base your data block on stored procedures instead of tables, adding a measure of object-orientation and data hiding to your system.

Lists

A *list* is a form item that lets you display a list of text items in a single place. The idea is to let the user choose among several mutually exclusive options by seeing the list of choices and choosing one. You've already seen two kinds of lists—the drop-down list from the WorkerHasSkills form in Chapter 4 and the list of values (LOV) that you've seen in the Designer, used to display choices, also in Chapter 4.

There are four types of lists, three of which are list items:

- *Poplist:* A drop-down list of text items that you activate through a small arrow in a box next to the list, causing the list to pop up on the window near the item.

- *Tlist:* A list box that displays all the text items in a scrolling list, like a separate canvas but within a single field in the form.

- *Combo box:* A combination of the poplist and a text item that lets you pull down a list of text items but also lets you type in a value.

- *List of values (LOV):* A dialog box that displays the text items and gives you pattern-matching capabilities for searching in the list. The dialog box returns the single list item you select and copies it into another block item. This is a completely separate object in Form Builder, not a list item, and you connect it to items with a special set of properties in each item. The LOV gives you the ability to use pattern matching in finding an item in a long list of values. See the section "Creating a LOV" in Chapter 4 for a tutorial on using the LOV Wizard to create LOVs for items.

All of these lists display a list of text items in some way. These strings are not necessarily the value for the item, however. The list transforms what you see on the screen, a *label,* into an actual *value* in the item, and it's that value that Forms stores in the database. Because of the level of indirection between the label and the value, you can use text for display and some other data type for the field. Lists thus give you a way to display nicely formatted, meaningful text on your form but still store meaningless, hard-to-use codes in your database.

For example, you may be using an older database that stores numbers as codes for different options. The number 1 could stand for Red, 2 for Green, 3 for Purple, and so on. The purpose of a list item is to show the user the text "Green" but to put the number 2 into the database. It also translates the 2 when you query the record from the database, displaying "Green" instead.

Effective Lists

Lists are powerful tools for displaying information in a useful way. There are some specific approaches to structuring lists that make them more usable.

I recommend using the string you display as the value in the database. Codes were useful when disk space was at a premium and programmers could only read numbers. Most developers have now learned to read text, (which means they've caught up with the rest of the world). There are reasons to use codes, but for the most part these have to do with adapting to "previously owned" databases that do not use modern design methods or optimizing space in very large databases with billions of instances of the values. If you have the choice, keep it simple by keeping the label and value the same in the list.

TIP

When you query a set of records, and for some reason the record that the database server returns violates a trigger or some other required condition in the form, Oracle Developer discards the record without telling you. Why do I bring this up here? One of those required conditions is that a list item value be in the list you've coded. If you query a record from the database that has a value that isn't in the list, Forms won't let you display that record but will just silently throw it away. Forms assumes that the database you are using has values consistent with the validation conditions you've built into the application. If that assumption doesn't hold, it can confuse the user. You should make sure your database consistently adheres to the set of business rules you are building into your applications.

The possibility of having data in the database with values not in the application list is the main reason for the existence of the Other Values property for list items (not including the LOV dialog box, though, because it is not a list item but a separate kind of object entirely). By default, this property of the list item is NULL. If you don't set it to a value, the Forms runtime throws away records with values not in the list. If you set it to a value, then the Forms runtime will display the record, but it displays the Other Values value instead of the value from the database. The Forms runtime displays this string for any value not in the list. You can make this value something like "Other," for example. You must add the value to the list as well, giving it an appropriate label.

NOTE
You aren't required to supply an Other Values setting. In the case where you have a check constraint on the database column corresponding to the item, for example, you know that no "other" values can come back from the database. In this case you can leave the Other Values setting NULL without causing any problems. If you can't guarantee that the values coming back will be in the list, however, it is a good idea to define the property, as the behavior of Forms is quite confusing otherwise.

The combo box creates another opportunity for validation issues. The whole idea of the combo box is to permit the user to enter free text into the field as well as drop down a list from which to choose a value. The consequence: Developer does not validate the text you enter against the list. If that's the behavior you want, fine. If not, you'll need to add validation code, either to interpret the database error that comes from violating a constraint or to interpret the text the user enters in some way. You can also use some of the built-in subprograms for managing list items to add the items the user enters to the list, which requires quite a lot of advanced coding. For these reasons, it is best to use combo boxes as suggestion lists rather than taking on the full load of validation programming.

Hard-Coded Lists

A *hard-coded list* is a list that you fully specify in Form Builder. You fill out a dialog box with the labels and their corresponding values, which become part of the client-side application. The advantages of this approach are simplicity and speed. You can create these lists very quickly, and they perform very well because the list is in memory when you open the application. The disadvantage is that you can't change the list without regenerating and redeploying the application. You would use hard-coded lists for simple lists that don't change.

To create a hard-coded list:

1. Create the list item in the block.

2. Display the Property Palette for the item.

3. Set the Item Type property to List Item, if you haven't done that already.

4. Set the Width property to the length of the longest label you intend to enter.

5. Go to the Functional section of the Property Palette. Set the List Style property to one of the three types of list (Poplist, TList, or Combo Box).

6. Double-click the Elements in List property.

You now see the List Elements dialog box, as shown here:

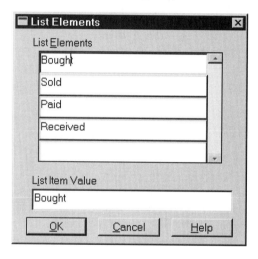

7. Enter the labels and corresponding values.

8. If you want the value to be NULL, leave the value cell blank.

9. Use the DOWN-ARROW key or the mouse to move to a new item in the list; use CTRL-K to see the list of function keys you can use in this dialog box. Use the CTRL-< key (don't forget to press SHIFT to get < instead of a comma) to delete the list item you have currently selected.

10. Click OK on the dialog box when you're finished.

11. Now enter one of the values (not a label) in the Other Values property, if you want to be able to handle values not in the list.

If you run the form, you see this item in the style you selected. You can see the labels you entered in the dialog box in the list when you display it, and you can select any item in the list.

NOTE
Sometimes you may get an extra blank line in the lists. This results from deleting the label and value without deleting the entire list element using CTRL-<. *Try that first.*

Dynamic Lists

A *dynamic list* is a list that you fill in at runtime. There are two ways to do this. The most common way is to build the list from a table in the database. The list gets its labels and values from a record group object that you create and fill with a SELECT statement. You then populate the list from the record group. The other way entails using the Add_List_Element built-in function to simply add the values. You'll learn more about this second way shortly. First let's look at building the list from a table.

BUILDING LISTS FROM TABLES　First, create the list item as you did in the previous section. Enter one label-value pair in the List Elements dialog box that you can use for the Other Values property, but only if you need to do this (see the discussion of Other Values in the previous section "Effective Lists").

This value unfortunately cannot be the NULL value. If you use the NULL value for the single hard-coded list element, you cannot remove it using Clear_List when you are ready to create the new dynamic list from the table. Instead, you get an error, and the list loading fails. The reason for this is apparently to address the release 1 problem with unwanted blank lines appearing in the drop-down list. The list no longer lets you delete the NULL element; thus it no longer needs to add it back in, producing the unwanted blank line. What this means is that you *must* choose a value from the database for your default value. For example, in the Person list in the Ledger form, I use the "General Store" value as my default list element. When the list loads from the table, this value will disappear, but the Other Values will still have this value. Thus, the value must appear in the list loaded from the database as well as in the hard-coded version.

One consequence of this requirement is that you can't just reuse a standard List SmartClass from the object library. You have to customize the List Elements and Other Values properties to the specific list item and its database values. It also means that if the value you choose changes in the database, you will have to change it in the hard-coded List Elements property as well. This is unfortunate, but you'll have to live with it for now.

Once you've set up your Other Values property, create a record group object for the form in the usual way. The Designer displays a dialog box asking whether to create the record group from a list of values or with a query, with query as the default. Just leave the radio button for query selected and enter a query in the text box. The query should select data corresponding to the label and value, in that order. If your value is a number or date, use the To_Char function to transform the values into strings. Use an ORDER BY clause to sort the list the way you want it to appear in the displayed list.

For example, if you wanted to create a list for the Ledger table's Action column, you could use the following query:

```
SELECT DISTINCT Action, Action
    FROM Ledger
ORDER BY 1
```

NOTE

Using the number 1 in the ORDER BY clause lets you order by the label regardless of the fact that there are two columns with the same name.

This query generates a record group with labels and values that are the same, using the unique values of Action in the Ledger table. You get the unique values using the GROUP BY clause. The GROUP BY also sorts the values by the label, but it is good coding practice to add the ORDER BY clause anyway so that you're not confused later should you need to change the GROUP BY.

Now, create the following as a procedure in the form or in an attached library. This is a good candidate for a systemwide library, as you can reuse the procedure in any form.

```
PROCEDURE Set_Up_List (pList in VARCHAR2, pGroup in VARCHAR2) IS
   vErrFlag NUMBER := 0;
   eListPopulationProblem EXCEPTION;
BEGIN
   vErrFlag := Populate_Group(pGroup);
   IF vErrFlag = 0 THEN
     Clear_List(pList);  -- remove anything already there
     Populate_list(pList, pGroup);
   ELSIF vErrFlag = 1403 THEN  -- no list elements found
     null;  -- do nothing and ignore the problem
   ELSE
     RAISE eListPopulationProblem;
   END IF;
EXCEPTION
   WHEN OTHERS THEN
     Message('Exception:  Could not populate '||pList
             ||' with query in group '||pGroup||'.');
END;
```

NOTE
You need only clear the list if you are calling the procedure several times for the same list. If you don't clear the list, you will just add values to the list that is already there. Also, carefully check the return code from Populate_Group, as that return code indicates any problems with your SQL query. Also, see the comments on the relationship between Clear_List, the List Elements property, and the Other Values property of the list item near the beginning of this section.

Now, you need to choose a trigger to build the list. You can build the list when you open the form through the When-New-Form-Instance trigger. Alternatively, you can wait until you are ready to display the list, perhaps in a When-New-Block-Instance trigger for the block in which the list appears. You can be quite creative about this to save some processing time when you load the form. Now, enter the following code in the trigger:

```
Set_Up_List('Action', 'LedgerActionGroup');
```

This procedure call fills up the LedgerActionGroup with its built-in query, then uses that group to populate the list.

NOTE
You may also want to rebuild the list as a separate action in your application. For example, if you have a subform that lets you modify the set of values that appears in the list, you need to run the code that builds the list again to reset the list to contain the new values. Unfortunately, doing that requires you to finish any existing transaction against the block in which the list item appears. A good way to do this is to issue a Clear_Block or Clear_Form statement in the code that rebuilds the list.

Radio Buttons

Ordinarily, if you want the user to choose among a series of alternative values, you would offer a list of choices. The radio button offers an alternative to lists. A *radio group* is a collection of radio buttons, with the radio button being a small circular button with a label (the exact format depends on the graphical user interface platform). When the user clicks a button, Oracle Developer deselects the current button and selects the chosen one. Thus, you can select only one of the radio buttons at a time. The name comes from the behavior of station-choice buttons on a radio, where pushing in one pops out the others (or the electronic equivalent on modern digital radios). In this example, it makes sense that only one choice is appropriate for each case:

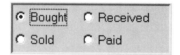

You use radio buttons when you have a relatively small number of mutually exclusive choices, usually two or three, that are unlikely to change with time. In the case of the above example, the four possible types of action are very stable.

NOTE
The radio group couples the structure of the application to the structure of the value constraints in the database. Therefore, the dynamic list is usually a preferable interface because you can extend it without changing the application code. If your list is static rather than dynamic, or if the values really won't change with time, the radio group does offer some advantages in presentation and ease of use for this kind of choice.

The radio group is a block item that corresponds to a column in a database table. The radio buttons correspond to possible values for that column. Thus, the radio buttons cluster together under the single radio group item. When the user clicks on a button, the Value property for that button object becomes the value for the radio group.

This logic has implications for the set of properties of these objects. Any property that affects all buttons at once is a property of the radio group, such as the default value, database-related properties, or navigational properties. Any property that affects only a single button is a button property, such as the button value, the button label, and the physical position of the button. To set the initial button that Oracle Developer shows as selected in a new record, you set the Default Value property of the radio group to the button's value (such as "Bought" in the example).

NOTE
Until you create a record in a block, the Default Value property for any item in that block doesn't have any effect. Even though you can see the items in the block, you haven't really created a record in the block until you navigate to it. The default value doesn't appear until you actually create a new record in the block.

To set up the individual buttons, create the button using the Create tool in the usual way, then change the Label and Radio Button Value properties. The Label is the text that Oracle Developer displays as a prompt; the Radio Button Value is the actual value Oracle Developer assigns to the radio group when a user clicks the button.

Just as for lists, if you retrieve a row from the database with a value that does not correspond to any of the radio button values, you have a problem, and Oracle Developer silently discards the record. The Other Values property of the radio group works just like the property with the same name for a list item. It lets you convert values that do not correspond to buttons to one of the button values for display purposes.

As a matter of user-interface design style, it is usually a good idea to distinguish the radio group visually in some way. The example just given uses a boilerplate graphics rectangle around the four radio buttons to separate them from the rest of the block's items on the canvas. The rectangle in this case has its Beveled property set to Lowered to give it a three-dimensional effect.

Calculated Items

A common task in creating a form is to create an item that represents some calculated value. For example, you could combine several database items into a concatenated string in a separate item that doesn't correspond to a column in the base table. In the Ledger form, you could replace the Amount field that comes from the database with a field you calculate as the Quantity multiplied by the Rate. Another common example is when a Total field is created that sums the records in another block.

In previous versions of Oracle Developer, you achieved these effects by using various triggers to calculate the values and display them by assigning the value to the item. Typically you would use the When-Validate-Item and Post-Query triggers for these effects. To calculate Amount, for example, you would set the Base Table Item property to False, make the item a display item by changing its type, then create When-Validate-Item triggers on Quantity and Rate, each of which had this code:

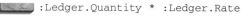 `:Ledger.Amount := :Ledger.Quantity * :Ledger.Rate;`

This handled inserts and updates to the two database items. You would also create a Post-Query trigger on the Ledger block with the same code to handle data coming back from the database.

You can create calculated fields very easily using the Calculation property group. You again create a display item not in the base table by setting the item property Database Item to No. Instead of creating triggers, however, you fill in the properties in the Calculation group. Setting Calculation Mode to Formula turns on the calculation feature. You then enter the formula just as though you were entering the PL/SQL code seen earlier:

`:Ledger.Quantity * :Ledger.Rate`

Whenever any change occurs in the record, Oracle Developer recalculates the field and displays the new value.

Totals are easy in Oracle Developer. You create the total item in the block you intend to aggregate. You must set the Precompute Summaries property in the Advanced Database group for that block to Yes, which tells Oracle Developer to calculate the summary before it does a query. Because you are aggregating, usually the block displays multiple records. You do not, however, want to display one total for each record. Set the Total item property Number of Items Displayed to 1 (usually it is 0, meaning the same number of items as records displayed in the block).

NOTE

You can set Query All Records in the Records group to Yes instead of setting Precompute Summaries to Yes to achieve the same effect. Rather than computing the summary separately, Oracle Developer then queries all the records instead of fetching them as needed. This lets it calculate the summary from the records in memory. For blocks with large result sets, this can cause some memory problems. The precomputation will also slow you down but not as much as Query All Records. Experiment with field performance testing to decide which alternative to use.

Now, you set four properties for the item. Calculation Mode set to Summary turns on summarization calculation for the item. Setting Summary Function to Sum tells Oracle Developer to add the record values. You can use any of the standard aggregation functions here, such as Count, Average, Min, Max, Stddev, or Variance. The Summarized Block and Summarized Item drop-down lists show all the blocks and all the items in the block you choose, respectively. For example, to create a Total item to total the Amount item in the Ledger block, you set Summary Function to Sum, Summarized Block to Ledger, and Summarized Item to Amount. Oracle Developer automatically displays the total for the block in a separate field on your canvas and handles all the calculations for changes to the summarized items, including clearing or removing the records.

Date and Time Items and Format Masks

Most people who deal with computers must now be aware of the "Year 2000" problem: when the clock strikes midnight on the last day of 1999, all the two-digit year fields will become "00," and the result, according to the media, will be chaos. This book is now officially Y2K compliant! It will still let you read after January 1, 2000.

However overstated this problem is, you definitely need to pay some attention to date and time fields. To ensure that you have no Year 2000 problems, you should always specify and display years as four-digit values. For date items in Oracle Developer, that translates into a format mask with some variation on "YYYY." Date format masks can handle all of the common date formats from around the world, so you need not write extensive triggers or procedures to format dates.

Most of the problems with dates and times come when you stray into the other half of the date-time arena. Dealing with time can be quite aggravating unless you bear in mind a few basic facts about Oracle Developer and Oracle times.

The foremost fact of life is that time and date are Siamese twins, inextricably linked. The date type DATE is common to Oracle Developer items and fields, PL/SQL variables, and Oracle columns and contains both the date and the time. Most problems occur when you try to deal with date and time separately. For example, you may want to present users with separately enterable date and time fields that let them set or see a time. You cannot do this without coding PL/SQL in Pre-Insert, Pre-Update, Pre-Delete, and Post-Query triggers to combine or split apart the elements of the date using the To_Char and To_Date conversion functions. To save yourself needless stress, use a format mask such as "MM/DD/YYYY" "HH:MI" in an Oracle Developer Date item instead of trying to separate them for "usability."

NOTE
Oracle Developer Forms also has the DATETIME and TIME data types for backward compatibility with previous versions of Forms. You should not use these data types, as the conversion to Oracle DATE can yield surprising effects.

Using a format mask in Oracle Developer does not affect the actual precision of the date and time, which always remains the same. What you see on the screen is not necessarily what gets into the database, as a result, and there is nothing you can do about that. For example, the fact that you do not see the time in a date item in a form does not mean it has no time or a time of 00:00, though that might be the effect you get by default. You can have PL/SQL code that sets a specific time:

```
:Ledger.ActionDate := To_Date(To_Char(:Ledger.ActionDate,
                               'MM/DD/YYYY')||' 12:00',
                               'MM/DD/YYYY HH:MI');
```

This code, for example, assigns the default value of 12 noon to all the dates you insert through the Ledger.ActionDate item instead of taking the default of midnight.

Table 6-3 shows the Oracle Developer format mask elements relating to years that you can combine into date-time format masks.

Table 6-4 shows the various time-related elements you can use in Oracle Developer format masks.

Element	Description
A.D.	Displays "B.C." for B.C. dates and "A.D." for A.D. dates.
AD	Displays "BC" for B.C. dates and "AD" for A.D. dates.
B.C.	Displays "B.C." for B.C. dates and "A.D." for A.D. dates.
BC	Displays "BC" for B.C. dates and "AD" for A.D. dates.
RR	Year with two digits that defaults to the "right" century; it is better to use four digits rather than two.
RRRR	Year with four digits, same as YYYY.
SYYYY	Year with four digits and a minus sign for B.C. dates.
Y	Year with one digit (not recommended).
Y,YYY	Year with four digits and a thousands separator comma.
YY	Year with two digits (not recommended).
YYY	Year with three digits (not recommended!).
YYYY	Year with four digits (recommended).

TABLE 6-3.   *Year-Related Format Mask Elements*

Element	Description
A.M.	"A.M." for ante-meridian times and "P.M." for post-meridian times.
AM	"AM" for ante-meridian times and "PM" for post-meridian times.
HH	The hour of the day in 12-hour format (1-12).
HH12	The hour of the day in 12-hour format (1-12).
HH24	The hour of the day in 24-hour format (0-23).
MI	The minute of the hour (0-59).
P.M.	"A.M." for ante-meridian times and "P.M." for post-meridian times.
PM	"AM" for ante-meridian times and "PM" for post-meridian times.
SS	The second of the minute (0-59).
SSSSS	The number of seconds since midnight (0-86399).

TABLE 6-4. *Hour-Related Format Mask Elements*

Table 6-5 shows the day- and month-related elements you can combine into your format masks.

You can place most punctuation anywhere in a format mask, and Oracle Developer will reproduce it in the displayed string. You can embed any text string in double quotes in the mask to display the string. For example, the mask "MONTH" "DD", "YYYY" displays the string "APRIL   18, 1999". Notice that the fixed-length MONTH mask element results in extra blanks in the month name. You can use the FM prefix to strip these out: "FMMONTH" "DD", "YYYY" displays the string "APRIL 18, 1999". You can specify case in the format element, using "Month" or "MONTH" depending on which you prefer.

Delimiters are the punctuation marks that separate the day, month, and year in dates. Usually this is a dash or a slash: 18-APR-1999 or 4/18/1999, for example. When you use these as part of the format mask, the user can enter different punctuation (4.18.1999, for example), and the mask translates it properly. To force use of specific punctuation and to force the user to supply all the numbers and characters in a date or time, you use the FX prefix. For example, the format mask FXDD-MON-YYYY HH:MM forces the user to enter 01-JAN-1999 12:00 in exactly that format, including the leading 0 and dash.

You can use the FX and FM prefixes together to relax the FX so it applies only to delimiters. For example, FMFXDD-MON-YYYY would allow the user to enter 1-JAN-1999 but not 1.JAN.1999.

Element	Description
D	Numeric day of the week (1-7, with 1 being Sunday, unless the current NLS language defines it as something else, such as Monday).
DAY	Fixed-length, nine-character day name ("SUNDAY ", "MONDAY ", and so on).
DD	Day of the month (1-31).
DDD	Day of the year (1-366).
DY	Three-letter day name (SUN, MON, TUE, and so on).
J	The number of days since January 1, 4712BC ("Julian" day); use only for specialty sorting applications; Oracle Corporation deprecates the use of this format, so don't use it.
MM	Month in number format (1-12).
MON	Three-letter month name (JAN, FEB, and so on).
MONTH	Fixed-length, nine-character month name ("JANUARY ", "FEBRUARY ", and so on).

TABLE 6-5. *Day- and Month-Related Format Mask Elements*

Procedural Encapsulation

The EXECUTE privilege gives you an interesting alternative to granting extensive privileges to objects: *procedural encapsulation.* One limitation of the discretionary approach of users, roles, and privileges is that, being server based, those privileges apply regardless of the mechanism by which you start a session. That is, data-changing privileges available to you when you log on through an application are just as available to you if you log on through SQL*Plus or some other program. If some or all of your validation processes exist only in your Oracle Developer code, going through these other programs can result in database problems due to lack of validation. If you rely on application-level security, the problem is even worse because the server doesn't enforce such security measures.

If you really want to restrict the ability of users in a high-security environment, you can encapsulate the allowed behavior in a stored procedure, then grant EXECUTE privilege on the procedure to the role or user. The user does not need any privileges on the underlying objects to execute the procedure. Only you need those privileges to create the procedure itself. Thus, a user logging in through an application that runs a procedure can do the necessary things, but the same user logging in through SQL*Plus cannot do those things directly with SQL (other than running the same procedure, of course, with all the restrictions that implies).

NOTE
This discussion applies to stored triggers as well as to procedures.

Oracle Developer has the ability to use stored procedures in the data block as data source. First, think about the data block and its base table as a class of objects in the database. What behaviors do you need to associate with the objects as a class?

- *Select:* Select some number of database objects and display them as records in the data block.

- *Insert:* Insert a database object from a record in the data block.

- *Update:* Change a database object from a changed record in the data block.

- *Delete:* Delete a database object from a record you've selected in the data block.

- *Lock:* Lock a database object corresponding to a record in the data block.

These five behaviors are the basis for most of what Oracle Developer does in the database. If you build stored procedures for each of these behaviors and then link them with the data block, you can get all the advantages of procedural encapsulation for your Oracle Developer application. Anyone running the application with the EXECUTE privilege on these procedures will see the application behave just as though using a standard data block. Anyone without these privileges won't be able to do anything in the application. Also, if you have extensive table lookup as part of the validation sequence of your data block, you can improve performance by moving all of this to the server as part of the stored procedures.

To use procedural encapsulation in this way, you must set up a special package for each table on which you are going to base a data block in an Oracle Developer application. For example, for the Skills table, you could define this package, connecting to the user that owns Skills:

```
CREATE OR REPLACE PACKAGE SkillPackage AS
     -- A record type with all the columns in the Skill table
  TYPE tSkill IS RECORD (
    rSkill Skill.Skill%TYPE,
    rDescription Skill.Description%TYPE);
```

```
  -- A record type with the primary key column in the Skill table
TYPE tSkillKey IS RECORD (rSkill Skill.Skill%TYPE);
  -- A ref cursor for a set of Skill rows
TYPE tSkillCursor IS REF CURSOR RETURN tSkill;
  -- A table type for a table of Skills
TYPE tSkillTable IS TABLE OF tSkill INDEX BY BINARY_INTEGER;
  -- A table type for a table of primary keys;
TYPE tSkillKeyTable IS TABLE OF tSkillKey INDEX BY BINARY_INTEGER;
  -- An exception for the row-locked error (Oracle error -54)
eRowLocked EXCEPTION;
PRAGMA EXCEPTION_INIT(eRowLocked, -54);
  -- Two query procedures, one by cursor and one by table
PROCEDURE SelectCursor (pSkillCursor IN OUT tSkillCursor,
                            pDescription IN VARCHAR2);
PROCEDURE SelectRows (pSkillTable IN OUT tSkillTable,
                        pDescription IN VARCHAR2);
  -- Data manipulation procedures
PROCEDURE InsertRows (pSkillTable IN tSkillTable);
PROCEDURE UpdateRows (pSkillTable IN tSkillTable);
PROCEDURE DeleteRows (pKeyTable IN tSkillKeyTable);
PROCEDURE LockRows (pKeyTable IN tSkillKeyTable);
END SkillPackage;
```

This package is an example of an abstract data type—a data structure accompanied by a set of behaviors that operate on the data structure. It resembles the object-oriented class, but it does not have inheritance.

NOTE

To make sense of the PL/SQL, you will need to refer to the chapters on PL/SQL, Chapters 11 and 12. These chapters discuss the various elements you see in the package specification. Chapter 12 also contains details about the structure and use of PL/SQL packages with Oracle Developer.

The procedure bodies can have any PL/SQL code you like, although they must generally function along the lines of what Oracle Developer expects from the procedure.

```
CREATE OR REPLACE PACKAGE BODY SkillPackage AS
  --
  -- Query by reference cursor
PROCEDURE SelectCursor (pSkillCursor IN OUT tSkillCursor,
                            pDescription IN VARCHAR2) IS
  vDescription VARCHAR2(80) := pDescription;
```

```
BEGIN
  IF vDescription IS NULL THEN  -- select all skills for NULL
    vDescription := '%';
  END IF;
  OPEN pSkillCursor FOR
    SELECT Skill, Description
      FROM Skill
     WHERE Description LIKE vDescription
     ORDER BY Skill;
END SelectCursor;
  --
  -- Query into table of records
PROCEDURE SelectRows (pSkillTable IN OUT tSkillTable,
                      pDescription IN VARCHAR2) IS
  vIndex NUMBER := 1;
  vDescription VARCHAR2(80) := Nvl(pDescription, '%');
  CURSOR cSkill IS
    SELECT Skill, Description
      FROM Skill
     WHERE Description LIKE pDescription
     ORDER BY Skill;
BEGIN
  OPEN cSkill;
  LOOP
    FETCH cSkill INTO pSkillTable(vIndex).rSkill,
                      pSkillTable(vIndex).rDescription;
    EXIT WHEN cSkill%NOTFOUND;
    vIndex := vIndex + 1;
  END LOOP;
END SelectRows;
  --
  -- Insert rows from a record table into database table
PROCEDURE InsertRows (pSkillTable IN tSkillTable) IS
  vIndex NUMBER := 1;
  vCount NUMBER := pSkillTable.Count;
BEGIN
  FOR vIndex IN 1..vCount LOOP
    INSERT INTO Skill (Skill, Description)
    VALUES (pSkillTable(vIndex).rSkill,
            pSkillTable(vIndex).rDescription);
  END LOOP;
END InsertRows;
  --
  -- Update rows from a record table into database table
PROCEDURE UpdateRows (pSkillTable IN tSkillTable) IS
  vIndex NUMBER;
  vCount NUMBER := pSkillTable.Count;
BEGIN
```

```
      FOR vIndex IN 1..vCount LOOP
        UPDATE Skill
          SET Description = pSkillTable(vIndex).rDescription
        WHERE Skill = pSkillTable(vIndex).rSkill;
      END LOOP;
   END UpdateRows;
   --
   -- Delete rows from a table of keys
   PROCEDURE DeleteRows (pKeyTable IN tSkillKeyTable) IS
      vIndex NUMBER := 1;
      vCount NUMBER := pKeyTable.Count;
   BEGIN
      FOR vIndex IN 1..vCount LOOP
        DELETE FROM Skill
              WHERE Skill = pKeyTable(vIndex).rSkill;
      END LOOP;
   END DeleteRows;
   --
   -- Lock rows from a table of keys
   PROCEDURE LockRows (pKeyTable IN tSkillKeyTable) IS
      vIndex NUMBER := 1;
      vCount NUMBER := pKeyTable.Count;
      vDummy VARCHAR2(1);
   BEGIN
      FOR vIndex IN 1..vCount LOOP
        SELECT 'X'
          INTO vDummy
          FROM Skill
         WHERE Skill = pKeyTable(vIndex).rSkill
         FOR UPDATE NOWAIT;
      END LOOP;
   END LockRows;
END SkillPackage;
```

NOTE

Using this kind of logic effectively makes it impossible to use the standard Oracle Developer query-by-example mechanism. You must build the query yourself by passing arguments to the select procedure. In the example just given, the two select procedures take the Description, which is the only column on which you could query. The WHERE clause in the procedure body assumes that you want to do a LIKE expression on what you enter for the value. You can get much more sophisticated than this, but the techniques are beyond the scope of this book.

1. Compile the package logged on as the package owner (Talbot, for example).

2. Grant the EXECUTE privilege on the package to every role that will need to call the procedures in the package (HRSkillRole, for example).

    ```
    GRANT EXECUTE ON SkillPackage TO HRSkillRole;
    ```

3. Log on as a DBA user or as a user with CREATE PUBLIC SYNONYM privilege, and create a public synonym for the package:

    ```
    CREATE PUBLIC SYNONYM SkillPackage FOR Talbot.SkillPackage;
    ```

NOTE
You must both grant the EXECUTE privilege and create the public synonym for the user to be able to access the packaged procedures through your application unless you code the owner user name as part of the procedure name, as for example, TALBOT.SKILLPACKAGE.SELECTCURSOR. This is not generally regarded as good coding practice, because it couples the application code to a particular user name.

You are now ready to create the data block.

4. Start the Data Block Wizard from Tools|Data Block Wizard.

5. In the first dialog box, choose the Stored Procedure radio button instead of the Table button. This tells the Wizard to ask you for the procedure information instead of the standard table-and-column information.

6. Click on the Next button to start defining the block.

7. The next dialog box asks for the query procedure. Enter the package name and cursor procedure name: "SKILLPACKAGE.SELECTCURSOR", for example. Unfortunately, this release does not let you browse the data dictionary for this information.

8. Click on the Refresh button to display the type column names (RSKILL and RDESCRIPTION, in this case).

9. Move the columns you need for your block with the > or >> button. Notice that the list of arguments at the bottom of the dialog box now shows the arguments to the procedure. Don't change these.

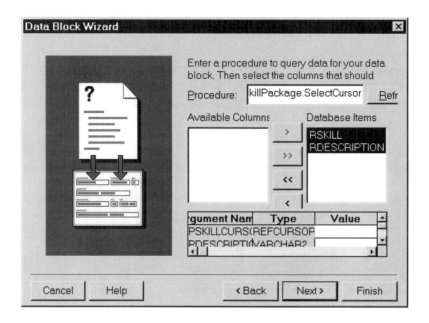

NOTE

Make sure you add the package name to the procedure name, or the Data Block Wizard will not be able to find the procedure. In the dialog box illustrated, the package name has scrolled off to the left of the entry field.

10. Click on Next to move to the next dialog, which asks for the insert procedure.

11. Enter the package name and the name of the insert procedure like this: "SKILLPACKAGE.INSERTROWS".

12. Click on the Refresh button again. This action displays the type columns and procedure arguments, although there is nothing you can do with them at this point.

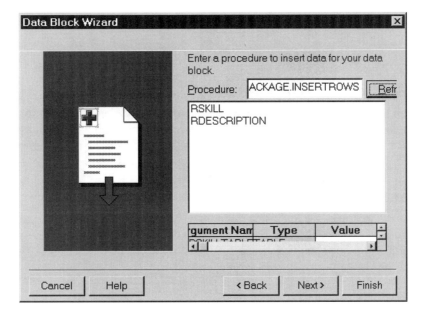

13. Repeat these steps for the update, delete, and lock procedures (UPDATEROWS, DELETEROWS, and LOCKROWS, respectively) in the following three dialogs boxes. If your data block structure makes it possible, you then see the standard master-detail relationship definition dialog box. This window lets you define any master-detail relationship between the new block and the other blocks you have defined previously.

14. Now you can proceed to the Layout Wizard as usual.

Using procedural encapsulation, you can limit access to clearly defined behaviors encapsulated in PL/SQL procedures rather than permitting broad SQL access to the objects.

Menus

The menu system in Form Builder lets you execute the different functions that make up the runtime system, such as Next_Record, Enter_Query, or Previous_Item. Most of these commands correspond directly to keypresses, and most have built-in procedure equivalents. You can use the menu that Oracle Developer displays by default, or you can build your own custom menu to add or change commands.

Using the Default Menu

The Form Builder system has a built-in command menu. When you execute your form application, if you do not define a custom menu, the system displays by default the menu shown in Figure 6-5. The form also displays the default menu toolbar if you are running in an MDI environment such as Windows 95 or NT.

Creating Custom Menus

The default menu you see in Oracle Developer is built into the code, and you cannot modify it. If you want to customize the menu by adding some commands to the default menu items, copy the MENUDEF.MMB file, which Oracle provides as a template, rather than starting from scratch.

NOTE
One consequence of supplying your own menu module is that the menu toolbars disappear. As the earlier section "Creating Toolbars" discussed, this toolbar gives you some of the standard operations, such as Enter Query and Next Record. You cannot display this default toolbar through your custom menu; you must build your own toolbar using the Visible in Horizontal Menu Toolbar (or Vertical Menu Toolbar) property of the menu item.

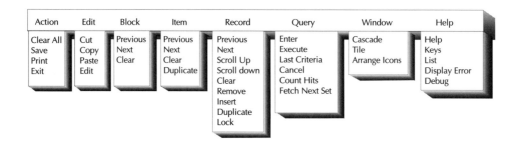

FIGURE 6-5.   *The default menu structure in Forms Runtime*

Creating Menus, Items, and Submenus

There are two kinds of objects in a menu module:

- *Menu:* The main menu, the individual menus (such as Action or Record), and submenus (hierarchical menus that pop up from a menu item).

- *Menu item:* The items on each individual menu or submenu that correspond to PL/SQL code or command text; the individual menu or submenu owns the items on the menu.

Each menu and menu item has a name that uniquely identifies it within the menu module. Menu items have, in addition, a label. The label string appears on the individual menu when you display the menu.

You should follow five guidelines in creating your menu structure.

First, any individual menu or submenu should have no more than nine separate menu items. Your menus will be much easier to use if you keep them short. Use submenus to gather several menu items into groups if necessary.

Second, if you do use submenus, try to use them only one level below the individual menus on the main menu. Having deep hierarchies of nested submenus just makes it difficult to find commands. For example, take the single Report submenu in the Query menu. It has two menu items, Ledger Summary and Mailing Labels. That means there are no more than three menu levels in the system. The user can easily find these menu commands.

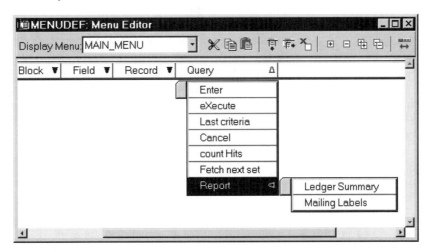

Third, don't even consider dynamic menus that change depending on the current state of the application. This guarantees a mystified user. Menus should be stable and unchanging.

Fourth, to help the user avoid mistakes, *disable* (gray out) the menu items that do not apply given the current state of the application. For example, if you display a particular modeless window that uses some commands but not others, disable the menu items that do not apply to it or to the application as a whole. You can do this with the Disable_Item built-in subprogram, which takes the menu name and the item name:

```
Disable_Item('Block', 'Previous');
```

This example disables the Block|Previous menu item. To enable the item, use Enable_Item with the same arguments.

NOTE
You can enable and disable items in the main menu by using the Set_Menu_Item_Property built-in subprogram or by using the menu name 'MAIN_MENU' in the Enable_Item and Disable_Item built-ins, respectively.

If you want to display a menu toolbar, the order of menu items determines the order of icons in the toolbar. Therefore, you have to balance the order from the menu perspective with the order from the toolbar perspective. Alternatively, you can display your own toolbars as separate canvases in your application.

If for any reason you can't adhere to these guidelines, you should consider a different kind of command interface to simplify your menus. For example, set up a group of control dialog boxes that lets you execute the commands by pushing buttons, or set up dialog boxes that let you enter choices as options rather than offering each command as a separate command on the menu. Instead of listing all your reports as menu items, for example, you might have a single menu item, Query|Run Report, and a dialog box that lets you specify which report to run with a series of radio buttons or check boxes. You might even benefit from a graphics display that represents your command structure. Get creative to make your application easier to use.

There are three kinds of menus, only one of which this book discusses in detail:

- *Pull-down menu:* A menu that you pull down by clicking on the individual menu name; this is the default style and the one this book uses.

- *Full-screen menu:* A menu occupying the complete character-mode screen that lets you navigate to a command by choosing items and displaying new screens; these menus only work for character-mode and block-mode applications.

■ *Bar-style menu:* A menu that replaces the main menu with the individual menu items when you click on it; this kind of menu occupies only the menu bar space and never extends into the content area of the application; again, this style suits character-mode applications better than GUI ones.

If you want to know more about full-screen or bar-style menus, see the online Forms documentation.

Before you can use a menu, you must compile the menu file into an MMX file. Use the File|Administration|Compile File in the Forms Designer to generate the MMX file before attempting to run any form that uses the file. You also need to recompile the MMX file after you make any changes. None of this happens automatically when you run a form.

NOTE
It is very common for developers to forget to compile menus before running the form. Whenever you work on a menu, get into the habit of automatically generating the form using the keypress that corresponds to File|Administration|Compile or Compile File, such as CTRL-T *on Windows.*

Editing Menus

The Menu Editor, which lets you directly see the menu system you're building, has several features to understand before you can fully edit your menus and menu items. The small tabs on the upper-left corner of each menu are selection tabs. Clicking on these tabs selects the menu object. You can also move a menu by clicking on the tab and dragging to the new location; CTRL-dragging copies the menu rather than moving it. Clicking on any menu item selects that item. As with forms, you can see the properties of any object in its Property Palette by choosing the Tools|Property Palette item or by double-clicking on the object's icon in the

Object Navigator. Double-clicking on a menu in the Menu Editor pulls down the menu; double-clicking on a menu item lets you edit its label. You can delete a selected object with the Delete tool.

Two special tools on the editor toolbar let you add menu items and submenus. The Create Down tool lets you add a menu item to the menu under the menu item

you select. The Create Right tool lets you create a submenu to the right of the selected menu item. These tools correspond to the Menu|Create Down and Menu|Create Right menu items.

You can change menu item names in the Object Navigator or Property Palette in the usual way. Changing the item name does not change the item label, however, and vice versa. If you change the name, the menu looks the same in the Editor because you have not changed the label. Change the label by double-clicking on the item or in the Property Palette with the Label property.

NOTE
Interface design guidelines often tell you to place an ellipsis (three dots) after the label: "Options...", for example. As most of these guidelines point out but many user-interface designers miss, you should do this only when displaying a dialog box that requests more information to perform the command. For example, you do not do this for submenus or for document windows that you invoke through a menu item.

Coding Menu Items

The Command Type property of a menu item lets you specify the kind of command you want to execute by choosing the item. See Table 6-6.

You refer to a menu item in PL/SQL using the menu name and item name in the dot-separated syntax menu_name.item_name. You can use this syntax to attach commands to menu items, initialize items, change startup code, or disable/enable menu items. Use the syntax main_menu.item_name to refer to an item on the main menu, such as Block or Query.

Value	Description
Null	Does nothing; you can use this to create a separator item or make an item null until you are ready to make it do something.
Menu	Invokes a submenu; the command text is the submenu name.
PL/SQL	Executes a block of PL/SQL code in the command text; the code cannot directly refer to form module variables but must use Name_In and Copy to refer to them indirectly.
Plus, Current Forms, Macro	Do not use these compatibility choices. Use the Host or Run_Product PL/SQL built-in procedures to run SQL*Plus, forms, or operating system commands.

TABLE 6-6. *Menu Item Command Type Property Values*

To create the code, double-click in the Command Text property in the Property Palette for the menu item and enter the code into the resulting PL/SQL editor. Compile it and close the editor.

NOTE
If you are executing a simple, standard command that corresponds to a keypress of some kind, use the Do_Key built-in procedure:

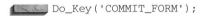

```
Do_Key('COMMIT_FORM');
```

This PL/SQL code implements the Save item. Using Do_Key lets you unify your menu items with your command keys so that you do not have to duplicate your efforts.

If you're using the Oracle Developer Server, you can use the Web.Show_Document built-in subprogram to run a report and display it in the Web browser. If you're deploying a fat client application, you can run an Oracle product with the Run_Product built-in procedure. For example, the Ledger Summary menu item runs the Ledger Summary report. The code for this menu item would look like this:

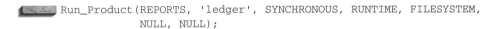

```
Run_Product(REPORTS, 'ledger', SYNCHRONOUS, RUNTIME, FILESYSTEM,
            NULL, NULL);
```

This command runs the Runform program with the Ledger.RDF file from the file system. It runs the report immediately (RUNTIME) instead of in batch mode, and it runs the report synchronously, which means that you must wait for the report to finish printing before you can continue work in the application. There are no parameters and no Graphics display.

NOTE
The two NULL values at the end are required. They represent arguments you are not using for this particular Run_Product call. Without them, PL/SQL won't recognize the call because of an invalid number of arguments.

You can run a report more directly using the Run_Report_Object built-in subprogram. First, you must define a report object in the form. Find the Reports heading under your form and click on the Create tool in the usual way. You now see the New Report dialog box, which lets you create a new report from scratch or by reading in a report module from a file. Chapter 7 gives more details on creating reports in forms using the Report Editor. Once you have a report object, you can use the Property Palette to give it a name and to set the Dev/2000 Integration property group properties Execution Mode and Communication Mode (Synchronous and Runtime, for example). You can also set the system parameters for the report, such as the Destination Type, Name, and Format.

Once you have set up the report object, regenerate the form. Now you can refer to the report object by name in the call to the Run_Report_Object built-in. For example, if you created a Ledger report object using the Ledger.RDF report file, you could place this code in the PL/SQL block for the Query|Ledger Summary menu item:

```
DECLARE
  vReturn VARCHAR2(100);
BEGIN
  vReturn := Run_Report_Object('Ledger');
  IF vReturn IS NOT NULL THEN
    Message('Ledger Summary Report: '||vReturn);
    Synchronize;
  END IF;
END;
```

To refer to an item value in the form to which you attach the menu, use the Name_In built-in function. For example, to compare the value of the WORKER block's NAME item to a specific name, you would use the following code:

```
IF Name_In('WORKER.NAME') = 'Adah Talbot' THEN
```

Similarly, use the Copy built-in procedure to assign a value:

```
Copy('Adah Talbot', 'WORKER.NAME');
```

If your PL/SQL is even moderately complex, you are better off putting the code into a separate program unit in a library that you associate with the menu module. For example, the code just given for running the report could be a procedure that takes the name of the report, as shown here:

```
PROCEDURE Run_Form_Report(pReport IN VARCHAR2) IS
  vReturn VARCHAR2(100) := Run_Report_Object(pReport);
BEGIN
  IF vReturn IS NOT NULL THEN
    Message(pReport||' Report: '||vReturn);
    Synchronize;
  END IF;
END;
```

This not only removes the complexity to a separately maintained procedure but standardizes your error-reporting mechanism for reports.

There is a Startup Code property for the menu module. Oracle Developer executes any code in this property when you start the form that loads the menu. This code can do various setup tasks in the rare cases where you need to do something menu related before displaying the form. You should rely on default property settings where you can, but sometimes you must enable different menu items depending on the platform, or something similar.

Using Special Menu Items

The Menu Item Type property lets you change the kind of menu item to display. There are five types of menu items, as shown in Table 6-7.

You can associate a command with check and radio menu items, but this produces counterintuitive effects for most uses, so you should avoid doing it. Checking a menu item should exhibit the same behavior as checking a check box, turning an option on and off. You are not starting a process but rather setting a property. Most user-interface guides such as *The Windows Interface: An Application Design Guide* (Microsoft Press, 1992) stress this behavior for these types of menu items.

The magic items Cut, Copy, Paste, Clear, Quit, and Window all have built-in functionality in Oracle Developer, which also handles their display in the manner

Value	Description
Plain	The default style with just a label.
Check	Displays a check mark against the label; sets the item state to TRUE or FALSE, which you can test through the GET_MENU_ITEM_PROPERTY built-in function with the CHECKED option and set through the SET_MENU_ITEM_PROPERTY
Radio	Makes the item one of a set of items in a radio-button group, where choosing one item sets that item to TRUE and the rest to FALSE; again you can test the stare through GET_MENU_ITEM_PROPERTY and set the state through SET_MENU_ITEM_PROPERTY.
Separator	Makes the item a separator line to create visual groupings of items.
Magic	One of several special menu items: Cut, Copy, Paste, Clear, Undo, About, Help, Quit, and Window.

TABLE 6-7. *Menu Item Type Property Values*

appropriate to the platform (position and style). You must set up command text or submenus for the other ones, such as Help, About, and Undo.

Setting Up Menus in Forms

To attach a menu to a form, compile the menu (File|Administration|Compile or Compile File), select the form in the Object Navigator, then enter the menu module name in the Menu Module property of the form.

You can tell Oracle Developer, when using the Call_Form procedure to start a form, to use the current menu instead of the menu attached to the form you are starting. This lets different forms share a single menu in a single application.

NOTE
You may also want to set up role-based security for menus. For details, consult the section "Menu Access Controls" in Chapter 9.

Keypress Assignments

There are three kinds of keypress assignments you can use in a form application: standard function keys, menu access keys, and accelerator keys.

A previous section alluded to the *standard functions,* such as Execute_Query or Next_Record. These functions have default key settings that you can change using the Oracle Terminal utility. By carefully using Do_Key in your menu PL/SQL command text, you can ensure that both a menu command and a function key have the same effects.

Most GUI platforms define a set of menu access keys. A *menu access key* is a keypress sequence (ALT-F-G, CTRL-D, COMMAND-Q, and so on) that selects a menu item without making the user go through the menu directly. The menu access key thus acts as a keyboard shortcut to execute the command that the menu item executes. The menu usually displays the menu access keys using a special notation that depends on the platform standards. In Windows, for example, the menu access key appears as an underlined capital letter. You execute it by a sequence of characters starting with ALT and navigating through the access keys on the menu bar and in the submenus. The Ledger Summary report menu item, for example, is ALT-Q-R-L (Query menu, Report submenu, Ledger Summary item).

You get these menu access keys without doing anything special. Oracle Developer uses the first uppercase letter, or the first letter if none is uppercase, in the label for the menu access key.

If you have menu labels for which the above rule produces two or more menu access keys that are the same, simply change the label to tell Oracle Developer which key to use. You can capitalize the specific letter you want to use—"rEport" instead of "Report," for example. If you do not like the funny capitalization, put an ampersand in front of the letter—"R&eport," for example. Oracle Developer removes the ampersand and makes the letter that follows it the menu access key. You can use a double ampersand to put a literal "&" into the menu item if you wish.

Oracle Developer also provides accelerator keys. An *accelerator key* is a key sequence you can assign to a menu item along with its menu access keys. Often you do this to shorten the key access sequence or to attach a standard key sequence to a standard function of some kind.

Oracle Developer provides for five logical accelerator keys, Accelerator1 through Accelerator5, that you set up with Oracle Terminal. (Chapter 15 gives the details.) You can only assign five accelerator keys in any given menu module. To assign a key, find the menu item in the Object Navigator and display its Property Palette. Put the logical name, such as Accelerator3, in the Accelerator property. Then, using Oracle Terminal, associate this logical key to a physical key sequence such as CTRL-X or SHIFT-CTRL-Y.

This chapter has completed your introduction to the advanced graphical design techniques available in the Form Builder. Using the triggers and other control features of the preceding chapter and the windows and menus you learned to customize in this chapter, you can create sophisticated GUI applications. The next two chapters extend your capabilities to reports and charts, and the following chapters give you some special tools to make your design more secure, robust, and reusable.

CHAPTER
7

Advanced Reports

ow that you understand forms completely, you can dive into the next big topic: reports. You can use Oracle Developer Reports to build both very simple and very sophisticated reports. While the number of different kinds of objects in the report is smaller than in the form, you can combine them in many different ways. In addition, Oracle Developer gives you the server tools to deploy your reports to the Internet, making it easy to distribute reports across your company or across the world. Chapter 4 took you through the details of producing HTML and Adobe Acrobat reports for Internet deployment using the Web Wizard. This chapter goes into detail on the major data modeling, layout, and reporting features of Developer Reports. It builds on the tutorial introduction of Chapter 4 and the report process overview of Chapter 5 to add details that will help you to build the several basic types of reports available.

NOTE
Oracle Developer Reports is a very flexible tool. This chapter outlines the tools and basic report strategies for some broad classes of report, but you can use the Report Builder to construct an enormous variety of reports. Take the tools you learn about here and experiment to figure out how to approach all the different reports you might need. You can buy the Reports product separately from Oracle Developer if you wish, so even if you don't need to build Forms, you can still cost effectively build reports using Oracle Developer technology. Oracle Reports also integrates with Oracle Express, the data exploration tool, giving you a powerful extension to the data mining features of Express.

Modeling Report Data

You saw in Chapter 4 how to build a basic data model with a single query and groups for adding summarization. This section goes into more detail on how to build and use groups, formula and summary columns, multiple queries, and data links in your data models. Later sections on specific types of reports will build on these details. To see the data model in graphics format, click on the Data Model Editor tool or choose the Tools|Data Model Editor menu item.

Groups

Every Oracle Developer report comprises some arrangement or structure of columns. The query relates some of those columns, the *database columns,* to data in the database. A *group* is a data model object that structures the columns of the report, including database columns, formula columns, summary columns, and placeholders.

For example, the Ledger report in Chapter 4 queried the Ledger table in the Talbot database. The query, in this case, collects the database columns from the Ledger table. There is a single group in the report consisting of all the rows in the Ledger table. The summary data giving the amount total is a summary column at the group level.

There are two types of groups—the record group and the break group. A *record group* corresponds to the records that a query returns. It is similar in many ways to a Forms base-table data block. A record group provides the cluster of columns that constitutes the fundamental data of your report. The *break group* is a group that sits between a record group and its query. The break group gives a hierarchical structure to the report. This is usually for the purpose of breaking up the records in the record group into segments for summarization. See the section "Summary Columns" that follows for more information. Every break group must have at least one column with the Break Order property (and its cohort, the Set Break Order property) set.

Figure 7-1 shows the data model from the Ledger Summary report of Chapter 4. The LedgerGroup is a record group that organizes the database columns ActionDate, Item, Quantity, Rate, and Amount, all of which come from the Ledger table. This record group contains the basic data for the report, which comes from the database through the LedgerQuery. The PersonGroup, which fits in between the LedgerGroup and the LedgerQuery, adds one hierarchical level to the report as a break group. The database column Person, with its Break Order property set, is the break column in that break group. The Subtotal column is a summary column that provides a subtotal for each break in the report (see "Summary Columns" later in the chapter).

If you double-click on the group, either in the Data Model Editor or in the Object Navigator, you see the very limited Property Palette for the group. Apart from the group Name and a Comment property, there is only one other property, the Filter Type. You can set this drop-down list to None, First, Last, or PL/SQL.

If you set the property to First or Last, you will see another property, Number of Records, magically appear. If you put a number in that property, Oracle Developer filters out all records except that number of first or last records. For example, if you set Number of Records to 10 and Filter Type to First, you see only the first ten records, no matter how many the query returns.

If you set the property to PL/SQL, another property appears: PL/SQL Filter. Clicking on this property displays the Program Unit Editor with a function template that returns a Boolean value (True or False). You can use whatever logic you wish to decide whether to return True or False. When Oracle Developer fetches a row, it calls this function. If the function returns False, Developer discards the record from

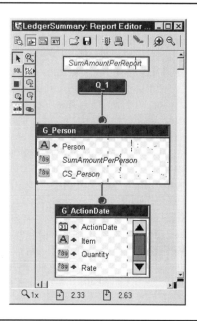

FIGURE 7-1. *The Ledger Summary data model*

the report; if True, it includes the record in the report. See Chapter 12's section "Functions" for more details on functions and their use in filters and formulas.

Formula Columns

The Ledger Summary report of Chapter 4 built a data model with the quantity and rate columns and a total amount column. Instead of getting this latter column from the database, you could calculate it as the quantity times the rate. A *formula column* is a column in a report that gets its value from a function rather than directly from the database. This section shows you how to build a formula column to get the amount.

You can do all kinds of fancy things with the PL/SQL that define the value of a formula column. Most of this you can do with SQL as well, or with database PL/SQL functions. You generally use PL/SQL when you want to do something that you cannot easily do with SQL, such as a calculation that requires a conditional (IF-THEN-ELSE) decision. If that is not the case, why do it in report functions? There are three reasons.

First, you will generally want to compute values of interest only to this application in the application itself. If the value is useful in several different applications, you may want to move the calculation to the server to share it instead of writing the code over and over. If you can calculate the value with Oracle SQL, though, you do not need a function to do it. For example, you could avoid the formula column by using this SQL:

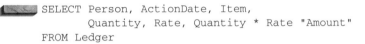

```
SELECT Person, ActionDate, Item,
       Quantity, Rate, Quantity * Rate "Amount"
FROM Ledger
```

Second, if you want your report to be independent of Oracle, you cannot use most of the advanced features of SQL that Oracle provides, such as the string and date functions. Putting the calculation into PL/SQL functions in the report makes it possible for even very sophisticated reports to use ODBC to access databases other than Oracle.

Third, moving the calculation to the server may improve client performance under some circumstances. Be sure to benchmark the application thoroughly if this is your reason for putting the PL/SQL in the database.

This short tutorial shows you how to make the Amount column a formula column in the Data Model Editor.

1. Double-click on and modify the LedgerQuery to look like this:

   ```
   SELECT Person, ActionDate, Item, Quantity, Rate
     FROM Ledger
   ```

   Modifying the query removes the database Amount column and invalidates any current summary fields based on it.

2. Double-click on the Formula Column tool in the Data Model Editor, and then click in the group box under the Rate column.

3. Double-click on the resulting column CF_1 to see the Formula Column Property Palette.

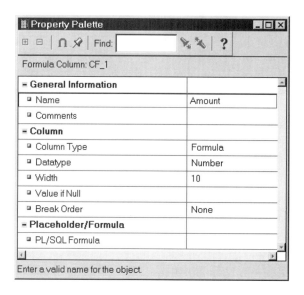

NOTE

If you don't see the tool palette with the Formula Column tool along the side of the Data Model Editor, choose the View/Tool Palette menu item with the Data Model Editor having the focus.

4. Change the name to Amount in the General group.

5. Click on the PL/SQL Formula property to display the Program Unit Editor for the PL/SQL function that computes the value.

6. Add a single statement to compute the amount:

```
return :Quantity * :Rate;
```

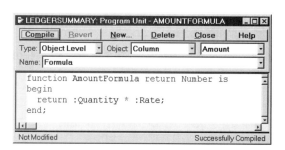

The colons indicate references to report items.

7. Click on Compile and deal with any errors; then click on Close.

When you click on OK in the property sheet, you see the new column Amount in the LedgerGroup. The Editor displays the column in italics so that you know it is a formula column.

Switch to the Object Navigator and find the new column under LEDGERGROUP in the Groups subsection of the Data Model section. The formula column has two icons, one representing the formula column and one representing the PL/SQL code. You can display the Property Palette for the column by clicking on the Formula Column icon, or the PL/SQL code for the formula by clicking on the PL/SQL icon.

NOTE
One use for a formula column is to act as a placeholder when all the data in a group is null and you want to suppress standard printing.

See Chapter 12's "Functions" section for more details on functions and their use in filters and formulas.

As the final step, you need to reestablish the relationship between the Amount column you've added and the summary columns that were invalidated by your changing the column. The following section tells you how to set the Source property for summary columns, as well as how to add new summary columns to your report.

TIP
To get the formatting right, it is usually best to go back into the Report Wizard and reestablish all the columns the way you want them; then reformat the new Amount column in the Live Previewer.

Summary Columns

A formula column lets you calculate and display a value based on a record at any place in a report. There are times, however, when you want to go beyond simple calculations to compute values based on a group of records in the report. The *summary column* is a data object that calculates an aggregate value.

A *break column* is a column you have moved from a record group into a higher-level break group. That column tells Developer to create a break, or group instance, for each different value of the column. That is, as the report fetches a record, it checks the value for the break column, and if it is different from the previous record, it breaks to take some special action. In the report layout, this corresponds to a repeating frame object. The break column and repeating frame let you take some action for each break. You can set the Break Order property to either Ascending or Descending depending on which way you wish to display the sorted data. Setting Break Order to None suppresses the breaking feature for the column—the usual setting in a record group.

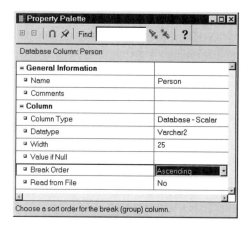

You put the summary column into the group that represents the level of aggregation you want. If you want to subtotal a group of records, you place it with the break column in the break group. If you want to total all the records in a report, you place the summary column outside any group, as in Chapter 4. To create most summary columns, you can use the Report Wizard, as in Chapter 4's Ledger Summary report. To create a summary column for a specific break group in a way that the Wizard cannot, first create the break group, then click on the Summary Column tool in the Data Model Editor's tool palette, then click in the break group. Double-clicking on the resulting column shows you the Property Palette for the summary column.

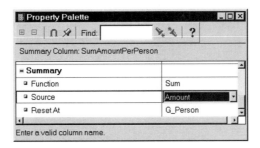

The Function property lets you set the kind of aggregation to perform. You can choose from the sum, average, minimum, maximum, count, first value, last value, percent of total, standard deviation, or variance.

The Source property has a drop-down list from which you choose the source of the data to aggregate. It automatically displays all the appropriate columns in the record group below the break group. In the case of the Subtotal column for the LedgerGroup, it displays not only Amount but also Quantity and Rate. If you look at the grand total column, which is outside any group, it offers all the possible columns: Amount, Rate, Quantity, and Subtotal. You could base the grand total on the Amount column or on the Subtotal column and get the same result in this case.

The Reset At property tells Developer where to start aggregating. Consider the subtotal for a break group. You want the subtotal to sum the values over all the rows in the group. The Reset At property thus specifies the break group, telling Oracle Developer to reset the value to zero before starting the next group. For a break-group summary column, the possible reset points are the break group, the Page, and the Report. If you choose the break group (G_Person for the Ledger Summary report), Oracle Developer calculates a value that starts with the first record in a break group instance and then resets the value to zero before continuing with the next group. The result is a subtotal for the group instance. If you choose Page, it resets the value before each page, even if the group spans pages or multiple groups appear on one page. You would usually use Page if you had some reason to calculate page-related counts. If you choose Report, Oracle Developer sets the value to zero at the beginning of the report and does not reset it thereafter, giving you a running total for each group instance. A *running total* sums the total through the whole report instead of restarting at the beginning of each group of records. You get this effect with a Reset At property of Report on a summary column that prints after a break group.

The Compute At property tells Developer where to compute the value for the percent-of-total aggregation function. Again, this can be at the Report, Page, or break group level. This lets you vary the total on which Developer calculates the percentage. Report means as a percentage of the total for the report; page means as a percentage of the total for the page; and group means as a percentage of the total for the group. This last choice may make more sense when you have multiple break groups and you are printing percent-of-totals for subgroups of a larger group of records.

Multiple Queries and Data Links

Sometimes a single query is all you need for a report, and sometimes you need more than one. Oracle Developer lets you use more than one query to achieve myriad complex reporting effects beyond what you can do with a single query, its break groups, and its summary and formula columns.

A familiar example is the master-detail report. Chapter 4 showed how to develop a master-detail form for the skill database that relates workers to their skills. How would you go about developing a similar report?

Oracle Developer reports use a structure very similar to the form objects for doing the same thing. Instead of two data blocks, you have two queries in your data model. Instead of a relation object in the master data block, you have a data link. A data link is just what it sounds like: a way to link two data sets. The reality is a bit more complex: what you're really doing in a master-detail report is linking a master group to a detail query, setting a WHERE clause for the query.

I. Create a new report, defining a query with the Report Wizard to query the workers from the database using the following SQL:

```
SELECT Name
  FROM Person
 WHERE Lodging IS NOT NULL
 ORDER BY 1
```

2. Display the query and its group in the Data Model Editor.

3. Click on the Query tool, and then click on the Data Model Editor canvas to the side of the Worker query.

4. Enter the following SQL:

```
SELECT Name, Skill, Ability
  FROM WorkerHasSkill
 ORDER BY 1
```

Notice that the Name database column in the new group that appears gets the name Name1 rather than Name to enable it to be unique.

5. Now click on the Data Link tool; then click and drag from the Worker Name to the Skill Name1 column. When you release the mouse, the link snaps up to the query and the column name appears under the query name.

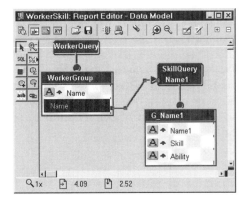

If you now go back to the Object Navigator and look under the Data Links heading, you will see the new data link.

If you double-click on the data link line in the Data Model Editor, or on the Data Link icon in the Object Navigator, you see the Property Palette for the object. You can set two different properties of the link:

- ■ *SQL Clause:* HAVING, START WITH, or WHERE: HAVING is the selection based on a GROUP BY; START WITH implements a CONNECT BY; and WHERE is the standard selection.

- ■ *Condition:* The relational operator to use to equate the columns.

If you have defined foreign key constraints between the tables, you can directly link the queries without referring to the groups and columns. In the case of the Worker-Skill link, you can get the same results as before by clicking on the Data Link tool, then clicking and dragging from the WorkerQuery to the SkillQuery. After some work with the data dictionary looking up constraints, the Data Model Editor draws the same data link from Name in the WorkerGroup to Name1 in the SkillQuery.

After linking your master and detail queries, you can use the Report Wizard to define a Group Left report that displays the two groups in a break-group style, as in Figure 7-2. You can also define a Group Above report that prints a series of Skill records under every worker record.

NOTE
You can also link two groups by dragging the group name to the other group name. In this case, the name of the master group appears as a column in the master group, and the name of the child group appears in the child query. The column information in the Property Palette is blank. This variety of link is rare. You can refer to the master columns in the detail query as bind variables. One use is to do a value-based lookup.

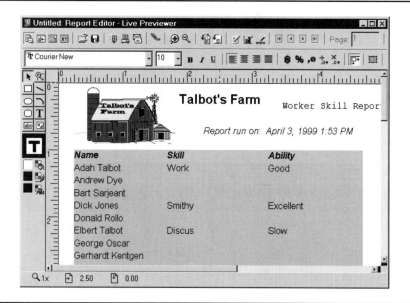

FIGURE 7-2. *The master-detail WorkerSkill report*

With data links, you now have the complete range of tools you need to create the data model for your reports. The next section shows you how to take the results of your data modeling and lay them out into the format you need.

Formatting Reports

Chapter 4 introduced you to the basics of formatting a report. This section exposes you to some of the formatting tools available in Oracle Developer Reports. The most important interface in the Report Builder is the Live Previewer, which both displays the actual report and gives you a way to format it directly. The Live Previewer makes it easy to format report layout and boilerplate, especially in the headers and margins of the report.

TIP

You can do virtually everything you need to do to a report through the Live Previewer or through properties. Sometimes you may want a finer level of control over frames; to do that, you should learn to use the Layout Editor, an older interface that shows the design format rather than a live view of the report. The Layout Editor is, however, much harder to work with than the Live Previewer for most purposes, so I don't go into much detail on it here.

The Live Previewer

The basis for virtually everything you can do in the Live Previewer is the selection of one or more fields. Just about everything you see in the Live Previewer is a field. Click on anything, and you see handles appear on all the objects that are part of the field. If the field is not within a repeating field, you see only the single field with handles. If the frame repeats, then you see all of the repetitions with handles, as in Figure 7-3.

You can multiselect in the usual way, with a SHIFT-click on the additional fields and frames to extend the selection. You can select the headers separately for different formatting and sizing. You can select the frame around the fields using the Edit|Select Parent Frame menu item or the Select Parent Frame tool. If you double-click on a field, you see its Property Palette.

If you use any of the formatting tools, you format everything you've selected. If you have not selected anything, you set the default formatting for future additions to the report. See the later section, "Formatting Tools," for details on what you can do.

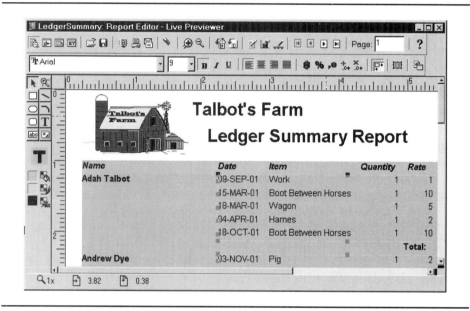

FIGURE 7-3. *The Live Previewer with the Ledger Summary report*

The handles give you three specific capabilities:

- You can drag the corner handles or the bottom or top handles to change the font size.

- You can drag the side handles to change the field or frame size without changing the font size.

- You can drag in the middle of the field to move the field to the left or right.

What happens to other fields and headings when you resize or move a field depends on the Flex Mode setting. The Flex Mode button on the toolbar shows this setting. If Flex Mode is off, resizing and moving has no effect whatever on other fields or headings. You can move the field anywhere you want, overlapping other fields. The header does not move along with it. If Flex Mode is on, however, and you resize or move a field to make it bigger or move it to the right, other fields move to accommodate the changed size or position of the field. If you move or resize a field right, and there is not enough room on the page to move the fields to the right of it, the mouse cursor changes to a "not" symbol. You cancel the moving or resizing when you release the mouse.

NOTE
You need to watch carefully for the dragging limits, or Oracle Developer may frustrate you in your efforts to reformat the layout. The process is like one of those games in which you move little squares around, shuffling the pieces to allow movement of other pieces. By moving several other fields or by resizing them, you open enough space for them to move when you resize another field.

The four page tools (First, Previous, Next, and Last) on the toolbar let you page through the report in the Live Previewer to inspect the various parts of the report. What you see in the Live Previewer is precisely what you get when you print the report. You must be able to see all the pages of the report to inspect things like report totals, charts on header pages, and so on.

TIP
It is a good idea when developing a report to have enough data in your test database to permit multiple-page reports in your Live Previewer. Otherwise, you may find the end result is unsatisfactory. On the other hand, working with too much data in your test database can result in many report pages that are structurally identical, forcing you to scroll through many pages before seeing what you want. You can go to a specific page by entering the page number in the Page field and pressing ENTER, as long as you know approximately where you want to go.

Modifying Reports

To modify a report, you can use the Live Previewer for most formatting tasks. You can also use the Report Wizard to redo the basic layout if you have major changes to make. There are some important properties you can change through property sheets that give you finer control over report formatting.

Using the Report Wizard to Reformat Your Report

Chapter 4 demonstrated the Report Wizard for a basic summary report. The Report Wizard not only gives you control over the most important parts of your layout, it lets you redo the layout while preserving formatting changes you've made. You can run the Report Wizard using the Report Wizard tool on the toolbar in any of the editors, or you can use the Tools|Report Wizard menu item.

NOTE

Choosing the style of the report layout in the Report Wizard has a major impact on your layout options. If you choose Group Left, for example, the Wizard adds tabs that let you define the grouping of columns. Since the tabs don't exist for styles that don't use them, new users of the Wizard can easily become confused about their options.

Frames Properties

A *frame* is a rectangular area of the report that contains a set of objects. Frames are the objects in a report that organize the layout by grouping fields and other frames. Frames separate sections of the report. Frames set up relative positioning relative to other frames. A *repeating frame* defines an iteration structure within which Developer lays out a group from the data model.

Frames are objects that appear in the Object Navigator as well as in the Live Previewer. Sometimes it seems that most of the objects in a report are frames, especially for complex reports. Frames appear in the Live Previewer as dashed lines. The frame object property sheet contains a set of layout properties divided into two groups, the General Layout and Advanced Layout properties.

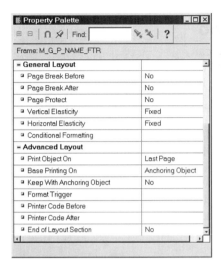

The page properties let you specify what happens when Oracle Developer formats the frame. Page Break Before and After let you specify how the report gets paginated relative to the frames. For example, to put each group of data on a separate page of a break report, you can set Page Break Before or After to Yes for the repeating frame for the group. Page Protect is like a Keep Together property in a word processor; it tells Oracle Developer to keep all the objects in the frame on the same page, if possible. The Keep With Anchoring Object property works like a Keep with Next feature in a word processor. If the frame and its anchoring object (usually another frame) cannot both fit on the logical page, Oracle Developer moves them to the following logical page.

Vertical and Horizontal Elasticity specify how to allow the frame to expand with its data; see the following section on "Elasticity and Sizing."

Conditional Formatting lets you apply format exceptions to the frame object. Using a format exception lets you hide the frame or change its fill and border colors based on a condition on the data elements within the frame.

The Print Object On and Base Printing On properties let you specify a printing relationship to the enclosing or anchoring object for the frame. You use this to modify the repetition of the printing of the frame. For example, you can suppress the printing of headings on all but the first page by setting Print Object On to First Page for the Anchoring Object.

NOTE
This example also shows you how to use the Live Previewer to deal with at least some aspects of frames. Select a heading in the Live Previewer, and then click on the Select Parent Frame tool. Now choose the Tools|Property Palette menu item. You can set the properties in the Property Palette, and Oracle Developer redisplays the report in the Live Previewer.

The Format Trigger property lets you specify a Boolean PL/SQL function (one that returns True or False). In the trigger, you can set any properties of the frame that you can access through built-in subprograms. If the trigger returns False, neither the frame nor its contents appear in the report. You can thus use additional frames and their format triggers to format or suppress certain areas of the report. For example, if you want to show a particular set of fields only for certain groups, you can add a frame around those fields and add a format trigger to it that checks the current group information and returns the appropriate Boolean value.

Repeating frames have an additional couple of sections in the Property Palette.

Property Palette	
⊞ ⊟ ∩ ✗ Find: ✗ ✗ ?	
Repeating Frame: R_G_ActionDate	
▪ Repeating Frame	
▫ Source	G_ActionDate
▫ Print Direction	Down
▫ Maximum Records per Page	0
▫ Minimum Widow Records	0
▫ Column Mode	No
▫ Horiz. Space Between Frames	0
▫ Vert. Space Between Frames	0

The Source for the frame is the name of the group from which the frame gets its data. The Print Direction property tells Oracle Developer whether to repeat the records down (the usual format for a tabular report) or across or a combination of both. Printing across/down means that Oracle Developer prints the records across until it can't print a record, then prints that record on the next line down and continues. Down/across prints in columns, with the records going down to the page bottom, then starting again at the top in the next column to the right. The Column Mode property lets you control combination print directions by aligning continuing records on subsequent pages so that you can cut and paste the pages together if necessary. You can see the print direction on the Layout Editor frame through a small arrow appearing on the frame border, as this illustration shows. To get a clear idea of their meaning, you should try these settings to see what happens.

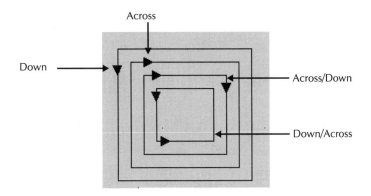

Maximum Records per Page limits the number of records Oracle Developer prints on a single page. You can use this property, for example, to print a single record on each page.

Minimum Widow Records specifies a minimum number of records; if the page can't contain that many records, Oracle Developer moves the records to the next page. This resembles widow control in a word processor, which specifies that each paragraph must have at least two lines, not one line, at the bottom of a page.

Horizontal or Vertical Space Between Frames lets you add a margin to each record, printing the amount of space you specify between repeating records.

Finally, the Filter Type property performs the same role for the frame as its corresponding property on the group. You can manage the filtering of records on a frame basis rather than on a group basis, however. If you filter records, you should by preference do it on the group unless you refer to the group from more than one frame with differing filtering requirements—a fairly rare occurrence.

Elasticity and Sizing

Horizontal and Vertical Elasticity properties describe how the object adjusts at runtime to the objects or data it contains. Different kinds of objects show different effects. Frames vary in size depending on the frame contents. Text objects vary with the size of the text. Images and graphical objects scale proportionately to the size of the containing object.

There are four kinds of elasticity:

- *Fixed:* The size of the containing object does not vary with the size of the contained objects, and the size cannot increase beyond what you specify in the Layout Editor or Live Previewer, truncating the contained objects.

- *Contracting:* The size of the containing object decreases vertically or horizontally to the size of the contained objects, but the size cannot increase beyond what you specify in the Layout Editor or Live Previewer. If you set Horizontal Elasticity to Contracting, Oracle Developer truncates the contained objects, but the objects overflow to the next page for Vertical Elasticity set to Contracting.

- *Expanding:* The size of the containing object increases vertically or horizontally to the size of the contained objects, but the size cannot decrease beyond what you specify in the Layout Editor or Live Previewer. If the object does not fit on one page, the object overflows onto the next page; if the object's size from the Editor does not fit onto the page, the object moves to the following page, then overflows if necessary.

- *Variable:* The size of the containing object expands or contracts to the size of the contained objects; the size of the containing object in the Layout Editor or Live Previewer has no relationship to the size at runtime. If the object does not fit on one page, the object overflows onto the next page.

Because you can set vertical and horizontal elasticity separately, you can have up to 16 possible combinations of these types of elasticity. Setting Horizontal Elasticity to Fixed and Vertical Elasticity to Expand for a text field, for example, gives you text that maintains the same width but expands downward as text exceeds the size you specified in the Editor. The field expands to the next page if it overflows the current page. Setting Horizontal Elasticity to Variable, for example, gives you a report that displays the fields of the record right next to one another instead of lining up the fields in a column.

Experiment with the settings on the Ledger report to see the effects of setting different combinations of these options on a text field, such as Item, that can wrap to multiple lines. You can see the effects immediately through the positioning of the field values and their selection handles.

NOTE
The rules for overflow printing are extremely complex.
See the online Reports documentation for details.

At some point you will probably encounter an error message if you use settings of anything but Fixed for fields that get their values from calculated sources such as page numbers. This problem occurs when the data source cannot provide a value until the formatting of the entire report. This in turn means that Oracle Developer must format the field without knowing precisely which data it will contain, which leads to the error. These fields must have Fixed-Fixed elasticity, and Oracle Developer will convert the field to that if needed. This problem happens for these situations:

- *Source:* The data source is one of &Total Logical Pages, &Total Physical Pages, &Total Panels, &Logical Page Number, &Physical Page Number, or &Panel Number.

- *Summary or Formula:* The summary or formula column has the Reset At or Compute At property set to Page or relies upon such a column.

Formatting Tools

The Live Previewer not only lets you see the immediate results of your formatting effort but also provides most of your formatting needs in easy-to-use tools in its toolbar.

The magnifying glass icons are the Zoom In and Zoom Out tools that let you magnify or reduce the magnification of the Editor so you can see finer distinctions or the bigger picture. The next two icons insert date/time and page number, followed by the three wizards (Report, Chart, and Web). The second line of the toolbar lets you specify the font and font size along with bold, italic, and underline settings instead of using the Format|Font menu item. The next three icons control the justification of the selection (Left/Start, Center, Right/End). Finally, there are several icons that let you change the characteristics of a number field: inserting a currency symbol, percent symbol, and thousands indicator, or inserting or removing a decimal place in the number. All of these tools have their equivalents on the Format menu, but using the tools is much easier. Just select the items you wish to format, and then click on the tool.

Other formatting options on the Format menu allow you to more precisely control your layout:

- *Text options:* Line spacing and flow direction

- *Line options:* Width, beveling, which borders to display, dash and arrowhead effects

- *Graphics options:* Various drawing options, such as image dithering or rounded corners

You also can use Format|Reduce Image Resolution to control the amount of image data you must store with the report. If you reduce the size of an image, you can often get as good quality from a reduced-resolution version of the image as from the original resolution. Reducing the resolution can save a good deal of space. You should experiment with your reports to determine the most effective resolution/space trade-off for your specific situation.

Buttons and Interactive Reports

Oracle Developer Reports does not limit you to static, printed reports. You can add buttons to your layout that the runtime user can press to execute multimedia or PL/SQL code. You can do whatever you wish with the code you associate with the button. A common use is to provide *drill-down reports*—reports that let you generate a second report with detailed data for the record. You can also play videos or sound files.

NOTE
While the button makes for an interesting and useful report, it certainly blurs the line between form and report applications. You may find developing active applications in the more flexible Oracle Developer Forms environment easier than using reports. Use buttons in a report where it seems natural and where you intend to produce the report online rather than printing it, such as on the Internet.

   1. Create the master report and the drill-down report. Create a master report that lists the total amount of money in the ledger for each person. Then create a drill-down report that lists the individual transactions for a single person, with summary information. The SELECT statement in the data model for the first report (Person.RDF) groups the people:

```
SELECT p.Name, SUM (Quantity*Rate) "Total Amount"
 FROM Ledger l, Person p
 WHERE l.Person = REF(p)
 GROUP BY p.Name
```

The query joins the Ledger and Person tables by joining the Person object reference in Ledger to references generated with a REF function on the Person table. Joining lets you refer to the person's name, which is not a column in the Ledger table.

The data model SELECT for the second report (PersonDetail.RDF) selects the data for a specific person supplied through a bind variable:

```
SELECT Action, Item, Quantity, QuantityType,
       Rate, Quantity * Rate "Amount"
  FROM Ledger l, Person p
 WHERE l.Person = REF(p) AND
       p.Name = :P_Person
 ORDER BY 1
```

When you create the data model in the Report Wizard or the Data Model Editor, Reports automatically creates the user parameter object named P_Person. You can include this on your parameter form and supply a list of values through the object's List of Values property using a SELECT statement such as this:

```
SELECT Name
  FROM Person
 ORDER BY 1
```

NOTE
Since you are not actually going to display the parameter form when you access the PersonDetail report through the Person report, you don't have to set up the form or the list of values. It's a good idea to do this to increase the reusability of the PersonDetail report. You may also want to display the parameter value somewhere in the header for the report, such as in the top margin.

2. Continue through the standard formatting steps in the Report Wizard until the two reports are ready for display.

3. In the Person report, you now add the button. Open the Layout Editor. Select the Amount field and resize it to leave room for a button next to it. The button will repeat for each record as long as it is inside the repeating frame for the person.

4. Click on the Button tool on the tool palette, and then draw the button rectangle within the frame.

5. Set the bevel style to Raised, using Format|Bevel.

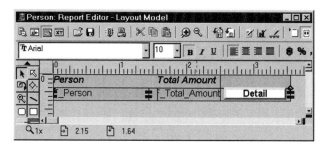

6. Display the Property Palette for the button by double-clicking it.

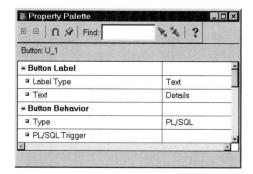

7. Enter the text for the label, such as "Details."

8. Check the Live Previewer or Layout Editor to see the font formatting, and correct it with the appropriate formatting tools.

9. Back in the Property Palette for the button, set the Type property in the Button Behavior section to PL/SQL.

10. Enter the following PL/SQL code for the button trigger by clicking on the PL/SQL Trigger property:

```
PROCEDURE U_1ButtonAction IS
BEGIN
  SRW.Run_Report(
    'PersonDetail.rdf P_Person="'||:Name ||'"');
END;
```

The PL/SQL Program Unit Editor supplies the PROCEDURE template; all you need to do is enter the procedure call to Run_Report. You will be passing one parameter on the command line, taking the value from the current record's Person database column.

11. Compile the trigger, and you are ready to try your report.

Use the View|Runtime Preview menu item, which becomes available when the Live Previewer is the top window, to run your report again with fresh data. You can't click on the button directly in the Live Previewer. Figure 7-4 shows the resulting report Previewer. If you click on the Detail button for any person, you will see the detail report in Figure 7-5.

What You Can Do with Reports

There are many varieties of reports. This section takes you through some of the basic variations, showing you how to use the tools introduced in previous sections to achieve your desired effects.

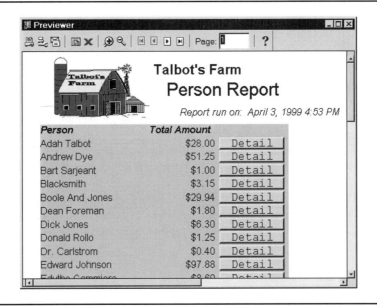

FIGURE 7-4. *The Person report in the Runtime Previewer*

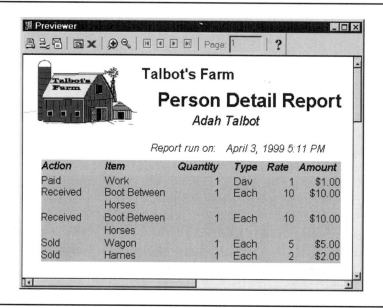

FIGURE 7-5. *The PersonDetail report in the Runtime Previewer*

Tabular and Group Reports

Recall from the previous section on "Modeling Report Data" that a group is a set of rows distinguished by a unique value in one or more columns. In the Ledger Summary report of Chapter 4, for example, the Person column groups the ledger rows. You represent the group in the data model through a group object that includes the group columns. This group object corresponds to a group frame in the layout. The query in the data model orders the results by the Person and ActionDate columns. As the report prints, Oracle Developer checks the value of the group columns in each row it prints. When the value changes, a *break* occurs, and Oracle Developer builds the group frame for the next group. The group frame displays the value of the group columns only once for all the rows in the group, making the rows stand out as a group in the report.

There are three styles in the Report Wizard that build tabular reports:

- *Tabular:* A simple table of columns and rows with no groups

- *Group Left:* A tabular report with one or more group columns that the group frame displays on the left of the grouped data records

- *Group Above:* A tabular report with one or more group columns that the group frame displays above the grouped data records

You can choose any of these styles for your report through the Style screen of the Report Wizard. Depending on which of these styles you choose, the Report Wizard displays a different set of screens (when creating the report) or tab pages (when modifying a report you've previously created). All three display these screens or tab pages:

- *Style:* The style of the report (tabular, Group Left, or Group Above radio buttons)

- *Data:* The SQL SELECT statement that defines the result table

- *Fields:* The columns to display on the report

- *Totals:* The columns to aggregate into group or report totals and the aggregation functions to use in doing that

- *Labels:* The labels and sizes of the fields for the report

- *Template:* The report template to use for laying out the report

Figure 7-6 shows the resulting report for the Ledger Summary report of Chapter 4 done in the Tabular style. The last page of this report has a single row for the total of the Amount column for the entire report, which the figure does not show. Also, in the break report, the report automatically ordered the rows by the break column, but that doesn't happen in the tabular report. In this case, since the Name column is part of the dereferenced REF to the Person table, there is no way to sort the output by name, as you cannot refer to the Name column in an ORDER BY statement.

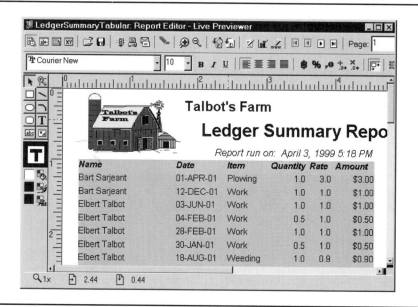

FIGURE 7-6. *The tabular Ledger report*

The Group Left and Group Above styles add another screen/tab page:

■ *Groups:* The columns with which to group the data

Figure 7-7 shows the Ledger Summary report using the Group Left style; Figure 7-8 shows it using the Group Above style.

All three reports include summary data. You will see in the figures that the Report Wizard produces subtotals for the groups as well as the report total for the group reports.

Form Reports

A *form report* is a report laid out to display a single record at a time, much as you would lay out a form. You can use form reports to print things like service orders, delivery bills, and other items that require a single record on a page. As an example,

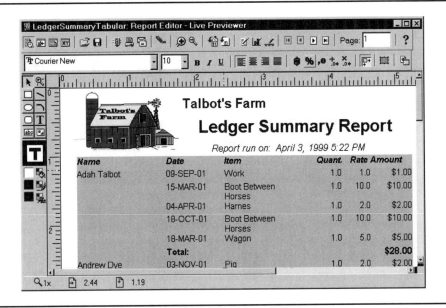

FIGURE 7-7. *The group-left Ledger Summary report*

consider a report that prints the lodging information in the Lodging table, with each lodging appearing as a cluster of fields.

1. Start the Report Wizard for a new report, and choose the Form-like style.

2. Enter this query:

```
SELECT Lodging, LongName "Full Name", Manager, Address
  FROM Lodging
ORDER BY 1
```

3. The rest of the screens need no changes, so just click on Finish.

   This builds a form report with one record per page, laying out the fields and their headings left-to-right and wrapping to the next line when there is an overflow. In this case, there is too little data to display one record per page.

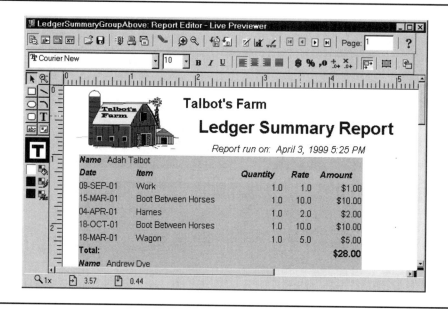

FIGURE 7-8. *The group-above Ledger Summary report*

4. Select the frame object (there is only one) and change its Maximum Records Per Page property to 0 from the default 1. That means display as many records on a single page as possible.

5. Also, change the Lodging field to display in boldface to emphasize each lodging.

Figure 7-9 is the result.

Mailing-Label Reports

Mailing labels let a business such as Talbot's Farm create mailings to groups of people. A mailing-label report prints sheets of such labels. Talbot's can use this report to generate labels for paychecks or mailings to its employees, for example.

A mailing-label report prints its repeating records without any headings in identically spaced chunks down a page. When you print the report, you generally do so on special adhesive mailing-label paper from which you peel off the labels after printing. This section shows you how to generate a speedy, simple prototype of such a report.

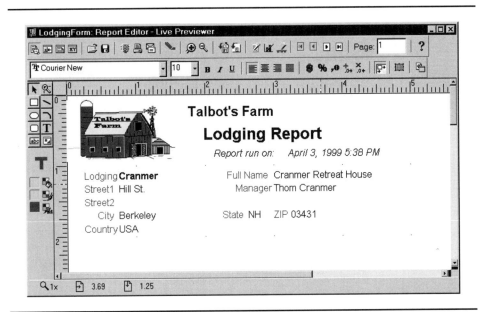

FIGURE 7-9. *A form report on the Lodging table*

I. Create a new report using the Report Wizard. The query for the report is slightly more complex than the previous example because it involves two joined tables instead of a single one. This gives you the name from the Person table and the LongName and Address of the lodging for the person from the Lodging table. The join is done by generating a reference for the Lodging rows and then joining them to the Lodging object reference in the Person table. The SQL also orders the result by the person's name.

```
SELECT p.Name, l.LongName, l.Address
  FROM Person p, Lodging l
 WHERE p.Lodging = REF(l)
 ORDER BY 1
```

The next screen (Figure 7-10) resembles the Fields screen for the other reports but has special features for mailing-label construction. This Text screen lets you position the fields in a prototype mailing label. It provides special buttons for the various punctuation marks that usually separate items in a mailing label (new lines, spaces, commas, dashes, and periods).

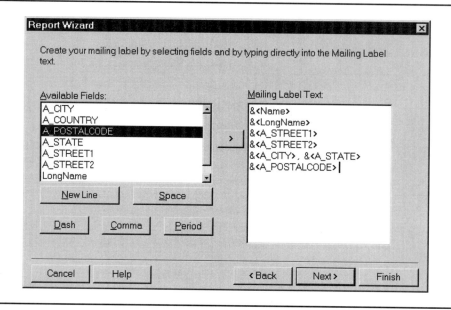

FIGURE 7-10. *The Report Wizard Text tab page for the Talbot mailing-label report*

2. To create the Talbot mailing label, for example, you select Name, click on the > button, click on the New Line button, and repeat for the Long Name and the A_Street1 and A_Street2 fields. Then add A_City, click Comma, Space; then add A_State, Space, Space; then add A_PostalCode. This last field wraps to a new line, but it will come out on the same line in the mailing label.

The only other available screen in the Wizard is the template screen. If you have a template set up for your mailing-label reports, you can use it.

3. Click on Next. Select the Draft template or no template.

TIP
It is a good idea to define templates for your standard mailing-label layouts. Otherwise, you will spend quite a bit of time fooling around with getting the margins, spacing, and positioning just right using the Live Previewer and Property Palettes.

Figure 7-11 shows the result of some basic layout work.

Matrix Reports

In a situation where you have two kinds of things and you want to tabulate some kind of aggregate value for each possible combination of the things, you need a matrix report. The matrix, also known in the statistical community as a *cross-tabulation* or *crosstab* report, relates two or more variables in a matrix. The possible values of some variables run along the top, and the possible values of other variables run down the side.

Oracle Developer Reports supports the matrix through a separate report style and some options that let you control the layout of the report. As an example, suppose an executive at Talbot's Farm wanted to see how much cash was flowing to workers on a weekly basis over the year. A matrix report with weeks as columns and workers as rows could display the sum of the amounts paid per week to each worker. Create a new report with the Report Wizard, setting the report style on the Style page to Matrix. This setting enables a structure of Wizard screens that lets you set up the row and column structure and the structure of the cells.

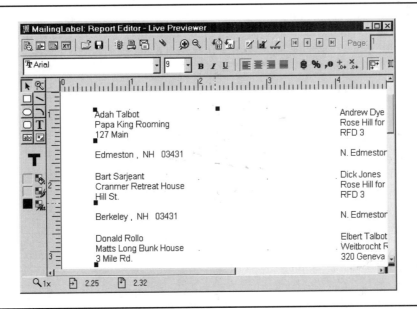

FIGURE 7-11. *A mailing-label report for Talbot workers*

First, enter this query in the Data screen as usual to set up the basic data model:

```
SELECT To_Char(l.ActionDate, 'MM')||'-
       '||To_Char(l.ActionDate, 'Mon') "Month",
       p.Name, l.Quantity*l.Rate "Amount"
  FROM Ledger l, Person p
 WHERE l.Person = REF(p) AND
       p.Lodging IS NOT NULL AND
       l.Action = 'Paid' AND
       To_Char(l.ActionDate, 'YYYY') = '1901'
```

This query retrieves three values: the month, the name of the worker, and the amount paid to the worker. The month consists of the numeric month (01, 02, and so on) and the three-character month name ('Jan', 'Feb', and so on) concatenated. The reason for adding the month number is that the matrix report sorts the columns alphabetically by the unique values. If you just had the character name, the months would come out not in month order but in alphabetical order.

The query joins to the Person table to restrict the query to workers, who are people with lodgings (Lodging IS NOT NULL). The REF joins the tables based on the Person object reference in the Ledger table. The action is 'Paid', and the query restricts the ledger entries to the year 1901 through the YYYY date format.

The next screen in the Report Wizard (Figure 7-12) asks you to specify which database column to use for the rows. The column you specify contributes its distinct values as the labels down the side of the report. You can specify more than one column. This nests the distinct values of the second column within those of the first,

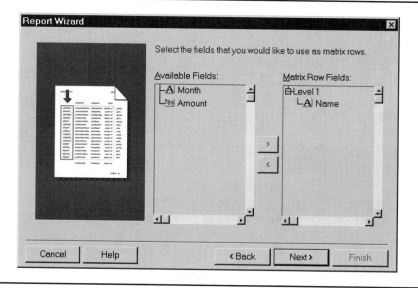

FIGURE 7-12. *The Report Wizard Row screen for the matrix report*

and so on, in a multiple-repetition structure, such as weeks within the months or action types within the person. For example, if you wanted to show the sum of the amounts bought, sold, paid, or received to or from each person, you could nest the action type as a level-two row variable under the person as the level-one row variable. The cells of the report would then have one sum for each combination of person and action.

The next screen (Figure 7-13) then asks you to specify which database column to use for the report columns, with that column contributing its distinct values as column headers. You can specify multiple levels here as well.

The next screen (Figure 7-14) lets you set up the structure of the cells. You generally use one of the standard aggregation functions such as Sum to sum a particular column into a value for each cell, as Figure 7-14 shows. This example sums the amount values for rows in the query for the worker and the month that identify the cell. If there are no such rows, the cell will have a null value.

NOTE
Many report developers are tempted to try to replace the null value for null aggregations with zeros. This can lead to unfortunate misinterpretations, especially for cases in which zero is a valid aggregate value. How can you distinguish the "real" zeros from the fake ones? In the case of our example, "nothing was paid this month" is really the same as "$0 was paid this month," but you can't always say that. One of the first things that elementary statistics classes teach is that an aggregation of rows including a null is a null, not a value treating the null as zero. Only in very restricted circumstances can you assert that a null is the same as zero. Try to avoid this confusing issue by leaving the nulls alone or by using zeros instead of nulls where it is appropriate. For example, instead of leaving commission NULL if someone doesn't get a commission, make the commission zero in that row in the database. Another reason to avoid doing it is that it is actually fairly hard to do in Oracle Developer. You must insert a boilerplate text '0' in the repeating cell frame, then set up the fill for the field to obscure the '0' when there is a value for the cell.

The standard Wizard Totals screen lets you specify which columns to total. Setting up a total displays totals rows along the right side of the matrix, columns along the bottom, and a grand total in the lower-right corner. You usually use a sum of the cell column or columns here.

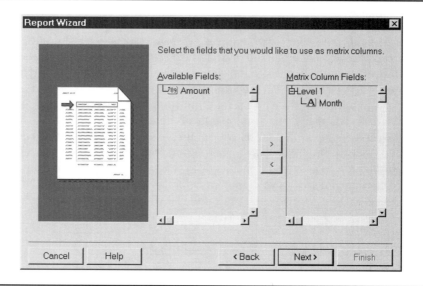

FIGURE 7-13. *The Report Wizard Column screen for the matrix report*

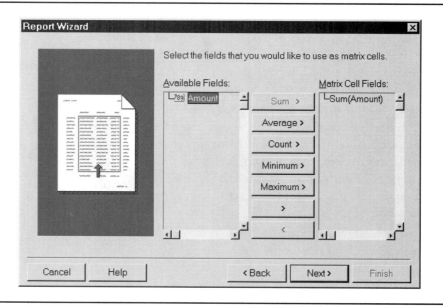

FIGURE 7-14. *The Report Wizard Cell screen for the matrix report*

The standard Wizard Labels screen lets you modify the labels for the various columns, which appear in unusual places in the matrix report, as the column and row labels come from the data. I prefer to eliminate the column label entirely, as it simply repeats under the data label. Finally, the usual Template screen lets you choose a template for report layout. Figure 7-15 shows the resulting report after some cleaning up of the cell sizes and the labels.

So that you have some idea of what's actually happening in this report, Figure 7-16 shows you the data model that the Report Wizard generates. You see the two groups that depend on the query, corresponding to the rows and columns of the matrix. The new thing in this data model is the group that encloses these two groups. This kind of group is a cross-product group, and its function is to produce the cross product of the distinct values of the groups within it. The elements of the cross-product group are the cells of the matrix report.

Data File Export Reports

Although it is not in the official set of report styles, the data file export report is well-used among Oracle Developer report designers. A data file export report is a report that comes out as a plain-text, ASCII file of data, usually for export to some other software system. For example, one purpose is to export data to a spreadsheet for further analysis; another is to export a report to a word processor for formatting. This report is moderately easy to produce, but involves more than just using the Report Wizard.

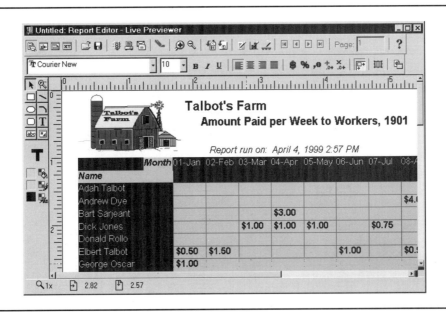

FIGURE 7-15. *The Worker Paid matrix report*

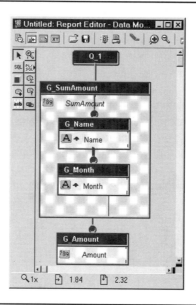

FIGURE 7-16. *The Worker Paid matrix report data model*

NOTE
There are several different ways to accomplish this task, but they all have limitations. The limitation of the report is that it can be quite difficult to produce given all the things you must set up correctly. You can also use Oracle Objects for OLE or a similar tool integration mechanism to get the data directly from the database, but only on systems that support such mechanisms. You can produce similar ASCII reports using Oracle's SQL*Plus, but its reporting capabilities are much more limited than Oracle Developer's, and you can integrate reports more tightly with your application through menus using Run_Report with a report object in your form. Finally, you could write a relatively simple system using PL/SQL stored procedures that puts data out in export format using the DBMS_FILE package.

Here's an example that produces a set of data from the Person table, listing the name, age, and lodging of all the people in the table. In the Report Wizard for the new report, choose a tabular report style in the Style screen, and then enter the following SQL SELECT statement in the Data screen:

```
SELECT '"'||p.Name||'", '||
         p.Age||',"'||l.Lodging||'"' Output
  FROM Person p, Lodging l
 WHERE p.Lodging = REF(l)
 ORDER BY Name
```

This SELECT produces a series of concatenated columns separated by commas, with each column value quoted using a double quote. This format, called a comma-separated data export format, is a common one for many software systems. The commas delimit the values, and the quotes ensure that the importing software handles blanks, commas, and nulls properly. The alias, "Output," gives you something to refer to in later Wizard screens.

NOTE
If you have embedded double quotes in your column values, you must translate them to something else using SQL functions.

1. In the fields and labels screen, include the Output field in the report and remove the label, leaving it null.

2. Give the Output field a length appropriate to the line, such as 80 or 132.

3. Use no template in the template screen, or use your data export file template, if you've developed one yourself.

4. Finish the report.

5. Select the report object in the Object Navigator and display its Property Palette.

6. Find the Character Mode heading and the Design in Character Units property, and set it to Yes.

7. Find the System Parameters heading under the Data Model object in the Object Navigator. Expanding that heading, you will see all the system parameters for the report. By double-clicking on these, you see the Property Palette for the parameter. You need to set an initial value that gives Oracle Developer the information it needs to create the output file, as Table 7-1 specifies.

System Parameter	Example Initial Value	Description
DESNAME	C:\DataFile.txt	The name of the output file, including a path if you wish.
DESTYPE	File	The "File" destination type tells Oracle Developer to produce file output instead of sending the file to the printer.
MODE	Character	The "Character" mode tells Oracle Developer to produce ASCII character output instead of standard printer output.
DESFORMAT	Delimited	The "Delimited" format tells Oracle to produce the file in a format suitable for input into programs that accept delimited-field formats; there is no drop-down list for this field, so make sure you type in the format correctly.

TABLE 7-1. *System Parameter Settings for a Data File Export Report*

Finally, you must remove the margins from the report.

8. Display the Layout Editor for the report and click on the Margin tool. This displays a heavy black line for the margin.

9. Click on this line with the mouse to select the margin and display its sizing handles.

10. Drag the middle handles on all four sides as far out as they will go to move the margins out to the edge of the "paper." For example, drag the top margin up to the top of the Editor, and drag the left margin to the left edge.

11. Save the report and run it by clicking on the Green-Light icon. If you now look in the output file you specified, you should find the following report:

```
"Adah Talbot", 23,"Papa King"
"Andrew Dye", 29,"Rose Hill"
"Bart Sarjeant", 22,"Cranmer"
"Blacksmith", ,""
"Boole And Jones", ,""
"Dean Foreman", ,""
"Dick Jones", 18,"Rose Hill"
"Donald Rollo", 16,"Matts"
"Dr. Carlstrom", ,""
```

```
"Edward Johnson", ,""
"Edythe Gammiere", ,""
"Elbert Talbot", 43,"Weitbrocht"
"Feed Store", ,""
"Fred Fuller", ,""
"Gary Kentgen", ,""
"General Store", ,""
"George August", ,""
"George B. McCormick", ,""
"George Oscar", 41,"Rose Hill"
"Gerhardt Kentgen", 55,"Papa King"
"Harold Schole", ,""
"Helen Brandt", 15,""
"Henry Chase", ,""
"Isaiah James", ,""
"James Cole", ,""
"Janice Talbot", ,""
"Jed Hopkins", 33,"Matts"
"John Austin", ,""
"John Pearson", 27,"Rose Hill"
"Kay And Palmer Wallbom", ,"Rose Hill"
"Lily Carlstrom", ,""
"Livery", ,""
"Manner Jewelers", ,""
"Methodist Church", ,""
"Mill", ,""
"Morris Arnold", ,""
"Palmer Wallbom", ,""
"Pat Lavay", 21,"Rose Hill"
"Peter Lawson", 25,"Cranmer"
"Phone Company", ,""
"Post Office", ,""
"Quarry", ,""
"Richard Koch And Brothers", ,"Weitbrocht"
"Robert James", ,""
"Roland Brandt", 35,"Matts"
"Sam Dye", ,""
"School", ,""
"Underwood Bros", ,""
"Verna Hardware", ,""
"Victoria Lynn", 32,"Mullers"
"Wilfred Lowell", 67,""
"William Swing", 15,"Cranmer"
```

This chapter has given you a solid overview of how to produce effective reports of several different types. When you're ready to deploy your reports, take a look at Chapter 14, which describes the Oracle Developer Server and its Report Server component. Don't neglect the techniques you learned in Chapter 4 for producing reports in HTML and Adobe Acrobat format for deployment on the Internet. The next chapter expands your knowledge even further with a similar overview of the Graphics component of Oracle Developer.

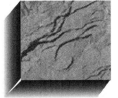

CHAPTER

8

Advanced Graphics

he third major component of Oracle Developer, Graphics, lets you add spice to your applications through active graphics. Multimedia is the name of the game in Internet publishing, and Graphics gives you the ability to take advantage of the new possibilities for great-looking applications. You can present these displays through the Graphics Runtime system as standalone applications or as embedded charts in forms or reports.

NOTE
If you love PL/SQL programming and are up for a challenge, you can use the programming system in Graphics to create just about any graphical display you can imagine. The hundreds of subprograms available in the Graphics library permit you to draw and manipulate any shape you desire, as long as you are willing to do your homework to figure out the geometry and logic required. See the online Graphics documentation for details on such advanced programming capabilities.

This chapter will give you a foundation on which to build your use of graphics in your applications. The first section focuses on the way you use graphics; the other sections go into more detail on how to use the Graphics Builder to create the charts you need.

Effectively Using Graphics

Everyone likes to see the flash of an application that makes heavy use of graphics and visual objects. A deeper understanding of their effectiveness and the structure by which they contribute their value can help you build objects you will want to reuse.

Graphics in applications are part of what you are *communicating* and are not there just for decoration. A graphic, like the written word, communicates its message effectively only if it communicates clearly. Most people receive at least minimal training in language skills and writing at some point in their careers, but few get any training in graphics and graphic construction. This section gives you a few pointers and several references in case you want to learn more. The chapter then focuses on graphics you can build with the Graphics component of Oracle Developer.

First, what about pictures? A picture is worth a thousand words, right? Unfortunately, only if you want to communicate the thousand words. If your concern is communicating a simple fact, showing a picture will almost always be overkill and will ultimately obscure the message you wish to communicate. Use a picture in an application only if the picture represents real information; for example, a picture of a house or apartment in a real-estate query system, a person in a personnel database, or a product in a sales application.

Next, what about bitmap logos and icons? A classic use for bitmaps is to display the corporate logo, as in the Talbot reports in Chapter 4. This is fine, as long as the people with whom you're communicating need to know graphically what company they should associate with the application. In an in-house application, however, these logos are probably superfluous. On memos, for example, corporate logos establish the "official" nature of the communication. These images come under the class of nice-to-have graphics rather than necessary ones.

Another major use for icons is to represent buttons that initiate some action, display another window, and so on. Using icons in toolbars, for example, has become extremely popular. If you build a lot of control bitmaps into your application, make sure they do not get in the way of the information the application communicates. Make them small and unobtrusive, or separate them into their own window (a toolbar is a good place for these icons). Do spend some time designing and testing the icons for usability.

Now, on to the more complicated realm of graphic displays. The first decision you must make is which kind of graphic is appropriate for your application. To do that, you must first determine what you want to communicate through the graphic. Just as you want to state your conclusion clearly in a piece of writing, you want your graphic to show the main point as clearly as possible. If you do not know what that main point is, you should not be using a graphic. You should also try to sum up the main point in the graphic's title or caption that tells the reader what the graphic contains.

Once you have figured out the main point, you next must determine how many components of information you need to convey. Are you comparing one thing with another? Two things compared by date? If you have more than three components, you probably will need more than one chart to show the information.

Now, for each component, you must determine whether the information is qualitative or quantitative. Qualitative data comes in categories; for example, the names of the people from whom Talbot bought goods. Quantitative data comes in numbers, such as dates or amounts. Some qualitative data can have an implicit order, such as names in alphabetical order, age groups, or economic classes.

Given all this information, you can now decide what kind of graphic to use. For example, to show a two-component graphic with one qualitative component and one quantitative component, you should construct a pie chart, bar chart, or histogram. The pie slices and bars in these graphics directly represent categories in an effective way.

The Sold pie chart of Chapter 4 (replicated here in Figure 8-1) represents this two-component qualitative/quantitative chart. The qualitative component is the person, and the quantitative component is the sum of the amounts for transactions by that person. The main point is to determine who the biggest customers of Talbot's Farms are compared with total sales, so the caption for the chart reads "Talbot Customers' Share of Total Sales."

If there is more than one quantitative component, you cannot use a pie chart but must use a double-barred chart or histogram. Stack the bars if the amounts are additive, or put them next to one another if you want to compare them. For example, if you want to compare the cash flows of the different types of ledger action (Sold, Received, Paid, or Bought), use the bar chart in Figure 8-2.

If you are comparing two quantitative components with no qualitative component, use a line or scatter graph to show trends or a table to show exact values. For example, Figure 8-3 shows the total sales at Talbot's Farm versus time in three varieties of line chart. Use shaded areas in a line chart to emphasize the size of total amounts, as opposed to the changes or trends in amounts.

As far as the graphics details go, the principle is to keep it simple. The point is the data, so make sure the details do not obscure the data. If there are too many labels, or you need a complicated legend, or you have too many components,

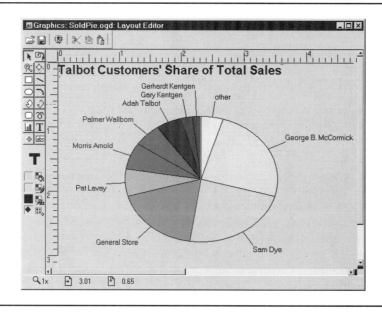

FIGURE 8-1. *Sold pie chart representing Talbot's customers' share of total sales*

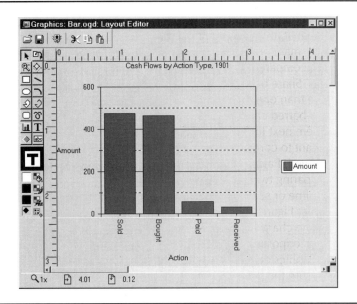

FIGURE 8-2. *Talbot's Farm cash flows by type*

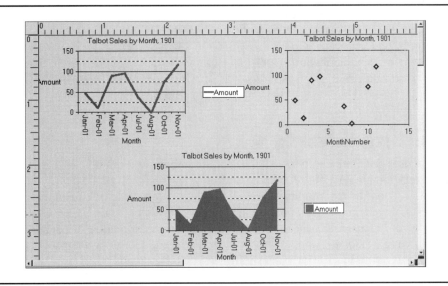

FIGURE 8-3. *Sales trend at Talbot's Farm*

simplify or you will not communicate your point. Make the data elements the prominent elements of the graphic. Surround the data area with scale lines, where appropriate, or with tick marks outside the data area to show gradations. Do not use too many tick marks; these will obscure the message. Use a reference line through the graphic to show an important value (a change point, a particular event date, and so on). Label individual data elements only if necessary to make your point. When possible, use graphical means to distinguish components rather than labels. You can achieve many of these effects using chart properties in Oracle Developer; others may require programming in format triggers, as the later section "Adding Triggers for Setup and Formatting" discusses.

To facilitate readers' understanding, if there is more than one component, include a caption or legend that tells them what the components are in the data area. Put the legend outside the data area. If you use special graphics, use a legend that tells the reader what the graphics represent. Use a scale that makes your point, but try to avoid fooling people with unusual scales. If you have more than one chart, use the same scale if the reader is going to compare them. Do not include zero on the scale just because it is there; only include it if it is meaningful and useful.

There are also a couple of practical issues you must consider. First, proofread or test your graphic displays to ensure they achieve your goals without obvious errors. Second, consider what might happen if someone needs to print a black-and-white copy of the graphic. Careers have fallen victim to the chart that looks great on the monitor but turns into a black smudge when it emerges from the printer. Not everyone enjoys getting their information from computer screens.

To learn more about how to produce effective graphic displays, consult *The Visual Display of Quantitative Information* by Edward R. Tufte (Graphics Press, 1983) and *The Elements of Graphing Data* by William S. Cleveland (Wadsworth Advanced Books and Software, 1985). To explore the depths of the possibilities in this field, consult the massive *Semiology of Graphics: Diagrams, Networks, Maps* by Jacques Bertin (University of Wisconsin Press, 1983).

Building Charts

You can use the Chart Genie to build any of a number of different charts. This wizard lets you create a query, then generates a quick version of the chart you want to display. You then can modify the result to your heart's content. You've already seen a simple example of this process in Chapter 4, which also shows you how to integrate your charts into your forms and reports. This section goes into detail on the individual types of queries and charts you can build and the properties you can set for each type of chart.

An Oracle Developer *display module* contains the queries and layouts that you define in the Graphics component. A chart is a particular object within a display, and displays can have more than one chart. Also, you can have multiple queries, with different charts using different queries, the same query, or filtered versions of the same query. For example, you could have a series of pie charts, each illustrating a different subset of the data; or a pie chart and a line chart illustrating different relationships of a variable to other variables. You define each chart separately in the Chart Genie. You then lay out the charts in the Layout Editor, adding the captions and legends you need to distinguish each chart's contribution to the whole display. When you embed graphics, you embed the entire display, not a single chart within the display.

Your query structures the data you will use to build your chart. Your chart's structure in turn comes from the structure of the data. A big part of building a chart is thus getting the structure of the query right, which can take quite a lot of thought. Focusing on the quantitative/qualitative distinction helps, as does experimenting with the granularity and grouping of the data. The sections below discuss building the query and then building specific classes of charts.

Getting Data for Your Charts

Chapter 4 showed you how to construct a basic query and data model for your charts using the Chart Genie and its New Query screen. This section goes into more detail on the construction process, giving you some alternatives to the simple Chart Genie query building process Chapter 4 demonstrated. The last subsection shows you an alternative method for filtering the data records for multiple charts associated with a single query.

Alternative Data Sources

Oracle Developer does not limit you solely to a SELECT statement that you type into the Chart Genie when you create a chart. There are a variety of ways to get data that serves as the basis for your chart.

NOTE
Advanced users can create queries directly as objects in the Object Navigator through the Property Palette for the query object. You can also create a query using PL/SQL's built-in subprograms such as OG_Make_Query and OG_Execute_Query. You can also type the data in through the Data tab page for a query you create manually, though this is a poor way of doing it.

USING EXTERNAL QUERIES   As in reports, you can use an external query to get the data for your chart. The Chapter 10 section "External Queries and the Query Builder" goes into detail on the external query module in the Reports component of

Oracle Developer. In Graphics, external queries are not modules but rather files that you access from the Chart Genie's New Query dialog box in its Query tab page.

There are two ways to use external files: importing the query and referring to an external file. Both require a single SELECT statement in an ASCII file. Do not terminate the statement with a semicolon or include programming options as you would in a SQL*Plus script.

To import the SQL into the query by copying the text of the statement, click on the Import SQL button to the right of the SQL Statement text field, as shown here:

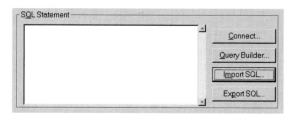

This button displays a standard Open dialog box that lets you select the file, then copies the contents of the file into the SQL Statement text field. You then proceed as though you had entered the SQL statement yourself.

NOTE
A limitation of this approach is that you don't see the SQL statement in the SQL Statement text field. You can see the resulting data by clicking on Execute and going to the Data tab. You can also export the SQL statement you enter yourself into an external file by clicking on the Export SQL button. This is an easy way of creating a statement you can reuse in other charts and reports.

A better way to use SQL in an external file is to use the Type drop-down list to make the query type an External SQL File. This choice activates the File field and Browse button, shown here, which again lets you choose the file through a standard Open dialog box.

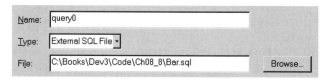

This time, instead of copying the SQL, the Chart Genie refers to the file when it needs to execute the SQL. That means if you change the file, your chart will pick up the changes, which enhances the reusability and maintainability of your query and chart (Chapter 10).

GETTING DATA FROM A FILE   You can also use raw data from a small variety of spreadsheet data file formats:

- SYLK: The old Microsoft Excel/Multiplan export file format.

- WKS: The old Lotus 1-2-3 export file format, also used by other spreadsheet and database programs.

- PRN: A generic printer output file with unknown structure (I don't recommend using this choice, since it isn't documented anywhere except as a "text file format").

Choose the appropriate format from the drop-down list, as shown here, and then use the activated Browse button to specify the file using the standard Open dialog box. The data will appear in the Data tab page.

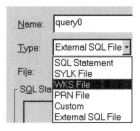

NOTE
Given the limited nature of the data formats you can use in queries, it's probably a better idea to import the data into an Oracle table rather than relying on non-SQL external file formats. You can use a product that converts these file formats to Oracle tables, such as Data Junction by Tools and Techniques, Inc., to automate the process.

GETTING DATA FROM A CALLING MODULE   When other modules embed the chart, often you want to query the same data for use in the chart as in the calling module. For example, a form or report may present a tabular display of the data that the chart represents graphically. In a form, you can create a parameter list for the OG.Open call. The section "Passing Parameters to Reports and Charts" in Chapter 10 goes into detail on using data parameters to pass Forms record groups into charts for use as the query.

To use these parameters effectively, you must coordinate the display module with the calling module:

■ On the Chart Properties dialog box of the Chart Genie, or in the Chart Properties property sheet, find the Data tab page and check the check box labeled "Update chart on query execution." This check box, shown here, tells the display module to update the display when the calling module passes control to the chart. Oracle Developer checks this box by default.

■ Make sure the columns in the record group you pass by data parameter have exactly the same names or aliases that the query columns have in your query. The display module matches these names. Your aliases in the display module query for a display you are going to control through embedding should therefore be easy to specify. You can label your chart axis using the Axis object property palette instead of using the default alias.

Filtering the Data

Usually, you use the WHERE clause in your SQL statement to filter the data for display in your chart. You can parameterize the WHERE clause using a lexical reference to a parameter, as Chapter 10 discusses. Under certain circumstances, however, you may want to filter the records using a PL/SQL filter function:

■ If you are using data from a non-SQL file format or data you have manually entered into the query.

■ If you are using data from a calling module and you want the chart to control the content of the set of records rather than the calling module.

■ If you have multiple charts in the display all using the same query but requiring different subsets of the data (this would require inefficient multiple queries of the same data from the database).

Go to the Data tab page on the Chart Properties dialog box and find the Filter field, shown here:

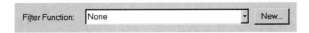

You can select from a list of existing filter functions, or you can create a new filter function by clicking on the New button. If you create a new function, Graphics displays the PL/SQL Program Unit Editor with a filter function template:

```
-- Query Filter Functions. Called for each row of a query
-- that is associated with the chart object
-- ARGUMENTS:
--    CHARTOBJ  The current chart object.
--    QUERY     The query associated with the chart object
-- RETURN:
--    TRUE   keep the row
--    FALSE  remove the row
FUNCTION OGQUERYFILTER0(chartobj IN og_object,
                        query IN og_query)
                        RETURN BOOLEAN IS
BEGIN

END;
```

You can then add code between the BEGIN and END statements that returns TRUE or FALSE based on the values of the data columns in your query. When you execute the query, Graphics executes the function for each record and filters out those for which the function returns a FALSE.

Building Line Charts

A *line chart* displays two or more quantitative components (Figure 8-4). The line connects the data points, and some of the variations on this type of chart represent various ways of connecting the points. For example, a scatter plot just displays the points; a line plot connects them with a line; and an area plot displays a solid area under the line. The x axis represents a single quantitative variable, while the y axis represents one or more quantitative variables that you are comparing. Figure 8-4 shows the relationship between time and amount sold at the granularity of a month in 1901 as a line chart, a scatter plot, and an area graph.

The key to building a line chart is getting both quantitative components at the right level of granularity. For example, in Figure 8-4, the x axis ticks are months.

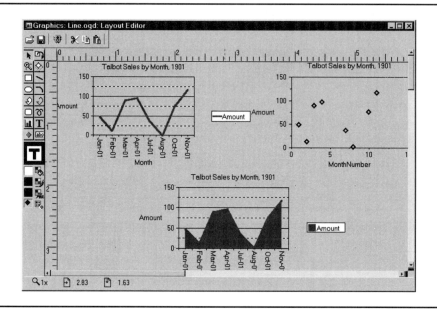

FIGURE 8-4. *Line charts, scatter plots, and area graphs*

The raw data in the Ledger table is the date. To aggregate into months and order properly, you use this query:

```
SELECT To_Char(ActionDate, 'Mon-YY') "Month",
       To_Number(To_Char(CctionDate, 'MM')) "MonthNumber",
       Sum(Amount) "Amount"
  FROM Ledger
 WHERE To_Char(ActionDate, 'YYYY') = '1901' AND
       Action = 'Sold'
 GROUP BY To_Char(ActionDate, 'Mon-YY'),
       To_Number(To_Char(ActionDate, 'MM'))
 ORDER BY 2
```

The MonthNumber column in the select list does not appear in the chart but rather orders the data, as ordering by the Month column would sort alphabetically rather than in month order. The WHERE clause subsets the data to retrieve only sales data for 1901. The GROUP BY clause includes both the Month and MonthNumber columns to enable the SELECT list to contain them both. SELECT lists for grouped SELECTs can contain only summary function expressions or elements from the GROUP BY clause. You use the Chart Properties screen in the Chart Genie to set up the category and value columns for the chart.

Now that you've gotten the basics, what do you do to modify the chart's formatting and layout?

Modifying Charts

The Chart Properties dialog box controls the basic characteristics of each chart. To see this dialog box, you must first select the chart by clicking on it. You can then display the Chart Properties dialog box with the Chart|Properties menu item or by right-clicking and choosing Properties on the pop-up menu. This dialog box lets you choose a default chart type and subtype. It sets up the relationship between the query and the chart through a series of tab pages that you've already seen, as they are part of the Chart Genie sequence you've gone through to create a line or pie chart.

Modifying Chart Frames and Axes

To get to the next level of chart formatting, you can choose the Frame or Axes menu items on the Chart or pop-up menu. When you select the chart and choose Frame, you see the Frame Properties dialog box, which lets you control aspects of the chart frame. The Frame tab page, shown here, lets you modify the basic frame:

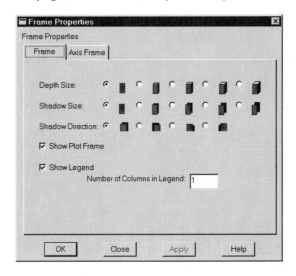

The three radio-button sequences control the three-dimensional appearance and shadowing characteristics of the frame. For example, you can make the frame appear to be a box with the chart appearing in the middle. The Show Plot Frame check box lets you hide or show the frame border, and the Show Legend check box lets you hide or show the legend box.

The Axis Frame tab page, shown here, lets you modify characteristics of the axes.

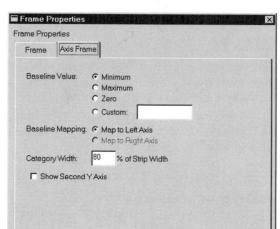

NOTE

The tab pages for the pie chart are totally different. Go to the later section "Building Pie Charts" for details.

The baseline value is the value at which the value axis starts. By default, this setting starts the baseline with the minimum value for your query, which is usually the correct setting. You can set it to maximum, zero, or some other custom value using this dialog box.

NOTE

Remember to scale the chart in the way least likely to confuse the user. You don't need to start the chart at zero, for example, but you might want to if zero is a valid baseline. For example, if you have several charts in a display, you may want to set their baselines to the same value, such as zero, to permit accurate comparison.

If you click on the Show Second Y Axis check box, the chart displays a second scale on the opposite side of the frame from the first *y* axis. The Baseline Mapping radio group lets you control the mapping of the values to the scales. You can use this feature to display two lines, for example, along different scales. You might do this to show the growth in two variables along completely different scales versus time for comparison of the rates rather than the absolute values. The Category Width setting controls the width of a category axis.

When you click on the Axes menu item, you see the Axis Properties dialog box with its Axis tab page and either a Continuous Axis or Discrete Axis tab page, depending on what kind of axis you've selected in the drop-down list. The Axis tab page shown here lets you control the labels and ticks on the axis.

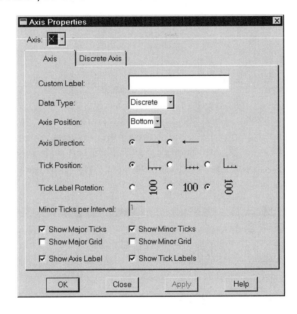

You can replace the automatic label with one of your own by typing it into the Custom Label field. You can specify whether the axis is continuous, discrete, or date using the Data Type drop-down list. The result must correspond to the data type of the column you've assigned to the axis in the Chart Properties dialog box. You can control the axis position (Bottom, Top, Left, or Right) through a drop-down list. You can control the axis direction through a radio button—left to right or right to left. The various settings for the ticks and labels give you a fine degree of control over the appearance of the axis and its labels.

The Discrete Axis tab page shown here lets you control the number of categories that a qualitative axis displays. It's usually best to leave this set to auto.

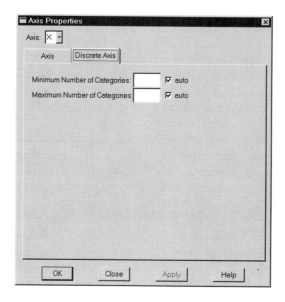

The Continuous Axis tab page shown next lets you control different quantitative characteristics of an axis. You can set the minimum and maximum values for the axis and the step size. These settings can be useful for setting up a comparative scale, but again bear in mind the clarity to the user. You can also use a logarithmic scale instead of a linear scale if necessary.

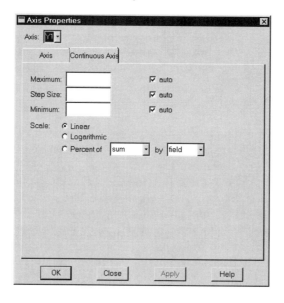

Now that you've seen all the ways of modifying the chart, what about modifying the contents of the chart—the individual graphical objects?

Modifying Chart Object Properties

To modify the object formatting properties, you must select the objects. You do this by selecting the chart, then clicking on the objects: lines, symbols, pie slices, or what have you. If you just click on the objects of a chart once, you will select the chart itself. Click again until you see all the chart elements appear with selection handles. You can now use the Format menu and the formatting tools in the tool palette (line, fill, and symbol) to format the elements of the chart: colors, line sizes, bevels, arrows, and so on, as well as font settings.

You can also modify certain properties of the fields through the field template. Select the chart or the fields and click on the Field Template menu item in the pop-up menu or Chart menu. Depending on the type of chart, you see a tabbed dialog box that lets you modify the template that formats the fields. Chapter 10 goes into detail on using and reusing field templates to control object formatting for multiple charts.

Building Bar Charts

A *bar chart* displays a qualitative component and one or more quantitative components (Figure 8-5). The size of the bars reflects the quantitative value. Variations show multiple quantitative components either with bars stacked on top of one another or side by side. Figure 8-5 shows a chart relating the types of cash flow (Bought, Sold, Paid, Received) to the amounts from 1901 as a bar chart.

The trick to building good bar charts is to identify the qualitative variable properly. The bar chart in Figure 8-5 requires only a relatively simple query:

```
SELECT Action "Action", Sum(Amount) "Amount"
  FROM Ledger
 WHERE To_Char(ActionDate, 'YYYY') = '1901'
 GROUP BY Action
 ORDER BY 2 DESC
```

The GROUP BY clause sets the category dimension for the bar chart, and the ORDER BY sorts the quantitative values in descending order. The WHERE clause subsets the year to 1901.

A *histogram* is a bar chart that you display sideways, with the bars going left to right on the *x* axis instead of bottom to top on the *y* axis as in the bar chart. Often, histograms represent two quantitative components to show a probability or frequency distribution. Figure 8-6 shows the frequency of cash sales over time, with each bar representing a week in 1901 and the data ordered by decreasing frequency. This histogram shows the single-tailed frequency distribution for cash

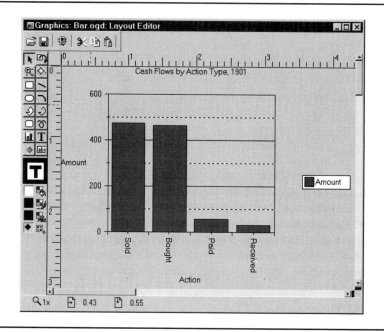

FIGURE 8-5. *A bar chart*

sales, giving you an idea of how the sales distribute themselves over the weeks of the year. The histogram looks pretty much like the half-bell curve you would expect from normally distributed random variations in sales.

Since a histogram displays frequencies versus a quantitative variable, you need to structure your query more like that of a line chart:

```
SELECT To_Number(To_Char(ActionDate, 'IW')) "Week",
       Count(*) "Count"
  FROM Ledger
 WHERE To_Char(ActionDate, 'YYYY') = '1901' AND
       Action = 'Sold'
 GROUP BY To_Number(To_Char(ActionDate, 'IW'))
 ORDER BY 2 DESC
```

The GROUP BY clause in this query aggregates the data by week using the ISO week number, which becomes the quantitative value. The frequency component comes from the Count(*) element of the SELECT list. The ORDER BY sorts by frequency in descending order.

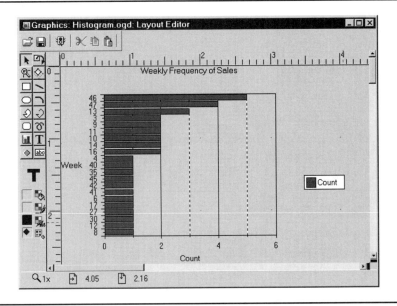

FIGURE 8-6. *A histogram of sales cash flows over time*

Building Pie Charts

A *pie chart* displays a qualitative component and a quantitative component. The size of the pie slices reflects the quantitative value, with the slice representing the ratio of the value to the sum of all the values. Variations reflect different styles of display, including a shadowed pie and a three-dimensional pie.

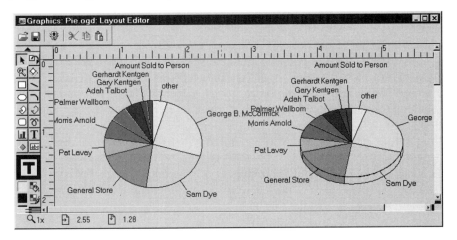

You can use the special pie chart Frame Properties dialog box shown here to modify the options for the pie chart. You set special pie options through the Pie Frame tab page.

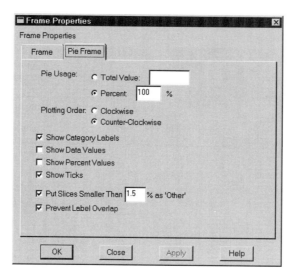

You've already seen the creation of the "other" pie slice in Chapter 4. The rest of the options control specific characteristics of the slices and their relationship with the pie. The options on the Pie Frame tab page control the content and spacing of the labels.

You control the depth and shadowing of the pie using the standard Frame tab page, as the prior section "Modifying Charts" described. The Show Legend check box has no effect for pie charts.

Building Drill-Down Charts

Sometimes, one chart is not enough. You can put as many charts into a single display as you wish. Sometimes you run into a situation where you want to go from a higher-level chart to a chart with more detail. For example, take the Sold pie chart. Perhaps you would like to see a line chart showing the trend for sales to a particular person. You could display this line chart right next to the pie, but for which person?

The solution to this requirement is to *drill down* from one chart to another. This technique lets you click on an object in a master chart to configure a detail chart parameterized by that object, usually to display details for that object. In the example, the object is the person slice, and you parameterize the line chart with the person that slice represents.

Building a drill-down relationship is quite easy in Oracle Developer. It does not require any Graphics programming, just two charts and a few property settings in the master chart. The key to the relationship is to modify the query for the detail chart to include a host variable that refers to a parameter based on a value from the master chart. When you click on a pie slice, for example, the Graphics Runtime system sets the parameter, executes the query, and redisplays the detail chart.

Starting with the Sold pie chart, add a line chart next to it, as shown here:

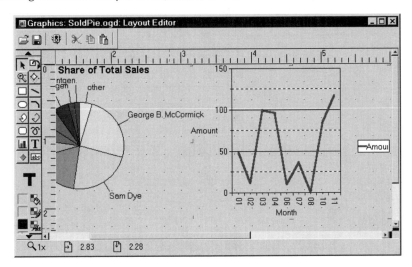

This chart is a standard line chart, unmodified except for changing the orientation of the labels on the x axis to horizontal from vertical through the Chart Properties dialog box. The query that drives this graph contains the following SQL:

```
SELECT To_Char(ActionDate, 'MM') "Month", Sum(Amount) "Amount"
  FROM Ledger
 WHERE To_Char(ActionDate, 'YYYY') = '1901' and
       Action IN('Sold', 'Received')
 GROUP BY  To_Char(ActionDate, 'MM')
 ORDER BY 1
```

This query generates one point on the graph for each month in 1901, summing the amounts sold to anyone. At this point, there is no qualification for the person in the pie chart.

  1. Now go to the pie chart in the Layout Editor, click on the chart to select it, and then click on the pie slices to select the pie slice object. You will see the selection handles appear on all the slices.

2. Right-click to get the pop-up menu and choose the Properties menu item, or choose the Tools|Properties menu item from the main menu.

3. Choose the Drill-down tab page:

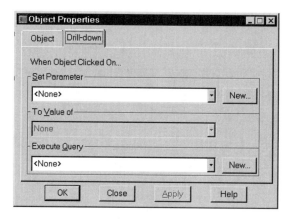

4. Click on the New button next to the Set Parameter field to create a new parameter. Oracle Developer displays the Parameters dialog box, as shown here:

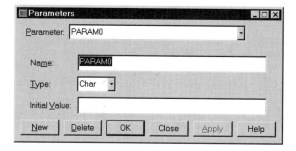

5. Change the name of the parameter to something readable, such as PERSON, and supply an initial value such as George B. McCormick, the largest buyer. In this case, the data type is already correct (CHAR), but you could change it to NUMBER or DATE if necessary.

6. Click on OK. Oracle Developer creates the parameter in the display module.

7. Back in the Drill-down tab page, drop down the To Value Of drop-down list to choose Person from the list of columns.

8. Drop down the Execute Query drop-down list to choose the query of the line chart (QUERY0) as the query to execute on drill-down. The resulting tab page now looks like this:

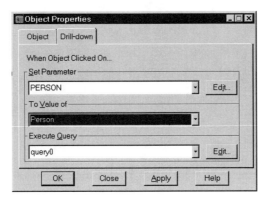

The New button next to the Execute Query field has changed to Edit instead of New.

9. Click on the Edit button to edit the query. Add a join to the Person table to get the Person Name column, and then compare that column to the :Person parameter:

```
SELECT To_Char(ActionDate, 'MM') "Month",
       SUM(Amount) "Amount"
  FROM Ledger l, Person p
 WHERE l.Person = REF(p) AND
       To_Char(ActionDate, 'YYYY') = '1901' AND
       Action IN ('Sold', 'Received') AND
       p.Name = :Person
 GROUP BY To_Char(ActionDate, 'MM')
 ORDER BY 1
```

10. Execute the query, and the query will pick up the values for the query from the default value you assigned to the parameter. In this case, George McCormick has bought quite a lot, but only in two months out of the year, as this refreshed display shows:

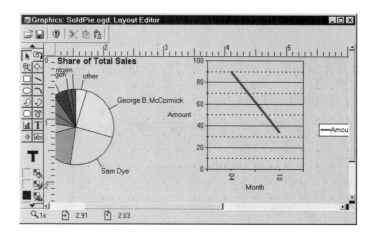

That's all there is to creating a drill-down chart. Now, when you run the chart in Graphics Runtime, you can click on a pie slice to see the monthly trend for any person. Try it by clicking on the Run tool in the Layout Editor.

Laying Out Displays

The Graphics Layout Editor has many tools available for adding to or changing your basic chart layout. The following sections introduce the range of things that you can do with the Editor.

Drawing Shapes, Images, and Sounds

You can add background shapes, bitmapped images, and sounds to emphasize or otherwise set off your basic chart, or you can compose an entire graphic of these elements without using any data model at all.

NOTE
There are two drawing tricks you should know. First, double-clicking on a tool in the tool palette sets that tool on for drawing multiple objects; single-clicking means the Editor resets the tool after you draw a single object. Second, whenever you draw a shape, you can usually SHIFT-click to draw a more regular version of the shape—a square instead of a rectangle, or a circle instead of an ellipse.

To add a shape, you click on the tool for the shape: Rectangle, Line, Ellipse, Arc, Polygon, Polyline, Rounded Rectangle, or Freehand. The *polyline* is a series of lines that leave a gap in the boundary rather than describing a full polygon. Freehand drawing lets you draw a sequence of pixels in any direction. Once you've clicked the tool, you draw the shape. To modify the characteristics of the shape, you select it by clicking on it, then use the appropriate tool or menu item to modify it. On the tool palette, you have these tools:

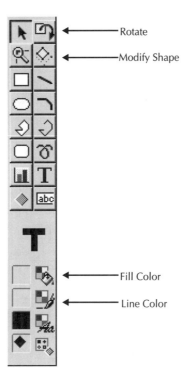

- **Rotate:** Rotates the shape by dragging the sizing handles; SHIFT-dragging moves by 45-degree increments.

- **Modify Shape:** Lets you modify the shape of polygons, polylines, or freehand drawings.

- **Fill Color:** Changes the color of the shape fill or makes the fill transparent (No Fill); you can also set a fill pattern, though this book recommends against using any fill patterns if you have any user-interface portability requirements.

- **Line Color:** Changes the color of the shape's lines or makes the lines transparent (No Line).

There is a tremendous array of menu items that affect shapes, all on the Format menu. You can adjust the line width, make the line one of several dashed patterns, add beveling, add arrowheads, or make symbols bigger or smaller. By choosing the Drawing Options menu item, you can access a series of dialog boxes that give you full control over the details of the shapes. There are also specific drawing options for arcs and rounded rectangles, which each have special characteristics.

Adding Triggers for Setup and Formatting

Chapter 5 went into some detail on the Graphics Runtime execution sequence, including the various triggers that fire at different points. This section acquaints you with some of the uses for these triggers, focusing on handling special setup and formatting tasks that go beyond the standard chart properties.

Graphics triggers aren't sequenced and named by specific processes, as in Forms. You create Graphics triggers by creating procedures and associating them with the trigger event on a specific graphic object that executes the procedure. For example, say you wanted to take an action when the user clicked on a data value in a scatter chart such as that shown in Figure 8-4.

1. First, display the Object Properties dialog box, shown here, for the symbol objects by selecting them and using the pop-up menu, double-clicking, or choosing the main menu's Tools|Properties menu item.

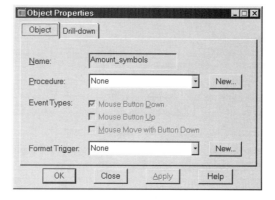

2. Pull down a list of available procedures using the Procedure drop-down list, or you can click on the New button next to the list. Either action displays the Program Unit Editor with the following code template:

```
PROCEDURE OGBUTTONPROC0 (buttonobj IN og_object,
                         hitobj IN og_object,
                         win IN og_window,
                         eventinfo IN og_event) IS
BEGIN

END;
```

You now add your own PL/SQL code to the template between the BEGIN and END, changing the names to suit your needs. The Format Trigger works in much the same way but runs whenever the Graphics runtime system formats the objects.

You can access different trigger events from different property sheets, and you can assign the Open and Close triggers through the Display Properties dialog box, which you open using the Tools|Display menu item. You can also assign the Post Execution triggers through the Object Navigator, where they appear as nodes under the query object. You can similarly assign a Timer trigger by selecting the timer you want to assign a procedure to, then clicking on the Timer Procedure node underneath it.

As you design your system of procedures, give some thought to making them as general as possible for later reuse. You can, for example, build PL/SQL libraries of trigger procedures that you include in multiple displays. Consult Chapters 10, 11, and 12 for advice on making your PL/SQL reusable in different displays.

When programming in Graphics, you will often need to refer to objects from your display module. Chapter 11 contains a complete explanation of the system that Oracle Developer gives you for finding and using object identifiers or handles, including a table of the built-in functions for obtaining the different kinds of handles available in Graphics.

NOTE
When a built-in subprogram calls for a dimension, you should supply the information relative to the system global variable OG_INCH instead of in any absolute value. This variable takes into account the display resolution and specifies the number of layout units in one inch for the current display. Thus, you can set an existing rectangle aRect to a specific size (2 inches by 4 inches) using this PL/SQL code:

```
aRect.width := 2 * OG_INCH;
aRect.height := 4 * OG_INCH;
```

Now you have seen the basic elements of all three major components of Oracle Developer. The following chapters in this part of the book describe some advanced programming issues relating to application security and reuse. The next part expands your ability to program, with an in-depth tutorial on PL/SQL.

CHAPTER

9

No Entry

afety is one of the basic human needs. Although seemingly far removed from the realm of personal safety, a database application must provide some degree of security from harm. What you do to achieve the level of safety you desire is your application's security policy.

Why Be Secure?

What is the point of security? Why should you spend any time on it? Does Oracle or Oracle Developer automatically guarantee the safety of your data? How can you protect your system from intrusion if it is publicly available through the Internet?

Here are some things that might happen through the intentional actions of some person:

- *Unavailability:* Your system could deny service to legitimate users because someone crashes or overloads it, particularly if the application is available through the Internet.

- *Unaccountability:* You might become unable to account for the accuracy or legitimacy of data in an application or database because of your inability to trace the source of a data item. When an application gets data entry through a Web page, for example, anybody in the world could enter the data, and you must have a way to know the source.

- *Uncontrollability:* You might become unable to control the operation of your application, leading to an inability to guarantee the legitimacy of its results.

- *Theft:* Someone might be able to steal data or even real money or goods through forgery or fraud. This includes stealing information for intelligence. Again, the Internet makes this easy.

This is not a book on computer security, which is a broad field with many sophisticated aspects. The point is that a lot can happen to your Oracle Developer software system if you do not protect it from harm. How can you best do that?

First, you must identify the risks that come from deliberate actions to harm your software. As with any risk, evaluate the probability of failure and its impact. For those risks you deem unacceptable, take actions that reduce the risk. This analysis lets you decide what is a security problem and what is not. You can eliminate many "security problems" by realizing that they are really not a problem. Never fall into the trap of believing that everything must be secure simply because it must.

NOTE
You should have already identified the risks that derive from unintentional acts that harm your system. An example might be the risk of a query that brings the system to its knees by querying huge amounts of data. Your database and application design should take such risks of technical failure into account. Security risks are a different beast.

Second, in taking action, your alternatives come down to stopping the unauthorized use of your software and stopping authorized use from leading to unauthorized use. If you believe you must ensure the safety of data through security measures, do not fool yourself: your tactics will involve preventing someone from using your software. Depending on the problem, it may even involve making your software harder to access and use for legitimate users. Again, justify the action before taking it if its consequences lower the quality of your work.

Third, you may want to extend your alternatives to forensic detection after the fact: auditing. Auditing is tracing events and activities in the database or in the application. Establishing an audit trail may help you simultaneously investigate and deal with any problems that arise and may prevent problems from arising by deterring intruders.

The universe of techniques for ensuring security is very broad. The discussion at the beginning of the chapter focuses on Oracle and Oracle Developer, which use discretionary access control and auditing. A later section summarizes a more secure approach—called mandatory access control—which you can use for highly secure applications.

Ultimately, the physical access that people have to your application may determine its true security. You must take physical measures as well as software measures into account in your risk analysis and management plan. For example, a security-conscious application should not be available through public telephone lines and certainly not through the Internet. You must limit physical access to machines running the software, including network connections.

This book does not recommend that every database application be extremely secure; just the reverse, in fact. A common security model is to limit access to only what is necessary for doing your job (the "need-to-know" approach). Although this yields excellent security, the consequences may be chilling for ease of use. If you are building applications for the Internet, this approach is simply not possible. The less security overhead you impose on your users, the more usable your application will be. You are the ultimate judge of your security needs and how much ease of use to forfeit to meet those needs. Be as paranoid as your risk tolerance demands, but not more so.

One place that insists on secure access is the Internet. If you are going to deploy your applications on the Internet, you have to be sure the application doesn't breach your firewalls and let hackers (or anyone else) into your databases. Oracle Developer Server supports firewalls by running outside the firewall and accessing servers on the other side of the firewall through secure Net8 tunneling.

Discretionary Access Control

Discretionary access control is the ability to control access to an application and its data through the granting of privileges to subjects (users and processes) that use the application and its data. This section summarizes the different kinds of discretionary access control available in Oracle Developer. It distinguishes standard SQL security controls from those that Oracle provides in addition to the standard. It also details the different mechanisms available in Oracle Developer for imposing discretionary access control.

NOTE
Many of the security measures described in the next few sections are server based, not part of Oracle Developer. The concepts are important enough, however, that this chapter deals with them in some detail. You can find more detail in books on SQL or in the Oracle documentation (see the following sections for specific references).

SQL Access Control

The ANSI SQL standard provides a primitive level of access control that is the base for Oracle's security system. If you want to develop a database-portable application in ODBC, you may have to limit yourself to ANSI security techniques; otherwise, you should definitely use the extended facilities of Oracle or whatever other database manager you want to use.

Schemas and Authorization

The ANSI security scheme starts with the schema and its accompanying authorization identifier. In ANSI SQL, the *schema* is an object that owns a specific set of tables, views, and privileges (views and privileges will be discussed presently). Any particular table, view, or privilege belongs to exactly one schema. Each schema has a name called an *authorization identifier*. This name also serves to identify a table, as different schemas can contain tables with the same name. That is, schemas provide a scope for the names of the objects they own.

In Oracle, these terms are equivalent to the *user* and its *user name*. Oracle permits you to have a password for the schema as well (you'll learn more about this in the following section on Oracle extensions).

The authorization identifier is the basic means for separating access to different parts of the database. Using this feature of SQL, you can partition the database into schemas with different access controls. Creative relationships between modules and schemas can produce sophisticated access control. For example, it is quite common to create the basic application data in a central schema, then create separate users for the different people who use the application, granting them the appropriate levels of access to the data.

The schema and its authorization identifier thus let you achieve the security objective of limiting access to part of the database by separating the database into sections rather than securing it as a whole.

Privileges

An ANSI *privilege* authorizes a category of action on a table or view by a specified authorization identifier. There are five actions:

- *INSERT:* Lets the grantee put new rows into the table or updateable view

- *DELETE:* Lets the grantee delete rows from the table or updateable view

- *SELECT:* Lets the grantee read rows from the table or view

- *UPDATE:* With an optional list of columns, lets the grantee change the values in the columns you specify for a table or updateable view

- *REFERENCES:* With an optional list of columns, lets the grantee refer to the column in an integrity constraint

You define a privilege with the GRANT statement, like this:

```
GRANT <privileges> ON <table name> TO <grantee> [{, <grantee>}...]
  [WITH GRANT OPTION]
```

The ANSI security system works by associating an authorization identifier with an abstraction it calls a *module*, which contains the SQL to execute against a database. You must have granted the privileges necessary to execute the SQL statements in the module to the authorization identifier. This provides a basic level of access control for each table and view in the database.

The WITH GRANT OPTION clause lets a grantee grant the privileges to another grantee; otherwise, only the owning authorization identifier can grant privileges for an object.

Oracle and the 1992 SQL standard add a REVOKE statement that drops a privilege, optionally cascading revocation from grantees of the grantee. The 1992 standard also extends privileges to all the objects it adds to the schema (domains, character sets, and so on). It adds a list of columns to the INSERT privilege along with DEFAULT values for columns. It also adds a new privilege, USAGE, for the new objects: the ability to use domains, character sets, translations, and collations.

Using schemas, you can achieve the following security objectives:

■ You can limit access to specific tables, columns, and views using privileges granted to other authorization identifiers.

■ You can limit the kind of access to those tables and views using the several types of privilege.

Views

A view is an object that looks like a table but is in fact a SELECT statement that defines the table. The view thus derives its data from one or more base tables or views. Certain views are not updateable—those with joins or grouping or expressions in the SELECT list, for example.

You can also use a view for security, because it can encapsulate references to underlying tables but does not require that you have any privileges on the underlying tables when you use it. That is, you can create a base table in one schema, create a view on that base table, and grant privileges only on the view to other authorization identifiers.

With a view, you can achieve the following security objectives:

■ You can limit access to specific columns of the base table or tables through the SELECT list of the view definition.

■ You can limit access to specific rows of the base table or tables through the WHERE clause of the view definition.

Oracle Access Control

Oracle extends the ANSI SQL standard in several different ways to provide a complete discretionary access control system for your database server.

See the *Oracle Server Concepts Manual* for a full description of the access control and auditing facilities of Oracle.

Authentication

Authentication is the process of confirming that the user is who he or she claims to be and hence can legitimately use the privileges granted to that user. As the previous section mentioned, Oracle provides a password system along with the standard authorization identifier, which Oracle calls a *user name.* Oracle takes the authorization identifier one step further and adds a CREATE USER command to SQL. This command lets you create a user (and hence a schema with no objects defined in it) with a password, default and temporary tablespaces, quotas, and a profile (the following sections discuss tablespaces and profiles).

Oracle provides two separate password mechanisms. The first assumes that the operating system provides a password scheme and thus disables password checking for Oracle sessions.

```
CREATE USER <user name> IDENTIFIED EXTERNALLY
```

The second scheme keeps the passwords in encrypted form in the database data dictionary on the server and checks it whenever you start a session. You can use either scheme or both at once in any given database through the CREATE USER statement.

```
CREATE USER <user name> IDENTIFIED BY <password>
```

If you use EXTERNALLY, Oracle uses a standard prefix, usually "OPS$," to prefix the operating system userid in Oracle operations. You should therefore use the same prefix in the <user name> for the CREATE USER command. See the OS_AUTHENT_PREFIX initialization parameter for your particular system.

Regardless of which scheme you use, the passwords are only as good as your password-changing practices. Every user should change passwords at least once a month, if not more often. Passwords should be words or jumbles that are not obvious (first names, and so on) and that include odd symbols ($, #, _, and so on). Also, people should not write the passwords on yellow stickies and put them on their terminals, and they should not tell the passwords to people passing by on the street or post the passwords on electronic bulletin boards. Your system's authentication security is only as strong as the degree of belief (and respect) your users put in it.

The Oracle authentication scheme achieves the security objective of verifying the user's identity when he or she starts up a session.

Roles

An Oracle *role* is a collection of privileges. You can grant privileges directly to a user, or you can grant a set of privileges to a role, then grant the role to the user (or to a number of users). This gives you the ability to manage very complicated privilege combinations with many different users.

For example, Talbot could hire a new accountant and just add his or her user name to the Accounting Role. If an application required a new table and hence privileges on that table, Talbot would just change the privileges for the role, and all the users for that role would get the correct privileges.

To set up a role, you must first identify your security objectives. Each role should be a coherent group of privileges that means something. For example, each application can have a single role established for it that contains all the privileges you need to run that application. For a complex application, you may be able to identify several different sets of users that use an application; each of these sets of users would get a different and perhaps overlapping set of privileges and would thus be assigned different roles. You should really do this as part of your application requirements analysis. If you identify different roles, you can more easily identify the access requirements for those roles.

You can grant roles to roles, so you can combine a role with additional privileges or other roles in a hierarchy of roles.

You can password-protect roles through an IDENTIFIED BY clause on the CREATE ROLE statement. This lets you require users to enable roles by supplying the role password before they get the privileges of the role. This adds one more layer of protection to the role but obviously doubles the difficulty of logging on for the user. You should only password-protect roles if you have a critical risk of some kind that justifies it.

Oracle also provides a special keyword, PUBLIC, that refers to all the users that the database currently has defined. By default, this user group provides access to data dictionary tables. By assigning privileges to PUBLIC, you grant those privileges to all users, which is sometimes useful. You can also create synonyms (described in the next section) and database links as PUBLIC synonyms or links, which means that any user can refer to them.

The role serves the security objective of making it easier to manage a complex set of privileges, leading to a finer granularity of access control because it is much less work to maintain the security structure. This in turn satisfies the objective of limiting access to only what is necessary for doing your job.

System and Object Privileges

Oracle adds several different kinds of privileges to the server security system. A primary reason for the additional privileges is the extensive set of additional schema objects that Oracle adds to the database besides the standard tables and views:

- *Synonym:* An alias for any object name

- *Cluster:* A storage structure for storing multiple tables together that share common information, such as tables related by a foreign key integrity constraint

- *Index:* A secondary storage structure that provides an alternative access path to data in a table

- *Sequence:* An object you can use to generate unique integers to use as primary keys

- *Procedure:* A stored PL/SQL procedure or function

- *Trigger:* A stored PL/SQL procedure you associate with a server event on a table, such as BEFORE or AFTER an UPDATE or INSERT

- *Snapshot:* A table that holds the results of a query on master tables, usually in a remote database

System privileges let you manage your schema and its operation by performing a particular action on a particular *type* of object. You may get the privilege to use the CREATE, ALTER, and DROP commands to add, change, or drop any of the different kinds of objects from your schema. Adding the keyword ANY to the privilege means that you can exercise your privilege on any schema, not just your own.

There are some specific system privileges beyond just managing schema objects. These privileges are mostly for database administration, but you may have occasion to grant them to an application role. These are explained in Table 9-1.

You can grant a system privilege only if another user has granted you that privilege with the ADMIN OPTION or if you have the GRANT ANY PRIVILEGE privilege.

An *object privilege* is the privilege to take some action on a specific, extant object. Table 9-2 describes the set of privileges.

The discretionary access system works by assuming initially that no privileges exist. Therefore, you must either grant a privilege explicitly to a user or to the role of that user for that person to be able to take the action in question.

See the *Oracle Server SQL Language Reference Manual* or a book on Oracle SQL such as Koch and Loney's *Oracle: The Complete Reference* (Osborne/McGraw-Hill, 1996) for a complete discussion of the syntax of the SQL GRANT and REVOKE commands that let you assign privileges to roles and users.

Using Oracle system and object privileges, you can achieve the following security objectives:

- You can limit access to specific Oracle objects of any variety using privileges granted to other users or roles.

- You can limit the kind of access to those objects using the several types of privilege.

- You can limit the administrative capabilities required in the practical maintenance of the database server and its databases.

Privilege	Description
BECOME USER	Lets you import objects from any schema
BACKUP ANY TABLE	Lets you export objects from any schema
EXECUTE ANY PROCEDURE	Allows executing any function or procedure or reference to any public package variable
FORCE [ANY] TRANSACTION	Lets you force COMMIT or ROLLBACK of your (or any) in-doubt transaction in a two-phase commit
GRANT ANY PRIVILEGE	Lets you grant any system or object privilege
GRANT ANY ROLE	Lets you grant any role to any user
SELECT/INSERT/UPDATE ANY TABLE	Lets you select, insert, or update data in any database table
LOCK ANY TABLE	Lets you lock any database table
MANAGE TABLESPACE	Lets you take tablespaces online and offline for backups
READUP	Lets you query data with a higher access class than that of the current session (see the later section on mandatory access control)
RESTRICTED SESSION	Lets you log on after restricting the server access mode
SELECT ANY SEQUENCE	Lets you refer to sequences
UNLIMITED TABLESPACE	Lets you override any assigned quota
WRITEDOWN	Lets you CREATE, ALTER, DROP, INSERT, UPDATE, or DELETE objects with access classes lower than the current session (see the later section on mandatory access control)
WRITEUP	Lets you CREATE, ALTER, DROP, INSERT, UPDATE, or DELETE objects with access classes higher than the current session (see the later section on mandatory access control)

TABLE 9-1. *Oracle System Privileges*

Profiles

Oracle *profiles* give you a way to control the resources that a user can consume in a session. Oracle establishes a default profile that applies to all users. If you set the initialization parameter RESOURCE_LIMIT to TRUE, you can then define and

Privilege	Table	View	Sequence	Procedure Function Package	Snapshot
ALTER	X		X		
DELETE	X	X			
EXECUTE				X	
INDEX	X				
INSERT	X	X			
REFERENCES	X				
SELECT	X	X	X		X
UPDATE	X	X			

TABLE 9-2.   *Oracle Object Privileges*

use additional profiles. You can use the CREATE USER statement to give a new user a specific profile, or you can assign profiles to existing users with the ALTER USER statement.

The CREATE PROFILE statement lets you define a profile that sets one or more limits on the resources a user can use in a session. These limits are explained in Table 9-3.

You can use the Oracle auditing facilities (discussed later in this chapter in the "Auditing" section) and the Oracle instance management and tracing facilities to gather resource information for different kinds of users. You should then analyze the risks associated with these resources and determine what policies you need to put in place to limit your risk.

User profiles let you achieve the security objective of limiting risks associated with server interactive resource use, such as overloading or crashing applications due to resource exhaustion.

Tablespaces and Quotas

Profiles let you control interactive resources, but what about storage? The CREATE USER statement also gives you the ability to control the amount of space a user can use in the database through quotas on tablespaces.

Resource Limit	Description
SESSIONS_PER_USER	Limits the user to a specific number of concurrent sessions; you can use this, for example, to limit the number of users of a specific application if you have everyone log on to that application with the same user name
CPU_PER_SESSION	Limits the amount of CPU time a session can use
CPU_PER_CALL	Limits the amount of CPU time a particular parse, execute, or fetch call can use
CONNECT_TIME	Limits the elapsed time of a session
IDLE_TIME	Disconnects the session after a specific amount of idle time (not counting time during execution of a query)
LOGICAL_READS_PER_SESSION	Limits the number of blocks the session can read from the database
LOGICAL_READS_PER_CALL	Limits the number of blocks the session can read from the database during a parse, execute, or fetch call
COMPOSITE_LIMIT	Limits the total cost of a session in composite units
PRIVATE_SGA	Limits the amount of space a session can allocate in the SGA as private space

TABLE 9-3.   *Oracle Profile Resource Limits*

A *tablespace* (CREATE TABLESPACE) is a set of operating system files and a storage specification that applies to the creation of tables, indexes, and clusters on disk.

A *quota* is a limit on the amount of space a user can create in a particular tablespace.

Using tablespaces, you can partition your data into specific parts of the physical database. Using the various CREATE statements, you can create objects belonging to users in specific tablespaces. Using quotas, you can then limit the amount of data that a particular user can add in that specific tablespace for those objects he or she creates in the tablespace.

For example, this statement creates the Talbot user with a quota on his default tablespace:

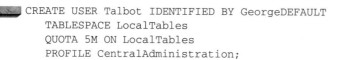
```
CREATE USER Talbot IDENTIFIED BY GeorgeDEFAULT
    TABLESPACE LocalTables
    QUOTA 5M ON LocalTables
    PROFILE CentralAdministration;
```

Quotas let you achieve the objective of limiting risks associated with consumption of physical storage resources.

Client Security

Column update controls and menu access controls give your Oracle Developer forms some needed security. The former lets you control the updating of columns through Oracle Developer. The latter uses the custom menu features to let Oracle roles enable and disable menu items.

NOTE
Both of these features depend on Oracle. If you have a requirement for database portability, neither of these features is relevant.

Column Updating

The section on the logon process in Chapter 5 detailed the process of starting a form. Part of that process was enforcing column security.

The Update Allowed property of a *block* lets you control whether the user can update block records. Updating a record implies querying the record, then changing one or more items. If you set Update Allowed to False, the user can query records but cannot change them.

The Update Allowed property of an *item* lets you control the updating of a particular column in a record. If you set the block property to True, you can set one or more of the item properties to False to stop the user from being able to change that item's value. The Update If Null property of an item lets you prevent the user from updating any value other than one that is NULL. That means the user can enter the value once but cannot change the value after leaving the item. For example, in a project management system, you can have the end date for a task as Update If Null. When the end date is entered, that means the task is completed, and the system prevents a user from later changing the date. You might not like the users' reaction to this kind of restriction, but sometimes security is a thankless job.

These features achieve the objective of preventing changes to table rows or values through a particular block in a form. You can set these properties when you design the form. You can also change them through PL/SQL calls in triggers at runtime.

Oracle Developer can do some of this work for you through the Column Security feature. You can set the Column Security property of the form to True. When a user logs on to a form, Oracle Developer queries the data dictionary for the update privileges on tables and columns in the form's blocks. It sets the Update Allowed property to False for any column for which the user does not have UPDATE privilege. If you use this feature, you can take advantage of the privileges you have set up on the server.

Menu Access Controls

If you create your own menus, you can use a special feature of Oracle Developer menu customization to disable or remove menu items through Oracle security roles. There is even a dialog box for setting up security roles and granting those roles to specific user names from within Oracle Developer (File|Administration|Database Roles menu item). However, you should do this with SQL scripts or through the administrative interfaces to the Oracle database in most cases, as it is easier to see what's going on. At the same time you are defining the roles, you should also install the FRM50_ENABLED_ROLES view in the data dictionary and grant SELECT on it to all the users who will be developing applications using menu security. You must do this by installing the Forms database tables through the Oracle Developer Build and Grant scripts in the Admin group.

Once you've defined the roles, go to the menu module in the Object Navigator and select the Module Roles property in the menu property sheet. Open the dialog box by clicking on the More button. You can now enter the roles that you want to control menu access for this module. This dialog box shows the roles you will create later, in the section at the end of this chapter called "Talbot's Application Security."

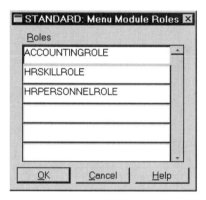

NOTE

This dialog box contains a simple text list. It does not give you any help in getting the roles from the database schema. Before setting up this list, you may want to write down the roles that you want to enter here so none are forgotten when you input the list.

Now, find the menu item in the Object Navigator that you want a role to control. Find the Item Roles property in the property sheet for the menu item. Clicking on the More button displays a dialog box that lets you toggle the roles that enable the menu item. When you select a role by clicking on it with the mouse, it means that a user granted that role sees the menu item enabled in his or her menu bar, but a user not granted that role sees the menu item disabled. Hold down the SHIFT key while you click to select several contiguous items, or hold down the CTRL key while clicking to select or deselect a specific item regardless of the status of the other items.

The Display Without Privilege property controls whether Oracle Developer disables the menu item or removes it completely. Yes means disable it, No means remove it. Set the Use Security flag to Yes in the menu property sheet. Now, regenerate the menu by choosing File|Administration|Compile File, and you are done. Using this feature of Oracle Developer, you can automate your security measures through the security features of Oracle.

NOTE
If you want to develop and test your application without the interference of menu security, keep Use Security set to No until you are ready to deliver the application. Then set it to Yes and regenerate the menu module.

Auditing

Auditing is the process of investigating the activities of a database system and its users. You can monitor database activities, then trace them back to their origin or collect statistics on them. You can also record historic information to make sure you can always reconstruct a chain of events. The information you record (regardless of the type of information it is) is called the *audit trail*.

Auditing in Oracle

Oracle provides extensive auditing facilities:

- *Statement auditing:* Tracing statements of a particular type for one or more users

- *Privilege auditing:* Tracing actions relating to specific system privileges for one or more users

- *Object auditing:* Tracing specific statements on a particular schema object for all users of the database

All of these options let you store the audit trail in a table, AUD$, that belongs to the SYS user. You access the information through data dictionary views. See the *Oracle Server Administrator's Guide* for details on this data dictionary support for auditing.

Auditing is a way for you to check whether your security policy is having its desired effects. If you identify specific risks that you regard as sufficiently serious, you can audit the actions that might cause the system to fail. If it does fail, you can then identify the sequence of actions that caused the failure, or you can trace the failure to its possibly illegitimate source and deal with that source. You can also isolate the failures by locating them in the audit trail. You can audit only successful or unsuccessful statements, if that is appropriate. How often have you confronted a problem with little information about its context? Auditing can provide that context.

You can best understand the impact of auditing by studying the different options and experimenting with them to understand how they apply to the security problems in your particular application.

Auditing lets you achieve the overall objective of ensuring that you meet your other security objectives.

Client Audit Trails

Oracle lets you audit the database activity, but it has no way to extend auditing to the meaningful events in your client application. Depending on your security issues, you may want to build additional auditing into your application.

One broad area is *application auditing.* This is the standard practice of maintaining transaction histories as part of the application data. For example, in an accounting application, you must ensure that an audit trail exists for all data changes. You must always be able to reconstruct a given value as it was at a given time, no matter what has happened to that value in the database. You must also be able to relate each object to its real-world counterpart; for example, an inventory record to the actual inventory item on a shelf. All of these requirements need to be explicit in the database design for the application.

You can also have requirements based on specific security issues; this is called *issue auditing*. For example, there may be some transactional issue that is so vital to your application that you want to verify that the transaction is legitimate and successful under all circumstances by storing traces of the transaction in separate audit trails. This is approximately what Oracle does, but it applies to the meaningful events in your application, not to the server events that Oracle auditing supports.

Generally, because of the sensitive nature of this kind of audit trail, you will want to encapsulate the auditing and the trace tables in separate database schemas and procedures so that clients cannot interfere with the auditing process. See the earlier sections on schemas and authorization, authentication, and procedural encapsulation. Also, see the extensive discussion in Chapter 13 on tracing, which you can use to track SQL execution and a great deal of other information about the runtime behavior of an application system.

Mandatory Access Control

Mandatory access control is a security system that puts much stronger controls on access to objects in the database by associating a security label with each object and with each session. The labels provide a classification scheme that permits the server to judge whether to grant access to the object based on the level in the classification rather than on specific privileges.

Why would such a scheme be necessary? Under discretionary access control, data is just data. If you move data somewhere else, the privileges on that data come from the place it is, not from the data itself. For example, if a user has SELECT privilege on a table without GRANT option, the user can still copy the data to another table he or she has created with the same structure, and can then grant others access to this table. There are many similar situations that limit the ability of discretionary access control to manage security risks.

Mandatory access control deals with most of these issues by associating the security constraint with the data. When you copy the data, you also copy the security constraint. You can do this with privileges, but it is much easier to handle through a security-level classification scheme.

Trusted Oracle

Oracle provides a mandatory access control scheme that makes Oracle conform to the U.S. B1 TCSEC criteria and the E3 assurance level for the European ITSEC standard. This is an optional product called Trusted Oracle. It only works on operating systems that provide similar features with similar conformance to security standards. Windows and Macintosh cannot be Trusted Oracle servers, for example, nor can you field applications on the World Wide Web unless the browser is running under a secure operating system.

See the *Trusted Oracle Server Administrator's Guide* for details on the mandatory access control scheme in Trusted Oracle. The following gives you a summary of how all this works.

Each label in this scheme has a classification component, a category component, and a marking component.

The Classification Component

A *classification* is a hierarchical level that identifies the sensitivity of labeled information. You define the classifications and orders at the operating system level. Here are some examples: TOP SECRET, SECRET, SENSITIVE, and UNCLASSIFIED.

The Category Component

A *category* is a division within a classification that makes the classification regional. This permits you to restrict access to particular areas, even within the classification scheme. For example, you could have categories for each project, breaking up classifications by project. Only those sessions with labels containing the project category could see information relating to the project.

The Marking Component

A *marking* is a further piece of information within a classification that gets associated with the data under different circumstances. You could mark a particular object as PROPRIETARY, for example, and your applications could ensure that printing always marks PROPRIETARY objects with a specific warning about dissemination.

The mandatory access control mechanism works by comparing the object label to the session label you establish through your operating system security clearance when you log on to the session. This comparison works through the process of domination: one label *dominates* another if its classification is greater than or equal to that of the other label, and its categories are a superset of the other's categories. The label strictly dominates another if it dominates but does not match the other label. The label is not comparable if neither label dominates the other due to differences in the categories and classification. Your *security clearance* is the range of labels for which you are authorized to read and write information. You can read an object only if your label dominates the label of the object, and you can write to an object only if your label *matches* that of the object.

There are several Oracle system privileges that get around these constraints:

- *READUP:* Lets you read data with a label that strictly dominates your label

- *WRITEUP:* Lets you write data with a label that strictly dominates your label

- *WRITEDOWN:* Lets you write data with a label that your label strictly dominates

See the "Discretionary Access Control" section near the beginning of this chapter for more on Oracle discretionary access controls through system and object privileges for the context of these privileges.

To summarize, if you need serious security, the government or other customer will almost certainly require that your application conforms to B1 or other security standard. The combination of operating system and Trusted Oracle may make it possible to use Oracle Developer to develop such applications. Note, however, that Oracle Developer must run on the Trusted operating system to conform to the security standard.

Keeping Talbot's Safe

As an example of using Oracle Developer and Oracle security, this section considers the development of Talbot's security policy from start to finish. The example is very simple; a real security policy would be much more extensive.

Talbot's Security Risks

There are several possible security risks that the risk analysis of Talbot's computer operations identifies.

The major risks of system intrusion and intelligence gathering do not exist for Talbot's. Talbot's isolates its database physically with no access other than through the farm workstations, which the Talbots keep in locked offices around the farm. There is an exposure to intrusion through the local intranet running on a local area network, as it is accessible in unsecured areas, but the impact analysis shows that even the impact of a full system failure would be minimal. The intranet has firewall protection with careful controls over external access through the Internet and modems. The risk assessment team in this case decided that daily backups stored in a secure location and a disaster recovery policy were sufficient to handle any risk of system failure due to intrusion. They also decided that the impact of information leaked to competitors was very low and did not require extraordinary measures to protect data from unauthorized access.

344   Oracle Developer Starter Kit

Because Talbot's uses an operating system that provides no security, the risk assessment team decided to rely on database server security: Oracle user names and passwords.

The risks relating to the database contents include the three following possibilities:

- Corrections or changes to ledger entries could lead to auditing problems, which could in turn lead to problems with tax audits and corporate audits.

- There is a regulatory requirement that workers' addresses be kept private; the risk is of regulatory penalty or employee lawsuit if an address becomes available through inadvertent information leakage or lack of security measures.

- Talbot's experience with maintaining a skills database suggests that giving full access to everyone will likely result in inaccuracies in the database, rendering it useless.

The risk assessment team considered two possibilities for managing corrections to the ledger. The first was to maintain an audit trail by double-recording all updates to the database ledger. The advantage to this would be that the ledger would always be as correct as possible, while auditors could reconstruct the history of changes from the audit trail. The second possibility would be to require corrections to be separate ledger entries, correcting entries. The advantage to this approach would be reduced complexity, reduced system overhead, and ease in auditing. (The second approach is a standard one in accounting practices.) The team decided to disallow updates to ledger entries and to require that all corrections be through additional ledger entries. As additional security, the team decided to separate the Ledger table from the other tables into a password-protected schema.

The risk assessment team noted that part of accounting's job was to maintain the accounts payable information in the Person table. This did not extend to managing addresses (which will be discussed shortly).

The risk assessment team decided to separate the Lodging table into a separate schema to make it as secure as possible from intrusion. Only authorized individuals in human resources would have access to this data.

The remaining tables (Person, Skill, WorkerHasSkill) all reside in a single schema, with human resources having manipulation access and all others having query access only.

Talbot's Oracle Security Architecture

Figure 9-1 shows the original UML class diagram with the additional schema information represented as *packages*—containers for the various classes. Each schema corresponds to a specific Oracle user name and password.

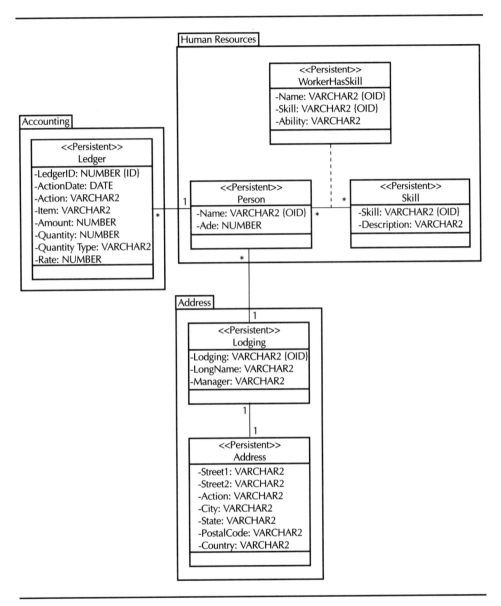

FIGURE 9-1. *Security schemas for Talbot's database*

Each actual user of the system will have an Oracle account with a distinct password. The security team recommended standard password maintenance procedures (changing passwords once a month, and so on).

The roles associated with these requirements are straightforward:

- *Accounting:* Needs to be able to query and insert ledger entries but not to update or delete them; needs to be able to query entries in the Person table; needs to be able to query, insert, update, and delete from the Person table, but cannot delete or update entries for individuals with addresses.

- *Address:* Owns and manages the private address table.

- *HR Skills:* Needs to be able to insert, update, and delete skills and relationships between people and skills.

- *HR Personnel:* Needs to be able to insert, update, and delete information from the Person table.

Besides these roles, there is the standard DBA role that Talbot assumes to create the schemas, users, roles, privileges, and so on.

To set up the database, Talbot logs on to Oracle through SQL*Plus as SYSTEM and executes the following six statements:

```
CREATE USER Human_Resources IDENTIFIED BY FT3R$27SD;
GRANT CONNECT, RESOURCE TO Talbot;
CREATE USER Accounting IDENTIFIED BY TYB##5X$5;
GRANT CONNECT, RESOURCE TO Accounting;
CREATE USER Lodging IDENTIFIED BY M45C$BHI_9Z;
GRANT CONNECT, RESOURCE TO Lodging;
```

Talbot then connects to each account and creates the schema for the account by running a script with the CREATE SCHEMA statement. When you create foreign key references to tables created by another user, you need to make sure you've already created those tables in that user. You thus need to create the tables in a specific order to allow foreign key definition. Alternatively, you can add all the foreign keys after creating all the tables by using the ALTER TABLE syntax for adding constraints.

First, create the Lodging schema, this way:

```
CREATE SCHEMA AUTHORIZATION Lodging
  CREATE TABLE Lodging (
    Lodging  VARCHAR(15) PRIMARY KEY, /* short name for lodging */
    LongName VARCHAR(40),             /* complete name */
    Manager  VARCHAR(25),             /* manager's name */
    Address  VARCHAR(30)              /* address of the lodging */);
GRANT REFERENCES ON Lodging to Human_Resources;
```

This last statement grants the REFERENCES privilege to the Human_Resources user, allowing the user to make a foreign key reference to the Lodging table in the Person table. Now, create the Human_Resources schema:

```
CREATE SCHEMA AUTHORIZATION Human_Resources
    CREATE TABLE Skill (
        Skill          VARCHAR(25) PRIMARY KEY, /* name of a capability */
        Description    VARCHAR(80)              /* description of the skill */
    )
    CREATE TABLE Person (
        Name           VARCHAR(25) PRIMARY KEY,      /* worker's name */
        Age            INTEGER,                      /* age in years */
        Lodging        VARCHAR(15) REFERENCES Lodging.Lodging
                            /* reference to short name of lodging */
    )
    CREATE TABLE WorkerHasSkill (
        Name           VARCHAR(25) REFERENCES Person, /* worker's name */
        Skill          VARCHAR(25) REFERENCES Skill,  /* capability name */
        Ability        VARCHAR(15),            /* how skilled is the worker? */
        PRIMARY KEY (Name, Skill)
    );
GRANT REFERENCES ON Person TO Accounting;
```

As before, this last statement allows the Accounting user to make a foreign key reference to the Person table from its Ledger table. Also, notice that the foreign key REFERENCES clause in the Person table uses the authorization identifier Lodging to prefix the name of the table Lodging. Finally, create the Accounting schema, along with the LedgerSequence for the Ledger primary key values:

```
CREATE SEQUENCE LedgerSequence /* sequence numbers for Ledger */;
CREATE SCHEMA AUTHORIZATION Accounting
    CREATE TABLE Ledger (
        LedgerID       INTEGER
                           PRIMARY KEY,/* sequence number, primary key */
        ActionDate     DATE,          /* when */
        Action         VARCHAR(8),    /* bought, sold, paid, received */
        Item           VARCHAR(30),   /* what */
        Quantity       INTEGER,       /* how many */
        QuantityType   VARCHAR(10),   /* quantity: lbs, bushels, etc. */
        Rate           NUMERIC(9,2),  /* how much per quantity type  */
        Amount         NUMERIC(9,2),  /* rate * quantity */
        Person         VARCHAR(25)
                           REFERENCES Human_Resources.Person /* who */
    );
```

With all the users and tables created, you can now set up the roles with their privileges. The SYSTEM user is the DBA, which already has all the needed privileges. Connect to SYSTEM to create the roles:

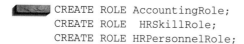

```
CREATE ROLE AccountingRole;
CREATE ROLE  HRSkillRole;
CREATE ROLE HRPersonnelRole;
```

Now connect to the Accounting user to grant privileges on Ledger to the Accounting role:

```
GRANT SELECT, INSERT ON Ledger TO AccountingRole;
```

Now connect to the Human_Resources user to grant privileges on the Person, Skill, and WorkerHasSkill tables:

```
GRANT SELECT, INSERT, UPDATE, DELETE ON Person to AccountingRole;
GRANT SELECT, INSERT, UPDATE, DELETE ON Skill to HRSkillRole;
GRANT SELECT, INSERT, UPDATE, DELETE ON WorkerHasSkill to HRSkillRole;
GRANT SELECT, INSERT, UPDATE, DELETE ON Person to HRPersonnelRole;
```

NOTE
Discretionary access control cannot use privileges to enforce the restriction of the Accounting role not being able to update users with addresses; you will have to enforce this constraint in database triggers. You could do this by creating a separate view that excludes those rows with a WHERE clause. That solution, however, does not allow the application to see those names, which violates another requirement to be able to query all the names. You could use the view for updating and the underlying table for querying, but this is hard to do given how Oracle Developer blocks work. You would need two separate blocks, one for query purposes and the other for query/update purposes.

Now, having created all the roles with all the required privileges, you can create the individual users and grant them their roles. For example, to set up an

accounting user and a personnel user, connect to SYSTEM in SQL*Plus and issue
the following statements:

```
CREATE USER User1 IDENTIFIED BY JU8##NMY78$;
GRANT CONNECT TO User1;
GRANT AccountingRole TO User1;
GRANT SELECT ON FRM50_ENABLED_ROLES TO User1;
CREATE USER User2 IDENTIFIED BY H#17_TH$5;
GRANT CONNECT TO User2;
GRANT HRPersonnelRole TO User2;
GRANT SELECT ON FRM50_ENABLED_ROLES TO User2;
```

TIP
*You can use the Security Manager, a part of the
Oracle Enterprise Manager suite, to create users and
grant privileges with a user-friendly interface.*

NOTE
*The grant of SELECT privilege on
FRM50_ENABLED_ROLES is necessary so that the
user can use the menu security feature of Oracle
Developer. Without it, you get the Forms error
message FRM-10256, "User is not authorized
to run Form Builder menu." This also assumes
you have installed the Forms database tables
from the Administration program group, which
is also required.*

Talbot's Application Security

The Ledger form must satisfy the requirement of not being able to update or delete
rows in the Ledger table. Through the AccountingRole security role, the Oracle
database enforces this restriction. If you try to update a value or delete a row in
Ledger, you will get an error when you save the changes to the database because
the SQL statements will fail.

Although this solves the problem, it is not as well designed as it might be. One
principle of a good interface is to give immediate feedback when you make a mistake.
Relying on database security gives you feedback only when you save, not when you
actually change a value or delete a record. To enforce this constraint with more
immediacy in the interface, you need to put a little extra code in the application.

To address these issues, all you need to do is turn off the Update Allowed and Delete Allowed properties in the Ledger block. This will stop users from updating or deleting any values queried from the database, and the feedback is immediate through a standard Forms error message.

NOTE

You could alternatively set the Column Security flag in the module to True, but in this case the Update Allowed flag on the block seems more direct. An alternative to raising an error might be to turn off the menu and key methods of removing a record (that is, the Record|Remove menu item and the standard keypress for [Delete Record]). This would yield a better interface by not permitting the action at all, but the work involved (creating custom menus, and so on) seems out of proportion to the additional benefits. If you already have your own menus and keypress definitions for these items, you should change them there.

In developing other applications, the Talbots could use the menu security system to configure the menus in their applications differently based on the Oracle roles. For example, the Ledger form could have data manipulation menu items (such as Create Record or Delete Record) enabled through the AccountingRole security role and disabled through the other roles. It could also have the Ledger Summary report enabled for AccountingRole users and disabled for other users. See the earlier section "Menu Access Controls" for details and examples on setting up menu security.

In summary, Oracle Developer, working in conjunction with Oracle or another DBMS, gives you strong security tools. Using them takes some thought and careful preparation, but when you finish you will be able to sleep at night, knowing that your applications are as secure as you can make them.

CHAPTER
10

Advanced Design
for Reuse

his last chapter in Part II deals with several topics relating to advanced design of applications. When you have mastered triggers and processes and understood the basic operations of forms, reports, and graphics, you are ready to optimize your architecture. Oracle Developer provides several tools by which you can make your applications adapt more easily to changes in the environment or to the differing needs of multifarious users.

Recycling: Everyone Should Do It

Reusability is the ability to use objects in different contexts. This translates directly into increased productivity through reducing the amount of code you must build for each new requirement you undertake. The more code you can reuse in new applications, the less time, effort, and money it will take to produce the new applications. Reusing code also makes your applications more consistent, yielding many benefits in ease of use and maintenance.

If you design your objects for optimum utility, you will make them more reusable by making the development team want to use the features. Part of this is a selling job: your objects must have the documentation and "public relations material" that will let the team know what the object does for them. The rest of the job is to make the object as flexible as possible, given constraints on the way your particular system works and the cost of building and testing the object. The following sections give you some tools to increase flexibility throughout your Oracle Developer code.

TIP

You will also benefit from reusing other teams' code, such as off-the-shelf Java Beans and ActiveX components you can buy rather than build. Chapter 15 goes into detail on the technology that Oracle Developer provides for integrating off-the-shelf components into your applications. Building a culture of reuse inside your company with respect to the code you develop is just as important as making appropriate build/buy decisions, however.

One of the strongest benefits of Oracle Developer is its object-based nature. Because each application comprises a set of objects, and because Oracle Developer makes it easy to reuse them, it encourages you to build compatible objects. As with any software system, you can find ways to make objects incompatible, and some objects are essentially incompatible for reasons often beyond your control. Oracle Developer gives you the tools to easily reuse code. If you follow the recommendations in the following sections, you should be able to optimize your ability to reuse objects in different applications.

The following sections summarize or introduce the elements of Oracle Developer that contribute to reuse in major ways. You should also consult Chapter 12 for approaches to packaging PL/SQL functions and procedures for reuse in different modules.

Modules

Oracle Developer structures its operations around a few major objects that you have already seen in action, the Oracle Developer modules:

- *Form:* A module that contains data blocks, records, and items that represent an interactive database application for presenting data in forms

- *Menu:* A module that contains menus and menu items that represent the interface to a set of command actions

- *Report:* A module that contains a data model and a layout for a report that you can generate from data in the database

- *Display:* A module that contains one or more charts or other graphics and one or more queries that represents a graphical display of data from the database

- *External query:* A query you build using the Report Builder to which you can refer in other modules

- *Library:* A library of PL/SQL code you build using the Form, Report, or Graphics Builders, to which you can refer in other modules

As you design your modules, you should think about them as reusable components of applications, not just as standalone applications. If you design your components in such a way that you can use them in other applications, you will optimize reusability in your development life cycle.

The key to module reusability is to *decouple* the modules as much as possible from their environment. *Coupling* is the degree to which a module uses data and operations external to the module. Here are some guidelines for decoupling modules.

Where possible, do not use variables from outside the module, such as global variables or variables in other modules. The more you use such variables, the less you will be able to reuse the module in different contexts. Also, it is hard to predict how other modules will use shared variables, so using them when interacting with other modules is likely to produce unpleasant surprises. A good alternative to using global variables is to create a package that exports a variable object. When you refer to a package attached to your module, Oracle Developer loads the package into memory for the duration of the session. This means you can use the variable from anywhere in the module, but nothing outside the module can access it. These variables are also an alternative to using the global parameters and can be faster to access under some conditions. Chapter 13 has more details on using packages.

Try to isolate application-specific or platform-specific components in procedures or libraries to decouple your module from the underlying dependencies on a specific application or platform. For example, if you only need certain text onscreen in a specific application, do it in a procedure you call from an instance trigger. If you want application-specific help, put it in a PL/SQL library and switch the library for different applications.

Avoid boilerplate text (text hard-coded into the canvas, report, or display) that ties the object into a specific application. Minimize the use of titles and especially help text in boilerplate. Use generic terminology, and use the database table and column names where possible instead of the application version. You can always modify it if it really does not work, and you can do some things to parameterize those parts of the application that need to be application specific. See the following sections.

NOTE
Much of the text you display in a form consists of the prompts for fields. Oracle Developer Forms provides prompt properties to contain such text, and the Oracle Translation Builder gives you tools to manage internationalization. What remains is miscellaneous text telling users what to do or identifying groups of items, for example. You should try to minimize such text.

If you use many PL/SQL procedures and functions, cluster these procedures and functions into packages and libraries with high cohesion. Design your modules in layers and subsystems that minimize the connections between each other. The more connections you make between layers through inadequate structuring, the less you will be able to decouple a module for partial reuse elsewhere. Also, the more you hide the functionality of your module in layers, the easier it will be for developers and designers to understand what your module does. The top layer will speak for the complex interactions hidden within the module.

Templates and Components

If you cannot reuse modules because they are too application specific, you can at least get some mileage from abstracting various elements into templates. A *template* is an object that you can use to format a module with basic options or contents. If you have standards and development guidelines, build them into templates that you can reuse in building modules. You can create a form, report, or display module, for example, that has all the standard settings that represent your standards and guidelines. Then the development team can copy that module as a template to start developing their own forms. For reports and charts, you can develop special template objects that represent default information in a structured way. This section goes into detail on all these topics and more.

Modules and templates are the basic building blocks of Oracle Developer. The more reusable you make your modules, and the more you can use standard templates, the more productive your development process will be.

Forms Templates

Oracle Developer Forms does not provide explicit templates, unlike the Reports and Graphics components (see the following sections "Reports Templates" and "Graphics Templates"). The Welcome window of the Form Builder lets you build a new form based on another form. Clicking on the "Build a New Form Based on a Template" radio button in the Welcome dialog box presents you with an Open Form dialog box that lets you choose an FMB file to use as a template. Oracle Developer then copies the form you choose into a new form in the Form Builder.

NOTE
There is no way to get to this dialog box other than through starting the Form Builder. This is the only way you can use this limited template feature of Forms. You can also open the template form using the Open tool in the usual way, then save it under another name using the File|Save As menu item.

You should build a standard form with the objects that you want to standardize. You can then use the Data Block Wizard and the Layout Wizard more effectively to build your blocks and to fill in your canvases. Table 10-1 suggests some possible uses for these standard objects.

Object	Suggested Uses
Form	Standard form settings in the Property Palette such as Coordinate System/Information, Menu Module, and option settings
Form trigger	When-New-Form-Instance to set up standard window sizes and other initializing PL/SQL
Alerts	Standard error and warning alerts
Attached libraries	Standard libraries that multiple forms share
Canvases	Standard canvases with appropriate ruler and layout settings
Parameters	Standard parameters that every form uses
Pop-up menus	Standard pop-ups that all applications share
Program units	Standard program units specific to the form, such as initialization procedures called from the When-New-Form-Instance trigger or standard procedures for sending messages to customer support about problems with the form
Reports	Standard reports that all forms share
Windows	Standard windows and dialog boxes

TABLE 10-1. *Uses for Forms Template Objects*

Reports Templates

About the third time you embed the corporate logo and name in a report, you start to wonder whether there's a better way. There is—the report template. Chapter 4 demonstrated its use with the Talbot.TDF standard report template. This section shows you how this template was built.

A report template is a special file that contains boilerplate text and graphics along with example fields using the different data types, character, number, and date. The Report Wizard templates screen lets you specify which template to reuse. The new report it creates uses the template boilerplate and fields to format your initial prototype. You can then customize the prototype in the Live Previewer to get exactly the report you want. Using a template thus standardizes the parts of the report you don't change and saves you the effort of redoing all the standard elements. This can mean a substantial increase in productivity for reports with extensive formatting.

Oracle Developer ships with a set of standard templates. Unfortunately, these are not "generic" templates; they are more like demonstration files, as they have embedded images and text for demo companies. These standard templates appear in a list in the Report Wizard automatically. You can use these as the basis for your templates, but you will need to modify them before you can use them.

1. To open a standard template, use File|Open to display the Open dialog box.

2. Set the Files of Type field to Report Templates (*.TDF) using the drop-down list.

3. Navigate to the template directory (usually an Admin folder and its subfolders somewhere under Oracle_Home) and select the file you want to open (CORP1 in the example here).

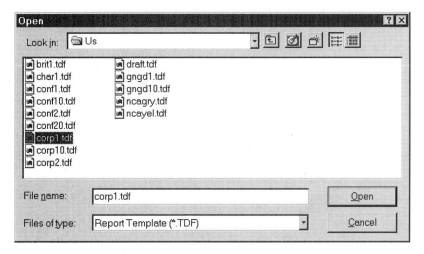

The template file opens in the Template Editor, as there is no Live Previewer for a template (you aren't looking at data, just data type fields).

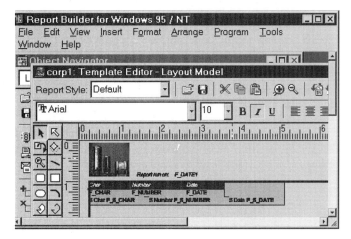

If you look at the Object Navigator, you have a new module under the Templates heading, CORP1. The CORP1 template is a moderately fancy layout with a bitmap logo, a corporate name, and some heading formatting and layout settings. To use it, you need to replace the image and the corporate name.

4. You will want to save the new template with a different name rather than replacing the standard template. Use File|Save As to do that.

5. Edit the boilerplate by removing the existing image and replacing it with your own logo, in this case that of Talbot's Farm.

6. Change the name of the company as well, and move the boilerplate around to suit the new logo graphic.

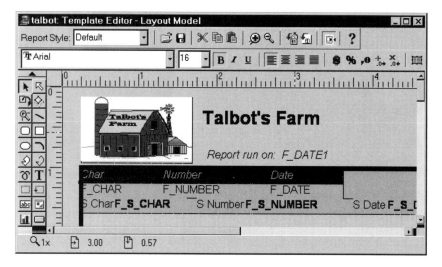

7. Save the template with the Save tool.

   Now you can create a report using the template.

8. Select the Reports heading and click on the Create tool to create a new report using the Report Wizard.

9. Create the Ledger Summary report as in Chapter 4, but instead of using the Draft template, use the Talbot template by clicking on the Template file radio button and browsing to the new Talbot.TDF file.

NOTE
The predefined templates in the Report Wizard are built into the system, and there is no way to add to them or to change the names of the files to which the choices point. In addition, you can't change the wizard thumbnail graphics that illustrate the report, as these are based on special bitmaps from the template directory. You are better off totally ignoring these predefined templates and using the Template file radio button to choose a specific file instead of modifying the standard templates.

The Template Editor, like the Layout Editor for a report, lets you look at the body, margins, header, and trailer of the template. Unlike the Layout Editor, when you look at the body of the template, you cannot draw fields, add graphics, or do anything but display the Property Palette for the default section frame. If you click on the Margin, Header, or Trailer tools, you see the various drawing and formatting tools appear, indicating you can draw a boilerplate or add fields as you wish. The template thus permits you to customize your margins, header pages, and trailer pages, but it does not permit customization of the boilerplate or field layout of the body. That's the job of the Report Wizard when you build a report from the template.

If you look at the structure of the template in the Object Navigator, as shown in Figure 10-1, you see five main sections in the template:

- *Data Model:* The system and user parameters of the report

- *Layout Model:* The body and margins of the report

- *Report Triggers:* The Before Report, After Report, Between Pages, Before Parameter Form, and After Parameter Form triggers

- *Program Units:* The PL/SQL program units of the report

- *Attached Libraries:* The PL/SQL libraries you want to use in program units of the report

Using the Data Model section, you can set up default values for the various system parameters such as DESFORMAT or ORIENTATION. For example, you could set DESFORMAT to Printer instead of Preview if you wanted to default all your reports to send the report to the printer rather than the Previewer. You can also add standard user parameters.

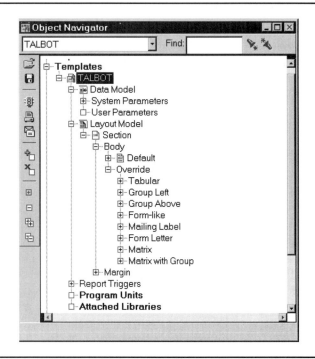

FIGURE 10-1. *Object Navigator with report template hierarchy*

You should use the Template Editor to modify the Margin object using the visual editor and drawing tools. The Body section, however, contains an extensive array of objects you can use to customize the different kinds of reports. Figure 10-2 shows the hierarchy of objects in the Body section. The first object is the Default section, which lays out the basic settings for the report body section. It consists of settings for the Frames, Field Labels/Headings, Fields, Summary Labels, and Summaries. Using these settings, you can control the default appearance of virtually every aspect of the report section.

The next object, Override, contains a set of objects that override the Default section settings for a specific type of report. Each of these objects corresponds to one type of report, such as the Tabular report, the Mailing Label report, or the Matrix report. Each of these objects in turn contains objects for the different report sections, each of which eventually contains the same five objects listed under the Default section. Using these objects, you can override the defaults in the Default section for each specific kind of section in each kind of report.

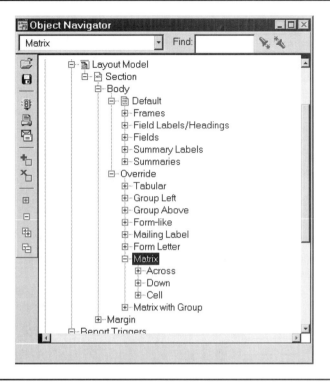

FIGURE 10-2. *Object Navigator with Body object hierarchy*

NOTE
There is no way to specify a default format mask in the template for fields of one type or another. All you can specify is their justification.

Finally, you can attach libraries and program units to the template to make them accessible to every report. This lets you build standard subprograms and packages, either in libraries or within the template, and use them automatically in any report you create without having to attach or import them.

If you invest some time in developing thorough report templates for your standard reporting situations, you will find your productivity improving dramatically over time. You will be able to build reports quickly without having to make extensive formatting changes to the basic layout.

Graphics Templates

If you start using the Graphics Builder extensively, you will find yourself doing the same kind of chart over and over again. You might also find yourself building many charts that look identical, such as drill-down charts or multiple-chart displays. Instead of individually customizing each chart, you should build a custom chart template that formats all charts with similar characteristics.

Setting up chart templates is as easy as setting up charts.

1. Start the Graphics Builder, open a display, and find the Templates category in the Object Navigator. (It is right under the Layout category for the display.)

2. Select the category and click on the Create tool or use the Navigator|Create menu entry to create a new template (template0).

Figure 10-3 shows the resulting Chart Template Editor.

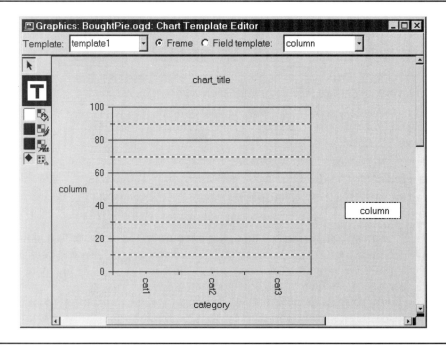

FIGURE 10-3. *The Chart Template Editor with frame template*

The Editor shows the frame editor with its *frame template,* which contains the title, axis labels, and legend position, set up for a column chart. Using the Type menu, you can select any of the over 50 default templates (line charts, column charts, bar charts, pie charts, Gantt charts, scatter charts, or tables, for example).

You can move around or change any of the frame elements in this editor. For example, you can select all the elements and change the font to Arial 10 Bold instead of using the system font. By double-clicking on any element, you can set various parameters to make the chart frame appear any way you want.

You can have one frame template in each chart template, but you can have multiple field templates. A *field template* is a specification for the display characteristics of a particular set of data in the chart. You can associate a different field template with different columns in the query to display the data from each column using a particular style. This lets you set up a standard set of line and fill colors, fonts, symbols, or any other characteristic of a data element display.

This is the default field template for a column chart:

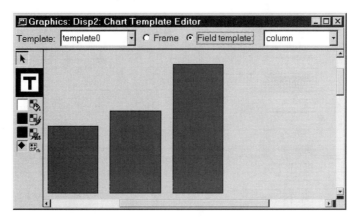

You can assign a particular chart template to a chart through the Chart Property Palette. Double-click on the chart object in the Object Navigator. The Template field at the bottom of the Chart tab (Figure 10-4) lets you pull down a list of the available chart templates, and the chart reconfigures according to the template when you click on OK.

You can assign a particular field template to a column through the Values tab of the Chart Property Palette (Figure 10-5). Select the column you want to format; then pull down the list of available field templates and assign the one you want to that column.

If you experiment with the template capabilities of Oracle Developer, you will find it much easier to develop large numbers of graphics using your graphics standards. Your goal in developing templates is to reduce the amount of custom work you need to do for a particular chart to only the changes that chart requires

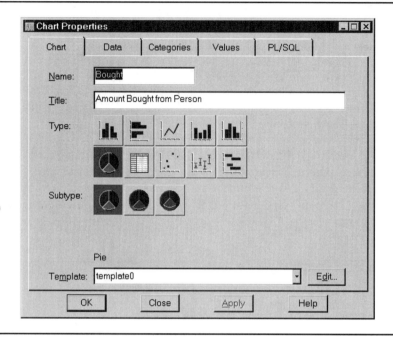

FIGURE 10-4. *The Chart Property Palette with chart template pull-down list*

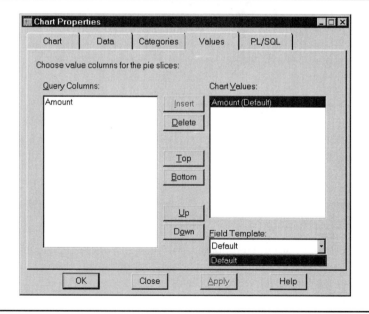

FIGURE 10-5. *The Chart Property Palette with field template pull-down list*

(such as the Other pie slice in the Talbot pie charts). Things such as fonts and colors should be standard, not decided on a chart-by-chart basis.

To get the maximum use from your templates, you should export them into separate template files.

1. Select the template you want to export in the Object Navigator.

2. Choose the File|Export|Template menu item. This displays the Export dialog box.

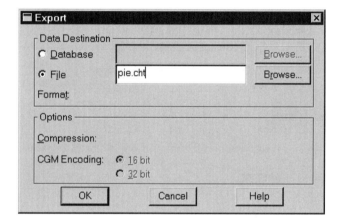

3. Enter a filename ("PIE.CHT," for example).

4. Click on OK to save the template in some central directory.

5. When you want to use the template in another display, import the template into the display. Select the Templates node under the display or display the Chart Template Editor and choose File|Import|Template to display the Import dialog box, which is very similar to the Export dialog box.

6. Find the file and click on OK to import the template.

External Queries and the Query Builder

An *external query* is a text file that contains an SQL SELECT statement. You can refer to this external query from the data model of any report. By separating the query into a module, you are making the query reusable to different reports.

NOTE
The Oracle Developer documentation consistently refers to this as an ANSI-standard SELECT, but Reports does not enforce this restriction on the SQL. The presence of Oracle comments and other elements in the published examples indicates that the query can be any SQL query that your target database can understand and process.

When you build a report data model, think hard about the queries you are creating and see whether you can build them as external queries that would be useful in other applications.

Creating and Using an External Query

1. To create an external query, locate and select the External Query heading in the Report Builder Object Navigator and click on the Add tool to create an Untitled external query.

2. Double-click on the External Query icon to display the External Query Definition Editor for the query you've just created:

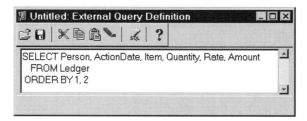

3. After you enter the query, close the Editor and select the UNTITLED object in the Object Navigator.

4. Save it to a file by clicking on the Save tool, giving the file the extension .SQL, such as "LEDGER.SQL."

5. To add the query using the Property Palette, find the Query icon and double-click on it.

6. Click on the More button in the External Query Source File property, or just double-click the property. This displays a standard Open dialog box

through which you can choose the Ledger.SQL file. You then see the SQL Query Statement dialog box with the statement.

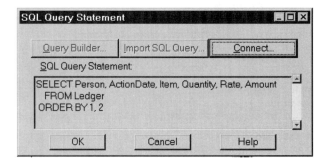

NOTE
Alternatively, you can open this dialog box directly by clicking on the More button in the SQL Query Statement property and then clicking on the Import SQL Query button to get the Open dialog box.

7. To use the Report Wizard, open the Wizard using the Tools|Report Wizard menu item; then choose the Data tab page.

8. Use the Import SQL Query button to open the Ledger.SQL file as before.

9. Click on Finish.

NOTE
Use the filename for the query and rely on the path in the registry variable REPORTS60_PATH to identify the directory in which you store the file. You can then move the file around to different file systems and different platforms without having to redo your Query Property Palette entries. Once you make the query refer to an external query, you cannot edit the query in the Property Palette, even though it displays it in the normal manner. You must select the external query object and edit it by double-clicking on its icon. When you click on OK to dismiss the Property Palette, Oracle Developer parses the query and reports any problems.

Now that you have defined the external query, you can refer to it from any report. For example, if you wanted to create a new report based on the ledger query but with a different layout, different summarization and grouping, and so on, you could build the new data model and refer to the external query in the Query Property Palette just as in the previous example.

Using the Query Builder

You can make use of the Query Builder through the Report Wizard. This interface lets you build an external query through the Query Builder that you can save for later reuse in other reports.

You get to the Query Builder from the SQL Query Statement dialog box or the Report Wizard Data tab page, just as for external queries. Instead of clicking on Import SQL Query, click on the Query Builder button. The Query Builder lets you build SQL queries using a graphical drawing approach. Figure 10-6 shows the Ledger query in the Query Builder. When you click on OK, the Query Builder creates the SQL SELECT statement and places it into your SQL window.

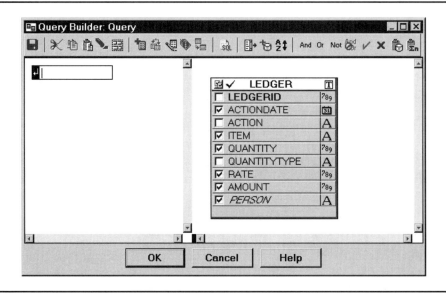

FIGURE 10-6. *The Query Builder with the Ledger query*

NOTE
Personally, I find developing queries through writing SQL much easier than all the dragging and dropping and drawing you have to do to use the Query Builder or other graphical tools, particularly with complex queries. Developers not comfortable with SQL or not having their database schema at their fingertips will probably find the Query Builder easier to use than coding the actual SQL. I highly recommend becoming totally comfortable with SQL coding (and with your schema) if you are going to develop even moderately sized client/server or Internet applications, however. Becoming familiar with the Query Builder is also a good idea.

Lexical References and Bind Variables

Sometimes, as with any piece of code, you could make the query reusable by parameterizing it. That is, if you could specify a placeholder in the query and replace it at runtime with a value, you could use the query in more places.

There are two ways to do this in Report Builder. You can use lexical references to replace chunks of text in the SQL statement, or you can include bind variables in the SQL statement. A *lexical reference* is a reference to a column or parameter in your report that you preface with an ampersand (&). Oracle Developer parses the SQL when you refer to the SQL statement and accept the Property Palette or when you run the report. At this time, it substitutes the value of the variable into the SQL statement as text.

A *bind variable* is a reference to a column or parameter in your report that you preface with a colon (:). Instead of substituting text, this construct tells the Reports Runtime engine to substitute a value.

NOTE
The references and variables are either to data model columns or to report parameters. This book recommends that external queries refer only to parameters; if you refer to report columns, you are coupling the query too closely to the application. To reuse the external query, the other reports would need to have the same column defined in the data model, which is too constraining for good reuse. See the later section, "Parameterizing Your Applications," for details on using parameters. Also, you will find the rules for referring to columns at different levels in your data model quite confusing, and this is always a good way to add defects to your application.

The difference between the lexical reference and the bind variable can seem mysterious until you have used each of them. The practical difference in a report is that you can use lexical references to substitute whole chunks of the SQL as *text,* such as an entire WHERE or GROUP BY clause. But you can only use a bind variable in a situation where you could put a literal value, such as a number, string, or date. You will usually use bind variables when you want to use a value in an SQL SELECT or WHERE clause comparison. You will usually use lexical substitution when you can figure out a way to make the statement more reusable by substituting pieces of the statement text on a report-by-report basis. Also, you do not have lexical substitution available in PL/SQL code, only in SQL statements.

For example, say you have a report that you want to parameterize with a specific type of ledger action, such as Bought or Sold. You might do this with lexical substitution:

```
SELECT Person, ActionDate, Item, Quantity, Rate
    FROM Ledger
&WHERE_CLAUSE
ORDER BY Person, ActionDate
```

In this case, however, you would usually just use a bind variable:

```
SELECT Person, ActionDate, Item, Quantity, Rate
    FROM Ledger
   WHERE Action = :ActionType
ORDER BY Person, ActionDate
```

The first example takes the parameter WHERE_CLAUSE and lets you substitute the entire text of the WHERE clause: "WHERE Action = 'Bought'". The format is so specific and regular, though, it makes more sense to structure it for users rather than requiring that they understand WHERE clause syntax. In the second example, all they need to do is supply the value for the ActionType parameter: 'Bought' or 'Sold', for example.

An instance of a good use of lexical reference is when you want to refer to different tables in different reports but with otherwise identical SQL. You could have several different tables with various kinds of people in them, all of which share the columns in the report. You could use the following external query to represent the SQL for the report query:

```
SELECT Name, Age
    FROM &PersonTable
ORDER BY Name
```

The parameter PersonTable would contain the precise name of the table from which you want the report to get its data. You could not use a bind variable in this case because there is nowhere in the FROM clause you could put a bind variable; it only contains table names, which are identifiers. "FROM 'WorkingPerson'", for example, would yield a syntax error because of the single quotes, and with a bind variable there is no way to remove the quotes and treat the string as a table name.

The rules for using lexical substitution and bind variables are quite complex, particularly if you refer to columns at different levels in your data model.

NOTE
You should define your parameters (or columns) and give them initial values before referring to them from an SQL statement. Accepting the Query Property Palette parses the query and also creates variables for you, but you may want more control over the process than that.

Named Visual Attributes

A *named visual attribute* is an object in a form or menu module that contains a set of visual attribute option settings. These objects act as formatting agents for the module objects to which you apply them. When you apply the named visual attribute, the object takes on only those aspects of the attribute that make sense for that object. When you change the values in the attribute, the corresponding values also change in the objects to which you have applied the attribute. Table 10-2 lists the properties you can set through named visual attributes.

If you carefully design your set of named visual attributes, you can copy them from module to module to apply your standard visual attributes with nothing more than setting the items to use the visual attribute object. This also lets you change a standard by just changing the named visual attributes rather than having to change all the object visual attributes throughout your modules. For example, in the form tutorial in Chapter 4, you had to convert all the text to use the MS Sans Serif font instead of the default font. You could change the default font in the initialization file, but another way to do this would be a named visual attribute that sets text to MS Sans Serif Medium 8.

You should consider the different combinations of visual attributes you are likely to use in your applications. Create a separate named visual attribute object for each combination of visual attributes you are likely to use. Put these into your form and menu templates so that developers start with the appropriate sets of attributes.

To create a named visual attribute through the Object Navigator, find the Visual Attributes heading under the module, right below the Reports heading, and click on the Create button. To apply the named visual attribute to an object, select the object

Property	Description
Font Name	The name of the font (MS Sans Serif, Arial, and so on)
Font Size	The font size in points
Font Weight	Weight of the font (Light, Medium, Bold, and every shade in between)
Font Style	Style of the font (Plain, Italic, Oblique, Underline, and so on)
Font Spacing	Spacing of font elements (Dense, Normal, Expand, and every width in between)
Foreground Color	Color of the foreground region or text
Background Color	Color of the background region
Fill Pattern	Pattern for the fill region in background and foreground colors (arrows, balls, carrot, chair, and many equally well-named patterns are available; don't use these if you want your application to be portable)
Character Mode Logical Attribute	The name of the logical attribute in the Oracle Terminal resource file to use as the basis of device attributes for a character mode version of your application, if any
White on Black	For monochrome displays, specifies white text on a black background if True or Yes

TABLE 10-2.   *Properties in the Named Visual Attribute Object*

and display its Property Palette; then set the Visual Attribute Name property to the name of the named visual attribute object.

Property Classes

The nature of named visual attributes limits their impact to fonts, colors, and patterns. Another kind of object provides a much more extensive level of shared property definition in form and menu modules: the property class. The *property class* is an object belonging to a module that contains a set of properties, *any* properties. Just as with a named visual attribute, when you base an object on a property class, you get all the properties of that class that make sense for the kind of object you are defining. Again, when you change the class, you change the properties of all the objects based on that class.

TIP
A property class can contain a named visual attribute, letting you make the most of both approaches to reuse.

Inheritance and the Property Class

The property class gives Oracle Developer a form of inheritance. *Inheritance* is a relationship between objects such that the child object has all the properties of the parent object plus whatever additional ones make it different. In most object-oriented programming languages, inheritance represents a typing hierarchy: the child is *a kind of* the parent. Figure 10-7 shows a simple example of an object-oriented inheritance hierarchy.

The root class is the Object class; every object has certain characteristics that its subclasses inherit. The next class down is the Person class; every Person has a name, an address, and a home phone number, as well as the attributes that it inherits from the Object class. The next class down from that is the Employee class, with each Employee having an extension, a department number, and a salary, as well as the attributes inherited from the Person class and the Object class. On the

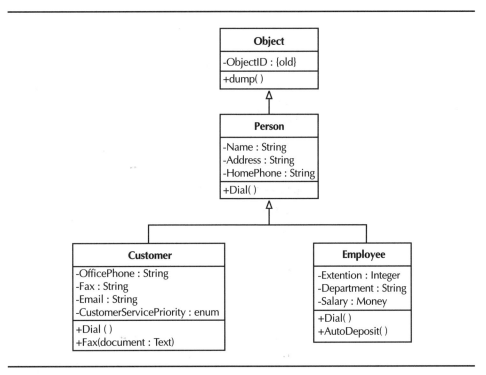

FIGURE 10-7. *An example inheritance hierarchy*

same level as Employee is Customer; a customer is also a kind of person (that is, inherits from the Person class). The Customer, however, has an office phone number, a fax number, an e-mail address, and a customer service priority ranking. Again, the Customer has all the attributes of a Person and an Object. All of these classes determine the structure of each object of the class. That is, you can create many different Customer and Employee objects, and each of these objects has the structure of its class of objects. The Object and Person classes are *abstract* classes, that is, classes that do not themselves correspond to objects. Their only purpose is to represent the shared properties of their subclasses.

The property class relationship to the object in Oracle Developer is somewhat different from the usual object-oriented way of doing things. In an object-oriented system, when you create an object from a class, the object gets its attributes and behavior from the class. You create different kinds of objects with different attributes and behavior by creating additional subclasses of the class. With property classes, on the other hand, when you associate an object with the property class, you take the values of the properties from the corresponding properties in the property class. Although similar to inheritance, this is in reality quite different.

Property classes let you assign default values to properties. In most object-oriented programming environments, you can also add properties to your objects; that is not the purpose of property classes. The property classes supply the initial values for the properties, which you can then override to customize the object to your needs. The object does not get all the properties from the property class, just the values for the ones the object already supports. On the other hand, when you supply triggers through property classes, the objects you subclass inherit those triggers and their behavior—a key reuse benefit. You can thus code triggers once in a property class and reuse them in its subclasses. See the following section, "Triggers in Property Classes," for details on using triggers in property classes.

The property class is an excellent way to build reusability into your modules. What you are doing is abstracting the property values into shared parents. As long as the values you assign in the parent class apply equally to all the children, you save yourself the coding of those properties in the child objects. Perhaps more importantly, when you change the parent, all the children pick up the change, as long as they actually share the default value and you have not overridden it in the object.

Another advantage of property classes is that you can inherit a property class in them. This lets you create parents of parents of parents in the same kind of inheritance hierarchy of abstract classes you find in object-oriented systems. You can use this hierarchical structure to get more exact combinations of properties, and this makes the property classes more reusable. For example, you could construct a huge property class with all the known attributes of all items in it. When you assigned this, the object to which you assigned it would pick up the relevant properties and ignore the rest. But if you had differences between objects, you would have a different, equally massive Property Palette. Instead, you could abstract the properties shared between the different property classes into a higher-level property class until you reached the highest level where all objects would share the properties. Then the lower-level classes would contain just those properties relevant to your object, which would be much easier to understand and to deal with.

NOTE
The ability to subclass objects gives you a more general way of inheriting properties. See the section "Subclassing" later in this chapter for details. Often, subclassing an object, and especially an Object Library object, is preferable to creating a property class.

Creating a Property Class Hierarchy

You can create a property class in either of two ways: by creating a new property class object and adding properties, or by using a current object as a template in the Property Palette to create a property class with all the properties and settings of the current object.

The Property Classes heading in the Object Navigator is right below Program Units for form or menu modules. To create a new property class, select the heading and click on the Create tool.

Once you have created the property class, double-click on its icon to display its Property Palette. The tools on the toolbar at the top of the Property Palette control the addition and removal of properties in different ways.

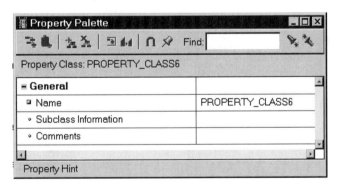

Click on the Add Property tool in the Property Palette toolbar to display the Properties LOV dialog box. Select a property from the list, and then set the property value to whatever you want.

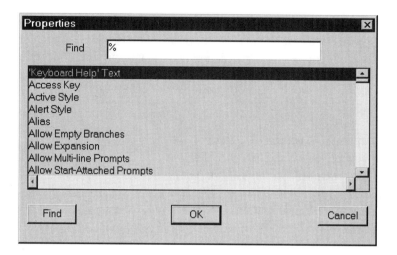

You can also copy properties into the Property Palette from an existing object. Select the object from which you want to copy all the properties and display the Property Palette for the object. Click on the Copy Properties tool in the Property Palette toolbar to copy all the object's properties and their settings.

Find and select the property class object and click on the Paste Properties tool to paste all the copied properties into the property class.

To remove unwanted properties, select the property you want to remove and click on the Delete Property tool to delete it.

You can create a property class directly from another object. First, select the object and display its Property Palette. Click on the Property Class tool to create a Property Palette by copying the properties and values from the object you are displaying. Oracle Developer informs you that it is creating a new property class and gives you the name of the class. You can then select that property class object in the Object Navigator and add more properties or remove ones that you know you

will not want to inherit in the objects based on the property class. Usually, these removed properties will be the ones that change for each object you create, such as the horizontal or vertical position in the canvas.

The final step is creating a property class that inherits its properties from another property class. You use the same techniques as before to create a property class from an object, but the object is another property class. If you are creating your hierarchy bottom up, you can remove properties from the superclass using the Delete Property tool. You then have the properties that two or more property subclasses share. For example, say you want to have two different kinds of text entry fields, one with a specific format mask and fixed text length and one with a different format mask and no fixed length. Say that both share all the other properties of a text entry item. You could create the FIXEDTEXTFORMAT property class from the fixed object, then remove all the properties that you will set for each object, such as X Position, Y Position, Primary Key, and so on. You could then do the same for VARIABLETEXTFORMAT. Finally, you could create TEXTFORMAT from either one of these property classes, removing the Fixed Length and Format Mask properties but leaving the shared ones such as Data Type and Maximum Length.

If you are creating your hierarchy top down, you can add properties using the Add Property tool and the Properties LOV dialog box to create the subclass. In this case, you would first create the TEXTFORMAT class, then the FIXEDTEXTFORMAT class and the VARIABLETEXTFORMAT class.

If your property class hierarchy would be useful in more than one module, you should define it in a template module as suggested earlier in this chapter. You can base your new modules on this module by using File | Save As to save the template as a new module. You can also copy the property classes you want to use from the template into a new module by dragging and dropping or cutting and pasting them. You can copy the property class to an object library that you can share between modules. See the upcoming section on subclassing, copying, and referring to objects.

Inheriting and Overriding Properties from the Property Class

For an object to inherit the properties from a property class, you need to assign the property class to the object. Each object has a property called Class. To assign the property class, set the Class property in the usual way by selecting the object in the Object Navigator and selecting the Class property in the Property Palette. The Property Palette provides a drop-down list of the property class names in the module that owns the object.

When you set the Class property, Oracle Developer copies the property values from the property class into the object properties that exist for the object. It marks these properties in the object with an equal sign. If there are properties in the object that have no corresponding values in the property class, Oracle Developer leaves them unchanged. If there are properties in the property class that have no corresponding properties in the object, Oracle Developer does not copy them.

NOTE
Property classes and subclassing are intimately related. The section "Subclassing, Copying, and Referring to Objects" goes into detail on this relationship. While property classes provide many reuse benefits by themselves, subclassing provides many more benefits.

You can override inherited properties in an object with a different value, making that property a *variant* property. Just set the value in the object, and the plus sign will disappear. Variant properties do not inherit changes in the property class.

You can also convert a variant property back to an inherited property by selecting the property in the object and clicking on the Inherit tool in the toolbar on the Property Palette for the object.

Triggers in Property Classes

A very nice feature of property classes is that they can not only have properties in their property palette but also triggers. This lets you inherit application behavior in your objects. The trick to using triggers in property classes is to write them to be reusable. Using bind variables can help here, but only a bit, because the names must refer to names in the form that owns the property class and trigger, thus coupling the trigger to the form. This feature works best to define behavior that does not require referring to actual values other than that in the field itself.

To create a property class trigger, expand the property class object in the Object Navigator, and then create a trigger of the appropriate kind in the usual way, using the Triggers LOV dialog box and the PL/SQL editor. When you assign the property class to an object, the object (a form, block, or item) inherits the trigger and runs it when the appropriate event occurs. If the event is not an appropriate event for the kind of object you associate the class with, the object ignores the trigger (as it would ignore the trigger if you put it directly on the object).

You can override an inherited trigger by adding a trigger for the same event to the object itself. If you expand the trigger heading under the object, you will see that it does not display the inherited trigger name. You can see that only under the property class.

Subclassing, Copying, and Referring to Objects

The Object Navigator in the Form Builder gives you an easy way to reuse objects: copying and referring to objects elsewhere in the system. For example, you can implement a block in at least seven ways:

- Create the block from scratch, as illustrated in Chapter 4.

- Copy the block from another block by dragging and dropping it.

- Copy the block from another block by copying and pasting it.

- Move the block by cutting and pasting it.

- Move the block within a module by dragging it while holding down the CTRL key.

- Refer to another block by dragging and dropping the block.

- Subclass a block through the Subclass Information property on the referring block.

Drag-and-Drop Moving, Copying, and Subclassing

When you select an object and drag it elsewhere in the Object Navigator, you are doing one of several possible things: copying the object, moving the object, or subclassing the object.

- *Moving* the object means you are removing the object from its starting location and physically moving it, with associations, to the new location in which you drop or paste it. You can move an object by simply dragging it to a new location with the mouse.

- *Copying* the object means you are creating a new object and initializing it with most of the contents and associations of the original object.

- *Subclassing* the object means you are creating a new object that refers to the original one in a new location. A *subclass* inherits the properties and associations of the object to which it refers, except for a few properties you can change. When you change the original object, the reference object or subclass also changes by inheriting the changes in the object to which it refers. You can subclass objects within the same form or between different forms, and you can subclass objects from an object library.

The easiest way to copy or subclass an object is to *drag and drop* it from its original location to a new location in the Object Navigator. Select the object, or several objects of the same type if you wish, hold down the CTRL key, and drag the object while holding down the left mouse button to a location suitable for that type of object. You then see an alert asking whether you want to copy or subclass.

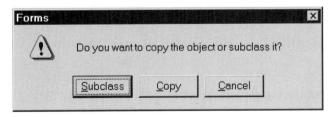

Objects you copy or subclass both own a set of objects and associate with another set of objects. For example, a block *owns* a set of items and triggers, but it *associates* with canvases through the items that it owns. The associations appear as properties in the Property Palette of the object, not as objects underneath the copied object in the Object Navigator. When you copy an object, Oracle Developer resolves the associations within the module by looking for objects with the names that exist in the Property Palette properties. When you cut or copy and paste an object, you lose all the associations.

NOTE

In a way, you increase coupling in the system when you reuse code by reference. For example, if you change trigger code in a module and other modules or applications refer to that code, and the code has problems, all your other modules inherit the problems with the new code. On the other hand, you only need to fix the problem in one place. Be careful when making changes to code to which you refer.

When you establish a reference between different modules, you should add a dependency to the project using the Project Builder. The section "Saving Your Form" in Chapter 4 showed you how to set up a dependency with the Add Files to Project tool in the Project Builder. To recap for the current case, when you have a dependency between two modules, add the FMB file for the source module to the FMX file for the reusing module. For example, say you had a series of applications that all used several items from the Skill module, Skill.FMB. If you did this in the HR form, there is a dependency between the HR form and the Skill form. To represent the dependency in the Project Builder, you find the HR.FMX file and click on the Add Files to Project tool; then select the Skill.FMB file from the Add File dialog box.

The benefit from these dependencies comes not when you make your reference but when you change the original objects to which you refer. If you are reusing the object in more than one module, you must rebuild all the reusing modules to make the change effective. You select the project and click on the Build Incremental tool. Project Builder uses the dependencies to decide which forms to rebuild.

Subclassing

Subclassing in Oracle Developer is the ability to inherit some or all of the properties of an object of the same type. For example, you can base a text item on another text item, or a canvas on another canvas. The subclass is the object making the reference, and the parent class is the object to which the subclass refers and from which it inherits properties.

Form Builder provides the Subclass Information property in the General property group for all form-module objects. Clicking on the More icon for this property displays the Subclass Information dialog box, which lets you choose between subclassing an object and subclassing a property class through a radio button.

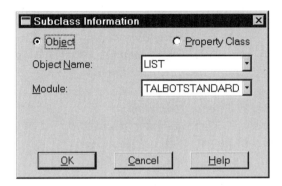

The illustrated dialog box is specific to block items. For item objects, you would also see the Block field. Each of the fields in the dialog box is a drop-down list that gets its values from the modules currently open in the Form Builder.

1. Choose the module that contains the object you want to subclass. This drop-down list contains all the open form modules and object libraries (see the section "The Object Library and SmartClasses" for details on object libraries). The module can be the same form that contains the subclass.

2. Choose the block that contains the item you want to subclass from the drop-down list of blocks in the module you've chosen. You can choose <NULL> for the block, in which case the drop-down list of objects lists all the items in the module. You can also choose a specific block, in which case the list contains only the objects in that block.

NOTE
You should not choose <NULL> for the block, as this can lead to problems if you have more than one object with the same name. This may work when you first do it, but as time goes on and you add more blocks to the application, you can easily add items with the same name. Always use the block name.

The drop-down list of objects contains only those objects of the same type as the subclass. If you click on the Subclass Information property for a list item, you see only list item objects to subclass. If you click on a canvas, you see only canvases.

TIP
You can also choose <NULL> for the object name. This choice lets you remove a subclass reference from an object that already has one. For example, if you have a list subclass of another list, and you want to redefine the item as a radio group without subclassing, you set the Object field to <NULL> and break the subclass relationship. You do this when you no longer want any properties of the object to inherit from any other object.

3. Clicking on OK subclasses the object.

   There are four kinds of properties in the subclass:

   ■ *Default:* The Form Builder sets the property from its internal defaults; the Property Palette displays a small circle next to the property name.

   ■ *Set:* The property comes from you or the Form Builder assigning a specific value (for example, the Layout Wizard can set the Height and Width properties of most objects, overriding any inherited property value); the Property Palette displays a small rectangle next to the property name.

   ■ *Inherited:* The property comes from the same property in the subclassed object or its parent objects; the Property Palette displays a right-angled arrow next to the property name.

   ■ *Overridden:* The property, originally inherited from a parent class, now has a value you or the Form Builder assigned, breaking the inheritance link; the Property Palette displays the inheritance arrow with a red "x" on it, indicating a broken link.

The subclass inherits only properties you have explicitly set in the parent class or in its parents. Any other property gets the Form Builder default (a circle rather than an inheritance arrow). As with property classes, you can build entire hierarchies of parent classes, adding and overriding properties down the hierarchy.

The Object Library and SmartClasses

An *object library* is a container for Form Builder objects. You can drag any number of individual objects, such as blocks, items, canvases, windows, or property classes, into a library for reuse in other modules.

NOTE
The object library contains only form-based objects. You cannot store menu, report, or graphics objects in object libraries. Also, you cannot store form modules in object libraries, only the objects within such modules.

You create an object library in the usual way: by selecting the Object Libraries heading in the Form Builder Object Navigator and clicking on the Create tool. This heading is sandwiched between the PL/SQL Libraries and Build-in Packages headings at the top level of the Object Navigator hierarchy. Like the PL/SQL library, the object library corresponds to a separate file (or database object, if you choose to store it on the database server). When you double-click on the New Object Library icon, Oracle Developer opens the Object Library Editor and displays two empty tab pages. It creates these tab page objects under the Library Tabs subheading under the new library in the Object Navigator.

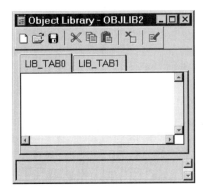

NOTE
You can also create an object library using the Tools/Object Library menu item in the main menu of the Form Builder or by clicking on the New tool on the Object Library toolbar.

Organizing your object libraries is totally up to you. There are no constraints on putting objects on any tab page you choose. Thinking a bit before you start can help make your libraries more useful, however.

You first should decide on the purpose of your library. For example, Talbot's Farm, in Chapter 4, uses a standard object library that all its applications share. This makes items, canvases, windows, and other objects consistent in formatting and basic property settings. Such a standard library contains a broad array of small, reusable objects organized into type-based tab pages. For example, you could have one tab page per type of object (one for blocks, one for items, one for property classes, and so on). Another kind of library might package a block and its items, or several blocks sharing a master-detail relationship, for reuse in several applications. For this kind of library, you might want to create one tab page per block that contains the block and any objects the block needs to do its job. This kind of library strongly resembles, and replaces, the object group, although you can still use groups to some advantage.

TIP

You can find a standard library in the demonstration materials that come with Oracle Developer. Try searching for files on the CD-ROM with the .olb extension. The one I've seen uses a Real Point coordinate system, so it won't work with the Talbot applications, which use Real Inch. Make sure the standard library and the target modules use the same coordinate system.

There are two other decisions you should make before dragging objects into your new library. First, limit the number of objects on any tab page to a number easily visible on one screen. Depending on the setup, you may also want to limit the number to make it easier for the developer to see all the objects at a glance. Second, the Object Library Editor does not permit you to rearrange objects once you drag them onto the library page. Therefore, you should have a good idea about how to arrange them, such as alphabetical order or some other ordering that makes sense given the objects.

You can change the name and label of the tab pages through the corresponding objects in the Object Navigator and their Property Palettes. To create new tab pages, use the Add tool on the Object Navigator toolbar after selecting a current tab page object or the Tab Page heading. You can select a tab page and remove it with the Remove tool in the Object Navigator toolbar.

To include objects in the library, just drag them onto the open tab page. You can also right-click on the object and use the Add Object to Library menu item on the pop-up menu. This copies the object onto the open tab page. When you finish copying objects into the library, save it using the Save tool, either in the Object Navigator toolbar or in the Object Library Editor toolbar. The result is a series of objects in the open tab:

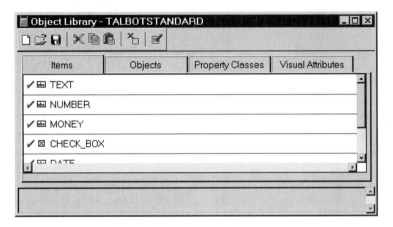

NOTE
When you include the object in the library, you are doing just that: copying. There is no link between the original object and the object in the object library. If you change the original object, the object in the object library does not inherit the change. If you need to change the object in the library to correct a problem or to make a new feature available, you must remove the current object in the library using the Remove Object tool and replace it with the new one. This requires some additional care in configuration management as you move forward through maintenance and new product versions of your application, and Oracle Developer does not have any tools to help you with this at present.

The lower box in the Object Library Editor displays the Comment property of the object. You can set the comment in the original object through the standard Property Palette, or you can use the Comment tool in the Object Library Editor to create a comment in the copy in the object library. If you maintain the objects in a form separate from the object library, it's a good idea to comment in the original form rather than in the object library, as you will have to redo the comment every time you replace the object in the library.

To reuse objects from an object library, you open the library in the usual way using the File Open tool, then drag and drop the objects into your forms. You get the same alert asking whether to copy or subclass the object that you do dragging objects between forms. Subclassing an object from an object library lets you inherit any changes to the library over time. Oracle Developer maintains a link between the Object Library objects and subclassed objects. This is an extremely powerful feature with many maintenance and reuse benefits.

Alternatively, you can create objects in your form, then subclass them from the object library. You can do this in two ways.

First, you can use the Subclass Information property of the new object to select a parent object from the object library.

1. If you create a text item in a block and want to make it a subclass of the NUMBER object in the TalbotStandard.OLB object library, click on the property's More button to see the Subclass Information dialog box.

2. Set the radio button to Object.

3. Choose the TalbotStandard module (that is, the object library).

4. Choose the NUMBER object from that library.

One disadvantage to this approach is that you see all the objects in the library in the drop-down list, not just the ones that are appropriate to the kind of object you are subclassing.

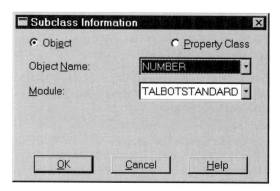

A second way to subclass from a library uses the new SmartClass feature. A SmartClass is a class in a library that you choose to make available through a pop-up menu. You can make any object in your library a SmartClass. Open the object library and select the object you wish to make into a SmartClass in the Object Library Editor. Now choose the Object|SmartClass menu item from the main menu of the Form Builder. You see a green checkmark appear next to the object in the Object Library Editor.

Select an object in the Object Navigator of the same type as the SmartClass object. Right-click on the object and choose the SmartClasses menu item. You now see a submenu that lists all the SmartClasses in open libraries of the same type of object as the object on which you right-clicked the mouse. This example shows four text item objects in the object library—a general text item, a number subclass, a money number subclass, and a date subclass:

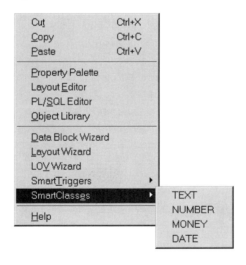

Choosing a SmartClass menu item subclasses the object from the SmartClass in the object library. This arrangement, like SmartTriggers, gives you a context-dependent menu that greatly speeds up subclassing from your object library.

Object Groups

Another feature of Oracle Developer lets you package your reusable objects for later copying or subclassing. The *object group* collects a set of objects in the module under a single heading. By copying or referring to the object group, you get all the objects it contains. You can group any objects down to the block level, but you cannot group items within a block. You have to include the entire block in the object group.

To create an object group, find the module's Object Group heading in the Object Navigator. Create the new group with the Create tool. Now drag and drop all the objects you want to gather into the group by dropping them on the Object Group Children node under the group you have created.

NOTE

You can use object libraries to replace object groups from prior versions of Oracle Developer. Libraries are much more flexible than groups, as they permit access to the individual objects from subclassing forms. On the other hand, you can also place object groups in your libraries as a kind of package within a package, creating a package of objects that you can drag and drop or subclass into a new application in one action. You should use it primarily when the package works as a unified system and its parts are not separately usable. You can also put both object groups and the objects in the group into the library separately to provide for both kinds of reuse, although this increases your configuration management worries because of the duplication.

When to Do What

How do you choose between using subclasses, named visual attributes, and property classes? When should you copy these objects and when should you refer to or subclass them?

- You can define only font, color, and pattern attributes in a named visual attribute but any property in a property class or subclass.

- You can define a property class or subclass to inherit from a property class or another object, respectively, but a named visual attribute stands alone.

■ You can change named visual attribute properties dynamically through PL/SQL, but you cannot change property class values in this way. You can inherit dynamic changes to parent objects in subclasses, but you cannot change all object properties, just the ones that Oracle Developer allows for the built-in subprogram that changes the value. You cannot change Object Library parent properties dynamically.

■ Named visual attributes take precedence over property class or parent object settings, so if you have both, the fonts, colors, and patterns will be those of the named visual attribute, not the property class or parent.

■ You can copy any objects you wish, but you cannot update all the copies in a single operation.

■ If you refer to an object, you must change the properties of this object in the original module to which it belongs; you cannot change them in the reference. On the other hand, if you subclass an object, you can override the properties in the subclass. Also, if you make an error in the original objects, all its references or subclasses pick up the error.

■ Object groups make available chunks of form modules, such as several blocks and triggers taken as a whole.

■ Object libraries make available objects from Forms modules of any kind.

These points lead to the following recommendations:

■ Use named visual attributes to represent visual information where possible (see Table 10-2 for a list of the properties you can define in visual attributes). Include the named visual attributes in your property classes, object library objects, and intended parent objects so that you can inherit them as properties.

■ Replace property classes where possible with references to parent objects, and preferably to objects in an object library.

■ Use subclassing anywhere you can to reuse major parts of modules in other modules, and use object groups to create packaged, reusable chunks of modules. Use object libraries rather than object groups, or place your object groups into object libraries for ease of reference.

■ Copy objects only to create an initial setup for making local changes. That is, if you intend to customize your objects a good deal in the local module, copy the objects rather than referring to them.

■ Use object library pages to hold clusters of objects in preference to object groups where possible.

Parameterizing Your Applications

Using parameters, you can customize forms, reports, and graphics when you run them, as well as when you code them. A *parameter* is a variable that you set when you activate the object by passing in values as *arguments* on the command line or calling procedure. Parameters let you construct objects to be flexible to external requirements by allowing the user of the object to configure the object dynamically.

Forms Parameters

A form parameter is a form variable to which you can assign values through arguments you pass when you start the form. You can pass arguments to a form either through the command line of the Forms Runtime program or through the various subprograms that start a form from another object, such as Call_Form, New_Form, Open_Form, or Run_Product. Each of these procedures takes a parameter list as an argument. Forms parameters can be any of three data types: CHAR, NUMBER, or DATE.

Creating Form Parameter Objects

A form parameter is an object that belongs to a form. To create one, find and select the Parameters heading in the Object Navigator, just below the Object Groups heading under the Form module, and click on the Create tool. Double-clicking on the icon displays the Property Palette for the parameter.

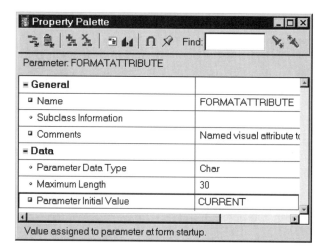

This particular parameter accepts a string that represents the name of a named visual attribute to use to set the Current_Record_Attribute property of the form when you start it. This lets you start up with one of a set of different visual attributes. You could do this for portability reasons (different fonts on different platforms) or for different projects with different visual standards (10-point type on one project but 12-point type on another, for example).

You need to set the Data Type (CHAR, NUMBER, or DATE), the Length for a CHAR parameter, and the internal Name of the parameter in the Property Palette. You also need to set the Initial Value, which the form uses when you do not supply an argument for the parameter. Leaving this variable uninitialized is not a good thing to do. In this case, the default value is "Current," which means the form will use the CURRENT named visual attribute for the form.

Using Form Parameters

You can use form parameters with bind variable syntax in PL/SQL code or in certain properties. To refer to a parameter, you prefix the name with ":PARAMETER" and a dot separator. For example, to use the parameter FormatAttribute to set the form property in a When-New-Form-Instance trigger, you would refer to :PARAMETER.FormatAttribute:

```
DECLARE
   vFormID FormModule;
BEGIN
   vFormID := Find_Form(:System.Current_Form);
   Set_Form_Property(vFormID, Current_Record_Attribute,
     :Parameter.FormatAttribute);
END;
```

You can refer to parameters, still prefacing the name with ":PARAMETER.", in the object properties in Table 10-3.

Object	Property
Block	WHERE Clause
Block	ORDER BY Clause
List of Values	Return Item (in Column Mapping dialog box)
Item	Default Value
Text Item	Range Low Value
Text Item	Range High Value

TABLE 10-3. *Object Properties That Accept Parameters*

Passing Arguments

To supply arguments to the WorkerSkill form, you could just put them on the
command line that sets up the Runform environment:

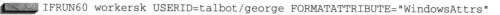
```
IFRUN60 workersk USERID=talbot/george FORMATATTRIBUTE="WindowsAttrs"
```

USERID is a system parameter valid in any form, and FORMATATTRIBUTE is a
user-defined parameter that the WorkerSkill form defines. The parameter takes on
the value WindowsAttrs when Oracle Developer initializes the form on startup.

PARAMETER LISTS   If you want to run a form from another form, and you
need to supply parameter arguments to the form, you do so by building a parameter
list before you call the built-in procedure to run the form. A *parameter list* is an
object that contains a list of parameters with their values. Parameter lists let you
build highly reusable modules by parameterizing elements. Such modules are useful
in widely varying domains controlled by the parameters, whereas modules without
parameters are much less flexible.

To create a parameter list, you call the Create_Parameter_List built-in function,
which returns a ParamList ID. You then call the Add_Parameter built-in procedure
for each parameter argument you want to add to the list. The actual list is created in
form memory and persists beyond the code block, so you need to create and add a
list only once for the form instance. You do this by getting the object ID for the ID
variable, then testing whether it is null. If the code gets called more than once in a
form session, you check the existence of the list, and if it is already there, you set
the parameters rather than adding them. Finally, you pass the ParamList ID to the
call to Call_Form, New_Form, Open_Form, or Run_Product. The following
anonymous PL/SQL block, for example, sets up a parameter list to pass a name,
'MotifFormVisualAttrs', to use for the FormatAttribute parameter:

```
DECLARE
  vListID ParamList :=
    Get_Parameter_list('WorkerSkillFormArguments');
BEGIN
  IF ID_Null(vListID) THEN  -- No list yet, create it
    vListID := Create_Parameter_List('WorkerSkillFormArguments');
    Add_Parameter(vListID, 'FormatAttribute', TEXT_PARAMETER,
                'MotifFormVisualAttrs');
  ELSE  -- List already created, just set parameter
    Set_Parameter_Attr(vListID, 'FormAttribute', TEXT_PARAMETER,
                'MotifFormVisualAttrs');
  END IF;
  Open_Form('WorkerSk', ACTIVATE, NO_SESSION, vListID);
END;
```

Oracle Developer automatically creates the DEFAULT parameter list when it initializes the form. This parameter list contains all the parameters you've created in the Form Builder. If you use multiple forms, you will usually want them to behave consistently, and you thus will want to pass through parameters using a parameter list. You can thus pass all the parameters directly to another form using this code:

```
DECLARE
   vListID ParamList :=
     Get_Parameter_list('Default');
BEGIN
   Open_Form('WorkerSk', ACTIVATE, NO_SESSION, vListID);
END;
```

AN ALTERNATIVE WAY OF PASSING ARGUMENTS   As an alternative for passing arguments into a form, you can create a control block (a block that does not correspond to a base table) with the items being the parameters, with appropriate defaults and other settings. You can then display the parameter form as a modal dialog window with a special canvas for the user to enter arguments. You should include a means in your application to display this dialog box at any time to set the parameters with different arguments. See Chapter 6 for details on creating dialog windows and canvases for them.

TIP
These dialog boxes would be excellent candidates for reusable object library objects. You could structure the parameters into several control blocks that represent cohesive clusters of parameters. You could then subclass these control blocks in different forms as you needed to include the particular sort of parameter. You could structure the entry of the arguments into separate options dialog boxes or into a single dialog box if that was appropriate.

Internally, you can refer to the parameters as you would any control block item. The only differences are the inability to specify the arguments on the command line and the need to preface the item name with the control block name rather than with PARAMETER.

PASSING PARAMETERS BACK WITH GLOBAL VARIABLES
Occasionally, you may want to pass data back into a calling form from a called form. Unfortunately, parameter lists pass parameters by value, not by reference,

so the called form is always dealing with a copy of the parameter and cannot change the value in the calling form directly. Also, unlike PL/SQL subprogram arguments, there is no such thing as an IN OUT or OUT parameter (see the section "Subprograms" in Chapter 12 for details on these parameters).

The only solution I've found to this is to create global variables that the called form sets. This solution clearly increases the coupling between your forms because both forms refer to the same global variables by name. You thus cannot reuse the forms independently of one another. Also, since code from anywhere can set the value of a global variable, you never really know what value is in the variable. You must thus take special care to manage the variable's value to prevent problems.

There are two kinds of global variables available in Oracle Developer. A Forms global variable is a special variable that any form can access using the prefix :Global. A package variable is a variable that is part of the public interface specification of a PL/SQL package. Any PL/SQL code, including code in reports and graphics, can access such variables by referring to the package variable using the package name (:MyPackage.vVariableName, for example). See Chapter 12 for details on using package variables.

NOTE
The advantage to using package variables instead of Forms globals is that they can span Oracle Developer components. You can even span applications if you create the package on the server.

The trick to using global variables safely is to initialize them when you start the application, then to reinitialize them whenever you finish using them. That way, they always reflect a known value. For example, say the WorkerSkill form lets you call the Skill form to choose a skill to associate with a worker rather than just providing a drop-down list of skills. You might do this if you wanted the user to be able to use the query-by-example features of the form to select the skill based on its description, or something similar. To pass back the skill name, you need a global variable called Skill that can hold the name. In the When-New-Form-Instance trigger for the WorkerSkill form, you add this statement:

```
:Global.Skill := NULL;  -- initialize the skill to NULL
```

In the Skill form, you can use any number of methods to permit the user to select a particular skill, such as using the current record on exit, using a push button, or using a check box on each skill record. Regardless of the method, the code that executes sets the global variable:

`:Global.Skill := :Skill.Skill;  --Copy current skill into global`

When you return to the WorkerSkill form, the global variable now reflects the skill set by the Skill form. For example, if you originally called the form from the When-Button-Pressed trigger, the code following the Call_Form statement trigger should then copy the global variable's value to the appropriate block item, then reinitialize the global to NULL. This ensures that you always know precisely what the global contains, even after the trigger completes and returns control to the user.

WARNING
For reusability and to reduce complexity and coupling, you should avoid using parameters as global variables in PL/SQL code. That is, do not pass information from one program unit to another by setting a parameter value unless you can find no other way to do this. Use PL/SQL program unit parameters to move data in and out of PL/SQL code, not global variables.

PASSING PARAMETERS TO REPORTS AND DISPLAYS   Form parameters give you a way to make forms more reusable through the ability to customize their behavior at runtime by passing in arguments. The same logic applies to reports and graphics displays. Most of the time, you pass arguments to reports and charts from forms. There are two kinds of parameters—the text parameter and the data parameter.

The *text parameter* lets you pass a string value for a named parameter, which can be a standard parameter in the called report or chart, a user-defined parameter, a bind variable, or a lexical reference. A standard parameter name, bind variable, or lexical reference name must correspond to the exact name, such as DESTYPE or COPIES. A text parameter lets you pass any standard command line parameter to the report or chart. Any parameter that you could pass on the command line can be a text parameter.

The *data parameter* lets you pass the name of a Forms record group that contains data records. You can pass data parameters to reports and graphics displays, but not to forms. If you pass a data parameter to a report, you can use it only in a master query, not in any child queries in the report data model.

WEB.SHOW_DOCUMENT   When you deploy your application on the Internet, you can use the special built-in subprogram Show_Document to hyperlink to a Web document, including documents that start Oracle Developer applications or Web-enabled reports. For example, to display a static report Talbot has generated and stored in a logical directory on your Web server, /reports, you might use the following code in a trigger associated with a hypertext link in a form displayed on the Web:

```
Web.Show_Document('http://www.talbotfarms.com/reports/ledger.html', _BLANK);
```

The first argument to the call is any valid Internet URL. The second argument can be one of several possibilities:

- _BLANK: Display the document in a new, top-level browser window.

- _PARENT: Display the document in the parent window or frame that contains the hypertext link that you clicked to display the document (same as _SELF for window or top-level-frame references).

- _SELF: Display the document in the same frame or window as the current document.

- _TOP: Display the document in the same window as the current document, replacing any frames that window currently displays.

See Chapter 15 for some additional techniques to use with Show_Document.

RUN_PRODUCT   You can run a report or display by constructing a parameter list and passing it using the built-in subprogram Run_Product. See Chapter 15 for more details on using Run_Product. The following code builds a parameter list and runs a report. It passes the data from the Ledger record group into the report.

```
DECLARE
   vListID ParamList := Get_Parameter_List('ReportArguments');
BEGIN
   IF ID_Null(vListID) THEN  -- No list yet, create it
     vListID := Create_Parameter_List('ReportArguments');
     Add_Parameter(vListID, 'DESTYPE', TEXT_PARAMETER, 'PRINTER');
     Add_Parameter(vListID, 'DESNAME', TEXT_PARAMETER, 'LPT2');
     Add_Parameter(vListID, 'LedgerQuery', DATA_PARAMETER, 'Ledger');
   ELSE
     Set_Parameter_Attr(vListID, 'DESTYPE', TEXT_PARAMETER, 'PRINTER');
     Set_Parameter_Attr(vListID, 'DESNAME', TEXT_PARAMETER, 'LPT2');
     Set_Parameter_Attr(vListID, 'LedgerQuery', DATA_PARAMETER, 'Ledger');
   END IF;
   Run_Product(REPORTS, 'Ledger', SYNCHRONOUS, RUNTIME, FILESYSTEM, vListID);
END;
```

This code might appear in the PL/SQL block for a menu item or in a When-Button-Pressed trigger. When the user chooses the menu item or presses the button, Oracle Developer builds the argument list and passes it to the report using

Run_Product. This runs the Reports Runtime, which communicates with the Reports Server to produce the report as requested.

REPORT OBJECTS AND CHART ITEMS   Although the Run_Product approach is perfectly OK, Oracle Developer provides a much tighter integration for reports and graphics with report objects and chart items, one of the many kinds of objects in a form module. The report object properties contain several of the report system parameters and the various Run_Product parameters as well. You set up these properties using the Property Palette or the Report Wizard, then run the report using the Run_Report_Object built-in subprogram, as Chapters 4 and 7 demonstrated. Alternatively, you can run the report with Web.Show_Document (see the previous section "Web.Show_Document").

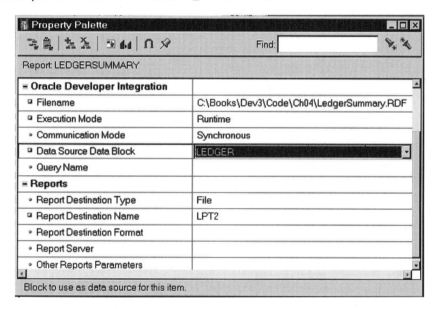

This example sets the Destination Type and Name properties as before. Instead of using a data parameter, you specify the data block that is the source of the data in the Data Source Data Block property. The report now gets its data directly from the Ledger block without your needing to build an intermediate record group. This approach gives the user more control over the report, as he or she can set up the data in the block using query by example in Forms Runtime.

TIP
You can specify any of the report parameters in the Other Reports Parameters property with a <keyword> = <value> syntax, such as DECIMAL=',.'.

You can use the Chart Wizard or the Property Palette for a chart item to set up a graphics display in a form. You can set up a data source for a graphics display through the Data Source Data Block property. The chart item adds the Data Source X Axis and Data Source Y Axis properties, which let you specify items from the data block to use for the two dimensions of the chart.

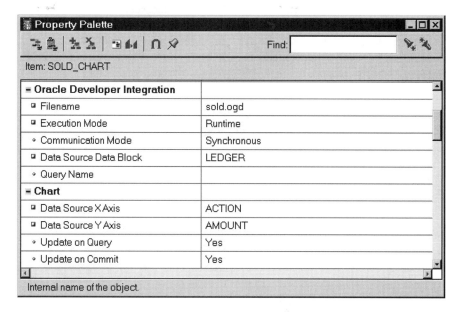

Report Parameters

Report parameters are similar to form parameters, but you have an additional option for using them: lexical references in SQL statements. You also have a built-in way to create a form for entering parameters.

Report Builder comes with a standard set of system parameters. You have already seen the parameters in Table 10-4 on the form that Reports displays when you previewed a report in the Chapter 4 tutorials.

Creating Parameters

You create parameters in the Object Navigator in much the same way as for Form Builder parameters. The heading to look for is User Parameters under the Data Model heading for the report (for example, Reports\LEDGER\Data Model\User Parameters). In the Parameter Property Palette, you can enter a name, a data type, a width for CHAR parameters, an input mask, an initial value, a validation trigger, a comment, a list of values (LOV) dialog box, or a combo box set of values. You should always enter an initial value, and you should try to use the input mask, LOV

Parameter	Description
Background	Whether to run the report in a background process
Copies	How many copies of the report to print
Currency	The symbol to indicate a monetary value, such as "$"
Decimal	The symbol to separate the decimal portion of a number, such as "," or "."
Destination Format	The format of the output device
Destination Name	Name of the output device (filename, printer name, and so on)
Destination Type	Where to send the output (screen, file, mail, printer, preview)
Mode	Bitmap or character
Orientation	Landscape or portrait
Printjob	Whether to display the Print Job dialog box
Thousands	The symbol to separate the groups of three digits in a number, such as "," or "."

TABLE 10-4. *Report System Parameters*

or combo box, and/or validation trigger where possible to make sure that the input arguments are acceptable.

You can also create a parameter automatically if you refer to a parameter as a bind variable in a query. Use the parameter in your code, and the Report Builder automatically creates it for you.

Creating a Parameter Form

You will find the Parameter Form object under the report object, right after the Layout object. Double-clicking on the object icon displays a special Parameter Form Editor that lets you add fields for the different parameters. If you do not build a form of your own, the default form comes with fields for the various system parameters. When you add one of your own from scratch, it is blank, so you have to create parameter fields for any system parameters you want the user to see. You can change the form title, add hint line text, add boilerplate text, add fields for argument entry, or break the form into two or more pages.

A better strategy is to use the Tools|Parameter Form Builder menu item to create a parameter form that includes the system parameters. This displays the

Parameter Form Builder dialog box, which lets you choose the system parameters you want to display.

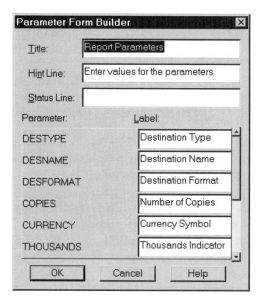

To select additional parameters or to deselect any selected ones, click on them. Scroll down to see the whole set of parameters. You can also enter a hint and status bar text if you wish.

When you click on OK after making your choices, Oracle Developer generates the layout and displays it in the Parameter Form Editor. You can then edit the boilerplate text and add other parameters.

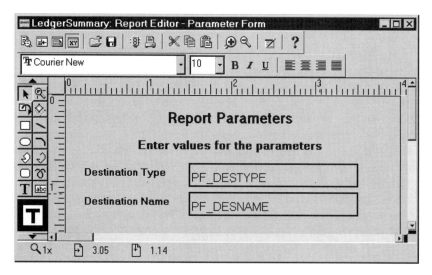

The Report Properties Property Palette has a Parameter Form Window section that lets you specify the number of pages in the parameter form. You can also specify the size of the pages and the title for the Previewer window.

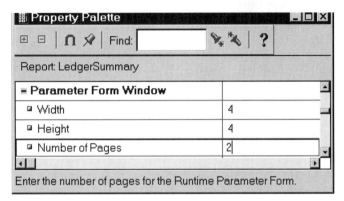

When you add a field, you access its Property Palette in the usual way by double-clicking on the field in the Editor or in the Object Navigator. Here, for example, is the very simple Property Palette for the PF_DESNAME field:

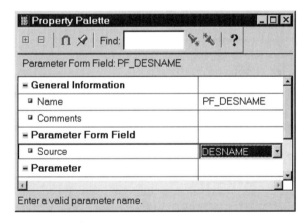

The drop-down list on the Source property provides all of the parameters, both system and user defined. By setting this, you specify the connection between the parameter and the field.

Using Parameters
You can use parameters in queries either as bind variables or as lexical references. See the "External Queries and the Query Builder" section earlier in this chapter for details on these alternatives. You can also use parameters as part of your drill-down report setup; see Chapter 7 for details.

Graphics Parameters

Graphics Builder parameters are very similar to form and report parameters, but they have a special role to play in the Graphics Builder: they are the basis for drill-down behavior, passing the value of chart elements or the name of a graphic object. You can also use them through bind variables in PL/SQL code or through bind variables or lexical references in queries, as in reports. As with Report Builder, when you refer to a parameter in PL/SQL or query code, Oracle Developer creates a parameter for you automatically if it does not already exist.

NOTE

For more information about creating drill-down relationships, see Chapter 8. You cannot create such relationships in a graphics display integrated with a form or report, only in a standalone one.

One difference in using Graphics Builder parameters is that because display modules have no items or fields, you just use the parameter name without further qualification. For example, to parameterize the query of amounts bought by Talbot's so that the user can control the ordering of the pie slices:

```
SELECT Person "Person", SUM(Amount) "Amount"
  FROM Ledger
 WHERE Action IN ('Bought', 'Paid')
GROUP BY Person
&Ordering
```

The Ordering parameter appears in lexical reference form. To sort by amount, set the parameter to "ORDER BY 2"; to sort by person, set the parameter to "ORDER BY Person" or "ORDER BY 1".

Graphics Builder provides no way for the end user to enter these values as parameters, unlike the Forms and Reports Runtimes, which provide parameter entry forms. You can write code for buttons or chart elements that sets the parameters when the user clicks on them. The user can also enter the parameters directly through the command line of the Graphics Runtime program.

Using Multiple Forms

When you build a form application, you often have the choice of building a large form with many blocks or a series of small forms. Although the large form may contain more functionality, it will serve a smaller range of possible applications because of its complexity. There will always be some part of the form you do not need. The smaller forms, although they are less functional, are more reusable because they offer their functions in smaller groups that you can reuse in more places.

In composing an application from multiple forms, there are a series of issues you must confront:

1. What kind of relationship is there between the forms?

2. What is the impact on transaction processing?

3. How do you exit the various forms?

The rest of this section gives you an overview of these issues.

TIP
I've been asked several times over the years how many forms you can stack up. I've never found any definitive answer to this question except "as many as your available memory will allow." The answer probably depends on which kinds of PL/SQL procedures you use to open the forms, as the next section, "Opening Forms," details. In general, it would be best to avoid two situations: letting the user determine how many forms to open at runtime or opening forms within code that loops. You should try to keep the stack as flat as possible.

Opening Forms

The most important issue in multiple-forms programming is the relationship between forms. In practical terms, this translates into a decision about which built-in subprogram you use to open the forms. The choice of behaviors ranges over these possibilities:

■ A set of independent forms between which you can navigate

■ A stacked set of modal forms, only the top one of which is enabled

■ A single form

■ A mixture of all of the above behaviors

While these last two choices seem contradictory to the others, they really aren't. The single-form style of multiple-form programming means replacing the current form with a new one, always leaving exactly one form in memory. The mixture of these behaviors lets you do this replacement for one form while leaving other forms in memory.

NOTE
You open forms using a built-in subprogram, usually in a trigger or a subprogram that a trigger calls. Depending on which subprogram you use, Oracle Developer behaves differently about the remaining code in the calling block. For example, Call_Form establishes a stack, and when the called form exits, you return to the calling code and continue execution.

The Open_Form built-in subprogram lets you open a form independently from all other open forms. Calling Open_Form leaves the current form accessible but replaces the current main menu with the called form's menu. You can navigate to items in other forms either with the mouse or with the Go_Form, Next_Form, and Previous_Form built-in subprograms (the order is the order in which you opened the forms). When you navigate, Oracle Developer does no validation and fires no triggers other than the When-Window-Deactivated trigger on the current form and the When-Window-Activated and When-Form-Navigate triggers on the target form. Each form has a current item, and when you navigate to any other item in that form, the usual validation occurs. When you specify the ACTIVATE parameter, Open_Form gives the called form the focus and ignores any statements following the Open_Form call in the calling PL/SQL block. When you specify the NO_ACTIVATE parameter, Open_Form keeps the focus on the calling form and continues executing the statements following the Open_Form call. Open_Form does not issue a savepoint (see the upcoming "Closing Forms" section for more details). Open_Form with the SESSION parameter opens the form in a new Oracle database session; NO_SESSION opens the form in the current database session (see the following section "Multiple-Form Transactions" for more details).

WARNING
Be very careful in using Open_Form. You should not create a situation in which end users can overload the deployment platform with too many forms open at the same time.

The Call_Form built-in subprogram lets you open a form by pushing the current form on a call stack. When you push a form onto the stack, you disable the form, giving the called form the focus and making it modal with respect to other forms on the stack. If you specify the DO_REPLACE parameter, Oracle Developer replaces the main menu with the called form's menu; NO_REPLACE leaves the current menu operational, ignoring any menu options set in the called form. If you specify the HIDE parameter, Oracle Developer hides the current form; NO_HIDE leaves it displayed. When you exit the form, execution continues after the Call_Form statement in the calling code. Call_Forms issues a savepoint and opens the new form in the same session. You can also specify the QUERY_ONLY parameter to disallow inserts, updates, and deletes in the called form. With Call_Form there is only one form active at a given time.

The New_Form built-in subprogram lets you replace the current form with a new one. Oracle Developer removes only the current form from memory, leaving others on the call stack or independent forms still operating. Oracle Developer ignores any PL/SQL statements after the New_Form call, as that form is no longer in memory. New_Form issues a savepoint and opens the new form in the same session. You can also specify the QUERY_ONLY parameter to disallow inserts, updates, and deletes in the new form.

NOTE
You should usually have the same main menu regardless of the form you are in. Changing the menu structure is a sure way to confuse users. With Open_Form and New_Form, for example, you cannot leave the menu in place as you can for Call_Form using NO_REPLACE, so you should make sure that all the forms use the same menu module (Form property Menu Module). You can also dynamically replace the menu using Replace_Menu if that makes more sense.

Multiple-Form Transactions

Recall from Chapter 1 that a transaction is a sequence of database operations. When you have multiple forms open, how those forms relate to one another has a major impact on your transactions. First, you can have forms open in different sessions. Second, which subprogram you use to open a form determines its validation and transaction processing behavior with respect to outstanding changes in the current form. Third, the subprogram also determines what happens when you exit the called form (see the following section "Closing Forms").

If you use Open_Form, you can open the called form in a new database session, and hence a different transaction, by using the SESSION parameter. The default is to open the new form in the same session as the calling one. You must also have the Forms Runtime parameter SESSION set to On or the Registry variable FORMS60_SESSION set to TRUE. This setting enables multiple sessions in forms. Opening separate forms in separate sessions keeps your transactions separate so that you can deal with them independently, decoupling the forms. On the other hand, if the forms use the same tables, you can get lock conflicts when both transactions try to access the same tables at once. Separate sessions are most useful when the forms do not share tables.

In a single transaction, the major issue becomes the status of existing changes to database-related data. Using New_Form or Call_Form requires that you commit or post data to the database before calling the new form. You might use code such as the following, for example:

```
DECLARE
   vCurrentMessageLevel VARCHAR2(2) := :System.Message_Level;
BEGIN
   IF :System.Form_Status = 'CHANGED' THEN
     :System.Message_Level := 5;  -- turn off undesirable messages
     Post;
     :System.Message_Level := vCurrentMessageLevel;
   END IF;

   IF :System.Form_Status <> 'QUERY' THEN
     Call_Form('NEW_FORM', NO_HIDE, NO_REPLACE);
   END IF;
END;
```

This example tests whether there is any changed data and posts it if there is; then it calls a form called "NEW_FORM," placing the current form on the stack. Setting the message level to 5 turns off the messages Oracle Developer displays so as not to confuse the end user. Remember that posting, as opposed to committing, writes the data to the database without ending the transaction. One consequence of calling Post or Commit_Form is the navigation to form level with validation (see the section "Transaction Processing" in Chapter 6). That means that, before moving to the called form, you validate all changes and post them to the database. This can cause problems if you are calling the new form to set data in the old one. For example, if you call a form to query an ID of some kind based on a complex query to set a required relationship in the current form, posting validates the relationship before it gets set, causing an error. You would want to use Open_Form in a case like this, as it does not require posting and validation.

Closing Forms

There are three ways to close a form:

- *Close_Form:* Closes the specified form; you use this to close any form in the application, including the current one, in which case it is equivalent to Exit_Form

- *Exit_Form:* Closes the current form; available as Action|Exit on the default menu; corresponds to the Key-Exit trigger

- *Clear_Form:* Rolls back and resets all forms in memory; available as Action|Clear All on the default menu; corresponds to the Key-ClrFrm trigger

The Call_Form and New_Form subprograms issue an Oracle savepoint, while Open_Form does not. A *savepoint* is a point in the transaction to which you may roll back without rolling back the entire transaction. Creating a savepoint when you move to a different form gives you more control over what happens when the called form closes. If there is a rollback, and there is a savepoint, Oracle only rolls the changes back to the point just before you called the new form, preserving all the changes you made and posted.

Exit_Form and Clear_Form have two parameters—the Commit mode and the Rollback mode. The exit process first commits any changes based on the Commit mode. This mode may have one of four values:

- *ASK_COMMIT:* Ask the user whether to commit changes; then validate changes and commit if the user approves (the default)

- *DO_COMMIT:* Validate changes, commit, and exit without asking the user

- *NO_COMMIT:* Validate changes and exit without committing

- *NO_VALIDATE:* Exit without validating, committing, or asking the user

When you exit the form with Exit_Form or Clear_Form, the Commit mode determines validation and commit behavior. After committing, the Rollback mode determines what happens. The Rollback mode may have one of three possible values:

- *TO_SAVEPOINT:* Roll back changes to the current form's savepoint, then exit (the default)

- *FULL_ROLLBACK:* Roll back changes to the beginning of the current transaction, then exit

- *NO_ROLLBACK:* Exit without rolling back any changes

The New_Form subprogram also has the Rollback mode, to enable it to handle changes from the form that it replaces with the new form.

NOTE
You can set up these options in the Key-Exit and Key-ClrForm triggers to redefine the default behavior of these processes. Just put the call to Exit_Form in the Key-Exit trigger, specifying the options you want to become standard.

One problem that many developers have is the behavior that Oracle Developer exhibits when you close a form. Action|Exit, for example, simply closes the current form. Most applications, however, exhibit different behavior for Exit—closing the application rather than just the current form. If you have multiple forms open, Oracle Developer does not close the application until you close the last form. You can change this behavior with a global flag. Initialize the flag to 'FALSE' in a When_New_Form_Instance trigger on your main form—the one you display first.

```
:Global.Exit_Flag := 'FALSE';
```

In the code that calls Exit_Form, such as a When-Button-Pressed trigger or a Key-Exit trigger, set the flag to 'TRUE' before calling Exit_Form:

```
:Global.Exit_Flag := 'TRUE';
```

In a When-Window-Activated trigger for each form, place the following code:

```
IF :Global.Exit_Flag = 'TRUE' THEN
   Exit_Form;
END IF;
```

Whenever you pop back to another form after exiting, that form in turn exits, until the last open form closes and the application closes as well. This is a good candidate for a When-Window-Activated trigger in your standard object library or form template.

Writing Code Once

Other chapters have briefly mentioned the possibility of building procedures, functions, and triggers in the database rather than in the application. What are the advantages of doing this for reuse?

If you are using Oracle as your database server, you have the choice of running your PL/SQL code in your applications or on the server. To make this decision, you must look at two issues: code/data cohesion and performance.

How does cohesion apply to triggers and procedures? As Chapter 13 details, you can use packages and libraries to group your procedures and functions into reusable, cohesive clusters. What role can the database play in this? Unlike a standard programming language, PL/SQL by its nature is a database programming language. Although you can and do use it for purely programmatic functions such as calculations and decision logic, you also use it to maintain database relationships. When you have a cluster of procedures or functions that work together with tables in your database, you need to consider the cohesion of both the data (the tables and columns) and the code (the procedures and functions).

This issue is similar in many ways to the integrity constraint mechanism in the database. Because Oracle and other ANSI-compliant database managers supply primary and foreign key constraints, you no longer need to place the code that maintains these relationships in your applications. You can define the tables with the constraints and let the database manager maintain the data. Using this feature increases the cohesion of the system by placing the constraints where they belong—with the table.

Similarly, when you have procedures and functions that interact with specific tables and columns to do specific things, you generally will want to place these procedures and functions on the server with the tables, not in your applications. You thus place the code closer to the data it uses and accrue all the benefits of the increased cohesion. You no longer have to move code around your network so that different applications can use it, and anyone with access to the database has access to the procedures. An example of this is when you use procedures as the basis for form data blocks. You could place your procedures in your applications; but because you intend for the procedures to encapsulate all references to your data, you should place them with the data and grant the appropriate privileges to them to guarantee your access control. Another example is when you have procedures that represent things that must happen when a database event happens, such as deleting a particular kind of row or some such server event. Again, you could do this in every application that initiates the event, but it is simpler and more straightforward to put the code into a database trigger.

As Chapter 6 already mentioned, if you want to prevent users from accessing data through tools other than your applications, triggers and other database procedures provide a way to encapsulate access to the data through privileges on the data and the procedures. Triggers also ensure full enforcement of the constraints they represent regardless of the tool a user uses to modify the data.

There are also performance implications. You may find that moving the code from the application server to the database server can improve performance substantially and can also reduce network traffic. This leads to the concept of *application partitioning,* which is the breaking up of your application server code into chunks running on different servers to improve resource usage, particularly over a network. One of the nicest features of Oracle Developer is the ability to drag code you write in your application to the database server, creating stored procedures. The availability of the same language system (PL/SQL and, in the future, Java) makes this possible.

You access database objects through the Database Objects heading in the Object Navigator. Once you connect to a database, this heading shows a list of all the user names the database defines. Each user name in turn shows the Stored Program Units, Libraries, Tables, and Views that belong to the user.

To create a stored procedure, you select the Database Objects|<USER NAME>|Stored Program Units heading in the Object Navigator and click on the Create tool. This displays the New Program Unit dialog box through which you enter the procedure name and type (Procedure, Function, Package Spec, or Package Body):

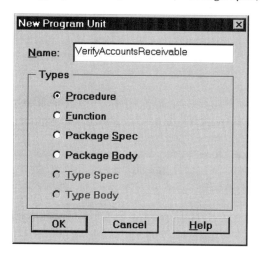

When you click on OK, Oracle Developer displays the Stored Program Unit Editor.

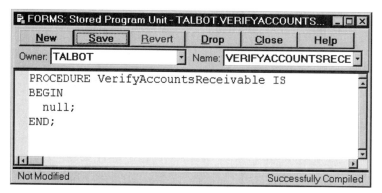

You can then enter the code for your program unit and compile it by clicking on the Save button. This issues a CREATE PROCEDURE (or whatever), which compiles the program unit on the server and returns any PL/SQL compilation errors after running it. You need to have CREATE privilege for the kind of program unit you are creating.

To create a database trigger for a particular table, expand the table object in the Object Navigator to see the Trigger heading under it. Click on Create just as before to see the Database Trigger Editor shown in Figure 10-8. Click on the New button to create a new trigger. The Editor contains several different radio button and check box fields to specify parts of the trigger, such as the trigger type (which kind of statement) and timing (Before or After the statement). In the case of Figure 10-8, the developer is defining a Before-Insert trigger on the Ledger table. As before, clicking on the Save button compiles the code by issuing a CREATE TRIGGER statement.

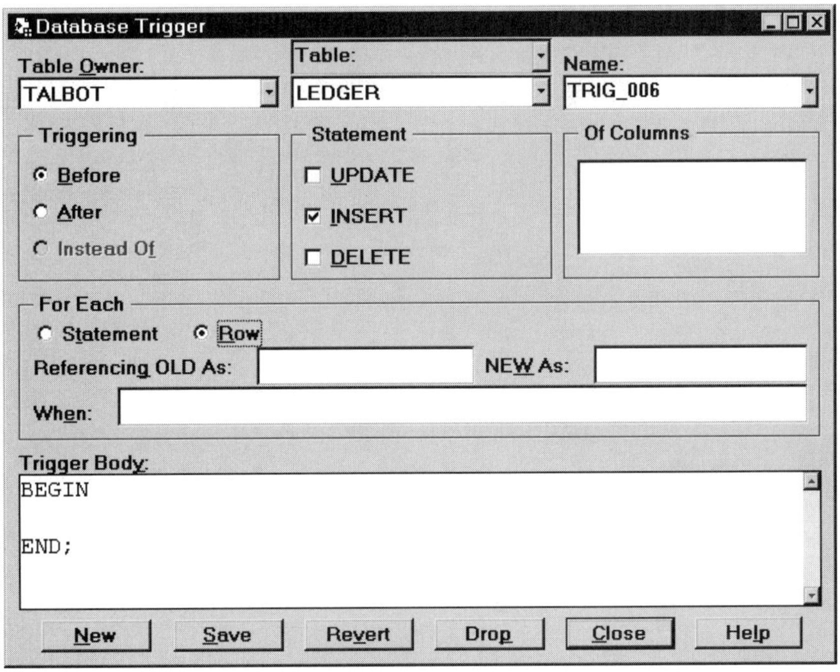

FIGURE 10-8. *The Database Trigger Editor*

NOTE

You cannot refer to any form items in your stored program unit or database trigger code. That is, you cannot refer to an item in a block through a bind variable. The client-side items are not available to the server that executes the PL/SQL. Instead, you must add the variable to the parameters of the program unit to pass information in and out of the program unit. This is generally a good way to structure program units within the module as well, as it makes them more reusable. You should note that database triggers do not have parameters.

Part II has taken you through the process of prototype and design. You are now at a point where you need to learn the details of producing a working, final application through coding, testing, and debugging techniques. If you apply what you have learned in this part of the book, you will find that coding, testing, and debugging are less time consuming and less likely to be rework instead of work.

PART
III

Programming with Developer

CHAPTER
11

PL/SQL Basics

he chapters in Part III teach you how to use Oracle Developer to build real, complete applications from your prototypes and designs. PL/SQL is Oracle's procedural extension to SQL. In other words, PL/SQL gives you the ability not only to execute SQL but also to embed it in control structures such as IF-THEN-ELSE and loops. This allows you to do much more sophisticated work in your applications than you could using only SQL. The PL/SQL syntax derives from the more complex Ada programming language but is in practice much simpler to use.

This chapter teaches you the fundamentals of the PL/SQL programming language: how it organizes data, how you program with control structures, and how to use SQL as a part of the language. The next chapter expands on this one with more complex program structures that let you organize your programs into robust collections of reusable code. Chapter 13 introduces you to the debugging facilities in Oracle Developer. When you have completed this part of the book, you will understand how to create, test, and debug your applications.

This chapter focuses on basic programming structures in PL/SQL. In Oracle Developer, you place your code into two kinds of structures: triggers and program units. Developer events fire the triggers, which in turn can call the program units. The material in this chapter tells you what you need to know to code basic triggers and program units; the next chapter tells you how to produce more complex program units (procedures, functions, and packages). You can also use the knowledge gained here to develop stored program units (database triggers, procedures, and packages) in your Oracle database. The last part of the next chapter discusses how to package your program units in program libraries that you can reuse in many different applications.

NOTE
Oracle Developer uses a local version of PL/SQL to compile your program units. The Oracle database server uses the version of PL/SQL current for the Oracle database server release to compile program units. These two versions of PL/SQL may not be the same, so some features may be available through the server PL/SQL that are not available through the Oracle Developer PL/SQL. For example, if you are using Oracle Developer with a version 7.3.4 Oracle server, the PL/SQL version on the server lacks many of the facilities available to you in Oracle Developer PL/SQL8. Usually, though, this will only impact you in fairly advanced uses, such as using nested tables in your code. You do need to understand the assumptions your code is making about what is underneath it.

The basic program unit structure in PL/SQL has the following structure:

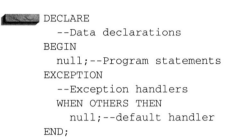

```
DECLARE
   --Data declarations
BEGIN
   null;--Program statements
EXCEPTION
   --Exception handlers
   WHEN OTHERS THEN
     null;--default handler
END;
```

A complete program with this structure is an anonymous block—a block of code without a name. The whole block is a single PL/SQL statement; hence, the END requires the semicolon statement terminator. If you have no data declarations, you can omit the DECLARE, BEGIN, and END keywords; and if you have no exception handlers, you can omit the EXCEPTION keyword and the WHEN clause. You usually will have a BEGIN-EXCEPTION-END sequence, not just an EXCEPTION clause. You must have at least one valid programming statement in the block, hence the use of the null statements in the preceding code listing. The code examples in this chapter always include a null statement so that the example compiles if there is no code in a block.

NOTE
A PL/SQL block is completely different from the Oracle Developer Forms data block. A PL/SQL block is an executable program (an anonymous block, a procedure, or a function), whereas a Forms data block is a collection of item definitions within a form that might or might not map to a base server table definition. You can also see a Forms data block as a list of records. A PL/SQL block can contain PL/SQL blocks nested within itself to any level, with the scope of names in each block restricted to the block in which you declare the nested block. PL/SQL is thus a block-structured programming language, as is Ada.

Here are some practical issues you should know about:

- Most PL/SQL expressions use the same syntax as SQL expressions, and you can use most of the Oracle SQL built-in functions. If you know SQL, you already know most of PL/SQL.

- PL/SQL is not case sensitive, so you can code using uppercase or lowercase letters, or use a mixture of the two for readability. Literals in quotes (characters taken as themselves rather than as symbols for something else) are case sensitive.

- PL/SQL identifiers must start with a letter and may contain only letters, numbers, underscores, number signs (#), and dollar signs ($). Identifiers can have up to 30 characters and cannot be any of the reserved words of the language, such as DECLARE or END.

- Use two single quotes to embed a single quote in a quoted string literal: 'Talbot''s Farm', for example.

- BOOLEAN type values can be TRUE, FALSE, or NULL. These are not quoted strings; they are values: IS_WINDOW_DISPLAYED := TRUE, not 'TRUE', for example.

- You can comment lines either with an inline comment starting with two dashes or with a multiple-line comment between a /*-*/ pair:

```
null;      -- This is an inline comment terminated by the line end
/* This is
a multiple-line
comment terminated by */
```

TIP
*Use inline comments in preference to multiple-line comments. It's easy to forget the terminating */ or to delete one side of the comment pair while you're working on the code.*

If you do much PL/SQL programming, see Scott Urman's book, *Oracle8 PL/SQL Programming* (Oracle Press, 1997). The reference contains a full list of the various built-in functions you can use.

A Brief Introduction to Data

Probably the single most important thing to understand about a programming language is how the language organizes data. Some programming languages have a tremendously complex type system, and some are quite simple. Some languages let you extend the type system, and others do not.

Data Types

A data type is the category of data into which a value falls, such as character, number, or date. PL/SQL unifies its programming language types with the SQL data types, extending the SQL types with special features. Because the primary purpose of PL/SQL is to embed SQL, it is logical to expect the language to map directly to SQL statements and the types of values therein. PL/SQL also adds some data types that are useful in block programming: BINARY_INTEGER, BOOLEAN, RECORD, and TABLE. Using PL/SQL with Oracle Developer also adds several types corresponding to the different objects in forms, such as windows and blocks.

NOTE

CURSOR and REF CURSOR are special data types you associate with SQL statements. See the later section "Using SQL in PL/SQL" for details.

SQL Types

PL/SQL provides a one-to-one mapping with the SQL type system, at least for the important SQL types. See the online documentation for details of these types: DECIMAL, FLOAT, INTEGER, NUMBER, REAL, SMALLINT, DATE, DATETIME, CHARACTER, LONG, RAW, STRING, VARCHAR, and VARCHAR2. You can use the standard Oracle SQL conversion functions to handle explicit conversion of these types in PL/SQL blocks.

PL/SQL Binary Integers and Booleans

PL/SQL adds three data types to handle signed integer numbers. When you use signed integer numbers in PL/SQL calculations, it does not need to convert the data to an internal format, as it does with NUMBER or any of the other SQL types. In blocks that do heavy integer arithmetic, you can increase performance by using signed integers instead of NUMBER data.

The basic signed integer type is BINARY_INTEGER, with which you can represent numbers in the range -2147483647 to 2147483647. The two subtypes represent smaller ranges. The NATURAL type represents numbers from 0 to 2147483647, and the POSITIVE type represents numbers from 1 to 2147483647. You use these to restrict data to nonnegative values.

The BOOLEAN type lets you handle TRUE and FALSE values directly. You can also set a BOOLEAN to NULL, meaning the value is undefined. This means that PL/SQL Boolean values have three possible states, TRUE, FALSE, and NULL, and that the logic is a three-valued logic.

NOTE
Three-valued logic can be counterintuitive. For example, if you compare two Boolean variables and either or both are NULL, the result is NULL, not TRUE. If you have a NULL expression in an IF statement, the statement executes the ELSE clause. A third example: NOT(NULL) evaluates to NULL. For a good discussion of three-valued logic and its use with SQL, see Chris Date's article "Null Values in Database Management" in Chapter 15 of his book Relational Database: Selected Writings *(Addison-Wesley, 1986). Database managers do not consistently implement any one model of three-valued logic, so consult the Oracle documentation carefully to understand what happens in specific situations.*

PL/SQL Records

A PL/SQL record lets you define a single variable that comprises several data elements, much like a database row. You can use the RECORD type to create structured data of any type. You can then refer to the data as a logical unit using dot notation.

To create records, you must first create the individual record type. For example, to create a type corresponding to part of the Ledger table, you could use the following statement in a DECLARE section:

```
DECLARE
   TYPE LedgerType IS RECORD (
     LedgerID VARCHAR(25) NOT NULL := 0,
     ActionDate DATE,
     Action VARCHAR(8),
     Amount NUMBER(9,2));
BEGIN
  null;
END;
```

In this case, the record represents only part of the table data. The NOT NULL clause is the same as the SQL NOT NULL, which prevents you from assigning NULL to the field. Although the obvious use for the RECORD type is to represent data that corresponds to table data, you can have fields of any type, including a RECORD type, in any combination. You can use records in packages, for example, to represent runtime objects that you do not store in the database, such as a particular time of day on the 24-hour clock. You could then package the type with a set of functions that operate on the data in the record. This lets you call the function Subtract with values for the time and the time interval to subtract from it.

```
PACKAGE Time24Package IS
   TYPE Time24Type IS RECORD (
      hour NATURAL NOT NULL := 0,
      minute NATURAL NOT NULL := 0,
      second NUMBER NOT NULL := 0);

FUNCTION Subtract(time Time24Type,
                  interval TimeIntervalPackage.tTimeInterval)
      RETURN Time24Type;
END;
```

You can declare two variables of Time24Type, pass them to the function, get back the difference, and assign it to a third variable of Time24Type. This kind of packaging, an abstract data type, lets you represent more complex objects than the simple PL/SQL types. Chapter 12 gives a complete discussion of packages and abstract data types.

NOTE
See the section "Using Type Attributes" for a way to make the field types correspond exactly to the database column types.

Once you define the type, you can then use the type to create a variable, also in a DECLARE section:

```
DECLARE
   TYPE tLedger IS RECORD (
      vLedgerID VARCHAR(25) NOT NULL := 0,
      vActionDate DATE,
      vAction VARCHAR(8),
      vAmount NUMBER(9,2));
   vLedgerItem tLedger;
BEGIN
  null;
END;
```

The resulting record has a LedgerID field with value 0 and the rest of the fields NULL. PL/SQL creates the variable when it executes the DECLARE section and destroys it when it reaches the END of the block in which you declared it. You can assign values to the fields and refer to the fields using dot notation, as in this code fragment:

```
IF vLedgerItem.vAction = 'Sold'
THEN vLedgerItem.vAmount := 0.0;
END IF;
```

Notice that the comparison operator is "=," whereas the assignment operator is ":=".

PL/SQL Tables

Although the RECORD type is powerful, it lacks one feature: the ability to represent more than one row of data at a time. That's the job of the TABLE type. Most programming languages have multiple-value data types such as this, and PL/SQL is no exception.

An *array* is a variable in a programming language that represents multiple values, called elements, that you access through an integer index. The first element of the array has index 1, the second element has index 2, and so on. Some languages start indexing at 0, others at 1, and still others at arbitrary values, including negative indexes. PL/SQL tables are like arrays in that you access them through an index. They are unlike most programming language array types in that you have complete control over the index values and the storage allocated for elements. When you assign a value to an element using some index, if that element does not exist, PL/SQL creates it. You can thus build an array with five arbitrary index values such as -4, 33, 1275, 2, and -43, and the array will have five elements. Accessing an element you haven't created in this way gives you Oracle error -1403, "no data found."

A *linked list* is a data structure in a programming language that represents elements that you access through pointers to the first, last, next, or previous element. PL/SQL tables are like linked lists in that the storage for the elements exists only for elements you've added to the table. There are table attributes that you use to navigate through the table, just as for a linked list. Unlike a linked list, however, you can go right to an element if you know its index.

The PL/SQL table thus combines the best aspects of arrays and linked lists. You can use tables for many different purposes. The major ones are to represent multiple-value data in PL/SQL subprograms and to represent result sets from queries in PL/SQL code. The table lets you build a complete result set in a stored procedure, for example, and to return it to the caller through an IN OUT parameter.

NOTE
Oracle Developer Forms has a similar construct called record groups. These objects exist only in a form, however, and as they are not integral to the PL/SQL language, you have to use built-in subprograms to access data elements. In general-purpose PL/SQL programming, use tables instead of record groups. Use record groups where some feature needs them, such as for building dynamic lists (Chapter 7) or passing Oracle Developer parameter lists (Chapter 10).

DECLARING TABLES   As with records, you declare a table by declaring a table type, then declaring variables of that type. This makes tables particularly suitable for package programming (see Chapter 12). You can export a table type through the package specification, then declare as many tables of that type as you need in the PL/SQL code that refers to the package.
You can declare a simple table of scalar values:

```
DECLARE
   TYPE tLedgerAction IS TABLE OF Ledger.Action%TYPE INDEX BY BINARY_INTEGER;
   vActionTable tLedgerAction;  --declare an action table
BEGIN
  null;
END;
```

The INDEX clause is required to be in this format, as PL/SQL does not yet support anything but BINARY_INTEGER indexing. You can also declare a more complex table using a record type:

```
DECLARE
   TYPE tLedger IS TABLE OF Ledger%ROWTYPE INDEX BY BINARY_INTEGER;
   vLedgerTable tLedger;  --declare a Ledger table
BEGIN
  null;
END;
```

You can use any record type in the OF clause of the TYPE declaration, not just a %ROWTYPE-derived record.

USING TABLES WITH INDEXES AND ATTRIBUTES   Once you have declared the table type and a variable of that type, you can create elements in the table by assigning values to them. Again, PL/SQL does not actually create any element until you assign a value to it using an index.

For example, say you want to create a list of possible values by directly assigning the four kinds of ledger action to the vLedgerTable variable:

```
DECLARE
    TYPE tLedgerAction IS TABLE OF Ledger.Action%TYPE INDEX BY BINARY_INTEGER;
    vActionTable tLedgerAction;  --declare an action table
BEGIN
   vActionTable(1) := 'Bought';
   vActionTable(2) := 'Sold';
   vActionTable(3) := 'Paid';
   vActionTable(4) := 'Received';
   -- Use the table in further processing
END;
```

You specify the index in parentheses after the table name to refer to a particular element of the table. In this example, you are creating four elements in the table with indexes 1, 2, 3, and 4.

NOTE

Again, you can use any index values, not just sequential ones or a sequence starting at 1. It is, however, a good idea to use such a series, as it is easy to remember and easy to program in loops. Alternatively, you can use SQL to fill in the table (see the later section "Using SQL in PL/SQL" for details on the CURSOR and the looping syntax):

```
DECLARE
    TYPE tLedgerAction IS TABLE OF Ledger.Action%TYPE INDEX BY BINARY_INTEGER;
    vActionTable tLedgerAction;  --declare an action table
    CURSOR cLedger IS SELECT DISTINCT Action FROM Ledger;
BEGIN
   FOR vLedgerAction IN cLedger LOOP
     vActionTable(cLedger%ROWCOUNT) := vLedgerAction.Action;
   END LOOP;
END;
```

This example selects the DISTINCT values of the Action column from the Ledger table through a cursor and a special cursor FOR loop, assigning the retrieved values to the action table using the special cursor ROWCOUNT attribute as the index. This would have the same result as the previous example, but it is more flexible. If the possible set of values in the table changes, you would have to redo the first example, but not the second.

You can also access tables through the table attributes listed in Table 11-1.

To use a table attribute, you attach it to the table name using dot notation. For example, to get the index to the element in the table previous to element 4, you would use this syntax:

```
vIndex := vActionTable.Prior(4);
```

For examples of using these attributes, see the PL/SQL User's Guide and Reference or Scott Urman's book, *Oracle PL/SQL Programming*.

Oracle Developer PL/SQL Object Types

When you use PL/SQL in Oracle Developer, you also have several types available that represent the different kinds of objects in Oracle Developer. Table 11-2 shows the different objects that Forms gives you.

When you call built-in subprograms with arguments, you can usually supply either the unique name of the object or the object ID. The object ID is a handle to the object—a value that uniquely identifies it. When you declare a variable with

Attribute	Type	Description
Count	NUMBER	Returns the number of elements in the table
Delete		Deletes all the elements of the table
Delete(index)		Deletes element specified by *index* from the table
Delete(index1, index2)		Deletes all elements between *index1* and *index2,* inclusive, from the table
Exists(index)	BOOLEAN	Returns whether the element specified by *index* exists in the table
First	BINARY_INTEGER	Returns the index of the first element in the table
Last	BINARY_INTEGER	Returns the index of the last element in the table
Next(index)	BINARY_INTEGER	Returns the index of the element next in the table after the element specified by *index*
Prior(index)	BINARY_INTEGER	Returns the index of the element prior in the table to the element specified by *index*

TABLE 11-1. *PL/SQL Table Attributes*

Object	Type	Lookup Function
Alert	ALERT	FIND_ALERT
Block	BLOCK	FIND_BLOCK
Canvas	CANVAS	FIND_CANVAS
Editor	EDITOR	FIND_EDITOR
Form	FORMMODULE	FIND_FORM
Item	ITEM	FIND_ITEM
List of Values	LOV	FIND_LOV
Menu Item	MENUITEM	FIND_MENUITEM
Parameter List	PARAMLIST	GET_PARAMETER_LIST
Record Group	RECORDGROUP	FIND_GROUP
Record Group Column	GROUPCOLUMN	FIND_COLUMN
Relation	RELATION	FIND_RELATION
Report	REPORT	FIND_REPORT
Tab Page	TAB_PAGE	FIND_TAB_PAGE
Timer	TIMER	FIND_TIMER
View	VIEWPORT	FIND_VIEW
Window	WINDOW	FIND_WINDOW

TABLE 11-2.   *Forms PL/SQL Object Types and Lookup Functions*

one of the types from Table 11-1, you are really declaring an object ID handle. You get the ID by calling the FIND function, which returns the ID when you pass in the name. You can thus use the name to find the ID, then use the ID for a series of subprogram calls. This can speed up processing if you are making many references to an object, because each time you pass in a name, Oracle Developer must look up the ID internally. For example, you might have some code that refers to an item value inside a processing loop. Instead of looking up the item by name during each loop iteration, you get the item ID using FIND_ITEM() before entering the loop, then use the resulting item ID to look up the item value while in the loop.

The parameter list object has a special ID type, PARAM_LIST, which corresponds to the GET_PARAMETER_LIST function rather than to a function starting with FIND.

Table 11-3 shows the Graphics data types and their corresponding GET functions, which work in much the same way as the Forms types despite the different naming conventions.

See Chapter 19 for detailed descriptions of the GET functions and the different subprograms that take object ID arguments.

NOTE
Reports has no object types and no object IDs.

Declaring Variables and Constants

You have already seen several declarations of variables earlier in this book. A variable declaration in a DECLARE section takes this form:

```
variable_name  type_name  [NOT NULL] [:= initial_value];
```

You can also declare variables in a parameter list of a subprogram (procedure or function); see Chapter 13.

The NOT NULL qualifier specifies that you cannot assign a NULL value to the variable. The assignment of an initial value sets the variable to the value you specify with a literal or an expression. If you specify NOT NULL, you must also specify the initial value. It is a good idea to initialize all variables to ensure that you have a

Object	Type	Lookup Function
Axis	OG_AXIS	OG_GET_AXIS
Button Procedure	OG_BUTTONPROC	OG_GET_BUTTONPROC
Chart Template	OG_TEMPLATE	OG_GET_TEMPLATE
Display	OG_DISPLAY	OG_GET_DISPLAY
Field Template	OG_FTEMP	OG_GET_FTEMP
Graphic Object	OG_OBJECT	OG_GET_OBJECT
Layer	OG_LAYER	OG_GET_LAYER
Query	OG_QUERY	OG_GET_QUERY
Reference Line	OG_REFLINE	OG_GET_REFLINE
Sound	OG_SOUND	OG_GET_SOUND
Timer	OG_TIMER	OG_GET_TIMER
Window	OG_WINDOW	OG_GET_WINDOW

TABLE 11-3. *Graphics Object Types and Lookup Functions*

valid value to which to refer the first time you use the identifier. You can also use the reserved word DEFAULT in place of the assignment operator: DEFAULT initial_value instead of := initial value.

You can refer to Oracle Developer objects through host variables. A host variable is a name from the embedding application that you reference by adding a colon (:) to the beginning of the name. You can use these host variables anywhere you can use a PL/SQL variable, inside a SQL statement or outside.

```
BEGIN
    /* Update the age in the block field and the database. */
    :Person.Age := :Person.Age+1;
    UPDATE Person SET Age = Age+1 WHERE Name = :Person.Name;
END;
```

PL/SQL has the same types as all the Oracle Developer products, so the host variables do not need a separate declaration in the PL/SQL procedure. PL/SQL treats them as though you had declared them with the type you specified in the item definition.

NOTE

Oracle Developer objects use the VARCHAR2 type to represent text values. The differences between CHAR, VARCHAR, and VARCHAR2 are important in certain cases. CHAR represents fixed-length data. If you assign a value to a CHAR variable with a length greater than the value's length, PL/SQL pads out the string to the length of the variable with blanks. VARCHAR and VARCHAR2 are the same and do not pad in this way. You may have problems with assignments and with comparisons. If you assign a value that is shorter than the size of the CHAR variable, PL/SQL pads the string. If you have trailing blanks in a VARCHAR2 variable and compare it to another string of any type, PL/SQL treats the blanks as valid characters and makes them part of the comparison, but it does not pad out the other string. If you compare two CHAR variables, PL/SQL pads out the shorter one to the length of the longer one before comparing. This means that if you have trailing blanks in the longer string, PL/SQL will effectively ignore them by comparing them to padded blanks in the shorter string. Generally, you should use VARCHAR2 in most circumstances and avoid using CHAR and VARCHAR.

A constant is an identifier that gets a value when you declare it and to which you cannot thereafter assign any values. You declare a constant with the CONSTANT keyword:

```
constant_name   CONSTANT   type_name   := value;
```

PL/SQL requires the initialization of the constant; this value is the value of the constant for its entire life cycle.

Using Type Attributes

A PL/SQL *type* attribute is a modifier that you can use to get information about an object for use in declaring other objects. The %TYPE attribute lets you get the type of a variable, a constant, or a database column. The %ROWTYPE attribute lets you get the types of all the columns in a database table or a SELECT cursor result table. Use the %TYPE as often as you can, as it improves maintainability greatly.

You can use %TYPE to declare variables with the same type as another variable or constant. You can also use it to declare variables with the same type as a database column, usually because you are going to store a value from that column in the variable.

The following example code retrieves a value from the database, increments the value, and assigns the result to a new variable with the same type.

```
DECLARE
   vDBAge      Person.Age%TYPE;    -- database column type
   vNewAge     vDBAge%TYPE;          -- type from dbAge
BEGIN
   SELECT Age INTO vDBAge FROM Person
    WHERE Person.Name = :Person.Name;
   vNewAge := vDBAge + 1;
END;
```

NOTE
Even when you declare a database column with the NOT NULL attribute, PL/SQL does not give the variable the NOT NULL qualifier. You must do that explicitly if you wish to prevent assignment of NULL to the variable.

You can use the %ROWTYPE attribute to create a record variable that can contain all the columns from a table. For example, say you want to retrieve skills and abilities from the database for further processing in a trigger. The following declarations create a record that will hold the columns of the WorkerHasSkill table:

```
DECLARE
   hasSkillRecord    WorkerHasSkill%ROWTYPE;
BEGIN
    -- Retrieve records and process; for example,
hasSkillRecord.Name := 'Gerhardt Kentgen';
END;
```

The %ROWTYPE attribute also applies to tables you create as the result of a cursor SELECT. Using %ROWTYPE, you can create a record that PL/SQL automatically formats correctly to hold whatever data the SELECT returns. If you use %ROWTYPE, you need not declare the individual variables with their types, making maintenance easier. For example, if you want to retrieve the sums of the amounts from the Ledger table grouped by person, you can declare the variable this way:

```
DECLARE
   CURSOR sumCursor IS SELECT Person, SUM(Amount) Total
      FROM Ledger GROUP BY Person;
   sumRecord    sumCursor%ROWTYPE;
BEGIN
   null;  -- Retrieve rows and process
END;
```

When you use %ROWTYPE this way, you must specify an alias for any expressions in the SELECT list, such as Total in the sumCursor SELECT. This alias becomes the variable name for the field in the record PL/SQL creates. See the section "Using SQL with PL/SQL," later in the chapter, for more details on cursors.

You can assign one %ROWTYPE variable to another if they both come from the same table or cursor. You cannot assign the record you create with %ROWTYPE to variables you create with a RECORD type. You can use RECORD types in much the same way as %ROWTYPE declarations except with cursors. The disadvantage of a RECORD is that you cannot automatically create its structure from the data dictionary. The advantage is that you can give it whatever structure you like, including additional fields that do not correspond to database columns.

An Even Briefer Introduction to Control

The control statements in a programming language are its primary reason for existing, which is especially true for PL/SQL. Control structures differentiate a procedural programming language from a declarative programming language such as SQL. When you embed SQL in PL/SQL, you combine the best aspects of the declarative language with the added benefits of the control structures with which you surround the SQL statements.

There are three kinds of control structures: sequential, conditional, and iterative.

A sequential structure is the simple order of program statements. PL/SQL executes them in order, one at a time. SQL works on a statement-by-statement basis; the language understands only a single statement at a time. PL/SQL processes a series of statements and has variables that connect the statements. This gives you much more flexibility to structure your processing by letting you break it into a series of steps, including multiple SQL statements.

A conditional structure is a statement that branches program flow based on the truth or falsity of a logical condition. You use conditional structures to make decisions about further processing, which you cannot do easily in SQL. The DECODE function gives you a limited ability to make decisions on a row-by-row basis, but complex conditions quickly get out of hand in the declarative syntax.

An iterative structure is a statement that controls a looping process that repetitively executes program statements. SQL, by its nature, provides for looping in several ways as an internal mechanism. Besides the simple iteration over the multiple rows of the result table, SQL has nested subqueries that let you loop in a highly structured, powerful way using predicate calculus operators (ANY and ALL, EXISTS and IN, for example). SQL even has the correlated subquery to let you test the row of an outer query to the rows of a nested subquery on a row-by-row basis. Still, even these capabilities are not flexible enough to easily handle all the possible iterative situations you will find yourself in during database application programming. Iterative control structures give you both the ability to retrieve rows from the database and to process them using more SQL. This can be much simpler and faster than the nested selects or joins in a single SQL statement. Iteration also lets you accomplish many standard programming tasks at the application level, for which SQL is not appropriate.

NOTE
PL/SQL also provides an unconditional branching statement (GOTO with a statement label), which you should avoid unless it makes the program clearer. For example, in lengthy procedures you can sometimes get very complex conditional and iterative procedures that, if replaced with a simple GOTO, would be much easier to understand. This is rare. The standard case of simplifying error handling, for example, by branching to an ERROR label, is better done with exceptions; see Chapter 12.

Conditional Control

PL/SQL provides the IF-THEN, IF-THEN-ELSE, and IF-THEN-ELSIF-ELSE structures for conditional control of program execution. The IF-THEN structure tests a condition and, if it is true, executes a block of code. For example, the following trigger block tests the age of the current worker and displays an alert, then causes the trigger to fail by raising the FORM_TRIGGER_FAILURE exception.

```
DECLARE
   vAlertButton NUMBER;
BEGIN
   IF :Person.Age < 16 THEN
     vAlertButton := Show_Alert('Under_Age_Alert'); --Display error
     RAISE FORM_TRIGGER_FAILURE;
   END IF;
END;
```

NOTE
See the section on exceptions and exception handling in Chapter 12 for more information on the RAISE statement.

If you have two program blocks, one for the TRUE decision and one for the FALSE, you can use the IF-THEN-ELSE structure:

```
DECLARE
   vAlertButton NUMBER;
BEGIN
   IF :Person.Age < 16 THEN
     vAlertButton := Show_Alert('Under_Age_Alert'); --Display error
     RAISE FORM_TRIGGER_FAILURE;
   ELSE
     vAlertButton := Show_Alert('Over_Age_Alert'); --Display error
   END IF;
END;
```

If your decision has several parts, you can use nested IF statements in your ELSE clause, but a better way is the ELSIF structure:

```
DECLARE
   vAlertButton NUMBER;
BEGIN
   IF :Person.Age < 16 THEN
     vAlertButton := Show_Alert('Under_Age_Alert'); --Display error
     RAISE FORM_TRIGGER_FAILURE;
   ELSIF :Person.Age > 70 THEN
     vAlertButton := Show_Alert('Over_Age_Alert'); --Display error
       RAISE FORM_TRIGGER_FAILURE;
   ELSE  -- Worker is between 16 and 70 years old, inclusive
   vAlertButton := Show_Alert('Age_OK_Alert'); --Display info alert
   END IF;
END;
```

In this control structure, the first condition identifies values under 17, the second identifies values over and including 17 but greater than 70, and the ELSE clause identifies values between 17 and 70, inclusive. The ELSIF clauses all imply that the conditions in prior IF and ELSIF clauses evaluated to FALSE.

NOTE
Rules for testing NULL values are the same as for SQL. Remember that NULL is not a value, it is the absence of a value. Therefore, you must use the IS NULL and IS NOT NULL expressions instead of equality comparisons to test whether some expression is or is not NULL, respectively.

Iteration Control

Oracle Developer builds in quite a bit of iteration control. Oracle Developer Forms retrieves sets of records automatically through blocks, executing triggers at all levels. Oracle Developer Reports loops over rows and groups with a very complex iteration structure that the report data model drives through its groups. Even Oracle Developer Graphics fetches data into a table for translation into charts in a looping process. Before using iteration in trigger code and program units with Oracle Developer, you should try to make use of what is already there. For example, you can put program statements into item or record triggers, and Forms will execute them automatically for each row in an iteration structure. This is much more efficient and easier to maintain than code that retrieves all the records, then loops through them in a PL/SQL block. You can put statements into page triggers in reports, and Reports will execute them after each page. The PL/SQL control structures give you some additional control within a particular trigger, but you should avoid the complexity if you can.

There are three kinds of iteration control statements in PL/SQL: LOOP, WHILE, and FOR.

The LOOP statement, in combination with the EXIT WHEN statement, lets you loop until a particular condition evaluates to TRUE. For example, to loop through all the records in a block, incrementing age by 1, you could use this block:

```
DECLARE
   vCurrentPosition   VARCHAR2(10)  := :SYSTEM.CURSOR_RECORD;
BEGIN
   FIRST_RECORD;
   LOOP
     :Person.Age := :Person.Age + 1;
     EXIT WHEN :SYSTEM.LAST_RECORD = 'TRUE';
     NEXT_RECORD;
   END LOOP;
   Go_Record(vCurrentPosition);    -- Reset cursor
END;
```

This structure executes the statements at least once, as the test for EXIT WHEN comes at the end of the statements. In this case, if the first record is a New record with NULL age, the result will be NULL, with no effective change even though there was one iteration of the loop.

If you nest LOOP statements within other LOOP statements, you can label them and refer to the label in the EXIT WHEN statement to specify what loop in the nested stack to exit.

The WHILE statement lets you control processing by evaluating a condition before executing the statements:

```
DECLARE
  vCurrentPosition  VARCHAR2 (10) := :SYSTEM.CURSOR_RECORD;
BEGIN
  FIRST_RECORD;
  WHILE :SYSTEM.LAST_RECORD != 'TRUE' LOOP
    :Person.Age := :Person.Age + 1;
    EXIT WHEN :SYSTEM.LAST_RECORD = 'TRUE';
    NEXT_RECORD;
  END LOOP;
  :Person.Age := :Person.Age + 1;
  Go_Record(vCurrentPosition);   -- Reset cursor
END;
```

This structure need not execute the statements within the control structure at all if the condition immediately evaluates to FALSE. In this case, the example would never update the last record, so there needs to be a final update after the loop. As before, if the age is NULL, the statement evaluates to and assigns NULL to the age, resulting in no change.

Finally, the FOR statement lets you put an explicit numeric limit on the number of iterations:

```
DECLARE
  vCurrentPosition  VARCHAR2(10) := :SYSTEM.CURSOR_RECORD;
  vLastRecord VARCHAR2 (10) := 0;
BEGIN
  LAST_RECORD;
  vLastRecord := :SYSTEM.CURSOR_RECORD;
  FIRST_RECORD;
  FOR I IN 1..To_Number(vLastRecord) LOOP
    :Person.Age := :Person.Age + 1;
    NEXT_RECORD;
  END LOOP;
  Go_Record(vCurrentPosition);   -- Reset cursor
END;
```

This structure executes the loop within the range of numbers you specify. It also gives you a value to use through the counter you declare in the FOR statement. You can use this value to look up specific records, to insert values into the database with an incremented number, and so on.

You can specify the lower and upper limits of the range with an expression, as in the example. You can use this feature to tie the range to some variable outside the loop, or you can use it to determine the range dynamically at runtime. For example, you could get a count of the number of rows in a table with a SQL statement, then loop through the fetching of the rows that number of times. This is not the most efficient use of loops, however, because you can more effectively use the %NOTFOUND attribute on the cursor (see the following section "Using SQL in PL/SQL") to exit a standard LOOP.

The example gets the number of the range end by setting the cursor to the last record and saving the record number. This lets you loop over the records precisely the right number of times. As in the LOOP example, if there is only one New record, it gets updated with NULL.

Looking at the three examples, none stands out from the others as being better, though perhaps the LOOP is the most straightforward. You can usually do the same thing with any of the three iteration control structures. You will usually have to judge which is better by the number of lines of code and your subjective judgment about which design is simpler. One way to make that judgment is to look at how easy the code would be to verify as correct: how many things would you need to look at? Do you have a single decision or multiple decisions? Do you have special cases you must take into account? For example, the preceding WHILE code must use a statement after the loop to update the last row, which seems like one thing too many given the alternatives.

NOTE
See the section "Using SQL in PL/SQL" for a special version of the FOR loop that automatically handles cursor fetching. This structure can save you much programming if its functionality does what you need.

Using SQL in PL/SQL

There are three reasons to use PL/SQL in Oracle Developer applications: to use control structures to change application behavior during event processing, to add special-purpose code that does calculations (outside of what calculated items can do), or to issue SQL statements to the server beyond what the Oracle Developer tools give you automatically (rarely useful). Oracle Developer also lets you base data blocks on packaged procedures on the server, as opposed to basing the data block on a table or view.

NOTE
SQL error handling in PL/SQL uses exceptions. Chapter 12 gives details on raising and handling exceptions, and tells you how to use the SQLCODE and SQLERRM built-in functions in error handlers.

Simple SQL

The simplest way to use SQL in PL/SQL is to just use it. PL/SQL treats SQL statements as programming language statements and will accept almost any standard SQL. Many triggers will consist of a simple INSERT, UPDATE, or DELETE statement, perhaps using host variables to connect the statement to items in the application.

There are some SQL statements that you cannot use in PL/SQL:

- DDL statements such as CREATE TABLE, GRANT, or ALTER VIEW, which imply the end of a transaction (but see the following section "Data Definition SQL" for some exceptions)

- Session control commands, such as SET ROLE

- ALTER SYSTEM

- EXPLAIN PLAN

You should avoid DML statements (INSERT, UPDATE, and DELETE) in triggers that can modify application items after committing data to the database, as this may lead to incorrect results. Refer to the trigger processing descriptions in Chapter 6.

WARNING
You can use COMMIT, ROLLBACK, and SAVEPOINT statements in PL/SQL programs, but it is not a good idea for client-side code. The Oracle Developer runtime systems have very specific ideas about transaction processing, and doing a COMMIT or ROLLBACK is likely to disrupt that processing. Oracle Developer Forms does interpret a COMMIT as an implicit call to the procedure COMMIT_FORM, but you should use it only in very high-level code that executes at a well-defined point in your program. Because Oracle Developer takes care of transaction processing for you, you can avoid the maintenance headaches associated with doing it yourself.

A special SELECT syntax lets you retrieve a single row of data: the implicit cursor or single-row select. The ANSI standard requires that the SELECT INTO statement actually return only one row; if the statement finds more than one row that qualifies, it must raise an error.

The implicit cursor adds an INTO clause after the select list, with host variables that map to the elements in the select list. You can declare these variables with %TYPE or use items that map to the data correctly.

```
DECLARE
   vDBAge NUMBER := 0;
BEGIN
   SELECT Age INTO vDBAge FROM Person WHERE Name = :Person.Name;
   -- Use vDBAge to do something here.
END;
```

NOTE
The INTO clause treats PL/SQL variables as identifiers rather than as host variables, so you do not put a colon (:) before the variable names. The host variable :Person.Name refers to the Name item in the Person data block, not to a PL/SQL variable.

WARNING
You should use INTO and the implicit cursor carefully. Each such statement generates two round-trips on the network, one to make sure only one row gets returned, and one to return the row. You can replace the implicit cursor with an explicit one and a FOR loop that fetches data into variables. This is more code, more complexity, and thus more maintenance, so you have to make a judgment. I use implicit cursors only when I'm sure the impact on performance is minimal. If you are deploying your application on the Internet, you should not use implicit cursors.

Using Explicit Cursors

The serious SQL work for PL/SQL programs begins when you need to work with queries that return more than one row. To do this, you must declare and use explicit cursors. An explicit cursor is a PL/SQL data structure that represents the position of a query in a result table deriving from execution of a SELECT statement. PL/SQL gives you many tools to make using cursors easier.

NOTE

Remember that blocks and their records in Oracle Developer Forms and data models in reports handle this kind of thing automatically. You can use these automatic facilities if you can develop blocks or data models that represent the iteration. Explicit cursors, although very useful in general PL/SQL programming, have less application in Oracle Developer programming, because Oracle Developer does most SQL work automatically. You can use explicit cursors to build more complex SQL than Oracle Developer can create automatically. The disadvantage is that you must rewrite all the automatic features you render useless.

The basic form for an explicit cursor looks like this example:

```
DECLARE
   CURSOR cSkill IS SELECT Skill, Description FROM Skill;
   vSkill cSkill%ROWTYPE;
BEGIN
   OPEN cSkill;
   LOOP
     FETCH cSkill INTO vSkill;
      EXIT WHEN cSkill%NOTFOUND;
      -- Process the row
   END LOOP;
   CLOSE cSkill;
END;
```

The two declarations set up the basic data structures for the block. The cursor contains the SELECT statement that retrieves all the data from the Skill table. The record declaration uses the %ROWTYPE attribute to create a record with the structure of the SELECT.

The OPEN and CLOSE statements execute and terminate the query. When you OPEN the cursor, you are executing the query; you must then fetch the rows. When you CLOSE the cursor, you can no longer fetch any more rows. Don't forget to close the cursors you have opened. Otherwise you will very quickly reach the maximum of open cursors allowed.

NOTE
There is a limit on the number of cursors you can open that is set by the Oracle database server OPEN_CURSORS initialization parameter. If you get Forms error FRM-40515, "Oracle error: unable to open cursor" as a SQL exception from your application, you may be exceeding this parameter. You can either increase this parameter value or you can set OPTIMIZETP=NO on the Forms Runtime command line to share cursors. This will slow down processing. Sharing cursors requires reparsing all the SQL statements that your application submits to the server. The OPEN_CURSORS parameter is operating-system dependent, so you may not be able to open as many cursors as you need on all operating systems.

The LOOP shows the basic structure of fetching. This variation uses the %NOTFOUND attribute of the cursor to test for an attempt to fetch beyond the end of the results table. It is the same as the SQL message ROW NOT FOUND.

There is a shortcut way to do all this using a special option to the FOR LOOP statement:

```
DECLARE
   CURSOR cSkill IS SELECT Skill, Description FROM Skill;
BEGIN
   FOR vSkill IN cSkill LOOP
     null;-- Process the row
   END LOOP;
END;
```

This block does exactly the same thing as the longer block above. You should use this shortcut syntax unless you have complex logic that requires that you have explicit control over fetching, opening the cursor, or closing the cursor.

NOTE
Remember that if you use expressions in the SELECT list, you must supply an alias that you can use as the field name in the record. Without the alias, you will not be able to refer to the field.

There are several cursor attributes that you can use to get information about the status of the cursor. Most of the attributes in Table 11-4 apply to both explicit and implicit cursors. For explicit cursors, you use the attributes by appending them to the cursor name. For implicit cursors, you use the implicit cursor name "SQL": for example, SQL%NOTFOUND or SQL%ISOPEN.

NOTE
You can use these attributes on the implicit cursors for data manipulation statements (INSERT, UPDATE, and DELETE) as well as for SELECT statements. %ROWCOUNT, for example, gives the number of rows inserted, updated, or deleted for an implicit cursor on these statements.

An important feature of cursors for reuse is the ability to parameterize cursors. You can use cursor parameters in the SELECT statement anywhere you could use a host variable or a literal value (see the section "Declaring Variables and Constants" for details). When PL/SQL opens the cursor, it accepts the values you supply for the parameters and inserts them into the SQL statement. The scope of the parameters is the

Attribute	Description
%NOTFOUND	TRUE when the last fetch failed to return a row; you use this attribute to test whether your loop has fetched the last row
%FOUND	TRUE when the last fetch did return a row; you use this attribute to test whether there is valid data from a fetch to execute some further action, such as inserting the data into another table
%ROWCOUNT	0 when you open the cursor, and increments by one for each row you fetch
%ISOPEN	TRUE if the cursor is open, FALSE otherwise; you use this attribute to test whether you need to open the cursor if there was some control action that might have closed it

TABLE 11-4. *PL/SQL Cursor Attributes*

cursor; you cannot use the parameter names anywhere other than the SELECT statement in the cursor. The following code illustrates the use of a parameterized cursor:

```
DECLARE
   CURSOR cSkill (pAbbrev IN VARCHAR2 DEFAULT '%') IS
     SELECT Skill, Description FROM Skill
      WHERE UPPER(Skill) LIKE UPPER(pAbbrev);
BEGIN
  FOR vSkill IN cSkill('%Horse%') LOOP
    null; -- Process the row
  END LOOP;
END;
```

This example expands the Skill query to handle subsets based on pattern lookups in the Skill table. You supply a LIKE operator expression, and the query finds those records that match the expression. In the example, the FOR LOOP passes in a pattern that tells the SELECT to look for any skill that contains the term "horse." Notice the conversions to uppercase in the SELECT; this makes it case insensitive for comparisons, making the cursor even more reusable. Also, notice the DEFAULT clause attached to the parameter; this clause supplies the obvious pattern to use when you pass no arguments, the "match any characters" pattern.

NOTE
Parameterized cursors are more useful when you declare them as part of a package specification, exporting the cursor and its parameters. This lets external programs use the cursor, supplying arguments as required for the particular purpose of the program. See Chapter 12 for details on packages.

Using Cursor Variables

A cursor variable is a pointer to a cursor. A PL/SQL cursor is not, strictly speaking, a variable. You cannot pass a cursor through a subprogram parameter list, nor can you assign different cursors to a single variable in your PL/SQL code. The cursor variable lets you do this. The major use for this feature in Oracle Developer is to pass a cursor as an IN OUT variable to a stored procedure. This lets you retrieve data on the client side while the procedure that executes the query is on the server side.

You can't just declare a variable to point to a cursor. First, you must declare a type, then you can declare variables. To declare a reference cursor type, use this syntax:

```
TYPE <type name> IS REF CURSOR [RETURN <record type>];
```

The type name is the name you use to declare your cursor variable. The optional record type in the RETURN clause corresponds to the structure of the cursor SELECT list. You usually construct the record type using the %ROWTYPE attribute. If you supply the RETURN clause, PL/SQL checks the SQL statements you open to ensure that the returned data corresponds to the type you've specified. Otherwise, it's up to you to match the SQL with your processing statements.

You open a cursor variable using a variant of the OPEN statement:

```
OPEN <cursor variable> FOR <select>;
```

The OPEN statement thus associates the variable with a particular select. With a regular cursor, you must declare the cursor in a declaration section with its SQL SELECT. With a cursor variable, you declare the SQL in your executing code.

NOTE

You cannot use a variable for the SELECT statement. That means you must code the SQL statement in its entirety in your PL/SQL code; you cannot construct it dynamically and pass it to the cursor. You can use the DBMS_SQL package with its dynamic SQL programming capabilities to parse and execute statements dynamically, though the techniques involved are beyond the scope of this book. See the following section, "Data Definition SQL," for an example of using DBMS_SQL.

As an example, say you want to query skill-related information through a Skills package (see Chapter 12 for details on package syntax):

```
CREATE OR REPLACE PACKAGE SkillsPackage AS
    -- A record type with all the columns in the WorkerHasSkill table
  TYPE tSkill IS RECORD (
    vSkill WorkerHasSkill.Skill%TYPE,
    vAbility WorkerHasSkill.Ability%TYPE);
    -- A record type with the primary key column in the Skill table
  TYPE tSkillCursor IS REF CURSOR RETURN tSkill;
```

```
    -- A table type for a table of Skills
  PROCEDURE SelectCursor (pcSkill IN OUT tSkillCursor,
                            pPerson IN VARCHAR2);
END SkillsPackage;
```

The package body just opens the cursor with a simple SELECT:

```
CREATE OR REPLACE PACKAGE BODY SkillsPackage AS
  PROCEDURE SelectCursor (pcSkill IN OUT tSkillCursor,
                            pPerson IN VARCHAR2) IS
  BEGIN
    OPEN pcSkill FOR
      SELECT Skill, Ability
        FROM WorkerHasSkill
        WHERE Name = pPerson;
  END SelectCursor;
END SkillsPackage;
```

This package puts together the record type, cursor type, and procedure for creating the cursor. To use it, you declare a record and a cursor variable and call the procedure:

```
DECLARE
  vSkill SkillsPackage.tSkill;
  vSkillCursor SkillsPackage.tSkillCursor;
BEGIN
  SkillsPackage.SelectCursor(vSkillCursor, 'Adah Talbot');
  LOOP
    FETCH vSkillCursor INTO vSkill;
    EXIT WHEN vSkillCursor%NOTFOUND;  -- exit after last row fetched
  -- Process the skills of Adah Talbot
  END LOOP;
  CLOSE vSkillCursor;
END;
```

Data Definition SQL

The SQL statements you can execute in PL/SQL blocks include only the SELECT, INSERT, UPDATE, and DELETE statements. PL/SQL does not permit the embedding of other SQL statements such as CREATE TABLE, DROP VIEW, COMMIT, GRANT, or ALTER SESSION. These are *data definition* (DDL) statements—statements that change the database schema or data dictionary.

PL/SQL binds SQL objects it encounters to the data dictionary when you compile it. This feature of the system gives you two major advantages: early feedback about problems with your SQL and enhanced performance due to the compile-time binding of SQL objects to the data dictionary. A limitation of this approach, however, is that the compiler cannot deal with objects that do not exist. That means PL/SQL cannot handle DDL statements, which create or destroy objects in the data dictionary.

In practice, this limitation doesn't mean much. Each of the Oracle Developer components has a subprogram that lets you execute any SQL statement as part of its standard program units. In addition, PL/SQL provides you with the DBMS_SQL package for dynamic SQL.

NOTE

While you can execute any SQL statement from your application using these program units, you must be clear on the impact on your transactions. DDL statements, in addition to affecting the data dictionary, signal the end of the current transaction. When you execute a DDL statement, Oracle commits any outstanding changes to the database and removes any locks the session holds against the database. From the application developer's perspective, that means you must be careful about the timing of your DDL statements. Only execute DDL when you can assure that there are no outstanding changes or locks against the database.

In Oracle Developer's Forms component, you can use the Forms_DDL procedure to execute DDL. For example, if you have a menu item that drops a utility table from the database using a simple DROP TABLE statement, you can code something like this in your menu PL/SQL block:

```
IF :System.Form_Status = 'CHANGED' THEN
  Message('Please save your changes before dropping the utility table.');
ELSE
  Forms_DDL('DROP TABLE UtilityTable');
  IF NOT Form_Success THEN
    MyErrorHandler(DBMS_Error_Code);
  END IF;
END IF;
```

Checking the form status ensures that there are no outstanding changes before executing the DDL statement. Calling the Form_Success built-in function tells you whether there is an outstanding error from the last statement. You need to pass this code to your standard error-handling mechanism, such as the My_Error_Handler procedure in the example, to inform the user about what happened.

NOTE
*You do not terminate the SQL statement with a semicolon when you use Forms_DDL. You can submit a PL/SQL block using Forms_DDL, using the standard syntax, but you don't terminate it with a slash as you do in SQL*Plus.*

In Oracle Developer Reports, you use the Do_SQL procedure in the SRW package to achieve similar results. For example, you might want to drop the utility table in the After Form trigger with this trigger function:

```
FUNCTION DropUtilityTable RETURN BOOLEAN IS
BEGIN
   SRW.Do_SQL('DROP TABLE UtilityTable');
   RETURN (TRUE);
EXCEPTION
   WHEN SRW.Do_SQL_Failure THEN
      SRW.Message(100, 'Error while dropping the utility table.');
      RAISE SRW.Program_Abort;
END;
```

For Oracle Developer Reports, there is no issue with committing pending changes. The major difference here is in the error handling. Instead of using functions and return codes, you use exception handling to deal with problems. When Do_SQL fails, it raises the SRW package exception Do_SQL_Failure. The exception handler (see Chapter 12 for details on exception handling) prints a message and aborts the report using the SRW built-in procedure Program_Abort.

In an Oracle Developer Graphics display module, you can execute DDL statements using the built-in Do_SQL procedure. The code is similar to the Reports example, but there is no standard exception for the procedure:

```
PROCEDURE DropUtilityTable IS
BEGIN
   Do_SQL('DROP TABLE UtilityTable');
END;
```

It is a good idea to use the DBMS_SQL package instead of the component-specific built-in subprogram for executing SQL. Using DBMS_SQL gives you a standard set of tools for managing your SQL. It also uses the standard SQL error-handling mechanisms, so you can code error handling based on the SQL error codes from the database.

The full scope of DBMS_SQL is too broad to discuss in this book. The example for this section would look like this when done using DBMS_SQL:

```
CREATE OR REPLACE FUNCTION DropUtilityTable RETURN BOOLEAN IS
   vCursorID INTEGER := DBMS_SQL.Open_Cursor; -- open a cursor for the DDL
   vDummy INTEGER; -- a dummy return value for Execute
BEGIN
   DBMS_SQL.Parse(vCursorID, 'DROP TABLE UtilityTable', DBMS_SQL.NATIVE);
   vDummy := DBMS_SQL.Execute(vCursorID);  -- return value not used for anything
   DBMS_SQL.Close_Cursor(vCursorID);
   RETURN (TRUE);
EXCEPTION
   WHEN OTHERS THEN
     DBMS_SQL.Close_Cursor(vCursorID);
     RAISE;
END;
```

Using DBMS_SQL, you open an explicit DDL cursor, parse the statement, execute the statement, and close the cursor. Any exception closes the cursor and propagates the exception (see Chapter 12 for details on exception propagation and handling). This procedure is fully general and can execute on the client or on the server as a stored function.

Chapter 11 has taken you through the basic parts of PL/SQL programming. You can now declare data structures, write basic procedural code, and integrate SQL into your code in reasonably complex ways. The next chapter will expand your horizons into the different ways that PL/SQL lets you structure your code.

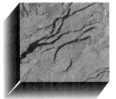

CHAPTER
12

Advanced PL/SQL

L/SQL is a simple language, but as with many simple things, it is most complex when it is simplest. In particular, you can use the tools described in Chapter 11 to create an infinite structure of badly organized code, duplicated over and over throughout your chaos of applications.

To reduce the complexity, PL/SQL offers a series of tools that let you structure your system of code in seemingly simple ways. Although the structure adds complexity to your initial programming task, you will find that judicious use of these facilities will make your system much more reusable and more easily maintained over its lifetime. These tools include exceptions for error handling, functions and procedures for organizing chunks of code, packages for clustering code into abstract data types using cursors and other data structures, and libraries for building easily reused systems of code.

Making Exceptions

Exceptions are gradually finding their way into mainstream database applications programming after many years of languishing on the sidelines. Anyone who has ever programmed large database applications knows that the error-handling code in database programming often grows to obscure the code it supports. The exception is the preferred way to do error handling in modern programming languages. You can also use it to replace most of the uses of the GOTO statement, because it implements a well-understood flow of control within a block.

An *exception* is a PL/SQL signal that the runtime system raises when your program identifies or encounters an anomalous condition. These signal events have names and a system for handling the signal: the exception handler.

There are three kinds of exceptions you can use in your programming:

■ *Built-in PL/SQL exceptions:* Exceptions that are part of the PL/SQL programming language.

■ *Built-in runtime exceptions:* Exceptions that are part of the Oracle Developer runtime environment (Forms, Graphics, and Reports all have different exceptions).

■ *User-defined exceptions:* Exceptions you define to handle Oracle error messages or other situations in your code.

Recall from Chapter 11 the basic form of a PL/SQL block:

```
DECLARE
  --Data declarations
BEGIN
  null;--Program statements
```

```
EXCEPTION
  --Exception handlers
  WHEN OTHERS THEN
    null;--default handler
END;
```

This section focuses on the last clause in the block, the EXCEPTION clause. The structure of your exception handlers within this clause looks like this:

```
EXCEPTION
WHEN <exception 1> THEN
  <statements>
... -- more exception handlers
WHEN OTHERS THEN
  <statements>
```

The EXCEPTION clause is a series of exception handlers, each of which begins with WHEN and the exception name. When the block raises an exception, PL/SQL stops executing the block and checks the EXCEPTION clause of the block for a handler for that exception. If there is one, PL/SQL jumps to the handler, executes it, and returns to the caller. If there is none, PL/SQL jumps out of the current block and goes to the exception handler in the block that encloses the first block. Either way, no further program statements in the main part of the block execute, and PL/SQL does not execute any statements between the one that raised the exception and the exception handler.

This handing off of the exception is called exception *propagation*. If the top-level subprogram does not handle the exception, control passes back to the caller's exception handler, and the exception propagates within the calling subprogram. Eventually, if nothing handles the exception, it propagates to the host environment, which handles it by some default action, usually rolling back. An Oracle Developer application will display an alert that prints a default message; then it will take the action appropriate to the exception. For example, on raising FORM_TRIGGER_FAILURE, Oracle Developer Forms will abort the trigger and the process driving it, usually leaving the cursor on the offending item or record.

You can explicitly raise any exception with the RAISE statement:

```
RAISE <exception-name>;
```

When PL/SQL executes this, it transfers control to the exception handler in the current block. If the block does not handle the exception, it propagates.

If you handle the exception, but you want the outer block or calling subprogram to see the exception, you can explicitly propagate it with just the RAISE statement:

```
RAISE;
```

This should be the last statement in your handler.

NOTE
If you raise an exception in a declaration section or in an exception section, the exception immediately propagates. You must put any exception handler for this exception in an outer block.

The following package represents a series of nested subprograms that will serve as an example for exception propagation. A later section goes into detail on the structure and use of packages. First, you must create the package specification.

```
CREATE OR REPLACE PACKAGE exceptionPackage IS
    eTest EXCEPTION;
    PROCEDURE OuterProc;
END exceptionPackage;
```

The package body implements the Outer_Proc procedure with a series of nested blocks and subprograms. The complexity of the block structure illustrates how exceptions propagate. The block Inner Block #2 raises a test exception, and the exception propagates through the exception handlers.

```
CREATE OR REPLACE PACKAGE BODY exceptionPackage IS
    PROCEDURE OuterProc IS
    BEGIN -- OuterProc block
      DECLARE -- Start of Inner Block #1
        PROCEDURE InnerProc IS
        BEGIN -- Inner Procedure
          BEGIN -- Inner Block #2
            RAISE eTest; -- explicitly raise the exception here
          EXCEPTION  -- Inner Block #2 exception handlers
            WHEN eTest THEN
              Message('Exception handled in Inner Block #2');
              RAISE;
          END; -- End of Inner Block #2
        EXCEPTION  --Inner Proc exception handlers
          WHEN eTest THEN
            Message('Exception handled in InnerProc');
            RAISE;
        END InnerProc;
      BEGIN -- Inner block #1
        InnerProc;
```

```
    EXCEPTION  -- Inner Block #1 exception handlers
      WHEN eTest THEN
        Message('Exception handled in Inner Block #1');
        RAISE;
    END;  -- End of Inner Block #1
  EXCEPTION  -- OuterProc exception handlers
    WHEN eTest THEN
      Message('Exception handled in OuterProc');
      RAISE;
  END OuterProc;
END exceptionPackage;
```

The following code calls the Outer_Proc procedure:

```
BEGIN
    exceptionPackage.OuterProc;
EXCEPTION
  WHEN exceptionPackage.eTest THEN
    Message('Exception handled in calling procedure');
END;
```

Running this code in Oracle Developer yields the following output messages:

```
Exception handled in Inner Block #2
Exception handled in InnerProc
Exception handled in Inner Block #1
Exception handled in OuterProc
Exception handled in calling procedure
```

The Inner Block #2 raises the exception. Its handler propagates the exception to the block that contains Inner Block #2, InnerProc. That procedure's handler propagates the exception to the block containing it, the Inner Block #1, which in turn propagates the exception to the containing OuterProc. That procedure is the top subprogram in the hierarchy, so it propagates the exception to the calling subprogram block.

NOTE
When you propagate the exception outside the subprogram, PL/SQL does not set the OUT parameters of the subprogram and automatically rolls back work done in the subprogram. If this is not what you want to happen, you should code a WHEN OTHERS clause in the outer block of the subprogram to handle the exception the way you want.

PL/SQL Built-in Exceptions

PL/SQL defines several exceptions as part of its STANDARD package. All PL/SQL programs can raise these exceptions. Common built-in exceptions you need to handle in your code are the NO_DATA_FOUND and VALUE_ERROR exceptions. NO_DATA_FOUND occurs when your single-row select (SELECT ... INTO) fails to return a row. VALUE_ERROR occurs when a statement has a problem with a value (arithmetic, conversion, truncation, or constraint). The most common problem that raises VALUE_ERROR is assigning a string that is too long to a variable. For example, if you define a variable as VARCHAR2(10) and try to assign the string "George E. Talbot" to it, you will raise VALUE_ERROR. The string has 14 characters, but the variable allows only 10.

Oracle Developer Built-in Exceptions

Each of the three Oracle Developer builders has a set of built-in exceptions appropriate to its own specific environment.

Form Builder provides a single built-in exception during normal runtime processing: FORM_TRIGGER_FAILURE. Forms raises this exception whenever a trigger fails during one of the many Forms processes. You can use this exception in your code within a trigger to tell PL/SQL that the trigger failed:

```
RAISE FORM_TRIGGER_FAILURE;
```

Form Builder also provides the DEBUG.BREAK exception, with which you can explicitly embed a debugger break through a RAISE statement in a block. See Chapter 15 for details.

Oracle Developer Reports packages its exceptions in the SRW package.

The two most common exceptions you will use in Reports code are the RUN_REPORT_FAILURE exception and the PROGRAM_ABORT exception. RUN_REPORT_FAILURE indicates to Reports that a report failed, so it prints a general message and ends the report. You can code an exception handler to display your own error message, say, when you are running a second report from within a report. You can raise PROGRAM_ABORT to stop report execution on some fatal error in your code with the appropriate error message.

Oracle Developer Graphics has a truly stupendous array of built-in exceptions—too many to detail here. See the online Graphics Builder reference for a complete list. If you code extensively in Graphics Builder, you will find yourself using many exception handlers to deal with the many exceptional situations that arise. There is a broad array of objects you can program in a Graphics display, each with a different set of possible error situations. There are about 200 such exceptions, one for each possible error you can get in programming with the OG and TOOLINT packages.

For example, Oracle Developer Graphics raises the exception OG_DATE_OVERFLOW when you try to display a date axis with OG_UPDATE_CHART but the data extends beyond the valid range of the axis. It raises OG_INVALID_POSITION when you specify an invalid position on an axis.

User-Defined Exceptions

There are two kinds of user-defined exceptions: Oracle error exceptions and user exceptions.

You can use the pragma EXCEPTION_INIT to set up a named exception for a particular Oracle error message. A pragma is a compiler directive that tells the compiler to do something while compiling. In this case, it tells the compiler to create an exception for the Oracle error code:

```
ePrivileges EXCEPTION;
PRAGMA EXCEPTION_INIT(ePrivileges, -1031);
```

This statement associates Oracle error -1031 with the name privilegesException. When the core Oracle database server engine sends that error to PL/SQL, PL/SQL raises the named exception and passes control to your exception handler. This PRAGMA saves you some code; otherwise, you would have to catch the general Oracle database server error condition and test the error code (SQLCODE) for the error number—additional code that you don't need to write.

To define a simple user exception, all you need to do is to declare the exception in a DECLARE block. For example, if a trigger did some internal validation for a ledger record, it might have a special exception for the failure of this validation so that you can report the problem:

```
DECLARE
   eValidation   EXCEPTION;
   vAlertButton NUMBER;
BEGIN
   null;   -- Do the validating.
EXCEPTION
   WHEN eValidation THEN
     vAlertButton := Show_Alert('LedgerValidationAlert');
     RAISE FORM_TRIGGER_FAILURE;
   WHEN OTHERS THEN
     RAISE FORM_TRIGGER_FAILURE;
END;
```

Exceptions are scoped just like variables. You can define an exception as many times as you want in different scopes. You may find it better to define a given exception just once in a package (see the following section), exporting it to the subprograms that use it. You can also define exceptions with different names. This ensures that an exception handler that handles the exception will in fact handle it.

WARNING

If you define two exceptions with the same name, they are two separate exceptions. This can be very confusing when you code your error handlers, particularly in subprograms with nested blocks. It is particularly unwise to declare your own exception with one of the built-in exception names, such as NO_DATA_FOUND.

Using Blocks to Control Exception Handling

In some situations, you will want to continue processing after handling an exception. Unfortunately, when PL/SQL raises an exception, it ends block processing and returns to the caller after executing any exception-handler code. This means that you cannot go back to the point in the block that raised the exception and continue. The usual situation is one in which you have several statements and you want to execute all of them even if one fails for some reason.

If you want to have full control of this sort over processing, you must divide your subprogram into nested blocks. See the following section on subprograms (functions and procedures) for more details on block nesting. What this lets you do is put the exception handler for each "nonfatal" exception in a separate block. After the handler executes, the block exits to the enclosing block and continues executing. It only skips the code in the nested block.

For example, say you want to look up a data value in a table, but also want to set up a default value to use in case the original data value isn't in the table. You could execute several SQL statements to determine the true state and branch accordingly, or you could have a structure like this:

```
DECLARE
   vLookupValue VARCHAR2(100);
BEGIN
   BEGIN
     SELECT lookupValue INTO vLookupValue FROM LookupTable;
   EXCEPTION
     WHEN NO_DATA_FOUND THEN
        vLookupValue := 'N/A';
   END;
   INSERT INTO AuditTable (currentDate, currentValue)
     VALUES (sysdate, vLookupValue);
END;
```

This block first executes the single-row select to find the lookup value. If the server returns no data, the nested block exception handler assigns a default value, and processing continues with the first statement below the END of the nested block: the INSERT statement.

Error-Handling Functions

There are two PL/SQL built-in functions that you can use in exception handlers to deal with database errors.

The SQLCODE function returns the error code of the last error. This code will be a negative number, or it will be +100 (NOT FOUND) or +1 for errors you define with PRAGMA EXCEPTION_INIT.

The SQLERRM is the text of the error message, including the error code.

Oracle Developer Forms also provides some built-in functions for error handling, which Table 12-1 describes.

Making Blocks Less Anonymous

Chapter 11 used the anonymous block to great effect in showing you how to build simple chunks of code for triggers. When you get to the stage of needing to reuse code, the anonymous block becomes less useful. You need to move on to more formal organizations that name the block and parameterize it.

Subprograms

PL/SQL provides two kinds of objects that perform this organizing role in the language: procedures and functions. Together, these two kinds of code organization are subprograms: named, parameterized blocks of code that you call with arguments to perform some operation. A function is a subprogram that computes a

Function	Returns	Description
ERROR_TYPE	CHAR	Returns the kind of error that last occurred: FRM for a Forms error or ORA for a database error.
ERROR_CODE	NUMBER	Returns the code of the last Forms error.
ERROR_TEXT	CHAR	Returns the text of the last Forms error.
DBMS_ERROR_CODE	NUMBER	Returns the code of the last database error message that Forms detected.
DBMS_ERROR_TEXT	CHAR	Returns the type and text of one or more database error messages; DBMS_ERROR_CODE is the first of these.

TABLE 12-1. *Oracle Developer Forms Built-in Error-Handling Functions*

value, whereas a procedure performs an action. In Oracle Developer, you can code these into each module under the Program Units heading, or you can add them to a library module. Either way, you must call the subprogram explicitly within trigger code or anywhere else that you refer to a subprogram name (group filters and formulas in Reports, for example, use functions). The subprogram call is a PL/SQL statement; hence, when you create a subprogram, you are extending the PL/SQL language by adding a new kind of statement.

You will typically program a function when you want to compute a single value as the result of the operation. You will program a procedure when you want to perform an operation rather than computing a value. However, all subprograms can have output parameters, which let you return a value through the parameter. Because you expect functions to return a single value, you should code functions without any OUT or IN OUT parameters. For error conditions and returns and the like, you should define and raise exceptions (see the preceding section). See the following section on parameters for more information about output parameters.

You can overload subprograms in a package or in another subprogram or block by having multiple subprograms with the same name. See the section "Creative Packaging," later in the chapter, for details.

Procedures

A procedure has a name, a set of parameters, and a block of code, as shown here:

```
PROCEDURE <name> [<argument list>] IS
   <declarations>
BEGIN
  <program statements>
END;
```

This syntax is the same as the anonymous block except for the replacement of the DECLARE keyword with the PROCEDURE ... IS sequence. The PROCEDURE ... IS sequence is the procedure specification, and the rest of the block is the procedure body. You can code the specification alone to forward declare a subprogram to another subprogram or block that uses it, then later code the entire subprogram.

Functions

A function has a name, a set of parameters, a return type, and a block of code. When you return from the function, the function returns to the caller a value of the type you specify. (This syntax is like the procedure's except for the RETURN clause in the specification.)

```
FUNCTION <name> [<argument list>] RETURN <type> IS
   <declarations>
BEGIN
  <program statements>
END;
```

To finish the function's processing and return a value, you use the RETURN statement with an expression that evaluates to the value to return.

NOTE
You can have as many RETURN statements as you like, but it is poor practice to have more than one. Having two or more exits from a subprogram leads to an explosion of possible control paths through the program, making unit testing difficult. When you get to integration testing, your tests must validate each return against each caller to ensure that the caller gets the correct value. Thus, saving a bit of coding with multiple returns leads to a tremendous increase in testing effort and in the potential for defects. One approach you can use is to raise internal exceptions and returns from the exception handler. In general, though, it is better to structure your code to avoid the necessity. You can use nested blocks to achieve this (described in the upcoming section "Nesting Blocks").

Parameters

To define a set of parameters to a subprogram, you have a list of declarations in parentheses:

 `( <variable> [ <mode> ] <type> [ := | DEFAULT <value>, ... )`

The <variable> is a standard PL/SQL identifier that names the parameter. The <mode> is one of three possibilities:

- *IN:* The parameter value is an input into the subprogram, and assignments to the variable do not change its value to the calling program. This is the default if you do not specify a mode. This kind of argument can be a variable, a constant, a literal, or an expression.

- *OUT:* The parameter value is an output from the subprogram, letting you assign a value to the variable that is accessible to the caller when the subprogram returns. You cannot use the variable until you assign a value to it. The variable in the caller (the argument) must be a variable you can modify, and it must be a variable, not a literal, because you assign a value to it.

■ *IN OUT:* The parameter value is both an input and an output variable. You can use the input value and you can assign an output value for the caller to see. This kind of argument must be a variable because you can assign a value to it.

Again, you should avoid specifying OUT or IN OUT parameters on functions, which should return only a single value as their return value.

The <type> can be any valid PL/SQL type, including the Oracle Developer objects or types that you define. You do not constrain the types with scale or precision, such as VARCHAR2(20); you use only the type name.

The ":= | DEFAULT <value>" clause means that you can use either the assignment operation := or the keyword DEFAULT to assign a default value to the parameter. This lets you call the subprogram without an argument for that parameter, in which case the subprogram assigns the default value as the argument. This works only for IN variables, not for OUT or IN OUT variables.

This sequence repeats in a comma-separated list.

If a subprogram has no parameters, it has no parentheses:

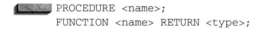

```
PROCEDURE <name>;
FUNCTION <name> RETURN <type>;
```

Calling Subprograms

A subprogram call is a PL/SQL statement, and you can put such a call anywhere you can put a PL/SQL statement. You can have the subprogram call as the only statement in the block:

```
Do_Key('NEXT RECORD');
```

You can have the subprogram call as part of an anonymous block or as part of a procedure:

```
DECLARE
   vAlertButton NUMBER;
BEGIN
   vAlertButton := Show_Alert('WarningAlert');
END;
```

TIP

When you call a function, as in the immediately preceding example, you must assign the result to a variable. If you do not, you will get an error saying that PL/SQL cannot find the procedure. The return type is part of how PL/SQL recognizes a function.

Where you define a subprogram determines where you can call that subprogram. If you define a subprogram in a module (a form, menu, report, or display), only the triggers and other subprograms you define in that module can call the subprogram. For example, if you define a procedure in a form module, only the form triggers and form subprograms can call that subprogram. If you define a function in a menu module, only the menu item commands and startup code can call that function.

 If you define a subprogram in a library module, you must first attach the library to the module to be able to call the subprogram. To do this, find the Attached Libraries header in the module, click on the Create button, and choose the library to attach through the resulting dialog box.

Calling stored subprograms (subprograms you define on the server instead of in a library or module) is a bit more complex. First, it's a good idea to define a public synonym for the subprogram. With a public synonym, callers need only specify the name of the subprogram.

Second, you must have the proper privileges to execute the procedure. If you log on with the user name of the user that owns the procedure, you have automatic EXECUTE privilege. Otherwise, the owner must grant your user or role that privilege:

```
GRANT EXECUTE ON Talbot.AddLedgerTransaction to AccountingRole;
```

Now any user granted the AccountingRole role can execute the AddLedgerTransaction subprogram.

NOTE
If you call a subprogram and PL/SQL does not recognize the name, check the type and number of your parameters carefully against the procedure specification. PL/SQL uses the subprogram name, the return type (for functions), and the existence and type of the parameters to identify a particular subprogram. If you miss one, or if you specify the wrong type, or if you pass in a bind variable of the wrong type, PL/SQL won't recognize the call as a call to the subprogram you intend to use. As already mentioned, if you are using a function, make sure you assign the return value to a variable, as PL/SQL uses this to recognize the function name.

POSITIONAL NOTATION   There are two ways to pass arguments to a subprogram. The first way is positional notation—big words that mean passing values for arguments in the same sequence as the subprogram defines the parameters. For example, say the procedure specification looks like this:

```
PROCEDURE testLedgerItem(pItemID NUMBER, pAmount NUMBER);
```

Your procedure call might look like this:

```
testLedgerItem(456, :Ledger.Amount);
```

This passes the value "456" for pItemID and the form item Ledger.Amount for the pAmount. Note the use of the bind variable syntax (the colon prefix) to pass the item object value.

NAMED NOTATION   The other way to pass parameters is named notation. Using this syntax, you can pass the values in any order by naming the parameter:

```
testLedgerItem(pAmount => :Ledger.Amount, pItemID => 456);
```

Named notation is particularly helpful with defaults. If you use defaults with positional notation, you can leave out trailing parameters that have defaults. If you use named notation, you can leave out any parameter with a default, not just trailing ones. That means you can leave out some parameters with defaults but include others that follow the ones left out in the subprogram specification.

Report Filters and Formulas

A major use for functions in Oracle Developer Reports is to implement filters and formulas, which Chapter 7 discusses in detail.

A report group filter is a function returning a Boolean value that Oracle Developer uses to select which records to display for the group. By setting the Filter property of the group to Condition and supplying a function, you tell Reports to display only those records in the group for which the function returns TRUE.

A report formula is a function you attach to a column with type property Formula that returns a value for each record in a group. You can use an expression instead of a function for this, but you cannot use the full facilities of PL/SQL without using a function. The function returns a single value with a data type corresponding to the column data type: number columns have functions that return NUMBER; date columns have functions that return DATE; and character columns return CHARACTER, VARCHAR, or VARCHAR2.

Nesting Blocks

The block-structured nature of PL/SQL gives you great control over the scope of the parts of your subprograms. The block structure of a program is the way in which you use PL/SQL blocks (DECLARE ... BEGIN ... END; sequences) to structure the availability of variables and exception handlers.

The basic idea of block structuring is that a block is a program statement. This statement executes in order, just as would any program statement. Within the statement, however, you can have an infinitely complex structure about which the outer block and its processing know nothing. This hiding, or encapsulation, permits you to uncouple the complex workings of the internal block from the sequence of the outer block. This in turn reduces the complexity of your program and makes it easier to understand, debug, test, and maintain. For example, you can defer coding the nested block body, making it a program stub. You can then continue with coding and testing of the rest of the subprogram. This way, you don't need to worry about the details of the nested block until you are ready.

The earlier section on exception handling provided an example of using nested blocks to control the flow of execution after exception handling. By putting the exception handler in an inside block, you can continue processing the outer block after handling the exception.

Block structure also lets you isolate logical clusters of code in a subprogram. For example, if you find yourself needing to have multiple returns from a subprogram, you should consider nesting the code you do not want to execute and executing that block conditionally. Then you can have a single point of exit from your subprogram. This clarifies the control structure of the program, especially for testing.

By declaring nested blocks, you can share data elements between blocks without using global variables. The nested blocks can refer to any variable you declare in the outer block.

You can nest entire subprograms within other subprograms by including them in the declarations section of the outer subprogram. You must declare nested subprograms after all other declarations (variables, types, or exceptions).

Positioning Blocks in the Navigator

Now you know how to code subprograms. The next question is where and how to do it. An earlier section noted two places in which you can code subprograms:

- *Program units:* Under the Program Units heading in a form, menu, display, or report module

- *Library:* In a library under the Libraries heading in Forms, Reports, or Graphics

There is a third choice as well:

■ *Stored:* Stored in the database using CREATE FUNCTION and CREATE PROCEDURE statements or by creating the subprogram under the Database Objects heading.

How do you decide where to define your subprogram?

Use a stored subprogram if you are using the subprogram to access data that you do not want to be generally available. This is the encapsulated procedure that the Chapter 6 section "Procedural Encapsulation" discusses. Use a stored subprogram if you are trying to accomplish a lot of database work in the subprogram. This will let you call the subprogram and have the (presumably) more powerful server execute everything. This also reduces network traffic. Use a stored subprogram if the operation is a general operation on a database object. This will let you share the operation among all the users of the object. This is the principle of cohesion—storing the operations near the data on which they operate.

NOTE

Because the server and client versions of PL/SQL may differ, you can build stored procedures that encapsulate functions of the server-side version of PL/SQL for use by the client-side version. For example, if you use Oracle Developer with both Oracle7 and Oracle8 databases, you aren't dealing with the same version of PL/SQL. You can build stored subprograms that use DBMS_SQL, parameterize them appropriately, then call them from the client-side PL/SQL. When you run against the Oracle7 database, you run Oracle7 PL/SQL on the server; when you run against the Oracle8 database, you run PL/SQL8.

Use a library if you want to make the subprogram available to more than one module. This usually applies to a general operation that is applicable to different situations. Also, the subprogram should use the database in only limited ways; a stored subprogram should be used for most database-related operations to minimize the network traffic and to facilitate reuse. One exception would be subprograms that need to call built-in subprograms for the module, since you can't call Oracle

Developer built-in subprograms from the database server. Another exception might be subprograms that need to refer to Oracle Developer module variables. However, you should pass these values as arguments to the subprogram rather than directly referring to them. This uncoupling of the subprogram from the data of the module is a basic tenet of good system architecture. The uncoupling means you can store the subprogram in the database and pass module data to it.

The "Checking Out the Library" section at the end of the chapter shows how to create subprograms in libraries. Once you have coded your subprograms, you can then attach the library to any module to use the subprograms in that module. To attach a library, find the Attached Libraries heading in the module, select it, and click on the Create tool. You can then choose the library through a standard Open File dialog box; don't forget to remove any path information from the filename.

That leaves subprograms in the module. You should put subprograms in modules only if the code is so specific to the module that you cannot conceive of its being of any use in any other module. Heavy use of many module items, logic relating solely to a specialized application, or heavy use of other module objects through built-in subprograms would indicate module specificity.

To create a module program unit, find the Program Units heading under the module. When you click on the Create tool, you see the New Program Unit dialog box and use the same PL/SQL Editor to define the subprogram, but Oracle Developer stores the code with the form, menu, display, or report module. The later section "Creating a Library" goes into detail on how to use these tools to create subprograms and packages.

Another situation would be the definition of an object group that included subprograms that operate on the objects in the group. This group acts as a kind of package, and it makes sense to include subprograms in that package for reuse in other modules. This is an alternative to PL/SQL packages or libraries; you'll learn more about this in the following sections.

When Oracle Developer looks for program units, it first checks the module's Program Units section. Next, it looks for the program unit in libraries you've attached in the Attached Libraries section of the module. Third, it looks on the database server. You can use this sequence to advantage by adding program units with the same name at a higher level in the hierarchy. For example, you may have a library subprogram that holds default behavior for most applications. Instead, you want a specific application to do something different. So you add a subprogram with the same name to the Program Units section of the module. When Oracle Developer runs the application and calls the subprogram, it finds the one you added first and never executes the library subprogram.

Creative Packaging

A package lets you combine other PL/SQL elements into a single whole: a package of data objects, types, cursors, exceptions, and subprograms. The package has a specification and a body. A package specification is the public face of the package: the specifications of the elements that the package lets you use. These elements are public elements. The package body is the implementation of the cursors and subprograms the package specifies, as well as any private elements you want to declare. You can replace the package body without recompiling the package specification.

NOTE
You cannot nest packages within program units.

Creating a Package

Why would you create a package? The package provides a way to combine PL/SQL elements into a cohesive system. The package is comparable to an object in an object-oriented system: it includes both state and behavior relating to some cohesive piece of the system. It provides for complete data abstraction and information hiding to improve the modularity of your program. This improved cohesion and uncoupling of the data abstraction leads directly to improved understanding of the code and improved ability to maintain the software. Also, once you execute a component of the package, Oracle loads the package into memory so that further processing with package components performs much better.

You can, for example, change a function in a package body without recompiling any of the callers of that function, because the interface specification does not change. You can also stub out the subprograms until you are ready to code them, or even not supply a body at all. This lets you compile and possibly unit-test program units that use the package without having to actually finish the package first.

The package also lets you define variables, constants, and cursors that persist throughout your session as either public or private elements. That gives you the ability to keep information around between procedure calls or transactions without having to rely on unstructured global variables. With a package, you have structured control of the data and operations. All such elements are NULL unless you initialize them in the declarations. You can also define subprograms entirely within the package body. You cannot access these subprograms outside the package.

Finally, PL/SQL's implementation of the package loads the entire package into memory when you use any part of it. That means additional calls to the programs in the package do not require any additional loading of code, which increases performance. This feature also suggests that it is a good idea to keep your packages relatively simple and cohesive rather than collecting large numbers of disparate things into a single package.

There are several kinds of cohesion that indicate you should be using a package:

- *Functional cohesion:* A set of elements that, taken together as a whole, represent a specific function of the application, such as an object type or a cluster of related object types.

- *Abstract cohesion:* A set of program units that work together as a layer of abstraction to provide a well-defined set of services is abstract cohesion. An application programming interface, or API, exhibits this kind of cohesion, and examples of it include the SRW package for Oracle Report Builder and the OG package for Graphics Builder.

- *Practical cohesion:* Using a set of objects and/or program units together, even though there are no service or functional aspects to such use, is practical cohesion. A specific case of practical cohesion is the packaging of a transaction and its elements, however diverse, into a single package of cursors and subprograms.

The logic for positioning packages is the same as for subprograms. (If necessary, review the "Positioning Blocks in the Navigator" section earlier in this chapter.) If you structure your packages well, you will easily distinguish database-related packages from purely client-oriented packages. For the sake of reusability, you should develop most application packages in libraries rather than in modules. The one exception to this rule is when you group a package with module objects such as blocks or charts. The process for creating your package is identical to that for subprograms. See the "Subprograms" section earlier in this chapter for details.

There are two package-related syntaxes, one for the specification and one for the body.

The Package Specification

```
PACKAGE <name> IS
  {<variable spec>|<type spec>|<cursor spec>|<exception spec>} ...
  <subprogram spec> ...
END;
```

See Chapter 11 for details on the specifications for variables and types. The specification includes a set of object specifications (variables and constants, types, cursors, and exceptions) followed by a set of subprogram specifications.

The cursor specification takes the following form:

```
CURSOR <name> <parameter list> RETURN <type>;
```

The cursor specification, because it does not include the SELECT statement, must provide the RETURN clause to identify the type of record the cursor fetches. The <type> can be any of the following types:

- *Record:* A previously defined record type

- *Variable%TYPE:* The type of a previously defined variable

- *Table.Column%TYPE:* The type of a database column

- *Table%ROWTYPE:* The record with types for all the columns in a table

If you are doing more than just selecting columns from a table, such as including a GROUP BY or an expression in the SELECT list, you must supply a record type. That type must match the type you specify in the cursor body, which you define in the package body. The objective of the cursor specification is to specify the interface of the cursor, which consists of the cursor name, parameter list, and return type.

The subprogram specification has the following syntax:

```
PROCEDURE | FUNCTION <name> <parameter list>
   [RETURN <type>];
```

See the "Parameters" section earlier in the chapter for the parameter list syntax. The RETURN clause applies only to the function. In a full subprogram definition, the statement continues with IS and the subprogram body. The objective of the subprogram specification is to export the interface of the subprogram, which consists of the name, the parameter list, and the return type. The subprogram specifications come after all the other declarations in the package specification.

You can overload subprograms in a package or in another subprogram or block by having multiple subprograms with the same name, as long as the number and/or type of the parameters differ. This lets you create alternative versions of the subprogram with different parameters. An example is the Oracle Developer built-in subprograms in the built-in packages that take either an object name or an object ID as the first argument. These are really two separate, overloaded subprograms in the built-in package (Forms STANDARD, Reports SRW, or Graphics OG). Subprogram overloading lets you create a very flexible array of operations for different uses, making the package much more reusable and easy to use.

NOTE
The types must differ completely; REAL and NUMBER and FLOAT are all the same type when considering subprogram overloading. This applies to the RETURN type for functions.

The following example of a package specification is the declaration of the interface of a package for handling 24-hour time values. The package includes a record type, a set of exceptions, and arithmetic functions that operate on the record type. It refers to another package, TimeIntervalPackage, that exports a time interval type (TimeIntervalType) and the functions for dealing with that type. It overloads the arithmetic addition operator for convenience in specifying the time and interval to add in either order. Subtraction is not symmetric.

```
CREATE OR REPLACE PACKAGE Time24Package IS
   TYPE tTime24 IS RECORD (
      vHour NATURAL NOT NULL := 0,
      vMinute NATURAL NOT NULL := 0,
      vSecond NUMBER NOT NULL := 0.0);
   eInvalidHour EXCEPTION;
   eInvalidMinute EXCEPTION;
   eInvalidSecond EXCEPTION;
   FUNCTION CurrentTime RETURN tTime24;
   PROCEDURE SetTime(pTime IN OUT tTime24, pHour IN NUMBER,
      pMinute IN NUMBER, pSecond IN NUMBER);
   FUNCTION Add(pTime IN tTime24,
               pInterval IN TimeIntervalPackage.tTimeInterval)
      RETURN tTime24;
   FUNCTION Add(pInterval IN TimeIntervalPackage.tTimeInterval,
               pTime IN tTime24)
      RETURN tTime24;
   FUNCTION Subtract(pTime IN tTime24,
               pInterval IN TimeIntervalPackage.tTimeInterval)
      RETURN tTime24;
   FUNCTION Format(pTime IN tTime24) RETURN VARCHAR2;
   PROCEDURE Validate(pTime IN tTime24);
END Time24Package;
```

This is an example of a package that represents an object. The TYPE declaration does not create an actual record, it merely defines what a record looks like. The functions all take an instance of the record type, or two instances. The package itself thus contains no data. You create the data object, a variable of the record type, in the subprogram that uses the package. You then call the functions on that variable to do things to it or to create new data by returning a new object of the type. The individual elements of the record are visible to the caller as part of the specification; good practice would ignore this and use only the functions to operate on the data.

> **NOTE**
> *There is only one copy of a package in memory, which means that if you define your variable as part of the package, you can have only one such variable. If that fits your needs, fine; the example above is clearly one case where it is inadequate. You have to be able to create multiple time values, not just one. That means, however, that you cannot fully encapsulate the structure of the record type within the package—at least not without a lot of programming, handle indirection, and some maintenance nightmares. This is a case where it is better to use what you have, rather than insisting on "doing it the right way." You can do what you want easily and with little effort, but you incur some risk that someone will abuse the privileges by accessing the structure directly.*

The Package Body

The package body has the following syntax:

```
PACKAGE BODY <name> IS
{<variable spec>|<type spec>|<cursor body>|<exception spec>} ...
   <subprogram body> ...
[BEGIN
   <statement>; ...
[EXCEPTION
   <exception handlers> ...]]
END;
```

Only the cursor and subprogram bodies correspond to subprograms you declare in the package specification. The rest of the declarations (variables and so on) are all private to the package body; you cannot use these elements in your external code.

The cursor body syntax is just like the cursor specification syntax except for the addition of the SELECT statement:

```
CURSOR <name> <parameter list> RETURN <type> IS <SELECT statement>;
```

The parameter list must exactly match the parameter list on the cursor specification, as must the RETURN type.

Package body initialization happens in the optional BEGIN ... END sequence at the end of the package body, after you have finished defining all the implementations of cursors and subprograms in the declarations section. This block of code executes once, when you first refer to an element of the package. You use it to initialize private or public variables in the package. The exception handlers handle any exceptions that the initialization code raises.

The following example shows the body for the package specified in the previous section.

```
CREATE OR REPLACE PACKAGE BODY Time24Package IS
   cSeparator CONSTANT CHAR(1) := ':';  -- format cSeparator hh:mm:ss
   cSecondModulus CONSTANT NUMBER := 60.0;
   cMinuteModulus CONSTANT NATURAL := 60;
   cHourModulus CONSTANT NATURAL := 24;
   cSecondsPerMinute CONSTANT NUMBER := 60.0;
   cSecondsPerHour CONSTANT NUMBER := 60*cSecondsPerMinute;
   cSecondsPerDay CONSTANT NATURAL := 24*cSecondsPerHour;
   eSecondsOverflow EXCEPTION;  -- internal error

   -- An internal Convert function to convert time values
   -- to and from seconds
   FUNCTION Convert(pTime tTime24) RETURN NUMBER IS
     vSeconds NUMBER := 0;
   BEGIN
     Validate(pTime);
     vSeconds := (pTime.vHour * cSecondsPerHour) +
                 (pTime.vMinute * cSecondsPerMinute) +
                  pTime.vSecond;
    IF vSeconds NOT BETWEEN 0 AND cSecondsPerDay THEN
       RAISE eSecondsOverflow;
    END IF;
    RETURN vSeconds;
    EXCEPTION
    WHEN eSecondsOverflow THEN
       DBMS_Output.Put_Line('Error converting seconds, number out of
range:  '||
               To_Char(cSecondsPerMinute));
       RETURN 0.0;
   END Convert;

   FUNCTION Convert(pSeconds NUMBER) RETURN tTime24 IS
     vTimeBuffer tTime24;  -- return value
     vSecondsBuffer NUMBER := pSeconds;
```

```
BEGIN
  IF pSeconds > cSecondsPerDay THEN
    RAISE eSecondsOverflow;
  END IF;
  vTimeBuffer.vHour := FLOOR(vSecondsBuffer / cSecondsPerHour);
  vSecondsBuffer := MOD(vSecondsBuffer, cSecondsPerHour);
  vTimeBuffer.vMinute := FLOOR(vSecondsBuffer / cSecondsPerMinute);
  vSecondsBuffer := MOD(vSecondsBuffer, cSecondsPerMinute);
  vTimeBuffer.vSecond := vSecondsBuffer;
  Validate(vTimeBuffer);
  return vTimeBuffer;
EXCEPTION
  WHEN eSecondsOverflow THEN
    DBMS_Output.Put_Line('Error converting seconds, number too large:
'||
            To_Char(cSecondsPerMinute));
    SetTime(vTimeBuffer, 0, 0, 0);
    RETURN vTimeBuffer;
END Convert;

FUNCTION Add(pTime tTime24,
             pInterval TimeIntervalPackage.tTimeInterval)
  RETURN tTime24 IS
  vTimeBuffer   tTime24;  -- Buffer for return value
  vCarry  NATURAL := 0;  -- carry digits to next component
BEGIN
  Validate(pTime);
  TimeIntervalPackage.Validate(pInterval);
  vTimeBuffer.vSecond := MOD(pTime.vSecond + pInterval.vSecond,
                          cSecondModulus);
  vCarry := FLOOR(pTime.vSecond + pInterval.vSecond /
cSecondModulus);
  vTimeBuffer.vMinute := MOD(pTime.vMinute + pInterval.vMinute +
vCarry,
                          cMinuteModulus);
  vCarry := FLOOR(pTime.vMinute + pInterval.vMinute + vCarry /
                cMinuteModulus);
  vTimeBuffer.vHour := MOD(pTime.vHour + pInterval.vhour + vCarry,
                        cHourModulus);
  Validate(vTimeBuffer);
  RETURN vTimeBuffer;
END Add;

FUNCTION Add(pInterval TimeIntervalPackage.tTimeInterval,
             pTime tTime24)
  RETURN tTime24 IS
BEGIN
  RETURN Add(pTime, pInterval);
END Add;
```

```
    FUNCTION Subtract(pTime tTime24,
                   pInterval TimeIntervalPackage.tTimeInterval)
       RETURN tTime24 IS
      vTimeBuffer tTime24;  -- Buffer for returned value
      vSeconds1 NUMBER := 0.0;
      vSeconds2 NUMBER := 0.0;
      vResultSeconds NUMBER := 0.0;
    BEGIN
      -- Convert the time and interval to seconds to simplify
      vSeconds1 := Convert(pTime);
      vSeconds2 := TimeIntervalPackage.Convert(pInterval);
      vResultSeconds := vSeconds1 - vSeconds2;
      IF vResultSeconds NOT BETWEEN -cSecondsPerDay AND cSecondsPerDay
        THEN RAISE eSecondsOverflow;
      ELSIF vResultSeconds < 0 THEN
        -- Add negative value to total seconds per day to get the
        -- "reverse" number of seconds
        vResultSeconds := cSecondsPerDay + vResultSeconds;
      END IF;
      vTimeBuffer := Convert(vResultSeconds);
      Validate(vTimeBuffer);
      RETURN vTimeBuffer;
    END Subtract;

    FUNCTION CurrentTime RETURN tTime24 IS
      vDateTime DATE := SYSDATE;
      vTime tTime24;  -- return value
    BEGIN
      vTime.vHour := To_Number(To_Char(vDateTime, 'HH24'));
      vTime.vMinute := To_Number(To_Char(vDateTime, 'MI'));
      vTime.vSecond := To_Number(To_Char(vDateTime, 'SS')); -- no
fraction
      Validate (vTime);
      return vTime;
    END CurrentTime;

    PROCEDURE SetTime(pTime IN OUT tTime24, pHour NUMBER, pMinute NUMBER,
                   pSecond NUMBER) IS
      vTimeCopy tTime24;
    BEGIN
      pTime.vHour := pHour;
      pTime.vMinute := pMinute;
      pTime.vSecond := pSecond;
      vTimeCopy := ptime;
      Validate(vTimeCopy);
    END SetTime;
    -- l 140
```

```
FUNCTION Format(pTime tTime24) RETURN VARCHAR2 IS
BEGIN
  Validate(pTime);
  RETURN To_Char(pTime.vHour)||cSeparator||
         To_Char(pTime.vMinute)||cSeparator||
         To_Char(pTime.vSecond);
END Format;

-- This internal procedure validates the time record
PROCEDURE Validate(pTime IN tTime24) IS
BEGIN
  IF pTime.vHour NOT BETWEEN 0 AND 23 THEN
    RAISE eInvalidHour;
  END IF;
  IF pTime.vMinute NOT BETWEEN 0 AND 59 THEN
    RAISE eInvalidMinute;
  END IF;
  IF pTime.vSecond NOT BETWEEN 0 AND 59.0 THEN
    RAISE eInvalidSecond;
  END IF;
END Validate;

END Time24Package;
```

NOTE

There are some restrictions on packages. First, when you call a packaged subprogram, Oracle executes an implied savepoint. If the subprogram fails with an unhandled exception, PL/SQL rolls back the transaction to this savepoint before raising the exception in the caller. Second, if you are using the package in a distributed transaction, you cannot include any transaction commands (COMMIT, ROLLBACK, or SAVEPOINT).

Using a Package

You refer to an element of a package with a dot-separated name consisting of the package name and the element name:

```
DECLARE
  vTime Time24Package.tTime24;
BEGIN
  vTime := Time24Package.CurrentTime;
END;
```

NOTE
If you are using a stored package on the server, you must again have EXECUTE privilege on the package. Unlike subprograms, however, you must grant EXECUTE privilege to a user, not to a role granted to the user. Again, defining a public synonym is a good idea, as it will enable applications to refer to the package without a user's name prefixing the package name.

Built-in Packages

Form Builder comes with several built-in packages that provide you with a very fine degree of control over your applications. Although the details of these packages are beyond the scope of this book, carefully reviewing the reference manual descriptions of the contents of these packages will pay off if you are going to do any significant amount of PL/SQL programming in your applications.

Form Builder provides the packages in Table 12-2. The packages themselves appear in the Object Navigator under the Built-in Packages node.

Report Builder has many of the same packages as Forms, but the main package of interest is the SRW package. The components of this package provide most of the access to report elements that you need in order to do special report programming.

Package	Description
DDE	Provides access to Microsoft DDE
DEBUG	Provides debugging subprograms you can use to find problems in your code
EXEC_SQL	Provides most of the DBMS_SQL package functions for use in application PL/SQL code
FTREE	Provides operations on hierarchical trees
OLE2	Provides access to Microsoft OLE version 2
ORA_FFI	Provides access to foreign functions
ORA_NLS	Provides information about the language environment
ORA_PROF	Provides timing subprograms for profiling your code
PECS	Provides performance evaluation tools (deprecated by Oracle Corporation)

TABLE 12-2. *Standard Packages in Oracle Developer Forms*

Package	Description
STANDARD	Provides PL/SQL built-in procedures and functions
STANDARD Extensions	Provides Oracle built-in procedures and functions to extend PL/SQL
TEXT_IO	Provides file I/O
TOOL_ENV	Provides access to environment variables
TOOL_ERR	Provides error-handling subprograms, including MESSAGE
TOOL_RES	Provides access to strings in resource files
VBX	Provides access to tools for dealing with VBX controls
WEB	Provides the Show_Document subprogram for displaying Web documents

TABLE 12-2. *Standard Packages in Oracle Developer Forms* (continued)

Graphics, again, uses many of the same packages as Forms, but in addition it has the two packages OG and TOOL_INT. The OG package provides an enormous number of components that do just about everything you can do to any element of a chart or display. The TOOL_INT package provides the tools for creating parameter lists to pass parameters to other products.

Checking Out the Library

Several of the preceding sections have mentioned the PL/SQL library. The library exists as a way to group and store PL/SQL program units into separately stored modules for easy reuse. Ordinarily, you store PL/SQL code as database objects. With the availability of PL/SQL as a client-side programming language, it became necessary to have a way to store the code as file system objects that you could attach to your application.

Libraries work the same way for all the Oracle Developer products. You create a library as a separate module in any of the products or with the Procedure Builder. You then attach the library to any Oracle Developer module (form, menu, report, or display) to make all its components available to any of the objects in the module. You can also attach a library to a library module. You do not need to prefix names with the library name to use the components.

Creating a Library

To create program units (procedures, functions, package specifications, or package bodies) in a library, find the library module header in the Object Navigator and select it. Create a new library by clicking on the Create tool, or open a previously saved library using the Open tool. Select the Program Units heading under the library name, and click on the Create tool to create a program unit. You first see the New Program Unit dialog box, which lets you choose which kind of program unit to create (procedure, function, package specification, or package body), as shown here:

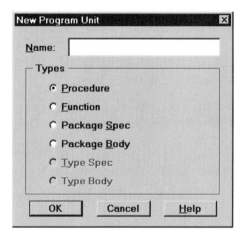

When you make your choice and click on OK, you see the standard PL/SQL Editor with a template for the specific type of program unit, as shown here:

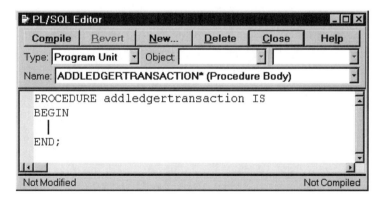

When you finish coding and compiling your unit, save it by saving the library module in the usual way with the Save tool. Saving the library also sets the name of the library; you cannot change it in the Navigator directly. Make sure you compile all the program units in the library; if you don't, modules using the library will have troubles. You can quickly check the status of the units by the presence or absence of special symbols on the unit names: an asterisk means uncompiled, and an at sign (@) means not saved to disk. Another strategy is to choose the File|Compile All menu item with the library name selected, which ensures that either you compile all units or you see errors for ones that do not compile.

There are three kinds of library files:

- *PLL:* A file that contains both PL/SQL source and compiled code that you can execute; Oracle Developer generates this file when you save the library.

- *PLX:* A file with just the compiled code.

- *PLD:* A text file with just the PL/SQL source; you can use this file as the input to source-control software or as an input script of PL/SQL that you can include and compile.

1. To create a PLX file, open the Forms Compiler.

2. Enter the name of the library in the File field.

3. Enter your user name, password, and database.

4. Set the Module type to FORM, MENU, or LIBRARY field to LIBRARY.

5. Enter the name of the output PLX file in the "Write output to file" field. Figure 12-1 illustrates the setup for the TalbotStandard library.

To create a PLD file, attach the library in the Procedure Builder and use the EXPORT command in the Interpreter to generate the library text file:

```
.EXPORT LIBRARY <library> FILE [<directory>]<name>.PLD
```

For more information on the GENERATE and EXPORT commands, see the *Procedure Builder Developer's Guide,* Chapter 7.

Attaching and Using a Library

To attach a library, find the Attached Libraries node under the module to which you want to attach the library. Click on the Create tool to see the Open File dialog box, and choose the library you want to attach.

Clicking on Attach attaches the library as a read-only object. You cannot change anything in the library through this object. Instead, open the library under the library module heading and change it there.

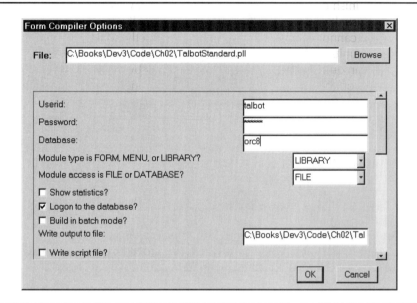

FIGURE 12-1. *Generating a PLX file for the TalbotStandard library*

TIP
You should always remove any path information from the library filename. Hard-coding the path means that if you move the library somewhere else, you must change and recompile the application. Instead, just change the registry variables FORMS60_PATH, REPORTS60_PATH, or GRAPHICS60_PATH to include the directory.

When you attach a library to another module, that module can then refer to any component of the library without using the library name. The order of the libraries under the Attached Libraries header in your module is the search order for the name. Oracle Developer first looks for a program unit in the Program Units section of the module. If the name is not there, it looks in each attached library in order. You can thus override specific program units by positioning them either in the module's Program Units section or by positioning an overriding library ahead of another library. You can use this strategy to extend or adapt a library to a specific use, rather than having to rewrite or repackage the whole library.

Attaching a library to another library lets you build structured layers of library code that other modules can use with just a click of the mouse. You can also use this strategy to build extensions of other libraries by attaching the base library to the extending library and recoding some of the program units.

To use Oracle Developer variables (such as globals, system variables, parameters, items), you have to use a subprogram parameter, a package variable, or indirection through the Name_In and Copy subprograms:

```
vAmount := Name_In('Ledger.Amount');
vSecurityLevel := Name_In('GLOBAL.SecurityLevel');
vCurrent := Name_In('SYSTEM.CURRENT_RECORD');
Copy(4.05, 'Ledger.Amount');
Copy('Secret', 'GLOBAL.SecurityLevel');
Copy('TRUE', 'SYSTEM.SUPRESS_WORKING');
```

The Name_In function takes a name (data block name plus item name in the block) and returns the value in the item. The Copy procedure assigns a value to an item identified by a data block name and an item name.

NOTE

It is much better to use subprogram parameters to pass values than to refer to variables using Name_In or Copy. You use bind variable syntax (:Ledger.Amount, for example) to do this. When you take the Name_In/Copy approach, you are coupling the two parts of the system by a direct link from the middle of the code, which is never a good idea. Use subprograms and packages and parameters to move data in a structured, easily maintained way, and you will find that your libraries are much more reusable. Also, if you are writing code that is specific to a module and thus requires many references to module variables, you should probably move the code into the module's Program Units section. This strategy gives you direct access to the variables. This code is not reusable, but with many module-specific references it probably is not reusable as a matter of design.

Combining what you have learned in this chapter with the basics of PL/SQL programming taught in Chapter 11 gives you just about everything you need to know to develop very sophisticated applications with Oracle Developer. The sophistication comes not so much from the whizzy things you can do on the screen, but from the many ways you can create a valuable application while building a set of reusable system components for future applications. By using the full set of features of PL/SQL, you simultaneously ensure that your applications can do what the user wants and that your code will serve you well in the future, increasing your productivity and the value you can deliver to your customers.

The next two chapters introduce the concepts you need to ensure that your components and applications do what they are supposed to do: they are all about testing and debugging.

CHAPTER
13

Debugging

You've created your application, you've run it, and something has failed. Sometimes, the failure is obvious—you left out a field in a block, or you crossed an "i" somewhere that you should have dotted instead. But much of the time the cause of a failure—the *fault*—is not obvious, and you have to track it down. This tracking process is *debugging,* or the art of solving a problem by finding and fixing a fault in the code.

Debugging is complementary to testing, though not exactly. You can find faults simply by inspecting your code, and that is a particularly effective way to debug. Testing combined with debugging is a powerful technique that lets you discover and fix problems early in the development process. If as a developer you test your objects thoroughly and use the techniques described in this chapter to find and fix the faults that cause the failures you run into, you will spend a lot less time doing debugging in alpha and beta tests.

Using Oracle Developer to produce software applications removes many sources of faults that you might meet in standard programming. Pointer and memory allocation errors do not exist, and even SQL syntax errors do not happen. Your SQL gets parsed immediately, and you get immediate feedback on errors. That means that if you learned to debug with another programming language, you will find many of the specific techniques you learned are irrelevant to Oracle Developer applications. There is still quite a bit of classic debugging art that applies, however.

The Art of Debugging

Building test models is a wonderful way to understand a piece of code—or a requirement or design component—thoroughly. As you will see in this section, understanding a piece of code is also the essence of what you do when you are debugging. You will find that if you build object test models for the component objects in your application, you will usually find many of the faults hiding in the component. You will find them, in fact, without either running the tests or even developing the test cases. The act of building the test model is often enough for a good developer to recognize logic and coding flaws in the object under test.

Some faults require more investigation, however. This usually happens because the fault involves something that is easy to overlook, something that is in more than one place or object, or something you base on a hidden assumption that is not a part of the test model you develop. That is when the art of debugging really kicks in.

The title of this section comes from a small book that is probably the best book in existence on testing and debugging software: Glenford Myers's *The Art of Software Testing* (Wiley, 1979). Despite its age and increasing obsolescence with respect to the technological and theoretical aspects of testing and debugging, this book provides a very practical introduction to its subject. No one who does software development for a living should continue doing it without reading this book. The rest of this section summarizes the points that Myers makes as an introduction to the art of debugging. The rest of the chapter shows you how to add Oracle Developer debugging tools to your artistic debugging palette and how to use them effectively to support your debugging.

Locating Faults by Induction

The process of induction reasons from the parts to the whole (Figure 13-1). That is, using data about the failure, you narrow down the nature of the fault.

1. *Locate the relevant data about the failure.* Do not just say, "There's a problem" and start fixing things. Specify exactly how the failure occurs by observing how it occurs, showing how to make it occur reproducibly, and showing how to avoid the problem with similar but different test cases. Explore the context in which the failure occurs.

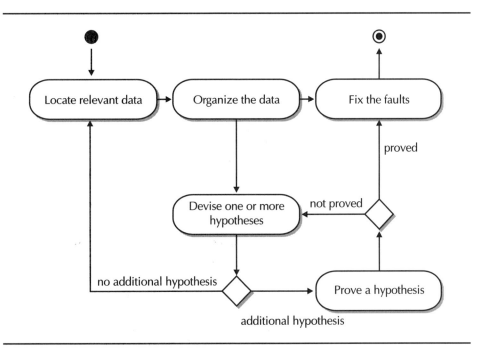

FIGURE 13-1.   *The inductive debugging process*

2. *Organize the data about the failure.* Induction proceeds by pattern analysis, and it is much easier to see the patterns and relationships in the data if the data is well organized. Myers has a table that shows what happens, where it happens, when it happens, and to what extent it happens versus the circumstances under which the failure does and does not occur. Organizing the events as a scenario can also be useful. Then, study the patterns of relationships that emerge from this data. One particularly effective way to do this is by *backtracking*: starting from a point where you have failed, work backward through the data about the process. Another possibility is to work through some additional test cases to see the patterns more clearly.

3. *Devise a hypothesis.* Having studied the relationships, propose one or more hypotheses about the fault. If you cannot devise a hypothesis that fits the facts, get more data.

4. *Prove the hypothesis.* Pick the hypothesis that seems the most likely; then prove it is correct by showing, first, how it fits the known data and second, how it works in the code.

5. *Fix the fault.* Change the code as your hypothesis suggests; then test the code again to prove that the fix does prevent the failure and that it does not cause any additional failures.

You use induction when you have a set of data and a relatively poor understanding of how the program works and/or of the nature of the failure. Induction requires thorough data analysis and much time and effort to do well compared to the deductive approach described in the next section.

Locating Faults by Deduction

The process of deduction reasons from the whole to the parts (Figure 13-2). That is, using your knowledge about the application and system, you deduce the nature of the fault by eliminating and refining hypotheses:

1. *List the possible faults that might cause the failure.* Brainstorm, preferably with other developers, the set of hypotheses about the fault that explain the failure. Even partial hypotheses are useful. Some hypotheses come from general programming theory, such as looking at recently changed code ("I only changed one thing; it can't possibly have caused the problem!"); code that is very complex ("I had to do it that way because otherwise it wouldn't have worked!"); or code that has a history of faults ("Not again!"). Some hypotheses come from programming practice, such as boundary condition errors or the standard misunderstandings of SQL constructs such as GROUP BY HAVING or outer joins ("Which one does the plus sign go on?").

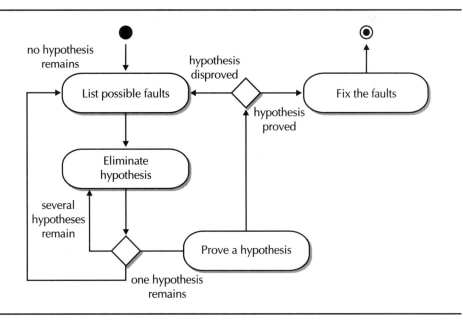

FIGURE 13-2.   *The deductive debugging process*

2. *Eliminate hypotheses.* Analyze the data and its relationships. If you cannot eliminate all but one hypothesis, gather more data with an eye toward the remaining hypotheses. Often, working through some additional test cases works well. If you eliminate all the hypotheses, go back to brainstorming new hypotheses.

3. *Refine and prove the hypothesis.* Make the theory about the fault as specific as possible using the available data. What exactly is going on? Show how the refined hypothesis fits the known data and how it works in the code.

4. *Fix the fault.* Change the code as your hypothesis suggests, and then test the code again to prove that the fix does prevent the failure and that it does not cause any additional failures.

You would use deduction when you have a good understanding of how the program works and of the nature of the failure. This good understanding lets you move right to a set of hypotheses. The key part of the method, however, is the elimination and refinement of hypotheses by data analysis. Skipping the data analysis will usually result in wild-goose chases. You may think you know exactly what's happening, but then so did George Washington's doctors when they bled him to death. Check your data; then prove the hypothesis.

Locating Faults by Tracing

The *brute force* method of finding faults is to *trace* through the program, event by event, until you find something wrong. Most developers get a good, intuitive feel for what to look for during a debugging (that is, tracing) session. It should be clear, however, that this method is *much* less efficient than induction or deduction, largely because you do not *think* during the process. You can generate truly massive amounts of data to process, most of it irrelevant. And the larger the application, the harder it is to do: the technique simply does not scale well.

Of course, if you do not understand what is happening in the program and you do not understand the failure well enough, this may be the only approach to finding the fault. For Oracle Developer programs, this would apply only if you do not understand how Oracle Developer is processing. For example, if you do not understand the processes in Chapter 5, and you cannot reproduce the failure reliably enough even to start an induction process, then you might as well step through the debugger until something unusual happens. Lay in supplies; it will take a while. If nothing else, the next time you will know how Oracle Developer works well enough to use deduction instead of brute force.

Fault Location Techniques

Here, in no particular order, are some thoughts about the practical details of induction and deduction.

- *Use your brain:* It may be your best programming asset.

- *Use your subconscious:* Let the problem rest a while and do something else. Often you will have a flash of insight that will save you much grief.

- *Use your friends:* Talk to someone about the problem. You may find that talking about it lets you see a new hypothesis, or you may find your peer can develop a different hypothesis.

- *Avoid the debugger:* See the comment about using your brain.

- *Avoid banging on it:* Specifically, try not to change parts of the application at random to see what happens. This is worse than tracing because it disrupts the playing field, potentially by adding new failures.

Fixing Faults

There is a bit more to the process of fixing faults than just changing the code.

- While you are fixing the problem, look around the code.

■ Make sure you have fixed the entire problem. By implication, this means that you need to understand what the entire problem was. In other words, do not fix the fault until you understand completely how the application failed and the full ramifications of that failure. The inductive and deductive approaches to debugging are much more likely to give you a full understanding of a failure. Also, do not simply fix a symptom rather than the disease. Software faults are easier to cure than human faults.

■ Make very sure that you have not broken something else. Especially as your applications get larger and/or more complex, the probability of introducing new failures gets quite high for each intervention. The best way to avoid doing this is with regression tests. These tests should demonstrate that everything works as it should. The next best way to do this is to inspect the code. In this case, you should inspect all code even indirectly related to the code you changed.

■ You should also study the pattern of faults in your code to learn from your mistakes. If your coding practices need to change to prevent certain faults, do it. If you find that certain kinds of faults seem to occur regularly in Oracle Developer code, put a standard in place to see if you can prevent them. If you find that certain kinds of failures are more frequent than others, focus your design efforts on ways to reduce those kinds of failures. An ounce of prevention...

Debugging Oracle Developer Objects

Having now thoroughly discredited the automated debugging tools as a method for debugging, the rest of the chapter tells you how to use these tools effectively and artistically. You should use these tools mainly in the hypothesis-proving stage of debugging.

The Oracle Developer environment lets you debug in several different ways. The built-in debugger lets you trace through your code and inspect virtually anything at will. Forms and Reports also let you debug using tracing facilities that tell you where you are in program execution.

The Debugger

The debugger lets you trace through the PL/SQL in your application using modern, interactive debugger techniques:

■ Interactive manipulation of breakpoints and triggers in the source code

■ Interactive inspection and manipulation of PL/SQL and variables

- Inspection of the PL/SQL calling stack

- Interactive execution of PL/SQL commands

Each tool sets up the application for the debugger in a different way.

The Forms Debugger

To use the debugger in an Oracle Developer Forms application, you must generate your form and menu executable files using the debug option. Click on the Run Form Debug tool on the Object Navigator Tool Palette, or use the Program|Run Form|Debug menu item to run in Debug mode. Whenever you generate your application, Oracle Developer/Forms embeds source code symbols in the application.

To run the debugger when you run your application, either run it from the Builder with the Run Form Debug tool or menu item, or use the Forms Runtime command line parameter DEBUG=YES with the special debugging executable IFDBG60 after compiling it with debugging information:

 `IFDBG60 workerskill talbot/george@orcl debug=YES`

The runtime system displays the debugger before loading the form to let you set any debugging actions.

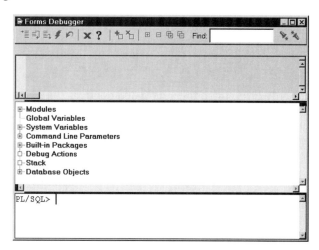

At this point, you can create a breakpoint in any trigger or program unit in the application, and you can create debugging triggers (triggers that fire on debugger events).

The top pane of the debugger shows the PL/SQL source from the currently executing block. This is the Source pane, which is blank because the debugger is not currently executing a block. You use this pane to set breakpoints, which exist only while you debug. The middle pane is the Object Navigator pane, which strongly resembles the Object Navigator but with fewer objects. This Object Navigator has a set of objects to use in runtime debugging; however, they are not the set of objects you see in the Builder Object Navigator. You use this pane to inspect debug actions and variables (global, system, local) and parameters in the call stack. The lower pane is the Interpreter pane, in which the commands you execute appear. The Interpreter pane lets you execute commands by typing them in.

NOTE
If you run into a situation where something seems to be going wrong but you are not seeing any errors or exceptions in Forms Runtime, check the On-Error triggers in the form. If these triggers catch all the exceptions in a WHEN OTHERS clause instead of properly handling specific exceptions and passing on the rest, the trigger absorbs all the errors without any feedback to you. Eliminate such clauses by commenting out the WHEN OTHERS clauses. Fix problems by inserting the appropriate exception handlers (consult Chapter 13 for details on such handlers).

The Report Debugger

Unlike Forms, the Reports debugger stores its debug actions in the report itself. In the Object Navigator in Report Builder, you can see two headings: Debug Actions and Stack. The former stores breakpoints and trigger actions; the latter represents the call stack at runtime.

To create breakpoints, you invoke the Report debugger with the Program| PL/SQL Interpreter menu item after selecting the program unit in the Report Builder Object Navigator. This displays a modeless, two-paned version of the debugger with the Source pane and the Interpreter pane:

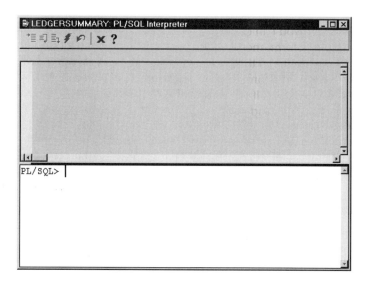

When you click on a program unit or trigger in the Object Navigator, the PL/SQL Interpreter displays the PL/SQL code. You can then set breakpoints anywhere in the code (see the following section), which you can then save with the report. When you run the report, the runtime debugger pops up when you reach the breakpoint and highlights the breakpoint (you don't need to scroll within the window).

NOTE

When you recompile program units, you need to reset any affected breakpoints to their new line numbers.

The Graphics Debugger

The Oracle Developer Graphics debugger works in much the same way as the Oracle Developer Reports one. You start the modeless debugger in the Graphics Builder with the Tools|PL/SQL Interpreter menu item.

Most of your debugging work will be figuring out which option you got wrong in the display or charts, and the debugger is not going to help much with that. You "test" various option settings by running the display as a standalone graphic display. By the time you integrate the display into a form or report, you should be confident in the internal consistency of the graphic.

If you get runtime errors in the display, you can use the debugger much as you would for a form or report. You can set breakpoints or debug triggers and inspect variables and parameters. Unless you have extensive use of PL/SQL in your displays, however, the debugger is not going to help much.

NOTE
If you correct program errors in the debugger and recompile there, you should choose the EditISynchronize Program Units menu item when you finish debugging. This synchronizes the changes in the version of the code that resides in the debugger with the code residing in the Designer or Builder.

The Source Pane and Breakpoints
You use the Source pane, which displays the source as read-only text, to set breakpoints and to see where you are in the execution process. This is a debugging session with a breakpoint set in a subprogram body:

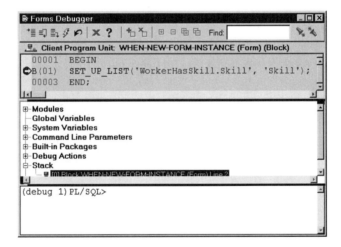

Notice the B(01) in the left margin of the pane, where the line numbers appear. This indicates that there is a breakpoint (breakpoint 1) at that line in the subprogram. You can set the breakpoint by double-clicking on the line in the Source pane. The arrow (pointing at the "B") indicates that the debugger has stopped execution just before executing that line.

When you see the initial debugger as Forms Runtime starts up, you enter a breakpoint at the place where you want to start debugging. Then you click on the Close tool to start the form. Action continues until the form reaches the breakpoint you have set. When the form breaks, it displays the debugger again. You can then examine the variables in the Navigator pane (see the following section), or you can start moving through the code using the Step commands.

By clicking on the Step Into tool, you can execute the next statement. If that statement is a subprogram call, you enter the subprogram and stop at the first executable line of that subprogram. The Step Over tool does the same thing but executes the subprogram and puts you on the next executable line after the subprogram call. The Step Out Of tool lets you continue executing until the current subprogram or block returns. The debugger then stops at the next executable line.

Step Over

Step Into   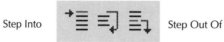   Step Out Of

By using these commands, you can navigate through the subprogram, statement by statement, tracing your execution path. At any point, you can examine the values of any variables to see what is going on.

You can use the Go tool to continue executing until the next break or until you exit the application.

The Reset tool exits the current debugging level and returns to the previous level; see the later section on the Interpreter pane for details.

The other kind of debug action is a debug trigger. A debug trigger associates a PL/SQL block with a specific line of code in a program unit. The debugger fires the trigger when execution reaches that line. You can also set triggers to fire when the debugger takes control or at every PL/SQL source line. By raising the DEBUG.BREAK exception as part of the trigger, you can cause a break. This lets you set conditional breakpoints:

```
IF DEBUG.GETN('RELDEF') = TRUE THEN
   RAISE DEBUG.BREAK;
END IF;
```

In the trigger code, you access variables in the current scope using the GETN and SETN subprograms. The Break exception causes the debugger to break and display the current source line (the line that fired the debug trigger).

WARNING
You can also make breaks persistent by using the Break procedure in your PL/SQL code. This book recommends against debug triggers and persistent breaks for at least two reasons. First, you should be using breaks and the debugger mainly to prove a hypothesis, not to extensively trace your code. Use the tracing facilities for that. Second, if you forget it and leave the break in your code, a customer can suddenly fall into the debugger. This is unlikely to help you to provide a quality application; instead, it actually adds a fault to your code. Debug triggers can help to speed up processing, particularly in loops, by automatically testing conditions for you, but your use for this will be rare.

The Navigator Pane and Variables

The Navigator pane lets you examine different kinds of variables. You can look at any item by navigating to it under the Modules heading. You can look at Global Variables, System Variables, and Command Parameters by navigating to them under those headings. The Stack heading provides the current state of the call stack for PL/SQL. This stack shows the hierarchy of PL/SQL blocks currently executing. This stack shows that the debugger is executing a trigger, ON-POPULATE-DETAILS, which in turn is calling a subprogram, QUERY_MASTER_DETAILS.

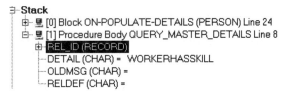

Each item in this stack represents an executing scope that defines variables, and you can navigate to those variables (parameters and local variables) under the Stack items. This illustration shows the variables in the running Set_Up_List subprogram, including the variable ERRFLAG, which was set by the call to Populate_Group:

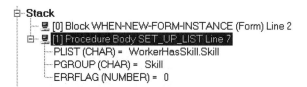

The Navigator pane shows the current values of all variables, including the parameters; PLIST, for example, has the value WorkerHasSkill.Skill, the data block and item names of the list item. You can also change these variables in the Navigator by selecting and entering the value directly after the equal sign.

NOTE
The debugger does not currently support package body variables, and there is no way to inspect the values of these variables. Package body variables are those you declare in the declarations section of a package body. They are inaccessible outside the package, but all the subprogram bodies in the package and the package initialization code share these variables. See Chapter 12 for details.

You can also inspect the details of your debug actions through the breakpoint and trigger dialog boxes. Under the Debug Action heading, you can select any breakpoint or debug trigger and double-click on its icon to see the dialog boxes. Here is the Breakpoint dialog box for the breakpoint from the previous section:

Using this dialog box, you can enable or disable the breakpoint with the Enabled check box. You can also enter some PL/SQL code as a trigger to execute whenever the break occurs.

The Interpreter Pane and Commands

The Interpreter pane lets you enter the textual versions of the debugger commands such as Step Into or Go. You can also see the debugging level. The debugging level is the nesting level of the breaks in program execution. That is, you can break, step over a subprogram, and hit a break in the subprogram. This then establishes debugging level 2 in the Interpreter pane. You can see the debugging level as a parenthesized expression in the Interpreter pane command prompt, such as "(debug 1)PL/SQL>". This nesting of debugging levels lets you reset the debugger back to the previous debugging level, thus restarting your debugging session.

For a complete list of Interpreter debugger commands and their syntax, consult the online help for the debugger in the Form Builder.

Tracing Forms

There are two separate tracing facilities in Oracle Developer Forms—one old and one new. First, the old one. You can turn on special debugging messages when you run your application. Whenever an event occurs that causes a trigger to execute, the runtime system displays a message on the message line and an alert. When you click on OK on the alert window, the application continues.

The debug message displays the name of the trigger and the name of the object that owns the trigger (form, block, or item).

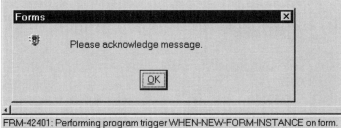

To display messages in Forms Runtime, add the DEBUG_MESSAGES parameter to the Forms Runtime command line:

```
IFRUN60 workerskill talbot/george@orcl debug_messages=YES
```

To display the same messages running a form from the Form Builder, choose the Tools|Preferences menu item and check the Debug Messages preference check box in the Runtime tab of the Preferences dialog box.

NOTE
You will find very quickly that the caution given in the last section about massive amounts of data and long debugging time holds true when using debugging messages. Try it at least once to see what happens on a form with a reasonable number of triggers. This gives new meaning to the term "last resort."

Now for the newer approach: Forms Runtime Diagnostics (FRD). The FRD facility provides a complete trace of Oracle Developer/Forms execution in a trace file that you can examine at your leisure. You need a lot of leisure, though, because this trace really is complete.

To start FRD, run the form you want to trace and supply the RECORD and LOG parameters to the command line:

```
IFRUN60 workerskill talbot/george@orcl RECORD=COLLECT LOG=WS.LOG
```

This command line runs the form, tracing all activity in the form into the WSLOG file in the current working directory. Here is an example of the first few trace elements in this file:

```
Forms Runtime Diagnostics Collection Log
Created: 13-MAR-1999 12:06:52

File Name: WS.LOG
Process ID: -946733
Forms 6.0 (Forms Runtime) Version 6.0.4.10.0 (Beta)
PL/SQL Version 8.0.5.0.0 (Production)
Oracle Virtual Graphics System Version 6.0.5.3.0 (Beta)
Oracle Multimedia Version 6.0.2.0.0 (Production)
Oracle Tools Integration Version 6.0.5.1.0 (Production)
Oracle Tools Common Area Version 6.0.5.3.0
Oracle CORE Version 4.0.5.0.0 - Production


Opened file: C:\BOOKS\DEV3\CODE\workerskill.fmx

WHEN-NEW-FORM-INSTANCE Trigger Fired:
```

```
Form: WORKERSKILL

State Delta:
FORM WORKERSKILL
  CURBLOCK    PERSON
  CURFIELD    NAME
  STATUS      NEW
  BLOCK PERSON
    RECCOUNT   1
    TOPREC     1
    CURREC     1
    STATUS      NEW
    RECSTATUS  NEW
    FIELD NAME
      CANVAS     CANVAS2
      GEOMETRY   499,67:1694,240
      MANDATORY  TRUE
      ENABLED    TRUE
      NAVIGABLE  TRUE
      INSERTABLE TRUE
      QUERYABLE  TRUE
      UPDATEABLE TRUE
  BLOCK WORKERHASSKILL
    RECCOUNT   1
    TOPREC     1
    CURREC     1
    STATUS      NEW
    RECSTATUS  NEW
    FIELD NAME
      MANDATORY  TRUE
      INSERTABLE TRUE
      UPDATEABLE TRUE
    FIELD SKILL
      CANVAS     CANVAS2
      GEOMETRY   0,544:1000,240
      MANDATORY  TRUE
      ENABLED    TRUE
      NAVIGABLE  TRUE
      INSERTABLE TRUE
      QUERYABLE  TRUE
      UPDATEABLE TRUE
    FIELD ABILITY
      CANVAS     CANVAS2
      GEOMETRY   1000,544:1069,240
      ENABLED    TRUE
      NAVIGABLE  TRUE
      INSERTABLE TRUE
      QUERYABLE  TRUE
```

```
        UPDATEABLE TRUE

Executing FIND_GROUP Built-in:
In Argument 0 - Type: String    Value: Skill
Out Argument 0 - Type: Integer   Value: 1

Executing POPULATE_GROUP Built-in:
In Argument 0 - Type: Integer  Value: 1
Out Argument 0 - Type: Number   Value: 0

Executing FIND_ITEM Built-in:
In Argument 0 - Type: String    Value: WorkerHasSkill.Skill
Out Argument 0 - Type: Integer   Value: 131075

Executing Clear_List Built-in:
In Argument 0 - Type: Integer  Value: 131075

Executing FIND_ITEM Built-in:
In Argument 0 - Type: String    Value: WorkerHasSkill.Skill
Out Argument 0 - Type: Integer   Value: 131075

Executing FIND_GROUP Built-in:
In Argument 0 - Type: String    Value: Skill
Out Argument 0 - Type: Integer   Value: 1

Executing Populate_List Built-in:
In Argument 0 - Type: Integer  Value: 131075
In Argument 1 - Type: Integer  Value: 1

# 1 - WORKERSKILL:PERSON.NAME - WINDOW
END

# 1 - WORKERSKILL:PERSON.NAME
WINDOW WORKERSKILL WINDOW1 ACTIVATE 1

# 2 - WORKERSKILL:PERSON.NAME - MENU
END

# 2 - WORKERSKILL:PERSON.NAME
MENU DEFAULT Query eXecute

ON-CLEAR-DETAILS Trigger Fired:
Form: WORKERSKILL

State Delta:

Executing FIND_BLOCK Built-in:
In Argument 0 - Type: String    Value: PERSON
```

```
Out Argument 0 - Type: Integer   Value: 1

Executing GET_BLOCK_PROPERTY Built-in:
In Argument 0 - Type: Integer  Value: 1
In Argument 1 - Type: Number  Value: 160
Out Argument 0 - Type: String   Value: PERSON_WORKERHASSKILL

Executing FIND_RELATION Built-in:
In Argument 0 - Type: String   Value: PERSON_WORKERHASSKILL
Out Argument 0 - Type: Integer   Value: 65537

Executing GET_RELATION_PROPERTY Built-in:
In Argument 0 - Type: Integer  Value: 65537
In Argument 1 - Type: Number  Value: 152
Out Argument 0 - Type: String   Value: WORKERHASSKILL

Executing FIND_BLOCK Built-in:
In Argument 0 - Type: String   Value: WORKERHASSKILL
Out Argument 0 - Type: Integer   Value: 2

Executing GET_BLOCK_PROPERTY Built-in:
In Argument 0 - Type: Integer  Value: 2
In Argument 1 - Type: Number  Value: 100
Out Argument 0 - Type: String   Value: NEW

Executing FIND_RELATION Built-in:
In Argument 0 - Type: String   Value: PERSON_WORKERHASSKILL
Out Argument 0 - Type: Integer   Value: 65537

Executing GET_RELATION_PROPERTY Built-in:
In Argument 0 - Type: Integer  Value: 65537
In Argument 1 - Type: Number  Value: 153
Out Argument 0 - Type: String   Value: NULL

ON-POPULATE-DETAILS Trigger Fired:
Form: WORKERSKILL
Block: PERSON

State Delta:
FORM WORKERSKILL
  STATUS     QUERY
  BLOCK PERSON
    STATUS     QUERY
    RECSTATUS  QUERY
    FIELD ROWID
      VALUE       0004B006.0000.0001
    FIELD NAME
      VALUE       "Bart Sarjeant"
```

You can see by examining this example that the tracing gives you every detail you need in order to know what Oracle Developer has done. Every trigger firing appears, and each event that could cause a change in data is accompanied by a *state delta*—a printout of any data elements changed since the last state delta.

Tracing Reports

You can turn on report tracing with the Tools|Trace menu item. Choosing this item displays the Trace Settings dialog box.

This lets you check the statistics that you want the trace log to display. This is the first part of the trace log for the Ledger Summary report that the full set of tracing options generates.

```
LOG :
      Report: Ledger
      Logged onto server:
      Username:


LOG :
      Logged onto server: orcl
      Username: talbot


15:33:48  APP   (  Header
15:33:48  APP  . (  Chart                     BOUGHTDISPLAY
15:33:53  APP  . )  Chart                     BOUGHTDISPLAY
15:33:53  APP   )  Header
15:33:56  APP   (  Frame
15:33:56  APP  . (  Generic Graphical Object B_1
15:33:56  APP  . )  Generic Graphical Object B_1
15:33:56  APP  . (  Text Boilerplate          B_DATE_BLULOGO1
```

```
15:33:57  APP . )  Text Boilerplate        B_DATE_BLULOGO1
15:33:57  APP . (  Text Boilerplate        B_TITLE_BLULOGO1
15:33:57  APP . )  Text Boilerplate        B_TITLE_BLULOGO1
15:33:57  APP . (  Text Boilerplate        OR$_BPAGENUM_BLULOGO1
15:33:57  APP . (  Text Boilerplate        OR$_BPAGENUM_BLULOGO1
15:33:57  APP . (  Text Field              F_DATE1
15:33:57  APP .. ( Database Column         Name unknown
15:33:57  APP .. ) Database Column         Name unknown
15:33:57  APP . )  Text Field              F_DATE1
15:33:57  APP )  Frame
15:33:57  APP (  Frame
15:33:57  APP . (  Frame                   M_G_PERSON_GRPFR
15:33:57  APP .. ( Repeating Frame         R_G_PERSON
15:33:57  APP ... ( Group                  G_Person  Local Break:  0  Global Break:  0
15:33:57  APP .... ( Query                 LedgerQuery
15:33:57  SQL             EXECUTE QUERY : select Person , ActionDate , Item , Quantity , Rate
                          from Ledger  ORDER BY 1 ASC , 1 , 2
15:33:57  APP .... ) Query                 LedgerQuery
15:33:57  PLS .... ( Function:        amountformula
15:33:57  PLS .... ) Function:        amountformula
15:33:57  APP ... ) Group                  G_Person
15:33:57  APP ... ( Text Field             F_PERSON
15:33:57  APP .... ( Database Column       Person
15:33:57  APP .... ) Database Column       Person
15:33:57  APP ... ) Text Field             F_PERSON
15:33:57  APP ... ( Frame                  M_G_ACTIONDATE_GRPFR
15:33:57  APP .... ( Repeating Frame       R_G_ACTIONDATE
15:33:57  APP ..... ( Group                G_ActionDate  Local Break:  0  Global Break:  0
15:33:57  APP ..... ) Group                G_ActionDate
15:33:57  APP ..... ( Text Field           F_RATE
15:33:57  APP ...... ( Database Column     Rate
15:33:57  APP ...... ) Database Column     Rate
15:33:57  APP ..... ) Text Field           F_RATE
15:33:57  APP ..... ( Text Field           F_QUANTITY
15:33:57  APP ...... ( Database Column     Quantity
15:33:57  APP ...... ) Database Column     Quantity
15:33:57  APP ..... ) Text Field           F_QUANTITY
15:33:57  APP ..... ( Text Field           F_ITEM
15:33:57  APP ...... ( Database Column     Item
15:33:57  APP ...... ) Database Column     Item
15:33:57  APP ..... ) Text Field           F_ITEM
15:33:57  APP ..... ( Text Field           F_ACTIONDATE
15:33:57  APP ...... ( Database Column     ActionDate
15:33:57  APP ...... ) Database Column     ActionDate
15:33:57  APP ..... ) Text Field           F_ACTIONDATE
15:33:57  APP ..... ( Group                G_ActionDate  Local Break:  1  Global Break:  1
15:33:57  PLS ...... ( Function:      amountformula
15:33:57  PLS ...... ) Function:      amountformula
15:34:05  APP ... ) Frame                  M_G_ACTIONDATE_GRPFR
15:34:05  APP ... ( Group                  G_ActionDate  Local Break:  1  Global Break:  225
15:34:05  APP ... ) Group                  G_ActionDate
15:34:05  APP ... ( Group                  G_Person  Local Break:  52  Global Break:  52
15:34:05  APP ... ) Group                  G_Person
15:34:05  APP .. ) Repeating Frame         R_G_PERSON
15:34:05  APP .. ( Frame                   M_G_PERSON_HDR
15:34:05  APP ... ( Text Boilerplate       B_RATE
15:34:05  APP ... ) Text Boilerplate       B_RATE
15:34:05  APP ... ( Text Boilerplate       B_QUANTITY
15:34:05  APP ... ) Text Boilerplate       B_QUANTITY
15:34:05  APP ... ( Text Boilerplate       B_ITEM
15:34:05  APP ... ) Text Boilerplate       B_ITEM
15:34:05  APP ... ( Text Boilerplate       B_ACTIONDATE
15:34:05  APP ... ) Text Boilerplate       B_ACTIONDATE
15:34:05  APP ... ( Text Boilerplate       B_PERSON
15:34:05  APP ... ) Text Boilerplate       B_PERSON
15:34:05  APP .. ) Frame                   M_G_PERSON_HDR
15:34:05  APP . )  Frame                   M_G_PERSON_GRPFR
```

```
15:34:05  APP  )  Frame

                    +------------------------------------+
                    | Report Builder Profiler statistics |
                    +------------------------------------+

        TOTAL ELAPSED Time:        60.00 seconds

        Reports Time:       60.00 seconds (100.00% of TOTAL)

             ORACLE Time:        0.00 seconds ( 0.00% of TOTAL)

                    UPI:      0.00 seconds
                    SQL:      0.00 seconds

TOTAL CPU Time used by process: N/A
```

Rather than tracing the entire report, you can use the SRW package to turn on tracing at specific spots in your report processing by calling SRW.TRACE_START() and SRW.TRACE_END() in report trigger code. You can set tracing options with SRW.TRACE_ADD_OPTIONS() and SRW.TRACE_REM_OPTIONS().

Tracing SQL and Client/Server Events

Although not strictly part of Oracle Developer, there are two other kinds of tracing that you may find useful under certain circumstances. Those circumstances are usually when you have no idea what is going on and you have to wade through enormous amounts of nearly useless material to figure it out. Unfortunately, this situation occurs more often than anyone would like to admit, so tracing tools at the client and server levels are still valuable, if time-consuming, tools of the application developer's trade. Again, the term "last resort" takes on new meaning.

SQL*Net Tracing on the Client

If you are using an Oracle7 database server and therefore SQL*Net version 2 as your connection from the client to the server, you can use SQL*Net tracing. This produces a hexadecimal dump of all the events of which SQL*Net is aware. You can see exactly which characters you are sending to the server from the client, and perhaps this will be enough to identify your problem. This kind of trace is more useful for debugging third-generation programs, where you can create bizarre situations by overwriting memory locations or attaching mysterious unwanted characters to the ends of strings by accident. That is very hard to do in Oracle Developer.

Turning on SQL*Net tracing requires you to set two parameters in the SQLNET.ORA file, which is in the Oracle_Home/Network/Admin directory: TRACE_LEVEL_CLIENT (value USER or ADMIN for summary or detailed network information, respectively, OFF to turn off tracing) and TRACE_DIRECTORY_CLIENT (value is the directory in which you want to create the trace file). This writes a file called SQLNET.TRC in the directory you specify.

NOTE
You should consult Oracle Corporation Technical Support for more information on using these techniques if the above description is not enough. These details are quite involved and are beyond the scope of this book, which focuses on Oracle8. Make sure you have enough disk space for the trace files, which can quickly grow very large (megabytes), and turn tracing off as soon as you get the trace information you need. Do not turn on tracing on a network basis, only locally (local variable setting or a local copy of SQLNET.ORA), or you will make your network administrator very unhappy as he or she struggles to figure out why there is no more disk space available on your system.

Net8 Tracing on the Client

If you are using an Oracle8 database server, and hence Net8 as your connection from the client to the server, you can use Net8 tracing to see the SQL you send to the server (among all the other network-related events as well). Net8 produces a hexadecimal dump of all the events of which it is aware. You can see exactly which characters you are sending to the server from the client, and perhaps this will be enough to identify your problem. This kind of trace is more useful when you debug custom Pro*C or Oracle Call Interface programs, where you can create bizarre situations by overwriting memory locations or attaching mysterious, unwanted characters to the ends of strings by accident. That is very hard to do in Oracle Developer.

Turning on Net8 tracing is easy. Find the SQLNET.ORA file in your client's Net8 Admin directory, usually somewhere like Oracle_Home\Net80\Admin. You will usually find one trace-related line in the file, TRACE_LEVEL_CLIENT = OFF. Change OFF to SUPPORT and add two lines to name the trace file:

```
TRACE_LEVEL_CLIENT = SUPPORT
TRACE_FILE_CLIENT = Net8_Trace
TRACE_DIRECTORY_CLIENT = C:\Orawin95\Net80\Trace
```

This example turns on SUPPORT-level tracing and puts the trace file in the file C:\Orawin95\Net80\Trace\Net8_Trace.trc. You can make the file name anything, but don't put an extension on it. You can make the directory anything, but make sure the directory exists before you run a client Oracle program. There are other levels for LEVEL, including USER and ADMIN, which limit the output. SUPPORT is probably the best choice, as it gives you all the information available and has a trace file formatting tool available, trcasst.

NOTE

Consult the Oracle8 Network Administration documentation for more information about using Net8 tracing and the trace assistant tool.

For example, if you start the Ledger application from Chapter 4 and press the Execute Query button to query all the records, you will find the following trace in the Net8 trace file:

```
(3ff2)  nspsend:  00  FD  00  00  06  00  00  00   |........|
(3ff2)  nspsend:  00  00  03  5E  0D  61  80  00   |...^.a..|
(3ff2)  nspsend:  00  00  00  00  00  98  F2  00   |........|
(3ff2)  nspsend:  01  84  00  00  00  C8  9F  00   |........|
(3ff2)  nspsend:  01  09  00  00  00  00  00  00   |........|
(3ff2)  nspsend:  00  EC  9F  00  01  00  00  00   |........|
(3ff2)  nspsend:  00  0A  00  00  00  1E  00  00   |........|
(3ff2)  nspsend:  00  00  00  00  00  00  00  00   |........|
(3ff2)  nspsend:  00  00  00  00  00  00  00  00   |........|
(3ff2)  nspsend:  00  00  00  00  00  00  00  00   |........|
(3ff2)  nspsend:  00  EE  9F  00  01  53  45  4C   |.....SEL|
(3ff2)  nspsend:  45  43  54  20  52  4F  57  49   |ECT ROWI|
(3ff2)  nspsend:  44  2C  4C  2E  50  45  52  53   |D,L.PERS|
(3ff2)  nspsend:  4F  4E  2C  4C  2E  4C  45  44   |ON,L.LED|
(3ff2)  nspsend:  47  45  52  49  44  2C  4C  2E   |GERID,L.|
(3ff2)  nspsend:  41  43  54  49  4F  4E  44  41   |ACTIONDA|
(3ff2)  nspsend:  54  45  2C  4C  2E  41  43  54   |TE,L.ACT|
(3ff2)  nspsend:  49  4F  4E  2C  4C  2E  49  54   |ION,L.IT|
(3ff2)  nspsend:  45  4D  2C  4C  2E  51  55  41   |EM,L.QUA|
(3ff2)  nspsend:  4E  54  49  54  59  2C  4C  2E   |NTITY,L.|
(3ff2)  nspsend:  51  55  41  4E  54  49  54  59   |QUANTITY|
(3ff2)  nspsend:  54  59  50  45  2C  4C  2E  52   |TYPE,L.R|
(3ff2)  nspsend:  41  54  45  2C  4C  2E  41  4D   |ATE,L.AM|
(3ff2)  nspsend:  4F  55  4E  54  2C  4C  2E  50   |OUNT,L.P|
(3ff2)  nspsend:  45  52  53  4F  4E  2E  4E  41   |ERSON.NA|
(3ff2)  nspsend:  4D  45  20  46  52  4F  4D  20   |ME FROM |
(3ff2)  nspsend:  4C  45  44  47  45  52  20  4C   |LEDGER L|
(3ff2)  nspsend:  20  01  00  00  00  01  00  00   | .......|
(3ff2)  nspsend:  00  00  00  00  00  00  00  00   |........|
(3ff2)  nspsend:  00  00  00  00  00  00  00  00   |........|
```

```
(3ff2) nspsend: 00 00 00 00 00 01 00 00   |........|
(3ff2) nspsend: 00 00 00 00 00 00 00 00   |........|
```

SQL Tracing on the Server

On the server side, you can trace the SQL statements and their performance characteristics using SQL tracing.

In Oracle Developer/Forms, you turn on SQL tracing with the Statistics option on the command line:

```
IFRUN60 workerskill talbot/george@orcl statistics=YES
```

NOTE
I was unable to start statistics tracing with the command line option to IFRUN60 in the version of Oracle Developer Forms component that I was running (6.0.5.0.2). Oracle Corporation verifies that the feature is supposed to work; try it.

In Reports, turn on tracing with an SRW procedure call in a Before-Parameter-Form trigger:

```
SRW.Do_SQL('ALTER SESSION SET SQL_TRACE TRUE');
```

In Graphics, use a similar call in an Open Trigger:

```
Do_SQL('ALTER SESSION SET SQL_TRACE TRUE');
```

NOTE
You can also turn on tracing for every session by setting the SQL_TRACE parameter of the Oracle instance to TRUE. You would not ordinarily want to do this; it is definitely overkill, since it traces every bit of SQL processing done by everyone using the server.

When you run your application with tracing on, the server produces an output trace file in a dump directory. You can identify this directory by running sysmgr and issuing the following command:

```
SHOW PARAMETER USER_DUMP_DEST
```

You can also get this information from the Instance Manager in the Initialization Parameters window.

On Windows NT, the trace file directory is likely to be Oracle_Home\ RDBMS80\Trace or something similar. Look in this directory for a file with extension .TRC and a unique identifier (process ID or similar number), such as ORA00075.TRC. Running the Ledger application, for example, generates this trace file:

```
Dump file D:\orant\rdbms80\trace\ORA00075.TRC
Mon Mar 29 09:50:48 1999
ORACLE V8.0.5.0.0 - Production vsnsta=0
vsnsql=c vsnxtr=3
Windows NT V4.0, OS V5.101, CPU type 586
Oracle8 Enterprise Edition Release 8.0.5.0.0 - Production
With the Partitioning and Objects options
PL/SQL Release 8.0.5.0.0 - Production
Windows NT V4.0, OS V5.101, CPU type 586
Instance name: orc8

Redo thread mounted by this instance: 1

Oracle process number: 10

pid: 4b


*** SESSION ID:(8.37) 1999.03.29.09.50.48.306
=====================
PARSING IN CURSOR #1 len=32 dep=0 uid=25 oct=42 lid=25 tim=22639233 hv=2162858323 ad='29e4478'
ALTER SESSION SET SQL_TRACE TRUE
END OF STMT
EXEC #1:c=3,e=3,p=0,cr=0,cu=0,mis=1,r=0,dep=0,og=4,tim=22639234
=====================
PARSING IN CURSOR #1 len=32 dep=0 uid=25 oct=42 lid=25 tim=22639503 hv=2162858323 ad='29e4478'
ALTER SESSION SET SQL_TRACE TRUE
END OF STMT
PARSE #1:c=1,e=1,p=0,cr=0,cu=0,mis=0,r=0,dep=0,og=4,tim=22639503
EXEC #1:c=0,e=0,p=0,cr=0,cu=0,mis=0,r=0,dep=0,og=4,tim=22639503
=====================
PARSING IN CURSOR #2 len=132 dep=0 uid=25 oct=3 lid=25 tim=22640182 hv=1199613752 ad='2a54244'
SELECT
ROWID,L.PERSON,L.LEDGERID,L.ACTIONDATE,L.ACTION,L.ITEM,L.QUANTITY,L.QUANTITYTYPE,L.RATE,L.AMOUNT,L.P
ERSON.NAME FROM LEDGER L
END OF STMT
PARSE #2:c=1,e=1,p=0,cr=0,cu=0,mis=0,r=0,dep=0,og=4,tim=22640183
EXEC #2:c=0,e=0,p=0,cr=0,cu=0,mis=0,r=0,dep=0,og=4,tim=22640183
=====================
PARSING IN CURSOR #4 len=47 dep=1 uid=0 oct=3 lid=0 tim=22640184 hv=1158616671 ad='2b6c630'
select metadata from kopm$  where name='DB_FDO'
END OF STMT
PARSE #4:c=1,e=1,p=0,cr=0,cu=0,mis=0,r=0,dep=1,og=4,tim=22640184
EXEC #4:c=0,e=0,p=0,cr=0,cu=0,mis=0,r=0,dep=1,og=4,tim=22640184
FETCH #4:c=0,e=0,p=0,cr=2,cu=0,mis=0,r=1,dep=1,og=4,tim=22640184
STAT #4 id=1 cnt=1 pid=0 pos=0 obj=240 op='TABLE ACCESS BY INDEX ROWID KOPM$ '
STAT #4 id=2 cnt=1 pid=1 pos=1 obj=241 op='INDEX UNIQUE SCAN '
FETCH #2:c=2,e=2,p=0,cr=21,cu=3,mis=0,r=11,dep=0,og=4,tim=22640185
---------------------
PARSING IN CURSOR #4 len=156 dep=0 uid=25 oct=3 lid=25 tim=22640616 hv=3424553781 ad='2a121cc'
SELECT L.PERSON,L.LEDGERID,L.ACTIONDATE,L.ACTION,L.ITEM,L.QUANTITY,L.QUANTITYTYPE,L.RATE,L.AMOUNT
FROM LEDGER L WHERE ROWID=:1 FOR UPDATE OF L.PERSON NOWAIT
END OF STMT
PARSE #4:c=1,e=1,p=0,cr=0,cu=0,mis=0,r=0,dep=0,og=4,tim=22640616
EXEC #4:c=0,e=0,p=0,cr=1,cu=3,mis=0,r=0,dep=0,og=4,tim=22640616
```

```
FETCH #4:c=0,e=0,p=0,cr=0,cu=0,mis=0,r=1,dep=0,og=4,tim=22640617
=====================
PARSING IN CURSOR #1 len=14 dep=0 uid=25 oct=46 lid=25 tim=22640800 hv=278968606 ad='2a112a8'
SAVEPOINT FM_1
END OF STMT
PARSE #1:c=1,e=1,p=0,cr=0,cu=0,mis=0,r=0,dep=0,og=4,tim=22640800
EXEC #1:c=0,e=0,p=0,cr=0,cu=0,mis=0,r=0,dep=0,og=4,tim=22640800
=====================
PARSING IN CURSOR #5 len=155 dep=0 uid=25 oct=6 lid=25 tim=22640801 hv=1725894326 ad='2a0eef4'
UPDATE LEDGER L SET
L.PERSON=:1,L.LEDGERID=:2,L.ACTIONDATE=:3,L.ACTION=:4,L.ITEM=:5,L.QUANTITY=:6,L.QUANTITYTYPE=:7,L.RA
TE=:8,L.AMOUNT=:9 WHERE ROWID=:10
END OF STMT
PARSE #5:c=1,e=1,p=0,cr=0,cu=0,mis=0,r=0,dep=0,og=4,tim=22640802
EXEC #5:c=0,e=0,p=0,cr=0,cu=1,mis=0,r=1,dep=0,og=4,tim=22640802
XCTEND rlbk=0, rd_only=0
EXEC #4:c=1,e=1,p=0,cr=1,cu=3,mis=0,r=0,dep=0,og=4,tim=22640937
FETCH #4:c=0,e=0,p=0,cr=0,cu=0,mis=0,r=1,dep=0,og=4,tim=22640937
=====================
PARSING IN CURSOR #1 len=14 dep=0 uid=25 oct=46 lid=25 tim=22641088 hv=278968606 ad='2a112a8'
SAVEPOINT FM_1
END OF STMT
PARSE #1:c=1,e=1,p=0,cr=0,cu=0,mis=0,r=0,dep=0,og=4,tim=22641088
EXEC #1:c=0,e=0,p=0,cr=0,cu=0,mis=0,r=0,dep=0,og=4,tim=22641088
EXEC #5:c=0,e=0,p=0,cr=0,cu=1,mis=0,r=1,dep=0,og=4,tim=22641089
XCTEND rlbk=0, rd_only=0
=====================
PARSING IN CURSOR #1 len=8 dep=0 uid=25 oct=45 lid=25 tim=22641236 hv=1470906206 ad='2a50020'
ROLLBACK
END OF STMT
PARSE #1:c=1,e=1,p=0,cr=0,cu=0,mis=0,r=0,dep=0,og=4,tim=22641237
XCTEND rlbk=1, rd_only=1
EXEC #1:c=0,e=0,p=0,cr=0,cu=0,mis=0,r=0,dep=0,og=4,tim=22641237
XCTEND rlbk=0, rd_only=1
STAT #2 id=1 cnt=11 pid=0 pos=0 obj=2488 op='TABLE ACCESS FULL LEDGER '
STAT #4 id=1 cnt=2 pid=0 pos=0 obj=0 op='FOR UPDATE '
STAT #4 id=2 cnt=2 pid=1 pos=1 obj=2488 op='TABLE ACCESS BY USER ROWID LEDGER '
STAT #5 id=1 cnt=0 pid=0 pos=0 obj=0 op='UPDATE LEDGER '
STAT #5 id=2 cnt=2 pid=1 pos=1 obj=2488 op='TABLE ACCESS BY USER ROWID LEDGER '
```

Although interesting, this file is somewhat hard to read. You can use the Oracle Toolkit profiler program (TKPROF) to format this trace into something you can easily work with. Supply the name of the input TRC file and the name of an output file on the TKPROF command line. You should also enter the user name and password to see execution plans for queries.

```
TKPROF80 c:\orant\rdbms80\trace\ora00075.trc c:\temp\output.trc
```

Formatting the trace for the LEDGER application yields this formatted trace file:

```
TKPROF: Release 8.0.5.0.0 - Production on Mon Mar 29 10:4:24 1999

(c) Copyright 1998 Oracle Corporation.  All rights reserved.

Trace file: ora00075.trc
Sort options: default

********************************************************************************
count    = number of times OCI procedure was executed
cpu      = cpu time in seconds executing
```

```
elapsed   = elapsed time in seconds executing
disk      = number of physical reads of buffers from disk
query     = number of buffers gotten for consistent read
current   = number of buffers gotten in current mode (usually for update)
rows      = number of rows processed by the fetch or execute call
*******************************************************************************

ALTER SESSION SET SQL_TRACE TRUE
```

call	count	cpu	elapsed	disk	query	current	rows
Parse	1	0.01	0.01	0	0	0	0
Execute	2	0.03	0.03	0	0	0	0
Fetch	0	0.00	0.00	0	0	0	0
total	3	0.04	0.04	0	0	0	0

```
Misses in library cache during parse: 0
Misses in library cache during execute: 1
Optimizer goal: CHOOSE
Parsing user id: 25
*******************************************************************************

SELECT ROWID,L.PERSON,L.LEDGERID,L.ACTIONDATE,L.ACTION,L.ITEM,L.QUANTITY,
  L.QUANTITYTYPE,L.RATE,L.AMOUNT,L.PERSON.NAME
FROM
 LEDGER L
```

call	count	cpu	elapsed	disk	query	current	rows
Parse	1	0.01	0.01	0	0	0	0
Execute	1	0.00	0.00	0	0	0	0
Fetch	1	0.02	0.02	0	19	3	11
total	3	0.03	0.03	0	19	3	11

```
Misses in library cache during parse: 0
Optimizer goal: CHOOSE
Parsing user id: 25
*******************************************************************************

select metadata
from
 kopm$  where name='DB_FDO'
```

call	count	cpu	elapsed	disk	query	current	rows
Parse	1	0.01	0.01	0	0	0	0
Execute	1	0.00	0.00	0	0	0	0
Fetch	1	0.00	0.00	0	2	0	1
total	3	0.01	0.01	0	2	0	1

```
Misses in library cache during parse: 0
Optimizer goal: CHOOSE
```

```
Parsing user id: SYS   (recursive depth: 1)
********************************************************************************

SELECT L.PERSON,L.LEDGERID,L.ACTIONDATE,L.ACTION,L.ITEM,L.QUANTITY,
  L.QUANTITYTYPE,L.RATE,L.AMOUNT
FROM
 LEDGER L WHERE ROWID=:1 FOR UPDATE OF L.PERSON NOWAIT
```

call	count	cpu	elapsed	disk	query	current	rows
Parse	1	0.01	0.01	0	0	0	0
Execute	2	0.01	0.01	0	2	6	0
Fetch	2	0.00	0.00	0	0	0	2
total	5	0.02	0.02	0	2	6	2

```
Misses in library cache during parse: 0
Optimizer goal: CHOOSE
Parsing user id: 25
********************************************************************************

SAVEPOINT FM_1
```

call	count	cpu	elapsed	disk	query	current	rows
Parse	2	0.02	0.02	0	0	0	0
Execute	2	0.00	0.00	0	0	0	0
Fetch	0	0.00	0.00	0	0	0	0
total	4	0.02	0.02	0	0	0	0

```
Misses in library cache during parse: 0
Optimizer goal: CHOOSE
Parsing user id: 25
********************************************************************************

UPDATE LEDGER L SET L.PERSON=:1,L.LEDGERID=:2,L.ACTIONDATE=:3,L.ACTION=:4,
  L.ITEM=:5,L.QUANTITY=:6,L.QUANTITYTYPE=:7,L.RATE=:8,L.AMOUNT=:9
WHERE
 ROWID=:10
```

call	count	cpu	elapsed	disk	query	current	rows
Parse	1	0.01	0.01	0	0	0	0
Execute	2	0.00	0.00	0	0	2	2
Fetch	0	0.00	0.00	0	0	0	0
total	3	0.01	0.01	0	0	2	2

```
Misses in library cache during parse: 0
Optimizer goal: CHOOSE
Parsing user id: 25
********************************************************************************

ROLLBACK
```

call	count	cpu	elapsed	disk	query	current	rows
Parse	1	0.01	0.01	0	0	0	0
Execute	1	0.00	0.00	0	0	0	0
Fetch	0	0.00	0.00	0	0	0	0
total	2	0.01	0.01	0	0	0	0

Misses in library cache during parse: 0
Optimizer goal: CHOOSE
Parsing user id: 25

```
****************************************************************************
```

OVERALL TOTALS FOR ALL NON-RECURSIVE STATEMENTS

call	count	cpu	elapsed	disk	query	current	rows
Parse	7	0.07	0.07	0	0	0	0
Execute	10	0.04	0.04	0	2	8	2
Fetch	3	0.02	0.02	0	19	3	13
total	20	0.13	0.13	0	21	11	15

Misses in library cache during parse: 0
Misses in library cache during execute: 1

OVERALL TOTALS FOR ALL RECURSIVE STATEMENTS

call	count	cpu	elapsed	disk	query	current	rows
Parse	1	0.01	0.01	0	0	0	0
Execute	1	0.00	0.00	0	0	0	0
Fetch	1	0.00	0.00	0	2	0	1
total	3	0.01	0.01	0	2	0	1

Misses in library cache during parse: 0

```
    8  user  SQL statements in session.
    1  internal SQL statements in session.
    9  SQL statements in session.
****************************************************************************
Trace file: ora00075.trc
Trace file compatibility: 7.03.02
Sort options: default

    1  session in tracefile.
    8  user  SQL statements in trace file.
    1  internal SQL statements in trace file.
    9  SQL statements in trace file.
    7  unique SQL statements in trace file.
   89  lines in trace file.
```

NOTE
You can turn on timing statistics by setting the TIMED_STATISTICS parameter of the Oracle instance to TRUE. If this parameter is FALSE, you will see only zeros in the statistics tables. Be aware, though, that turning on this parameter will definitely slow your system down, so don't do it on a production system unless you want to deal with the groans of all the affected users! Also, you should look at the new Oracle Trace option to the Enterprise Manager, part of the Performance Pack option, which gives you even more facilities for tracing Oracle applications.

Part III has shown you how to use the sophisticated tools of Oracle Developer to code and debug your applications. Applying these tools methodically, you will create a system of high-quality, reusable code on which you can build many applications. The next part of the book will help you move your application from the development environment to the real world, getting it into the hands of your customers and keeping it there by effective maintenance. It also shows you how to combine your applications with other software out there in the real world to leverage others' work in creating value with your own.

PART
IV

Advanced Tools

CHAPTER
14

Deploying and
Configuring Applications

ou have done your prototype, surveyed your users, redesigned and made secure your application, coded it, and tested and debugged it. What could possibly be left to do?

What happens after you finish doing your work on the application is really the critical part of the process—getting the application into the hands of its users and keeping it there. It is the difference between creating something for your own pleasure and education and producing a product. You've been running the application from your Builder tool; now it's time to set up your application server and run it over the Internet.

Deploying Your Application

To *deploy* a software product is to distribute the product to its users. Deployment includes everything from packaging your software to installing it on the user's workstation or network.

The first decision you must make is the deployment style: client/server versus three-tier deployment. Three-tier deployment uses an application server as a third tier between the client and the database server.

- *Client/server deployment* requires an installation package that you must install on each client that contains the Oracle Developer client runtime engines, the application executables, and any other miscellaneous files the client needs to run your application.

- *Three-tier deployment* requires installing the Oracle Developer Server engine on a central server along with the application executables and their associated files, and an HTTP listener as part of the Oracle Application Server or any other Web server.

The deployment benefits of the three-tier approach are dramatic, and they get better the more clients you have using your applications. Because there is only a single installation, you are no longer in the business of building installation systems and running around to all the clients installing the system. In addition, the client machines only need a Web browser or Java applet viewer to run the application rather than all the Oracle Developer and application-related software. That leaves room on the computer for other things, and you don't need to maintain the software on the clients, resulting in lower maintenance and administration costs for your system.

The Tangled Web

Imagine what it would be like if all you had to do to deploy an application was to tell users what name to type. That's the promise of the Internet, and it's a capability that Oracle Developer delivers with its multitiered deployment platform: Oracle Developer Server.

A *Web browser* is an application that connects to a network, usually the Internet or an intranet, and uses *Hypertext Markup Language* (HTML) pages to navigate through documents. Sun Microsystems added *Java,* a network-oriented programming language, to this recipe to produce a truly effective means of deploying software. Now, you can use an application by navigating to an HTML Web page and clicking on a button that runs a Java applet.

Oracle Developer Server is a platform that gives you a way to deploy your applications through a Web browser. This simultaneously makes it much easier and cheaper to deploy your applications and lets you create much more dynamic and capable Web applications. Oracle Developer Server lets you take advantage of all the benefits of the Web while giving you all the strengths of client/server computing. With Web-based applications, you can achieve a high degree of platform independence, running your applications on any machine that runs a browser rather than having to recompile under all the different operating systems you have in operation. You get the full array of capabilities for forms and reports, including interactive forms, HTML and Adobe Acrobat reports, drill-down reporting and graphics, dynamic reports, and report queue monitoring.

Figure 14-1 illustrates the Developer Server Forms architecture. The client workstation runs a Java-enabled Web browser. The user enters the URL for the HTML page through which the application starts (http://www.talbotfarms.com/hr, for example). When the user runs a form from the browser, the browser downloads the Oracle Developer Forms Java Client applet (a small bit of application code that handles user-interface instructions) and runs it. The applet sends a request to the Forms Server Listener, asking the server to run the application. The Listener connects to the Forms Runtime Server and passes it any runtime parameters, including the user name and password for the database server.

At this point, the Listener bows out. It sends the connection information back to the applet, which then establishes a connection directly with the Forms Runtime Server. The applet and the Runtime Server now communicate directly back and forth, with the applet handling display functions for the form and the server

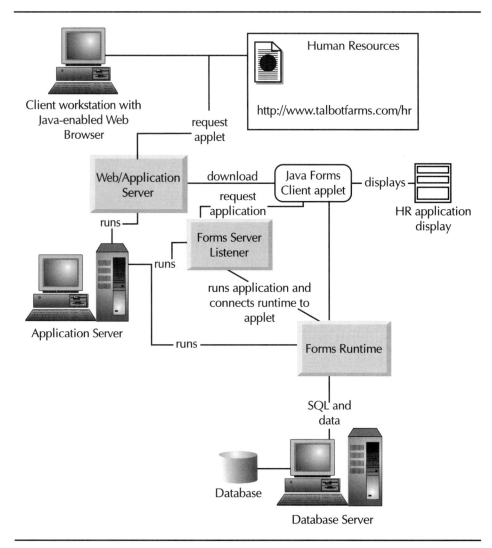

FIGURE 14-1. *Oracle Developer Server—Forms Server architecture*

handling everything else in the application. The Listener is now free to listen for other application requests. The Runtime Server runs the application, communicating with the Database Server through SQL and getting back data; then it passes the data on to the applet for display.

Reports are a bit different. There are two ways to get to the Reports Server: the Reports Web Cartridge and the Reports Web CGI (Common Gateway Interface). The Web Cartridge integrates with the Oracle Application Server; the CGI connects any Web server to the Reports Server. Figure 14-2 illustrates the architecture of the Reports Server system.

The client workstation runs a Web browser. The user enters the URL for the HTML page through which he or she can request a report (http://www.talbotfarms.com/reports, for example). The user clicks on a button or hypertext link that requests the report. If you're using the cartridge approach, the Application Server uses the Reports Cartridge to build a Reports Server command line. The Application Server submits the command synchronously (waiting for output) to the Reports Server. The Server in turn runs the report using the runtime system to produce the output file. The Web Cartridge then tells the browser where the output file is by passing back its URL. Alternatively, if you've used CGI, the CGI script in the Web server creates and submits the command line, then tells the browser where the output file is. The browser displays the report as HTML, HTML CSS (for HTML cascading style sheet), or Adobe Acrobat PDF, whichever you've generated.

Graphics has an even simpler architecture, as Figure 14-3 illustrates.

The client workstation runs a Web browser. The user enters the URL for the HTML page through which he or she can request a graphic display image (http://www.talbotfarms.com/images, for example). At this point, you can do one of two things: either display links that display specific images, or display a link that starts the Oracle Graphics Builder Web interface toolbar. The toolbar gives the browser user a way to connect to the database and to display a list of available images from which to choose. The difference between these approaches is that with the direct URL approach you must specify all the parameters in the URL, whereas the toolbar generates all the parameters for you. Also, using direct URLs gives you more control over display in custom HTML pages. Whatever method you choose, the URL passes the request for a display to the Web server, which invokes the Oracle Web Request Broker, which invokes the Graphics Server Cartridge to produce the display. The Cartridge accesses the database server through SQL and gets back data for the display. The Broker and Web server then return the image in an HTML page.

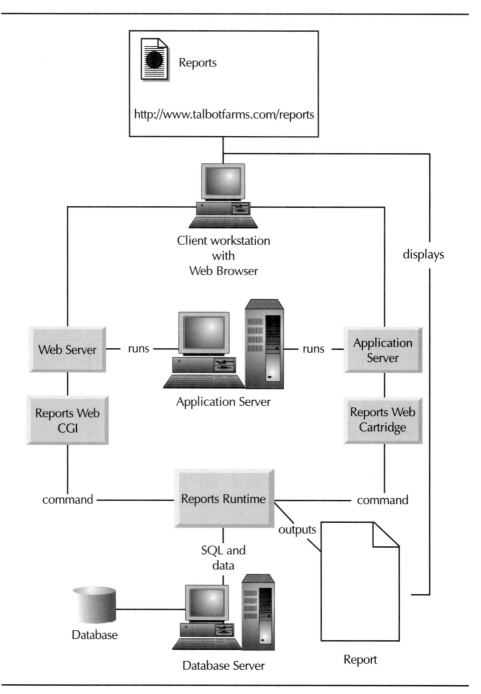

FIGURE 14-2. *Oracle Developer Server—Reports Server architecture*

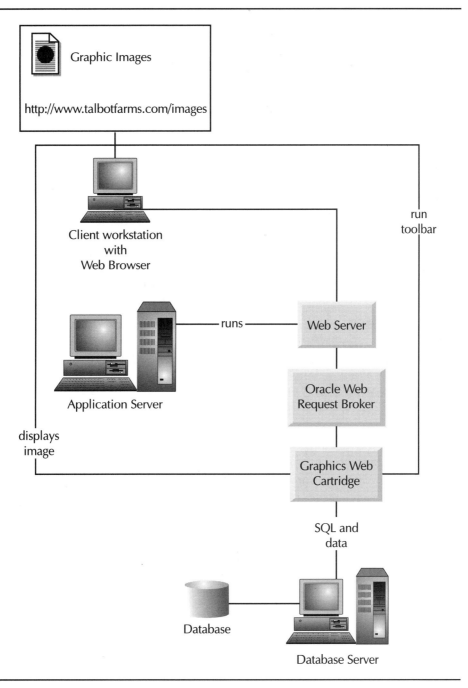

FIGURE 14-3. *Oracle Developer Server—Graphics Server architecture*

Installing Oracle Developer Server

Installing the Developer Server components requires you to accomplish several tasks:

- Install Oracle Developer Server on the middle-tier application server from the Oracle Developer Server CD-ROM, using the Oracle Installer with the server deployment option.

NOTE
Oracle sells the Oracle Developer Server separately from the Oracle Developer development system.

- Set up the Forms Listener and the Reports Server as services.

- Configure the Web server that you will be using in combination with Oracle Developer Server.

- Configure the HTML file that the server downloads to the client browser and any environment options.

- Configure the client machines with the JInitiator software.

NOTE
Many of the files involved in the various servers are in the Oracle installation directory hierarchy. If you're not already aware of the convention, the root directory of this hierarchy is known as the Oracle Home, and the root directory appears in all the following tutorials as Oracle_Home. Wherever you see Oracle_Home, substitute your local root, such as G:\Orant for a Microsoft Windows NT system.

Before you start this process, you need to have your Web server installed. You can theoretically use any Web server to run Oracle Developer applications in a multitiered environment, but you may want to use the Oracle Application Server for better integration and better performance. Each Web server has its own methods for setting up virtual directories; please consult the server's documentation for instructions.

NOTE
Oracle Application Server is a general-purpose application server that lets you deploy applications in a multitiered environment. Please refer to the Oracle Web Application Server Handbook by Dynamic Information Systems, LLC (Oracle Press, 1998). The following sections focus primarily on the Windows NT version of Oracle Developer Server, with differences for UNIX versions noted as required.

You should set up the virtual directories in Table 14-1 on the Web server, using whatever names you like in place of the ones here.

Installing the Software

The first step in deploying your application for the Internet is to install the Oracle Developer Server on your middle-tier application server. You should choose a

/codebase/	The physical directory containing Java class files, such as Oracle_Home\forms60\java. If you are using the load-balancing features of the Forms Server, you should define the same directory on each server in the server pool. This allows the cartridge to parameterize the name of the server, filling it in at runtime with the least-loaded server.
/jars/	The physical directory containing the Oracle (and other) JAR (Java Archive) files, usually the same as /codebase. Again, define this directory on all servers in a load-balancing pool.
/html/	The physical directory where the Web server will look for both static and cartridge HTML files.
/cache/	The physical directory containing the output from the Reports Runtime (Reports Server only).
/temp_image/	The physical directory, such as Oracle_Home\Forms60\Temp_Image, containing the JPEG temporary images the Forms Server generates while sending images or icons to the browser. You enter this virtual directory name in the FORMS60_MAPPING environment variable (see the later section "Configuring the Environment"), and you enter this physical directory name in the FORMS60_OUTPUT environment variable.
/web_reports/	The physical directory containing report output from the Forms Server; reports run from a form.

TABLE 14-1. *The Web Server's Virtual Directories for the Oracle Developer Server*

machine for your application server that will do very little else but run the Developer Server. You can install the system on your general Web server machine, but you may find that heavy general Web activity can affect the performance of your applications unless you have a very light application load or small number of users.

If you have many users or many applications, you may find it beneficial to distribute your processing over several application servers. Oracle Developer Server includes a load-balancing system that lets you configure your Forms application processing across multiple servers. A Forms Client request gets routed to the system most capable of running the application, based on the number of processes running on the servers.

NOTE
Consult the installation documentation for Developer Server for more information about setting up load balancing. Consult Appendix B for information on configuring your installation to work with the Oracle Application Server as cartridges. The Graphics Server only works in that context, so this section does not discuss installation of the Graphics Server.

1. Start the Oracle Developer Server installation on the machine you want to use as your application server. You will see this dialog:

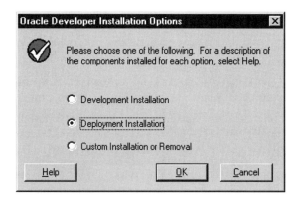

2. Choose the Deployment Installation radio button. You then see this dialog:

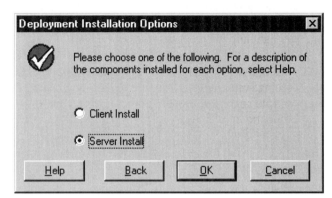

3. Choose the Server Install radio button, and then complete the installation. This installs all the various components of Oracle Developer Server onto the application server machine.

Configuring the Form Server

The Forms Listener and the Reports Server are both separate processes that you must start manually. You can configure the Reports Server as a service that starts automatically when the server starts.

1. Start the Forms Listener from the Windows NT task bar: Start|Programs|Oracle Developer 6.0|Forms Server Listener. (On UNIX, issue the command ifsrv60 -listen port=5555 &.)

2. Verify you've successfully started the Listener by looking at the Task Manager Processes display (right-click on the task bar to display Task Manager) for IFSRV60.EXE. (On UNIX, type ps -ef | grep ifsrv60.)

3. Modify TNSNAMES.ORA in the directory $Oracle_Home\Net80\Admin to contain the following TNS name specification, where <hostname> is the server name or IP address, such as 191.191.191.5:

```
repsvr.world=(ADDRESS=(PROTOCOL=tcp)(HOST=<hostname>)(PORT=1949))
```

4. Start the Reports Server as an NT service (UNIX background process with command "rwmts60 name=repsvr.world &"), using the TNS name you've added to TNSNAMES.ORA:

```
rwmts60 -install repsvr.world tcpip
```

5. Open the Services window with Start|Settings|Control Panel|Services, select the Report Server service, and click on the Start button. You may want to use the Startup button to make the service start automatically whenever the server starts, and you can specify any parameters in the Startup Parameters field.

CONFIGURING THE FORMS SERVER WITH A STATIC HTML PAGE

You run form applications with any Web server by creating a static HTML file that contains all the parameters and instructions the Forms Server needs to run your application.

1. Create the STATIC.HTM file in your /html virtual directory; give it any name you like. Copy the file from its installed version ($ORACLE_HOME\Tools\ Devdem60\Web\STATIC.HTM) and modify it with the following substitutions:

- *codebase:* The virtual directory for the Java code that you have defined when configuring your Web server.

- *archive:* Paths and files for any JAR files to download at application startup, including the Oracle-supplied ifsrv60.jar.

- *serverPort:* Forms Server Listener port (9000 is the default).

- *serverArgs:* Form parameters and user parameters.

- *serverApp:* Name of the application class that specifies fonts and icon path settings (see the cartridge documentation for details); "default" means to use the default fonts and icon path.

Here is an example of a modified template that runs the LEDGER application:

```
<HTML>
<HEAD><TITLE>Talbot Farms Ledger</TITLE></HEAD>

<BODY><CENTER>
      <BR>Welcome to Talbot Farms.
      <BR>Loading application…
<P>

<APPLET CODEBASE="/codebase/"
      CODE="oracle.forms.engine.Main"
      ARCHIVE="/jars/f60all.jar"
      HEIGHT=20 WIDTH=20>
<PARAM NAME="serverPort" VALUE="9000">
<PARAM NAME="serverArgs" VALUE="Module=Ledger userid=Talbot/george@orcl">
<PARAM NAME="serverApp" VALUE="default"
</APPLET>
```

```
</BODY>
</HTML>
```

This page parameterizes the module name as Ledger, so running the applet runs the LEDGER.FMX application. You need to have one static page for each application you want to run.

You may want to try the new Oracle look and feel, which provides a different look to applications run with Oracle Developer Server. Add the following code to the HTML:

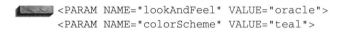
```
<PARAM NAME="lookAndFeel" VALUE="oracle">
<PARAM NAME="colorScheme" VALUE="teal">
```

You can use a number of different colorScheme values to change the colors that Oracle assigns to the window components.

CONFIGURING THE CLIENT WITH JINITIATOR   The Oracle JInitiator is an Oracle Corporation Java plug-in that runs Java applets or JavaBeans in an HTML page. It sets up a special Java Virtual Machine optimized for use with Oracle Developer applications. You can either let users download it from their client machines at runtime, or you can preinstall it on client machines:

1. Find the file jinit.exe in your Oracle Developer installation (Oracle_Home), copy it to the client machines, and run the program. This is an InstallShield executable that installs the plug-in for you.

USING APPLICATION CLASSES FOR ICONS AND FONTS ON THE INTERNET   Working with GIF images and fonts gives you a challenge when deploying your forms on the Internet. You can use the standard Form Builder settings if you want to define specific fonts and icons, but if you have several variations on a theme, you may want to use application classes. The most common case for this is when you want specific fonts to appear on different GUI platforms such as Windows, Motif, and the Macintosh.

An application class is a collection of font mappings and an icon path with specific fonts and icons. You can switch between several such configurations depending on the HTML serverApp parameter in your cartridge or static HTML base file (see the section "Configuring the Forms Server with a Static HTML Page" for details on this parameter). At runtime, the Forms Server first uses any settings in the named application class; if you have not named an application class in the serverApp parameter, the Forms Server uses the default fonts and icons. The default fonts are built into the Forms environment; the default icons come from the same directory as the base HTML page.

To build application classes, you need to edit the text of the file REGISTRY.DAT, which you can find in

```
Oracle_Home\forms60\java\oracle\forms\uiClient\v1_4\util
```

1. For each font mapping you want to add, put a line in REGISTRY.DAT containing the application class name, a font parameter name, and the font parameter value, such as the following Windows_Form application class:

```
Windows_Form.appFontNames=Courier,Terminal,Arial
Windows_Form.javaFontNames=MonoSpaced,Dialog,Helvetica
```

2. To specify the default Java font, which the form displays when no font matches the application font, add these lines for the Std_Form application class:

```
Windows_Form.DefaultFontname=Helvetica
Windows_Form.DefaultSize=12
Windows_Form.DefaultStyle=BOLD
```

3. To specify an icon directory, add a line like this for the Windows_Form application class:

```
Windows_Form.iconpath=/temp_image
```

In this case, the value is a virtual directory, /temp_image/, that you've defined in your Web server; see Table 14-1. You can also specify a URL or a directory relative to the HTML page; the virtual directory is your best bet because you can change it in the Web server if you move it without altering the REGISTRY.DAT file.

CONFIGURING THE REPORTS SERVER CGI   Configuring the Reports Server CGI is simple:

1. Find the file rwcgi60.exe in Oracle_Home\bin and copy it into your Web server CGI script directory, such as Oracle_Home/ows/40/bin. (On UNIX, copy the file rwcgim60.)

Setting Up the Forms and Reports Servers as NT Services

Now you've installed and configured the servers, but you need to install them as NT services (or UNIX background processes). To do this, it's best to log on to NT with administrator privileges; consult your NT system administrator for assistance.

1. First, create a TNS entry for the Reports Server. Edit the TNSNAMES.ORA file in the Oracle_Home\Network\Admin directory for Oracle7 SQL*Net or

the Oracle_Home\Net8\Admin directory for Oracle8 Net8. Add this entry at the bottom of the file:

```
repserver.world=(ADDRESS=(PROTOCOL=tcp)(HOST=<server>)(PORT=1949))
```

Here, <server> is the name or TCP/IP address of the server that will run the Reports Server, such as WAVERLY or 127.100.100.100. You can use any TNS name as long as you add the proper domain, such as reports.world or news_of_the.world.

2. Create an NT service for the Forms Server. You should be logged on to Windows NT with administrator privileges. Start a DOS shell from the task bar with Start|Programs|MSDOS Prompt. Execute the following command:

```
ifsrv60 -install forms60
```

3. Create an NT service for the Reports Server in the same DOS shell with the following command:

```
rwmts60 -install repserver.world tcpip
```

The service name, repserver.world, is the TNS name you specified in the TNSNAMES.ORA file.

4. Run the Services applet: choose Start|Settings|Control Panel, and then double-click on the Services icon. Find the Forms Server60 entry and click Startup. On the resulting dialog, find the Log On As section and choose This Account. Type in the current user name and password. This runs the service under this account. You may want to choose the System account— a good choice—or some other account; consult your NT administrator. Finally, click on Automatic to have NT start the Forms Server automatically when it boots.

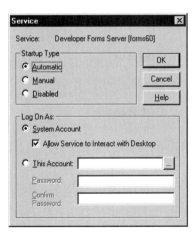

TIP
It's generally a good idea to run this kind of service under the System account along with all the other standard services, as it simplifies your security and configuration issues. However, there may be security or other reasons why this can't be done for your particular NT server.

5. Repeat the last step for the Reports Server60 entry in the Services dialog.

NOTE
You may want to read over the help file on creating NT services to see the extensive issues involved in setting up your Reports Server. There are more than a few items to consider that are beyond the scope of the basic installation covered here.

Configuring the Environment

Once you've set up your servers, you now must configure the various environment options for them. On Windows NT, that means editing the system registry.

I. On the task bar, choose Start|Run. Type in the following command and click OK:

```
regedit
```

2. Navigate down the registry tree to HKEY_LOCAL_MACHINE|SOFTWARE|ORACLE. Click on the ORACLE key folder to display all the Oracle keys.

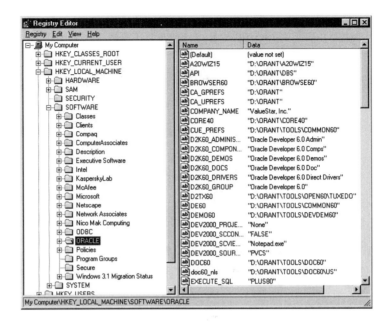

Now create the keys listed in Table 14-2. For each key in the table, perform the following steps:

3. Right-click on the key display panel and choose New|String Value or New|DWORD Value, as Table 14-1 indicates. The Editor creates a new key and positions you to rename the key.

4. Rename the key to the key name in Table 14-2.

5. Double-click the key to display the Edit String dialog box, and enter the appropriate value as Table 14-2 explains; then click OK.

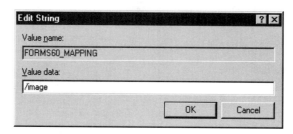

6. Exit from the Registry Editor with File|Exit.

Deploying Internet Applications

To complete the deployment of your applications for use with Web browsers, you must accomplish three more tasks:

- Install the application code for forms, reports, and displays on the server.
- Install the HTML access pages on the server.
- Give users the URLs for the access pages.

When you compile your applications, the output consists of executable files (FMX, RDF, and OGD files). You have to compile these executables using the builder or compiler that runs on the same operating system that your Developer Server runs on. For example, if you're going to run Developer Server on Windows NT, you must compile your applications using the builders or compilers for Windows NT, not for Windows 98 or Sun Solaris.

To install the code for forms (FMX executables), put them in any directory you wish and refer to them in the dynamic or static HTML page with complete path and file name. To install the code for reports (RDF executables), place them in any directory on the server, but put that directory into the server registry variable REPORTS60_PATH.

NOTE
The Graphics executables must be in a known place to allow the Graphics Server to provide its toolbar with a drop-down list of graphics displays to run.

Key Name	Key Type	Value
FORMS60_MAPPING	String Value	If you use images or icons in your applications, you must create a temporary directory and a virtual directory on the Web server that the Forms Server uses for storing JPEG images temporarily while sending them to the client browser. Enter the virtual directory name, such as "/image," here (no trailing slash here).
FORMS60_OUTPUT	String Value	A physical directory corresponding to the FORMS60_MAPPING virtual directory, such as G:\Orant\Forms60\temp_image.
FORMS60_PATH	String Value	A list of physical directories on the server separated by semicolons that the Forms Server looks in for FMX form executables. The Oracle Installer should create this automatically during installation; so you just need to enter your specific directories here.
FORMS60_REPFORMAT	String Value	Use the string "HTML," which tells the Forms Server to generate reports as HTML pages, or "PDF," which tells the server to generate Adobe Acrobat reports.
FORMS60_TIMEOUT	DWORD Value	Enter the number of minutes for the Forms Server to wait for input before timing out. It should be an integer number between 3 and 1440; try 15 minutes initially.
REPORTS60_WEBLOC	String Value	The virtual directory where the Web server looks for report output files, such as /web_reports/.
REPORTS60_WEBLOC_TRANSLATED	String Value	The physical directory to which the Reports Server transfers the Reports Runtime output if the Reports Server and Web server do not share a file system, such as G:\ORANT\web_reports.
REPORTS60_PATH	String Value	The list of physical directories in which the Reports Server looks for report definition (RDF) files.

TABLE 14-2.   *Registry Keys for Oracle Developer Server*

Place your dynamic or static HTML base pages in a standard virtual directory such as /html, and then give the appropriate URL to your users. So, for example, Talbot Farms has a WorkerSkill form static base page called WorkerSkill.html. Talbot users run the form by typing in this URL:

```
http://www.talbotfarms.com/html/WorkerSkill.html
```

The World of Client/Server Computing

The advantages of deploying your application on a multitier server are overwhelming. However, if for some reason your environment demands it, you can also deploy your applications as client/server applications, installing the Oracle Developer Deployment software on each client that you want to be able to run your applications. This section takes you through the steps of creating a client/server deployment package.

The user must obtain specific information from the database or system administrator, such as the host connect string with the network file server and database server names. Your documentation and deployment materials must tell users what information they need. You should also be careful about telling users what additional software (including the Oracle Developer runtimes and Oracle SQL*Net software), in what specific versions, your application requires in order to run.

Packaging Your Application

Two dimensions determine the scope of your effort in creating the installation system for your application: the degree of personal involvement in the installation process and the complexity of the installation process.

Usually, personal involvement directly relates to the nature of the application. Applications you yourself always install are typically personal or departmental tools or single-project applications. Corporate applications tend to require some personal involvement and some ability to turn it over to others. Applications the end user must install, with or without system engineering support (but certainly without your support), are usually products you sell to the end user.

The complexity of the installation process depends on several things. First, you may need to break the installation into *several parts*: client workstation versus server, several cooperating workstations, several distributed servers, a Web server, and so on. Second, you may need to install portions of the package *conditionally*. For example, the user can choose to install only part of the package, or the installation process detects a specific configuration to determine which parts of the package to install, or it detects whether it is updating or newly installing. Third, you may need to perform some kind of *processing* on the package: decompression;

checking for files already present and those that are newer; compiling; generating options files; or any number of creative ways to add complexity to the user's life.

If you have a product with no personal involvement in installation and with a relatively high degree of complexity, you should invest in a professional installation software package. These packages give you all the tools you need to make even the most complex installation look easy and professional to end users and to their managers, the ones who buy the product.

Otherwise, just be sure you pay attention to the details so you understand everything that needs doing and you have everything you need in one place. One general rule for packaging is the oldest rule in the world: keep it simple. Install only the files the user needs. Do not clutter up the disk with compressed versions, 23 README files for different parts of the product, or 600 special icon bitmaps that the user can install to customize the application. Leave these on disk for special access.

Also, you must decide whether to ship source with your object files. This decision will usually depend on the nature of the contract between you and the user. If you need to protect users from their own mistakes, do not ship source. If you need to protect your proprietary rights to the system, do not ship source code. If the user has no need or desire for source, do not ship source.

Here is a list of the Oracle Developer application components from the perspective of packaging. Table 14-3 tells you what components must ship as part of a package and what components are optional. You should carefully specify the purpose and nature of all the files in a README file or document that you ship with the package.

There are also many miscellaneous types of files that you might package with the system, such as icons, bitmaps, sound files, video files, and so on.

NOTE
Your executable files must be compatible with the operating system on which they run. That means specifically that you must compile your source on that operating system. For example, you cannot compile a form on a UNIX system, then deploy the resulting executable file to a Windows 98 client.

You also need to consider what files to ship for an upgrade. You can ship a complete system, including all files, or you can ship just the changed files. If you take the latter approach, you will need to expand system testing to cover different configuration possibilities, and you must manually configure the Project Builder component of Oracle Developer Server to deliver only the specific files you

Product	File	Source or Executable	Optional or Required	Comments
Application system	PRF	Source	Optional	Ship a model preferences file with the application or build one that contains the runtime options the system needs to run, if these differ from the defaults that Oracle builds using ORAINST.
	EXE	Executable	Required	The Oracle runtime executables, suitably licensed, and any executable tools you add; the user installs these from the Oracle-supplied installation CD using ORAINST.
	DLL	Executable	Required	The Oracle runtime dynamic link libraries, suitably licensed and installed through ORAINST, and any libraries your application system needs (user exits, foreign functions, and such).
Forms	FMB	Source	Optional	The source for the forms; ship only if you want the customer to be able to modify the application.
	FMX	Executable	Required	Executable code without source.
Menus	MMB	Source	Optional	The source for the menus; ship only if you want the customer to be able to modify the application menus.
	MMX	Executable	Required	Executable menu code without source.
PL/SQL	PLL	Source	Optional	The source for the PL/SQL libraries; ship only if you want the customer to be able to modify the program units.
	PLX	Executable	Required	Executable program units in the library.
Reports	RDF	Source	Optional	The source for the reports; ship only if you want the customer to be able to modify the reports.
	REP	Executable	Required	Executable reports.
Graphics	OGD	Source	Optional	The source for graphics displays; ship only if you want the customer to be able to modify the displays.
	OGR	Executable	Required	Executable displays.

TABLE 14-3. *File Components of Oracle Developer*

designate. You must ensure that the subset of files works for all the different, interesting configurations of your system.

NOTE
As a practical and legal matter, you must use the Oracle Installer to install the client/server deployment option. See Appendix B for complete details on installing the deployment software.

You can generate FMX files using the Form Compiler by clicking on its icon and entering the appropriate information. However, there's an easier way. With Project Builder, you can easily compile all of your files with one click of the mouse. You need to set up the project as the section on "Developer Project Management" in Chapter 3 discussed. First, find the node in the Project Navigator for the project you want to compile. Select that node, and then choose the Build All menu item from the pop-up menu for the node (right mouse button), or choose the Tools|Build All menu item from the main menu.

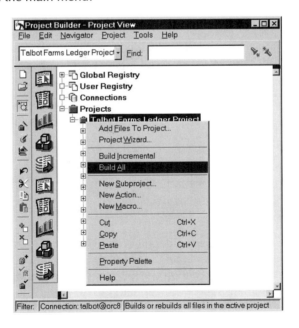

You can generate text-only versions of FMB and MMB files for documentation or compression. Oracle Developer supports incremental compilation to reduce the time that generation requires. If you make a small change to some PL/SQL and then regenerate the form, Oracle Developer does not recompile all the PL/SQL in the form; it recompiles just the changed trigger or program unit. To do this, Oracle

Developer stores additional information in the FMB file, such as all of the PL/SQL
source text, intermediate representation code, and the compiled code. It creates
intermediate representations and compiled code only when you generate the form
or compile a trigger or program unit. Converting to an FMT file and then back to
an FMB file shrinks the FMB file, since the FMT file does not store intermediate or
compiled code. The FMX file you generate only contains the compiled code, and
this is the file you should deploy.

You can generate FMT and MMT form and menu source text files using the
File|Administration|Convert menu item in the Form Builder, which displays the
Convert dialog box:

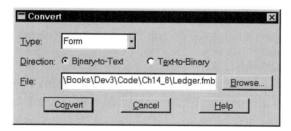

To generate an FMT form source file, set Type to Form, browse for the form file
(FMB), and set the Direction field to Binary-to-Text. To generate an MMT menu
source file, set Type to Menu, browse for the menu file (MMB), and set the Direction
field to Binary-to-Text. When you click Convert, the Builder produces a source text
file for the form or menu.

NOTE
*You can generate form and menu text-only files
using the Form Compiler; check the "Write script
file?" check box, which tells the generator to
generate a text script rather than object code.*

You can generate REP files (report definitions in object-only format) in two ways
in the Report Builder. You can generate the file with File|Administration|Generate,
or you can convert the database or RDF version of the report definition to a REP
version through File|Administration|Convert and the Convert dialog box. Set Source
Type to RDF and browse for the report definition (RDF) file in the Source field; set
Destination Type to REP and fill in the filename for the Destination field. You can
use the Convert dialog box to create REX files (report definitions in source-only
text format) as well, by selecting the Destination Type of REX instead of REP.

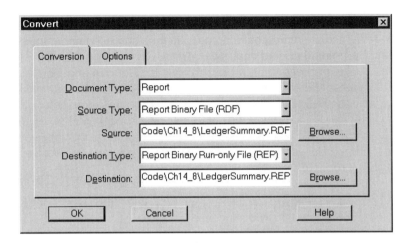

You can generate an OGR file (object-code-only graphics display) using the File|Administration|Generate menu item.

Client/Server Deployment

You can deploy your package to clients in a number of different ways. Not so long ago, you only had to choose between different types of floppy disks or tapes, depending on the target operating system or systems.

Recently, the CD-ROM has been gaining favor, especially with large, commercial products such as Oracle or Oracle Developer. With the rapid decline in prices and the technological improvements in CD-ROM mastering tools, you should seriously consider this option.

Even more recently, the Internet and other online services and commercial bulletin boards have become a source for software packages. You connect to the appropriate server and FTP or otherwise download the package onto your workstation and then install it. This is particularly popular for distributing low-cost software, free trial software, and upgrades. You could also use this mechanism effectively to distribute in-house applications if your corporate sites all connect to the Internet or to a central local or wide area network.

The newer Web technologies such as Java even let you download the application transparently and run it, as the prior section, "The Tangled Web," detailed.

Most commercial installation products handle the creation of packages on all these different media. On floppies, for example, the system provides compression and packing of the files onto disks and the setup and processing of the compressed files as part of the installation process on the workstation. You can cheaply and easily package your files using a standard disk compression utility such as the ubiquitous PKZIP from PKWARE, Inc. Using larger-capacity media such as tapes, you can just dump your entire file hierarchy to tape and back again to a new workstation. The possibilities are endless.

Oracle Developer makes this easy with Project Builder. You must have your project set up with all the deliverable files identified. Project Builder knows to deliver target files such as FMX files and not to deliver source files such as FMB files. If you want to tell it to deliver (or not to deliver) a specific file, select the file and display its Property Palette using the pop-up menu or the Tools|Property Palette menu item. Find the Deliver file property in the Property Palette and set the value to Yes or No, as appropriate.

1. When you are ready to deliver your project, select the project node and choose the menu item Tools|Delivery Wizard.

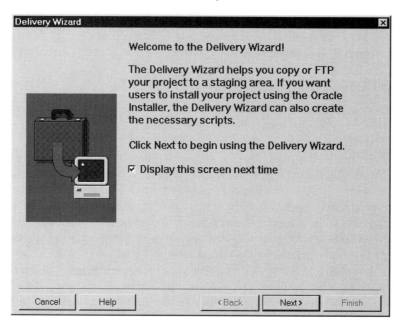

This Wizard will copy or FTP the deliverables in the project to a staging area. You can also tell the Wizard to create scripts so that you can combine your project with the runtime installation through the Oracle Installer. This makes it very easy for you to deploy both the Oracle Developer runtime and the application code together.

You can use the Delivery Wizard in two ways: to deliver a complete system or to deliver a system update. The next screen lets you deliver all the deliverables in the project or just those changed since the last delivery.

2. Click Next. If you're delivering a complete system, choose Deliver all files; otherwise, choose "Deliver files that have changed since the last delivery."

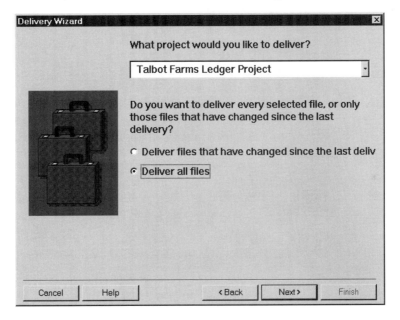

3. Click Next. Choose the type of delivery you want to build, and then enter the path or FTP address of the staging area:

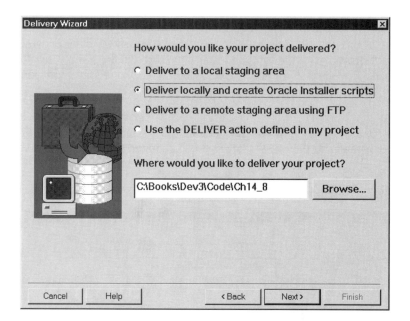

- *Local:* Deliver the project to a local staging area on your hard disk or on the network.

- *Local installer:* Deliver the project locally, but also create Oracle Installer scripts as part of the package. If you make this choice, the Wizard displays a screen asking for script details.

- *FTP:* Deliver the project remotely using FTP, a TCP/IP tool for transferring files to a remote location specified by ftp:// address.

- *Deliver:* Deliver the project using a custom Deliver action you define (see the Project Builder documentation for details on this advanced feature).

4. Click Next. The files screen lets you choose which files of the selected project to deliver. Generally, you will want to deliver all the files, so do nothing and click Next.

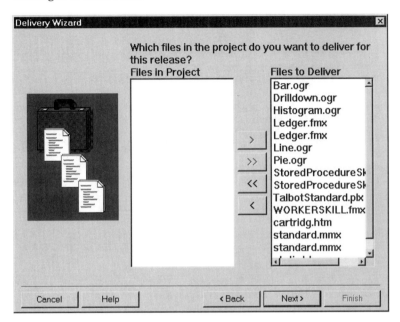

Now the Wizard moves into producing the Oracle Installer scripts.
The first screen describes the location where you want to install the files.
Generally, you should install all your project files into a single directory.
Not doing so means quite a lot of work downstream keeping track of where to put things.

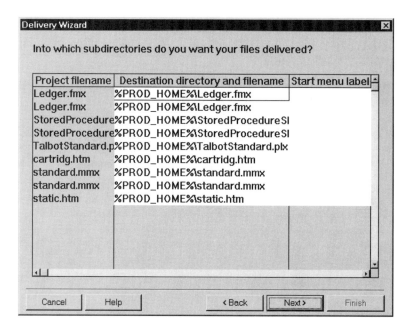

5. If you want an application to appear in the Start menu within a Program Group, specify the labels; then click Next.

6. Click Finish to deliver your project.

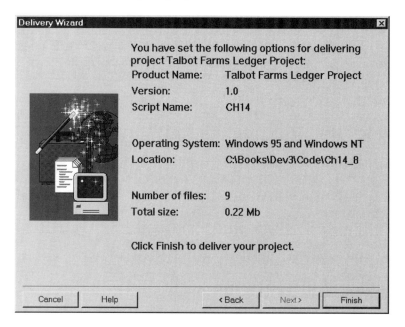

You now have your staging area directory containing all the files needed to deploy your project. The next logical step is to compress the files into a ZIP file or some other format for distribution on a floppy or network, or to burn the files onto a CD-ROM. The next topic is how to manage things going forward from deployment.

Configuration Management

When you enter the maintenance life cycle of an application, it is vital to have the application under control of a configuration management system. If you have somehow managed to avoid configuration management or version control to this point, now is the time to bite the bullet. However, you should seriously consider version control at every step in your development process, including putting the requirements and design documents under version control.

Oracle Developer integrates with multiple version control and configuration management tools such as Intersolv PVCS, Rational Clear Case, or Starteam from Starbase. You can use these tools from every single builder component of Oracle Developer Server, but you should use the Project Builder interface to manage the configuration of your files. You can use the File|Administration menu with its Check-In, Check-Out, and Source Control Options items or the Check In and Check Out options on the pop-up menu for the items.

This interface works by generating ASCII text for storing in the version control archive. You create the archive through the File|Administration|Source Control Options menu item and the Source Control Options dialog box, in which you specify the location and name of the archive directory.

The File|Administration|Check-In menu item displays the Check-In dialog box, which lets you check a module into the archive. The File|Administration|Check-Out menu item displays the Check-Out dialog box, which lets you check a module out of the archive. If you want to modify the module, you must check the Lock This File check box; otherwise, you get a read-only copy of the module file.

The configuration management life cycle within Oracle Developer proceeds as follows:

1. Create the archive directory.

2. Check in initial versions of the modules.

3. Check out modules that you want to modify.

4. Check modified modules back into the archive with new version numbers.

Using the windows of the configuration management software itself, you can manage the more sophisticated features of the configuration management system, such as declaring a release baseline across several modules. You can also generate difference reports (reports showing the difference between two files) using the

File|Administration|Source Control Options menu item and Source Control Options dialog box.

You can always use other configuration management systems, such as Source Integrity on Windows or rcs and sccs on UNIX, by exporting the text files into those systems, though you cannot check files in and out directly through Oracle Developer. You may be able to add actions for basic features to types in the Project Builder if the system provides a command line interface similar to that of PVCS. This slight disadvantage will not get in your way too much.

Version numbers can be arbitrarily complex in most configuration management systems. For most application software, a simple two-part version number is sufficient: <Release>.<Version>. The <Release> number changes with major upgrades to the product, and the <Version> number changes with every upgrade. For example, 1.0 might be the initial release of the product, 1.5 might be the fifth minor upgrade, and 2.3 might be the third minor release after the Release 2 major release. "Might be" describes all of these because you cannot count on this kind of simple logic with version numbers. There is Management involvement here. You will find all kinds of reasons to skip minor releases, to have parallel releases under two major release numbers, and a myriad of other confusing but perfectly reasonable (at least to the Marketing people) situations. All this will probably provide jobs for hundreds of archaeologists and historians in the year 3000 as they try to figure out our counting system for our primitive software organisms!

You've now learned about all the basic components of developing and deploying systems using Oracle Developer. The final chapter in this part goes into some advanced tools for integrating your applications with tools from outside the Oracle Developer product.

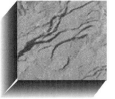

CHAPTER
15

Oracle Developer and
Open Systems

n *open system* is one that permits the use of tools from different vendors. UNIX became the archetypal open system: there are many different UNIX operating systems that you can use interchangeably (well, reasonably so). Tool integration in the late 1980s started in the software tools market with the repository technology and tool integration architectures such as the Atherton Backplane that let programmers integrate multiple software tools into a coherent work process. Then came Dynamic Data Exchange (DDE) and Publish and Subscribe for PCs and Macintoshes, which let system designers communicate with other tools at runtime.

With the development of the Object Linking and Embedding (OLE) interface and its successors ActiveX and the Component Object Model (COM), on the one hand, and the Common Object Request Broker Architecture (CORBA) and networked Java ("run anywhere") on the other, the open systems movement is beginning to create software architectures that are open all the way down to the object level. Using these architectures, you can create objects and share their use among many applications and servers.

This chapter outlines some of the ways in which Oracle Developer gives you an open systems environment. You have now reached the stage of having your application out in the real world as a system. How can you develop applications that use all the Oracle Developer tools working together? What does it take to open that system to systems beyond Oracle Developer? How can you create something that acts as part of a system community rather than just an island? How can you make your application global in scope rather than being tied to a single locale or language?

Integrating Oracle Products

The Oracle Developer tools can use one another as a first step toward open systems. You have seen such use in Chapter 4, which presented a couple of basic scenarios for mixing forms, reports, and graphics displays. There are other possible combinations, such as displaying a report within a graphics display or running a form from a report, and other possible ways to build the integration. You could click on a pie chart slice and generate a report on the subject (although the technical details of drill-down activity like this are beyond the scope of this book).

This part of the chapter gives you an overview of the basics of how to integrate the Oracle Developer products. You can refer to the individual manuals for each product for the details of the PL/SQL packages and how to use these packages in programming your applications. Oracle Developer also integrates with the Oracle Express data mining tools and with the Oracle Designer system, which permits you to integrate your systems requirements and design with Oracle Developer implementation.

The Forms component of Oracle Developer has the broadest array of tools for integrating other Oracle Developer products. The first question to ask is whether you are running a client/server system or a three-tier system with Oracle Developer Server. A client/server system runs the Reports Runtime or Graphics Runtime as a local program that accesses the database server. You install the runtime executables on every client that runs the reports and charts. A three-tier system uses the Reports Server or Graphics Server running on the middle-tier server to run the report or graphics display. The architecture under which your application runs thus has implications for your integration of other Oracle Developer tools.

If you want the report or graphic display to run transparently whether your architecture is client/server or three-tier, you should use the Run_Product built-in procedure to run the program. If you are running as a client/server program only, you should use either Run_Product or Run_Report_Object, which is a built-in subprogram that works with Form Builder report objects to integrate reports with forms. If you are running three-tier, you can use these two subprograms, but you can also use Web.Show_Document—the built-in that lets you submit a Uniform Resource Locator (URL) to the middle-tier application server and get back a page to display in your Web browser. The following sections show you how to use these three built-in subprograms to integrate components into your form applications.

You can also run graphics from forms using chart items. The section "Creating a Graphics Display in a Form" in Chapter 4 gives a detailed example of using a chart item to create a graphics display.

Integrating Products with Run_Product

The Run_Product built-in procedure is the mechanism in Oracle Developer Forms that lets you run other Oracle products using a two-tier approach.

NOTE
In Graphics, the Run_Product procedure is part of the TOOLINT package, so you must add the package name to the procedure name: TOOLINT.Run_Product.

This is the syntax of the Run_Product built-in procedure:

```
Run_Product(<product>, <module>, <communication mode>,
          <execution mode>, <location>, <list>, <display>);
```

Table 15-1 shows the possible values and meanings of these seven parameters.

Parameter	Possible Values	Description
<product>	FORMS, REPORTS, GRAPHICS, BOOK	The Oracle Developer component to run: Forms, Reports, Graphics, or Book.
<module>	String	The name of the module or document to open when you run the product.
<communication mode>	SYNCHRONOUS, ASYNCHRONOUS	A synchronous call returns control to Forms after you exit the product you call; an asynchronous call returns control immediately, running the product you call in parallel.
<execution mode>	BATCH, RUNTIME	A batch product call runs a report or display in the background with no user interaction; a runtime product call runs the product in the foreground, allowing interaction; only Reports and Graphics can run in batch mode.
<location>	FILESYSTEM, DATABASE	This parameter tells the procedure where the module resides, in the file system or in the database.
<list>	Param_List object	The parameter list contains a set of parameters to pass to the product; you pass its name or its object ID.
<display>	String	This is the name of the block chart item that will contain the display you are requesting from Graphics.

TABLE 15-1. *Run_Product Parameters*

NOTE
You must use a SYNCHRONOUS communication mode when you pass a record group from the form to the product you are calling or when you expect to view HTML, HTML CSS, or PDF output in a client browser. You must use RUNTIME execution mode when calling a form or a book document. You use the display parameter only when the product is the Graphics component of Oracle Developer.

For example, you might want to run a report when the user clicks on a button. You would place the following code in the button's When-Button-Pressed trigger:

```
Run_Product(Reports, 'LedgerSummary', RUNTIME, FILESYSTEM,
            NULL, NULL);
```

TIP
You should not qualify the module name with the path name. Use the REPORTS60_PATH registry variable on the middle-tier server to identify the directories that contain the reports you will run. This makes it easy to relocate the report modules to other directories, because you don't have to touch the module, just the registry key.

To run a report in a three-tier architecture with Run_Product, you must set the registry variables REPORTS60_PATH (the list of directories that contain reports), FORMS60_OUTPUT (the directory that will hold the report output), FORMS60_MAPPING (the virtual directory for the FORMS60_OUTPUT directory, such as /report_output/), and FORMS60_REPFORMAT ("PDF" or "HTML" depending on whether you want Adobe Acrobat output or HTML output).

Chapter 10, in the section "Run_Product," also contains some examples and an extended explanation of how to use the parameter list capabilities of the Run_Product subprogram.

Integrating Reports with Run_Report_Object

The Run_Report_Object built-in subprogram uses the setup information in a form report object you create in the Form Builder. You first create the report object and set up its properties, and then you use it in code in a menu item or a form trigger. The following tutorial sets up the LedgerSummary report in a report object, then codes a When-Button-Pressed trigger to run the report.

I. In the Form Builder Object Navigator, select the Reports node and click on the Add tool.

The Form Builder displays a dialog box that either lets you build a new report using the Report Builder or lets you enter a report name.

2. Enter the name "LedgerSummary.RDF," or browse to the LedgerSummary.RDF file using the Browse button; then click OK.

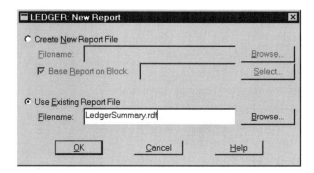

3. Change the name of the new object by clicking on it and typing "LedgerSummaryReport"; then press ENTER.

4. Double-click on the object to display the Property Palette.

5. Set the Execution Mode property to Runtime, the Communication Mode property to Synchronous, Report Destination Type to File, Report Destination Name to LedgerSummary.html, Report Destination Format to HTML, and Report Server to repsvr.world (the TNS name of the Reports Server).

TIP
You can supply any report parameters in the Other Report Parameters property as a command line string, such as "PERSON_NAME='Adah Talbot'" to set the Person_Name parameter.

6. Create a button item on a canvas and add a When-Button-Pressed trigger.

You use the report object together with Run_Report_Object, Report_Object_Status, and Copy_Report_Object_Output to set up and process a report run on a server or locally.

```
DECLARE
   vReportID REPORT_OBJECT;
   vReportName VARCHAR2(100);
   vReportStatus VARCHAR2(20);
BEGIN
   vReportID := Find_Report_Object('LedgerSummaryReport');
   vReportName := Run_Report_Object(vReportID);
   vReportStatus := Report_Object_Status(vReportName);
   IF vReportStatus = 'FINISHED' THEN
     Message('Report ready.');
     Copy_Report_Object_Output(vReportName,
            'C:\TempReports\Ledger.htm');
   ELSIF vReportStatus IN ('RUNNING', 'OPENING_REPORT', 'ENQUEUED')
     THEN Message('Report running, please check for output later.');
   ELSE
     Message('Error when running report: '||vReportStatus||'.');
   END IF;
END;
```

The Report_Object_Status function can return any of these values: finished, running, canceled, opening_report, enqueued, invalid_job, terminated_with_error, or crashed. These functions let you deal with reports that run on the Reports Server rather than in your current process. You can wait for the report output, you can report status and move on (as in the example code), or you can check on status at time intervals using the report status to tell the user when the report is available for use.

Integrating Reports and Graphics with Web.Show_Document

Using Web.Show_Document lets your form send a URL to an application server. The URL can be the address of any Web page or file to display, but it can also be a cartridge or CGI command string that tells the server to execute the Reports or Graphics Runtime.

For example, if the Ledger form has a button that runs the LedgerSummary report and displays it in a Web browser, the When-Button-Pressed trigger for the button contains this code:

```
Web.Show_Document(
    'http://www.talbotsfarm.com/reports/Reports60Cartridge?
    server=repsvr&report=LedgerSummary.rdf&userid=talbot@orcl&
    DESTYPE=CACHE&DESFORMAT=HTML', '_self');
```

The quoted string needs to be a single line of text in your program unit; the display here wraps it due to length restrictions. The CGI version of this command is very similar:

```
Web.Show_Document('http://www.talbotsfarm.com/cgi-bin/rwcgi60.exe?
    server=repsvr&report=LedgerSummary.rdf&userid=talbot@orcl&
    DESTYPE=CACHE&DESFORMAT=HTML''_self');
```

The CGI version replaces the report cartridge virtual directory with the CGI virtual directory and uses rwgi60.exe rather than the cartridge name (Reports60Cartridge). The second argument to the Web.Show_Document procedure tells the Forms Runtime where to display the report output:

- *_SELF:* Loads the report in the same frame or window as the form.

- *_PARENT:* Loads the report in the parent window or frame of the form. If the form is the top level, _PARENT is the same as _SELF.

- *_TOP:* Loads the report in the window containing the form and replaces the form display.

- *_BLANK:* Opens a new, nameless, top-level window and loads the report there.

Displaying a graphic with Web.Show_Document is very similar:

```
Web.Show_Document(
    'http://www.talbotsfarm.com/graphics/Graphics60Cartridge?
    &module=AmountTrend.ogd&userid=talbot@orcl', '_self');
```

For a graphics display, you supply the MODULE and the name of the Oracle Graphics cartridge you've defined on your application server.

Using Other Database Managers with ODBC

The Open Data Base Connectivity (ODBC) standard is a de facto standard application programming interface (API) for database managers. This API lets you write applications that you can move from one DBMS to another without rewriting or even recompiling your code. To use Oracle Developer with a DBMS other than Oracle, you need to know how it can access that DBMS through ODBC.

The Oracle Open Client Adapter (OCA) is an interface to ODBC that lets you make ODBC calls instead of Oracle calls in Oracle Developer. You access this software layer by using a special database logon string:

 `user_name/password@odbc:data_source`

The user_name and password are the standard name and password for your database, and the data_source is the ODBC name for your database. By prefixing "odbc:" to the data_source, you tell Oracle Developer to use the OCA. You can also use an asterisk as the data_source, in which case ODBC prompts you with a list of the registered data sources on your machine.

To set up a data source, you use the ODBC Administrator or other database-vendor-supplied program. Consult your database manager documentation or the ODBC driver documentation for details on setup.

NOTE
The OCA supports any ODBC-compliant data source. Oracle has documentation for several specific ODBC drivers and databases, but the OCA supports any compliant driver.

Oracle supplies scripts that create data dictionary views similar to those in the Oracle RDBMS. Running these scripts lets you use the various tools in Oracle Developer that access the data dictionary. You can create your own scripts for systems other than those for which Oracle supplies scripts; just copy one of the scripts and modify it with the system-specific differences you find.

There are several Oracle Developer features that will not work if you use an ODBC driver with the OCA to connect to the target database:

■ You cannot store modules in the database.

■ You can't access information about triggers for columns in the Database Objects group of the Object Navigator.

■ You can see stored procedures in the Database Objects group only for data sources that support such things, and you can't edit them.

■ You can't drag and drop procedures to or from the Database Objects group.

■ Oracle Developer can't use constraint information to generate master-detail relationships or primary key enforcement.

■ If optimizer hints appear in your SQL statements, the OCA ignores them.

Oracle Developer makes available two tools to help you make the best use of differences between specific data sources. The OCA PL/SQL library contains several subprograms that let you determine what the target database is and what functions it supports. The EXEC_SQL library lets you issue SQL statements that use syntax specific to the server you are accessing. In general, your PL/SQL code must conform to the standard Oracle PL/SQL and to the syntax of the specific database server you are accessing. You can set OCA_DEBUG_SQL=TRUE and OCA_DEBUG_ERROR=TRUE in the ORACLE.INI file or in the System Registry to debug the SQL statements you are sending to the data source.

Oracle Developer automatically adjusts its object properties to the situation, modifying them as needed to produce consistent results. There are certain properties you must take care of yourself:

■ You have to set the item's Primary Key property to Yes for those items that correspond to primary key columns, as OCA cannot get that information from the data source.

■ You may have to set the Update Changed Columns data block property to Yes if you get errors about not being able to update primary key columns.

■ You may have to adjust the Records Fetched data block property if you are trying to fetch more records than the data source supports at once.

■ You must quote any object names that the data source stores in mixed case. Most data sources are insensitive to case, but some, such as Sybase, let you distinguish between "Ledger" and "ledger." If you are using these data sources, and you use any lowercase in the names, you must quote the names in your SQL statements with double quotes (").

The OCA gives you a powerful tool for opening up your applications to data in data sources other than Oracle.

Integrating Components into Oracle Developer Forms

A component is a software system that you can combine with other components into a complete, working software system. Components have always been around in one form or another, but as object-oriented architectures have become more widespread, the concept is taking on a new importance. Oracle Developer supports several major component standards; the two major ones are JavaBeans and ActiveX. The next two sections show you how to reuse Java and ActiveX components, respectively, with Oracle Developer form applications.

Integrating Java Components into Forms

Java is a programming language developed and standardized by Sun Microsystems in an ongoing and contentious process. One aspect of the Java standardization is the JavaBean—a component specification that lets you use systems of Java classes as components in Java *applets* (code that runs in a Web browser), *servlets* (code that runs on an application server), and *applications* (code that runs on its own). Java gets much of its syntax from the C++ programming language, with various departures and additions. The JavaBean specification standardizes the ways that JavaBeans make their system properties available to clients.

NOTE

Using JavaBeans in your application could require some Java programming skills if you want to build your own JavaBeans or Java classes. For example, to use a JavaBean in a bean area, you must write a wrapper class in Java that extends (inherits from) the VBean class provided by Oracle with the Developer Server. All this Java code goes into the /codebase/ virtual directory on the application server (see Chapter 14 for details on this virtual directory). As teaching the Java skills and techniques is beyond the scope of this introductory text, and because of space limitations, this section does not present the actual Java code you need to write to integrate a JavaBean. Consult the Oracle Developer help files for some example code you can use, and go through the Oracle Developer Demo examples that ship with the Oracle Developer system.

You can purchase JavaBeans from a third-party vendor, or you can write your own using Oracle JDeveloper or any other Java development environment.

You can use a JavaBean in two ways:

- *Linking:* You can create special Bean Area items in a data block and use the Implementation Class property to link to the JavaBean and the When-Custom-Item-Event trigger to handle events in the Bean Area.

- *Customizing:* You can replace specific controls (check boxes, list items, push buttons, radio groups, and text items) with JavaBeans by writing the JavaBean implementing the IView interface, either directly or by extending VBean or one of the other Oracle JavaBean classes such as VButton.

To link a JavaBean control to your application, follow these steps in the Form Builder:

1. Open the canvas that will display the control, click on the Bean Area tool, and drag out a rectangular area that will display the control.

2. Write a wrapper class that extends the VBean class, such as VCalendar (a calendar bean). Put the Java and class files into the /codebase/ virtual directory on the application server, making it accessible to the form at runtime.

The wrapper class provides some specific methods that the Forms applet calls to set properties and get mouse events; it also registers the specific events that the form recognizes.

3. Navigate to the Bean Area item in the Object Navigator and double-click on the item to display its Property Palette. Change the Implementation Class property to the name of the wrapper class. Use the fully qualified name, including the entire package name, such as "oracle.forms":

| ▫ Implementation Class | oracle.forms.Calendar |

4. Write an event trap procedure and store it in a library. Attach the library to the form that uses the JavaBean. This procedure gets parameters from the System variable CUSTOM_ITEM_EVENT_PARAMETERS and the event information from the System variable CUSTOM_ITEM_EVENT. The code looks something like this:

```
PROCEDURE EventTrap IS
  vBean ITEM;
  vBeanParamList PARAMLIST;
  vParamType NUMBER;
  vEvent VARCHAR2(20);
BEGIN
  vBeanParamList := Get_Parameter_List(:SYSTEM.CUSTOM_ITEM_EVENT_PARAMETERS);
  vEvent := :SYSTEM.CUSTOM_ITEM_EVENT;
  vBean := Find_Item('CONTROL.CALENDAR'); -- gets the CALENDAR bean item from the
CONTROL block
-- Process the supported events registered through the wrapper Java class
  END;
```

TIP
You can write this procedure in the Program Units section of the application. It's a good idea when thinking about reusable components, however, to package the procedure in a library that you can reuse in other applications. You probably want to have a library that corresponds to a collection of JavaBeans so that when you use a bean you attach the library and have the event-trapping procedure ready and waiting.

5. Call the EventTrap procedure from a When-Custom-Item-Event trigger on the Bean Area item:

```
EventTrap;
```

You can set properties in the JavaBean object in PL/SQL code using the Set_Custom_Item_Property built-in procedure. This takes the Bean Area item name, the name of the property (check the Bean documentation), and the value. Values may be VARCHAR2, INT, or BOOLEAN.

```
Set_Custom_Item_Property('Control.Calendar', 'enabled', TRUE);
```

To develop a custom version of a standard form control, just substitute the control for the Bean Area in the preceding steps. In a text item, for example, specify the Implementation Class property as the replacement JavaBean name and add a When-Custom-Item-Event trigger to the text item.

Integrating ActiveX Components into Forms

ActiveX is a Microsoft-specific suite of technologies that enable Windows applications to use standardized interfaces for all kinds of different aspects of system development. An ActiveX control is a component that provides a well-defined interface (program and graphical interface) and sends events to clients (your application, for example, or other applications on the network). The ActiveX control, previously known as the OCX control, is based on the Component Object Model (COM) standard, which is also a Microsoft technology.

NOTE
You can use ActiveX controls only in applications that will run under Microsoft Windows.

You link ActiveX controls into your application by defining an ActiveX Control item in a data block. Oracle Developer imports the control methods and events, creating code skeletons that will interface to the control. You then write the code inside the generated procedures. When the control fires an event, it calls the procedure that corresponds to the event.

NOTE
You can do some sophisticated programming using the On-Dispatch-Event trigger, which permits you to work around the fact that the event procedures are by default restricted (that is, you cannot call unrestricted form procedures that navigate). See the help files for more information about these advanced ActiveX programming techniques.

To include an ActiveX component in your application, perform the following steps in the Form Builder:

1. Select the Program|Import OLE Library Interfaces menu item. The Form Builder displays the Import OLE Library Interfaces dialog box.

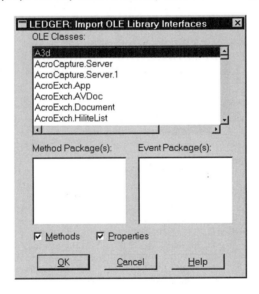

2. Scroll through the list of registered ActiveX components until you find the one you're looking for. This tutorial uses the OracleSpreadTable component. The dialog box then displays all the methods and events available from the component.

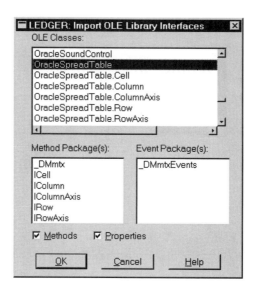

3. Select the methods and events you want to use in your application. Use the standard CTRL-click method of selecting multiple items. Click OK when you have selected all the methods and events.

   Oracle Developer now creates the procedure skeletons for the events and methods you've selected. It generates a series of packages in the Program Units section of your application:

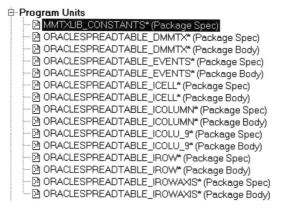

4. Display the canvas on which you want to display the control. Click on the ActiveX Control tool and draw a rectangle on the canvas in which to display the control.

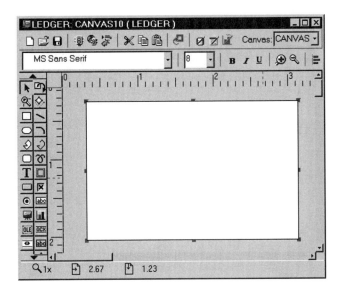

5. Double-click on the control rectangle on the canvas to display the control's
Property Palette. Click on the ... button to display the OLE Classes dialog
box. This is an LOV, so you can use standard LOV pattern matching to find
the control you want (the same one you found in the pick-list dialog box
when importing the events and methods).

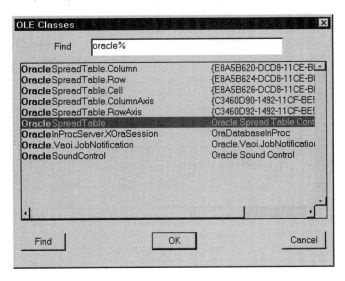

6. Select the name and click OK.

7. Click right on the control in the canvas and choose Insert Object from the pop-up menu. The Form Builder displays the Insert Object dialog box. Make sure the Create Control radio button is selected, and then click OK.

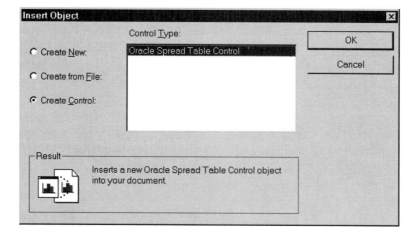

You now see the control filled in with the Spreadtable object.

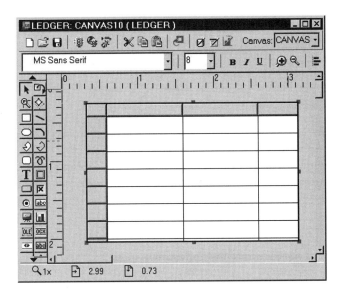

TIP
*Once you've "tenanted" the control, you should
look over any documentation available for the
component to understand what each event and
method does and what you need to do to respond to
an event. You can access internal documentation
through the control's Property Palette by using the
Control Help property: just click on the … button
once you've set the name of the control. You can
use the Control Properties property to set any
properties in the control as well.*

Now you need to go into each of the packages in the Program Units section and
replace the NULL bodies with code that implements the interfaces you've imported.
You can also write other subprograms and packages that use the methods you've
imported to do the various things you need to do. You can refer to component
properties with bind variable syntax in PL/SQL procedures:

```
vVar := :Item('<block>.<item>').ocx.<server>.<property>
```

where <block>.<item> is the name of the ActiveX Control item in the data block; <server> is the name of the ActiveX server (OracleSpreadTable.1, for example); and <property> is the name of the property. Alternatively, you can use the code generated for you by the OLE importer:

```
vVar := <package>.<property>(:Item('<block>.<item>').interface);
```

where <package> is the generated package name (OracleSpreadTable_IColumn, for example); <property> is the package function corresponding to the property (position, for example, for the column object); and <block> and <item> are the data block and ActiveX Control item names as before. There is a corresponding syntax for the procedures you use to set values:

```
<package>.<property>(:Item('<block>.<item>').interface, <value>);
```

where <value> is a data value of the appropriate type specified in the procedure argument list.

Modifying Key Assignments

The final topic of this chapter deals with a small but significant portion of the Oracle Developer Forms interface to the world. Form users perform many actions through keys on their keyboards. You can control these key assignments to make them whatever you want. If you are using the Developer Forms Server, you edit the key resource file in a text editor. For client/server forms, Oracle Terminal lets you change the keys you use to execute commands, both in the Builder and in the Runtime program.

Editing the Web Key Assignments

When you install Developer Server, the Oracle Installer adds a resource file to your installation called FMRWEB.RES:

```
#  FMRWEB.RES is the key definition file for webforms. The syntax is:
#
#    JFN : JMN : URKS : FFN : URFD    (whitespace ignored)
#
#     JFN = Java function number
#     JMN = Java modifiers number
#    URKS = User-readable key sequence (double-quoted)
#     FFN = Forms function number
#    URFD = User-readable function description (double-quoted)
#
#  JAVA FUNCTION NUMBER
```

```
#          33 = PageUp
#          34 = PageDown
#          35 = End
#          36 = Home
#          37 = LeftArrow
#          38 = UpArrow
#          39 = RightArrow
#          40 = DownArrow
#     65 - 90 = Ctrl+A thru Ctrl+Z (These will always have the control
#               modifier explicitly included, as well as any other
#               modifiers that might be used.)
#    112 - 123 = F1 thru F12
#           9 = Tab (Ctrl+I, without the control modifier)
#          10 = Return (Ctrl+J, without the control modifier)
#
#    JAVA MODIFIERS NUMBER
#    Equal to the sum of the values for the modifier keys:
#       0 = None
#       1 = Shift
#       2 = Control
#       4 = Meta
#       8 = Alt
#
#    FORMS FUNCTION NUMBER
#    The Forms function numbers match the function numbers found in a
#    typical Forms key binding file.
#
#    USER-READABLE STRINGS
#    The double-quoted strings appear when users click [Show Keys], and
#    are used for this purpose only. These strings can be translated as
#    needed. Note that the strings do not affect what actually happens
#    when end users press a particular key sequence.
#
9      : 0 : "Tab"           : 1  : "Next Field"
9      : 1 : "Shift+Tab"     : 2  : "Previous Field"
116    : 0 : "F5"            : 3  : "Clear Field"
38     : 0 : "Up"            : 6  : "Up"
40     : 0 : "Down"          : 7  : "Down"
33     : 0 : "PageUp"        : 12 : "Scroll Up"
34     : 0 : "PageDown"      : 13 : "Scroll Down"
69     : 2 : "Ctrl+E"        : 22 : "Edit"
10     : 0 : "Return"        : 27 : "Return"
76     : 2 : "Ctrl+L"        : 29 : "List of Values"
115    : 0 : "F4"            : 32 : "Exit"
75     : 2 : "Ctrl+K"        : 35 : "Show Keys"
83     : 2 : "Ctrl+S"        : 36 : "Commit"
118    : 1 : "Shift+F7"      : 61 : "Next Primary Key"
117    : 0 : "F6"            : 62 : "Clear Record"
```

```
38    : 2 : "Ctrl+Up"          : 63 : "Delete Record"
117   : 1 : "Shift+F6"         : 64 : "Duplicate Record"
40    : 2 : "Ctrl+Down"        : 65 : "Insert Record"
119   : 1 : "Shift+F8"         : 66 : "Next Set of Records"
1005  : 0 : "Down"             : 67 : "Next Record"
1004  : 0 : "Up"               : 68 : "Previous Record"
118   : 0 : "F7"               : 69 : "Clear Block"
66    : 2 : "Ctrl+B"           : 70 : "Block Menu"
34    : 1 : "Shift+PageDown"   : 71 : "Next Block"
33    : 1 : "Shift+PageUp"     : 72 : "Previous Block"
116   : 1 : "Shift+F5"         : 73 : "Duplicate Field"
119   : 0 : "F8"               : 74 : "Clear Form"
122   : 0 : "F11"              : 76 : "Enter Query"
122   : 2 : "Ctrl+F11"         : 77 : "Execute Query"
69    : 3 : "Shift+Ctrl+E"     : 78 : "Display Error"
80    : 2 : "Ctrl+P"           : 79 : "Print"
123   : 0 : "F12"              : 80 : "Count Query"
85    : 2 : "Ctrl+U"           : 81 : "Update Record"
121   : 3 : "Shift+Ctrl+F10"   : 82 : "Function 0"
112   : 3 : "Shift+Ctrl+F1"    : 83 : "Function 1"
113   : 3 : "Shift+Ctrl+F2"    : 84 : "Function 2"
114   : 3 : "Shift+Ctrl+F3"    : 85 : "Function 3"
115   : 3 : "Shift+Ctrl+F4"    : 86 : "Function 4"
116   : 3 : "Shift+Ctrl+F5"    : 87 : "Function 5"
117   : 3 : "Shift+Ctrl+F6"    : 88 : "Function 6"
118   : 3 : "Shift+Ctrl+F7"    : 89 : "Function 7"
119   : 3 : "Shift+Ctrl+F8"    : 90 : "Function 8"
120   : 3 : "Shift+Ctrl+F9"    : 91 : "Function 9"
```

Using any text editor, such as Notepad, you can edit the codes and key descriptions to assign any key to any function. You can remap any of the keys in the file by changing the code in the first column (the Java Function Number) and second column (Java Modifiers Number), which combine to create the complete key setup. You will see the definitions for these codes up near the top of the file. Leave the Forms Function Number (column 4) alone. You can modify what appears in the Key help screen by changing the two strings, the first of which is the key description and the second of which is the function description.

Assigning Keys with Oracle Terminal

Oracle Developer's Forms component run as a client/server application gets its key assignments from a resource file, such as the FMRUSW.RES file on Windows. The Oracle Terminal program lets you edit parts of that file to define a key binding. You can bind keys to application functions or to key triggers. This lets you modify the keyboard interface of your form applications to suit your needs. You can also modify the interface of the Form Builder to suit your own tastes.

NOTE
If you are running your applications through a Web browser, you cannot change the key assignments with Oracle Terminal.

1. When you run Oracle Terminal, it prompts you for a file. Find the resource file for Forms (usually fmrusw.res) and click OK. On Windows, it is in the FORMS60 directory. If you try some other resource files, you will find these files do not have the right structure for use with Oracle Terminal. Terminal then displays the main terminal window:

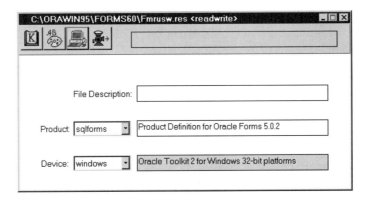

This window lets you set the product and device if the file defines more than one, which does not appear to be true for the current product.

2. Click on the Key Binding tool to edit the key bindings with the Key Binding Editor.

The Key Binding Editor displays a tree of key categories (Figure 15-1). Each of these categories contains a set of key bindings relating to a particular type of action. The intermediate categories (runform and design) have actions that apply to all situations in the product, such as Show Keys, Help, Cancel, and Exit. The leaf categories have actions that apply in specific situations.

3. To see the key bindings, double-click on the category's circle.

The Editor displays a table of bindings (Figure 15-2 displays the "normal" category node). This table shows the Action, such as [Next Block] or [Scroll Up], and the key to which it binds, such as CONTROL+D or SHIFT+F9. You can have duplicate rows for an action, indicating that you get the action by pressing any of a group of keys. Each key for an action takes a separate row in the table.

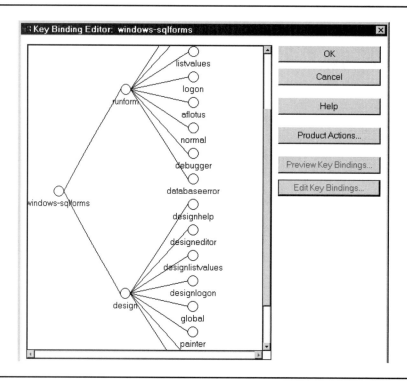

FIGURE 15-1.   *The Key Binding Editor*

4. To change a binding, find the action and change the key by typing over it.

You can manipulate the rows with the Row buttons (Duplicate, Insert, and Delete Row). You can also enter the key by placing the cursor in the key field and clicking on Macro Mode. You can then enter the keys by pressing the actual keys rather than spelling out words such as "Control" and "Shift." Follow the instructions in the resulting dialog box for finishing the macro recording.

Setting up a key trigger is a bit more involved because you need to define the action. You do this at the top level, windows-sqlforms, in the Key Binding Editor.

5. Double-click on the windows-sqlforms node. You see an empty action table.

6. Click on the Insert Row button to insert a row.

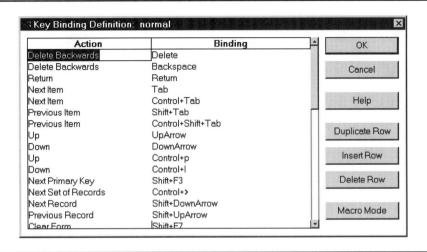

FIGURE 15-2. *The Key Binding Definition Editor*

7. Insert the action that corresponds to the key trigger (KEY-F3, for example). Then enter the key binding just as you did previously.

8. Now click on the Product Actions button to invoke the Product Actions Editor, which is very similar to the Key Binding Editor graphically.

9. Double-click on the sqlforms category to see the Product Action Definition window (Figure 15-3).

10. Enter the action ([User Defined Key 3], for example); its corresponding numeric code (from 82 for key 0 through 91 for key 9, Code (85) for Key 3 in this case); and a description to display in the list of key bindings. Click on OK.

11. When you finish defining bindings, click on OK to dismiss the Key Binding Editor and return to the main window.

12. Save the key bindings.

13. Click on the Generate tool to generate a new resources file with the new bindings.

14. Save again to complete the process.

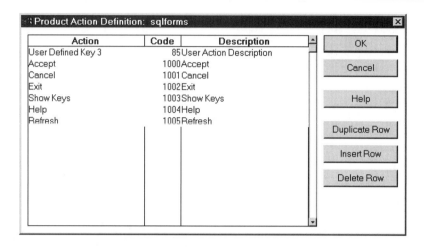

FIGURE 15-3.   *The Product Action Definition Editor with new key trigger action*

Internationalizing Your Applications with Oracle Translation Builder

With the Internet, the world is getting pretty small. As a rule of thumb, you are always going to be better off if you make linguistic portability a requirement for the application from the beginning. The world has gotten drastically smaller in the 1990s, and the next century promises to squeeze it even more. If you start out believing you will have to support applications in Norwegian, Russian, Arabic, or Kanji, you are likely to design an application that can accommodate these languages, however diverse their requirements.

To facilitate translation of your Oracle Developer applications into different languages, you need to understand three areas:

- National Language Support (NLS)
- Layout design
- String translation

National Language Support in Oracle

Oracle provides an extensive facility, called National Language Support (NLS), for dealing with linguistic differences. See the discussion of this facility in the *Database Administrator's Guide*. If you are going to work with multiple character sets and languages, you should start by reading everything about NLS in the Oracle documentation, because you definitely need to know what Oracle does for you.

Briefly, NLS provides support for these linguistic issues:

■ Text and character sets for different languages stored in the database

■ Messages from Oracle and the runtime programs in different languages

■ Format masks defaulting to appropriate formats for different languages

■ Sorting or collation sequences for different alphabets used with relational operators in SQL expressions and in ORDER BY clauses

■ Bidirectional formatting of displayed items in forms, reports, and graphs

By "support," Oracle in this case means handling everything transparently. As an application developer, you do nothing except to tell Oracle what language and territory you wish to use; it takes care of everything else. You specify the language with the NLS_LANG environment variable in the System Registry.

You can use the ALTER SESSION statement (an Oracle SQL extension to the ANSI standard) to change any of the parameters for NLS. If you wish, you can exercise a fine level of control over language support. This book advises you to go lightly with this, both because the NLS facility does not conform to the emerging ANSI standard and because with this kind of feature you are generally better off accepting the defaults. You can endlessly tweak and fix and investigate to get the behavior just right for Libyan Arabic, or you can go with the flow...

Another place for going with the flow is to use default format masks. All of the Oracle Developer products use format masks to format number and date data. Various examples in this book recommend setting the format masks to specific values for dates, numbers, and monetary values. If you are going to provide language-independent applications, ignore this advice. Use the default format masks. NLS automatically uses the right mask for the language you specify in NLS_LANG. If you use an explicit format, you lose this automatic handling. You then must code around everything, which, as you undoubtedly know, can get tedious.

There are some specific format mask characters you can use that Oracle interprets correctly using NLS:

Character	Meaning
C	The international currency symbol
L	The local currency symbol
D	The decimal separator in numbers
G	The thousands separator in numbers

L999G999D99, for example, is an internationally portable version of $999,999.99. NLS also interprets various date components in local versions, such as the names of months or days of the week. See the Oracle Developer Forms, Reports, and Graphs online documentation on format masks for details.

There is a special case you must watch for: PL/SQL expressions. If you use date constants in PL/SQL for any reason, wrap them in a To_Date function to make sure PL/SQL handles them correctly. For example, here is a language-dependent expression:

```
:Ledger.ActionDate := '1/1/01';
```

This is language dependent because PL/SQL converts the string using the standard "American" format mask, 'dd-MON-yy', regardless of the current language. Instead, you should use this kind of code:

```
:Ledger.ActionDate := To_Date('01/01/01', 'DD/MM/YY');
```

Layout Design

The key issue in layout design is precisely the issue that you have in windowing system portability: you have to accommodate different sizes for objects at different times. With a windowing system, buttons are different sizes, as are default fonts. Some buttons have double lines around them on one system and none on another.

With different languages, there are several layout issues:

■ The size of text strings varies with the translated string length.

■ The size of formatted strings (format mask territory) varies with the language.

■ The size of "widgets"—the various graphical objects you display onscreen that include text, such as radio buttons—varies with the language.

■ The location of labels varies with the size of the fields they label, which in turn depends on language.

Oracle recommends a rule-of-thumb value of 30 percent expansion room for all these cases. If you can, you should develop the original application in the language that takes up the most room.

Also, you should design your screen, report, and graph layout for linguistic portability. Use less boilerplate; this static material will get in the way when you need to expand fields, and every bit of text you add will require translation. Do not clutter the boilerplate with graphics that will interfere with expansion. Arrange the fields so that different languages will look reasonable, even if the reading direction is the reverse of the language in which you develop the application.

String Translation

Any application you develop is going to have a lot of strings. To minimize string translation, you should use as few strings as possible in boilerplate. For example, for applications that need to be internationally portable, do not put a lot of text directions for use into the boilerplate. Put directions in the database and display them in a display-only field.

There are two kinds of strings to worry about in Oracle Developer applications:

■   Boilerplate text, including labels and titles

■   String constants and variables in PL/SQL procedures

Boilerplate Text

Boilerplate text is any text in your forms, reports, or graphics that you type in through an editor rather than fill in from the database. The designer saves this text in various formats in your application files (or in the database if you save the application there).

Translation of boilerplate text is a matter of finding the text and translating it into the language or languages in which you wish it to appear. There are at least a couple of ways to approach the problem. First, you can make one application file (form, report, graphic) for each language. Second, you can replace the boilerplate with display fields and fill them in from the database, using special PL/SQL code to figure out the correct language and data location. This book recommends the former approach. Although slightly more tedious, maintaining the application data is a lot easier than maintaining the relatively complex code you would have to add to your applications.

Again, limiting the amount of such text is a good strategy for international applications, although it is difficult to eliminate entirely.

Oracle Translation Builder

The job of Oracle Translation Builder is to translate all the string resources in an Oracle Developer application from a base language into multiple target languages. It does this through a set of database tables you create on your database server.

To use the Oracle Translation Builder, you must first install its tables into the database (see Appendix B for details on installing the database tables). Once you've created the database, you start the Translation Builder from the task bar.

1. Choose Start|Oracle Developer 6.0|Translation Builder. This menu item starts the Builder, which displays an initial screen prompting whether to work on a project or to run the Quick Tour. Choose to work on a project.

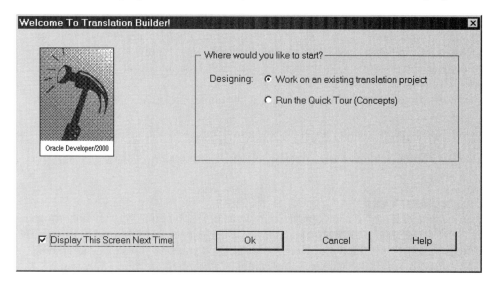

2. Your first task is to establish a standard connection by choosing File|New|DB Connection from the main menu. This illustration shows the Navigator with the Talbot connection:

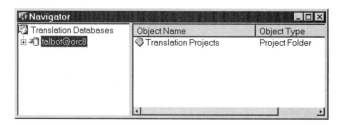

3. Now you need to create a project. The project corresponds to the set of
modules that you tie together into a single application or to whatever other
grouping of Forms modules you want to consider as a system. Click on
File|New|Project to create a project under your database connection. You
see the New Project dialog box:

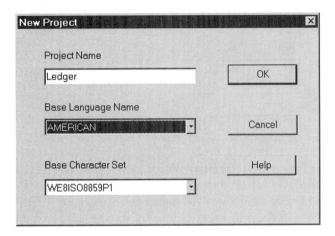

4. To create the project, you must specify a name and the base language and
character set. A good choice for the latter two items is the current setting of
the NLS_LANG environment variable, which you'll find in the System
Registry with all the other Oracle variables. In this case, for example, Talbot
uses the American language and the WE8ISO8859P1 character set. Click
on OK, and you see the new project under the project folder.

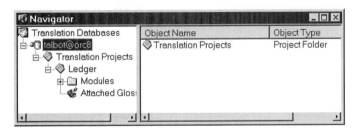

5. The first step in creating a translation is to import the base version into your
project. Open the project, and then click on Module|Import Strings or the
Import Strings tool to see this Import Strings dialog box:

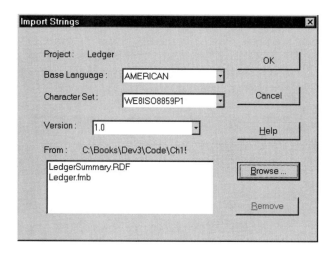

6. The project language and character set appear, but you can change them if necessary. Enter the version (any string, but a good choice is a version number such as 1.0) and the name of the file you want to import. Click on the Browse button to enter the path name for the files you are going to import, and choose the files (here, the Ledger form module and the LedgerSummary report module) from the Open File dialog box that appears. You see a list of the files you've chosen and the path to those files. Click on OK to finish. The Navigator now contains the new modules, as this illustration shows, and you can start translating:

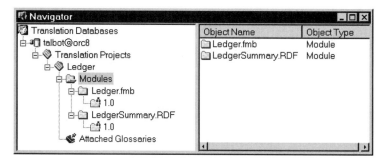

7. Open the version folder for a module. Add a translation of the module with the menu item Module|Add Translation or the Add Translation tool. This displays the Add Translation dialog box:

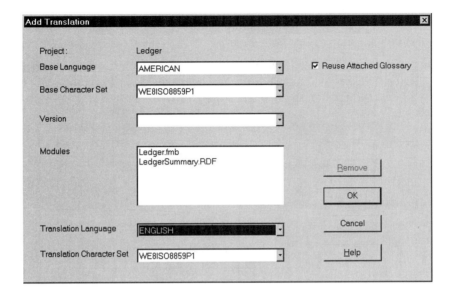

8. In this case, Talbot is doing a translation to the British dialect of English, so only the language changes, from American to English. Pull down the Translation Language list and choose English. The character set stays the same. Click on OK to create the new translation, which appears under the version in the Navigator:

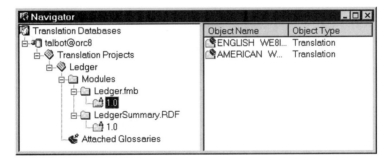

NOTE

Consult your Oracle documentation on the NLS features of Oracle for a complete list of languages and character sets.

The right pane of the Navigator now displays the two translations, American and English.

9. Double-click the English translation, indicating you want to create the translated version. The Navigator displays a dialog box prompting for the base version; enter American.

You now see the Translation Editor with its side-by-side listing of the strings:

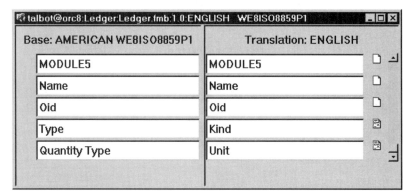

10. Change the strings that need translation. For strings you change, you see the Translated icon next to the string. In this case, Talbot has changed "Type" to "Kind" and "Quantity Type" to "Unit," as these terms will be more easily recognized by a British user. When you're finished editing, click on the Save tool, and then close the Editor with the window close control in the title bar of the Editor window.

Now you take the last step—integrating the translation back into the module.

11. Select the Ledger node in the Navigator. Click on the Module|Export Strings menu item or the Export Strings tool. You see the Export Strings dialog box, which resembles the Import Strings dialog box:

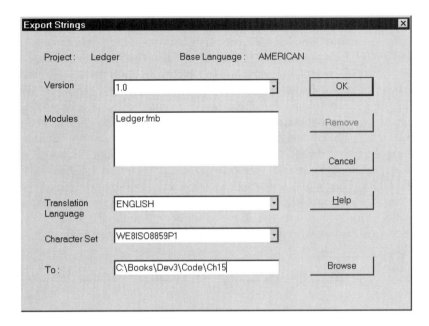

12. Select and remove with the Remove button any modules you don't want to export. In this example, Talbot has removed the LedgerSummary report, as it isn't yet translated.

13. Select the version to export from the drop-down list. Enter the language and character set for the translation to export (English, the translated language). Click on OK.

The Translation Builder writes out the translation to the module file, which now contains both sets of strings. When you run with NLS_LANG set appropriately, you see the translated strings rather than the base strings.

PL/SQL Strings

At various times, your PL/SQL code is going to display error, warning, or advisory messages through alerts or other mechanisms, such as display fields. Often, you will construct these messages by concatenating automatically generated strings. If you want an internationally portable application, you have to take measures to make sure these strings appear in the right language. You can code them dynamically to check the current language and respond correctly, but there are better ways to achieve the same results.

The most effective method centralizes your string handling in a PL/SQL library. You can code simple, constant messages with message number lookups, or you can develop specific functions that take parameterized input and produce an appropriate message. You build one library for each language you want to support; each library contains the same set of functions. When you install your system, you use the FORMS60_PATH, REPORTS60_PATH, and GRAPHICS60_PATH environment variables to point to the language directory in which your translated library resides. You can even switch languages by resetting this path, though you cannot do this dynamically if you are running the application in a Web browser. When you load a form, report, or graph, the runtime program looks for the attached libraries in the directories in the path. It loads the first version it finds. When your application calls one of the string functions, PL/SQL calls the one defined for the current language. Thus, all you need to do is to make sure that the correct directory is first in the path.

Using NLS in Oracle gets you a long way toward linguistic portability in your applications because it makes many of the character set issues you face transparent: it just works. With careful screen layout and rigorous string management in your applications, you are well on the way to having applications that will work around the world.

PART
V

Reference

CHAPTER
16

Object and
Property Reference

his chapter contains a complete reference to all the objects in Oracle Developer. There is one section for each of the three major components of the Oracle Developer environment: Form Builder, Report Builder, and Graphics Builder.

Form Builder

Form Builder integrates several modules: the form, the menu, the PL/SQL library, and the object library. The two library modules do not contain any internal objects. Form Builder also contains a list of the built-in subprograms in the Object Navigator under the Built-in Packages heading. Finally, Report Builder lists the database objects, giving you access to the database server data dictionary (users, tables, columns, compilation units, and triggers). See Chapter 2 for an overview of how these Object Navigator nodes work; see the section "Writing Code Once" in Chapter 10 for a tutorial on using the Database Objects node to define compilation units and to move them from client to server.

The Form Module

Figure 16-1 gives a graphical overview of the structure of the form module. The section "The Form Module" in Chapter 2 summarizes the structure and function of the objects in the form module.

Form Module Objects

Table 16-1 lists the form module objects and describes their function in a form application. Certain of these objects are objects nested within the main objects in Figure 16-1; Table 16-1 lists all the objects that have properties in Table 16-2, whether or not they appear explicitly in Figure 16-1 or in the Object Navigator. Table 16-1 lists the objects in alphabetical order for easy reference, not in the order in which they appear in the Object Navigator.

Form Module Properties

Table 16-2 lists all the properties in a form module in alphabetical order. As well as describing the property, the table shows which objects use each property. If the values are restricted, the description lists the possible values. If you see the word "whether," it means the property is a Boolean property with the values Yes and No

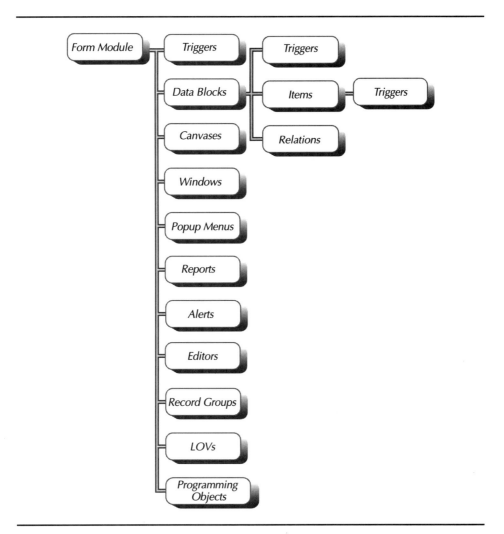

FIGURE 16-1.   *Object hierarchy for a form module*

as choices. The Get/Set column tells you whether you can use the appropriate Get or Set built-in subprogram to manipulate the property (Get_Form_Property,

Object	Description
Alert	A modal window that displays a message or asks a simple question that elicits a yes/no type of response from the user by means of up to three buttons, such as Yes, No, Cancel.
Arc	A graphic consisting of a curved line nested within the canvas object.
Attached Library	A PL/SQL library you have attached to another module; the order of libraries lets you replace program units with variations.
Canvas	The background within a window on which you place boilerplate text and items.
Data Block	An object that holds a collection of records and comprises a set of items that make up each record.
Editor	An object that displays as a text editor window for entering text into a text item.
Form	A module that presents data in an online format consisting of a series of items laid out in one or more windows.
Frame	An object within a canvas that contains the layout properties for a group of block items taken as a whole.
Graphic	A canvas graphic element (line, and so on); nested within the canvas object.
Image	A rectangular picture graphic nested within the canvas object.
Line	A kind of graphics object on a canvas; nested within the graphics object.
LOV	An object that displays as a special dialog box for selecting a single value from a list of values as a pick-list; you can associate an LOV with a record group and with an item to check for valid input into the item; it also has a search feature that makes it easy to find items in a large list.
Object Group	An object that lets you package your reusable objects for later copying or reference; it collects a set of objects under a single heading.
Parameter	An object to which you can assign a value by passing it in through the runtime system for the module; the parameter lets you customize a module at runtime, enhancing its reusability under different situations; see also system parameter and user-defined parameter.

TABLE 16-1. *Form Module Objects*

Object	Description
Popup Menu	A floating menu that pops up when you click the right mouse button on a canvas or item.
Program Unit	A PL/SQL package, function, or procedure.
Property Class	An object that collects any kind of property.
Record Group	An object that represents a special data structure that resembles a table, with rows and columns.
Relation	An object that represents a master-detail relationship, with the relation expressing the mapping between two data blocks; nested within the Data Block object that serves as the master in the relationship.
Report	An object that interfaces the form to an Oracle Developer Reports module, allowing the form to run the report with the Run_Report_Object built-in subprogram. There are other ways to run a report as well (the Run_Product and Web.Show_Document built-in subprograms).
Tab Page	An individual tab layout in a tabbed canvas.
Text	A graphic object nested under the canvas representing boilerplate text on the canvas.
Trigger	An anonymous PL/SQL block attached to another object that executes when a specific event happens in the context of that object; the name of the trigger reflects the type of event that triggers the PL/SQL block.
Visual Attribute	An object that collects a set of display properties to which you can refer from another object. This object controls several individual properties: font name, font size, font style, font spacing, font weight, foreground color, background color, fill pattern, character mode logical attribute, and white on black.
Window	An object that defines a rectangular area of the application display maintained by the GUI platform.

TABLE 16-1. *Form Module Objects* (continued)

Set_Item_Property, and so on). "G" means Get only, "S" means Set only, and "GS" means both Get and Set are possible. "Blank" means you cannot manipulate the property programmatically.

Property	Objects	Description	Get/Set
About Control	ActiveX Control Item	Displays an about screen for the ActiveX control; available only after you "tenant" the control by inserting an object (see Chapter 15).	
Access Key	Button, Radio Button, Check Box Item	The single character representing the key you can use to select an item; entering the ALT (or COMMAND) key plus this key is the same as clicking on the item with the mouse.	
Alert Style	Alert	Stop, Caution, or Note; specifies the icon the alert displays next to the message.	
Alias	Data Block	The SQL alias for the table corresponding to the data block; use this for Oracle8 tables with REF or object-type columns when you need to refer to the columns in a WHERE clause or ORDER BY clause property; automatically set by the Data Block Wizard.	
Allow Empty Branches	Hierarchical Tree	Whether branch nodes may exist without children: default No means that Form Builder converts branch nodes without children to leaf nodes, while Yes means that the Forms Runtime displays an empty branch as a collapsed node.	
Allow Expansion	Frame	Whether Form Builder can expand the frame when its contents grow beyond the current border; defaults to No, but I generally change this to Yes.	
Allow Multi-Line Prompts	Frame	Whether Form Builder can split a prompt into multiple lines to save space; defaults to No.	
Allow Start-Attached Prompts	Frame	In a tabular frame, whether to attach the prompt to the start side instead of the top side if there is room; default No.	

TABLE 16-2. *Form Module Properties*

Property	Objects	Description	Get/Set
Allow Top-Attached Prompts	Frame	In a form frame, whether to attach the prompt to the top side instead of the start side if there is room; default No.	
Application Instance	Form, Block, Item	Not something you enter, this property contains a reference to an instance of a Microsoft Windows application (NULL on other platforms) that you can access with Get_Application_Property. You can use this reference as a handle when calling the Windows API from PL/SQL.	
Arrow Style	Line	Where to place arrowheads on the line: None (the default), Start, End, Both ends, Middle to Start, Middle to End.	
Audio Channels	Sound Item	The number of channels to store in the database for this sound item: Automatic, Mono, or Stereo. The Write_Sound_File built-in also uses this property to write the sound data with the indicated channel style to a file system file.	
Automatic Column Width	LOV	Whether to set the LOV column width automatically; Yes means set the width to the greater of the Display Width property or the size of the text in the Column Title property; No (the default) means set the width to Display Width.	
Automatic Display	LOV	Whether to display the LOV immediately when the user navigates into an item to which the LOV attaches.	
Automatic Position	LOV	Whether to display the LOV near the item to which the LOV attaches.	

TABLE 16-2. *Form Module Properties* (continued)

Property	Objects	Description	Get/Set
Automatic Query	Relation	When the Deferred property is Yes (the default), Automatic Query set to Yes means that the Forms Runtime automatically executes the query when the user navigates to the detail block; No means the user must explicitly initiate the Execute Query function.	
Automatic Refresh	LOV	Whether to execute the query that populates the LOV every time the user invokes the LOV (Yes, the default). No permits you to manipulate the record group with built-in subprograms rather than automatically querying the LOV columns from the database or to avoid repopulating the LOV too frequently because multiple LOVs use the record group. It's usually better to set the property to No unless the data changes quite often in the database. The LOV always queries if the internal flag indicating that the record group has records is set, which is true for the first use of the record group or if an LOV with Automatic Refresh set to Yes uses the group and closes, clearing the records in the group. For data that can change in the database, I generally keep this set to Yes to avoid the coupling and interaction behavior that ensues when you set this property to No. If you do set it to No, carefully test varying sequences of LOV use to ensure that everything works as you anticipate.	GS
Automatic Select	LOV	Whether to dismiss the LOV automatically when the choices reduce to a single record (Yes) or to wait for the user to dismiss the LOV (No, the default).	

TABLE 16-2.   *Form Module Properties (continued)*

Property	Objects	Description	Get/Set
Automatic Skip	Text Item, LOV	Whether to move the cursor to the next item after entering the last character of the item (default No); for an item with an LOV, whether to move the cursor after picking a record in the LOV.	GS
Background Color	Item, Tab Page, Canvas, Window, Radio Button	The color of the object's background.	GS
Bevel	Text, Chart, Image, or Custom Item, Canvas	The beveling style of the object border: LOWERED (default), RAISED, INSET, OUTSET, or NONE. If the canvas or item has a scroll bar, you should set the border style to RAISED or LOWERED for best results.	GS
Block Description	Data Block	The text to display in the data block menu, if you use Listed in Block Menu to enable display of this data block in the menu; defaults to the initial name of the data block.	
Bottom Title	Editor	A title that appears at the bottom of the editor window (72 characters or fewer).	
Bounding Box Scalable	Graphic Text	Whether to scale the text object bounding box (the invisible box around the text) when scaling the text; Yes (default) or No.	
Button 1 Label	Alert	The text label that the alert displays for the first of three buttons; default OK; if you set the label to NULL, the alert does not display this button.	S
Button 2 Label	Alert	The text label that the alert displays for the second of three buttons; default Cancel; if you set the label to NULL, the alert does not display this button.	S

TABLE 16-2. *Form Module Properties* (continued)

Property	Objects	Description	Get/Set
Button 3 Label	Alert	The text label that the alert displays for the third of three buttons; default NULL; if label is NULL, the alert does not display this button.	S
Calculation Mode	Item	Specifies whether the item is a calculated item and, if so, what kind of calculated item: None (the default) means the item is not calculated, Formula means the item calculates its value based on the formula in the Formula property, and Summary means the item calculates its value based on the summary operation in the Summary Function property. The function calculates a value using data from a data block item specified in the Summary Data Block and Summary Item properties.	
Canvas	Item	The canvas on which to display the item; NULL means the item has no canvas. Without belonging to a specific canvas, Forms Runtime does not display the item anywhere; this is referred to as being displayed on the Null canvas. The Layout Wizard sets this to the canvas in the Wizard's canvas screen, and the Layout Editor sets it if you create the item with the tool palette, but the value is NULL by default if you create the item with the Add button.	
Canvas Type	Canvas	The kind of canvas: Content (the default), Stacked, Vertical Toolbar Canvas, Horizontal Toolbar Canvas.	
Cap Style	Graphic	The style of the edge cap in a graphic: Butt (the default), Round, or Projecting.	

TABLE 16-2. *Form Module Properties* (continued)

Property	Objects	Description	Get/Set
Case Insensitive Query	Text Item	Whether Forms Runtime ignores case for this item during a query by example (default No); Oracle Developer optimizes the query to enable use of indexes, unlike the usual case with an uppercase conversion query.	GS
Case Restriction	Text Item	The case of text entered into the text item: MIXED (the default), UPPER, or LOWER; use this property to ensure, for example, that all text goes into the database in uppercase or displays in uppercase (dates, for example).	GS
Character Cell WD/HT	Form	The width and height of a character cell when Coordinate System is Real; the width and height unit is in the Real Unit property; specified through the Coordinate System dialog.	
Chart Subtype	Chart Item	A variation on the chart type: Column (default, applies to Column chart type).	
Chart Type	Chart Item	A base chart type: Column (the default), Pie, Bar, Table, Line, Scatter, Mixed, High-low, Double-y, Gantt.	
Check Box Mapping of Other Values	Check Box Item	How to interpret a value from the database that is neither the value in the Value When Checked property or the Value When Unchecked Property: Not Allowed (the default), Checked, or Unchecked.	
Clip Height	Image	The height in Coordinate System units of the image after clipping from the bottom; the default is the original image height. If you make the measurement smaller than the default height, Forms clips the image from the bottom until it is the new height.	

TABLE 16-2. *Form Module Properties* (continued)

Property	Objects	Description	Get/Set
Clip Width	Image	The width in Coordinate System units of the image after clipping from the right side; the default is the original image width. If you make the measurement smaller than the default width, Forms clips the image from the right side until it is the new width.	
Clip X Position	Image	The amount in Coordinate System units to clip from the left side of the image; default 0.	
Clip Y Position	Image	The amount in Coordinate System units to clip from the top of the image; default 0.	
Close Allowed	Window	Enables (default) or disables the window system menu Close command through the window menu or iconic close box; you also need to write a When-Window-Closed trigger that calls Hide_Window or Exit_Form to actually close the window. On Microsoft Windows, the MDI main window automatically calls Exit_Form.	
Closed	Arc	Whether an arc graphic is closed.	
Column Mapping Properties	LOV	Clicking on More displays the Column Mapping dialog box, which lets you enter the column mapping information for the LOV: Column Name (relates to the name in the record group from which the LOV gets its data), Column Title (the string the LOV displays on top of the column), Display Width (the width of the column in Coordinate System units), and Return Item (the name of the item to which the LOV assigns the column's value when the user selects a value and clicks OK). The return item can be a data block item (block.item), a parameter (Parameter.name, no colon in front), or a global variable (Global.name, no colon in front).	

TABLE 16-2. *Form Module Properties* (continued)

Property	Objects	Description	Get/Set
Column Name	Items except Push Button, Chart, VBX Control, or ActiveX Control	Links the item to a column in the data block table. If the column is an object-type column or a REF column, the name uses dot notation to qualify the name fully, such as Address.Zip for the Zip column in the Address object in the Person table.	G
Column Specifications	Record Group	Clicking on the More button displays the Column Specification dialog box. The Column Names list displays the set of column names in the record. The Column Type displays the type (the default Char, Number, Date, Long) and length (defaults to database width or to 30 for static groups) for the currently selected column. The Column Values list displays the record values for the selected column for a static Record Group Type.	
Comments	All	A text that you can use for any purpose; it is purely internal, Forms Runtime never displays it, but it prints out if you generate documentation for the form. You usually put information about the object here that will be useful in maintaining the object.	
Communication Mode	Report, Chart Item	The style of communication— asynchronous or synchronous. Asynchronous communication returns control to the form immediately, and the report or graphic runs in a separate thread or process. Synchronous communication runs the report or graphic and does not return control until the report or graphic program has finished. For a chart item, the mode must be synchronous if you are updating the chart item in the form.	

TABLE 16-2. *Form Module Properties* (continued)

Property	Objects	Description	Get/Set
Compress	Sound Item	Whether to compress the sound object when reading it into the form. The default is to use the compression setting in the sound data file, if any.	
Compression Quality	Image Item	The level of compression to use when reading an image into the image item: None (the default), Minimum, Low, Medium, High, Maximum.	GS
Conceal Data	Text Item	Hides the characters the user types into the item. You use this property for passwords and the like. The default is No.	GS
Console Window	Form	The name of the window that displays the console or status bar at the bottom of the window. On Windows, the MDI application window always displays the console; however, you still must set this property in the form object to display the console status bar, even though it doesn't actually display in the named window. Setting the property to NULL suppresses the console. The default is WINDOW1.	
Control Help	ActiveX Control Item	Clicking on More displays the OCX help documentation, if any.	
Control Properties	ActiveX Control Item	Clicking on More displays the property sheet for the control.	
Coordinate System	Form	Clicking on More displays the Coordinate System dialog box, which lets you specify the type of coordinates (Character or the default Real), the Real Units (the default Point, Pixel, Inches, or Centimeters), and the Character Width and Height (default depending on the units). Use the character type only for character mode applications or if you require total portability between character and GUI systems.	

TABLE 16-2. *Form Module Properties* (continued)

Property	Objects	Description	Get/Set
Copy Value from Item	Item except for Push Button, Chart, and Image	The source of the value the Forms Runtime puts into the item when it creates the item. Use the <data block>.<item> notation. In a detail block item, the foreign key that maps to the master has this property specified with the name of the master item. The relation query then uses the master value to query the detail rows.	G
Current Record Visual Attribute Group	Form, Data Block, Item	The visual attribute to use to format an item when the item is part of the currently displayed data block record. Setting the property in a data block or form applies the property to all the items within the data block or form, respectively. You should avoid specifying the property at the form level, as it also affects toolbars and all other form elements.	GS
Cursor Mode	Form	Obsolete; do not use this property. Open, the default, keeps cursors open across transactions; Close closes cursors on commit or rollback.	GS
Custom Spacing	Text (Graphic)	Spaces the text on the canvas using Coordinate System units; default 0.	
Dash Style	Graphic	The style of the graphic's edge: Solid (the default), Dotted, Dashed, Dash Dot, Double Dot, Long Dash, or Dash Double Dot.	
Data Block Description	Data Block	Text describing the data block.	
Data Query	Hierarchical Tree	The query-based data source for the tree; default NULL.	
Data Source Data Block	Chart Item, Report	The source for report or graphics display data, replacing any internal data model in the report or graphics display module. A null value tells Forms Runtime to rely on the called module to get its own data for display.	

TABLE 16-2. *Form Module Properties* (continued)

Property	Objects	Description	Get/Set
Data Source X Axis	Chart Item	The data block column from which to take the values for the *x* axis of the graphic display.	
Data Source Y Axis	Chart Item	The data block column from which to take the values for the *y* axis of the graphic display.	
Data Type	Record Group, Parameter, various item types	Form Builder data type for the item or parameter or for a column in the record group. You specify a type for Check Box, Display, List, Radio Group, Text, and Custom Items. You should use only the CHAR, DATE, DATETIME, and NUMBER types (and BLOB, CLOB, NCLOB, and BFILE blob types). If the column is a database column, the types must be compatible. CHAR corresponds to VARCHAR2 but supports only 2000 characters. DATE is any valid date. DATETIME is any valid date and time. NUMBER corresponds to the database NUMBER type. The type is floating point, and you cannot put commas into the number.	
Database Block	Data Block	Whether the block gets data from the database (style depends on the DML Data Target Type property).	
Default Alert Button	Alert	Which alert button is the default button, the button visually distinguished from the others and the one that activates when the user takes the "default" action, whatever the platform defines as the Select action. Button 1 is the default, with Button 2 or Button 3 being alternatives.	
Default Button	Push Button Item	Whether this button item is the default button, the button visually distinguished from the others and the one that activates when the user takes the "default" action, whatever the platform defines as the Select action. The default is No.	

TABLE 16-2. *Form Module Properties* (continued)

Property	Objects	Description	Get/Set
Default Font Scaling	Form	Whether the form font uses the relative character scale of the display; default Yes.	
Defer Required Enforcement	Form	Whether to defer enforcing the item property Required until record validation occurs, allowing the user to navigate to other items but not out of the record or block. The default is No, but setting this to Yes can substantially improve the usability of your application.	GS
Deferred	Relation	Whether to defer fetching detail records when a coordination-causing event occurs. This property interacts with the Automatic property to determine coordination behavior.	
Delete Allowed	Data Block	Whether the user can delete records from the data block.	GS
Delete Procedure Arguments	Data Block	When the DML Data Target Type property is set to Procedure, this property contains the names, data types, and values of the arguments to pass to the stored procedure named in the Delete Procedure Name property for deleting data. Forms Runtime calls this procedure for the Delete Record action instead of generating an SQL DELETE statement. The default value is NULL.	
Delete Procedure Name	Data Block	When the DML Data Target Type property is set to Procedure, this property contains the name of the stored procedure to execute to delete a record. The Forms Runtime calls this procedure instead of generating an SQL DELETE statement. The default value is NULL. See the section "Procedural Encapsulation" in Chapter 6 for details on using procedures for deleting.	

TABLE 16-2. *Form Module Properties* (continued)

Property	Objects	Description	Get/Set
Delete Procedure Result Set Columns	Data Block	When the DML Data Target Type property is set to Procedure, clicking More on this property displays the Delete Procedure Result Set Columns dialog, which contains the names of the columns into which Forms Runtime copies the result set of the stored procedure. You would specify these if your delete stored procedure returned values, such as the deleted values or a result code.	
Delete Record Behavior	Relation	How Forms Runtime propagates a delete in the master record to its detail records: Non-Isolated (the default), Isolated, or Cascading. Non-Isolated means that the user cannot delete a master record while a detail record exists. Isolated means that the user can delete a master record without affecting the detail records (generally not a good idea). Cascading means that if the user deletes a master record, the Forms Runtime deletes the master's detail records.	GS
Detail Block	Relation	The name of the detail block.	G
Detail Reference Item	Relation	The REF item in the detail block that links to the master data block when Relation Type is REF.	GS
Direction	Various	Specifies the direction of the layout for the object: Default, Right-to-Left, Left-to-Right. Applies to Form, Alert, Data Block, LOV, Window, Canvas, Check Box, Button, Radio Group, and List Item.	GS

TABLE 16-2. *Form Module Properties* (continued)

Property	Objects	Description	Get/Set
Display Hint Automatically	Item except for Chart, Display, and Custom Items	Whether to display the text from the Hint property automatically when the input focus enters the item; default Yes. If you set this to No, the Forms Runtime displays the hint only when the input focus is on the item and the user selects Help. If the Hint property is NULL, this property has no effect.	GS
Display in 'Keyboard Help'	Trigger	Whether to display the text in the Keyboard Help Description field in the Forms Runtime Keys help screen; default No.	
Display Quality	Image Item	The level of quality Forms Runtime uses to display the image: High (the default), Medium, or Low. If you are having resource limitation problems such as low GDI resources on Windows systems, you can reduce resource consumption by setting this property to Medium or Low.	
Distance Between Records	Item	The amount of space in Coordinate System units between instances of items in a multiple-record data block (Number of Records Displayed is greater than 1); default 0.	
Dither	Image (Graphic)	Whether to dither (smooth gradations of color) in a boilerplate image.	

TABLE 16-2. *Form Module Properties* (continued)

Property	Objects	Description	Get/Set
DML Array Size	Data Block	The maximum size of the array the Forms Runtime uses to send data to the database during an insert, update, or delete; default 1. The larger the array size, the less network traffic occurs but the more memory gets used. If you have lots of memory and many multiple-record transactions, increase this property value to the expected number of records a user modifies in a single transaction. If Insert Allowed is Yes and you set array size greater than 1, you must specify a primary key using the Enforce Primary Key and Primary Key properties because Forms Runtime can't get a rowid when doing array data manipulation. Also, the Update Changed Columns Only property is always No if you set the array size greater than 1, since the array must have all the columns for each record. Finally, if there is large-object or image data in the record, the size may prevent the Forms Runtime from using an array.	
DML Data Target Name	Data Block	The name of the table you want to insert into, delete from, and update; default NULL, and the value is valid only if you set the DML Data Target Type property to Table. You use this property to manipulate a table while querying from a view or procedure in the data block. You can also use the Get and Set built-in subprograms to change the table name at runtime (though you need to be pretty careful with this kind of programming).	GS

TABLE 16-2. *Form Module Properties* (continued)

Property	Objects	Description	Get/Set
DML Data Target Type	Data Block	The kind of target for insert, update, and delete for the data block: Table (the default), Procedure, or Transactional Trigger. You can set the table name in the DML Data Target Name property. If you specify Procedure, you must supply procedure names and arguments in the Insert, Update, and Delete Procedure properties.	G
Edge Background Color	Graphic	The background color of the graphic's edge; default NULL.	
Edge Foreground Color	Graphic	The foreground color of the graphic's edge; default NULL.	
Edge Pattern	Graphic	The pattern of the graphic's edge; default NULL.	
Editor	Text Item	The editor to use when editing the text, default NULL meaning use the default Forms Runtime editor. If you specify SYSTEM_EDITOR, the Forms Runtime looks up the FORMS60_EDITOR registry variable and uses the program you specify there to edit the text. Otherwise, you can specify the name of an editor object you've defined in the form module.	G
Editor X Position	Text Item	The horizontal, x-axis coordinate of the upper left corner of the text editor in the Editor property, overriding the Editor object's Position property value. The default value 0 means use the Editor Position property.	G
Editor Y Position	Text Item	The vertical, y-axis coordinate of the upper left corner of the text editor in the Editor property, overriding the Editor object's Position property value. The default value 0 means use the Editor Position property.	G

TABLE 16-2. *Form Module Properties* (continued)

Property	Objects	Description	Get/Set
Elements in List	List Item	Clicking on More displays the Elements in List dialog box, which lets you enter labels and values for each list element. If a List Item Value is blank, the value is NULL.	
Enabled	Tab Page	Whether to display the tab page as usual (Yes, the default) or to gray it out (No).	GS
Enabled (Item)	Item except for Push Button, Chart, and Display Items	Whether the user can manipulate the item with the mouse; default Yes. Setting this property to No grays out the item. If you want the item not grayed but not changeable, use the Insert Allowed and Update Allowed properties set to No. Setting Enabled to No also sets the Keyboard Navigable property to No.	GS
End Angle	Arc	The ending angle of the arc using the horizontal axis as an origin; default 180.	
Enforce Column Security	Data Block	Whether Forms Runtime should look in the database for the user's update privileges on a column to determine whether to allow the user to update the corresponding item in the data block by turning off the Update Allowed item property when starting up the form; default No.	G
Enforce Primary Key	Data Block	Whether to check the values of the designated primary key before inserting or updating the row in the database; default No. You use this when the underlying table does not have a PRIMARY KEY constraint defined but one must be enforced, or when you set the DML Array Size greater than 1 and allow inserts. If you set this property to Yes, you must set the Primary Key property for at least one item in the data block to Yes.	GS

TABLE 16-2. *Form Module Properties* (continued)

Property	Objects	Description	Get/Set
Enterable	Data Block	Whether the user can navigate to an item in the block; this property defaults to Yes but is automatically set to No if there is no enterable item in the block (an item with Keyboard Navigable set to Yes).	
Execution Hierarchy	Trigger	When to execute the current trigger when there are other triggers with the same name at a higher level in the object hierarchy: Override (the default), Before, or After. Override executes the current trigger only. Before executes the current trigger, then the higher-level triggers. After executes the higher-level triggers, then executes the current trigger. Oracle recommends using this feature only with lots of care and testing, as it can produce applications that are difficult to maintain.	
Execution Mode	Chart Item or Report	The way Forms Runtime executes a report or graphic display: Batch (the default) or Runtime. Batch mode executes the report or display with no user interaction, while Runtime enables user interaction.	
Filename	Form, Chart Item	The name of the form or graphics display module file. You can't set this; Form Builder sets it when it reads the form module from the file. It corresponds to the application property Current_Form.	G
Fill	Arc	The fill shape of the arc: Pie (the default) or Chord. The Pie fill renders the arc from the center point of the circle. The Chord fill renders the arc from a line segment drawn from one end point to the other end point.	

TABLE 16-2. *Form Module Properties* (continued)

Property	Objects	Description	Get/Set
Fill Pattern	Item, Tab Page, Canvas, Window	The pattern to use to fill the object (defaults to no pattern).	GS
Filter Before Display	LOV	Whether to display a Query Criteria dialog box before displaying the LOV (default No). The user can enter values into the dialog box to further restrict the query, and the LOV appends the criterion to the SQL statement from the record group.	
Fire in Enter-Query Mode	Trigger	Whether to execute the trigger in Enter Query mode; default No. This property takes effect only for certain triggers: Key-<function key>, On-Error, On-Message, and When-<event> triggers except for When-Database-Record, When-Image-Activated, When-New-Block-Instance, When-New-Form-Instance, When-Create-Record, When-Remove-Record, When-Validate-Record, and When-Validate-Item	
First Navigation Data Block	Form	The name of the block to which Forms Runtime navigates when it opens the form; defaults to the first block in the form in the Object Navigator. You can either arrange the blocks in the order you like or set this property, but generally you set this property programmatically in the When-New-Form-Instance trigger to change the behavior of the form module.	GS
Fixed Bounding Box	Text (Graphic)	Whether the text's bounding box should remain fixed; default No (it expands to contain the text you enter). If this property is Yes, the Width and Height properties determine the size of the bounding box.	

TABLE 16-2. *Form Module Properties* (continued)

Property	Objects	Description	Get/Set
Fixed Length	Text Item	Forces the user to enter the number of characters that the Maximum Length property specifies, making the field a specific, constant length field. Default is No.	GS
Font Name	Item, Tab Page, Canvas, Window	The font family to use for text in the object.	GS
Font Size	Item, Tab Page, Canvas, Window	The font size to use for text in the object.	GS
Font Spacing	Form	If the Coordinate System is set to Character, this property specifies whether the form fonts default to the relative character scale of the display device at runtime.	
Font Spacing	Item, Tab Page, Canvas, Window	The width of the font. The default is Unspecified, meaning use the default font setting.	GS
Font Style	Item, Tab Page, Canvas, Window	The style of the font: Plain, Italic, Oblique, Underline, Outline, Shadow, Inverted, Overstrike, or Blink. The default is <Unspecified>, meaning use the default font setting.	GS
Font Weight	Item, Tab Page, Canvas, Window	The font weight: Ultralight, Extralight, Light, Demilight, Medium, Demibold, Bold, Extrabold, or Ultrabold. The default is <Unspecified>, meaning use the default font setting.	GS
Foreground Color	Item, Tab Page, Canvas, Window	The color of the object's foreground; for items, the color of the text the item displays.	GS

TABLE 16-2.   *Form Module Properties* (continued)

Property	Objects	Description	Get/Set
Form Horizontal Toolbar Canvas	Form	The canvas that displays as a horizontal toolbar on the MDI application window (Microsoft Windows only). The canvas must have Canvas Type set to Horizontal Toolbar.	
Form Vertical Toolbar Canvas	Form	The canvas that displays as a vertical toolbar on the MDI application window (Microsoft Windows only). The canvas must have Canvas Type set to Vertical Toolbar.	
Format Mask	Text Item	The format in which the item displays text; also the format in which the item requires text to be for input. See the later section "Format Masks" for a detailed reference to the syntax of format masks.	GS
Formula	Item	A PL/SQL expression (not a statement—don't enter a semicolon or create an assignment statement here) that Forms Runtime uses to calculate a value for the item when Calculation Mode is Formula. There is no default expression.	
Frame Alignment	Frame	How to align objects within the width of the frame: Fill (the default), Start, End, Center, or Column. Only takes effect when Layout Style is Form.	
Frame Title	Frame	The text that the frame displays in its border; default NULL.	
Frame Title Alignment	Frame	The alignment of the text from the Frame Title property: Start (the default), End, Center. Relative to the canvas Direction property.	
Frame Title Font Background Color	Frame	The color in which to display the background of the text from the Frame Title property. The default is the standard operating system color, usually black.	

TABLE 16-2. *Form Module Properties* (continued)

Property	Objects	Description	Get/Set
Frame Title Font Foreground Color	Frame	The color in which to display the text from the Frame Title property. The default is the standard operating system color, usually black.	
Frame Title Font Name	Frame	The name of the font in which to display the text from the Frame Title property. The default is the standard operating system font.	
Frame Title Font Size	Frame	The size of the font in which to display the text from the Frame Title property. The default is the standard operating system font size.	
Frame Title Font Spacing	Frame	The spacing between characters of the font in which to display the text from the Frame Title property. The default is the standard operating system font spacing.	
Frame Title Font Style	Frame	The style of the font in which to display the text from the Frame Title property (Italic, for example). The default is the standard operating system font style.	
Frame Title Font Weight	Frame	The weight of the font in which to display the text from the Frame Title property (Bold, for example). The default is the standard operating system font weight.	
Frame Title Offset	Frame	The distance of the frame title (see the Frame Title property) from the corner of the frame; defaults to 2 characters in the Coordinate System units.	
Frame Title Reading Order	Frame	The direction in which the frame title displays (see the Frame Title property): Default, Left-to-Right, or Right-to-Left.	

TABLE 16-2.   *Form Module Properties* (continued)

Property	Objects	Description	Get/Set
Frame Title Spacing	Frame	The amount of space to reserve on each side of the frame's title; default is 1 character in the Coordinate System's units. This space does not visually overlay the frame border, which extends right up to the edge of the text, but the text starts further along from the frame edge by this amount of space.	
Frame Title Visual Attribute Group	Frame	The named visual attribute from which to obtain the various font, color, and fill settings for the frame title. See the section "Named Visual Attributes" in Chapter 10.	
Graphics Type	Graphics	The type of graphic: Arc, Chart, Group, Image, Line, Polygon, Rectangle, Rounded Rectangle, Symbol, Text.	
Height	Canvas, Item, Editor, LOV, Window	The height of the object in Coordinate System units; the default varies with the kind of object.	GS
Hide on Exit	Window	For a modeless (as opposed to modal) window, whether to hide the window when the user navigates to an item in another window; default No.	GS
Highest Allowed Value	Text Item	The maximum value the user can enter (alphabetical, numeric, or date/time order); default NULL.	G
Hint	Item	Text that Forms Runtime displays on the console or status bar when the input focus is in the item. The default is "Enter value for: <item>" if you created the item with the Data Block Wizard, or NULL if not.	G
Horizontal Justification	Graphic Text	Justification of the text object: Start (the default), End, Left, Right, Center.	

TABLE 16-2. *Form Module Properties* (continued)

Property	Objects	Description	Get/Set
Horizontal Margin	Frame	The distance between the left and right borders of the frame and the objects within the frame (the margin); default is 1 character in the Coordinate System's units.	
Horizontal Object Offset	Frame	The horizontal distance between objects; default is 2 characters in the Coordinate System's units.	
Horizontal Origin	Graphic Text	The horizontal position of the text object relative to the origin point: Left (the default), Right, Center.	
Horizontal Toolbar Canvas	Window	The canvas to display as a horizontal toolbar on the window. The canvas must have its Canvas Type property set to the Horizontal Toolbar and must have its Window property set to this window. Default NULL.	
Icon Filename	Push Button Item, Window	The name of the icon file that contains the bitmap icon to display. Don't add an extension, and use the UI60_ICON registry variable to specify a path for all the icon files.	GS
Iconic	Push Button Item	Make the button an iconic button—a button with an icon instead of text on the button; default No. If this property is Yes, the Icon Filename property determines the icon to display.	G
Image Depth	Image Item	The style of image to display: Original (the default), Monochrome, Gray, LUT (lookup table), RGB.	GS
Image Format	Image Item	The format in which to store the image in the database: TIFF (default), BMP, CALS, GIF, JFIF, PICT, RAS, TPIC. This format replaces the original format of the item.	G

TABLE 16-2.   *Form Module Properties* (continued)

Property	Objects	Description	Get/Set
Implementation Class	Bean Area, Check Box, List, Push Button, Radio Group, Text Items	The class name of a JavaBean for the Bean Area or a custom implementation for any of the other items. There is no default.	
Include REF Item	Data Block	For a master data block, include a special, hidden item called REF in this block to coordinate a master-detail relationship built on a REF link; default No.	
Inherit Menu	Window	Whether the window should display the form menu; applies on platforms that support window menus. Default Yes.	
Initial Keyboard State	Display, Text Items	Sets the keyboard state so the user can begin to type immediately without switching keyboard state: Default (see Reading Order property), Local (right-to-left), Roman (left-to-right).	
Initial Menu	Form	The name of the menu in the menu module to use as the form menu; default blank. Specifying a name here lets you override the default menu in the menu module in the Main Menu property with another menu in that module, giving you a way to display different menus for different invocations of the form.	
Initial Value	Check Box, Display, List, Radio Group, Text, and User Area Items	The default value to assign to the item when creating a New record; default NULL. You can supply a value (number, string, date), a form item (:<block name>.<item name>, a global variable (:GLOBAL.<name>), a parameter (:PARAMETER.<name>), or a sequence (:SEQUENCE.<name>.NEXTVAL).	

TABLE 16-2. *Form Module Properties* (continued)

Property	Objects	Description	Get/Set
Insert Allowed (Block)	Data Block, Item	Whether the user can insert records in a data block or modify the item in a New record; default Yes. Setting this property to No for an item lets you prevent users from entering or changing the field without having to disable that field.	GS
Insert Procedure Arguments	Data Block	When the DML Data Target Type property is set to Procedure, this property contains the names, data types, and values of the arguments to pass to the stored procedure named in the Insert Procedure Name property for inserting data. Forms Runtime calls this procedure for the Insert Record action instead of generating an SQL INSERT statement. The default value is NULL.	
Insert Procedure Name	Data Block	When the DML Data Target Type property is set to Procedure, this property contains the name of the stored procedure to execute to insert a record. Forms Runtime calls this procedure instead of generating an SQL INSERT statement. The default value is NULL. See the section "Procedural Encapsulation" in Chapter 6 for details on using procedures for inserting.	
Insert Procedure Result Set Columns	Data Block	When the DML Data Target Type property is set to Procedure, clicking More on this property displays the Insert Procedure Result Set Columns dialog, which contains the names of the columns into which Forms Runtime copies the result set of the stored procedure. You would specify these if your insert stored procedure returned values, such as the new values or a result code.	

TABLE 16-2.   *Form Module Properties* (continued)

Property	Objects	Description	Get/Set
Interaction Mode	Form	How the user interacts with the form during a query: Blocking (the default) or Non-Blocking. Blocking prevents users from resizing or doing anything else to the form until the query results are fetched. Non-Blocking lets the user interact with the form during fetching. It is most useful for queries that take a long time to return records.	G
Isolation Mode	Form	How to conduct a transaction: Read Committed (the default) or Serializable. You will almost always want to leave this property set to Read Committed. If you set it to Serializable, Forms Runtime sets the database session isolation so that the transaction is guaranteed to be serializable with respect to all other transactions. Practically speaking, this means that if one user queries and updates a row without committing it, and another user comes along and updates the row and commits it before the first user, when the first user commits, he or she gets Oracle error ORA-08177: Cannot serialize access. You should set Locking Mode to Delayed if you want to use Serializable. You should use Serializable only if there isn't much chance of overlapping updates.	
Item Type	Item	The kind of item: Text Item (the default), ActiveX Control, Bean Area, Chart Item, Check Box, Display Item, Hierarchical Tree, Image, List Item, OLE Container, Push Button, Radio Group, Sound, Text Item, User Area, VBX Control.	

TABLE 16-2. *Form Module Properties* (continued)

Property	Objects	Description	Get/Set
Join Condition	Relation	An expression that defines the link between a master data block and a detail data block.	
Join Style	Graphic	The way two lines join together in a graphic: Mitre (the default), Bevel, or Round.	
Justification	Display and Text Items	The text justification within the item: Start (the default), End, Left, Center, Right.	GS
Keep Cursor Position	Text Item	Saves the position of the cursor when the user leaves the text item and restores it when the user returns to the item; default No.	GS
Key Mode	Data Block	How Forms Runtime identifies a row in the database (the key) for non-Oracle data sources: Automatic (the default), Non-Updateable, Unique, Updateable. Oracle uses the ROWID to identify rows; other databases use primary key values. Automatic uses ROWID if available and primary key if no. Non-Updateable key mode does not include primary key columns in an UPDATE SET clause, so you can't update the primary key columns in the database. Unique always uses the ROWID. Updateable lets the user update primary key values. If you are using Non-Updateable or Updateable, you need to set Enforce Primary Key to Yes, and you must designate at least one item as part of the primary key with the Primary Key property of the item set to Yes. Use this property when you are using non-Oracle databases.	GS

TABLE 16-2. *Form Module Properties* (continued)

Property	Objects	Description	Get/Set
'Keyboard Help' Text	Trigger	The text that appears in the Keys help screen if you set Display in Keyboard Help to Yes; default blank, meaning display the default description of the key.	
Keyboard Navigable	Item except Chart and Display Items	Whether the user or Forms Runtime can move the focus to the item during navigation; default Yes. If you set this property to No, Forms Runtime skips over the item and enters the next navigable item in the navigation sequence. If you set the Enabled property to No, the Form Builder also sets Keyboard Navigable to No. The reverse is not true, however; setting Enabled to Yes does not set Keyboard Navigable to Yes, so you have to change it explicitly or you won't be able to navigate into the item. You can use Go_Item to navigate to an item with Keyboard Navigable set to No. If you use the built-in subprograms to set Keyboard Navigable at an instance level, it has no effect unless the Item level property is set to the same value.	GS
Keyboard State	Item	Sets the supported international keyboard states: Any (the default), Roman Only, or Local Only. The user can use a key to toggle between keyboard states.	
Label	Push Button, Check Box, and Radio Button Items, Tab Page	The text label that a button, check box, or radio button displays or that a tab page displays in its tab.	GS

TABLE 16-2. *Form Module Properties* (continued)

Property	Objects	Description	Get/Set
Last Query	Data Block	The SQL statement that Forms Runtime issued for the last query of the data block.	G
Layout Data Block	Frame	The data block that owns the items that the frame arranges; there can be only one frame per block and one block per frame; default NULL.	
Layout Style	Frame	The way the frame lays out the items: Form (the default) or Tabular. In Form style, the frame arranges the items in two columns with prompts to the left of each item. In Tabular style, the frame arranges the items next to each other across the row with prompts above each item.	
Line Spacing	Graphic Text	The line spacing within the text object: Single (the default), One-and-a-half, Double, Custom (see the Custom Spacing property).	
Line Width	Graphic	The width of the edge of the graphic object in points.	
List Item Value	Radio Button Item	The value of the radio group item when this radio button in the group is set; default NULL (a NULL value).	
List Style	List Item	The kind of list item: Poplist (the default), Combo Box, or Tlist. The poplist is a drop-down list, the combo box is a standard combo box drop-down list, and the Tlist is a scrolling list of elements. The data structure remains the same for all types of lists.	
List Type	LOV	How to refer to the record group: Record Group (the default) or Old (an old-style LOV, no longer supported for new applications). If the value is Record Group, you must choose the record group in the Record Group property.	

TABLE 16-2. *Form Module Properties* (continued)

Property	Objects	Description	Get/Set
List of Values	Text Item	The name of the LOV to display for the text item when the user presses the LOV key or menu item. When you associate an LOV with an item, Forms Runtime displays a message on the console status line indicating that there is an LOV for the item.	G
List X Position	Text Item	For an item with an LOV in the List of Values property, the horizontal position of the upper left corner of the LOV with respect to the screen; default 0. If both X and Y positions are 0, the display coordinates of the LOV object take precedence.	G
List Y Position	Text Item	For an item with an LOV in the List of Values property, the horizontal position of the upper left corner of the LOV with respect to the screen; default 0. If both X and Y positions are 0, the display coordinates of the LOV object take precedence.	G
Listed in Block Menu/ Block Description	Data Block	Whether to list the data block in the block menu the user can access by pressing the Block Menu key. The menu permits the user to navigate to the first item in the block by choosing it from this menu. The text comes from the Block Description property.	

TABLE 16-2. *Form Module Properties* (continued)

Property	Objects	Description	Get/Set
Lock Procedure Arguments	Data Block	When the DML Data Target Type property is set to Procedure, this property contains the names, data types, and values of the arguments to pass to the stored procedure named in the Lock Procedure Name property for locking a row of data. Forms Runtime calls this procedure for the Lock Record action instead of generating an SQL SELECT FOR UPDATE statement. The default value is NULL.	
Lock Procedure Name	Data Block	When the DML Data Target Type property is set to Procedure, this property contains the name of the stored procedure to execute to lock a row. Forms Runtime calls this procedure instead of generating an SQL SELECT FOR UPDATE statement. The default value is NULL.	
Lock Procedure Result Set Columns	Data Block	When the DML Data Target Type property is set to Procedure, clicking More on this property displays the Lock Procedure Result Set Columns dialog, which contains the names of the columns into which Forms Runtime copies the result set of the stored procedure. You would specify these if your locking stored procedure returned values, such as a result code.	

TABLE 16-2.   *Form Module Properties* (continued)

Property	Objects	Description	Get/Set
Lock Record	Text Item	Whether to try to lock the database row when the user or a trigger modifies the item value; default No. You use this property to lock the database row for changes to an item that is not a database item.	GS
Locking Mode	Data Block	When Forms Runtime tries to acquire database locks on rows: Automatic (the default), Immediate, or Delayed. Automatic and Immediate are the same for an Oracle server: Forms Runtime locks the row as soon as the user changes the value in a text item or presses the Lock Record key. Delayed means that the Forms Runtime locks the row only when actually in the process of posting the record to the database. Mostly, you should use Automatic, the default. However, if you run into locking issues in high-transaction-rate environments or you want to set Isolation Mode to Serializable, you should set Locking Mode to Delayed. If another transaction modifies the value between the query and the commit, however, Forms Runtime will give the user an error message and fail to commit. The user will then need to execute the commit again.	GS
Lowest Allowed Value	Text Item	The low value in a range constraint on the text. If the value entered is less than this value, the Forms Runtime validation process fails. The value can be a constant, a form item (:block name>.<item name>), a global variable (:GLOBAL.<name>), or a parameter (:PARAMETER.<name>).	G

TABLE 16-2. *Form Module Properties* (continued)

Property	Objects	Description	Get/Set
Mapping of Other Values	List and Radio Group Items	The value to set the item to when something assigns a value not in the list or not one of the associated radio button values; default blank, meaning that the Forms Runtime should not allow other values. Note: If you leave this choice blank and a query returns a value not in the list or radio buttons, Forms Runtime silently rejects the record, and the user never sees it. This can be confusing if you allow entry of other values through some other method.	
Maximize Allowed	Window	Whether the user can zoom, or maximize, the window by using the window manager function to do that; default Yes.	
Maximum Length	Parameter, Items except Push Button, Image, and Chart Items	The maximum length in characters of a parameter of type CHAR or items of any type. The default is 30 for parameters. For items, the default depends on the type and state of other properties. Generally, for database items the default is the size of the corresponding database column. If the type is NUMBER, Form Builder adds 2 to accommodate the sign and decimal point. LONG items default to 240 bytes. If there is a Format Mask, or if there is an implicit format mask such as for dates, the Forms Runtime extends the maximum length to accommodate the size of the mask. If you are using a multiple-byte character set, the length is in bytes, not characters, but truncation occurs to the nearest character and Forms Runtime displays a warning.	

TABLE 16-2.   *Form Module Properties* (continued)

Property	Objects	Description	Get/Set
Maximum Objects Per Line	Frame	The greatest number of objects that may appear on each line in the frame; default 0, meaning that there is no maximum. For this property to be valid, you must set the Frame Style property to Form and the Vertical Fill property to No. You can use this property to achieve greater control over the layout of the frame.	
Maximum Query Time	Form, Data Block	If the Query All Records property is set to Yes, this property tells Forms Runtime to give the user the option to cancel a query when the elapsed time exceeds the value of this property.	
Maximum Records Fetched	Form, Data Block	If the Query Allowed and Query All Records properties are set to Yes, this property aborts the query at runtime when the number of records fetched exceeds the value given. This puts a limit on a potentially intractable query.	
Menu Module	Form	The name of the menu module to use with this form. If you set this to Default, Forms Runtime runs the built-in menu. If you set it to NULL, Forms Runtime does not display a menu. If you set Menu Source to Yes, the Menu Module property is the name of the compiled .MMX file. If you set Menu Source to No, this property specifies the name of the menu module in the database. See also the Initial Menu property to set a specific menu within the menu module as the main menu.	

TABLE 16-2.   *Form Module Properties* (continued)

Property	Objects	Description	Get/Set
Menu Role	Form	The security role that Form Builder should use to run the menu; obsolete. Set the Use Security property to No to turn off menu security instead of setting the role to a special "testing" role.	
Menu Source	Form	Whether to use direct reference to the .MMX file (Yes, the default) or to look up the menu in the database (No). If you set this property to Yes, you should supply the name of the .MMX menu module file in the Menu Module property. If you set it to No, you use the menu module properties to specify the filename of the .MMX file.	
Menu Style	Form	The kind of menus to display: Pull-down (the default), Full-Screen, or Bar. You should usually leave this property set to Pull-down. Full-Screen is a 3270-style full-screen menu that character-mode applications use; Bar is a Lotus 1-2-3, old-style DOS-type menu.	
Message	Alert	The text of the message to display (no default).	S
Minimize Allowed	Window	Whether the user can iconify the window; default Yes.	
Minimized Title	Window	The text that appears before an iconified/minimized window.	
Modal	Window	Whether the user can change the focus to another window without dismissing this one; default No. You use this property to create a modal dialog box along with the Window Style property set to Dialog.	

TABLE 16-2.   *Form Module Properties* (continued)

Property	Objects	Description	Get/Set
Mouse Navigate	Push Button, Check Box, List, and Radio Group Items	Whether to navigate to an item (move the cursor focus to the item) when the user clicks on the item with a mouse. If you set this property to No, Forms Runtime does not perform any navigation (and hence validation) processes, just the When-Button-Pressed or similar triggers. You can use this behavior, for example, to create arrays of buttons that issue commands without doing any navigation, similar to a toolbar.	GS
Mouse Navigation Limit	Form	How far outside the item with the current focus the user can navigate with the mouse: Form (the default), Block, Record, Item. Block means the user can navigate only to items within the current data block with the mouse. Record means the user can go only to items within the current record in the data block. Item means the user can't navigate out of the current item with the mouse.	
Move Allowed	Window	Whether the user may move the window to another location on the screen (or whether code in a trigger may do so).	
Multi-Line	Text Item	Whether the text item allows multiple lines (Yes) or not (No, the default). If you set the item to multiple lines, you must size it and set the font and Maximum Length properties to display the appropriate amount of text. You should also look at the Wrap Style and the Show Vertical Scroll Bar properties. Also, you can only set this for CHAR, ALPHA, or LONG data types. Finally, if you press ENTER in a single-line item, you navigate out of the item; in a multiple-line item, you insert a line return and do not navigate out of the item.	

TABLE 16-2. *Form Module Properties* (continued)

Property	Objects	Description	Get/Set
Multi-Selection	Hierarchical Tree	Whether the user can select multiple nodes at once; No (the default) means that selecting a node deselects the currently selected node, Yes means the user can select multiple nodes.	
Name	All Objects	The name of the object; no default. The name can be up to 30 characters, must begin with a letter, and may contain letters, numbers, and the special characters $, #, @, and _. Case does not matter. Names are unique within the kind of object.	
Navigation Style	Data Block	On Next Item or Previous Item operations, how to proceed when the focus is on the last or first navigable item in the data block, respectively: Same Record (the default), Change Record, Change Block. Same Record moves the focus to the first navigable item in the same data block and in the same record. Change Record moves the focus to the first navigable item in the same data block in the next record (or in a new record if there is no next record). Change Block moves to the first navigable item in the next or previous block.	GS
Next Navigation Block	Data Block	The name of the data block to which Forms Runtime will navigate when the focus moves to the next data block. By default, the next data block is the next one in the order they appear in the Object Navigator. You use this property to change the navigation order without reordering the data blocks in the Navigator. You use this property primarily programmatically to change data block navigation order at runtime.	GS

TABLE 16-2. *Form Module Properties* (continued)

Property	Objects	Description	Get/Set
Next Navigation Item	Data Block	The name of the item to which Forms Runtime will navigate when it moves the focus to the next item. By default, the next item is the one next in sequence in the Object Navigator. You set this property programmatically or in Form Builder if you want to redefine the sequence without reordering the items within the data block.	GS
Number of Items Displayed	Item	The number of item instances (individual item fields) that the multiple-record data block displays. This number overrides the Number of Records Displayed for the data block, allowing you to create a single button within a multiple-record data block. You usually don't want to make this item a database item.	
Number of Records Buffered	Data Block	The minimum number of records that Forms Runtime buffers in memory during a query in the data block; default is NULL, meaning that Forms Runtime uses the Number of Records Displayed property plus a constant of 3. Additional records get buffered to a temporary disk file. You can trade off memory versus disk performance using this property, or you can manage data blocks that have a large number of records to improve performance by increasing this property. You can also manage data blocks with large items (controls, charts, and the like) by reducing the property and hence the memory consumption for the set of records.	

TABLE 16-2. *Form Module Properties* (continued)

Property	Objects	Description	Get/Set
Number of Records Displayed	Data Block	The maximum number of records the data block displays at once; default 1. If you set this property to a number greater than 1, you create a multiple-record data block.	
OLE Activation Style	OLE Container	The event that activates the OLE containing item: Double Click (the default), Focus-in, Manual. Double Click activates the object by double-clicking anywhere in the object. Focus-in means that navigating into the OLE object activates the object. Manual means that the user activates the object by an explicit Edit or Open menu item from the OLE pop-up menu, and you must set the Show OLE Popup Menu property to Yes and the Object menu to display in the menu module.	
OLE Class	OLE Container	What class of OLE objects may reside in the item: NULL (the default) or a named class. NULL means that the user may insert any kind of OLE object from the OLE registration database at runtime. Specifying a class limits the user to that class rather than permitting any kind of OLE class.	
OLE In-place Activation	OLE Container	Whether to make in-place activation available; default No. Setting the property to Yes turns on the ability to edit embedded OLE objects; No forces external activation using the object server.	

TABLE 16-2. *Form Module Properties* (continued)

Property	Objects	Description	Get/Set
OLE Inside-Out Support	OLE Container	If OLE In-place Activation is set to Yes, this property turns on inside-out object support in the OLE server, allowing for more than one embedded object to have an active editing window within the OLE container item.	
OLE Popup Menu Items	OLE Container	Which OLE pop-up menu commands to display, selected from a list. You must set the Display and Enable options, where Display puts the command in the menu and Enable allows the user to choose it.	GS
OLE Resize Style	OLE Container	How the Forms Runtime displays the OLE object in the item: Clip (the default), Scale, Initial, and Dynamic. Clip crops the OLE object to fit the container item. Scale scales the object to fit into the container. Initial resizes the object to fit only when the user creates the object; Dynamic resizes the object whenever its size changes.	
OLE Tenant Aspect	OLE Container	How an OLE object appears in the container: Content (the default), ICO, or Thumbnail. Content displays the object contents. ICO displays an icon representing the object. Thumbnail displays a "thumbnail," or reduced view, of the object. The property must have the same value that existed when the OLE object was saved when you query the saved object into the container, or the object is automatically locked.	

TABLE 16-2.   *Form Module Properties* (continued)

Property	Objects	Description	Get/Set
OLE Tenant Types	OLE Container	The type of OLE objects that the user has permission to set into the container: Any (the default), None, Static, Embedded, or Linked. The Any setting means that any object may tenant the container. None means that no object may tenant the container. Static means that only snapshot images of linked OLE objects may tenant the container (the link is broken and the user cannot modify the object). Embedded means that only an embedded OLE object may tenant the container. Linked means that only a linked OLE object may tenant the container.	
Optimizer Hint	Data Block	A hint string that Forms Runtime adds to the query; consult the Oracle SQL reference and database administrator documents for details on optimizer hint syntax.	GS
Order By	Data Block	A string to append to the SQL SELECT that the Forms Runtime generates to add an ORDER BY clause. You can list any database item in the data block in a comma-separated list of items on which to sort the queried data. You can prefix the list with the words "ORDER BY," but this is not required.	GS
Other Reports Parameters	Report Object	A list of parameters to include in the running of the report; default blank. Each element of the list is in the format <keyword>=<value>, where <keyword> is any of the Reports Runtime command line keywords.	

TABLE 16-2. *Form Module Properties* (continued)

Property	Objects	Description	Get/Set
Parameter Data Type	Parameter	The data type of the parameter: CHAR (the default), DATE, or NUMBER. See the Data Type property for details.	
Parameter Initial Value	Parameter	The literal value to assign to the parameter when the form starts up. The value must be compatible with the Parameter Data Type property.	
PL/SQL Library Location	Attached Library	The path to the attached library; if the property contains only the library name, Forms Runtime uses the FORMS60_PATH variable to resolve the reference to the library; if the property contains the full path, Forms Runtime looks only in that one location. This property is informational only; you cannot change it.	
PL/SQL Library Source	Attached Library	Whether the attached library comes from a file (File) or from the database (Database). This property is informational only; you cannot change it.	
Popup Menu	Item, Canvas	The name of the pop-up menu object to display for the canvas or item; default NULL (no pop-up menu).	
Precompute Summaries	Data Block	Whether to compute the value of any summarized item before issuing a query on the block; default No. Forms Runtime issues a special query with the summary operations (count, sum, and so on) to select all the records in the block and compute the summary value. You must set this property to Yes if the block contains summarized items and the Query All Records property is No. Forms Runtime fires the Pre-Select trigger twice, once just before executing the summary query and again before executing a normal query. The Pre-Query trigger fires only once, before the special query.	

TABLE 16-2. *Form Module Properties* (continued)

Property	Objects	Description	Get/Set
Prevent Masterless Operation	Relation	Whether the user can query or insert records in a detail data block when there is no master record in the master block; default No. If you set this property to Yes, and there is no queried master record, the user cannot query detail records.	GS
Previous Navigation Block	Data Block	The name of the data block to which Forms Runtime will navigate when the focus moves to the previous data block. By default, the previous data block is the prior one in the order they appear in the Object Navigator. You use this property to change the navigation order without reordering the data blocks in the Navigator. You use this property primarily programmatically to change data block navigation order at runtime.	GS
Previous Navigation Item	Item	The name of the item to which Forms Runtime will navigate when it moves the focus to the previous item. By default, the previous item is the one prior in sequence in the Object Navigator. You set this property programmatically or in Form Builder if you want to redefine the sequence without reordering the items within the data block.	GS
Primary Canvas	Window	The name of the canvas that the Forms Runtime will try to display first in the window; default NULL. If you navigate to an item in another canvas, the Forms Runtime displays that canvas, not this primary canvas. You only need to set this property if you are displaying a window using Show_Window rather than through standard navigation. Generally, you should use navigation to display windows.	

TABLE 16-2.   *Form Module Properties* (continued)

Property	Objects	Description	Get/Set
Primary Key	Items except Push Buttons, Chart Items, and Image Items	Whether the item is a primary key column in the base table for the data block; default No. The item must be a database item. The Enforce Primary Key property for the data block must be set to Yes. Forms Runtime will query the table to ensure that the combination of items marked as primary key items is unique in the table. You would usually not specify this property; instead, you should use PRIMARY KEY constraints on the server to enforce the primary key. This property does give you the ability to enforce the constraint when you cannot use the server constraint (for example, if you are using a legacy database to which you cannot add the constraint). See the Key Mode property; if you set this to Non-Updateable or Updateable, you will need to set Primary Key to Yes for at least one item in the data block. Also, if you set DML Array Size greater than 1 and Insert Allowed is Yes, you must specify a primary key using the Enforce Primary Key and Primary Key properties because Forms Runtime can't get a rowid when doing array data manipulation.	GS
Program Unit Text	Program Unit	Clicking on More displays the PL/SQL code that a program unit contains in the PL/SQL Editor.	
Prompt	Item	The text label Forms Runtime displays for an item; default blank, but the wizards usually fill it in using the name of the database column.	GS

TABLE 16-2.   *Form Module Properties* (continued)

Property	Objects	Description	Get/Set
Prompt Alignment	Item	How the prompt aligns with the item's edge: Start (the default), End, or Center. Start lines up the prompt with the starting edge, End lines it up with the ending edge, and Center puts it over the center (usually for multiple-record data blocks).	GS
Prompt Alignment Offset	Item	The distance from the center point of the item at which to align the prompt; default 0, meaning center the prompt with the item. If alignment is Center, this moves the prompt right or left; if alignment is Start or End, this moves the prompt up or down.	GS
Prompt Attachment Edge	Item	To which edge of the item the prompt should attach: Start (the default), End, Top, or Bottom.	GS
Prompt Attachment Offset	Item	The distance from the edge of the item at which to align the prompt; default 0, meaning put the prompt right next to the item.	GS
Prompt Background Color	Item	The color of the background region for the item's prompt. The default is <Unspecified>, meaning use the default font setting.	
Prompt Display Style	Item	The way the prompt displays in multiple-record blocks: First Record (the default) or All Records. First Record displays the prompt once for the block. All Records displays the prompts for each record in the block. You usually use All Records when you wrap the record onto multiple lines in a multiple-record data block.	GS
Prompt Fill Pattern	Item	The pattern to use to fill the background region of the item's prompt.	

TABLE 16-2. *Form Module Properties* (continued)

Property	Objects	Description	Get/Set
Prompt Font Name	Item	The font in which to display the text in the Prompt property.	
Prompt Font Size	Item	The font size for the item's prompt in points. The default is Unspecified, meaning use the default font setting.	
Prompt Font Spacing	Item	The space between characters for the item's prompt in points. The default is Unspecified, meaning use the default font setting.	
Prompt Font Style	Item	The font style for the item's prompt: Plain, Italic, Oblique, Underline, Outline, Shadow, Inverted, Overstrike, Blink. The default is Unspecified, meaning use the default font setting.	
Prompt Font Weight	Item	The font weight for the item's prompt: Ultralight, Extralight, Light, Demilight, Medium, Demibold, Bold, Extrabold, or Ultrabold. The default is <Unspecified>, meaning use the default font setting.	
Prompt Foreground Color	Item	The color of the text for the item's prompt. The default is <Unspecified>, meaning use the default font setting.	
Prompt Justification	Item	Where to display the prompt text within the prompt region: Start (the default), End, Left, Right, Center. As far as I can tell, this property has no effect because you can't set the size of the text region, which therefore always tightly wraps the prompt text.	
Prompt Reading Order	Item	The direction in which to display the item's prompt: Default, Left to Right, or Right to Left.	
Prompt Visual Attribute Group	Item	The named visual attribute that sets the various visual attributes for the item's prompt.	

TABLE 16-2. *Form Module Properties* (continued)

Property	Objects	Description	Get/Set
Property Class	All	The name of the property class from which the object inherits property settings; default NULL (not subclassed).	
Query All Records	Data Block	Whether Forms Runtime should fetch all the records for a query result set into the data block when the user executes a query; default No, which fetches only the number of records specified by the Query Array Size property. If a data block contains summary items and Precompute Summaries is set to No, you must set Query All Records to Yes.	GS
Query Allowed	Data Block, Items except Push Buttons, Charts, and Images	Whether to allow the user to execute a query in the block or whether the item becomes part of the SELECT statement that Forms Runtime generates when the user executes a query. If the item is part of the foreign key in a detail block that participates in a relation, Form Builder automatically sets this property to No. If you set the item property to Yes, you must also set the item's Visible property to Yes. Items with the data type LONG never participate in a query.	GS
Query Array Size	Data Block	The maximum size of the array Forms Runtime uses to fetch data from the database during a query; default 1. The larger the array size, the lower the network traffic and the higher the memory usage. If you have lots of memory and large queries, and many users, set this value greater than 1. Response time for each user will be a bit slower the larger the value, but overall response will degrade much more slowly on the network with array fetches.	G

TABLE 16-2.   *Form Module Properties* (continued)

Property	Objects	Description	Get/Set
Query Data Source Arguments	Data Block	When the Query Data Source Type property is set to Procedure, this property contains the names, data types, and values of the arguments to pass to the stored procedure named in the Query Data Source Name property for querying data. Forms Runtime calls this procedure for the Execute Query action instead of generating an SQL SELECT statement. The default value is NULL.	
Query Data Source Columns	Data Block	When the Query Data Source Type property is set to Table, Sub-query, or Procedure, clicking More on this property displays the Query Data Source Columns dialog, which contains the names of the columns into which Forms Runtime copies the result set of the query.	
Query Data Source Name	Data Block	When the Query Data Source Type property is set to Table, Sub-query, or Procedure, this property contains the name of the table or subquery or the stored procedure to execute for the Execute Query action. Forms Runtime calls this procedure instead of generating an SQL SELECT statement. The default value is NULL.	

TABLE 16-2. *Form Module Properties* (continued)

Property	Objects	Description	Get/Set
Query Data Source Type	Data Block	The kind of source that Forms Runtime uses to get data records for the block: Table (the default), Procedure, Transactional Trigger, or FROM Clause Query. Most data blocks are based on a Table. See the section "Procedural Encapsulation" in Chapter 6 for details on using procedures for query; you can't use array fetching (Query Array Size > 1) or query by example if you set this property to Procedure or Transactional Trigger. The latter choice uses the On-Query trigger to perform the query. You can also specify a FROM clause of any complexity as a source; the Forms Runtime uses that FROM clause in the SELECT it generates. This approach is similar to defining a view on the server and using it instead of a table as the base for the data block, but it doesn't require actually defining the view on the server.	G
Query Length	Text Item	The number of characters the user may enter in Enter Query mode. You can set this property to a value greater than the Maximum Length property when you want the user to be able to enter relational operators (!=, >, <, and so on) to specify the query. This feature extends query by example to let you enter complex query conditions rather than only equality comparisons. The maximum value is 255 characters.	

TABLE 16-2. *Form Module Properties* (continued)

Property	Objects	Description	Get/Set
Query Name	Report Object, Chart Item	The name of the query object in the report or graphics display module to replace with the data block you specify in the Data Source Data Block property. The default is blank.	
Query Only	Item	Whether to include the item in INSERT or UPDATE statements (No) or not to include it (Yes).	GS
Radio Button Value	Radio Button Item	The value of the Radio Group item with which this radio button item associates when the user clicks on this button; default blank.	
Raise on Entry	Canvas	Whether to always raise the canvas to the front of the window when the user navigates to an item on the canvas (Yes) or to raise the canvas to the front only if the target item is behind another canvas already displayed in the window (No, the default).	
Reading Order	Display and Text Items	If the application uses bidirectional National Language Support, the reading order for groups of words in the same language within a single text item: Default, Right-to-Left, Left-to-Right. Reading Order controls the display of bilingual text items—text items that include word groups in both Roman and Local languages. If the text item has only words from a single language, this property has no effect.	
Record Group	LOV, Hierarchical Tree	The name of the record group from which the object gets its values.	GS

TABLE 16-2. *Form Module Properties* (continued)

Property	Objects	Description	Get/Set
Record Group Fetch Size	Record Group	If Record Group Type is Query, the number of records to fetch into the record group in a single fetch; default 20. Increasing this number uses more memory but can reduce overall network traffic if the record groups are large and if there are a large number of users running the application and querying the records into the record group.	
Record Group Query	Record Group	The SELECT statement that the Forms Runtime uses to populate the record group if Record Group Type is Query.	
Record Group Type	Record Group	Whether to use the SELECT statement in the Record Group Query property to populate the record group (Query) or to construct the group with a dialog box of column names and values.	
Record Orientation	Data Block	Whether to lay out the record items in Vertical (the default) or Horizontal format. You should generally use the Frame object to format data blocks rather than using record orientation.	
Relation Type	Relation	Whether the link between the master and detail block is a Join (the default, a relational join) or a REF (a REF column in the master pointing to referenced rows in the detail block). For a Join, use the Join Condition property to specify the join. For a REF, use the Detail Reference property to specify the REF item.	
Rendered	Display and Text Items	Whether to display the item as a rendered object; default Yes. If you set this property to No, the Forms Runtime releases the resources required to display the item when the item loses focus. Using this setting can reduce your system resource usage.	

TABLE 16-2. *Form Module Properties* (continued)

Property	Objects	Description	Get/Set
Report Destination Format	Report Object	The driver to use when the Report Destination Type property is File (in bitmapped environments) or the characteristics of the printer in the Report Destination Name property for character-mode environments: PDF, HTML, HTMLCSS, HTMLCSSIE, RTF, DELIMITED. PDF is Adobe Acrobat format, using the Acrobat printer driver. HTML produces HTML 3.0 output. HTMLCSS produces HTML 3.0 with cascading style sheets. HTMLCSSIE is similar to HTMLCSS but specifically for Internet Explorer. RTF produces Rich Text Format, which most standard word processors can read. DELIMITED produces delimited output suitable for input into spreadsheets or database programs. Unfortunately, I can't find anywhere to specify the delimiter to use for this latter choice.	
Report Destination Name	Report Object	The file, printer, or e-mail name to which to send the report output. If Report Destination Type is File, this is a filename. If Report Destination Type is Printer, this property is a printer name. If Report Destination Type is Mail, this property is an e-mail address or a distribution list name. You can specify a list of e-mail names with a parenthesized list: (name, name, …, name). The default is blank.	

TABLE 16-2. *Form Module Properties* (continued)

Property	Objects	Description	Get/Set
Report Destination Type	Report Object	The kind of output you want to generate: File (the default), SCREEN, PRINTER, PREVIEW, MAIL, or INTEROFFICE. File sends the output to a file named in Report Destination Name with a format specified in Report Format. Screen sends the output to a previewer without performing font aliasing. Printer routes the output to the printer in Report Destination Name. Preview is the same as Screen but performs font aliasing in formatting the output as PostScript output. Mail sends the report to the e-mail addresses specified by Report Destination Name. Interoffice sends the report to Oracle InterOffice mail users, sending the output to the Interoffice repository.	
Report Server	Report Object	The report server that should run the report; specify the standard server name from the TNSNAMES.ORA file on the server, for example, repserver.world.	
Required	List and Text Items	Whether to regard the item as invalid in a New record if its value is NULL; default No. When the user attempts to navigate out of the item, Forms Runtime reports an error and refuses to navigate until the user enters a non-NULL value. You can use the Defer Required Enforcement property to defer validation until leaving the record. Alternatively, you can set Initial Value to a valid value if you set Required to Yes, ensuring that there is always a value in the item. If a poplist has Required set to No, the Forms Runtime attaches an extra blank line to the list, allowing the user to enter a NULL value into the item. For a Tlist, if Required is set to Yes, you can't unselect the current value; just select another value.	GS

TABLE 16-2.   *Form Module Properties* (continued)

Property	Objects	Description	Get/Set
Resize Allowed	Window	Whether to allow the user to resize the window; default Yes.	
Rotation Angle	Graphics	The number of degrees by which to rotate the graphic; the default angle is 0.	
Runtime Compatibility Mode	Form	Whether to use Forms 4.5 or Oracle Developer 6 behavior. If you create the form in Oracle Developer/2000 release 2 or Oracle Developer 6.0, the value is 5.0; if you convert a form from Developer/2000 release 1 (Forms 4.5), the value is 4.5. You can then change it to 5.0 to convert the behavior to Oracle Developer 6 behavior with respect to several things: validation, initialization of items, date conversions, setting the Required property, and dealing with null values in poplists and Tlists.	
Savepoint Mode	Form	Whether to issue Oracle savepoints; default Yes. The savepoint is a feature of Oracle that marks a point in a transaction to which you can roll back if necessary without rolling back the entire transaction. Oracle Developer uses savepoints in several internal processes, such as Post. If you are running the form against a non-Oracle data source, you can turn off savepoints by setting this property to No.	GS
Scroll Bar Alignment	Frame	Whether to display the multiple-record scroll bar at the Start of the frame or at the End (the default).	
Scroll Bar Canvas	Data Block	The name of the canvas on which to display the data block's scroll bar enabled by the Show Scroll Bar property; default is <Null>, meaning don't display the scroll bar.	

TABLE 16-2. *Form Module Properties* (continued)

Property	Objects	Description	Get/Set
Scroll Bar Height	Data Block	The height of the scroll bar.	
Scroll Bar Orientation	Data Block	Whether to display the scroll bar enabled by the Show Scroll Bar property as a Horizontal or Vertical scroll bar; default Vertical.	
Scroll Bar Reverse Direction	Data Block	Whether to reverse the direction of scrolling records from the usual; default No. You should only do this for horizontal scroll bars, but even then you're likely to confuse users if you set this property to Yes.	
Scroll Bar Visual Attribute Group	Data Block	The name of the Named Visual Attribute to apply to the scroll bar to set font, color, and pattern attributes.	
Scroll Bar Width	Data Block	The width of the scroll bar.	
Scroll Bar X Position	Data Block	The horizontal X coordinate of the data block's scroll bar enabled by the Show Scroll Bar property; default 0.	
Scroll Bar Y Position	Data Block	The vertical Y coordinate of the data block's scroll bar enabled by the Show Scroll Bar property; default 0.	
Show Fast Forward Button	Sound Item	Whether the sound item displays the fast-forward control; default No.	GS
Show Horizontal Scroll Bar	Canvas, Window, Editor, Image Item	Whether to display a horizontal scroll bar with the object; default No. For a window, you must also set the Modal property to No. The window manager must support horizontal scroll bars.	
Show OLE Popup Menu	OLE Container Item	Whether right-clicking should display a pop-up menu of commands for interacting with the OLE object; default Yes.	GS
Show OLE Tenant Type	OLE Container Item	Whether to display a border defining the OLE object type around the container item; default Yes.	

TABLE 16-2. *Form Module Properties* (continued)

Property	Objects	Description	Get/Set
Show Palette	Image Item	Whether to display an image-manipulation palette next to the image item; default No. The image palette offers three commands: Zoom (click the image to increase its size), Pan (use a grabbing hand cursor to move the image around within the item view, where some of it may be hidden); Rotate (rotate the image clockwise in 90-degree increments by clicking on it).	GS
Show Play Button	Sound Item	Whether the control for the sound item displays the Play button; default Yes. If you set this property to No while the Show Record Button property is also set to No, the Forms Runtime automatically displays the Play button anyway.	GS
Show Record Button	Sound Item	Whether the control for the sound item displays the Record button; default No. If you set this property to No while the Show Play Button property is set to No, the Forms Runtime displays the Play button anyway.	GS
Show Rewind Button	Sound Item	Whether the sound item control displays the Rewind button; default No.	GS
Show Scroll Bar	Data Block	Whether to display a scroll bar for the records in the data block; default No.	
Show Slider	Sound Item	Whether the sound item control displays the slider position control to set the place in the sound to start playing; default Yes.	GS
Show Symbols	Hierarchical Tree	Whether the tree displays + or – symbols in front of each branch node to indicate whether the node is expanded (-) or collapsed with children (+); default Yes.	

TABLE 16-2. *Form Module Properties* (continued)

Property	Objects	Description	Get/Set
Show Time Indicator	Sound Item	Whether the sound item control displays a time indicator showing where the user is in playing the sound; default Yes.	GS
Show Vertical Scroll Bar	Canvas, Window, Editor, Image Item	Whether to display a vertical scroll bar with the object; default No. The window manager must support horizontal scroll bars. For a text item, the Multi-Line property must be Yes.	
Show Volume Control	Sound Item	Whether the sound item control displays a volume control; default Yes.	GS
Shrinkwrap	Frame	Whether to enclose the items within the frame tightly, removing all blank space between the frame border and the item edges; default No. You cannot resize a Shrinkwrap frame.	
Single Object Alignment	Frame	The way a single object on a line aligns when the Frame Alignment property is set to Fill: Start (the default), End, Center.	
Single Record	Data Block	Whether to force Forms Runtime to create a single record in a control block (a block not based on a database table). You use this feature to handle summary items, VBX controls, and ActiveX controls in the control block.	
Sizing Style	Image Item	The kind of action to take when the size of the image does not match the size of the item (Width and Height): Crop (the default) or Adjust. Crop displays only the portion of the image that fits, cropping the edges. Adjust scales the image to fit entirely within the image item.	
Sound Format	Sound Item	The format to store the sound in the database: AU, AIFF, AIFF-C, or WAVE (the default).	

TABLE 16-2. *Form Module Properties* (continued)

Property	Objects	Description	Get/Set
Sound Quality	Sound Item	The level of quality to use in storing the sound in the database: Automatic (the default), Highest, High, Medium, Low, or Lowest.	
Start Angle	Arc Graphic	The starting angle of the arc in degrees with the horizontal axis as the origin; default 90.	
Start Prompt Alignment	Frame	Where to align the prompt to the item's horizontal edge when the Layout Style property is set to Form: Start (the default), Center, or End.	
Start Prompt Offset	Frame	The distance in characters between the prompt and the item when Start Prompt Alignment is Start; default 0.	
Subclass Information	All referenced objects	Clicking on More displays the name of the source module, the source module type (Form or Menu) and location (File System or Database), and the name of the source object in the source module.	
Summarized Block	Items except for Push Button, Chart, Image, Sound, and VBX Control Items	The data block that contains the data to summarize for an item with Calculation Mode set to Summary; default blank. If you have a Summary item, that item contains an aggregate value (count, minimum, and so on) based on the records in this data block.	
Summarized Item	Item	The item to summarize for an item with Calculation Mode set to Summary; default blank. You can't summarize a summary item.	

TABLE 16-2. *Form Module Properties* (continued)

Property	Objects	Description	Get/Set
Summary Function	Item	The function to use to summarize data in the Summarized Block property for an item with Calculation Mode set to Summary: Avg, Count, Max, Min, Stddev, Sum, Variance. There is no default value.	
Synchronize with Item	Items except OLE Containers	The name of the item from which the current time should derive its value. The values of the two items then mirror each other; when one changes, the other changes.	
Tab Attachment Edge	Tab Canvas	The location where tabs will be attached to the tab canvas: Top (the default), Bottom, Start, End, Left, Right.	
Tab Page	Item	The tab page on which to place the item when the canvas referred to by the item's Canvas property is a tab canvas.	G
Tab Page X Offset	Tab Canvas	The distance between the left edge of the canvas and the left edge of the tab page in Coordinate System units.	G
Tab Page Y Offset	Tab Canvas	The distance between the top edge of the canvas and the top edge of the tab page in Coordinate System units.	G
Tab Style	Tab Canvas	The shape to use when displaying the tab: Chamfered (default), Square, or Rounded.	
Title	LOV, Window	The title to display in the LOV or window title bar; default NULL, meaning display the default name (the object name for the window). The allowed length of this title depends on the display resolution (800 × 600, for example).	GS

TABLE 16-2. *Form Module Properties* (continued)

Property	Objects	Description	Get/Set
ToolTip	Item	The text to display in a small box that appears beneath an item when the mouse enters the item; default blank.	GS
Tooltip Background Color	Item	The color of the tool tip background region; default Unspecified.	GS
Tooltip Fill Pattern	Item	The pattern for the item's fill region; default Unspecified.	
Tooltip Font Name	Item	The name of the font in which the Forms Runtime displays the tool tip; default Unspecified, meaning use the default font setting.	GS
Tooltip Font Size	Item	The font size for the item's tool tip in points. The default is Unspecified, meaning use the default font setting.	GS
Tooltip Font Spacing	Item	The space between characters for the item's tool tip in points. The default is Unspecified, meaning use the default font setting.	GS
Tooltip Font Style	Item	The font style for the item's tool tip: Plain, Italic, Oblique, Underline, Outline, Shadow, Inverted, Overstrike, Blink. The default is Unspecified, meaning use the default font setting.	GS
Tooltip Font Weight	Item	The font weight for the item's tool tip: Ultralight, Extralight, Light, Demilight, Medium, Demibold, Bold, Extrabold, or Ultrabold. The default is <Unspecified>, meaning use the default font setting.	GS
Tooltip Foreground Color	Item	The color of the tool tip text; default Unspecified.	GS
Tooltip Visual Attribute Group	Item	The name of the Named Visual Attribute to apply to the item's tool tip to set font, color, and pattern attributes.	

TABLE 16-2. *Form Module Properties* (continued)

Property	Objects	Description	Get/Set
Tooltip White On Black	Item	On a monochromatic display, whether to display the tool tip as white text on a black background (Yes) or as black text on a white background (No).	GS
Top Prompt Alignment	Frame	Where to align the item prompts with their items' edges when the Layout Style property is set to Tabular: Start (the default), End, or Center.	
Top Prompt Offset	Frame	How many character cells to displace the item prompts from their items' edges when the Layout Style property is set to Tabular; default 0.	
Top Title	Editor	Text to appear in the editor title bar.	
Transactional Triggers	Data Block	For a non-Oracle data source, whether the block is a transactional control block that includes transaction triggers. The Base Table property must be NULL. Setting this property to Yes also sets the Enforce Primary Key and Enforce Column Security properties to Yes. If you are using Oracle, leave this property set to No.	
Trigger Style	Trigger	Whether the trigger is a PL/SQL trigger (the default) or a V2-style trigger. This is read-only in release 6 and no longer permits V2 triggers.	
Trigger Text	Trigger	Clicking on More displays the PL/SQL code for the trigger in the PL/SQL Editor.	
Trigger Type	Trigger	Whether the trigger is Built-in (the default) or User-named. Built-in triggers are the Oracle Developer-provided triggers; User-named triggers are named by you and executed with the Execute_Trigger built-in procedure.	

TABLE 16-2.   *Form Module Properties (continued)*

Property	Objects	Description	Get/Set
Update Allowed	Data Block, Item except Push Button, Chart, and Image Items	Whether the user can modify the value of any item in the data block or of the specific item; default Yes. Setting the data block value overrides any settings in the items in the data block.	GS
Update Changed Columns Only	Data Block	Whether to generate an UPDATE statement that includes SET clauses for only those items actually changed; default No. If DML Array Size is greater than 1, Forms Runtime ignores this property. You use this property to reduce network traffic when applications update rows with very large items (LONG, BLOB, and so on) that are seldom updated. If this situation doesn't describe your case, don't set this property to Yes, as you lose the ability to reuse the parsed UPDATE statement for every update; this overhead of reparsing can be significant if there are many updates in a session.	GS
Update on Commit	Chart Item	Whether to update the graphics display when the source block changes due to committing new or updated records; default Yes.	
Update Layout	Frame	When to update the frame layout: Automatically (the default), Manually, or Locked. Automatically updates the frame layout whenever you move or resize the frame or modify a frame layout property. Manually updates after running the Layout Wizard or after you choose the Update Layout button or menu option. Locked never updates.	

TABLE 16-2. *Form Module Properties* (continued)

Property	Objects	Description	Get/Set
Update Only if NULL	Image, List, Sound, and Text Items	Whether to disallow changes to the item unless the value is NULL; default No, meaning the user may modify the item in all cases. Yes means the user cannot modify the item unless it is NULL.	GS
Update Procedure Arguments	Data Block	When the DML Data Target Type property is set to Procedure, this property contains the names, data types, and values of the arguments to pass to the stored procedure named in the Update Procedure Name property for updating data. Forms Runtime calls this procedure for the Update Record action instead of generating an SQL UPDATE statement. The default value is NULL.	
Update Procedure Name	Data Block	When the DML Data Target Type property is set to Procedure, this property contains the name of the stored procedure to execute to update a record. Forms Runtime calls this procedure instead of generating an SQL UPDATE statement. The default value is NULL. See the section "Procedural Encapsulation" in Chapter 6 for details on using procedures for updating.	
Update Procedure Result Set Columns	Data Block	When the DML Data Target Type property is set to Procedure, clicking More on this property displays the Update Procedure Result Set Columns dialog, which contains the names of the columns into which Forms Runtime copies the result set of the stored procedure. You would specify these if your update stored procedure returned values, such as the new values or a result code.	

TABLE 16-2. *Form Module Properties* (continued)

Property	Objects	Description	Get/Set
Update on Query	Chart Item	Whether to update the graphics display when the source block changes through a query; default Yes.	
Use 3D Controls	Form	Whether to display forms running under Windows with a 3-D, beveled look and feel; default Yes. This property disables the beveling properties in the items in the form; each item automatically appears lowered. If you upgrade a form from a previous version of the Form Builder, this property is set to No.	
Validate from List	Text Item	Whether to validate the text item against the list of values in the LOV from the List of Values property; default No. Forms Runtime automatically displays the LOV if the value does not match any list elements.	
Validation	Form	Whether to enable default validation processing (Yes, the default) or to disable it (No). You should not set this property to No except for short periods of time during which you want to avoid the validation processing. When you set the value to Yes again through a trigger calling Set_Form_Property, validation occurs.	GS
Validation Unit	Form	The scope of form validation: Default, Form, Block, Record, Item. See the section "Validation Units and States" in Chapter 5 for a complete explanation of validation scope. The Default setting can have different scopes on different platforms; for example, if you run a form in a block mode environment such as the 3270 (application property User_Interface is BLOCKMODE), the validation unit defaults to Block. Mostly it defaults to Item.	GS

TABLE 16-2. *Form Module Properties* (continued)

Property	Objects	Description	Get/Set
Value When Checked	Check Box Item	The value in the item when the user checks the check box; no default. The value must be compatible with the data type of the item. If a program unit assigns the value to the item, the visual check box is checked.	
Value When Unchecked	Check Box Item	The value in the item when the user unchecks the check box; no default. The value must be compatible with the data type of the item. If a program unit assigns the value to the item, the visual check box is unchecked.	
VBX Control File	VBX Control Item	The file that makes VBX controls available to the application; no default. Avoid specifying a path.	
VBX Control Name	VBX Control Item	The name of the control from the file identified by the VBX Control File property; no default.	
VBX Control Value	VBX Control Item	The value property of the VBX control—the property that returns the "value" of the item. The default is the default VBX value property, if any; if there is none, the default is "value."	GS
Vertical Fill	Frame	Whether the Layout Wizard may use the empty space in the frame to arrange objects; default Yes. Yes means that the Layout Wizard should use all available space, thus ignoring the Maximum Objects Per Line property. No means that the Layout Wizard does not use the space and wrapping objects go to the next frame line.	
Vertical Justification	Graphic Text	The vertical positioning of the text in the text region: Top (the default), Center, or Bottom.	

TABLE 16-2.   *Form Module Properties* (continued)

Property	Objects	Description	Get/Set
Vertical Margin	Frame	The vertical distance between the border of the frame and the objects within the frame; default 1 character. This property controls both the top and bottom border distances.	
Vertical Object Offset	Frame	The vertical distance between objects in the frame; default 0.	
Vertical Origin	Graphic Text	The position of the text object relative to its origin point: Top (the default), Center, or Bottom.	
Vertical Toolbar Canvas	Window	The canvas to display as a vertical toolbar in the window; default NULL. The canvas must have its Canvas Type property set to the Vertical Toolbar. On Windows, this property has no effect if you display the canvas using the Form Vertical Toolbar Canvas property.	
Viewport Height	Canvas	The height of the view of a stacked canvas, controlling the amount of the canvas that displays in the window at runtime; default 0.	S
Viewport Width	Canvas	The width of the view of a stacked canvas, controlling the amount of the canvas that displays in the window at runtime; default 0.	S
Viewport X Position	Canvas	The X coordinate for the upper left corner of the stacked canvas relative to the upper left corner of the content view of the window; default 0.	GS
Viewport X Position on Canvas	Canvas	The X coordinate of the view's upper left corner relative to the upper left corner of the canvas; default 0. This is the position of the view of the stacked canvas relative to the stacked canvas itself rather than the position of the view on another canvas (Viewport X Position).	GS

TABLE 16-2. *Form Module Properties* (continued)

Property	Objects	Description	Get/Set
Viewport Y Position	Canvas	The Y coordinate for the upper left corner of the stacked canvas relative to the upper left corner of the content view of the window; default 0.	GS
Viewport Y Position on Canvas	Canvas	The Y coordinate of the view's upper left corner relative to the upper left corner of the canvas; default 0. This is the position of the view of the stacked canvas relative to the stacked canvas itself rather than the position of the view on another canvas (Viewport Y Position).	GS
Visible	Canvas, Window, Tab Page	Whether the canvas or window is initially or currently visible; default Yes. If the user navigates to an item on the canvas, the Forms Runtime makes the canvas visible, setting this property to Yes. You can make a window invisible regardless of the visibility of a canvas in the window. Windows are visible even if they are completely obscured or iconified/minimized; canvases are visible only when some part of the view is visible. A stacked view is not visible when it is behind the content view in the window or a *single* stacked view completely obscures it.	GS
Visual Attribute Group	All visual objects	The method for setting the Font properties of the object: Default or a named visual attribute. The Default setting displays the object with default color, pattern, and font settings. If you specify a named visual attribute, that attribute object determines the settings. See the description of the Visual Attribute object in Table 16-1 for details on the properties the object controls. See Chapter 10 for a discussion of named visual attributes and how to use them effectively.	

TABLE 16-2. *Form Module Properties* (continued)

Property	Objects	Description	Get/Set
Visual Attribute Type	Visual Attribute	The type of visual attribute: Common (the default), Prompt, or Title. A Common visual attribute applies to most objects. You can also create special visual attributes for item prompts (Prompt) or frame titles (Title); choosing these latter types changes the set of attributes to the Prompt and Title attributes.	
Where Clause	Data Block	A standard SQL clause that the Forms Runtime will add to the SELECT statement that it generates when the user executes a query. You can prefix the SQL expressions with the WHERE keyword, but it's optional. You can refer to data block columns from the data block or to form parameters (:PARAMETER.<name>). You cannot embed SQL comments. The maximum length of the WHERE clause is 32KB.	GS
White On Black	Item, Tab Page, Canvas, Window, Radio Button	For monochromatic displays, whether to display the object with white text on a black background (Yes) or not (No); default <Unspecified>.	
Width	Canvas, Item, Editor, LOV, Window	The width of the object in Coordinate System units; the default varies with the kind of object.	GS
Window	Canvas	The window in which to display the canvas at runtime; default is the first Window node listed in the Object Navigator.	

TABLE 16-2. *Form Module Properties* (continued)

Property	Objects	Description	Get/Set
Window Style	Window	Whether the window is a Document window (the default) or a Dialog window. MDI applications display document windows within the application window frame but dialog windows as free-floating on the display screen.	
Wrap Style	Text Item, Editor	How to display text when a line of text extends beyond the width of the item or editor window: Word (default), Character, or None. Word breaks the text following the last complete word and wraps to the next line. Character breaks the text following the last character on the line and wraps, chopping up the text. None suppresses display of all but the first line of text.	G
Wrap Text	Graphic Text	Whether to wrap the text in the text object to the next line to fit it within the text box boundary; default Yes.	
X Corner Radius	Graphic Rounded Rectangle	The amount of horizontal rounding in Coordinate System units of the corners of the rounded rectangle; default 10.	
X Position	Item, Editor, LOV, Window, Canvas	The horizontal (*x*-axis) position of the upper left corner of the visual representation of the object on the screen in Coordinate System units; default 0, but mostly the value comes from the result of running the various wizards. You can override LOV and canvas positions by properties in items that display the LOV or in canvases that display the other canvas.	GS
Y Corner Radius	Graphic Rounded Rectangle	The amount of vertical rounding in Coordinate System units of the corners of the rounded rectangle; default 10.	

TABLE 16-2. *Form Module Properties* (continued)

Property	Objects	Description	Get/Set
Y Position	Item, Editor, LOV, Window, Canvas	The vertical (*y*-axis) position of the upper left corner of the visual representation of the object on the screen in Coordinate System units; default 0, but mostly the value comes from the result of running the various wizards. You can override LOV and canvas positions by properties in items that display the LOV or in canvases that display the other canvas.	GS

TABLE 16-2. *Form Module Properties* (continued)

Format Masks

The following sections give you a reference to the various characters you can use to construct format masks in the Format Mask property for items. To embed characters such as a hyphen or a comma, surround the character with double quotes. You don't see these appear in the text that goes to the database, and the item adds these embedded characters when it displays the text from the database. You can generally use the FM prefix to allow the user to enter the mask with or without these embedded characters.

CHARACTER FORMAT MASKS   You can use the following characters in format masks for strings:

- *FM:* Lets the user enter a string of any length without padding it out with blanks. Not using this prefix means you want the user to enter exactly the number of characters you specify in the mask.

- *X:* Any alphabetic, numeric, or special character.

- *9:* Numbers only.

- *A:* Alphabetic characters only.

NUMBER FORMAT MASKS   You can use the following characters in format masks for numbers:

- *9:* Display number with leading zeros as blanks.

- *0:* Display leading zeros (prefix) or display zero value as zero, not blank (suffix).

- *$:* Insert a dollar sign (used as a prefix).

- *B:* Display a zero value as blank (used as a prefix).

- *MI:* Display "-" *after* a negative value (used as a suffix).

- *PR:* Display negative values in angle brackets, accounting style (used as a suffix).

- *,:* Display a comma in this position; use "G" if you want to internationalize this as a thousands separator (see the section "International Format Masks").

- *.:* Display a decimal point in this position; use "D" if you want to internationalize this as a decimal separator (see the section "International Format Masks").

- *EEEE:* Display in scientific notation (format must contain exactly four "E"s).

- *FM:* Accept the string as typed; do not right justify.

NOTE
There is always room for a minus sign on a number. For positive numbers, this may result in the appearance of a blank before the number. If the user enters a number that is longer than the format mask, the item rejects the entry. However, if a number from the database is longer than the format mask, the item displays to fit the mask using rounding, even though it retains its actual value. This is likely to confuse users, however, so try to avoid it if possible.

DATE FORMAT MASKS   You can use the following characters in format masks for dates:

- *YYYY or SYYYY:* Four-digit year; "S" prefixes "BC" date with "-".

- *YYY or YY or Y:* Last three, two, or one digits of year.

- *Y,YYY:* Year with comma in this position.

- *BC or AD:* BC/AD indicator.

- *B.C. or A.D.:* BC/AD indicator with periods.

- *RR:* Two-digit year; deduces the century from a date entered by comparing the two-digit year entered with the year and century to which the computer's internal clock is set. Years 00–49 will be given the 21st century (the year 2000), and years from 50–99 will be given the 20th century (the year 1900).

- *MM:* Month (01–12; JAN = 01).

- *MONTH:* Name of month, padded with blanks to length of nine characters.

- *MON:* Name of month, three-letter abbreviation.

- *DDD:* Day of year (1–366).

- *DD:* Day of month (1–31).

- *D:* Day of week (1–7; Sunday = 1).

- *DAY:* Name of day, padded with blanks to length of nine characters.

- *DY:* Name of day, three-letter abbreviation.

- *J:* Julian day; the number of days since January 1, 4712 BC.

- *AM or PM:* Meridian indicator.

- *A.M. or P.M.:* Meridian indicator with periods.

- *HH or HH12:* Hour of day (1–12).

- *HH24:* Hour of day (0–23).

- *MI:* Minute (0–59).

- *SS:* Second (0–59).

- *SSSSS:* Seconds past midnight (0–86399).

- */. , :* Punctuation is reproduced in the result.

- *FM:* Allow the user to enter the string without requiring an exact length.

- *FX:* Force the user to enter the string exactly matching the format mask.

NOTE
Using double quotes lets you add characters other than the supported punctuation, slash (/), period (.), and comma (,).

INTERNATIONAL FORMAT MASKS   Use these characters in number format masks you intend for fully internationalized applications. The actual values that the Forms Runtime substitutes come from the National Language Support (NLS) parameter settings (NLS_LANG, for example) in the registry or in the Oracle initialization file.

- *C:* As a prefix, adds the international currency symbol.

- *L:* As a prefix, adds the local currency symbol.

- *D:* Adds the decimal separator at the position specified.

- *G:* Adds the thousands separator at the position specified.

The Menu Module

Figure 16-2 gives a graphical overview of the structure of the menu module. The section "The Menu Module" in Chapter 2 summarizes the structure and function of the objects in the menu module.

Menu Module Objects

Table 16-3 lists the menu module objects and describes their functions in a form application.

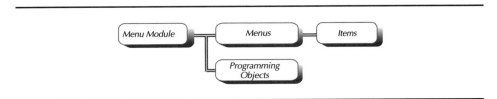

FIGURE 16-2.   *Object hierarchy for a menu module*

Object	Description
Attached Library	A PL/SQL library you have attached to another module; the order of libraries lets you replace program units with variations.
Menu	A list of text items that the user accesses by clicking on a row of text headers (menu names).
Menu Item	A text header in a menu that the user chooses.
Object Group	An object that lets you package your reusable objects for later copying or reference; it collects a set of objects under a single heading.
Parameter	An object to which you can assign a value by passing it in through the runtime system for the module. The parameter lets you customize a module at runtime, enhancing its reusability under different situations.
Program Unit	A PL/SQL package, function, or procedure.
Property Class	An object that collects any kind of property.
Visual Attribute	An object that collects a set of display properties to which you can refer from another object. This object controls several individual properties: font name, font size, font style, font spacing, font weight, foreground color, background color, fill pattern, character mode logical attribute, and white on black.

TABLE 16-3. *Menu Module Objects*

Menu Module Properties

Table 16-4 lists all the properties in a menu module in alphabetical order. As well as describing the property, the table shows which objects use each property.

Application Properties

The Get_Application_Property and Set_Application_Property built-in subprograms get and set the various global properties that apply to the Oracle Developer form application as a whole. Table 16-5 lists these properties and explains what they do.

Property	Object	Description	Get/Set
Associated Menus	Parameter	The name of the menu to which the parameter applies; the Forms Runtime prompts users to enter a value in a parameter dialog box when they navigate to this menu.	
Case Restriction	Parameter	The case for text in the parameter: MIXED (the default), UPPER, or LOWER.	GS
Checked	Menu Item	The state of the check-style menu item: CHECKED, UNCHECKED, or null (the default).	
Command Text	Menu Item	The text of the command to execute when the user selects the menu item. If Command Type is MENU, the command text is the submenu name. If Command Type is PL/SQL, the command text is an anonymous PL/SQL block.	
Command Type	Menu Item	The kind of menu item command to execute. Null does nothing; you can use this to turn off menu items or to stub them out until you're ready to add code, or for separator menu items that do nothing. Menu invokes a submenu with the name in the Command Text property. PL/SQL (the default) executes a PL/SQL block in the Command Text property. The other choices (Plus, Current Forms, and Macro) are for backward compatibility; you should not use these types.	
Conceal Data	Parameter	Whether to conceal the parameter value when the user types it into the prompting screen; default No. You can use this property to set up a password parameter for the menu.	

TABLE 16-4. *Menu Module Properties*

Property	Object	Description	Get/Set
Display without Privilege	Menu Item	Whether to display the menu item when the user is not a member of a role with access privileges to the item: No (the default) means the Forms Runtime does not display the menu item, while Yes means it displays a grayed-out menu item.	
Enabled	Menu Item	Whether the Forms Runtime displays the menu item (Yes, the default) or grays it out (No).	G
Fixed Length	Parameter	Forces the user to supply the number of characters for the parameter value that the Maximum Length property specifies.	
Help	Menu Item	In character mode, contains the help text for the menu item. When the user presses the Help key while selecting the menu item, the Forms Runtime displays this text.	
Hint	Menu Item, Parameter	Text to display when selecting a menu item or when entering a value for a parameter.	
Icon Filename	Menu Item	The name of the icon file that contains the bitmap icon to display for the menu item. Don't add an extension, and use the UI60_ICON registry variable to specify a path for all the icon files. Takes effect if the Icon in Menu property is set to Yes.	GS
Icon in Menu	Menu Item	Whether to display an icon in the menu beside the item text; default No.	
Item Roles	Menu Item	Which menu roles have access to a menu item; displays a list of roles you've set up for access in the Module Roles property on the menu object.	

TABLE 16-4.   *Menu Module Properties* (continued)

Property	Object	Description	Get/Set
Keyboard Accelerator	Menu Item	A logical function key to associate with the menu item: ACCELERATOR1–ACCELERATOR5. You use Oracle Terminal to change the physical key mappings to the logical names. You can also add more logical keys. See Chapter 15 for details on Oracle Terminal.	
Label	Menu Item, Parameter	The text label for the menu item (which is different from the name of the item and appears in the menu) or the prompt for a value in the parameter dialog for the parameter.	
Magic Item	Menu Item	Which of several predefined menu items this item represents: Cut (the default), Copy, Paste, Clear, Undo, About, Help, Quit, or Window. Forms Runtime displays the magic items in the native style for the GUI platform with appropriate accelerator key. The Form Builder supplies the functionality for Quit, Cut, Copy, Paste, and Clear. You must supply the functionality for Undo and About. The Help item is a submenu item, so the Command Type property must be Menu, and you must define the submenu of help choices. The Window item may be a submenu or it may be NULL, in which case the menu item displays a list of windows when the user selects it.	
Main Menu	Menu Module	The name of the menu object in the module that is the default menu that the Forms Runtime displays when you do not specify the Initial Menu property in the Form module. If you set that property to the name of a different menu object, Forms Runtime displays that menu as the main menu and does not permit the user to see other menu items not under the designated menu.	

TABLE 16-4. *Menu Module Properties* (continued)

Property	Object	Description	Get/Set
Maximum Length	Parameter	The maximum size in characters of the parameter; default 30.	
Menu Description	Menu Module	The string that identifies the menu module; default is the module name. If the form is running in character mode, the string displays on the message line when the user navigates to the menu.	
Menu Directory	Menu Module	When looking up the menu in the database, this property identifies the location of the compiled version of the menu module, the .MMX file; the default is blank. You should generally leave this property blank and use the standard FORMS60_PATH registry variable to identify the directory. The Forms Runtime gets the filename from the Menu Filename property.	
Menu Filename	Menu Module	When looking up the menu in the database, this property identifies the location of the compiled version of the menu module, the .MMX file; the default is the module name. The Forms Runtime gets the directory from the Menu Directory property.	
Menu Item Radio Group	Menu Item	The name of the radio group to which the current radio menu item belongs; no default. You must specify the same radio group name for all radio menu items belonging to the group between which you want to alternate choices.	

TABLE 16-4. *Menu Module Properties* (continued)

Property	Object	Description	Get/Set
Menu Item Type	Menu Item	The type of menu item: Plain (the default), Check, Magic, Radio, or Separator. A Plain item is a standard text menu item. A Check item is a Yes/No Checked or Unchecked menu item. A Magic item is one of the standard window menu choices (see the Magic Item property for details). The Radio item is a part of a group of such items that constitute a set of mutually exclusive choices (see the Menu Item Radio Group property). A Separator item is a line that divides items from other items; it has no menu command.	GS
Module Roles	Menu Module	Clicking on More displays a list of security roles from which you can pick the roles available for menu items in this module. In each item, you can specify Menu Item Roles to choose which roles have access to the menu item.	
Parameter Menu Initial Value	Parameter	The value Forms Runtime assigns to the parameter at form startup.	
Required	Parameter	Whether the user must enter a value for the parameter; default No.	
Secure	Parameter	Whether to hide characters that the user enters for the parameter.	
Share Library with Form	Menu Module	Whether to share any package data in attached libraries within the currently active form; default Yes.	

TABLE 16-4. *Menu Module Properties* (continued)

Property	Object	Description	Get/Set
Startup Code	Menu Module	PL/SQL code that Forms Runtime executes when it loads the menu module; this is essentially a When-New-Menu-Instance or Pre-Menu trigger, although menus don't have triggers.	
Submenu Name	Menu Item	The name of the submenu associated with a main menu when the Command Type property is set to Menu. The default is NULL.	
Tear-off Menu	Menu	Whether the menu is a tear-off menu that the user can drag off the menu display area; default No.	
Use Security	Menu Module	Whether the Forms Runtime should enforce the security scheme using the Menu Module Roles property. You can set this property to No while developing the module, then set it to Yes before you deploy it; this lets you develop without having to fuss with database roles.	
Visible In Horizontal Menu Toolbar	Menu Item	Whether the current form should display the menu item as an icon on the horizontal toolbar of the form; default No.	
Visible in Menu	Menu Item	Whether the menu displays the menu item at runtime; default Yes.	GS
Visible In Vertical Menu Toolbar	Menu Item	Whether the current form should display the menu item as an icon on the vertical toolbar of the form; default No.	

TABLE 16-4. *Menu Module Properties* (continued)

Property	Description
Builtin_Date_Format	The format mask that the application uses to convert strings to dates. It applies to strings that are not potentially visible to the user, mostly during processing of built-in subprograms.
Calling_Form	The name of the form from the form module Name property that called the Call_Form built-in subprogram to display the form with the current focus.
Connect_String	The SQL*Net or Net8 connect string (talbot/george@orc8, for example). You can access the individual pieces of the connect string separately through the Username and Password properties.
Current_Form	The name of the executable file (.FMX) that ran the form that has the focus; this is the name in the File_Name property of the form.
Current_Form_Name	The name of the form that has the focus. This is the name from the Name property of the form.
Cursor_Style	The shape of the application's mouse cursor: BUSY, CROSSHAIR, DEFAULT, HELP, INSERTION. The Forms Runtime will display the BUSY cursor for long operations regardless of this setting, but you can replace the BUSY cursor with something else once it is displayed.
Datasource	The name of the database server: ORACLE (the default), DB2, NULL, NONSTOP, TERADATA, NCR/3600, NCR/3700, and SQLSERVER.
Display_Height	The height of the current display in Coordinate System units. You can use this height to calculate where to place windows for best appearance.
Display_Width	The width of the current display in Coordinate System units. You can use this width to calculate where to place windows for best appearance.

TABLE 16-5. *Form Application Properties*

Property	Description
Operating_System	The name of the current operating system: WINDOWS, WIN32COMMON, UNIX, Sun OS, MACINTOSH, VMS, and HP-UX. Other values may be available; check your platform-specific documentation.
Password	The password that the user entered. You cannot change this value. You can access the entire connect string (user name, password, and host name) using the Connect_String application property.
PLSQL_Date_Format	The format mask that converts date values if you use To_Date with no explicit format mask or when you assign a CHAR value to a DATE variable or vice versa. You should set this format to contain the full century and the time, and you should set this mask to be the same as the Builtin_Date_Format application property. You can also set a date format as an NLS registry variable and access it through the User_NLS_Date_Format property for globalized applications.
Savepoint_Name	The name of the savepoint to which the Forms Runtime can roll back. In the On-Savepoint or On-Rollback triggers, you can get this name to be able to roll back explicitly to the savepoint (a very unusual requirement). See Chapter 5 for a description of savepoint behavior in the Post process. You can use the Savepoint Mode property of the form to turn off savepoints entirely.
Timer_Name	The name of the most recently expired timer.
User_Interface	The name of the current window manager: BLOCKMODE, CHARMODE, MACINTOSH, MOTIF, MSWINDOWS, MSWINDOWS32, PM, WIN32COMMON, WEB, X, UNKNOWN.
User_NLS_Character_Set	The current NLS character set from the NLS_Lang registry variable.
User_NLS_Date_Format	The current NLS date format mask. You can use this property to set other application date format properties, such as PLSQL_Date_Format.

TABLE 16-5. *Form Application Properties* (continued)

Property	Description
User_NLS_Lang	The complete value of the NLS_Lang registry variable, concatenating User_NLS_Language, User_NLS_Territory, and User_NLS_Character_Set.
User_NLS_Language	The NLS language component, from the NLS_Lang registry variable.
User_NLS_Territory	The NLS territory component, from the NLS_Lang registry variable.
Username	The user name of the current operator. Use the Connect_String property to get the entire connect string required to log on to the database.

TABLE 16-5.   *Form Application Properties* (continued)

Report Builder

Figure 16-3 gives a graphical overview of the structure of the report module. The section "Reports" in Chapter 2 summarizes the structure and function of the objects in the report module.

Report Module Objects

Table 16-6 lists the report module objects and describes their functions in a form application.

Report Module Properties

Table 16-7 lists all the properties in a report module in alphabetical order. As well as describing the property, the table shows which objects use each property.

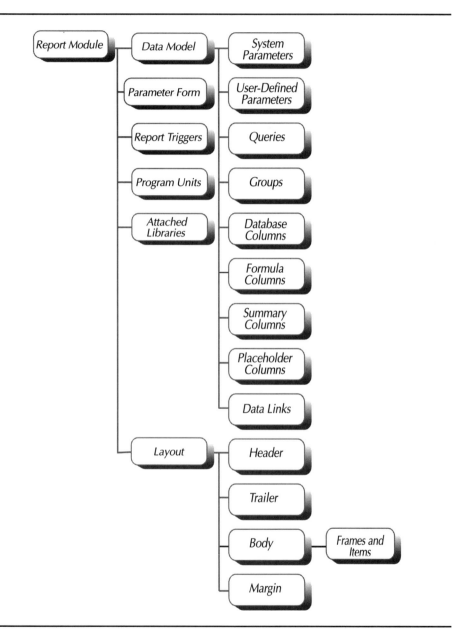

FIGURE 16-3. *Object hierarchy for a report module*

Object	Description
Anchor	A layout object that fixes one object to another object, ensuring that the first object is always positioned relative to the second object. For example, you can anchor a field to a frame to center the field within the frame.
Chart Item	A layout object that displays an Oracle Developer graphics display module in the report. The data for the graphics display may come from the display module or from the report.
Column	An object in a data model group that corresponds to a report field in the layout.
Data Link	An object that links master groups to detail queries in a master-detail report.
External SQL Query	A module that contains a single SQL statement that you can import into the report data model.
Field	A layout object that contains a value.
Formula Column	A special column in a group that you compute using PL/SQL blocks rather than getting data directly from the database.
Graphic Object	One of several layout objects that do not contain values but instead present pictures or graphic elements: rectangle, line, ellipse, arc, polygon, polyline, rounded rectangle, or freehand. These objects are also known as boilerplate graphics.
Group	An object that identifies the records that a query returns as a repeating group of records in the report. There is a hierarchy of groups in a report that represents the nesting of records within each other. The group also contains the set of fields and columns that make up the record structure.
Group Frame	A layout container that corresponds to a group and displays once for the group as a whole.
Layout Object	One of several kinds of objects you position on the report layout: fields, text, chart items, and graphics.
Parameter Form Boilerplate	A text, graphic, or image object placed in a parameter form.

TABLE 16-6.   *Report Module Objects*

Object	Description
Parameter Form Field	A field in a parameter form (the form that Oracle Developer presents to the user to gather parameters at runtime).
Placeholder Column	A column in a group you define to fill in from a trigger, formula, or user exit instead of from database values or standard summarization.
Query	An SQL SELECT statement.
Repeating Frame	A layout container that corresponds to the repeating sequence of records in a group and displays once for each record in the group.
Section	A header section, main section, or trailer section in a report. Each section contains a body and a margin.
Summary Column	A special column in a group that Developer computes by aggregating report data, such as totals or counts.
System Parameter	An Oracle-Developer-supplied variable for which the user can supply a value at runtime.
Template	An object that contains layout settings for the various frames and other objects within a report from which the report takes its initial layout settings.
Text Object	A layout object that contains text, as opposed to a field or text field that contains a value from the data model. This object is also known as boilerplate text.
User Parameter	A user-supplied variable for which the user can supply a value at runtime.

TABLE 16-6.   *Report Module Objects* (continued)

Graphics Builder

Figure 16-4 gives a graphical overview of the structure of the graphics display module. The section "Graphics" in Chapter 2 summarizes the structure and function of the objects in the display module.

Property	Object	Description
Additional Hyperlink Attributes	Layout Objects	Additional HTML tags for the hyperlink defined by the Hyperlink property.
After Form Type	Report	The type of footer to display at the end of the runtime parameter form when the report destination is an HTML file destined for a Web browser: Text (the default) or File. Text means display the string in After Form Value; File means get the text or graphics from the file named in the After Form Value property.
After Form Value	Report	The HTML text, or a valid filename for a file containing HTML text, or a graphic image to display at the end of the parameter form. You can use this property to place an image or standard links at the end of the parameter form.
After Page Type	Report	The type of footer to display at the end of each page when the report destination is an HTML file destined for a Web browser: Text (the default) or File. Text means display the string in After Page Value; File means get the text or graphics from the file named in the After Page Value property.
After Page Value	Report	The HTML text, or a valid filename for a file containing HTML text, or a graphic image to display at the end of each page.
After Report Type	Report	The type of trailer to display at the end of the report document when the report destination is an HTML file destined for a Web browser: Text (the default) or File. Text means display the string in After Report Value; File means get the text or graphics from the file named in the After Report Value property.

TABLE 16-7. *Report Module Properties*

Property	Object	Description
After Report Value	Report	The HTML text, or a valid filename for a file containing HTML text, or a graphic image to display at the end of the report document. You can use this property to put standard links or other material at the end of the report.
Align Summaries with Fields	Template	If the Style property is set to Form, whether the Report Builder puts summary fields under the fields that are the source of the summarized data; default Yes.
Alignment	Template	If the Style property is set to Form, this property tells the Report Builder how to position labels and fields across the page: Left (the default), Right, Center, Flush, or Column. Left aligns the leftmost label or field with the left side of the page, Right does the same with the right side of the page. Center centers the labels and fields across the page. Flush spaces the labels and fields evenly across the page; the leftmost label or field aligns with the left side of the page and the rightmost label or field with the right side. Column aligns the labels and fields in evenly spaced columns with size based on the width of the largest label and field.
Application Command Line (PDF)	Layout Object	A command to execute when the user clicks on the object in a PDF (Adobe Acrobat) report. This command executes instead of the action in the Hyperlink property.
Background Color	Template	Sets the default background color for the fill region of a layout object. If the Fill Pattern property is Transparent or Solid, Form Builder ignores this property.

TABLE 16-7. *Report Module Properties* (continued)

Property	Object	Description
Base Printing On	Layout Object	Whether to trigger display of the layout object based on the Anchoring Object (the default) or on the Enclosing Object. This property operates in conjunction with the Print Object On property to define the exact triggering of layout object display. Example: Anchoring Object and Print Object On set to All Pages triggers display on every page on which the anchoring object appears.
Before Form Type	Report	The type of header to display at the beginning of the runtime parameter form when the report destination is an HTML file destined for a Web browser: Text (the default) or File. Text means display the string in Before Form Value; File means get the text or graphics from the file named in the Before Form Value property.
Before Form Value	Report	The HTML text, or a valid filename for a file containing HTML text, or a graphic image to display at the beginning of the parameter form. You can use this property to place an image or standard links at the beginning of the parameter form.
Before Page Type		The type of header to display at the beginning of each page when the report destination is an HTML file destined for a Web browser: Text (the default) or File. Text means display the string in Before Page Value; File means get the text or graphics from the file named in the Before Page Value property.
Before Page Value		The HTML text, or a valid filename for a file containing HTML text, or a graphic image to display at the beginning of each page.

TABLE 16-7. *Report Module Properties* (continued)

Property	Object	Description
Before Report Type		The type of header to display at the beginning of the report document when the report destination is an HTML file destined for a Web browser: Text (the default) or File. Text means display the string in Before Report Value; File means get the text or graphics from the file named in the Before Report Value property.
Before Report Value		The HTML text, or a valid filename for a file containing HTML text, or a graphic image to display at the beginning of the report document. You can use this property to put standard links or other material at the beginning of the report.
Between Field and Labels (Horizontal)	Template	When Style is Form, the amount of horizontal space between a field and its label; default 0, units in the measurement unit for the report.
Between Frame and Fields (Horizontal)	Template	The amount of space between the side frame borders and the fields they enclose; default 0. Snapping to grid overrides the precise measurement here, as fields always snap to the grid when this option is on.
Between Frame and Fields (Vertical)	Template	The amount of space between the top and bottom frame borders and the fields they enclose; default 0. Snapping to grid overrides the precise measurement here, as fields always snap to the grid when this option is on.
Between Master and Detail (Horizontal)	Template	The amount of horizontal space between the master frame and the detail frame, default 0. Snapping to grid overrides the precise measurement here, as fields always snap to the grid when this option is on.

TABLE 16-7. *Report Module Properties* (continued)

Property	Object	Description
Between Master and Detail (Vertical)	Template	The amount of vertical space between the master frame and the detail frame, default 0. Snapping to grid overrides the precise measurement here, as fields always snap to the grid when this option is on.
Between Page and Frames (Horizontal)	Template	The amount of horizontal space between the page edge and the top-level frame, default 0. Snapping to grid overrides the precise measurement here, as fields always snap to the grid when this option is on.
Between Page and Frames (Vertical)	Template	The amount of vertical space between the page edge and the top-level frame, default 0. Snapping to grid overrides the precise measurement here, as fields always snap to the grid when this option is on.
Between Sibling Frames (Horizontal)	Template	The amount of horizontal space between frames at the same group level; default 0. There is no restriction on group parentage (that is, you can have groups in different parts of the group tree). Snapping to grid overrides the precise measurement here, as fields always snap to the grid when this option is on.
Between Sibling Frames (Vertical)	Template	The amount of vertical space between frames at the same group level; default 0. There is no restriction on group parentage (that is, you can have groups in different parts of the group tree). Snapping to grid overrides the precise measurement here, as fields always snap to the grid when this option is on.

TABLE 16-7. *Report Module Properties* (continued)

Property	Object	Description
Bookmark	Layout Object	A link that appears in an HTML bookmark frame or the table of contents area of the Acrobat Reader; clicking on the bookmark displays the layout object. You can either put in the bookmark name alone or prefix it with an outline number and the pound sign (#). Using the name alone orders the bookmark by the order of the object's appearance in the file. Adding the number reorders the bookmarks according to the outline numbers. If you put a bookmark on a frame, it automatically refers to the visible object nearest the left corner of the frame.
Borders	Template	Which borders to display for objects: All (the default), Top Only, Bottom Only, Left Only, Right Only, Top and Bottom, Left and Right, Top and Right, Top and Left, Bottom and Right, Bottom and Left, All but Top, All but Bottom, All but Left, All but Right, None.
Break Order	Column	Whether to display this column's values in Ascending order (the default) or Descending order. This property applies to break group columns—columns that identify distinct values for break groups.
Character Justification	Template	The method to use to align the text of a field or label of a CHARACTER data source field: Start (the default), End, Left, Center, Right.

TABLE 16-7. *Report Module Properties* (continued)

Property	Object	Description
Chart Column	Chart	A column or list of columns in the graphics display module that corresponds to the column or parameter in the Report Column property. If you supply a comma-separated list of columns, the Reports Runtime maps the report column to each of the display columns in the list.
Chart Filename	Chart	The name of the display module file from which to get the graphics display; the OGD extension is optional. You should not specify a path; use the REPORTS60_PATH registry variable to specify the search path.
Chart Hyperlink	Chart	A link you can specify for each chart, with the value being any valid hyperlink destination; default blank.
Chart Parameter	Chart	A parameter in the graphics display module that you want to set through the report column or parameter in the Report Column property.
Chart Query	Chart	The name of the graphics display query that the records from the Report Column property replace.
Child Column	Link	The name of a column in the child query that links to a parent group column. This column must be a database column, not a summary or formula column, and you cannot use a lexical reference here.
Child Edge Percent	Anchor	The percentage down or across the edge of the anchor's child object, specifying the position of the anchor on the edge. This must be an integer between 0 and 100, inclusive.

TABLE 16-7. *Report Module Properties* (continued)

Property	Object	Description
Child Edge Type	Anchor	The edge of an object on which to locate the anchor: Top, Bottom, Left, or Right.
Child Object Name	Anchor	The name of the anchored object (read-only).
Child Query	Link	The name of the query you define as the child linked to a parent query in the data model (read-only).
Collapse Horizontally	Anchor	Whether the anchor should have zero width if the parent object does not print; this causes the child object to move horizontally into the space where the parent would have appeared.
Collapse Vertically	Anchor	Whether the anchor should have zero height if the parent object does not print; this causes the child object to move vertically into the space where the parent would have appeared.
Column Mode	Repeating Frame	How the Reports Runtime gets and formats data in repeating frame; default No. Setting this property to Yes forces formatting to begin before completing the previous instances, causing the second page output to align with the first page. The No setting suppresses formatting until each instance completes, causing the instances not to align on subsequent pages. See the online help for graphical examples of this output option.
Column Type	Column	The kind of column this is: Database – Object, Database – Ref, Database – Scalar, Database – Unknown (an unsupported column type), Formula, Placeholder, or Summary.

TABLE 16-7.   *Report Module Properties* (continued)

Property	Object	Description
Comments	Object	A text field with any text you want that cannot exceed 64KB.
Compute At	Summary Column	The group over which to calculate a % of Total summary column: Report, Page, or group name. Report, the default, means compute the total for the report; Page means compute the total for each page; naming a group means compute the total for that group. In other words, the group you specify here specifies the total by which the Reports Runtime divides the value to get a percentage of total value.
Condition	Link	An SQL operator that relates parent column to child column: = (the default), <, <=, <>, >, >=, LIKE, NOT LIKE.
Conditional Formatting	Layout Object	Clicking on More displays the Conditional Formatting dialog box to set up output formatting for the object when the condition is true.
Dash	Template	The line dash style for the object (the drop-down list displays the various patterns); defaults to solid line.
Datatype	Column, Parameter, Parameter Form Field	The data type of the value: Character, Date, Long, Long Raw, Number, Raw, Varchar, or Varchar2. The default value for a database column comes from the database column it represents. For a summary column, the type is the type of the column in the Source property. For other columns, the default is Number. Parameters can be Character, Date, or Number, and Character is the default. For the parameter form field, this property is the data type of the parameter you specify in the Source property, and the property is read-only.

TABLE 16-7. *Report Module Properties* (continued)

Property	Object	Description
Date Justification	Template	The method to use to align a date field's text: Start (the default), End, Left, Center, Right.
Design in Character Units	Report	Whether to design the report using a character-cell grid (Yes) or a measure unit (No, the default). Using this with Include Borders displays character-mode borders for objects.
Direction	Report	The reading order for the entire report: Left to Right or Right to Left, with the default set according to the direction of the language. This property provides the default value for the layout objects in the report and controls the layout direction in the report editors.
Disable Host Menu Item	Report	Whether to disable the File|Host menu item in the Runtime Parameter Form and Live Previewer; default No.
Disable Split Screen Key	Report	Whether to disable the Split Vertical and Split Horizontal function keys; default No.
Disable Zoom Key	Report	Whether to disable the Zoom and Unzoom function keys in the Live Previewer; default No.
Display Name	Image	Text that the Reports Runtime displays when the cursor moves over the image in HTML or HTMLCSS report output; default blank.
Distribution	Section	Clicking on More lets you specify the distribution settings for the section.
Edge Background Color	Template	The background color of the pattern you define in the Edge Pattern property; default white. Setting Edge Pattern to transparent or solid makes the Reports Runtime ignore this property.

TABLE 16-7. *Report Module Properties* (continued)

Property	Object	Description
Edge Foreground Color	Template	The foreground color of the pattern you define in the Edge Pattern property; default black. Setting Edge Pattern to transparent makes the Reports Runtime ignore this property.
Edge Pattern	Template	The pattern to use for object borders; set with the pattern palette, default transparent.
External Query Source File	Query	The module name of an external query module (a filename or module name in the format DB:<name> in the database) to use as the source of the query for the report data model; default blank. Use the REPORTS60_PATH registry variable to specify the path rather than embedding the path in the filename.
Fields Per Line	Template	For a report with Style set to Form, the maximum number of fields that may appear on a line; default 0, meaning there is no limit.
File Format	Column	The format of the column value for columns with Read from File set to Yes: Text (the default), Image, CGM, Oracle Format, Sound, Video, OLE2, Image URL. Text is text in ASCII format; Image is a bitmapped image; CGM is a line drawing in CGM format; Oracle Format is a line drawing in Oracle format; Sound and Video are objects in longraw format; OLE2 is an OLE object to embed in the report; Image URL is a link to an image.
Fill Pattern	Template	The pattern to use for space enclosed by objects; chosen from the pattern palette. Use the Foreground Color and Background Color settings to control pattern colors.

TABLE 16-7. *Report Module Properties* (continued)

Property	Object	Description
Filter Type	Group	The kind of selection to use on the group's records: None (no selection, the default), First, Last, or PL/SQL. The First and Last settings retrieve a number of records you specify in the Number of Records property. First retrieves the first *n* records, while Last retrieves the last *n* records. PL/SQL defines a PL/SQL function that returns True or False for each record, with True meaning to include the record and False meaning not to include the record.
Font	Template	The text font to use for layout objects; default Courier 10-point regular. You can use any font defined on your system, accessible through the Font menu and dialog box.
Foreground Color	Template	The foreground color of the pattern you define in the Fill Pattern property; default black.
Format Mask	Field	The way to display date and number values in the field; default blank. See the earlier section "Format Masks" for the syntax of numeric and date format masks. There are some additional number formatting characters you can use in reports: () prints parentheses around negative values; Y removes the sign symbol; V multiplies the number by 10N, where N is the number of 0, 9, *, and S tokens that appear to the right of the V; and * prints one digit unless that digit is a leading zero to the left of the decimal point, when it prints an asterisk, and also prints any trailing zeros to the right of the decimal point.

TABLE 16-7. *Report Module Properties* (continued)

Property	Object	Description
Format trigger	Layout Object	A PL/SQL function to execute before formatting the object, thus allowing you to change the formatting properties of the object at runtime. The function returns True or False. False means to exclude the current object instance from the report, giving you a way to prevent display of a value given a condition. See the Chapter 5 section "Format Trigger" for details on using format triggers.
Function	Summary Column	The aggregation operator to execute when calculating the value: Average, Count, First, Last, Maximum, Minimum, % of Total, Std. Deviation, Sum, Variance.
Height	Report, Section	The height of the parameter form page in the unit specified by the Unit of Measurement property; default 4 inches/10cm/300pts for a parameter form page. For a section, the height of the section.
Horiz. Space Between Frames	Repeating Frame	The space to insert horizontally between instances of the repeating frame in the unit specified by the Unit of Measurement property; default 0.
Horizontal Elasticity	Layout Object	How the width of the object changes to accommodate the data within it: Contract, Expand, Fixed, Variable. Contract decreases the size but doesn't expand it beyond the original size. Expand does the reverse. Fixed keeps the same width. Variable lets the field expand or contract to fit the data. For a graphic, the Reports Runtime scales the image to fit if you specify Fixed.

TABLE 16-7. *Report Module Properties* (continued)

Property	Object	Description
Horizontal Panels per Page	Section	The width of the section's logical page with respect to the physical page; default 1.
Hyperlink	Layout Object	A URL that displays a location within a document when the user clicks on it; default blank. If you specify Hyperlink for a frame, the value becomes the hyperlink for all objects within the frame not possessing their own Hyperlink URL. For an Adobe Acrobat PDF document, the Application Command Line overrides the Hyperlink. If you specify this property for an object in a frame, navigating the link replaces the frame with an entire window displaying the hyperlink destination. To replace only the frame, set Additional Hyperlink Properties to target=<filename>, where <filename> is the name of the frame to replace. A destination within the current document is in the format #<destination>, where <destination> is the destination name in the Hyperlink Destination property. A destination within a local document is in the format file:/<path>/<filename>#<destination>. Removing the destination opens the document without going to a destination within it. A document on a remote machine (with or without a destination) is a simple HTTP URL possibly including #<destination>.
Hyperlink Destination	Layout Object	A unique name that you can use in a Hyperlink property to link an object to this object with a hyperlink; default blank. The name must use only ASCII letters, numbers, or the underscore. If the object is a frame, the link is to the object nearest the upper left corner of the frame.

TABLE 16-7. *Report Module Properties* (continued)

Property	Object	Description
Icon Name	Button	For buttons with Label Type set to Icon, the name of the file with the icon that you want to appear on the button; default blank. The file must be in the directory from the UI_ICON registry variable.
Image	Template	The text file to substitute for images to which external boilerplate objects in the template refer.
Include Bitmapped Objects	Report	Whether to convert all bitmapped objects to boxes when the report runs in Character Mode; default No, which deletes the objects instead of displaying boxes.
Include Borders	Report	Turns on borders in Character Mode for any objects with a line width greater than zero; default No. Using this property with the Design in Character property tells the Report Builder to display borders.
Initial Value	Parameter	The default value for the parameter. Certain system parameters have specific defaults: DESTYPE=Screen, DESFORMAT=dflt, COPIES=1; otherwise, the default is blank. The value must be appropriate given the Datatype property for the parameter.
Input Mask	Parameter	The format mask the Reports Runtime uses to validate the value the user enters through the command line or parameter form. See the Format Mask property for possibilities.
Inter-Field (Horizontal)	Template	The amount of horizontal space in units specified by the Unit of Measurement property between fields in a group; for a report with Style set to Form, the property is the amount of space between the end of one field-and-label combination and the next. Objects snap to the grid, so the exact space may be different.

TABLE 16-7. *Report Module Properties* (continued)

Property	Object	Description
Inter-Field (Vertical)	Template	The amount of vertical space between fields in a group in units specified by the Unit of Measurement property; default 0. Objects snap to the grid, so the exact measurement may be different.
Inter-Frame (Horizontal)	Template	The amount of horizontal space between frames in a group in units specified by the Unit of Measurement property; default .0087 inches or the equivalent.
Inter-Frame (Vertical)	Template	The amount of vertical space between frames in a group in units specified by the Unit of Measurement property; default .0136 inches or the equivalent.
Justify	Template	The way to align text in the title: Start (the default), End, Left, Center, Flush, Right.
Keep with Anchoring Object	Layout Object	Whether to keep the object with its anchoring object on the same page; default No. If the object is a repeating frame, this keeps the frame with its object. The anchor may be an implicit anchor.
Label Type	Button	The kind of button: Text (the default) or Icon. Use the Icon Name property to specify the icon file.
Line Stretch with Frame	Graphic Line	The name of a frame with which to associate the line, anchoring the line at the frame end points; default NULL. When the report formats, the line stretches with the frame. The frame must completely enclose the line and must be either horizontal or vertical, not sloped.

TABLE 16-7.   *Report Module Properties* (continued)

Property	Object	Description
List of Values	Parameter	Clicking on More displays the List of Values dialog box, which lets you create a list of values for entering the parameter value. You can check the Hide First Column check box to hide a column of data from the user while setting the value to it, or you can check the Restrict List to Predetermined Values to prevent the user from entering a value not in the list.
Max. Horizontal Body Pages	Report	The maximum number of body pages in the physical page width that may appear in the report; default 10.
Max. Vertical Body Pages	Report	The maximum number of body pages in the physical page height that may appear in the report; default 10.
Maximum Records Per Page	Report	The maximum number of repeating frame instances that the Reports Runtime can format on a logical page; default blank, meaning that the Reports Runtime can put as many instances on the page as will fit.
Maximum Rows to Fetch	Report	The maximum number of rows that the Reports Runtime will fetch and display for the query. You can use this to limit large queries during report development. Summary calculations ignore the rows not fetched.
Minimum Widow Lines	Boilerplate, Field	The least number of lines that must appear on the logical page where the Reports Runtime starts to print the object; default 0, meaning print the text that fits.
Minimum Widow Records	Repeating Frame	The least number of frame instances that must appear on a logical page where the Reports Runtime starts to print the frame; default blank, no minimum. This ensures that you have at least this number of records on each page.

TABLE 16-7.   *Report Module Properties* (continued)

Property	Object	Description
Multimedia Column	Button	The name of a database column in the report to run when the user presses the button; default blank.
Multimedia Column Type	Button	The format of the multimedia object specified in the Multimedia Column property: Image, Video, Sound. Defaults to the database column type.
Multimedia File	Button	The name of a file containing a multimedia object that the Reports Runtime executes when the user presses the button. Use the REPORTS60_PATH registry variable to set the path rather than embedding it in the filename.
Multimedia File Type	Button	The format of the file in the Multimedia File property: Image (the default), Video, Sound.
Name	Object	The name of the object; 30 characters or fewer. The Report Builder creates the names using a default naming scheme with prefixes indicating the type of object, such as G_ for group.
Number Justification	Template	The method to use to align field text when the Source is a number column: Start (the default), End, Left, Center, Right.
Number of Pages	Report	The total number of pages in the Runtime Parameter Form.
Number of Records	Group	The number of records to include in a group limited with a Filter Type property of First or Last; default 0, meaning all records.
Orientation	Section	Whether to output the section in Portrait or Landscape orientation, with the default set by system parameter ORIENTATION or the Page Setup dialog box setting.

TABLE 16-7. *Report Module Properties* (continued)

Property	Object	Description
Page Break After	Layout Object	Whether to move all the children of an anchor to this object to the next page; default No. This property doesn't affect sibling objects—objects at the same level that aren't anchored to one another.
Page Break Before	Layout Object	Whether to put the object on the page after the one on which the Reports Runtime started to format it; default No. This doesn't affect objects that may be below the object on the page but aren't anchored in any way to the object.
Page Navigation Control Type	Report	What the Page Navigation Control Value property is: Text (the default) or a File.
Page Navigation Control Value	Report	The HTML command string or filename that contains such commands that implement navigation buttons in HTML page-streamed report output. If you code your own script, you must add two variables: &TotalPages and &file_name (the name of the output destination file).
Page Numbering	Field	For fields with one of the page number types, clicking on More displays the Page Numbering dialog box that lets you set up the method for calculating page numbers for the field.
Page Protect	Layout Object	Whether to try to keep the entire object and everything it contains on the same logical page; default No. The object moves to the next page if it cannot fit entirely on the page where formatting started. If the result would leave a page nearly or completely blank, the Reports Runtime doesn't apply the property.

TABLE 16-7.   *Report Module Properties* (continued)

Property	Object	Description
Panel Print Order	Report	The order in which to print the physical pages that make up a logical page; default Across/Down, meaning print the pages left-to-right, then top-to-bottom, or Down/Across, meaning print the pages top-to-bottom, then left-to-right.
Parent Column	Link	A column in the parent group that relates to a column in the child query (read-only).
Parent Edge Percent	Anchor	The location of the anchor on the edge of the parent in terms of percentage down or across the edge specified in the Parent Edge Type property.
Parent Edge Type	Anchor	The edge of the parent object to which the anchor attaches; Top, Bottom, Left, or Right.
Parent Group	Link	The name of the group you defined as the parent when creating the link (read-only).
Parent Object Name	Anchor	The name of the parent object (read-only) to which the anchor attaches.
PL/SQL Filter	Group	Clicking on More displays the PL/SQL Editor for modifying the group filter function; when this function returns false for a group instance, the Reports Runtime does not display the instance. You must set the Filter Type property to PL/SQL.
PL/SQL Formula	Formula and Placeholder Column	Clicking on More displays the PL/SQL Editor, into which you place the PL/SQL expression that evaluates to the value of the column.

TABLE 16-7. *Report Module Properties* (continued)

Property	Object	Description
PL/SQL Statement	Query	Clicking on More displays the PL/SQL Editor for editing a function that returns data for the query through a ref cursor rather than relying on an SQL statement.
PL/SQL Trigger	Button	The procedure that executes when the user clicks on the button in the Live Previewer.
Place Labels Above Fields	Template	When Style is set to Form, whether to put field labels above their fields rather than to the left; default No.
Previewer Hint Line Text	Report	Text to display as the second-to-last line in the Live Previewer when you set the Use Previewer Hint Line property to Yes.
Previewer Status Line Text	Report	Text to display on the last line of the Live Previewer when you set the Use Previewer Status Line Text property to Yes.
Previewer Title	Report	The text that appears at the top of the Live Previewer; default null, meaning use the default previewer title.
Print Direction	Repeating Frame	The direction in which to display successive instances of the repeating frame: Down (the default), Across, Across/Down, Down/Across. Picking one of these choices lets you implement the various kinds of down and across report formats (see Chapter 7).
Print Object On	Layout Object	The frequency with which the object appears in the report: All Pages, All but First Page, All but Last Page, Default, First Page, Last Page. This property is relative to the Base Printing On property.

TABLE 16-7.   *Report Module Properties* (continued)

Property	Object	Description
Printer Code After	Layout Object	The printer-escape sequence to execute after each line of the object in a Character Mode report. The format is &number, where number is a number assigned to a sequence in the printer definition file.
Printer Code Before	Layout Object	The printer-escape sequence to execute before each line of the object in a Character Mode report. The format is &number, where number is a number assigned to a sequence in the printer definition file.
Product Order	Summary, Formula, and Placeholder Column	The order in which to evaluate groups for a summary, formula, or placeholder column in a matrix report. If the summary does not have its Reset At property set to Report, Product Order must be a subset of its source column's Product Order. The summary Product Order should be a subset of the source column's Product Order. If the Reset At property is set to Report, Product Order must be a prefix of the source column's Product Order.
Read from File	Column	Whether to get the image or text value for the column from a file (Yes) or from the database (No). You specify the file format using the File Format property.
Report Group	Chart	The group in the report summarized by the graphics display.
Report Height	Section	The height of the report page in character units; default 80.
Report Width	Section	The width of the report page in character units; default 66.

TABLE 16-7.   *Report Module Properties* (continued)

Property	Object	Description
Reset At	Summary Column	The group at which to reset the summary value to zero or null. Reset At may be Report, Page, or a group name. Report lets you calculate a summary column for the entire report. Page calculates the column for each page. Group calculates the summary over each group record.
Role Name	Report	Clicking on the More button displays the Set Role dialog box. The text is the name of the database security role with which to run the report at runtime. Setting this role allows users who do not have access to the tables in the report data model queries to run the report.
Set Break Order	Column	Whether to set the order in which to display the column values with the Break Order property; default Yes.
Source	Summary Column, Repeating Frame, Parameter Form Field, Field	The name of the column to summarize, or the name of the group that contains the data elements to repeat in the frame, or the parameter name for the parameter form field, or the column, parameter, or special value from which the field gets its value. Special values include &Current Date, &Logical Page Number, &Panel Number, &Physical Page Number, &Total Logical Pages, &Total Panels, &Total Physical Pages. For page numbers, you can use the Page Numbering property to control how page numbering is done.
Source Datatype	Field	The data type of the data source for the field (read-only).
Source File Format	Boilerplate	For boilerplate linked to an external file, the format of the file: Text, Image, CGM, Oracle Drawing Format, or Image URL.

TABLE 16-7. *Report Module Properties* (continued)

Property	Object	Description
Source Filename	Boilerplate	The name of the external file to which to link the boilerplate. You should use the REPORTS60_PATH to specify the path.
SQL Clause	Link	The type of SQL that relates the parent to the child: HAVING, START WITH, or WHERE. If you specify HAVING, the SELECT statement of the child query must have a GROUP BY clause; if you specify START WITH, it must have a CONNECT BY clause.
SQL Query Statement	Query	The SQL SELECT statement that implements the query.
Start in Zoom	Report	Whether to display the Live Previewer without the border, showing the report output only; default No.
Style	Template	Whether the group has a Tabular or Form styled layout. In a Tabular layout, labels are above fields and are outside the repeating frame. In a Form layout, labels are to the left of the fields and are inside the repeating frame. Group Above with a child group and Form-like layout styles use Form style, while Tabular, Group Left, Group Above with no child group, Matrix, and Matrix Breakall use Tabular style.
Suppress Previewer Title	Report	Whether to suppress the title in the Character Mode previewer; default Yes.
Text	Button, Template	The text label that appears on a button for a Label Type of Text (center justified), or the name of a text substitution file to use for boilerplate text objects in the template display.

TABLE 16-7. *Report Module Properties* (continued)

Property	Object	Description
Text Color	Template	The color of text for objects; default black.
Type	Boilerplate, Button, Query	The format of the boilerplate (read-only): the kind of button (Multimedia File named in the Multimedia File property, the default; Multimedia Column, a database column from the Multimedia Column property; or PL/SQL in the PL/SQL Trigger property) or the type of the query (read-only).
Unit of Measurement	Report	The metric unit the Report Builder uses to specify dimensions for various objects in the report: Inch (the default), Centimeter, or Point.
Use Previewer Hint Line	Report	Whether to display the text in the Previewer Hint Line property; default No.
Use Previewer Status Line	Report	Whether to display the text in the Previewer Status Line property; default No.
Use Vertical Spacing	Template	Whether to move objects to occupy unused space on previous lines; default Yes.
Validation Trigger	Parameter	Clicking on More displays the PL/SQL Editor to write a block that validates and/or modifies the parameter.
Value If Null	Column	The value to substitute for a NULL; default blank, meaning no substitution. If you set this on a break column, the Reports Runtime fetches all the rows in the group at once, which could degrade performance; in this case, use the NVL function in the query to substitute values for NULL.

TABLE 16-7.   *Report Module Properties* (continued)

Property	Object	Description
Vert. Space Between Frames	Repeating Frame	The amount of vertical space in a unit specified in the Unit of Measurement property between instances of the repeating frame; default 0.
Vertical Elasticity	Layout Object	How the height of the object changes to accommodate the data within it: Contract, Expand, Fixed, Variable. Contract decreases the size but doesn't expand it beyond the original size. Expand does the reverse. Fixed keeps the same height. Variable lets the field expand or contract to fit the data. For a graphic, the Reports Runtime scales the image to fit if you specify Fixed.
Vertical Panels per Page	Section	The height of the section's logical page in physical pages; default 1.
Visible	Field	Whether to display the field; default Yes. You can refer to the value in a hidden field in boilerplate text using the syntax &name, or &<name> with angle brackets to embed the value in other text without appending leading and trailing spaces.
Width	Column, Parameter, Parameter Form, Report, Section	The amount of text in characters a column or parameter can display; the width of the parameter form page in units specified in the Unit of Measurement property; the width of the physical page of the report; the width of the section.

TABLE 16-7. *Report Module Properties* (continued)

Display Module Objects

Table 16-8 lists the display module objects and describes their functions in a form application.

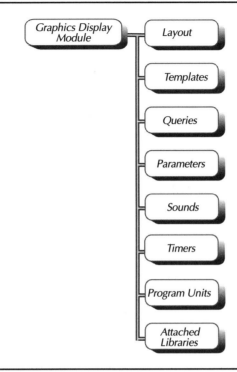

FIGURE 16-4.   *Object hierarchy for a graphics display module*

Display Module Properties

Graphics Builder differs from the other two major components, Form Builder and
Report Builder, in that you don't have Property Palettes and long lists of properties
to set through the Object Navigator. Instead, each object has a dialog box with
which you manipulate its properties. Table 16-9 lists all the properties in these
dialog boxes in alphabetical order. As well as describing the property, the table
shows which objects, and thus which dialog box, uses the property.

Object	Description
Layout Object	A graphic element of the chart.
Parameter	A variable you can set through the command line or by passing in parameters from a form or report.
Query	An SQL SELECT that defines the set of data that is the basis for the chart.
Sound	An object that represents sound data.
Template	A customized set of options for a chart.
Timer	An object that acts as a kind of alarm clock for the graphics display.

TABLE 16-8. *Graphics Display Module Objects*

Property	Object	Description
Active	Timer	Whether the timer is currently active (that is, whether the timer is to fire or not when the display executes).
Active Layer	Layer	The name of the currently active layer.
Begin	Chart	If Mapping Type is Gantt, the column to plot as the begin value.
Chart Category	Chart	The columns to plot on the category (x) axis.
Chart Values	Chart	If Mapping Type is General, the columns to plot on the value (y) axis.
Close	Chart	If Mapping Type is High-Low, the column to plot as the close value.
Custom Execute Procedure	Query	For custom queries, the PL/SQL procedure to invoke. Only procedures that have a valid custom query trigger procedure header appear in the drop-down list for this property.

TABLE 16-9. *Graphics Display Module Properties*

Property	Object	Description
Data Range	Chart	Which rows of data the chart plots: Plot All Rows (default) or Plot Rows (only those that fall within the specified range).
Data Type	Sound	The kind of sound file: 8 Bit Mono, 8 Bit Stereo, 16 Bit Mono, 16 Bit Stereo.
Date Format	Query	The Oracle date format the Graphics Runtime uses to recognize date data from a file (see the File property).
Device	Sound	The device on which to record or play back the sound.
Encoding	Sound	The kind of sound encoding: Signed/2's Complement PCM is the only choice.
End	Chart	If Mapping Type is Gantt, the column to plot as the end value.
Event Types	Chart	The mouse events that invoke the button procedure in the Procedure property: Mouse Button Down, Mouse Button Up, Mouse Move with Button Down, Mouse Move with Button Up (or any combination of these checked). Button Up applies only to layers.
Execute On	Query	When to execute the query automatically: Opening Display (default) or Timer (on a timer firing at a specific interval).
Execute Query	Layout Object	The query to execute when the user selects the object.
Existing Layers	Layer	The tree of layers in the display.
Field Template	Chart	If Mapping Type is General, the template that sets up the structure of the column you select in the Chart Values list.
File	Query	The name of the file from which to obtain the query.
Filter Function	Chart	A PL/SQL function that returns True for included records from the query in the Query property and False for records not to include.

TABLE 16-9.   *Graphics Display Module Properties* (continued)

Property	Object	Description
Format Trigger	Layout Object	The name of the procedure that executes when the Graphics Runtime formats the object. Only procedures that have a valid format trigger procedure header appear in the drop-down list for this property.
High	Chart	If Mapping Type is High-Low, the column to plot as the high value.
Initial Value	Parameter	The value to assign to the parameter variable when the Graphics Runtime creates it.
Interval	Timer	The amount of time in minutes and seconds that passes between executions of the PL/SQL procedure in the Procedure property for the timer.
Low	Chart	If Mapping Type is High-Low, the column to plot as the low value.
Mapping Type	Chart	The layout of the Values property page: General (the default, a single list of values), Gantt (begin and end values), or High-Low (high, close, and low values).
Maximum Number of Rows	Query	When the New Data property is Appends to Old Data, the greatest number of rows the query may return; the Graphics Runtime discards any additional rows.
Name	Layout Object, Chart, Query, Parameter, Timer	The object name.
New Data	Query	How to treat newly retrieved data: Replaces Old Data means discard all previous data, Appends to Old Data means retain previous data and add the new data to it.
New Name	Layer	The name with which to rename the layer when you click on the Rename button.

TABLE 16-9. *Graphics Display Module Properties* (continued)

Property	Object	Description
Parameter	Parameter	The name of the parameter to modify in the Parameter dialog box.
Post-Execution Trigger	Query	The PL/SQL procedure to invoke after executing the query. Only procedures that have a valid post-query trigger procedure header appear in the drop-down list for this property.
Procedure	Layout Object, Chart, Timer	The name of the PL/SQL button procedure for the object or chart. When a specified mouse event in the Event Types property occurs, the procedure executes. For a timer, this is the procedure to execute when the timer fires at the specified interval. Only procedures that have a valid button or timer trigger procedure header appear in the drop-down list.
Query	Chart	An SQL SELECT statement that returns the data to use as the basis for the chart.
Query Columns	Chart	Columns that you can use as chart categories (x axis) or chart values (y axis).
Rate	Sound	The rate at which to play back the sound in kHz.
Save Old Data	Query	When the New Data property is Replaces Old Data, whether to stored previously retrieved data in a buffer that you can access with PL/SQL built-in subprograms.
Set Parameter	Layout Object	When the object is selected, the parameter whose value is set.
SQL Statement	Query	The text of the SQL SELECT statement to execute for the query.
Subcategory	Chart	The column to use as a subcategory in a break chart.
Subtype	Chart	The particular kind of chart within the kind you select in the Type property.
Template	Chart	The chart template to use to structure the chart.

TABLE 16-9. *Graphics Display Module Properties* (continued)

Property	Object	Description
Timer	Timer	The timer to modify in the Timer dialog box.
Title	Chart	The text to display as a title for the chart.
To Value of	Layout Object	The value to which a parameter is set on object selection; the parameter is in the Set Parameter property.
Type	Chart, Parameter	The basic kind of chart: Column, Pie, Bar, Table, Line, Scatter, Mixed, High-Low, Double-Y, or Gantt. For a parameter, the data type: Number, Char, or Date.
Type	Query	The kind of query: SQL Statement, SYLK file (Excel spreadsheet), WKS file (Lotus 1-2-3 spreadsheet), PRN File (text file), External SQL File (a SELECT in a file). The file name appears in the File property.
Update Chart on Query Execution	Chart	Whether to update the chart automatically when the user executes the query; default checked.
Volume	Sound	The volume at which to record or play back the sound.

TABLE 16-9.   *Graphics Display Module Properties* (continued)

APPENDIX
A

The Database

his appendix contains the full Oracle8 SQL definition for the Talbot database. See Chapter 3 for an explanation of the different tables and for a full, graphical data model of the database showing the relationships between the tables.

You should use these commands by logging on as a single Oracle user with CONNECT and RESOURCE privileges. You may want to add workspace constraints to the tables if you wish to closely control the size of the data, although this is not a very large database.

Dropping the Tables

The first set of SQL commands drops the tables, sequences, and types, destroying any data in the database. These commands make sure you start with a clean example database.

```
DROP TABLE WorkerHasSkill;
DROP TABLE Skill;
DROP TABLE Ledger;
DROP TABLE Person;
DROP TABLE Lodging;
DROP SEQUENCE LedgerSequence;
DROP TYPE WorkerHasSkill_TP;
DROP TYPE Skill_TP;
DROP TYPE Ledger_TP;
DROP TYPE Person_TP;
DROP TYPE Lodging_TP;
DROP TYPE Address_TP;
```

Creating the Physical and Logical Schemas

The following commands create the storage structures and schema (the physical and conceptual databases). If you type in the commands, don't forget to put the slashes (/) after the CREATE TYPE statements. Because they can have PL/SQL in them, you need the slash as well as the semicolon terminator to execute the statement.

```
CREATE SEQUENCE LedgerSequence;
CREATE TYPE Address_TP AS OBJECT (
    Street1    VARCHAR2(100), -- first part of street address
    Street2    VARCHAR2(100), -- second part of street address
    City       VARCHAR2(100), -- city name
    State      VARCHAR2(2),   -- two-letter state abbreviation
    PostalCode VARCHAR2(15),  -- postal code of address
    Country    VARCHAR2(50)   -- country
);
/
CREATE TYPE Lodging_TP AS OBJECT (
```

```
  Lodging        VARCHAR2(15),  -- short name for the lodging
  LongName       VARCHAR2(40),  -- complete name
  Manager        VARCHAR2(25),  -- manager's name
  Address        Address_TP     -- address of the lodging
);
/
CREATE TYPE Person_TP AS OBJECT (
  Name           VARCHAR2(25),      -- worker's name
  AgeNUMBER,              -- age in years
  Lodging        REF Lodging_TP -- reference to person's lodging
);
/
CREATE TYPE Ledger_TP AS OBJECT (
  LedgerID       NUMBER,        -- sequence number, primary key
  ActionDate     DATE,          -- when
  Action         VARCHAR2(8),   -- bought, sold, paid, received
  ItemVARCHAR2(30),   -- what
  Quantity       NUMBER,        -- how many
  QuantityType   VARCHAR2(10),  -- type of quantity: lbs, bushels, etc.
  RateNUMBER(9,2),    -- how much per quantity type
  Amount         NUMBER(9,2),   -- total amount (extension) rate * quantity
  Person         REF Person_TP  -- reference to subject of transaction
);
/
CREATE TYPE Skill_TP AS OBJECT (
  Skill          VARCHAR2(25),  -- name of a capability
  Description    VARCHAR2(80)   -- description of the skill
);
/
REM Note that you cannot have a REF attribute as part of the primary key
CREATE TYPE WorkerHasSkill_TP AS OBJECT (
  Name           VARCHAR2(25),  -- worker's name, part of key
  Skill          VARCHAR2(25),  -- capability name, part of key
  Ability        VARCHAR2(15)   -- how skilled is the worker?
);
/
CREATE TABLE Ledger OF Ledger_TP (
  PRIMARY KEY (LedgerID)
);
CREATE TABLE Lodging OF Lodging_TP (
  PRIMARY KEY (Lodging)
);
CREATE TABLE Skill OF Skill_TP (
  PRIMARY KEY (Skill)
);
CREATE TABLE Person OF Person_TP (
  PRIMARY KEY (Name)
);
CREATE TABLE WorkerHasSkill OF WorkerHasSkill_TP (
  PRIMARY KEY (Name, Skill),
  FOREIGN KEY (Name) REFERENCES Person(Name),
  FOREIGN KEY (Skill) REFERENCES Skill(Skill)
);
```

Creating the Data

The following INSERT statements build the actual database. You must load the tables in the following order so that you satisfy all the integrity constraints. For example, if you insert a Person with a Lodging without having already inserted the Lodging, you violate an integrity constraint.

The Lodging Table

```
INSERT INTO Lodging VALUES (
'Cranmer','Cranmer Retreat House','Thom Cranmer',
Address_TP('Hill St.', NULL, 'Berkeley' , 'NH', '03431', 'USA'));
INSERT INTO Lodging VALUES (
'Matts','Matts Long Bunk House','Roland Brandt',
Address_TP('3 Mile Rd.', NULL, 'Keene', 'NH', '03431', 'USA'));
INSERT INTO Lodging VALUES (
'Mullers','Mullers Coed Lodging','Ken Muller',
Address_TP('120 Main', NULL, 'Edmeston', 'NH', '03431', 'USA'));
INSERT INTO Lodging VALUES (
'Papa King','Papa King Rooming','William King',
Address_TP('127 Main', NULL, 'Edmeston', 'NH', '03431', 'USA'));
INSERT INTO Lodging VALUES (
'Rose Hill','Rose Hill for Men','John Peletier',
Address_TP('RFD 3', NULL, 'N. Edmeston', 'NH', '03431', 'USA'));
INSERT INTO Lodging VALUES (
'Weitbrocht','Weitbrocht Rooming','Eunice Benson',
Address_TP('320 Geneva', NULL, 'Keene', 'NH', '03431', 'USA'));
```

The Skill Table

```
INSERT INTO Skill VALUES ('Woodcutter',
'Mark And Fell Trees, Split, Stack, Haul');
INSERT INTO Skill VALUES ('Combine Driver',
'Harness, Drive, Groom Horses, Adjust Blades');
INSERT INTO Skill VALUES ('Smithy',
'Stack For Fire, Run Bellows, Cut, Shoe Horses');
INSERT INTO Skill VALUES ('Grave Digger',
'Mark And Cut Sod, Dig, Shore, Fill, Resod');
INSERT INTO Skill VALUES ('Discus',
'Harness, Drive, Groom Horses, Blade Depth');
INSERT INTO Skill VALUES ('Work','General Unskilled labor');
```

The Person Table

```
INSERT INTO Person
   SELECT 'Bart Sarjeant', 22, REF(L)
```

```
      FROM Lodging L
   WHERE Lodging = 'Cranmer';
INSERT INTO Person
   SELECT 'Elbert Talbot', 43, REF(L)
      FROM Lodging L
   WHERE Lodging = 'Weitbrocht';
INSERT INTO Person
   SELECT 'Donald Rollo', 16, REF(L)
      FROM Lodging L
   WHERE Lodging = 'Matts';
INSERT INTO Person
   SELECT 'Jed Hopkins', 33, REF(L)
      FROM Lodging L
   WHERE Lodging = 'Matts';
INSERT INTO Person
   SELECT 'William Swing', 15, REF(L)
      FROM Lodging L
   WHERE Lodging = 'Cranmer';
INSERT INTO Person
   SELECT 'John Pearson', 27, REF(L)
      FROM Lodging L
   WHERE Lodging = 'Rose Hill';
INSERT INTO Person
   SELECT 'George Oscar', 41, REF(L)
      FROM Lodging L
   WHERE Lodging = 'Rose Hill';
INSERT INTO Person
   SELECT 'Kay And Palmer Wallbom', NULL, REF(L)
      FROM Lodging L
   WHERE Lodging = 'Rose Hill';
INSERT INTO Person
   SELECT 'Pat Lavay', 21, REF(L)
      FROM Lodging L
   WHERE Lodging = 'Rose Hill';
INSERT INTO Person
   SELECT 'Richard Koch And Brothers', NULL, REF(L)
      FROM Lodging L
   WHERE Lodging = 'Weitbrocht';
INSERT INTO Person
   SELECT 'Dick Jones', 18, REF(L)
      FROM Lodging L
   WHERE Lodging = 'Rose Hill';
INSERT INTO Person
   SELECT 'Adah Talbot', 23, REF(L)
      FROM Lodging L
   WHERE Lodging = 'Papa King';
INSERT INTO Person
   SELECT 'Roland Brandt', 35, REF(L)
      FROM Lodging L
```

```
      WHERE Lodging = 'Matts';
INSERT INTO Person
  SELECT 'Peter Lawson', 25, REF(L)
    FROM Lodging L
    WHERE Lodging = 'Cranmer';
INSERT INTO Person
  SELECT 'Victoria Lynn', 32, REF(L)
    FROM Lodging L
    WHERE Lodging = 'Mullers';
INSERT INTO Person VALUES ('Wilfred Lowell', 67, NULL);
INSERT INTO Person VALUES ('Helen Brandt', 15, NULL);
INSERT INTO Person
  SELECT 'Gerhardt Kentgen', 55, REF(L)
    FROM Lodging L
    WHERE Lodging = 'Papa King';
INSERT INTO Person
  SELECT 'Andrew Dye', 29, REF(L)
    FROM Lodging L
    WHERE Lodging = 'Rose Hill';
INSERT INTO Person VALUES ('Blacksmith', NULL, NULL);
INSERT INTO Person VALUES ('Boole And Jones', NULL, NULL);
INSERT INTO Person VALUES ('Dean Foreman', NULL, NULL);
INSERT INTO Person VALUES ('Dr. Carlstrom', NULL, NULL);
INSERT INTO Person VALUES ('Edward Johnson', NULL, NULL);
INSERT INTO Person VALUES ('Edythe Gammiere', NULL, NULL);
INSERT INTO Person VALUES ('Feed Store', NULL, NULL);
INSERT INTO Person VALUES ('Fred Fuller', NULL, NULL);
INSERT INTO Person VALUES ('Gary Kentgen', NULL, NULL);
INSERT INTO Person VALUES ('General Store', NULL, NULL);
INSERT INTO Person VALUES ('George August', NULL, NULL);
INSERT INTO Person VALUES ('George B. McCormick', NULL, NULL);
INSERT INTO Person VALUES ('Harold Schole', NULL, NULL);
INSERT INTO Person VALUES ('Henry Chase', NULL, NULL);
INSERT INTO Person VALUES ('Isaiah James', NULL, NULL);
INSERT INTO Person VALUES ('James Cole', NULL, NULL);
INSERT INTO Person VALUES ('Janice Talbot', NULL, NULL);
INSERT INTO Person VALUES ('John Austin', NULL, NULL);
INSERT INTO Person VALUES ('Lily Carlstrom', NULL, NULL);
INSERT INTO Person VALUES ('Livery', NULL, NULL);
INSERT INTO Person VALUES ('Mill', NULL, NULL);
INSERT INTO Person VALUES ('Manner Jewelers', NULL, NULL);
INSERT INTO Person VALUES ('Methodist Church', NULL, NULL);
INSERT INTO Person VALUES ('Morris Arnold', NULL, NULL);
INSERT INTO Person VALUES ('Palmer Wallbom', NULL, NULL);
INSERT INTO Person VALUES ('Phone Company', NULL, NULL);
INSERT INTO Person VALUES ('Post Office', NULL, NULL);
INSERT INTO Person VALUES ('Quarry', NULL, NULL);
INSERT INTO Person VALUES ('Robert James', NULL, NULL);
```

```
INSERT INTO Person VALUES ('Sam Dye', NULL, NULL);
INSERT INTO Person VALUES ('School', NULL, NULL);
INSERT INTO Person VALUES ('Underwood Bros', NULL, NULL);
INSERT INTO Person VALUES ('Verna Hardware', NULL, NULL);
```

The WorkerHasSkill Table

```
INSERT INTO WorkerHasSkill
VALUES ('Dick Jones','Smithy','Excellent');
INSERT INTO WorkerHasSkill
VALUES ('John Pearson','Combine Driver',NULL);
INSERT INTO WorkerHasSkill
VALUES ('John Pearson','Smithy','Average');
INSERT INTO WorkerHasSkill
VALUES ('Helen Brandt','Combine Driver','Very Fast');
INSERT INTO WorkerHasSkill
VALUES ('John Pearson','Woodcutter','Good');
INSERT INTO WorkerHasSkill
VALUES ('Victoria Lynn','Smithy','Precise');
INSERT INTO WorkerHasSkill
VALUES ('Adah Talbot','Work','Good');
INSERT INTO WorkerHasSkill
VALUES ('Wilfred Lowell','Work','Average');
INSERT INTO WorkerHasSkill
VALUES ('Elbert Talbot','Discus','Slow');
INSERT INTO WorkerHasSkill
VALUES ('Wilfred Lowell','Discus','Average');
```

The Ledger Table

```
INSERT INTO Ledger
SELECT LedgerSequence.NEXTVAL,'01-APR-01','Paid','Plowing',1,
      'Day',3,3,REF(P)
  FROM Person P
 WHERE Name = 'Richard Koch And Brothers';
INSERT INTO Ledger
SELECT LedgerSequence.NEXTVAL,'02-MAY-01','Paid','Work',1,
      'Day',1,1,REF(P)
  FROM Person P
 WHERE Name = 'Dick Jones';
INSERT INTO Ledger
SELECT LedgerSequence.NEXTVAL,'03-JUN-01','Paid','Work',1,
      'Day',1,1, REF(P)
  FROM Person P
 WHERE Name = 'Elbert Talbot';
INSERT INTO Ledger
```

```
    SELECT LedgerSequence.NEXTVAL,'04-JAN-01','Paid','Work',1,
           'Day',1,1, REF(P)
      FROM Person P
     WHERE Name = 'Gerhardt Kentgen';
    INSERT INTO Ledger
    SELECT LedgerSequence.NEXTVAL,'04-FEB-01','Paid','Work',.5,
           'Day',1,.5, REF(P)
      FROM Person P
     WHERE Name = 'Elbert Talbot';
    INSERT INTO Ledger
    SELECT LedgerSequence.NEXTVAL,'05-APR-01','Paid','Work',1,
           'Day',1,1, REF(P)
      FROM Person P
     WHERE Name = 'Dick Jones';
    INSERT INTO Ledger
    SELECT LedgerSequence.NEXTVAL,'06-AUG-01','Paid','Plowing',1,
           'Day',1.8,1.8, REF(P)
      FROM Person P
     WHERE Name = 'Victoria Lynn';
    INSERT INTO Ledger
    SELECT LedgerSequence.NEXTVAL,'07-OCT-01','Paid','Plowing',.5,
           'Day',3,1.5, REF(P)
      FROM Person P
     WHERE Name = 'Richard Koch And Brothers';
    INSERT INTO Ledger
    SELECT LedgerSequence.NEXTVAL,'09-SEP-01','Paid','Work',1,
           'Day',1,1,REF(P)
      FROM Person P
     WHERE Name = 'Adah Talbot';
    INSERT INTO Ledger
    SELECT LedgerSequence.NEXTVAL,'09-OCT-01','Paid','Work',.5,
           'Day',1.25,.63, REF(P)
      FROM Person P
     WHERE Name = 'Donald Rollo';
    INSERT INTO Ledger
    SELECT LedgerSequence.NEXTVAL,'10-NOV-01','Paid','Work',1,
           'Day',1.25,.63, REF(P)
      FROM Person P
     WHERE Name = 'John Pearson';
    INSERT INTO Ledger
    SELECT LedgerSequence.NEXTVAL,'10-AUG-01','Paid','Work',1,
           'Day',1,1, REF(P)
      FROM Person P
     WHERE Name = 'Helen Brandt';
    INSERT INTO Ledger
    SELECT LedgerSequence.NEXTVAL,'11-AUG-01','Paid','Work',1,
           'Day',2,2, REF(P)
      FROM Person P
```

```
 WHERE Name = 'Helen Brandt';
INSERT INTO Ledger
SELECT LedgerSequence.NEXTVAL,'11-SEP-01','Paid','Work',1,
       'Day',.75,.75, REF(P)
  FROM Person P
 WHERE Name = 'Roland Brandt';
INSERT INTO Ledger
SELECT LedgerSequence.NEXTVAL,'12-DEC-01','Paid','Work',1,
       'Day',1,1, REF(P)
  FROM Person P
 WHERE Name = 'Bart Sarjeant';
INSERT INTO Ledger
SELECT LedgerSequence.NEXTVAL,'12-JAN-01','Paid','Work',1,
       'Day',1,1, REF(P)
  FROM Person P
 WHERE Name = 'George Oscar';
INSERT INTO Ledger
SELECT LedgerSequence.NEXTVAL,'13-JUN-01','Paid','Work',1,
       'Day',1,1, REF(P)
  FROM Person P
 WHERE Name = 'Peter Lawson';
INSERT INTO Ledger
SELECT LedgerSequence.NEXTVAL,'14-JUL-01','Paid','Work',1,
       'Day',1.2,1.2, REF(P)
  FROM Person P
 WHERE Name = 'Wilfred Lowell';
INSERT INTO Ledger
SELECT LedgerSequence.NEXTVAL,'15-JUL-01','Paid','Work',1,
       'Day',2.25,2.25, REF(P)
  FROM Person P
 WHERE Name = 'Kay And Palmer Wallbom';
INSERT INTO Ledger
SELECT LedgerSequence.NEXTVAL,'03-OCT-01','Sold','Boot Between Horses',1,
       'Each',12.5,12.5, REF(P)
  FROM Person P
 WHERE Name = 'Gary Kentgen';
INSERT INTO Ledger
SELECT LedgerSequence.NEXTVAL,'01-NOV-01','Bought','Calf',2,
       'Each',2,4, REF(P)
  FROM Person P
 WHERE Name = 'Gary Kentgen';
INSERT INTO Ledger
SELECT LedgerSequence.NEXTVAL,'02-NOV-01','Bought','Mare',1,
       'Each',5,5, REF(P)
  FROM Person P
 WHERE Name = 'James Cole';
INSERT INTO Ledger
SELECT LedgerSequence.NEXTVAL,'03-NOV-01','Bought','Pig',1,
```

```
              'Each',2,2, REF(P)
      FROM Person P
     WHERE Name = 'Andrew Dye';
   INSERT INTO Ledger
   SELECT LedgerSequence.NEXTVAL,'04-NOV-01','Bought','Hay',1,
              'Wagon',5,5, REF(P)
      FROM Person P
     WHERE Name = 'Andrew Dye';
   INSERT INTO Ledger
   SELECT LedgerSequence.NEXTVAL,'05-NOV-01','Bought','Hay',4,
              'Wagon',5,20, REF(P)
      FROM Person P
     WHERE Name = 'Andrew Dye';
   INSERT INTO Ledger
   SELECT LedgerSequence.NEXTVAL,'05-NOV-01','Bought','Line',1,
              'Set',.75,.75, REF(P)
      FROM Person P
     WHERE Name = 'Andrew Dye';
   INSERT INTO Ledger
   SELECT LedgerSequence.NEXTVAL,'06-NOV-01','Bought','Colt',2,
              'Each',4.5,9, REF(P)
      FROM Person P
     WHERE Name = 'Andrew Dye';
   INSERT INTO Ledger
   SELECT LedgerSequence.NEXTVAL,'06-AUG-01','Paid','Plowing',2,
              'Day',2,4, REF(P)
      FROM Person P
     WHERE Name = 'Andrew Dye';
   INSERT INTO Ledger
   SELECT LedgerSequence.NEXTVAL,'07-NOV-01','Paid','Sawed Wood',1,
              'Day',.5,.5, REF(P)
      FROM Person P
     WHERE Name = 'Andrew Dye';
   INSERT INTO Ledger
   SELECT LedgerSequence.NEXTVAL,'09-NOV-01','Bought','Colt',1,
              'Each',10,10, REF(P)
      FROM Person P
     WHERE Name = 'Andrew Dye';
   INSERT INTO Ledger
   SELECT LedgerSequence.NEXTVAL,'10-NOV-01','Sold','Hefer',1,
              'Each',28,28, REF(P)
      FROM Person P
     WHERE Name = 'Pat Lavay';
   INSERT INTO Ledger
   SELECT LedgerSequence.NEXTVAL,'11-NOV-01','Sold','Boot Between Horses',1,
              'Each',6,6, REF(P)
      FROM Person P
     WHERE Name = 'Pat Lavay';
```

```
INSERT INTO Ledger
SELECT LedgerSequence.NEXTVAL,'11-NOV-01','Sold','Butter',1,
       'Pound',.15,.15, REF(P)
  FROM Person P
 WHERE Name = 'Pat Lavay';
INSERT INTO Ledger
SELECT LedgerSequence.NEXTVAL,'12-NOV-01','Paid','Work',2,
       'Day',.75,1.5, REF(P)
  FROM Person P
 WHERE Name = 'Pat Lavay';
INSERT INTO Ledger
SELECT LedgerSequence.NEXTVAL,'13-NOV-01','Paid','Cut Logs',.5,
       'Day',.5,.25, REF(P)
  FROM Person P
 WHERE Name = 'Pat Lavay';
INSERT INTO Ledger
SELECT LedgerSequence.NEXTVAL,'13-NOV-01','Paid','Drawed Logs',1.5,
       'Day',.5,.75, REF(P)
  FROM Person P
 WHERE Name = 'Pat Lavay';
INSERT INTO Ledger
SELECT LedgerSequence.NEXTVAL,'13-DEC-01','Paid','Sawed Wood',1,
       'Day',.5,.5, REF(P)
  FROM Person P
 WHERE Name = 'Pat Lavay';
INSERT INTO Ledger
SELECT LedgerSequence.NEXTVAL,'14-NOV-01','Sold','Hefer',1,
       'Each',35,35, REF(P)
  FROM Person P
 WHERE Name = 'Morris Arnold';
INSERT INTO Ledger
SELECT LedgerSequence.NEXTVAL,'15-NOV-01','Sold','Beef',37,
       'Pound',.04,1.48, REF(P)
  FROM Person P
 WHERE Name = 'Fred Fuller';
INSERT INTO Ledger
SELECT LedgerSequence.NEXTVAL,'16-NOV-01','Sold','Butter',5,
       'Pound',.16,.8, REF(P)
  FROM Person P
 WHERE Name = 'Victoria Lynn';
INSERT INTO Ledger
SELECT LedgerSequence.NEXTVAL,'18-NOV-01','Sold','Butter',6,
       'Pound',.16,.96, REF(P)
  FROM Person P
 WHERE Name = 'John Pearson';
INSERT INTO Ledger
SELECT LedgerSequence.NEXTVAL,'20-NOV-01','Sold','Heifer',1,
       'Each',30,30, REF(P)
```

```
   FROM Person P
  WHERE Name = 'Palmer Wallbom';
INSERT INTO Ledger
SELECT LedgerSequence.NEXTVAL,'21-NOV-01','Sold','Beef',116,
       'Pound',.06,6.96, REF(P)
   FROM Person P
  WHERE Name = 'Roland Brandt';
INSERT INTO Ledger
SELECT LedgerSequence.NEXTVAL,'22-NOV-01','Sold','Beef',118,
       'Pound',.06,7.08, REF(P)
   FROM Person P
  WHERE Name = 'Gerhardt Kentgen';
INSERT INTO Ledger
SELECT LedgerSequence.NEXTVAL,'01-DEC-01','Bought','Beef',138,
       'Pound',.05,6.9, REF(P)
   FROM Person P
  WHERE Name = 'Victoria Lynn';
INSERT INTO Ledger
SELECT LedgerSequence.NEXTVAL,'01-DEC-01','Bought','Beef',130,
       'Pound',.06,7.8, REF(P)
   FROM Person P
  WHERE Name = 'George B. McCormick';
INSERT INTO Ledger
SELECT LedgerSequence.NEXTVAL,'03-DEC-01','Bought','Beef',130,
       'Pound',.05,6.5, REF(P)
   FROM Person P
  WHERE Name = 'Peter Lawson';
INSERT INTO Ledger
SELECT LedgerSequence.NEXTVAL,'03-DEC-01','Bought','Beef',125,
       'Pound',.06,7.5, REF(P)
   FROM Person P
  WHERE Name = 'Helen Brandt';
INSERT INTO Ledger
SELECT LedgerSequence.NEXTVAL,'05-DEC-01','Bought','Beef',140,
       'Pound',.05,7, REF(P)
   FROM Person P
  WHERE Name = 'Robert James';
INSERT INTO Ledger
SELECT LedgerSequence.NEXTVAL,'05-DEC-01','Bought','Beef',145,
       'Pound',.05,7.25, REF(P)
   FROM Person P
  WHERE Name = 'Isaiah James';
INSERT INTO Ledger
SELECT LedgerSequence.NEXTVAL,'07-DEC-01','Bought','Horse',1,
       'Each',30,30, REF(P)
   FROM Person P
  WHERE Name = 'George August';
```

```
INSERT INTO Ledger
SELECT LedgerSequence.NEXTVAL,'07-DEC-01','Bought','Reaper/Binder',1,
       'Each',47.5,47.5, REF(P)
  FROM Person P
 WHERE Name = 'Janice Talbot';
INSERT INTO Ledger
SELECT LedgerSequence.NEXTVAL,'03-JAN-01','Bought','Hominy',1,
       'Bushel',1.25,1.25, REF(P)
  FROM Person P
 WHERE Name = 'General Store';
INSERT INTO Ledger
SELECT LedgerSequence.NEXTVAL,'09-JAN-01','Bought','Lice Killer',1,
       'Each',.5,.5, REF(P)
  FROM Person P
 WHERE Name = 'General Store';
INSERT INTO Ledger
SELECT LedgerSequence.NEXTVAL,'11-JAN-01','Bought','Mending Brace',1,
       'Each',.15,.15, REF(P)
  FROM Person P
 WHERE Name = 'General Store';
INSERT INTO Ledger
SELECT LedgerSequence.NEXTVAL,'11-JAN-01','Bought','Stove Blacking',1,
       'Each',.05,.05, REF(P)
  FROM Person P
 WHERE Name = 'General Store';
INSERT INTO Ledger
SELECT LedgerSequence.NEXTVAL,'13-JAN-01','Bought','Grinding Bat',10,
       'Each',.03,.3, REF(P)
  FROM Person P
 WHERE Name = 'General Store';
INSERT INTO Ledger
SELECT LedgerSequence.NEXTVAL,'14-JAN-01','Sold','Beef Hide',1,
       'Each',5.46,5.46, REF(P)
  FROM Person P
 WHERE Name = 'General Store';
INSERT INTO Ledger
SELECT LedgerSequence.NEXTVAL,'14-JAN-01','Sold','Cheese Flat',13,
       'Each',3.15,40.95, REF(P)
  FROM Person P
 WHERE Name = 'General Store';
INSERT INTO Ledger
SELECT LedgerSequence.NEXTVAL,'14-JAN-01','Bought','Lantern Globe',1,
       'Each',.1,.1, REF(P)
  FROM Person P
 WHERE Name = 'General Store';
INSERT INTO Ledger
SELECT LedgerSequence.NEXTVAL,'15-JAN-01','Bought','Stamp For Letter',1,
       'Each',.02,.02, REF(P)
```

```
    FROM Person P
 WHERE Name = 'Post Office';
INSERT INTO Ledger
SELECT LedgerSequence.NEXTVAL,'15-JAN-01','Bought','Stocking',2,
       'Pair',.15,.3, REF(P)
    FROM Person P
 WHERE Name = 'General Store';
INSERT INTO Ledger
SELECT LedgerSequence.NEXTVAL,'16-JAN-01','Bought','Oil',4,
       'Gallon',.1,.4, REF(P)
    FROM Person P
 WHERE Name = 'General Store';
INSERT INTO Ledger
SELECT LedgerSequence.NEXTVAL,'16-JAN-01','Bought','Sugar',25,
       'Pound',.07,1.75, REF(P)
    FROM Person P
 WHERE Name = 'General Store';
INSERT INTO Ledger
SELECT LedgerSequence.NEXTVAL,'16-JAN-01','Bought','Molasses',1,
       'Gallon',.6,.6, REF(P)
    FROM Person P
 WHERE Name = 'General Store';
INSERT INTO Ledger
SELECT LedgerSequence.NEXTVAL,'16-JAN-01','Bought','Card Of Thanks',1,
       'Each',.3,.3, REF(P)
    FROM Person P
 WHERE Name = 'General Store';
INSERT INTO Ledger
SELECT LedgerSequence.NEXTVAL,'17-JAN-01','Bought','Horse Shodding',1,
       'Each',.85,.85, REF(P)
    FROM Person P
 WHERE Name = 'Livery';
INSERT INTO Ledger
SELECT LedgerSequence.NEXTVAL,'17-JAN-01','Bought','Corn',230,
       'Pound',.01,2.3, REF(P)
    FROM Person P
 WHERE Name = 'Feed Store';
INSERT INTO Ledger
SELECT LedgerSequence.NEXTVAL,'18-JAN-01','Bought','Corn Meal',213,
       'Pound',.01,2.13, REF(P)
    FROM Person P
 WHERE Name = 'Feed Store';
INSERT INTO Ledger
SELECT LedgerSequence.NEXTVAL,'18-JAN-01','Bought','Paper',50,
       'Sheets',.01,.5, REF(P)
    FROM Person P
 WHERE Name = 'General Store';
INSERT INTO Ledger
```

```
SELECT LedgerSequence.NEXTVAL,'18-JAN-01','Bought','Coffee',1,
       'Pound',.3,.3, REF(P)
  FROM Person P
 WHERE Name = 'General Store';
INSERT INTO Ledger
SELECT LedgerSequence.NEXTVAL,'18-JAN-01','Bought','Seeded Raisins',1,
       'Pound',.12,.12, REF(P)
  FROM Person P
 WHERE Name = 'General Store';
INSERT INTO Ledger
SELECT LedgerSequence.NEXTVAL,'18-JAN-01','Bought','Cotton Stocking',3,
       'Pair',.08,.24, REF(P)
  FROM Person P
 WHERE Name = 'General Store';
INSERT INTO Ledger
SELECT LedgerSequence.NEXTVAL,'19-JAN-01','Bought','Cotton Stocking',3,
       'Pair',.08,.24, REF(P)
  FROM Person P
 WHERE Name = 'General Store';
INSERT INTO Ledger
SELECT LedgerSequence.NEXTVAL,'19-JAN-01','Bought','Grinding Bat',24,
       'Each',.03,.72, REF(P)
  FROM Person P
 WHERE Name = 'General Store';
INSERT INTO Ledger
SELECT LedgerSequence.NEXTVAL,'19-JAN-01','Bought','Telephone Call',1,
       'Each',.15,.15, REF(P)
  FROM Person P
 WHERE Name = 'Phone Company';
INSERT INTO Ledger
SELECT LedgerSequence.NEXTVAL,'19-JAN-01','Bought','Tea',.5,
       'Pound',.5,.25, REF(P)
  FROM Person P
 WHERE Name = 'General Store';
INSERT INTO Ledger
SELECT LedgerSequence.NEXTVAL,'19-JAN-01','Bought','Hat',1,
       'Each',.1,.1, REF(P)
  FROM Person P
 WHERE Name = 'General Store';
INSERT INTO Ledger
SELECT LedgerSequence.NEXTVAL,'19-JAN-01','Bought','Salt Peter',1,
       'Each',.08,.08, REF(P)
  FROM Person P
 WHERE Name = 'General Store';
INSERT INTO Ledger
SELECT LedgerSequence.NEXTVAL,'19-JAN-01','Bought','Envelopes',6,
       'Each',.02,.12, REF(P)
  FROM Person P
```

```
      WHERE Name = 'General Store';
    INSERT INTO Ledger
    SELECT LedgerSequence.NEXTVAL,'19-JAN-01','Bought','Creoal',2,
           'Qaurt',.37,.74, REF(P)
      FROM Person P
     WHERE Name = 'General Store';
    INSERT INTO Ledger
    SELECT LedgerSequence.NEXTVAL,'23-JAN-01','Sold','Wood',1,
           'Cord',2,2, REF(P)
      FROM Person P
     WHERE Name = 'Methodist Church';
    INSERT INTO Ledger
    SELECT LedgerSequence.NEXTVAL,'24-JAN-01','Bought','Schooling',1,
           'Each',1,1, REF(P)
      FROM Person P
     WHERE Name = 'School';
    INSERT INTO Ledger
    SELECT LedgerSequence.NEXTVAL,'24-JAN-01','Bought','Hominy',186,
           'Each',.01,1.86, REF(P)
      FROM Person P
     WHERE Name = 'General Store';
    INSERT INTO Ledger
    SELECT LedgerSequence.NEXTVAL,'28-JAN-01','Bought','Grinding',1,
           'Each',.9,.9, REF(P)
      FROM Person P
     WHERE Name = 'Mill';
    INSERT INTO Ledger
    SELECT LedgerSequence.NEXTVAL,'28-JAN-01','Bought','Popcorn',5,
           'Pound',.04,.2, REF(P)
      FROM Person P
     WHERE Name = 'General Store';
    INSERT INTO Ledger
    SELECT LedgerSequence.NEXTVAL,'02-FEB-01','Bought','Sulpher',5,
           'Pound',.25,1.25, REF(P)
      FROM Person P
     WHERE Name = 'General Store';
    INSERT INTO Ledger
    SELECT LedgerSequence.NEXTVAL,'03-FEB-01','Bought','Oil',4,
           'Gallon',.13,.52, REF(P)
      FROM Person P
     WHERE Name = 'General Store';
    INSERT INTO Ledger
    SELECT LedgerSequence.NEXTVAL,'03-FEB-01','Bought','Swamp Root',1,
           'Each',.75,.75, REF(P)
      FROM Person P
     WHERE Name = 'General Store';
    INSERT INTO Ledger
    SELECT LedgerSequence.NEXTVAL,'04-FEB-01','Bought','Shoeing Ned',1,
```

```
           'Each',.5,.5, REF(P)
   FROM Person P
  WHERE Name = 'Blacksmith';
INSERT INTO Ledger
SELECT LedgerSequence.NEXTVAL,'04-FEB-01','Bought','Grinding',1,
           'Each',.47,.47, REF(P)
   FROM Person P
  WHERE Name = 'Mill';
INSERT INTO Ledger
SELECT LedgerSequence.NEXTVAL,'05-FEB-01','Bought','Pills',1,
           'Each',.25,.25, REF(P)
   FROM Person P
  WHERE Name = 'General Store';
INSERT INTO Ledger
SELECT LedgerSequence.NEXTVAL,'07-FEB-01','Bought','Thread',2,
           'Each',.05,.1, REF(P)
   FROM Person P
  WHERE Name = 'General Store';
INSERT INTO Ledger
SELECT LedgerSequence.NEXTVAL,'08-FEB-01','Bought','Shirts',2,
           'Each',.5,1, REF(P)
   FROM Person P
  WHERE Name = 'General Store';
INSERT INTO Ledger
SELECT LedgerSequence.NEXTVAL,'10-FEB-01','Sold','Butter',9,
           'Pound',.25,2.25, REF(P)
   FROM Person P
  WHERE Name = 'General Store';
INSERT INTO Ledger
SELECT LedgerSequence.NEXTVAL,'18-FEB-01','Bought','Horse Medison',1,
           'Each',.13,.13, REF(P)
   FROM Person P
  WHERE Name = 'General Store';
INSERT INTO Ledger
SELECT LedgerSequence.NEXTVAL,'18-FEB-01','Bought','Elbo Stove Pipe',1,
           'Each',.15,.15, REF(P)
   FROM Person P
  WHERE Name = 'General Store';
INSERT INTO Ledger
SELECT LedgerSequence.NEXTVAL,'18-FEB-01','Sold','Calf',1,
           'Each',4,4, REF(P)
   FROM Person P
  WHERE Name = 'Lily Carlstrom';
INSERT INTO Ledger
SELECT LedgerSequence.NEXTVAL,'25-FEB-01','Sold','Butter',21,
           'Pound',.25,5.25, REF(P)
   FROM Person P
  WHERE Name = 'General Store';
```

```
INSERT INTO Ledger
SELECT LedgerSequence.NEXTVAL,'28-FEB-01','Bought','Swamp Root',1,
       'Each',.75,.75, REF(P)
  FROM Person P
 WHERE Name = 'General Store';
INSERT INTO Ledger
SELECT LedgerSequence.NEXTVAL,'28-FEB-01','Bought','Liver Pills',1,
       'Each',.2,.2, REF(P)
  FROM Person P
 WHERE Name = 'General Store';
INSERT INTO Ledger
SELECT LedgerSequence.NEXTVAL,'28-FEB-01','Sold','Butter',3,
       'Pound',.25,.75, REF(P)
  FROM Person P
 WHERE Name = 'Helen Brandt';
INSERT INTO Ledger
SELECT LedgerSequence.NEXTVAL,'01-APR-01','Bought','Grinding',1,
       'Each',.45,.45, REF(P)
  FROM Person P
 WHERE Name = 'Mill';
INSERT INTO Ledger
SELECT LedgerSequence.NEXTVAL,'06-MAR-01','Bought','Medison For
       Indigestion',1,
       'Each',.4,.4, REF(P)
  FROM Person P
 WHERE Name = 'Dr. Carlstrom';
INSERT INTO Ledger
SELECT LedgerSequence.NEXTVAL,'06-JUN-01','Bought','Breading Powder',1,
       'Each',.9,.9, REF(P)
  FROM Person P
 WHERE Name = 'Mill';
INSERT INTO Ledger
SELECT LedgerSequence.NEXTVAL,'06-MAR-01','Bought','Pants',1,
       'Pair',.75,.75, REF(P)
  FROM Person P
 WHERE Name = 'General Store';
INSERT INTO Ledger
SELECT LedgerSequence.NEXTVAL,'07-APR-01','Bought','Hominy',200,
       'Pound',.01,2, REF(P)
  FROM Person P
 WHERE Name = 'Mill';
INSERT INTO Ledger
SELECT LedgerSequence.NEXTVAL,'08-MAR-01','Bought','Tobacco For
       Lice',1,
       'Each',.25,.25, REF(P)
  FROM Person P
 WHERE Name = 'Mill';
INSERT INTO Ledger
```

```
SELECT LedgerSequence.NEXTVAL,'07-MAR-01','Bought','Shoeing',1,
       'Each',.35,.35, REF(P)
  FROM Person P
 WHERE Name = 'Blacksmith';
INSERT INTO Ledger
SELECT LedgerSequence.NEXTVAL,'07-APR-01','Bought','Pins',1,
       'Each',.05,.05, REF(P)
  FROM Person P
 WHERE Name = 'General Store';
INSERT INTO Ledger
SELECT LedgerSequence.NEXTVAL,'07-MAR-01','Bought','Mail Box',1,
       'Each',1,1, REF(P)
  FROM Person P
 WHERE Name = 'Post Office';
INSERT INTO Ledger
SELECT LedgerSequence.NEXTVAL,'10-MAR-01','Bought','Stove Pipe Thimbles',2,
       'Each',.5,1, REF(P)
  FROM Person P
 WHERE Name = 'Verna Hardware';
INSERT INTO Ledger
SELECT LedgerSequence.NEXTVAL,'13-MAR-01','Bought','Thermometer',1,
       'Each',.15,.15, REF(P)
  FROM Person P
 WHERE Name = 'General Store';
INSERT INTO Ledger
SELECT LedgerSequence.NEXTVAL,'14-MAR-01','Bought','Lot In Cemetery No. 80',1,
       'Each',25,25,REF(P)
  FROM Person P
 WHERE Name = 'Methodist Church';
INSERT INTO Ledger
SELECT LedgerSequence.NEXTVAL,'14-MAR-01','Paid','Digging Of Grave',1,
       'Each',3,3, REF(P)
  FROM Person P
 WHERE Name = 'Jed Hopkins';
INSERT INTO Ledger
SELECT LedgerSequence.NEXTVAL,'16-APR-01','Bought','Grinding',1,
       'Each',.16,.16, REF(P)
  FROM Person P
 WHERE Name = 'Mill';
INSERT INTO Ledger
SELECT LedgerSequence.NEXTVAL,'16-MAR-01','Bought','Grinding',1,
       'Each',.16,.16, REF(P)
  FROM Person P
 WHERE Name = 'Mill';
INSERT INTO Ledger
SELECT LedgerSequence.NEXTVAL,'23-MAR-01','Bought','Cloth For Dress Lining',2,
       'Yard',.27,.54,REF(P)
  FROM Person P
```

```
    WHERE Name = 'General Store';
 INSERT INTO Ledger
 SELECT LedgerSequence.NEXTVAL,'18-AUG-01','Bought','SYRUP Thermometer',1,
        'Each',1,1, REF(P)
   FROM Person P
  WHERE Name = 'General Store';
 INSERT INTO Ledger
 SELECT LedgerSequence.NEXTVAL,'25-MAR-01','Bought','Boots For Shirley',1,
        'Pair',2.5,2.5, REF(P)
   FROM Person P
  WHERE Name = 'General Store';
 INSERT INTO Ledger
 SELECT LedgerSequence.NEXTVAL,'27-APR-01','Bought','Syrup Cans',2,
        'Dozen',1.07,2.14, REF(P)
   FROM Person P
  WHERE Name = 'Verna Hardware';
 INSERT INTO Ledger
 SELECT LedgerSequence.NEXTVAL,'22-MAR-01','Bought','Milk Cans',2,
        'Each',2.5,5, REF(P)
   FROM Person P
  WHERE Name = 'Verna Hardware';
 INSERT INTO Ledger
 SELECT LedgerSequence.NEXTVAL,'23-APR-01','Bought','Dubble Strainer',1,
        'Each',.95,.95, REF(P)
   FROM Person P
  WHERE Name = 'Verna Hardware';
 INSERT INTO Ledger
 SELECT LedgerSequence.NEXTVAL,'25-JUN-01','Bought','Milk Stirrer',1,
        'Each',.25,.25, REF(P)
   FROM Person P
  WHERE Name = 'Verna Hardware';
 INSERT INTO Ledger
 SELECT LedgerSequence.NEXTVAL,'27-MAR-01','Bought','Hominy',77,
        'Pound',.01,.77, REF(P)
   FROM Person P
  WHERE Name = 'Mill';
 INSERT INTO Ledger
 SELECT LedgerSequence.NEXTVAL,'28-APR-01','Bought','Corn',104,
        'Pound',.01,1.04, REF(P)
   FROM Person P
  WHERE Name = 'Mill';
 INSERT INTO Ledger
 SELECT LedgerSequence.NEXTVAL,'06-APR-01','Bought','Funeral',1,
        'Each',3.19,3.19, REF(P)
   FROM Person P
  WHERE Name = 'Underwood Bros';
 INSERT INTO Ledger
 SELECT LedgerSequence.NEXTVAL,'30-APR-01','Bought','Brush',1,
```

```
          'Each',.05,.05, REF(P)
    FROM Person P
   WHERE Name = 'General Store';
INSERT INTO Ledger
SELECT LedgerSequence.NEXTVAL,'30-APR-01','Bought','Sand',5,
          'Bushel',.03,.15, REF(P)
    FROM Person P
   WHERE Name = 'Quarry';
INSERT INTO Ledger
SELECT LedgerSequence.NEXTVAL,'31-MAR-01','Sold','Molasses',3,
          'Gallon',1,3, REF(P)
    FROM Person P
   WHERE Name = 'Harold Schole';
INSERT INTO Ledger
SELECT LedgerSequence.NEXTVAL,'28-MAR-01','Sold','Molasses',1,
          'Gallon',1,1, REF(P)
    FROM Person P
   WHERE Name = 'Gerhardt Kentgen';
INSERT INTO Ledger
SELECT LedgerSequence.NEXTVAL,'30-MAR-01','Bought','Fixing Shirleys Watch',1,
          'Each',.25,.25,REF(P)
    FROM Person P
   WHERE Name = 'Manner Jewelers';
INSERT INTO Ledger
SELECT LedgerSequence.NEXTVAL,'04-APR-01','Sold','Butter',9,
          'Pound',.23,2.07, REF(P)
    FROM Person P
   WHERE Name = 'Harold Schole';
INSERT INTO Ledger
SELECT LedgerSequence.NEXTVAL,'05-APR-01','Bought','Soda',1,
          'Each',.05,.05, REF(P)
    FROM Person P
   WHERE Name = 'General Store';
INSERT INTO Ledger
SELECT LedgerSequence.NEXTVAL,'05-MAR-01','Bought','Telephone Call',1,
          'Each',.2,.2, REF(P)
    FROM Person P
   WHERE Name = 'Phone Company';
INSERT INTO Ledger
SELECT LedgerSequence.NEXTVAL,'06-APR-01','Bought','Gloves',1,
          'Pair',.25,.25, REF(P)
    FROM Person P
   WHERE Name = 'General Store';
INSERT INTO Ledger
SELECT LedgerSequence.NEXTVAL,'06-APR-01','Bought','Shoes For Shirley',1,
          'Pair',2,2, REF(P)
    FROM Person P
   WHERE Name = 'General Store';
```

```
INSERT INTO Ledger
SELECT LedgerSequence.NEXTVAL,'09-APR-01','Bought','Peanuts',1,
       'Each',.05,.05, REF(P)
  FROM Person P
 WHERE Name = 'General Store';
INSERT INTO Ledger
SELECT LedgerSequence.NEXTVAL,'11-APR-01','Bought','Bran',300,
       'Pound',.01,3, REF(P)
  FROM Person P
 WHERE Name = 'General Store';
INSERT INTO Ledger
SELECT LedgerSequence.NEXTVAL,'15-APR-01','Bought','Shoeing',2,
       'Each',.3,.6, REF(P)
  FROM Person P
 WHERE Name = 'Blacksmith';
INSERT INTO Ledger
SELECT LedgerSequence.NEXTVAL,'17-APR-01','Bought','Hominy',173,
       'Pound',.01,1.73, REF(P)
  FROM Person P
 WHERE Name = 'General Store';
INSERT INTO Ledger
SELECT LedgerSequence.NEXTVAL,'17-APR-01','Bought','Bran',450,
       'Pound',.01,4.5, REF(P)
  FROM Person P
 WHERE Name = 'General Store';
INSERT INTO Ledger
SELECT LedgerSequence.NEXTVAL,'17-APR-01','Bought','Calf Meal',110,
       'Pound',.01,1.1, REF(P)
  FROM Person P
 WHERE Name = 'General Store';
INSERT INTO Ledger
SELECT LedgerSequence.NEXTVAL,'22-APR-01','Bought','Hominy',454,
       'Pound',.01,4.54, REF(P)
  FROM Person P
 WHERE Name = 'General Store';
INSERT INTO Ledger
SELECT LedgerSequence.NEXTVAL,'22-APR-01','Bought','Bran',300,
       'Pound',.01,3, REF(P)
  FROM Person P
 WHERE Name = 'General Store';
INSERT INTO Ledger
SELECT LedgerSequence.NEXTVAL,'22-APR-01','Sold','Calf',1,
       'Each',1,1, REF(P)
  FROM Person P
 WHERE Name = 'Pat Lavay';
INSERT INTO Ledger
SELECT LedgerSequence.NEXTVAL,'25-APR-01','Bought','Calf Meal',100,
       'Each',.01,1, REF(P)
```

```
   FROM Person P
 WHERE Name = 'General Store';
INSERT INTO Ledger
SELECT LedgerSequence.NEXTVAL,'27-APR-01','Bought','Shoeing Ned',1,
       'Each',.5,.5, REF(P)
   FROM Person P
 WHERE Name = 'Blacksmith';
INSERT INTO Ledger
SELECT LedgerSequence.NEXTVAL,'07-JUN-01','Received','Breaking Colt',1,
       'Each',5,5, REF(P)
   FROM Person P
 WHERE Name = 'Sam Dye';
INSERT INTO Ledger
SELECT LedgerSequence.NEXTVAL,'07-JUN-01','Received','Keeping Colt',1,
       'Each',4,4, REF(P)
   FROM Person P
 WHERE Name = 'Sam Dye';
INSERT INTO Ledger
SELECT LedgerSequence.NEXTVAL,'17-JUN-01','Bought','School Tax',1,
       'Each',6.56,6.56, REF(P)
   FROM Person P
 WHERE Name = 'School';
INSERT INTO Ledger
SELECT LedgerSequence.NEXTVAL,'17-JUN-01','Received','Threshing',2,
       'Day',1,2, REF(P)
   FROM Person P
 WHERE Name = 'Henry Chase';
INSERT INTO Ledger
SELECT LedgerSequence.NEXTVAL,'18-JUN-01','Paid','Threshing',.5,
       'Day',1,.5, REF(P)
   FROM Person P
 WHERE Name = 'William Swing';
INSERT INTO Ledger
SELECT LedgerSequence.NEXTVAL,'18-JUN-01','Bought','Sheep',22,
       'Each',.87,19.14, REF(P)
   FROM Person P
 WHERE Name = 'Boole And Jones';
INSERT INTO Ledger
SELECT LedgerSequence.NEXTVAL,'15-MAR-01','Sold','Potatoes',5,
       'Bushel',.25,1.25, REF(P)
   FROM Person P
 WHERE Name = 'General Store';
INSERT INTO Ledger
SELECT LedgerSequence.NEXTVAL,'15-MAR-01','Sold','Cow',2,
       'Each',33,66, REF(P)
   FROM Person P
 WHERE Name = 'Sam Dye';
```

```
INSERT INTO Ledger
SELECT LedgerSequence.NEXTVAL,'15-MAR-01','Received','Boot Between Horses',1,
       'Each',10,10, REF(P)
  FROM Person P
 WHERE Name = 'Adah Talbot';
INSERT INTO Ledger
SELECT LedgerSequence.NEXTVAL,'18-MAR-01','Sold','Wagon',1,
       'Each',5,5, REF(P)
  FROM Person P
 WHERE Name = 'Adah Talbot';
INSERT INTO Ledger
SELECT LedgerSequence.NEXTVAL,'04-APR-01','Sold','Harnes',1,
       'Each',2,2, REF(P)
  FROM Person P
 WHERE Name = 'Adah Talbot';
INSERT INTO Ledger
SELECT LedgerSequence.NEXTVAL,'16-APR-01','Sold','Cow',3,
       'Each',30,90, REF(P)
  FROM Person P
 WHERE Name = 'George B. McCormick';
INSERT INTO Ledger
SELECT LedgerSequence.NEXTVAL,'09-JUN-01','Bought','Use Of Pasture',1,
       'Each',10,10, REF(P)
  FROM Person P
 WHERE Name = 'George B. McCormick';
INSERT INTO Ledger
SELECT LedgerSequence.NEXTVAL,'28-JUN-01','Bought','Sheep And Bull',1,
       'Lot',97.88,97.88, REF(P)
  FROM Person P
 WHERE Name = 'Edward Johnson';
INSERT INTO Ledger
SELECT LedgerSequence.NEXTVAL,'03-JUL-01','Sold','Heifer',1,
       'Each',35,35, REF(P)
  FROM Person P
 WHERE Name = 'Sam Dye';
INSERT INTO Ledger
SELECT LedgerSequence.NEXTVAL,'18-MAY-01','Bought','Middlings',180,
       'Pound',.01,1.8, REF(P)
  FROM Person P
 WHERE Name = 'Dean Foreman';
INSERT INTO Ledger
SELECT LedgerSequence.NEXTVAL,'20-MAY-01','Bought','Middlings',450,
       'Pound',.01,4.5, REF(P)
  FROM Person P
 WHERE Name = 'George Oscar';
INSERT INTO Ledger
SELECT LedgerSequence.NEXTVAL,'22-MAY-01','Bought','Middlings',640,
       'Pound',.01,6.4, REF(P)
  FROM Person P
 WHERE Name = 'Edythe Gammiere';
INSERT INTO Ledger
```

```
SELECT LedgerSequence.NEXTVAL,'23-MAY-01','Bought','Middlings',110,
       'Pound',.01,1.1, REF(P)
  FROM Person P
 WHERE Name = 'John Austin';
INSERT INTO Ledger
SELECT LedgerSequence.NEXTVAL,'28-MAY-01','Bought','Comb',1,
       'Each',.07,.07, REF(P)
  FROM Person P
 WHERE Name = 'General Store';
INSERT INTO Ledger
SELECT LedgerSequence.NEXTVAL,'29-MAY-01','Bought','Buttons',1,
       'Each',.1,.1, REF(P)
  FROM Person P
 WHERE Name = 'General Store';
INSERT INTO Ledger
SELECT LedgerSequence.NEXTVAL,'05-JUL-01','Bought','Beans',6,
       'Pound',.03,.18, REF(P)
  FROM Person P
 WHERE Name = 'General Store';
INSERT INTO Ledger
SELECT LedgerSequence.NEXTVAL,'29-MAY-01','Bought','Raisons',3,
       'Pound',.08,.24, REF(P)
  FROM Person P
 WHERE Name = 'General Store';
INSERT INTO Ledger
SELECT LedgerSequence.NEXTVAL,'29-MAY-01','Bought','Cheese',3,
       'Pound',.09,.27, REF(P)
  FROM Person P
 WHERE Name = 'General Store';
INSERT INTO Ledger
SELECT LedgerSequence.NEXTVAL,'04-JUN-01','Bought','Beer',1,
       'Each',.2,.2, REF(P)
  FROM Person P
 WHERE Name = 'General Store';
INSERT INTO Ledger
SELECT LedgerSequence.NEXTVAL,'04-JUN-01','Bought','Cough Syrup',1,
       'Each',.25,.25, REF(P)
  FROM Person P
 WHERE Name = 'General Store';
INSERT INTO Ledger
SELECT LedgerSequence.NEXTVAL,'26-JUN-01','Bought','Shoe String',2,
       'Pair',.04,.08, REF(P)
  FROM Person P
 WHERE Name = 'General Store';
INSERT INTO Ledger
SELECT LedgerSequence.NEXTVAL,'26-JUN-01','Bought','Close Pins',1,
       'Each',.05,.05, REF(P)
  FROM Person P
 WHERE Name = 'General Store';
INSERT INTO Ledger
SELECT LedgerSequence.NEXTVAL,'26-JUN-01','Bought','Close Brush',1,
```

```
              'Each',.1,.1, REF(P)
       FROM Person P
      WHERE Name = 'General Store';
     INSERT INTO Ledger
     SELECT LedgerSequence.NEXTVAL,'06-MAR-01','Sold','Eggs',14,
              'Dozen',.12,1.68, REF(P)
       FROM Person P
      WHERE Name = 'General Store';
     INSERT INTO Ledger
     SELECT LedgerSequence.NEXTVAL,'06-MAR-01','Sold','Hens',12,
              'Each',.5,6, REF(P)
       FROM Person P
      WHERE Name = 'General Store';
     INSERT INTO Ledger
     SELECT LedgerSequence.NEXTVAL,'15-APR-01','Sold','Eggs',13,
              'Dozen',.1,1.3, REF(P)
       FROM Person P
      WHERE Name = 'General Store';
     INSERT INTO Ledger
     SELECT LedgerSequence.NEXTVAL,'27-APR-01','Paid','Plowing',1,
              'Day',3,3, REF(P)
       FROM Person P
      WHERE Name = 'Richard Koch And Brothers';
     INSERT INTO Ledger
     SELECT LedgerSequence.NEXTVAL,'16-APR-01','Paid','Plowing',1,
              'Day',3,3, REF(P)
       FROM Person P
      WHERE Name = 'Richard Koch And Brothers';
     INSERT INTO Ledger
     SELECT LedgerSequence.NEXTVAL,'17-DEC-01','Paid','Sawing',1,
              'Day',.75,.75, REF(P)
       FROM Person P
      WHERE Name = 'Dick Jones';
     INSERT INTO Ledger
     SELECT LedgerSequence.NEXTVAL,'28-JUL-01','Paid','Sawing',1,
              'Day',.75,.75, REF(P)
       FROM Person P
      WHERE Name = 'Dick Jones';
     INSERT INTO Ledger
     SELECT LedgerSequence.NEXTVAL,'18-AUG-01','Paid','Weeding',1,
              'Day',.9,.9, REF(P)
       FROM Person P
      WHERE Name = 'Elbert Talbot';
     INSERT INTO Ledger
     SELECT LedgerSequence.NEXTVAL,'29-SEP-01','Paid','Work',1,
              'Day',1,1, REF(P)
       FROM Person P
      WHERE Name = 'Gerhardt Kentgen';
     INSERT INTO Ledger
     SELECT LedgerSequence.NEXTVAL,'19-JAN-01','Paid','Work',1,
              'Day',1,1, REF(P)
```

```
  FROM Person P
 WHERE Name = 'Gerhardt Kentgen';
INSERT INTO Ledger
SELECT LedgerSequence.NEXTVAL,'30-JAN-01','Paid','Work',.5,
       'Day',1,.5, REF(P)
  FROM Person P
 WHERE Name = 'Elbert Talbot';
INSERT INTO Ledger
SELECT LedgerSequence.NEXTVAL,'28-FEB-01','Paid','Work',1,
       'Day',1,1, REF(P)
  FROM Person P
 WHERE Name = 'Elbert Talbot';
INSERT INTO Ledger
SELECT LedgerSequence.NEXTVAL,'20-MAR-01','Paid','Work',1,
       'Day',1,1, REF(P)
  FROM Person P
 WHERE Name = 'Dick Jones';
INSERT INTO Ledger
SELECT LedgerSequence.NEXTVAL,'21-JUL-01','Paid','Work',1,
       'Day',1,1, REF(P)
  FROM Person P
 WHERE Name = 'Victoria Lynn';
INSERT INTO Ledger
SELECT LedgerSequence.NEXTVAL,'22-OCT-01','Paid','Plowing',1,
       'Day',1.8,1.8, REF(P)
  FROM Person P
 WHERE Name = 'Dick Jones';
INSERT INTO Ledger
SELECT LedgerSequence.NEXTVAL,'23-SEP-01','Paid','Discus',.5,
       'Day',3,1.5, REF(P)
  FROM Person P
 WHERE Name = 'Richard Koch And Brothers';
INSERT INTO Ledger
SELECT LedgerSequence.NEXTVAL,'22-AUG-01','Paid','Sawing',1,
       'Day',1,1, REF(P)
  FROM Person P
 WHERE Name = 'Peter Lawson';
INSERT INTO Ledger
SELECT LedgerSequence.NEXTVAL,'23-AUG-01','Paid','Sawing',1,
       'Day',1,1, REF(P)
  FROM Person P
 WHERE Name = 'Peter Lawson';
INSERT INTO Ledger
SELECT LedgerSequence.NEXTVAL,'24-MAY-01','Paid','Work',1,
       'Day',1.2,1.2, REF(P)
  FROM Person P
 WHERE Name = 'Wilfred Lowell';
INSERT INTO Ledger
SELECT LedgerSequence.NEXTVAL,'11-MAY-01','Paid','Work',1,
       'Day',1.2,1.2, REF(P)
```

```
   FROM Person P
 WHERE Name = 'Wilfred Lowell';
INSERT INTO Ledger
SELECT LedgerSequence.NEXTVAL,'26-JUN-01','Paid','Painting',1,
       'Day',1.75,1.75, REF(P)
   FROM Person P
 WHERE Name = 'Kay And Palmer Wallbom';
INSERT INTO Ledger
SELECT LedgerSequence.NEXTVAL,'02-JUL-01','Bought','Middlings',220,
       'Pound',.01,2.2, REF(P)
   FROM Person P
 WHERE Name = 'Edythe Gammiere';
INSERT INTO Ledger
SELECT LedgerSequence.NEXTVAL,'03-JUL-01','Bought','Pig',1,
       'Each',3,3, REF(P)
   FROM Person P
 WHERE Name = 'John Austin';
INSERT INTO Ledger
SELECT LedgerSequence.NEXTVAL,'08-JUL-01','Bought','Cheese',1,
       'Pound',.09,.09, REF(P)
   FROM Person P
 WHERE Name = 'General Store';
INSERT INTO Ledger
SELECT LedgerSequence.NEXTVAL,'09-JUL-01','Bought','Beer',1,
       'Each',.2,.2, REF(P)
   FROM Person P
 WHERE Name = 'General Store';
INSERT INTO Ledger
SELECT LedgerSequence.NEXTVAL,'02-AUG-01','Bought','Milk Cans',3,
       'Each',2.5,7.5, REF(P)
   FROM Person P
 WHERE Name = 'General Store';
INSERT INTO Ledger
SELECT LedgerSequence.NEXTVAL,'05-AUG-01','Bought','Hominy',120,
       'Pound',.01,1.2, REF(P)
   FROM Person P
 WHERE Name = 'General Store';
INSERT INTO Ledger
SELECT LedgerSequence.NEXTVAL,'08-AUG-01','Bought','Brush',1,
       'Each',.06,.06, REF(P)
   FROM Person P
 WHERE Name = 'General Store';
INSERT INTO Ledger
SELECT LedgerSequence.NEXTVAL,'12-AUG-01','Bought','Corn',90,
       'Pound',.01,.9, REF(P)
   FROM Person P
 WHERE Name = 'General Store';
INSERT INTO Ledger
SELECT LedgerSequence.NEXTVAL,'25-MAR-01','Sold','Molasses',5,
       'Gallon',1,5, REF(P)
   FROM Person P
```

```
WHERE Name = 'Sam Dye';
INSERT INTO Ledger
SELECT LedgerSequence.NEXTVAL,'29-AUG-01','Sold','Butter',5,
       'Pound',.23,1.15, REF(P)
  FROM Person P
 WHERE Name = 'Gerhardt Kentgen';
INSERT INTO Ledger
SELECT LedgerSequence.NEXTVAL,'06-SEP-01','Bought','Telephone Call',1,
       'Each',.2,.2, REF(P)
  FROM Person P
 WHERE Name = 'Phone Company';
INSERT INTO Ledger
SELECT LedgerSequence.NEXTVAL,'09-SEP-01','Bought','Peanuts',1,
       'Each',.05,.05, REF(P)
  FROM Person P
 WHERE Name = 'General Store';
INSERT INTO Ledger
SELECT LedgerSequence.NEXTVAL,'12-SEP-01','Bought','Bran',170,
       'Pound',.01,1.7, REF(P)
  FROM Person P
 WHERE Name = 'General Store';
INSERT INTO Ledger
SELECT LedgerSequence.NEXTVAL,'13-SEP-01','Bought','Shoeing',4,
       'Each',.3,1.2, REF(P)
  FROM Person P
 WHERE Name = 'Blacksmith';
INSERT INTO Ledger
SELECT LedgerSequence.NEXTVAL,'15-SEP-01','Bought','Hominy',144,
       'Pound',.01,1.44, REF(P)
  FROM Person P
 WHERE Name = 'General Store';
INSERT INTO Ledger
SELECT LedgerSequence.NEXTVAL,'20-APR-01','Bought','Bran',370,
       'Pound',.01,3.7, REF(P)
  FROM Person P
 WHERE Name = 'General Store';
INSERT INTO Ledger
SELECT LedgerSequence.NEXTVAL,'17-JUL-01','Bought','Calf Meal',90,
       'Pound',.01,.9, REF(P)
  FROM Person P
 WHERE Name = 'General Store';
INSERT INTO Ledger
SELECT LedgerSequence.NEXTVAL,'20-JUL-01','Bought','Hominy',300,
       'Pound',.01,3, REF(P)
  FROM Person P
 WHERE Name = 'General Store';
INSERT INTO Ledger
SELECT LedgerSequence.NEXTVAL,'25-JUL-01','Sold','Calf',1,
       'Each',1,1, REF(P)
  FROM Person P
 WHERE Name = 'Sam Dye';
```

```
INSERT INTO Ledger
SELECT LedgerSequence.NEXTVAL,'19-SEP-01','Bought','Bran',100,
       'Pound',.01,1, REF(P)
  FROM Person P
 WHERE Name = 'General Store';
INSERT INTO Ledger
SELECT LedgerSequence.NEXTVAL,'23-SEP-01','Bought','Calf Meal',110,
       'Pound',.01,1.1, REF(P)
  FROM Person P
 WHERE Name = 'General Store';
INSERT INTO Ledger
SELECT LedgerSequence.NEXTVAL,'25-SEP-01','Bought','Hominy',80,
       'Pound',.01,.8, REF(P)
  FROM Person P
 WHERE Name = 'General Store';
INSERT INTO Ledger
SELECT LedgerSequence.NEXTVAL,'07-OCT-01','Paid','Work',1,
       'Day',1,1, REF(P)
  FROM Person P
 WHERE Name = 'Jed Hopkins';
INSERT INTO Ledger
SELECT LedgerSequence.NEXTVAL,'12-OCT-01','Bought','Sheep',12,
       'Each',.9,10.8, REF(P)
  FROM Person P
 WHERE Name = 'Boole And Jones';
INSERT INTO Ledger
SELECT LedgerSequence.NEXTVAL,'15-OCT-01','Sold','BEEF',935,'Pound',.03,28.05, REF(P)
  FROM Person P
 WHERE Name = 'General Store';
INSERT INTO Ledger
SELECT LedgerSequence.NEXTVAL,'18-OCT-01',
       'Received','Boot Between Horses',1,'Each',10,10, REF(P)
  FROM Person P
 WHERE Name = 'Adah Talbot';
INSERT INTO Ledger
SELECT LedgerSequence.NEXTVAL,'12-OCT-01','Sold','Heifer',1,
       'Each',35,35, REF(P)
  FROM Person P
 WHERE Name = 'George B. McCormick';
```

APPENDIX
B

Installing Oracle Developer

he CD-ROM that comes with this book is a complete trial copy of Oracle Developer release 6. This appendix provides basic installation instructions for the Development and Deployment software on the CD-ROM. For details on installing and configuring Oracle Developer Server, see Chapter 14; you only get the choice of installing a Server Installation if you install on Windows NT or UNIX. The final section in this appendix contains instructions for configuring the cartridge versions of the Oracle Developer Servers (Forms, Reports, and Graphics).

NOTE
Once you install the software, you should read the release notes. To access these from the task bar, choose Start|Oracle Developer 6 Doc|Release Notes.

Installing the Developer Software

To use Oracle Developer for building applications, you need to run the Development Installation from the CD-ROM. You also have the choice of running the Deployment Installation option; see the later section "Installing the Deployment Software" for details on deployment installation.

1. Insert the CD-ROM in the CD drive of the system on which you're going to deploy your applications. If you have Autorun turned on, the CD starts and the language dialog box prompts you for your default language. Choose the appropriate language and proceed by clicking on OK.

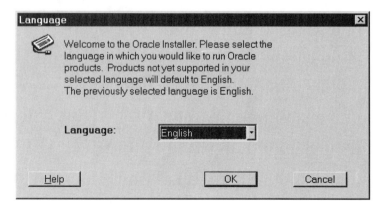

If you have Autorun turned off, navigate in the Explorer to the Setup program in the root folder of the CD-ROM and double-click it to start the Oracle Installer.

2. The Oracle Installer displays the Oracle Installation Settings dialog box. Enter the Oracle Home directory in which you want to install Oracle Developer. Click on OK.

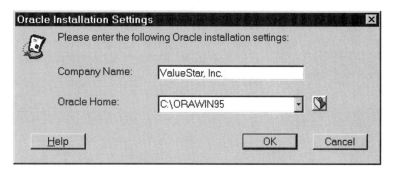

TIP
You must install Oracle Developer in the same Oracle Home directory as all your other Oracle software on Windows, although you can have separate Oracle Homes on your system running under UNIX.

3. The Oracle Installer displays a choice of Oracle Developer systems to install. Accept the default choice, Development Installation, and click on OK.

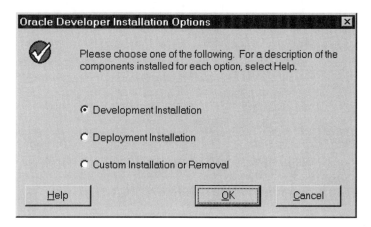

The Oracle Installer now installs all the software for the Developer environment. Depending on your configuration, there may be several prompts asking you to resolve specific issues during the installation, such as whether to install files in the Microsoft Windows system directory (for the OLE/ORA_FFI features). All of these prompts are self-explanatory. The following steps install tables into the SYSTEM user and are optional unless you are going to use features of Oracle Developer that require them. One such feature is saving your applications or program libraries to the database (see the section "Saving Your Form" in Chapter 4 for an analysis of when you should do this). Another feature that requires these tables is menu security (see the section "Menu Access Controls" in Chapter 9). The Translation Builder also requires some of these tables (see the section "Internationalizing Your Applications with Oracle Translation Builder" in Chapter 15).

1. From the task bar, choose Start|Oracle Developer 6.0 Admin|Oracle Developer Build. In response to the prompts, log in as the SYSTEM user with the user's password (default MANAGER, but the system administrator should have changed this). The script installs all the Developer-related tables you need in order to store applications in the database and to use menu security.

2. From the task bar, choose Start|Oracle Developer 6.0 Admin|Oracle Developer Grant. In response to the prompts, log in as the SYSTEM user with the user's password; then enter the name of the user to whom you want to grant access. This script lets the user access the Oracle Developer tables. You can either grant one user and have all developers log on as that user, or you can grant separate users for each developer or group of developers.

Installing the Deployment Software

If you are deploying Oracle Developer applications, you need to install the runtime system those applications use with the Deployment Installation choice on the CD-ROM. Deployment installation offers the choice of installing the client/server runtime system on a workstation or installing the Server Deployment software that lets you run the Oracle Developer Server on a server. For more details on this latter choice, see Chapter 14.

1. Insert the CD-ROM in the CD drive of the system on which you're going to deploy your applications. If you have Autorun turned on, the CD starts and the language dialog box prompts you for your default language. Choose the appropriate language and proceed by clicking on OK.

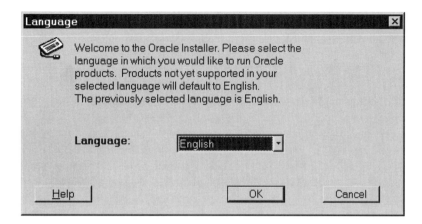

If you have Autorun turned off, navigate in the Explorer to the Setup program in the root folder of the CD-ROM and double-click it to start the Oracle Installer.

2. The Oracle Installer displays the Oracle Installation Settings dialog box. Enter the Oracle Home directory in which you want to install Oracle Developer. Click on OK.

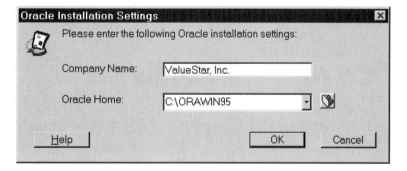

TIP
You must install Oracle Developer in the same Oracle Home directory as all your other Oracle software on Windows, although you can have separate Oracle Homes on your system running under UNIX.

3. The Oracle Installer displays a choice of Oracle Developer systems to install. Choose the Deployment Installation radio button and click on OK.

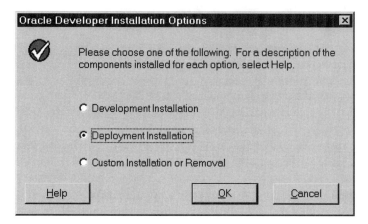

The Oracle Installer now installs all the software for the Developer runtime deployment. It installs all the Developer runtime executables and some additional components, such as the Query Builder, that users may find useful. Depending on your configuration, there may be several prompts asking you to resolve specific issues during the installation, such as whether to install files in the Microsoft Windows system directory. All of these prompts are self-explanatory.

Configuring Cartridge-Based Developer Servers

The Oracle Application Server (OAS) lets you create and configure versions of the Oracle Developer Server components that can be more effective in deploying and using Internet applications. These servers are known as *cartridges* in the language of the OAS. These cartridges dynamically generate the HTML pages you need to implement your forms and reports. The Graphics Server cartridge generates a menu of graphics for the user to display in client browsers. The trade-off you make over the static HTML and CGI techniques laid out in Chapter 14 is that the dynamic servers are more complicated to set up. This section takes you through the basics of setting up the three cartridge implementations of the Forms Server, the Reports Server, and the Graphics Server.

NOTE
*Consult the online help that comes with the Oracle
Developer Server for complete details on installation.
You should also check the release notes for any
modifications in a particular release of the software.
The cartridge configuration process is part of the
standard administration interface in Oracle
Application Server; for details, consult the Oracle
Web Server documentation or the* Oracle Web
Application Server Handbook *by Dynamic
Information Systems, LLC (Oracle Press, 1998).
Also note that Oracle Corporation says that most
of its customers are using the static HTML approach,
not the cartridge approach.*

The benefits of the dynamic approach include parameterization of the HTML
page and load balancing. Parameterization means you don't need to code a different
page for each application. The dynamic quality of the page lets the cartridge fill in
the module name. Also, if you want to use Forms Server load balancing, you must
use a dynamic page and a cartridge approach. Oracle does not support load
balancing using static HTML. The dynamic quality of the page lets the server fill
in the name of the least-loaded server at runtime.

Configuring the Forms Server with a Cartridge

The following tutorial shows you how to configure the dynamic Forms
Server cartridge.

1. Start the Oracle Application Server Manager from the task bar: Start|
Programs|Oracle Application Server|Oracle Application Server Manager.

2. Enter the administration user name and password (you must define these in
the installation of the Oracle Application Server and use the same name
and password here).

The Oracle Application Server Manager is a Web page that displays a tree
of components and a separate frame containing the settings for the currently
selected component.

3. The tutorial assumes your site has the default name "website40." Open the website40 Site tree item by clicking on its icon, and navigate to website40 Site|Applications. Click on the Add tool to add the application.

4. On the resulting Add Application page, set the Application Type field to "CWEB."

5. Click on Apply. On the resulting Add page, specify the name of the application, the display name, and a version number.

6. Click on Apply, and then wait until you see a Success window appear.

7. Click on the Add Cartridge to this Application button to display the Add CWEB Cartridge page. Put "Forms60Cartridge" into both the Cartridge and Display Name fields. The Cartridge Name is the name of the virtual directory for the cartridge, which you will use as part of the URL that runs the application. Enter the Web cartridge DLL path and name in the Cartridge Shared Object field (G:\ORANT\BIN\IFWKBC60.DLL, for example, if your Oracle_Home is G:\ORANT. Set the Entry Point (Shared Object) field to "form_entry."

8. Click on Apply, and then click the Reload tool while holding down the SHIFT key to redisplay the tree. Navigate to the web40site|Applications| <app>|Configuration folder (where <app> is your application's name); then click on Web Parameters. Specify a listener in the Listener List field.

9. Click on Apply. Navigate to the web40site|Applications|<app>|Cartridge Configuration folder; then click Cartridge Parameters.

10. Set the following parameters:

■ *code:* The entry point for the cartridge, "oracle.forms.engine.Main."

■ *codebase:* The virtual directory for the Java code that you have defined when configuring your Web server.

■ *baseHTML:* The physical directory and filename for the base HTML file your cartridge accesses at runtime as a template for building the dynamic HTML page. This is not a virtual directory but an actual operating system path and file name, such as G:\ORANT\webhtml\forms60cart.htm. Your virtual html directory should point to this directory as well.

■ *HTMLdelimiter:* A single character that serves as a substitution indicator in the base HTML file template, such as "%."

■ *Minimum # of Instances:* The smallest number of users that may simultaneously connect to the cartridge—best set to 0.

■ *Maximum # of Instances:* The greatest number of users that may simultaneously connect to the cartridge, such as 100.

■ *archive:* Paths and files for any JAR files to download at application startup, including the Oracle-supplied ifsrv60.jar.

■ *serverApp:* The name of the application class that specifies fonts and icon path settings; see the section "Using Application Classes" in Chapter 14 for details.

II. Click on Apply. Now, create the base HTML file in your /html virtual directory. Copy the file from its installed version ($ORACLE_HOME\Tools\ Devdem60\Web\CARTRIDG.HTM), rename it to the filename you specified in the baseHTML parameter, and modify it with the following substitutions:

■ *serverPort:* Set the Forms Server Listener port (9000 is the default).

■ *serverArgs:* Add form parameters and user parameters.

You can also set any of the parameters you set for the cartridge in the HTML template, but the server takes the values from the parameters, not from the HTML template. Here is an example of a modified template (carriage returns are for clarity only, don't add them to the template):

```
<HTML>
<HEAD><TITLE>Talbot Farms Web Applications</TITLE></HEAD>

<BODY><CENTER>
     <BR>Welcome to Talbot Farms.
     <BR>Loading application...

<APPLET CODEBASE="%LEASTLOADEDHOST%/codebase/"
     CODE="oracle.forms.uiClient. engine.Main"
     ARCHIVE="%LEASTLOADEDHOST%/jars/f60all.jar"
     HEIGHT=20 WIDTH=20>
<PARAM NAME="serverPort" VALUE="9000">
<PARAM NAME="serverArgs" VALUE="Module=%Module%">
PARAM NAME="serverApp" VALUE="default"
</APPLET>

</BODY>
</HTML>
```

This page parameterizes the module name as %Module%, letting the user add a module name to run. If you use the Forms Server load-balancing features, the Forms Server replaces the parameter %LEASTLOADEDHOST% with the least-loaded server name.

Configuring the Reports Server Cartridge

This section gives you a tutorial on setting up a Reports Server cartridge.

1. Start the OAS Manager from the task bar: Start|Programs|Oracle Application Server|Oracle Application Server Manager.

2. Enter the administration user name and password (you must use the name and password you specified when installing the OAS).

   The OAS Manager is a Web page that displays a tree of components and a separate frame containing the settings for the currently selected component.

3. The tutorial assumes your site has the default name "website40." Open the website40 Site tree item by clicking on its icon, and navigate to website40 Site|Applications. Click on the Add tool to add the application.

4. On the resulting Add Application page, set the Application Type field to "D2KWEB."

5. Click on Apply. On the resulting Add page, specify the name of the application, the display name, and a version number.

6. Click on Apply, and then wait until you see a Success window appear.

7. Click on the Add Cartridge to this Application button to display the Add D2KWEB Cartridge page. Put "Reports60Cartridge" into both the Cartridge and Display Name fields, and then enter the Web cartridge DLL path and name in the Cartridge Shared Object field (G:\ORANT\BIN\ RWOWS60.DLL, for example, if your Oracle_Home is G:\ORANT). Set the Entry Point (Shared Object) field to "rwows_entry."

8. Click on Apply, and then click the Reload tool while holding down the SHIFT key to redisplay the tree. Navigate to the web40site|Applications| <app>|Configuration folder (where <app> is your application's name); then click on Web Parameters. Specify a listener in the Listener List field.

9. Click on Apply. Navigate to the web40site|Applications|<app>|Cartridge Configuration folder, and then click Cartridge Parameters.

10. Set the following parameters, and then click on Apply.

   ■ *REPORTS60_WEBLOC:* The virtual directory where the Web server looks for report output files, such as /web_reports/.

   ■ *REPORTS60_WEBLOC_TRANSLATED:* The physical directory to which the cartridge transfers the Reports Runtime output if the Reports Server and Web server do not share a file system, such as "G:\ORANT\Reports."

   ■ *Minimum # of Instances:* The smallest number of users that may simultaneously connect to the cartridge—best set to 0.

   ■ *Maximum # of Instances:* The greatest number of users that may simultaneously connect to the cartridge, such as 100.

Configuring the Graphics Server

This section gives you a tutorial on setting up a Graphics Server cartridge. Unlike the Forms and Reports Servers, you have no other options with Graphics, and you can run the Graphics Server only with the Oracle Application Server.

1. Start the OAS Manager from the task bar: Start|Programs|Oracle Application Server|Oracle Application Server Manager.

2. Enter the administration user name and password (you must use the same names you specified when installing the OAS).

3. The tutorial assumes your site has the default name "website40." Open the website40 Site tree item by clicking on its icon, and navigate to website40 Site|Applications. Click on the Add tool to add the application.

4. On the resulting Add Application page, set the Application Type field to "D2KWEB."

5. Click on Apply. On the resulting Add page, specify the name of the display, the display name, and a version number.

6. Click on Apply, and then wait until you see a Success window appear.

7. Click on the Add Cartridge to this Application button to display the Add D2KWEB Cartridge page. Put "Graphics60Cartridge" into both the Cartridge and Display Name fields, and then enter the Web cartridge DLL path and name in the Cartridge Shared Object field (G:\ORANT\BIN\GO60.DLL, for example, if your Oracle_Home is G:\ORANT). Set the Entry Point (Shared Object) field to "GWWRBMain."

8. Click on Apply, and then click the Reload tool while holding down the SHIFT key to redisplay the tree. Navigate to the web40site|Applications| <app>|Configuration folder (where <app> is your application's name); then click on Web Parameters. Specify a listener in the Listener List field.

9. Click on Apply. Navigate to the web40site|Applications|<app>|Cartridge Configuration folder, and then click Cartridge Parameters.

10. Set the following parameters, and then click on Apply.

- *GW_TIMEOUT:* The number of minutes the display remains open in the browser.

- *Minimum # of Instances:* The smallest number of users that may simultaneously connect to the cartridge—best set to 0.

- *Maximum # of Instances:* The greatest number of users that may simultaneously connect to the cartridge, such as 100.

Glossary

Term	Definition
accelerator key	A key sequence you can assign to a menu item along with its menu access keys, usually to provide a shortcut to a complex t of menu access keystrokes
action state	A state with an internal action and at least one outgoing transition; corresponds to a Developer process in an activity diagram
ActiveX	A Microsoft technology based on COM that lets you develop and reuse component controls in applications and browsers running on Microsoft Windows
activity diagram	A UML diagram that represents the dynamic flow of a process, similar to a flowchart but based on state-transition logic
alert	A modal window that displays a message or asks a simple question that elicits a yes-no type of response from the user with up to three buttons, such as Yes, No, Cancel
anonymous block	A PL/SQL block that is not a subprogram and thus has no name
applet	A chunk of code that a web browser downloads and runs; a free-standing software component
application class	A collection of font mappings and an icon path with specific fonts and icons to use when displaying a form application in a web browser
application window	The master window that owns multiple document windows in the MDI user interface standard
association	A relationship between objects of two or more classes
attached library	A PL/SQL library you have attached to another module; the order of libraries lets you replace program units with variations
authentication	The process of confirming that the user is who he or she claims to be and hence can legitimately use the privileges granted to that user
bar chart	Shows data groups as horizontal bars in a display module
base-table data block	A data block that maps to a table in the database, with each record in the data block corresponding to a row in the table
block	*See* data block and PL/SQL block
body	The middle part of a report, which contains the report data in repeating frames and other report structures
boilerplate text	Characters that appear on a canvas in addition to the items that belong to data blocks
bookmark	An Acrobat tag that shows up in a special bookmark pane in Acrobat as a hyperlink to a point in the PDF document
break column	A column in a report break group that creates a break for each different value of the column; implies a sort by the column so that all similar values come together in the report

Term	Definition
break group	A group in a report that sits between a record group and its query, giving the report a hierarchical structure with breakpoints between the levels
built-in package	A PL/SQL package program unit that Oracle supplies as part of the Developer installation
built-in triggers	Triggers that the Developer framework supplies
canvas	The background within a window on which you place boilerplate text and items
cartridge	An Oracle Application Server module that serves as an interface to a software system, enabling users to run the software through their Web browser connecting to the Application Server; part of the Oracle Network Computing Architecture (NCA)
CASE	Computer Aided Software Engineering, tools for assisting software developers in building software systems
category	A division within a classification in a mandatory access control scheme label that makes the classification regional
chart	(1) A pictorial representation of data; (2) a single graphic element in a display module that shows data groups or values from a data model
check menu item	A menu item that represents a toggled option, displaying a check mark if toggled on and no mark if toggled off
class	In a UML diagram, a rectangle representing a type; objects are instances of the class, and classes correspond to object types or tables
classification	A hierarchical level in a mandatory access control scheme that identifies the sensitivity of labeled information
client/server	A style of deploying software that employs two logical machines, a client and a server; for Oracle Developer, the server is a database server and the client is the client workstation that runs Oracle Developer applications
column chart	Shows data groups as vertical bars in a display module
columns	Database objects representing properties of each row of a table; report objects corresponding to such database objects, as opposed to formula, summary, or placeholder columns
COM	Common Object Model, a Microsoft technology underlying the OLE technology; permits the accessing of objects and data through standard interfaces
combo box	A control that is a combination of the poplist and a text item that lets you pull down a list of text items but also lets you type in a value
commit	A successful-termination command for a transaction

Term	Definition
concurrency	The capability of a database manager or application to permit multiple users to access data or run the application at once
console	The area in which Forms displays messages, record counts, lamps, and any other status reports
content canvas	A canvas that displays the basic content of a window
control block	A data block that does not map to a table in the database; usually the control block has only one record, with the items in that record being variables to which you can refer from subprograms in the application (effectively, package variables with data block scope)
copy	To create a Developer object from another object without creating a subclass relationship between them
CORBA	The Common Object Request Broker standard, a standard of the Object Management Group that provides an object model and a set of interfaces and tools for building distributed object systems on networks
coupling	The degree to which a module uses data and operations external to the module
crosstab report	A cross-tabulation of two columns showing some aggregate or other value for the combination of each value from each column; also known as a matrix report
current record	(1) The record in the data block on which the end user has positioned the cursor; all activity in a data block happens on the current record; (2) the record that has the focus (see focus)
cursor	(1) A user interface abstraction that points at the focus object (see focus); (2) a SQL object that lets a programmer iterate through the rows that result from a query; (3) an Oracle object that contains a SQL statement (any SQL statement) and information about its result
data block	A Developer object that holds a collection of records and comprises a set of items that make up each record; see also base-table data block and control block
data file report	A comma-separated or other variety of delimited data file; you use this to transfer data into other tools
data link	A report data model object that links master groups to detail queries in a master-detail report
data model	A Developer report or graphics object that represents the data structure of the report or display, including data mappings to the database, relationships between the data objects, and grouping structures
data type	The category of data into which a value falls, such as character, number, or date

Term	Definition
database application	A program that uses data from a database management system such as Oracle8i
database object	A developer object that represents some object in the target database, such as a table, index, user, or other schema object
database portability	How independent the application is of its underlying database manager
debug actions	Breakpoints with attached code in PL/SQL code in reports and graphics
decision	A diamond shape in an activity diagram that represents the splitting of a flow of control based on a decision
declarative tool	A tool that lets you build an application by telling the system what you want rather than how to give it to you
default	A value assigned to a property, variable, or column object by the runtime system when you create the object
default behavior	The behavior a process exhibits "out of the box;" that is, without any additional coding by you that would change its standard behavior
deploy	To distribute a product to its users
dialog box	(1) A generally modal window that displays options or other ways to control application operation; (2) a window that is independent of the application window in the MDI user interface standard
discretionary access control	The ability to control access to an application and its data through the granting of privileges to subjects (users and processes) that use the application and its data
display module	A Developer module that contains one or more charts
document	A generally modeless window that displays an application "document" object, usually a content canvas related to a major part of the application
document window	A window contained entirely within the application window in the MDI user interface standard
domination	In a mandatory access control scheme, one label dominates another if its classification is greater than or equal to that of the other label, and its categories are a superset of the other's categories
double-y chart	In a display module, shows two y-axis data values for each x-axis value, with both the scales showing; you can use this to display two variables that differ over time, for example
editor	A Developer object that displays as a text editor window for entering text into a text item
entry transition	A transition in an activity diagram that represents the start of the activities in the diagram

Term	Definition
event driven process	A process that executes when an event occurs; events may be sequential, or they may occur as a result of external actions by the user in any order, yielding a very different style of programming than a standard sequential process
exception	A signal that the PL/SQL runtime system raises when your program identifies or encounters an anomalous condition
exit transition	A transition in an activity diagram that represents the end of the activities in the diagram; labeled with either "success" or "failure" to indicate the result of the activity
external query	SQL text in a separate file that you can share between applications; a Developer module that reports and displays can include for reuse of the SQL
fire	To execute a process when an event occurs; the event is said to "fire" the process
flexibility	The degree to which users with different needs can adapt your application to their intended use
focus	The single Forms object to which a user action applies at any given time; the window in which events occur at any given time from the perspective of the graphical user interface
foreign key	A column that refers to the primary key of a table from another table, creating a link between the tables
form	An application that presents data in an online format consisting of a series of items laid out in one or more windows
form letter report	Boilerplate text surrounding data from a record that fills in blanks in the text, such as recipient's name and address
form report	A report laid out to display a single record at a time, usually on a single page but not always
formula column	Special columns in a report group that you compute using PL/SQL blocks rather than getting data directly from the database
frame	A Developer Forms object within a canvas that contains the layout properties for a group of block items taken as a whole; a Developer Reports object that contains the layout of a set of fields and other frames
framework	A reusable system of objects that work together to define the basic abstractions required by a particular application domain
FTP	File Transfer Protocol, an Internet protocol for transferring files from one location to another
function	A PL/SQL subprogram that executes and returns a value

Term	Definition
gantt chart	In a display module, shows horizontal bars that represent start and end values; usually represents a schedule, with the x axis representing time and the y axis representing the set of tasks in the schedule
graph report	A report that includes a chart or graph of the data in addition to or in place of displaying the data itself
graphics	Pictorial representations of data
group	A report module structure that identifies the records that a query returns as a repeating group of records in the report; there is a hierarchy of groups in a report that represents the nesting of records within each other
group above report	A tabular report with one or more group columns that the group frame displays above the grouped data records
group left report	A tabular report with one or more group columns that the group frame displays on the left of the grouped data records
guard condition	A logical expression that evaluates to true or false attached to a transition coming out of a decision in an activity diagram; the flow of control moves through the transition if the expression evaluates to true
header	The first part of a report, which does not contain report data, but contains boilerplate text, non-repeating graphics, and other such display items
high-low chart	In a display module, shows each data element as a combination of three values: high, low, and close (as for stock-market prices)
horizontal toolbar	A canvas that displays along the top of a window to display tool buttons
HTML	Hypertext Markup Language, a derivative of the Generalized Markup Language (GML) that uses tags to mark up text and graphics for display as well as to run applets
interface	The specific methods by which you access a system such as the database manager
Internet	The global wide area network that supports the World Wide Web and internet-worked access between computers
intranet	A network inside a company that uses Internet technology but protects the network from access from the full Internet through firewalls or other access protection schemes
item	A single value definition in a data block; each item has a native data type such as character or number and a set of properties that differs depending on the type of item

Term	Definition
Java	(1) A programming language from Sun Microsystems that most Internet web browsers run to enable sophisticated applications beyond the capabilities of HTML; (2) A programming language oriented toward web browser applets and components
JavaBean	A java module that conforms to the JavaBean specification from Sun Microsystems
key	A keyboard key or its logical equivalent, such as ENTER or F1
key triggers	Triggers that fire when you press a standard key, such as F2
label	A combination of classification, category, and marking in a mandatory access scheme; every piece of information has a label, and every user has a label that defines their security clearance
label, list	The label of a list value for display purposes
lamp	A small status control on the console in a form that indicates the presence of some feature such as an LOV for a text item
layout, display	The graphic elements of the display module
layout, report	The graphical structure of a report
library	*See* object library or PL/SQL library
line chart	Shows data values as points relating x and y values in a display module
list	A Developer block item that represents a set of values and value labels (see value, list, and label, list)
list of values	*See* LOV
LOV	A Developer object that displays as a special dialog for selecting a single value from a list of values that the dialog displays; you can associate an LOV with a record group and with an item to check for valid input into the item; it also has a search feature that makes it easy to find items in a large list
magic menu item	A special menu item that has built-in behavior, as opposed to menu items for which you supply the code for the action
mailing label report	A series of regularly repeating records formatted on each page in a certain area
mandatory access control	A security system that puts much stronger controls on access to objects in the database by associating a security label with each object and with each session
many-to-many association	An association with many objects of one class relating to many objects of another class
margin	The part of a report outside the text boundaries of the report

Term	Definition
marking	A further piece of information within a classification and category in a mandatory access control scheme label that gets associated with the data under different circumstances
master-detail form	Divides the form into a parent record and several child records
Master-detail report	A master record with two or more related detail records displayed together
master-master report	Two groups of unrelated records displayed together
matrix report	A cross-tabulation of two columns showing some aggregate or other value for the combination of each value from each column; also known as a crosstab report
maximize	To expand the size of a window to the entire screen or to the size of the application window in the case of an MDI document window
MDI	Multiple Document Interface
menu	A list of text items that you access by clicking on a row of text headers (menu names)
menu access key	A key that has the same effect as choosing a menu item and usually involves pressing an escape key such as ALT plus one letter for each submenu
menu item	A menu item that displays another menu, a submenu
menu module	A Developer module that represents one or more menus in your applications and contains the menu and menu item definitions and the code that executes when you choose a menu item
minimize	To reduce a window to an icon
mixed chart	Shows data values as both points and as a line relating x and y values in a display module
moat	The border around a button control in a graphical user interface that indicates that a button is the default button in a window, the button that executes when you press the Enter key
modal window	A window that requires the user to respond and dismiss the window before doing anything in any other window in the application
modeless window	(1) A window that lets the user move to another window in the application without first dismissing the modeless window; (2) a window from which the user can move the focus at any time
module	A top-level building block for a Developer application; the runtime programs run modules, and the module collects all the objects for a form, report, menu, code library, object library, and so on
move	To change the location of a Developer object in the Object Navigator, either between modules or within a module

Term	Definition
Multiple Document Interface	A Windows standard for graphical user interfaces that organizes an application into a master application window and multiple document windows that it contains. The MDI window owns the menu for the application; it also displays the console.
multiplicity	The number of objects participating in an association; see one-to-one, one-to-many, and many-to-many association
named visual attribute	A Developer object that collects a set of display properties to which you can refer from another object; see also property class
navigability	The ability to move the focus from control to control in a graphical user interface
navigation	Moving the focus from object to object (see focus and navigability)
non-updateable view	A view with a join or expressions in the select list that prevent Oracle from being able to update the underlying tables through the view
null menu item	A menu item with no associated code; a separator is a null menu item, but you may make any menu item null by setting the command type to null
object group	A Developer object that lets you package up your reusable objects for later copying or reference; it collects a set of objects under a single heading
object library	A Developer module that packages Developer Forms objects for reuse in different applications
object type	An Oracle8 object that defines the structure and behavior of a class of objects; you use object types to create tables or columns in tables
ODBC	The Open Data Base Connectivity standard, a Microsoft de facto standard that provides a uniform SQL language and programming interface for any database manager that cares to write a driver for it
OLE	Object Linking and Embedding, a Microsoft technology for embedding documents in other documents
one-to-many association	An association with a single object of one class relating to several objects of another class
one-to-one association	An association with a single object of one class relating to a single object of another class
open system	A system that permits the use of tools from different vendors
Operating system (OS) portability	The portability of the tools and database manager itself
package	(1) A PL/SQL program unit that contains other PL/SQL objects, including subprograms, types, and attributes; (2) a UML object that represents a container of classifiers such as classes and other packages; in a persistent database diagram, the package represents a schema

Term	Definition
parameter	A form, menu, report, or display data object that the module defines, and to which you can assign a value by passing it in through the runtime system for the module; the parameter lets you customize a module at runtime, enhancing its reusability under different situations; see also system parameter and user-defined parameter
parameter form	The form that displays for entry of the values you want to assign to a set of parameters
parent class	An object to which a subclass refers
PDF	Portable Document Format, an Adobe Systems standard document format for transferring printed documents between users
pie chart	Shows data groups as slices of a circular pie in a display module
PL/SQL	A block-structured programming language that includes Oracle SQL as well as standard sequence, condition, and looping control statements and other modern structured programming concepts such as subprograms, packages, and exception handling
PL/SQL block	A series of PL/SQL programming statements, optionally including a set of data declarations and exception handlers; a block may be anonymous, or it may be a subprogram (procedure or function)
PL/SQL library	A Developer module that comprises a set of PL/SQL program units and attached libraries that you can attach to any module for reuse
PL/SQL menu item	A menu item with PL/SQL code that performs the action
placeholder column	Report columns you define to fill in from a trigger, formula, or user exit instead of from database values or standard summarization
poplist	A drop-down list of text items that you activate through a small arrow in a box next to the list, causing the list to pop up on the window near the item
pop-up menu	A floating menu that pops up when you click the right mouse button on a canvas or item
portability	The capability of running on different systems; see database portability and operating system portability
post	To write any pending changes in a form to the database through a series of INSERT, UPDATE, and DELETE statements without committing the transaction in which the posting takes place
primary key	One or more columns with values that uniquely identify each row of the table
privilege	Authorizes a category of action on a database object by a specified user
procedure	A PL/SQL subprogram that executes without returning a value
process	A sequence of tasks or subprocesses, events, and triggers

Term	Definition
program unit	A PL/SQL package or subprogram
propagation	The process of passing control to an exception handler when an exception occurs in a PL/SQL program
property	A quality associated with all the objects of a class; corresponds to a column in an object type or table
property class	A Developer object that comprises a collection of any kind of property; see also named visual attribute
query	A SQL statement that returns the data values that are the basis for a report or display; see also external query
query by example	A style of query specification that lets the user develop a query by supplying example records with values (and logical conditions) representing the desired data
radio button	A collection of small circular buttons, each with a label; choosing one button turns all the others off, creating a set of mutually exclusive choices
radio menu item	A menu item that represents one of several choices for a single option, with the other choices displayed as nearby menu items
record group	(1) A Developer Forms object that represents a special data structure that resembles a table, with rows and columns; (2) a Developer Reports data model object that represents the records that a query object returns
record type	A series of data fields—a single row of data
recovery	The capability of a database manager to protect the data from system crashes
referential integrity	The ability of the database and/or applications to make sure that when a row refers to another row, that second row exists
relation	A Developer object that represents a master-detail relationship, with the relation expressing the mapping between two data blocks
repeating frame	A Developer Reports frame that contains a repeating sequence of fields, with each repetition coming from a report group row
report	A page-oriented display of data
report module	A Developer module that defines a report
reusability	The ability to use objects in different contexts
role	(1) One side of an association between classes; (2) an Oracle security feature that collects a set of privileges and is assigned to some number of Oracle users
rollback	An unsuccessful-termination command for a transaction
rowid	A unique Oracle internal row identifier

Term	Definition
running total	A total that sums through the entire report
savepoint	A feature of Oracle that marks a point in a transaction to which you can roll back if necessary without rolling back the entire transaction
scatter chart	Shows data values as points relating x and y values in a display module
schema	An object that owns a specific set of tables, views, and privileges
scope, trigger	The set of objects that fire the trigger; scope consists of the object that owns that trigger and any objects belonging to that object
scroll bar	A user interface control that lets the end user move a set of records or a window that doesn't fit entirely within the visible display (the computer screen, another window, the application window, or whatever)
security	The capability of a database manager or application to protect data or application from unauthorized use
security clearance	The range of labels in a mandatory access control scheme for which you are authorized to read and write information
separator menu item	A menu item that separates other menu items and has no associated action
sequence	An Oracle object that generates a sequential integer on demand
servlet	A chunk of code that an application server runs; opposed to applet, which runs in a client web browser
SmartTriggers	A feature of the Form Builder that identifies the most likely triggers that you might want to attach to the object you have selected, making them available through a popup menu
specification	The procedure or function parameters, or function return type
stacked canvas	A canvas that displays over other canvases to show conditional or separable contents
standard function key	One of the programmable keyboard keys or logical equivalents, usually ranging from F1 to F12 or F24
static structure diagram	A UML diagram that represents the static, as opposed to dynamic, structure of a system, consisting primarily of types and classes and associations between them
status bar	*See* console
subclass	(1) An object that refers to another object (its parent class) and inherits its properties and associations; (2) to create such an object
submenu	A menu displayed from another menu
subprogram	A PL/SQL program unit that is either a procedure (a subprogram that executes without returning a value) or a function (a subprogram that executes and returns a value)

Term	Definition
summary column	Special columns in a report group that Developer computes by aggregating report data, such as totals or counts
system parameters	Parameters that Developer defines automatically, such as report destination
tab page	An individual tab layout in a tabbed canvas
tabbed canvas	A canvas that displays the basic content of a window in a series of overlapping canvases with labeled tabs
table chart	Shows data values in a tabular format in a display module
tabular report	A simple table of data
tag	A component of a markup language that describes the nature of the following text or graphics; HTML uses tags to mark up text and graphics for display in Web browsers and also to set options or to run applets within the browser
template	An object that you can use to format a module with basic options or contents; forms, reports, and charts all have different kinds of templates
template, chart	A customized set of options that lets you build several charts that all have identical formatting, possibly in the same display module
three-tier	A style of application deployment in which an application runs mainly on an application server, which in turn accesses a database server, and which manages only user-interface functions through the client workstation; the three tiers are the thin client, the application server(s), and the database server(s); opposed to client/server, a two-tier approach
timer	A display module element that acts as a kind of alarm clock for the display; allows for special effects, repeating queries, and so on
t-list	A list box that displays all the text items in a scrolling list, like a separate canvas but within a single field in the form
toolbar	A strip of icons along the top or left side of a window
trailer	The last part of a report, which does not contain report data but contains boilerplate text, non-repeating graphics, and other such display items
transaction	A logical unit of work; begins with a data-related action and ends with commit or rollback
transition	A flow of control from one action state to another action state or to a decision in an activity diagram

Term	Definition
trigger	(1) An anonymous PL/SQL block attached to a Developer object that executes when a specific event happens in the context of that object; the name of the trigger reflects the type of event that triggers the PL/SQL block; (2) a database object corresponding to an Oracle database trigger on the server; (3) an Oracle schema object that executes a PL/SQL block on a specific event on a table, such as an insert, update, or delete
trigger, report	Blocks of PL/SQL code that execute at well-defined points in report processing (before and after the report, between each page, before and after the parameter form)
two-tier application	An application that runs on a workstation and accesses a database server
UML	Unified Modeling Language, an Object Management Group standard system for representing object-oriented design through diagrams
user-defined parameters	Parameters that you create and initialize, as opposed to system parameters that Developer creates and initializes automatically
user-defined triggers	Triggers that you name with your own name rather than with a standard trigger event name; you fire the trigger from PL/SQL code with a procedure call
validation	The process of making sure that an object satisfies all the constraints you put on it in defining the form
value, list	One element of a list item
vertical toolbar	A canvas that displays along the left side of a window to display tool buttons
view	A rectangle within a window that covers part or all of a canvas
web browser	A light-weight software system that runs on a client computer and accesses applications over a network through Universal Resource Locators (URLs), often using Hypertext Markup Language (HTML) and Java applets downloaded from a server to implement applications
window	A rectangular area of the application display maintained by the GUI platform
World Wide Web	The worldwide system of interlinked HTML pages accessible through the Internet http protocol

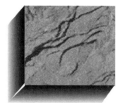

Index

Think you're
smart?

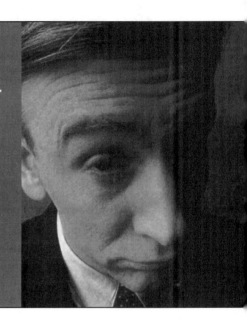

Think you're ready to wear this badge?

Get Your **FREE** Subscription to Oracle Magazine

Stay informed and increase your productivity with every issue of *Oracle Magazine.* Inside each FREE, bimonthly issue you'll get:

- Up-to-date information on Oracle Data Server, Oracle Applications, Network Computing Architecture, and tools
- Third-party news and announcements
- Technical articles on Oracle products and operating environments
- Software tuning tips
- Oracle customer application stories

Three easy ways to subscribe:

1 MAIL Cut out this page, complete the questionnaire on the back, and mail it to: *Oracle Magazine,* P.O. Box 1263, Skokie, IL 60076-8263.

2 FAX Cut out this page, complete the questionnaire on the back, and fax it to **+ 847.647.9735.**

3 WEB Visit our Web site at **www.oramag.com.** You'll find a subscription form there, plus much more!

If there are other Oracle users at your location who would like to receive their own subscription to *Oracle Magazine,* please photocopy the form and pass it along.

SIGNATURE (REQUIRED) ✓ _____   **DATE** _____

NAME _____   TITLE _____

COMPANY _____   E-MAIL ADDRESS _____

STREET/P.O. BOX _____

CITY/STATE/ZIP _____

COUNTRY _____   TELEPHONE _____

You must answer all eight questions below.

1 What is the primary business activity of your firm at this location? *(circle only one)*
- 01 Agriculture, Mining, Natural Resources
- 02 Architecture, Construction
- 03 Communications
- 04 Consulting, Training
- 05 Consumer Packaged Goods
- 06 Data Processing
- 07 Education
- 08 Engineering
- 09 Financial Services
- 10 Government—Federal, Local, State, Other
- 11 Government—Military
- 12 Health Care
- 13 Manufacturing—Aerospace, Defense
- 14 Manufacturing—Computer Hardware
- 15 Manufacturing—Noncomputer Products
- 16 Real Estate, Insurance
- 17 Research & Development
- 18 Human Resources
- 19 Retailing, Wholesaling, Distribution
- 20 Software Development
- 21 Systems Integration, VAR, VAD, OEM
- 22 Transportation
- 23 Utilities (Electric, Gas, Sanitation)
- 24 Other Business and Services _____

2 Which of the following best describes your job function? *(circle only one)*
CORPORATE MANAGEMENT/STAFF
- 01 Executive Management (President, Chair, CEO, CFO, Owner, Partner, Principal)
- 02 Finance/Administrative Management (VP/Director/Manager/Controller, Purchasing, Administration)
- 03 Sales/Marketing Management (VP/Director/Manager)
- 04 Computer Systems/Operations Management (CIO/VP/Director/Manager MIS, Operations)
- 05 Other Finance/Administration Staff
- 06 Other Sales/Marketing Staff

IS/IT Staff
- 07 Systems Development/Programming Management
- 08 Systems Development/Programming Staff
- 09 Consulting
- 10 DBA/Systems Administrator
- 11 Education/Training
- 12 Engineering/R&D/Science Management
- 13 Engineering/R&D/Science Staff
- 14 Technical Support Director/Manager
- 15 Webmaster/Internet Specialist
- 16 Other Technical Management/Staff

3 What is your current primary operating platform? *(circle all that apply)*
- 01 DEC UNIX
- 02 DEC VAX VMS
- 03 Java
- 04 HP UNIX
- 05 IBM AIX
- 06 IBM UNIX
- 07 Macintosh
- 08 MPE-ix
- 09 MS-DOS
- 10 MVS
- 11 NetWare
- 12 Network Computing
- 13 OpenVMS
- 14 SCO UNIX
- 15 Sun Solaris/SunOS
- 16 SVR4
- 17 Ultrix
- 18 UnixWare
- 19 VM
- 20 Windows
- 21 Windows NT
- 22 Other _____
- 23 Other UNIX _____

4 Do you evaluate, specify, recommend, or authorize the purchase of any of the following? *(circle all that apply)*
- 01 Hardware
- 02 Software
- 03 Application Development Tools
- 04 Database Products
- 05 Internet or Intranet Products

5 In your job, do you use or plan to purchase any of the following products or services? *(check all that apply)*

SOFTWARE	Use	Plan to buy
01 Business Graphics	☐	☐
02 CAD/CAE/CAM	☐	☐
03 CASE	☐	☐
04 CIM	☐	☐
05 Communications	☐	☐
06 Database Management	☐	☐
07 File Management	☐	☐
08 Finance	☐	☐
09 Java	☐	☐
10 Materials Resource Planning	☐	☐
11 Multimedia Authoring	☐	☐
12 Networking	☐	☐
13 Office Automation	☐	☐
14 Order Entry/Inventory Control	☐	☐
15 Programming	☐	☐
16 Project Management	☐	☐
17 Scientific and Engineering	☐	☐
18 Spreadsheets	☐	☐
19 Systems Management	☐	☐
20 Workflow	☐	☐
HARDWARE		
21 Macintosh	☐	☐
22 Mainframe	☐	☐
23 Massively Parallel Processing	☐	☐
24 Minicomputer	☐	☐
25 PC	☐	☐
26 Network Computer	☐	☐
27 Supercomputer	☐	☐
28 Symmetric Multiprocessing	☐	☐
29 Workstation	☐	☐
PERIPHERALS		
30 Bridges/Routers/Hubs/Gateways	☐	☐
31 CD-ROM Drives	☐	☐
32 Disk Drives/Subsystems	☐	☐
33 Modems	☐	☐
34 Tape Drives/Subsystems	☐	☐
35 Video Boards/Multimedia	☐	☐
SERVICES		
36 Computer-Based Training	☐	☐
37 Consulting	☐	☐
38 Education/Training	☐	☐
39 Maintenance	☐	☐
40 Online Database Services	☐	☐
41 Support	☐	☐
42 None of the above	☐	☐

6 What Oracle products are in use at your site? *(circle all that apply)*
SERVER/SOFTWARE
- 01 Oracle8
- 02 Oracle7
- 03 Oracle Application Server
- 04 Oracle Data Mart Suites
- 05 Oracle Internet Commerce Server
- 06 Oracle InterOffice
- 07 Oracle Lite
- 08 Oracle Payment Server
- 09 Oracle Rdb
- 10 Oracle Security Server
- 11 Oracle Video Server
- 12 Oracle Workgroup Server

TOOLS
- 13 Designer/2000
- 14 Developer/2000 (Forms, Reports, Graphics)
- 15 Oracle OLAP Tools
- 16 Oracle Power Object

ORACLE APPLICATIONS
- 17 Oracle Automotive
- 18 Oracle Energy
- 19 Oracle Consumer Packaged Goods
- 20 Oracle Financials
- 21 Oracle Human Resources
- 22 Oracle Manufacturing
- 23 Oracle Projects
- 24 Oracle Sales Force Automation
- 25 Oracle Supply Chain Management
- 26 Other _____
- 27 None of the above

7 What other database products are in use at your site? *(circle all that apply)*
- 01 Access
- 02 BAAN
- 03 dbase
- 04 Gupta
- 05 IBM DB2
- 06 Informix
- 07 Ingres
- 08 Microsoft Access
- 09 Microsoft SQL Server
- 10 Peoplesoft
- 11 Progress
- 12 SAP
- 13 Sybase
- 14 VSAM
- 15 None of the above

8 During the next 12 months, how much do you anticipate your organization will spend on computer hardware, software, peripherals, and services for your location? *(circle only one)*
- 01 Less than $10,000
- 02 $10,000 to $49,999
- 03 $50,000 to $99,999
- 04 $100,000 to $499,999
- 05 $500,000 to $999,999
- 06 $1,000,000 and over

OMG

ORACLE SOFTWARE LICENSE AGREEMENT

YOU SHOULD CAREFULLY READ THE FOLLOWING TERMS AND CONDITIONS BEFORE BREAKING THE SEAL ON THE DISC ENVELOPE. AMONG OTHER THINGS, THIS AGREEMENT LICENSES THE ENCLOSED SOFTWARE TO YOU AND CONTAINS WARRANTY AND LIABILITY DISCLAIMERS. BY USING THE DISC AND/OR INSTALLING THE SOFTWARE, YOU ARE ACCEPTING AND AGREEING TO THE TERMS AND CONDITIONS OF THIS AGREEMENT. IF YOU DO NOT AGREE TO THE TERMS OF THIS AGREEMENT, DO NOT BREAK THE SEAL OR USE THE DISC. YOU SHOULD PROMPTLY RETURN THE PACKAGE UNOPENED.

LICENSE: ORACLE CORPORATION ("ORACLE") GRANTS END USER ("YOU" OR "YOUR") A NON-EXCLUSIVE, NON- TRANSFERABLE DEVELOPMENT ONLY LIMITED USE LICENSE TO USE THE ENCLOSED SOFTWARE AND DOCUMENTATION ("SOFTWARE") SUBJECT TO THE TERMS AND CONDITIONS, INCLUDING USE RESTRICTIONS, SPECIFIED BELOW.

You shall have the right to use the Software (a) only in object code form, (b) for development purposes only in the indicated operating environment for a single developer (one person) on a single computer, (c) solely with the publication with which the Software is included, and (d) solely for Your personal use and as a single user.

You are prohibited from and shall not (a) transfer, sell, sublicense, assign or otherwise convey the Software, (b) timeshare, rent or market the Software, (c) use the Software for or as part of a service bureau, and/or (d) distribute the Software in whole or in part. Any attempt to transfer, sell, sublicense, assign or otherwise convey any of the rights, duties or obligations hereunder is void. You are prohibited from and shall not use the Software for internal data processing operations, processing data of a third party or for any commercial or production use. If You desire to use the Software for any use other than the development use allowed under this Agreement, You must contact Oracle, or an authorized Oracle reseller, to obtain the appropriate licenses. You are prohibited from and shall not cause or permit the reverse engineering, disassembly, decompilation, modification or creation of derivative works based on the Software. You are prohibited from and shall not copy or duplicate the Software except as follows: You may make one copy of the Software in machine readable form solely for back-up purposes. No other copies shall be made without Oracle's prior written consent. You are prohibited from and shall not: (a) remove any product identification, copyright notices, or other notices or proprietary restrictions from the Software, or (b) run any benchmark tests with or of the Software. This Agreement does not authorize You to use any Oracle name, trademark or logo.

COPYRIGHT/OWNERSHIP OF SOFTWARE: The Software is the confidential and proprietary product of Oracle and is protected by copyright and other intellectual property laws. You acquire only the right to use the Software and do not acquire any rights, express or implied, in the Software or media containing the Software other than those specified in this Agreement. Oracle, or its licensor, shall at all times, including but not limited to after termination of this Agreement, retain all rights, title, interest, including intellectual property rights, in the Software and media.

WARRANTY DISCLAIMER: THE SOFTWARE IS PROVIDED "AS IS" AND ORACLE SPECIFICALLY DISCLAIMS ALL WARRANTIES OF ANY KIND, EITHER EXPRESS OR IMPLIED, INCLUDING, BUT NOT LIMITED TO, THE IMPLIED WARRANTIES OF MERCHANTABILITY, SATISFACTORY QUALITY AND FITNESS FOR A PARTICULAR PURPOSE. ORACLE DOES NOT WARRANT, GUARANTEE OR MAKE ANY REPRESENTATIONS REGARDING THE USE, OR THE RESULTS OF THE USE, OF THE SOFTWARE IN TERMS OF CORRECTNESS, ACCURACY, RELIABILITY, CURRENTNESS OR OTHERWISE, AND DOES NOT WARRANT THAT THE OPERATION OF THE SOFTWARE WILL BE UNINTERRUPTED OR ERROR FREE. ORACLE EXPRESSLY DISCLAIMS ALL WARRANTIES NOT STATED HEREIN, NO ORAL OR WRITTEN INFORMATION OR ADVICE GIVEN BY ORACLE OR OTHERS SHALL CREATE A WARRANTY OR IN ANY WAY INCREASE THE SCOPE OF THIS LICENSE, AND YOU MAY NOT RELY ON ANY SUCH INFORMATION OR ADVICE.

LIMITATION OF LIABILITY: IN NO EVENT SHALL ORACLE OR ITS LICENSORS BE LIABLE FOR ANY DIRECT, INDIRECT, INCIDENTAL, SPECIAL OR CONSEQUENTIAL DAMAGES, OR DAMAGES FOR LOSS OF PROFITS, REVENUE, DATA OR DATA USE, INCURRED BY YOU OR ANY THIRD PARTY, WHETHER IN AN ACTION IN CONTRACT OR TORT, EVEN IF ORACLE AND/OR ITS LICENSORS HAVE BEEN ADVISED OF THE POSSIBILITY OF

SUCH DAMAGES. SOME JURISDICTIONS DO NOT ALLOW THE EXCLUSION OF IMPLIED WARRANTIES OR LIMITATION OR EXCLUSION OF LIABILITY FOR INCIDENTAL OR CONSEQUENTIAL DAMAGES SO THE ABOVE EXCLUSIONS AND LIMITATION MAY NOT APPLY TO YOU.

TERMINATION: You may terminate this license at any time by discontinuing use of and destroying the Software together with any copies in any form. This license will also terminate if You fail to comply with any term or condition of this Agreement. Upon termination of the license, You agree to discontinue use of and destroy the Software together with any copies in any form. The Warranty Disclaimer, Limitation of Liability, and Export Administration sections of this Agreement shall survive termination of this Agreement.

NO TECHNICAL SUPPORT: Oracle is not obligated to provide and this Agreement does not entitle You to any updates or upgrades to, or any technical support or phone support for, the Software.

EXPORT ADMINISTRATION: You acknowledge that the Software, including technical data, is subject to United States export control laws, including the United States Export Administration Act and its associated regulations, and may be subject to export or import regulations in other countries. You agree to comply fully with all laws and regulations of the United States and other countries ("Export Laws") to assure that neither the Software, nor any direct products thereof, are (a) exported, directly or indirectly, in violation of Export Laws, either to countries or nationals that are subject to United States export restrictions or to any end user who has been prohibited from participating in the Unites States export transactions by any federal agency of the United States government; or (b) intended to be used for any purposes prohibited by the Export Laws, including, without limitation, nuclear, chemical or biological weapons proliferation. You acknowledge that the Software may include technical data subject to export and re-export restrictions imposed by United States law.

RESTRICTED RIGHTS: The Software is provided with Restricted Rights. Use, duplication or disclosure of the Software by the United State government is subject to the restrictions set forth in the Rights in Technical Data and Computer Software Clauses in DFARS 252.227-7013(c)(1)(ii) and FAR 52.227-19(c)(2) as applicable. Manufacturer is Oracle Corporation, 500 Oracle Parkway, Redwood City, CA 94065.

MISCELLANEOUS: This Agreement and all related actions thereto shall be governed by California law. Oracle may audit Your use of the Software. If any provision of this Agreement is held to be invalid or unenforceable, the remaining provisions of this Agreement will remain in full force.

YOU ACKNOWLEDGE THAT YOU HAVE READ THIS AGREEMENT, UNDERSTAND IT, AND AGREE TO BE BOUND BY ITS TERMS AND CONDITIONS. YOU FURTHER AGREE THAT IT IS THE COMPLETE AND EXCLUSIVE STATEMENT OF THE AGREEMENT BETWEEN ORACLE AND YOU.
Oracle is a registered trademark of Oracle Corporation.

Register for the *Oracle Technology Network* (*OTN*)

Oracle Technology Network ("OTN") is the primary technical source for developers building Oracle-based applications. As an OTN member, you will be part of an online community with access to technical papers, code samples, product documentation, self-service technical support, free software, OTN-sponsored Internet developer conferences, and discussion groups on up-to-date Oracle technology. Membership is FREE! Register for OTN on the World Wide Web at

```
http://technet.oracle.com/register/oraclepress_xml/
```